Introduction to Pascal
and Structured Design

THIRD EDITION

Turbo Version

Nell Dale
The University of Texas at Austin

Chip Weems
University of Massachusetts at Amherst

D. C. HE

Lexington

Address editorial correspondence to:
D. C. Heath
125 Spring Street
Lexington, MA 02173

Acquisitions Editor: John Carter Shanklin
Developmental Editor: Katherine T. Pinard
Production Editor: Andrea Cava
Designer: George McLean
Production Coordinator: Lisa Merrill
Photo Researcher: Billie Ingram
Text Permissions Editor: Margaret Roll

Trademark Acknowledgments: Turbo Pascal is a trademark of Borland International, Inc. IBM is a registered trademark of International Business Machines, Inc.

Photo Credits: 1-10(a), page 21 (bottom right) Courtesy of Apple Computer, Inc.; 1-10(b), 1-10(c), 1-10(d), 1-10(e), 1-10(g), 1-10(i), page 21 (top), page 21 (bottom left), Courtesy of International Business Machines Corporation; 1-10(f) Courtesy of Microsoft Corporation; 1-10(h) Courtesy of Hewlett-Packard Company; page 20 Courtesy of Digital Equipment Corporation; page 22 Courtesy of Intel; page 23 (left) Courtesy of Sun Microsystems, Inc.; page 23 (right) Courtesy of Cray Research, Inc., photo by Paul Shambroom; 2-3, © 1991 by Cameramann Int'l., Ltd.; page 108 Courtesy of BASF; page 369 Courtesy of Beech Starship/Beech Aircraft Corporation.

Cover: CIRCA, 86, Inc.

hed simultaneously in Canada.

the United States of America.

ndard Book Number: 0-669-26951-4

Catalog Card Number: 91-70833

This book is dedicated to you,
and to all of our other students for whom it
without whom it would never have been completed.

PREFACE

Since its debut in 1983, *Introduction to Pascal and Structured Design* has led the field in introducing new topics and pedagogy because our philosophy of revision is to be proactive rather than reactive. We have consistently set trends instead of following them. In this edition of *Turbo Pascal,* we again have made many important changes. One thing, however, has not changed—our commitment to students.

As always, our efforts are directed toward making the sometimes difficult concepts of computer science more accessible. There are many new topics in this edition, but new material is of little value unless it is presented so that students can use it.

The previous edition of this book has been widely accepted as a model for textbooks for the ACM recommended curriculum for CS1 and the first section of the AP exam in computer science. We believe that this edition will also become a model because it reflects our view of the future direction of computer science education—more rigor, more theory, greater use of abstraction, and earlier application of software engineering.

The previous edition has shown that topics once considered advanced, such as loop invariants, testing, and abstract data types, can be taught in the first course. This edition addresses metalanguages explicitly as the formal means of specifying programming language syntax. Big-O notation is introduced early and used to compare algorithms in later chapters. Finite state machines are presented as one model for designing certain programs. Modular design is now discussed in terms of abstract steps, concrete steps, functional equivalence, and functional cohesion. Preconditions and postconditions are used both in the context of the algorithm walk-through and in the development of testing strategies. Procedure interface design has been expanded to include encapsulation, control abstraction, and communication complexity.

This edition of *Turbo Pascal* includes many more exercises and examples than the previous edition. We also introduce four types of special sections: Theoretical Foundations, Software Engineering Tips, Matters of Style, and Background Information. The last includes biographies and other cultural information of interest and value to every computer science student. In response to users' suggestions, we have streamlined the presentation and made it more direct. We have also reorganized each chapter so that the chapter discussion, which now includes only short examples, is followed by complete case studies.

The standard version uses ISO Standard Pascal and covers the system dependent aspects of program development in a generic manner, allowing the book to be used with a wide variety of computer systems and compilers. However, the popularity of Borland International's Turbo Pascal™ has made it, in essence, a second standard for Pascal. Thus we have written this new Turbo Pascal version specifically to address the features of Turbo Pascal, the Turbo Integrated Development Environment, and DOS. We explain differences between Turbo Pascal and ISO Pascal throughout the text so that students will be aware of extensions specific to Turbo Pascal.

The discussion of how to use the Turbo Environment now includes step-by-step instructions for entering the environment, using the editor to enter a program, and using the menu system to compile and run a program. Turbo Pascal version 6.0 with a mouse is treated as the standard environment, but Turbo Pascal 5.5 and keyboard interaction also are covered.

The Turbo Debugger is given extensive coverage once students have reached the required level of sophistication. Simple tracing and watched variables are treated early in the text, whereas tracing into subprogram calls and setting breakpoints are covered later.

The USES clause is introduced early to permit students to take advantage of the units supplied with Turbo Pascal or special units provided by the instructor. The construction of units is examined in Chapter 19, which may be assigned after Chapter 10. Units are discussed as a mechanism for building abstract data types.

Turbo Pascal file I/O and the peculiarities of keyboard I/O are treated fully. The programming style of the text has been revised to make use of the extended character set allowed for identifiers. As in the previous edition, strings and graphical output receive extensive coverage.

Synopsis

The overall organization of this Turbo version is similar to that of the third edition of the standard version, with the exception of the sections on the environment, the debugger, and the string data type. Chapters on graphics and units have also been added.

Chapter 1 is still designed to create a comfortable rapport between the student and the subject. However, because many students now enter the introductory course with prior exposure to computers, Chapter 1 moves more quickly into meaty topics. It now includes an expanded section on problem-solving techniques and applies these techniques immediately in a case study. By the end of Chapter 1, students should have a basic knowledge of computers, programming, and algorithmic problem-solving techniques.

Because Chapter 2 is the student's first look at syntax, we have added a section on metalanguages that includes both BNF and syntax diagrams. Research at the University of Texas at Austin has shown that students miss many subtleties of Pascal syntax when it is presented by the traditional syntax diagrams. More generally, beginners have trouble translating from a metalanguage to Pascal constructs when the metalanguage is formulated much differently than the programming language. Thus Chapter 2 also introduces the syntax template—a metalanguage every bit as rigorous as the syntax diagram but one that closely resembles Pascal constructs. For instructors who feel that students must learn to read syntax diagrams in the first course, Appendix E presents the Pascal syntax diagrams side-by-side with syntax templates.

Chapter 2 aims to enable students to design a simple program of their own. They should be able to attain this goal after reading the first half of the chapter. Because there are so many concepts and rules to learn before even the simplest program may be written, the middle of the chapter includes a discussion of program entry, correction, and execution using the Turbo Pascal Integrated Development Environment. Students then can reinforce the new concepts by trying them on the computer. The remainder of the chapter fleshes out the details of Pascal syntax for more complex expressions and output.

The top-down design methodology, rewritten here with greater formalism, is a major focus of Chapter 3. The chapter also covers Input and Text files other than Input and Output, including the Turbo Pascal extensions required to use files. The early introduction of files permits the assignment of programming problems that require the use of sample data files. However, because many instructors postpone the use of files until loops are introduced, the section is designed to be optionally covered anywhere prior to the end of Chapter 5.

Procedures, first mentioned in Chapter 1, are further discussed in Chapter 2. Chapter 3 introduces the basic concepts of subprogram calls, parameter passing, and subprogram libraries. Chapter 3 also relates subprograms to the implementation of modular designs and begins the discussion of interface design that is essential to writing proper procedures.

Chapter 4 begins with the Boolean data type (and a biographical sketch of George Boole), but its main purpose is to introduce the concept of flow of control. Selection, using IF-THEN and IF-THEN-ELSE, is used to demonstrate the distinction between physical ordering of statements and logical ordering. The concept of nested control structures is also developed. Chapter 4 concludes with a lengthy Testing and Debugging section that expands upon the modular design discussion by introducing preconditions and postconditions. The algorithm walk-through and code walk-through are introduced as a means of preventing errors, and the execution trace (both with and without the Turbo Debugger) is used to find errors that crept into the code. Data validation and testing strategies also are covered extensively in this section.

Chapter 5 focuses on looping structures. As in the previous edition, all of the structures are introduced using the syntax of the WHILE statement. Rather than confuse students with multiple syntactical structures, we teach the concepts of looping using only the WHILE. However, because many instructors have told us that they prefer to show students the syntax for all of Pascal's loops at once, we have rewritten the discussion of FOR and REPEAT in Chapter 9 to be optionally covered after Chapter 5.

We first introduce students to the basic loop control strategies and common looping operations. We then describe how to design loops using a checklist of seven questions. The checklist leads naturally to a discussion of the loop invariant as a means of validating a loop design. Because of the introduction of preconditions and postconditions in Chapter 4, the loop invariant now can be covered at a higher level. Chapter 5 also introduces the topics of Big-O notation and finite state machines.

Because there are so many new concepts associated with designing and writing user-defined subprograms, we have devoted three chapters to this topic. Chapter 6 covers flow of control in procedures, formal and actual parameters, local variables, and interface design. The last topic now includes control abstraction, encapsulation, and physical versus conceptual hiding of an implementation. Chapter 7 expands the discussion to consider value parameters, nested scope, stubs and drivers, and more on interface design, including side effects. Chapter 8 covers user-defined functions and briefly introduces recursion. Because of Chapter 8's numerical orientation, we also take the opportunity to discuss the problems of representation and precision associated with Real numbers.

Chapter 9 represents a transition between the control structures orientation of the first half of the book and the abstract data type orientation of the second half. The chapter begins by introducing the first new data type since Chapter 3 (Sets) and ends by covering the remaining "ice cream and cake" control structures in Pascal (CASE, REPEAT, and FOR). Chapter 9 is a natural ending point for the first quarter of a two-quarter introductory programming course.

In keeping with the emphasis on abstraction, simple data types are given a chapter of their own, Chapter 10. The built-in simple data types are examined in terms of the set of values that variables or constants of that type can contain and the allowable operations on values of that type. Enumerated and subrange types are explained in detail. The functions Pred, Succ, and Ord are defined as Pascal implementations of the corresponding operations on scalar data types. Type compatibility is defined, and anonymous typing is strongly discouraged. This is a likely point from which to expand into the area of abstract data type implementation and can be followed by the first part of Chapter 19, which discusses Turbo Pascal Units.

The array data type is introduced in Chapter 11. Arrays are the last big conceptual hurdle for students: a variable to access another variable? Three case studies and numerous small examples successfully help readers make the jump. Three typical types of array processing (subarray processing, parallel arrays, and indexes with semantic content) and patterns of array access (randomly, sequentially, and as a single object) are treated.

The purpose of Chapter 12 is to broaden students' experience with array processing and to introduce the list as an abstract data type. Algorithms that are commonly applied to lists are developed and coded as general purpose Pascal procedures. The Turbo Pascal String type is described as a variation of the array. A case study uses strings to demonstrate their applicability. Big-O notation is used to compare the various searching and sorting algorithms that were developed.

Multidimensional arrays are discussed in Chapter 13. Records, along with a discussion on how to choose an appropriate data structure, are presented in Chapter 14. Data abstraction is demonstrated by creating an abstract data type Date and several useful operations on dates.

Chapter 15 discusses the remaining data types, files and pointers. Pointers are presented as a way to make programs more efficient. Chapter 16 is devoted completely to the use of pointers to create dynamic data structures. Linked lists in general and linked-list representations of stacks, queues, and binary trees are described. Following the presentation of a tree sort, the discussion returns to a comparison of sorting algorithms using Big-O.

Chapter 17 deals with recursion. There is no consensus regarding the best place to cover recursion. We personally feel that this topic requires more maturity than many first-semester students possess. We have included it, however, for two reasons: many instructors have requested it, and there are those students for whom recursion seems natural. The examples are divided into two parts: those requiring only simple data types and those requiring structured data types. The first part is appropriate after Chapter 8. The second part contains examples from simple arrays to binary trees. These examples may be used singly after the appropriate chapter or as a unit after Chapter 16.

From among our colleagues, we especially thank Suzy Gallagher at Austin and W. Richards Adrion, Alan Hanson, Edward Riseman, William Verts, Conrad Wogrin, and Beverly Woolf at Amherst. We also extend a special thanks to Jeff Brumfield at Austin for designing the syntax templates.

For their many helpful suggestions, we thank the lecturers, teaching assistants, consultants, and student proctors who run the courses for which this book was written, and the students themselves.

We would also like to thank the following people who reviewed the manuscript: Charles Burchard, Pennsylvania State University at Erie—Behrend College; Ronald S. Curtis, State University of New York at Buffalo; Edmund Deaton, San Diego State University; Virginia Eaton, Northeast Louisiana University; Norman Gibbs, Carnegie-Mellon University; Ghodra Habibishad, Barstow College; Michael Hennessey, University of Oregon; Martin Holoien, University of California at Santa Barbara; William Kraynek, Florida International University School of Computer Science; Lynn Krell, University of Southern Mississippi; K. W. Loach, State University of New York at Plattsburgh; Lawrence Malloy, Oakland Community College at Orchard Ridge; Andrea Martin, Louisiana State University; Robert Martin, Middlebury College; Scott McLeod, University of California at Los Angeles; Chris Nevison, Colgate University; Mike Olan, University of Wisconsin at LaCrosse; E. K. Park, United States Naval Academy; James C. Pleasant, East Tennessee State University; Eleanor S. Quinlan, Ohio State University; Robert Redding, Worcester State College; Glenn A. Richard, State University of New York at Stony Brook; David C. Rine, George Mason University; Peter Schleppenbach, Los Angeles Pierce College; David Teague, Western Carolina University; Ralph Tomlison, University of Nebraska at Omaha; Marilyn Weiner, Texas Tech University. We would like to thank especially Ernest Ferguson, Southwest Baptist University, for his suggestions to the Testing sections in Chapters 4 and 5, and Robert Sterling, Tidewater Community College, for providing us with additional exercises and programming assignments.

Our thanks also go to Tom Parks for his numerous contributions to the Turbo edition.

For this impressive list of reviewers, as well as her tremendous support, we must thank our developmental editor, Kitty Pinard. To all the others at D. C. Heath who contributed so much, especially Carter Shanklin, Andrea Cava, and Dave Serbun, we are indeed grateful.

Anyone who has ever written a book—or is related to anyone who has—knows the amount of time involved in such a project. To our families who learned this firsthand, all we can say is: "To all the Dale clan and the extended Dale family (too numerous to name) and to Lisa, Charli, and Carol, thanks for your tremendous support and indulgence."

B R I E F
C O N T E N T S

CONTENTS

4 *Conditions, Boolean Expressions, and Selection Control Structures*   141

7 *Value Parameters, Nesting Procedures, and More on Interface Design*   297

Overview of Programming and Problem Solving

GOALS

- To understand what a computer program is.
- To be able to list the basic stages involved in writing a computer program.
- To know what an algorithm is.
- To know what a high-level programming language is.
- To be able to describe what a compiler is and what it does.
- To understand the compilation and execution processes.
- To learn the history of the Pascal programming language.
- To learn what the major components of a computer are and how they work together.
- To be able to distinguish between hardware and software.
- To be able to choose an appropriate problem-solving method for developing an algorithmic solution to a problem.

Overview of Programming

com·put·er \kəm-'pyüt-ər\ *n. often attrib* (1646): one that computes; *specif*: a programmable electronic device that can store, retrieve, and process data*

What a brief definition for something that has in just a few decades changed the way of life in industrialized societies! Computers touch all areas of our lives: paying bills, driving cars, using the telephone, shopping. In fact, it would be easier to list those areas of our lives that are *not* affected by computers.

It is sad that a device that does so much good is so often maligned and feared. How many times have you heard someone say, "I'm sorry, our computer fouled things up" or "I just don't understand computers; they're too complicated for me"? The very fact that you are reading this book, however, means that you are ready to set aside prejudice and learn about computers. But be warned: This book is not just about computers in the abstract. This is a text to teach you how to program them.

What Is Programming?

Much of human behavior and thought is characterized by logical sequences. Since infancy, you have been learning how to act, how to do things. And you have learned to expect certain behavior from other people.

A lot of what you do every day you do automatically. Fortunately, it is not necessary for you to consciously think of every step involved in a process as simple as turning this page by hand:

1. Lift hand.
2. Move hand to right side of book.
3. Grasp corner of top page.
4. Move hand from right to left until page is positioned so that what is on the other side can be read.
5. Let go of page.

Think how many neurons must fire and how many muscles must respond, all in a certain order or sequence, to move your arm and hand. Yet you do it unconsciously.

Much of what you do unconsciously you once had to learn. Watch how a baby concentrates on putting one foot before the other while learning to walk. Then watch a group of three-year-olds playing tag.

On a broader scale, mathematics could never have been developed without logical sequences of steps for solving problems or proving theorems. Mass production would

*By permission. From *Webster's Ninth New Collegiate Dictionary* © 1989 by Merriam-Webster, Inc., publishers of the Merriam-Webster® Dictionaries.

never have worked without certain operations taking place in a certain order. Our whole civilization is based on the order of things and actions.

We create order, both conscious and unconscious, through a process we call **programming.** This book is concerned with the programming of one of our tools, the **computer.**

Programming   Planning, scheduling, or performing a task or an event.

Computer   A programmable device that can store, retrieve, and process data.

Computer Programming   The process of planning a sequence of steps for a computer to follow.

Just as a concert program lists the actions the players perform, a **computer program** lists the steps the computer performs. From now on, when we use the words *programming* and *program,* we mean *computer programming* and *computer program.*

Computer Program   A list of instructions to be performed by a computer.

The computer allows us to do tasks more efficiently, quickly, and accurately than we could do them "by hand"—if we could do them by hand at all. In order to use this powerful tool, we must specify what we want done and the order in which we want it done. We do this through programming.

How Do We Write a Program?

To write a sequence of instructions for a computer to follow, we must go through a two-phase process: *problem solving* and *implementation* (see Figure 1-1).

Problem-Solving Phase

1. *Analysis and Specification.*   Understand (define) the problem and what the solution must do.
2. *General Solution (Algorithm).*   Develop a logical sequence of steps to be used to solve the problem.
3. *Verify.*   Follow the steps exactly to see if the solution really does solve the problem.

Implementation Phase

1. *Specific Solution (Program).*   Translate the algorithm into a programming language (code).
2. *Test.*   Have the computer follow the instructions, and then manually check the results. If you find errors, analyze the program and the algorithm to determine their source, and then make corrections.

Once a program has been written, it enters a third phase: maintenance.

Figure 1-1
*Programming
Process*

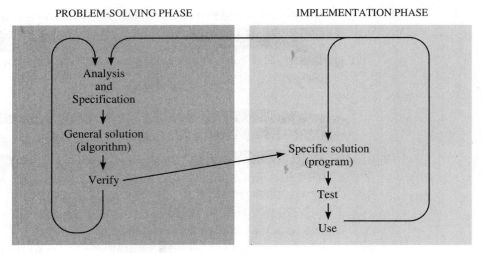

Maintenance Phase

1. *Use.*   Use the program.
2. *Maintain.*   Modify the program to meet changing requirements or to correct any errors that show up in using it.

Each time the program is modified, it is necessary to repeat the problem solving and implementation phases for those aspects of the program that will change. Together, the problem solving, implementation, and maintenance phases constitute the program's *life cycle*.

A computer is not intelligent. It cannot analyze a problem and come up with a solution. The programmer must analyze the problem, arrive at the solution, and then communicate it to the computer. What's the advantage of using a computer if it can't solve problems? Once we have a solution for a problem and have prepared a version of it for the computer, the computer can repeat the solution quickly, again and again. The computer frees people from tasks that require great speed or consistency, or that are repetitive and boring.

The programmer begins the programming process by analyzing the problem and developing a general solution, called an **algorithm.** Understanding and analyzing a problem take up much more time than Figure 1-1 implies. They are the heart of the programming process.

Algorithm   A step-by-step procedure for solving a problem in a finite amount of time.

If our definitions of a computer program and an algorithm look similar, it is because all programs are algorithms. A program is simply an algorithm that has been written for a computer.

An algorithm is a verbal or written description of a logical sequence of actions. We use algorithms every day. Recipes, instructions, and directions are all examples of algorithms that are not programs.

When you start your car, you follow a step-by-step procedure. The algorithm might look something like this:

1. Insert the key.
2. Make sure the transmission is in Park (or Neutral).
3. Depress the gas pedal.
4. Turn the key to the start position.
5. If the engine starts within six seconds, release the key to the ignition position.
6. If the engine doesn't start in six seconds, release the key, wait ten seconds, and repeat steps 3 through 6, but not more than five times.
7. If the car doesn't start, call the garage.

Without the phrase "but not more than five times" in step 6, you could be trying to start the car forever. Why? Because if something is wrong with the car, repeating steps 3 through 6 over and over again will not start it. This kind of never-ending situation is called an infinite loop. If we leave the phrase "but not more than five times" out of step 6, the procedure does not fit our definition of an algorithm. An algorithm must terminate in a finite amount of time for all possible conditions.

Suppose a programmer needs an algorithm to determine an employee's weekly wages. The algorithm reflects what would be done by hand:

1. Look up the employee's pay rate.
2. Determine the number of hours worked during the week.
3. If the number of hours worked is less than or equal to 40, multiply the number of hours by the pay rate to calculate regular wages.
4. If the number of hours worked is greater than 40, multiply 40 by the pay rate to calculate regular wages, and then multiply the difference between the number of hours worked and 40 by one and a half times the pay rate to calculate overtime wages.
5. Add the regular wages to the overtime wages (if any) to determine total wages for the week.

The steps the computer follows are often the same as those you would use to do the calculations by hand.

After developing a general solution, the programmer tests the algorithm, "walking through" each step mentally or manually. If the algorithm doesn't work, the programmer repeats the problem-solving process, analyzing the problem again and coming up with another algorithm. Often the second algorithm is just a variation of the first. When the programmer is satisfied with the algorithm, he or she translates it into a **programming language.** We use the Pascal programming language in this book.

Programming Language   A set of rules, symbols, and special words used to construct a program.

A programming language is a simplified form of English (with math symbols) that adheres to a strict set of grammatical rules. English is far too complicated a language for today's computers to follow. Programming languages, because they limit vocabulary, are much simpler.

Although a programming language is simple in form, it is not always easy to use. Try giving someone directions to the nearest airport using a vocabulary of no more than 36 words, and you'll begin to see the problem. Programming forces you to write very simple, exact instructions.

Translating an algorithm into a programming language is called *coding* the algorithm. The product of that translation—the program—is tested by running *(executing)* it on the computer. If the program fails to produce the wanted results, the programmer must *debug* it: determine what is wrong and then modify the program or even the algorithm to fix it. The combination of coding and testing an algorithm is called *implementation*.

There is no single way to implement an algorithm. For example, an algorithm can be translated into more than one programming language. Each translation produces a different implementation. Even when they translate an algorithm into the same programming language, different people are likely to come up with different implementations (see Figure 1-2). Why? Because every programming language allows the programmer some flexibility in how an algorithm is translated. Given this flexibility, people

Figure 1-2
Differences in
Implementation

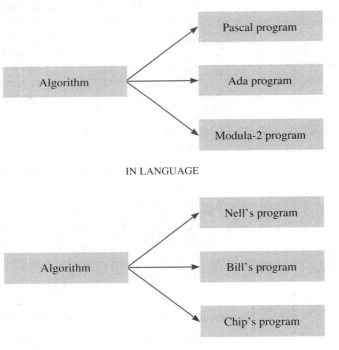

IN LANGUAGE

IN PERSONAL PROGRAMMING STYLE

Figure 1-3
Programming
Shortcut?

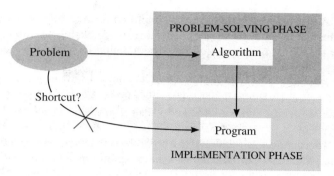

adopt their own *styles* in writing programs, just as they do in writing short stories or essays. Once you have some programming experience, you will develop a style of your own. Throughout this book, we offer tips on good programming style.

Some people try to speed up the programming process by going directly from the problem definition to coding the program (see Figure 1-3). A shortcut here is very tempting and at first seems to save a lot of time. However, for many reasons that will become obvious to you as you read this book, this kind of shortcut actually takes *more* time and effort. Developing a general solution before you write a program helps you manage the problem, keep your thoughts straight, and avoid mistakes. If you don't take the time at the beginning to think out and polish your algorithm, you'll spend a lot of extra time debugging and revising your program. So think first and code later! The sooner you start coding, the longer it takes to write a program that works.

In addition to solving the problem, implementing the algorithm, and maintaining the program, **documentation** is an important part of the programming process. Most programs are used by many different people over a long period of time. Each of those people must be able to read and understand your code.

Documentation The written text and comments that make a program easier for others to understand, use, and modify.

After you write a program, you must give the computer the information or data necessary to solve the problem. **Information** is any knowledge that can be communicated, including abstract ideas and concepts. **Data** is information in a form the computer can use—for example, numbers and letters.

Information Any knowledge that can be communicated.

Data Information that has been put into a form a computer can use.

---

*T*heoretical Foundations

Data Representation

In a computer, data is represented electronically by pulses of electricity. Electric circuits, in their simplest form, are either on or off. Usually a circuit that is on is represented by the number 1; a circuit that is off is represented by the number 0. Any kind of data can be represented by combinations of enough 1s and 0s. We simply have to choose which combination represents each piece of data we are using. For example, we could arbitrarily choose the pattern 1101000110 to represent the name *Pascal*.

Data represented by 1s and 0s is in *binary form*. The binary (base-2) number system uses only 1s and 0s to represent numbers. (The decimal [base-10] number system uses the digits 0 through 9.) The word *bit* (short for <u>bi</u>nary dig<u>it</u>) often is used to refer to a single 1 or 0. So the pattern 1101000110 has 10 bits. A binary number with 10 bits can represent 2^{10} (1024) different patterns. A *byte* contains 8 bits; it can represent 2^8 (256) patterns. Inside the computer, each character is usually represented by a byte. Four bits, or half of a byte, is called a *nybble*—a name that was originally proposed with tongue in cheek but is now standard terminology. Groups of 16, 32, and 64 bits are generally referred to as *words* (although the terms *short word* and *long word* are sometimes used to refer to 16-bit and 64-bit groups, respectively).

The process of assigning bit patterns to pieces of data is called *coding*—the same name we give to the process of translating an algorithm into a programming language. In the early days of computers, programming meant translating an algorithm into patterns of 1s and 0s because the only language the first computers could work with was binary in form.

Binary coding schemes can be used to represent both the instructions that the computer follows and the data that it uses. For example, 16 bits can represent the decimal integers from 0 to $2^{16} - 1$ (65535). More complicated coding schemes are necessary to represent negative numbers, real numbers, and numbers in scientific notation. Characters also can be represented by bit combinations. In one coding scheme, 01001101 represents *M* and 01101101 represents *m*.

The patterns of bits that represent data and instructions vary from one computer to another. Even on the same computer, different programming languages can use different binary representations for the same data. A single programming language may even use the same pattern of bits to represent different things in different contexts. (People do this too. The four letters that represent the word **tack** have different meanings depending on whether you are talking about upholstery, sailing, sewing, paint, or horseback riding.) The point is that patterns of bits by themselves are meaningless. It is the way the patterns are used that gives them their meaning.

Fortunately we no longer have to work with binary coding schemes. Today the process of coding is usually just a matter of writing down the data in letters, numbers, and symbols. The computer automatically converts these letters, numbers, and symbols into binary form. Still, as you work with computers, you will continually run into numbers that are related to powers of 2—numbers like 256, 32768, and 65536—reminders that the binary number system is lurking somewhere nearby.

What Is a Programming Language?

In the computer, all data, whatever its form, is stored and used in binary codes, strings of 1s and 0s. When computers were first developed, the only programming language available was the primitive instruction set built into each machine, the **machine language,** or *machine code*.

Machine Language   The language, made up of binary-coded instructions, that is used directly by the computer.

Even though most computers perform the same kinds of operations, their designers choose different sets of binary codes for each instruction. So the machine code for one computer is not the same as for another.

When programmers used machine language for programming, they had to enter the binary codes for the various instructions, a tedious process that was prone to error. Moreover, their programs were difficult to read and modify. In time **assembly languages** were developed to make the programmer's job easier.

Assembly Language   A low-level programming language in which a mnemonic is used to represent each of the machine language instructions for a particular computer.

Instructions in an assembly language are in an easy-to-remember form called a *mnemonic* (pronounced "ni-'män-ik"). Typical instructions for addition and subtraction might look like this:

Assembly Language	*Machine Language*
ADD	100101
SUB	010011

The only problem with assembly languages was that instructions written in them could not be executed directly by computers. So a program called an **assembler** was written to translate the instructions written in assembly language into machine code.

Assembler   A program that translates an assembly language program into machine code.

The assembler was a step in the right direction, but programmers still were forced to think in terms of individual machine instructions. Eventually high-level programming languages were developed. These languages are easier to use than assembly languages or machine code because they are closer to English and other natural languages (see Figure 1-4).

*Figure 1-4
Levels of
Abstraction*

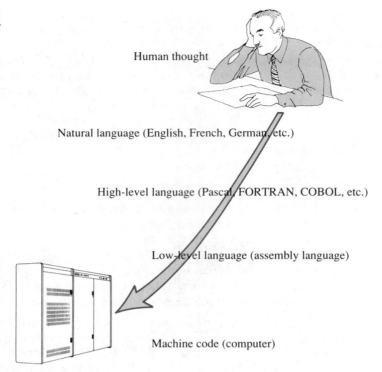

Human thought

Natural language (English, French, German, etc.)

High-level language (Pascal, FORTRAN, COBOL, etc.)

Low-level language (assembly language)

Machine code (computer)

Programs in high-level languages (Pascal, FORTRAN, COBOL, Modula-2, and Ada, for example) must be translated into machine language by a program called a **compiler.** If you write a program in a high-level language, you can run it on any computer that has the appropriate compiler. This is because most high-level languages are *standardized,* that is, an official description of them exists.

Compiler   A program that translates a high-level language into machine code.

The International Standards Organization (ISO) established an official description of Pascal in 1981. Whenever a program is written according to the ISO standard for Pascal, it can be executed by any computer with a compiler that also adheres to the ISO standard. Unfortunately not all compilers adhere strictly to that standard; for one reason or another, some recognize slightly different versions of the Pascal language.

Turbo Pascal, for example, is very similar but not quite identical to ISO standard Pascal. There are three general ways in which Turbo Pascal differs from ISO standard Pascal. First, ISO Pascal has a few features not found in Turbo Pascal. Second, there are a few features of ISO Pascal that Turbo Pascal also provides but in a different way. Third, many special features of Turbo Pascal are not found in ISO Pascal.

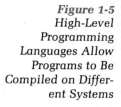

*Figure 1-5
High-Level
Programming
Languages Allow
Programs to Be
Compiled on Differ-
ent Systems*

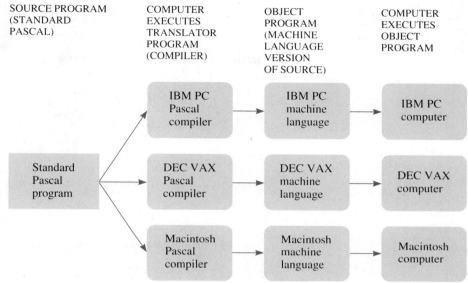

SOURCE PROGRAM (STANDARD PASCAL) | COMPUTER EXECUTES TRANSLATOR PROGRAM (COMPILER) | OBJECT PROGRAM (MACHINE LANGUAGE VERSION OF SOURCE) | COMPUTER EXECUTES OBJECT PROGRAM

Throughout this book, we use the ISO standard for Pascal unless we specifically say otherwise. Whenever there is a difference between Turbo Pascal and the ISO standard, we first will describe the Turbo Pascal approach and then show how standard Pascal differs. We also will discuss many of the special features of Turbo Pascal so that you can take advantage of them in writing your programs. It is important to remember that these special features are not available on most other systems. That is, whenever you write a program for a system that does not use Turbo Pascal, you won't be able to use these features. When we discuss such special features, we will identify them clearly as Turbo-Pascal specific.

A program in a high-level language is called a **source program.** To the compiler, a source program is just input data. It translates the source program into a machine language program called an **object program** (see Figure 1-5). Some compilers also output a listing—a copy of the program with error messages and other information inserted.

Source Program   A program written in a high-level programming language.

Object Program   The machine language version of a source program.

Notice in Figure 1-6 that compilation and execution are two distinct processes. During compilation, the computer runs the compiler program. During execution, the object program replaces the compiler program in the computer's memory. The computer then runs the object program, doing whatever the program instructs it to do.

Figure 1-6
Compilation/
Execution

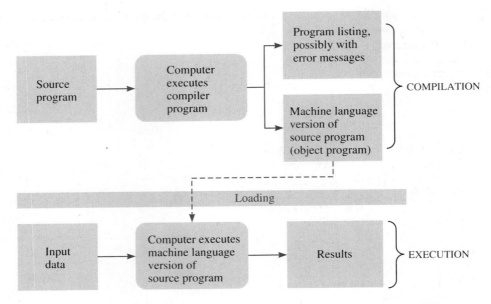

The instructions in a programming language reflect the functions a computer can actually perform:

- A computer can transfer data from one place to another.
- A computer can input data from an input device (a keyboard, for example) and output data to an output device (a screen, for example).
- A computer can store data in and retrieve data from its memory and secondary storage.
- A computer can compare two data values for equality or inequality.
- A computer can perform arithmetic operations (addition and subtraction, for example) very quickly.

Programming languages require that we use certain structures to express algorithms as programs. There are four basic ways of structuring statements (instructions) in Pascal and other languages: sequentially, conditionally, repetitively, and procedurally (see Figure 1-7). A *sequence* is a series of statements that are executed one after another. *Selection*, the conditional structure, executes different statements depending on certain conditions. The repetitive structure, the *loop*, repeats statements while certain conditions are met. And the *procedure* allows us to structure a program by breaking it into smaller subprograms.

Assume you're driving a car. Going down a straight stretch of road is like following a *sequence* of instructions. When you come to a fork in the road, you must decide which way to go and then take one or the other branch of the fork. This is what the

Figure 1-7   *Basic Structures of Programming Languages*

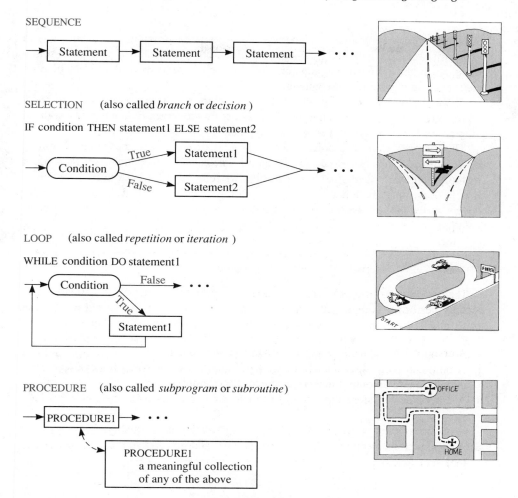

SEQUENCE

SELECTION   (also called *branch* or *decision*)

IF condition THEN statement1 ELSE statement2

LOOP   (also called *repetition* or *iteration*)

WHILE condition DO statement1

PROCEDURE   (also called *subprogram* or *subroutine*)

PROCEDURE1
a meaningful collection
of any of the above

computer does when it encounters a *selection* (sometimes called a *branch* or *decision*) in a program. Sometimes you have to go around the block several times to find a place to park. The computer does the same sort of thing when it encounters a *loop* in a program.

A *procedure* is a process that consists of multiple steps. Every day, for example, you follow a procedure to get from home to work. It makes sense, then, for someone to give you directions to a meeting by saying, "Go to the office, then go four blocks west"—without repeating all the steps you have to take to get to the office. Procedures allow us to write parts of our programs separately and then assemble them into final form. They can greatly simplify the task of writing large programs.

What Is a Computer?

You can learn a programming language, how to write programs, and how to run (execute) programs without knowing much about computers. But if you know something about the parts of a computer, you can better understand the effect of each instruction in a programming language.

There are five basic components in most computers: the memory unit, the arithmetic/logic unit, the control unit, input devices, and output devices. Figure 1-8 is a stylized diagram of the basic components of a computer.

The **memory unit** is an ordered sequence of storage cells, each capable of holding a piece of data. It is like an old-fashioned post office with pigeonholes for mail. Each memory cell has a distinct address to which we refer in order to store information in it or retrieve information from it. These storage cells are called *memory cells,* or *memory locations.** The memory unit holds data (input data or the product of computation) and instructions (programs) (see Figure 1-9).

Memory Unit   Internal data storage in a computer.

The part of the computer that follows instructions is called the **central processing unit (cpu).** The central processing unit is actually two components. The **arithmetic/logic unit (ALU)** performs arithmetic operations (addition, subtraction, multiplication, and division) and logical operations (comparing two values). The **control unit** controls the actions of the other components, so that programs are executed in sequence.

*The memory unit is also referred to as RAM, an acronym for random access memory (because we can access any location at random).

Figure 1-8
Basic Components
of a Computer

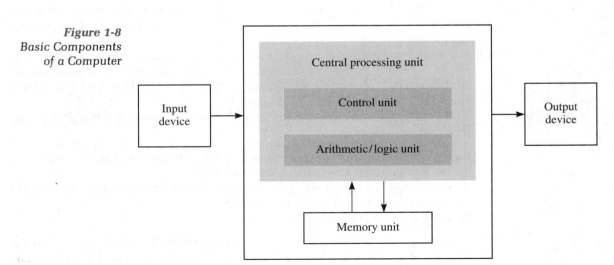

Figure 1-9
Memory

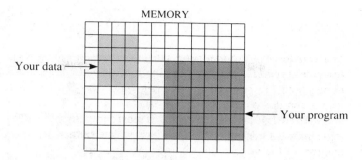

MEMORY

Your data

Your program

Central Processing Unit (CPU)   The part of the computer that executes the instructions (program) stored in memory; made up of the arithmetic/logic unit and the control unit.

Arithmetic/Logic Unit (ALU)   The component of the central processing unit that performs arithmetic and logical operations.

Control Unit   The component of the central processing unit that controls the actions of the other components so that instructions (the program) are executed in sequence.

For us to use computers, we must have some way of getting data into and out of them. **Input/Output (I/O) devices** accept data to be processed (input) and present data that have been processed (output).

Input/Output (I/O) Devices   The parts of the computer that accept data to be processed (input) and present the results of that processing (output).

A keyboard is a common input device. Another is a *mouse*, a "pointing" device. A video display is a common output device, as are liquid crystal display (LCD) screens and printers.

For the most part, computers simply move and combine data in memory. The differences among various computers basically involve the size of their memories and the speed with which data can be recalled, the efficiency with which data can be moved or combined, and limitations on I/O devices.

When a program is executing, the computer proceeds through a series of steps, the *fetch-execute cycle:*

1. The control unit retrieves *(fetches)* the next coded instruction from memory.
2. The instruction is translated into control signals.
3. The control signals tell the appropriate unit (arithmetic/logic unit, memory, I/O device) to perform *(execute)* the instruction.
4. The sequence repeats from step 1.

Computers can have a wide variety of **peripheral devices** (see Figure 1-10). An **auxiliary storage device,** or *secondary storage device,* holds coded data for the com-

Figure 1-10
Peripheral
Devices

(a) Keyboard

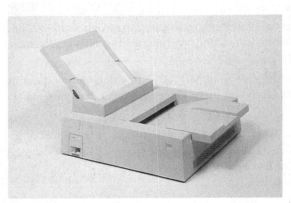

(b) Scanner

(c) 3.5" Disk Drive

(d) Magnetic Tape Drive

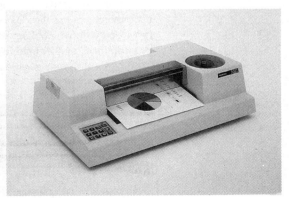

(e) Plotter

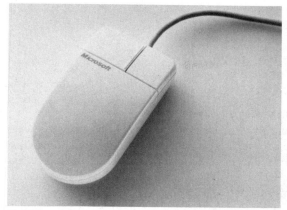

(*f*) Mouse

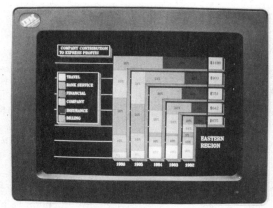

(*g*) Monitor

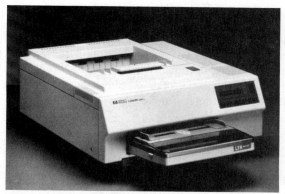

(*h*) Laser Printer

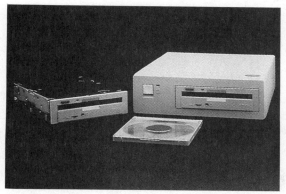

(*i*) CD Rom Drives

puter until we actually want to use the data. Instead of inputting data every time, we can input it once and have the computer store it on an auxiliary storage device. Whenever we need to use the data, we tell the computer to transfer the data from the auxiliary storage device to its memory. Typical auxiliary storage devices are magnetic tape drives and disk drives. A *magnetic tape drive* is like a tape recorder. A *disk drive* is a cross between a compact disk player and a tape recorder. It uses a thin disk made out of magnetic material. A read/write head (similar to the record/playback head in a tape recorder) travels across the spinning disk, retrieving or recording data.

Together, all of these physical components are known as **hardware.** The programs that allow the hardware to operate are called **software.** Hardware is usually fixed in design; software is easily changed. In fact, the ease with which software can be manipulated is what makes the computer such a versatile, powerful tool.

*B*ackground Information

The Origins and Features of Pascal

Pascal was designed by Swiss computer scientist Niklaus Wirth in 1968, then revised in 1972. In 1984 Wirth received the prestigious Turing Award, the highest honor in computer science, in part for his work on Pascal.

Wirth created Pascal to avoid the problems of the programming languages in widespread use in the late 1960s. It includes their better features and more, in a streamlined format that is easy to use. He named the language after the famous French mathematician Blaise Pascal (1623–1662), who is credited with designing an early mechanical calculating machine, a forerunner of the modern computer.

Originally intended as a teaching tool for programming concepts, Pascal is widely used today in business, industry, and personal computing. The language is simple to learn, yet embodies a wide range of programming concepts. Pascal encourages programmers to write programs that are clear and that can be easily understood by other programmers.

Once you've learned Pascal, you will find it easy to learn FORTRAN, COBOL, BASIC, Modula-2, Ada, and other programming languages. Modula-2 and Ada are relatively new languages based directly on Pascal. In fact Wirth designed Modula-2 as a successor to Pascal. Both Modula-2 and Ada incorporate sophisticated features that go well beyond the scope of an introductory programming course.

Peripheral Device   An input, output, or auxiliary storage device attached to a computer.

Auxiliary Storage Device   A device that stores data in encoded form outside the computer's main memory.

Hardware   The physical components of a computer.

Software   Computer programs; the set of all programs available on a computer.

In addition to our programs, there are programs in the computer that are designed to simplify the user/computer **interface,** making it easier for us to use the machine. The interface between user and computer is a set of I/O devices—for example, a keyboard and screen—that allows the user to communicate with the computer. We work with the keyboard and screen on our side of the interface boundary; wires attached to the keyboard and screen carry the electronic pulses that the computer works with on its side of the interface boundary. At the boundary itself is a mechanism that translates information for the two sides.

Interface   A connecting link at a shared boundary that allows independent systems to meet and act on or communicate with each other.

When we communicate directly with the computer through a keyboard and screen, we are using an **interactive system.** Interactive systems allow direct entry of programs and data and provide immediate feedback to the user. In contrast, *batch systems* require that all data be entered before a program is run, and provide feedback only after a program has been executed. In this text we focus on interactive systems, although in Chapter 3 we discuss file-oriented programs, which share certain similarities with batch systems.

The set of programs that simplifies the user/computer interface and improves the efficiency of processing is called *system software*. It includes the compiler as well as the operating system and the editor (see Figure 1-11). The **operating system** manages all of the computer's resources. It can input programs, call the compiler, execute object programs, and carry out any other system commands. The **editor** is an interactive program used to create and modify source programs or data.

Interactive System   A system that allows direct communication between user and computer.

Operating System   A set of programs that manages all of the computer's resources.

Editor   An interactive program used to create and modify source programs or data.

Figure 1-11
User/Computer
Interface

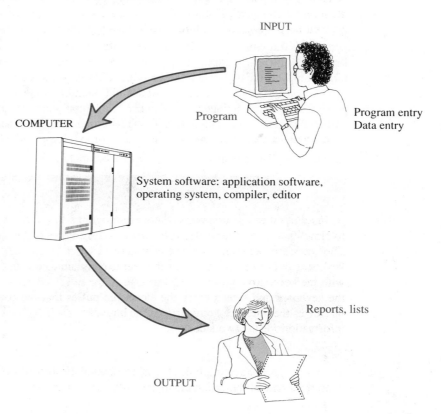

INPUT

COMPUTER

Program

Program entry
Data entry

System software: application software,
operating system, compiler, editor

Reports, lists

OUTPUT

*B*ackground Information

Micros, Minis, and Mainframes

There are many different sizes and kinds of computers. *Mainframes* are very large (they can fill a room!) and very fast. A typical mainframe computer consists of several cabinets full of electronic components. Inside those cabinets are the memory unit, the central processing unit, and input/output units. It's easy to spot the various peripheral devices: Separate cabinets are labeled "disk drive" and "tape drive." Other units are obviously terminals and printers.

At the other end of the spectrum are *microcomputers,* or *personal computers (PCs).* These are so small that they fit comfortably on top of a desk. Because of their size, it can be difficult to spot the individual parts inside personal computers. Many PCs are just a single box, with a screen, a keyboard, and sometimes a mouse. You have to open up the case to see the central processing unit, which is usually just a large integrated circuit.

Personal computers rarely have tape drives; most operate with disk drives and printers. The disk drives for personal computers typically hold much less data than those used with mainframes. Similarly, the printers that are attached to personal computers typically are much slower than those used with mainframes.

Between mainframes and personal computers are *minicomputers.* These intermediate-sized computer systems are less expensive than mainframes and more powerful than personal computers. Minicomputers are sometimes set up for use primarily by one person at a time, in a form called a *workstation.* A typical workstation looks very much like a PC. In fact, as PCs have grown more powerful and workstations have become more compact, the distinction between them has begun to fade.

One last type of computer that we should mention is the *supercomputer,* the most powerful class of computer in existence. Supercomputers typically are designed to perform scientific and engineering calculations on immense sets of data with great speed. They are very expensive, and so are not in widespread use.

Mainframe Computer

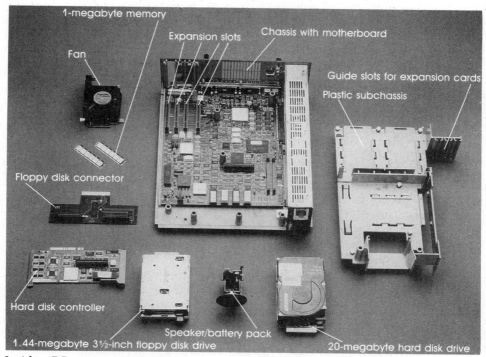

1-megabyte memory

Fan

Expansion slots

Chassis with motherboard

Guide slots for expansion cards

Plastic subchassis

Floppy disk connector

Hard disk controller

Speaker/battery pack

1.44-megabyte 3½-inch floppy disk drive

20-megabyte hard disk drive

Inside a PC, system unit broken down

Personal Computer, IBM PS/2 Model 50Z

Personal Computer, Mac II

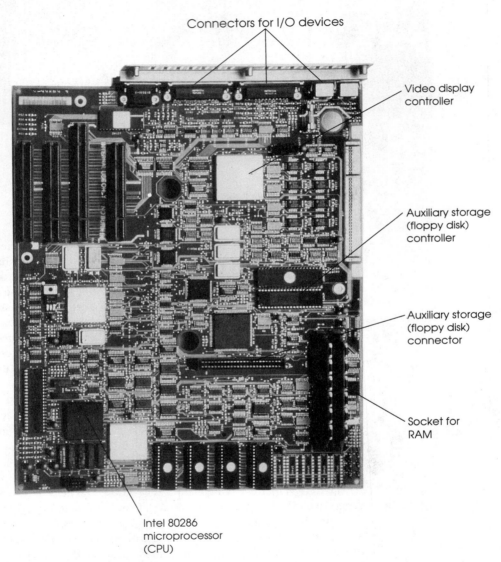

Connectors for I/O devices

Video display controller

Auxiliary storage (floppy disk) controller

Auxiliary storage (floppy disk) connector

Socket for RAM

Intel 80286 microprocessor (CPU)

Inside a PC, close-up of a system board

Workstation

Supercomputer

Problem-Solving Techniques

You solve problems every day, often unaware of the process you are going through. In a learning environment, you usually are given most of the information you need: a clear statement of the problem, the necessary input, the required output. In real life, the process is not always so simple. You often have to define the problem yourself, and then decide what you have to work with and what the results should be.

After you understand and analyze a problem, you must come up with a solution—an algorithm. Earlier we defined an algorithm as a step-by-step procedure for solving a problem in a finite amount of time. Although you work with algorithms all the time, most of your experience with them is in the context of *following* them. You follow a recipe, play a game, assemble a toy, take medicine.

In the problem-solving phase of computer programming, you will be *designing* algorithms, not following them. This means you will have to be conscious of the strategies you use to solve problems in order to apply them to programming problems.

Ask Questions

If you are given a task orally, you ask questions—When? Why? Where?—until you understand exactly what you have to do. If your instructions are written, you might put question marks in the margin; underline a word or sentence; or in some other way indicate that the task is not clear. Your questions may be answered by a later paragraph, or you might have to discuss them with the person who gave you the task.

These are some of the questions you will be asking in the context of programming:

- What do I have to work with; that is, what are my data?
- What does the data look like?
- How much data is there?
- How will I know when I have processed all the data?

- What should my output look like?
- How many times is the process going to be repeated?
- What special error conditions might come up?

Look for Things That Are Familiar

Never reinvent the wheel. If a solution exists, use it. If you've solved the same or a similar problem before, just repeat your solution. People are good at recognizing similar situations. We don't have to learn how to go to the store to buy milk, then to buy eggs, then to buy candy. We know that going to the store is the same; only what we buy is different.

In programming you will see certain problems again and again in different guises. A good programmer immediately recognizes a subtask he or she has solved before and plugs in the solution. For example, finding the daily high and low temperatures is really the same problem as finding the highest and lowest grades on a test. You want the largest and smallest values in a set of numbers (see Figure 1-12).

Solve by Analogy

Often a problem reminds you of a similar problem you have seen before. You may find solving the problem at hand easier if you remember how you solved the other problem. In other words, draw an analogy between the two problems. For example, a solution to a perspective projection problem from an art class might help you figure out how to compute the distance to a landmark when you are on a cross-country hike. As you work your way through the new problem, you will come across things that are different than they were in the old problem, but usually these are just details that you can deal with one at a time.

Figure 1-12
Look for Things
That Are Familiar

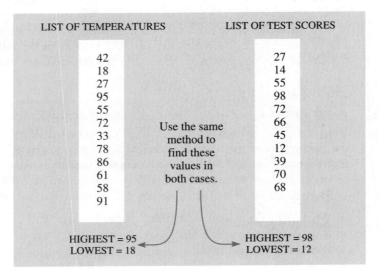

LIST OF TEMPERATURES

LIST OF TEST SCORES

42	27
18	14
27	55
95	98
55	72
72	66
33	45
78	12
86	39
61	70
58	68
91	

Use the same method to find these values in both cases.

HIGHEST = 95
LOWEST = 18

HIGHEST = 98
LOWEST = 12

Figure 1-13
Analogy

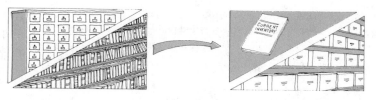

A library catalog system may give some insight into how to organize a parts inventory.

Analogy is really just a broader application of the strategy of looking for things that are familiar. When you are trying to find an algorithm for solving a problem, don't limit yourself to computer-oriented solutions. Step back and try to get a larger view of the problem. Don't worry if your analogy doesn't match perfectly—the only reason for starting with an analogy is that it gives you a place to start (see Figure 1-13). The best programmers are people who have broad experience solving all kinds of problems.

Means-Ends Analysis

Often the beginning state and the ending state are given; the problem is to define a set of actions that can be used to get from one to the other. Suppose you want to go from Boston, Massachusetts, to Austin, Texas. You know the beginning state (Boston) and the ending state (Austin). The problem is how to get from one to the other.

In this example, you have lots of choices. You can fly, walk, hitchhike, ride a bike, or whatever. The method you choose depends on your circumstances. If you're in a hurry, you'll probably decide to fly.

Once you've narrowed down the set of actions, you have to work out the details. It may help to establish intermediate goals that are easier to meet than the overall goal. Let's say there is a really cheap, direct flight to Austin out of Newark, New Jersey. You might decide to divide the trip into legs, Boston to Newark and then Newark to Austin. Your intermediate goal is to get from Boston to Newark. Now you only have to examine the means of meeting that intermediate goal (see Figure 1-14).

The overall strategy of means-ends analysis is to define the ends and then to analyze your means of getting between them. The process translates easily to computer pro-

Figure 1-14
Means-Ends
Analysis

Start: Boston **Goal:** Austin	**Means:** *Fly*, walk, hitchhike, bike, drive, sail, bus
Start: Boston **Goal:** Austin	**Revised Means:** Fly to Chicago, then Austin; *fly to Newark, then Austin;* fly to Atlanta, then Austin
Start: Boston **Goal:** Austin **Intermediate goal:** Newark	**Means:** *Commuter flight,* walk, hitchhike, bike, drive, sail, bus
Solution: Take commuter flight to Newark and then catch cheap flight to Austin	

Figure 1-15
Divide and Conquer

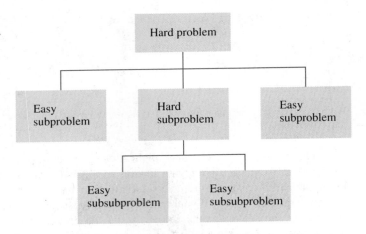

gramming. You begin by writing down what the input is and what the output should be. Then you consider the actions a computer can perform and choose a sequence of actions that can transform the data into the results.

Divide and Conquer

We often break up large problems into smaller units that are easier to handle. Cleaning the whole house may seem overwhelming; cleaning the rooms one at a time seems much more manageable. The same principle applies to programming. We break up a large problem into smaller pieces that we can solve individually (see Figure 1-15). In fact the top-down methodology we describe in Chapter 3 is based on the principle of divide and conquer.

The Building-Block Approach

Another way of attacking large problems is to see if there are any existing solutions for smaller pieces of the problem. It may be possible to put some of these solutions together end to end to solve most of the big problem. This strategy is really just a combination of the look-for-familiar-things and divide-and-conquer approaches. You look at the big problem and see that it can be divided into smaller problems for which solutions already exist. Solving the big problem is just a matter of putting the existing solutions together, like mortaring together blocks to form a wall (see Figure 1-16).

Merging Solutions

Another way to combine existing solutions is to merge them on a step-by-step basis. For example, to compute the average of a list of values, we must both sum and count the values. If we already have separate solutions for summing values and for counting values, we can combine them. But if we first do the summing and then do the counting, we have to read the list twice. We can save steps if we merge these two solutions: read a value and then add it to the running total and add 1 to our count before going on to

Figure 1-16   *Building-Block Approach*

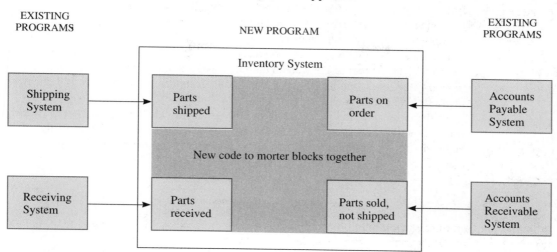

the next value. Whenever the solutions to subproblems duplicate steps, you should think about merging them instead of joining them end to end.

Mental Blocks: The Fear of Starting

Writers are all too familiar with the experience of staring at a blank page, not knowing where to begin. Programmers have the same difficulty when they first tackle a big problem. They look at the problem and it seems overwhelming.

Remember that you always have a place to begin solving any problem: Write it down on paper in your own words, so that you understand it. Once you begin to try to paraphrase the problem, you can focus on each of the subparts individually instead of trying to tackle the entire problem at once. This process gives you a clearer picture of the overall problem. It helps you see pieces of the problem that look familiar or that are analogous to other problems you have solved. And it pinpoints areas where something is unclear, where you need more information.

As you write down a problem, you tend to group things together into small understandable chunks, which may be natural places to split the problem up, to divide and conquer. Your description of the problem may collect all of the information about data and results into one place for easy reference. Then you will be able to see the beginning and ending states necessary for means-ends analysis.

Most mental blocks are caused by not really understanding the problem. Rewriting the problem in your own words is a good way to focus on the subparts of the problem, one at a time, and to understand what is required for a solution.

Algorithmic Problem Solving

Coming up with a step-by-step procedure for solving a particular problem is not always cut and dried. In fact it is usually a trial-and-error process requiring several attempts and refinements. We test each attempt to see if it really solves the problem. If it does, fine. If it doesn't, we try again. You will typically use a combination of all of the techniques we've described to solve any nontrivial problem.

Remember that the computer can only do certain things (see p. 12). Your primary concern, then, is how to make the computer transform, manipulate, calculate, or process the input data to produce the wanted output. If you keep in mind the allowable instructions in your programming language, you won't design an algorithm that is difficult or impossible to code.

In the case study below we develop a program for calculating employees' weekly wages. It will give you an idea of the thought processes involved in writing an algorithm and coding it as a program, and will show you what a complete Pascal program looks like.

PROBLEM-SOLVING CASE STUDY

An Algorithm for a Company Payroll

Problem: A small company needs an interactive program (the payroll clerk will input the data) to figure its weekly payroll. The input data and each employee's wages should be saved in a secondary storage file, and the total wages for the week should be displayed on the screen so that the payroll clerk can transfer the appropriate amount into the payroll account.

Discussion: At first glance, this seems like a simple problem. But if you think about how you would do it by hand, you see that you need to ask questions about the specifics of the process: What employee data is input? How are wages computed? In what file should the results be stored? How does the clerk indicate that all of the data has been entered?

- The data for each employee includes an employee identification number, the employee's hourly pay rate, and the hours worked that week.
- Wages equal the employee's pay rate times the number of hours worked up to 40 hours. If an employee worked more than 40 hours, wages equal the employee's pay rate times 40 hours, plus one and a half times the employee's regular pay rate times the number of hours worked above 40.
- The results should be stored in a file called Pay_File.
- There is no employee number 0, so the clerk can indicate the end of the data by entering a 0 when asked for an employee number.

Let's apply the **divide-and-conquer** approach to this problem. There are three obvious steps in almost any problem of this type:

1. Get the data.
2. Compute the results.
3. Output the results.

First we need to get the data. We need three pieces of data for each employee: employee identification number, hourly pay rate, and number of hours worked. So that the clerk will know when to enter each value, we must have the computer output a message that indicates when it is ready to accept each of the values (this is called a *prompting message,* or a *prompt*). To input the data, then, these steps must be taken:

Prompt the user for the employee number (put a message
   on the screen)
Read the employee number
Prompt the user for the employee's hourly pay rate
Read the pay rate
Prompt the user for the number of hours worked
Read the number of hours worked

The next step is to compute the wages. Let's apply **means-ends analysis.** Our starting point is the set of data values that was input; our wanted ending, the payroll for the week. We know that if there is no overtime, wages are simply the pay rate times the number of hours worked. If the number of hours worked is greater than 40, however, wages are 40 times the pay rate, plus the number of overtime hours times one and a half times the pay rate. The number of overtime hours is computed by subtracting 40 from the total number of hours worked. To figure the wages, then, the following steps must be taken:

If hours worked is greater than 40.0,
   then
      wages = (40.0 × pay rate) +
             (hours worked − 40.0) × 1.5 × pay rate
   otherwise
      wages = hours worked × pay rate

The last step, outputting the results, is simply a matter of having the computer write the employee number, the pay rate, the number of hours worked, and the wages onto Pay_File:

Write the employee number, pay rate, hours worked, and wages on the list.

There are two things we've overlooked. This process must be repeated for each employee, and the total wages for the week must be computed. Let's use the **building-block approach** to combine our three main steps (getting the data, computing the wages, outputting the results) with a structure that repeats the steps for each employee as long as the employee number is not 0. When the employee number is 0, this structure will skip to the end of the algorithm. Next we'll insert a step just after the wages are computed that adds them to a running total.

Finally, there are a couple of housekeeping chores that we must take care of. Before we can start processing, we must prepare the output file to receive the results and set the running total to zero; and at the end of the algorithm, we must tell the computer to stop processing.

What follows is the complete algorithm. Calculating the wages is written as a separate procedure that is defined before the start of the main algorithm. Notice that the algorithm is simply a very precise description of the same steps you would follow to do this process by hand.

Procedure for Calculating Pay

If hours worked is greater than 40.0,
>   then
>>   wages = (40.0 × pay rate) +
>>   (hours worked − 40.0) × 1.5 × pay rate
>   otherwise
>>   wages = hours worked × pay rate

Main Algorithm

Prepare to write a list of the employees' wages (open File Pay_File)
Set the total payroll to zero
Prompt the user for the employee number (put a message on the screen)
Read the employee number
As long as the employee number is not 0, repeat the following steps:
>   Prompt the user for the employee's hourly pay rate
>   Read the pay rate
>   Prompt the user for the number of hours worked
>   Read the number of hours worked
>   Perform the procedure for calculating pay (above)
>   Add the employee's wages to the total payroll
>   Write the employee number, pay rate, hours worked, and wages on the list (File
>   Pay_File)
>   Prompt the user for the employee number
>   Read the employee number
When an employee number equal to 0 is read, continue with the following steps:
>   Write the total company payroll on the screen
>   Indicate that the list of wages is complete (close Pay_File)
>   Stop

Before we implement this algorithm, it should be tested. Programming Warm-Up Exercise 3 asks you to carry out the test.

What follows is the Pascal program for this algorithm. It's here just to give you an idea of what you'll be learning. If you've had no previous exposure to programming, you probably won't understand most of the program. Don't worry; you will soon. In fact, throughout this book as we introduce each new construct, we refer you back to Program Payroll. One more thing. The statements enclosed in the symbols (* and *) are called comments. They are here to help you understand the program; the compiler ignores them.

```
PROGRAM Payroll (Input, Output, Pay_File);

(* This program computes each employee's wages and the total company payroll *)

CONST
   Max_Hours = 40.0;      (* Maximum normal work hours *)
   Overtime = 1.5;        (* Overtime pay rate factor  *)

VAR
   Pay_Rate,              (* Employee's pay rate    *)
   Hours,                 (* Hours worked           *)
   Wages,                 (* Wages earned           *)
   Total:                 (* Total company payroll  *)
     Real;
   Emp_Num:               (* Employee ID number     *)
     Integer;
   Pay_File:              (* Company payroll file   *)
     Text;


(* ******************************************************************* )


PROCEDURE Calc_Pay(    Pay_Rate,   (* Employee's pay rate *)
                       Hours:      (* Hours worked        *)
                         Real;
                   VAR Wages:      (* Wages earned        *)
                         Real);

(* Calc_Pay computes wages from the employee's pay rate *)
(* and the hours worked, taking overtime into account   *)

BEGIN (* Calc_Pay *)
  IF Hours > Max_Hours                       (* Check for overtime *)
    THEN                            (* Compute wages if overtime *)
      Wages := (Max_Hours * Pay_Rate) +
              (Hours - Max_Hours) * Pay_Rate * Overtime
    ELSE
      Wages := Hours * Pay_Rate      (* Compute wages if no overtime *)
END;  (* Calc_Pay *)


(* ******************************************************************* )
```

PROBLEM-SOLVING CASE STUDY cont'd.

```
BEGIN (* Payroll *)
  Assign(Pay_File, 'PAYFILE.DAT');        (* Open file Pay_File *)
  Rewrite(Pay_File);                      (* Open File Pay_File *)
  Total := 0.0;                      (* Initialize Total to zero *)
  Write('Enter employee number: ');                 (* Prompt *)
  Readln(Emp_Num);                  (* Read employee ID number *)
  WHILE Emp_Num <> 0 DO          (* While employee number <> 0 *)
    BEGIN
      Write('Enter pay rate: ')                      (* Prompt *)
      Readln(Pay_Rate);               (* Read hourly pay rate *)
      Write('Enter hours worked: ');                 (* Prompt *)
      Readln(Hours);                     (* Read hours worked *)
      Calc_Pay(Pay_Rate, Hours, Wages);    (* Compute wages *)
      Total := Total + Wages;          (* Add wages to total *)
      Writeln(Pay_File, Emp_Num, Pay_Rate,  (* Put results in Pay_File *)
              Hours, Wages);
      Write('Enter employee number: ');              (* Prompt *)
      Readln(Emp_Num)                     (* Read ID number *)
    END;
  Writeln('Total payroll is ',         (* Print total payroll on screen *)
          Total:10:2);
  Close(Pay_File)                       (* Close file Pay_File *)
END.  (* Payroll *)
```

Summary

We think nothing of turning on the television and sitting down to watch it. It's a communication tool we use to enhance our lives. Computers are becoming as common as televisions, just a normal part of our lives. And like televisions, computers are based on complex principles but are designed for easy use.

Computers are dumb; they must be told what to do. A true computer error is extremely rare (usually due to a component malfunction or an electrical fault). Because we tell the computer what to do, most errors in computer-generated output are really human errors.

Computer programming is the process of planning a sequence of steps for a computer to follow. It involves a problem-solving phase and an implementation phase. After analyzing a problem, we develop and test a general solution (algorithm). This general solution becomes a specific solution, our program, when we write it in a high-level programming language. The sequence of instructions that makes up our program is then compiled into machine code, the language the computer uses. After correcting any errors or "bugs" that show up during testing, our program is ready to use.

Add 3 eggs plus 1 extra egg yolk to the bowl

Melt 3 squares of unsweetened chocolate and add to the mixture in the bowl

Beat the mixture for 1 minute at medium speed

Pour the batter into the tube pan

Put the pan into the oven and bake for 1 hour and 10 minutes

Perform the test for doneness described in the introduction to the chapter on cakes

Repeat the test once each minute until the cake is done

Remove the pan from the oven and allow the cake to cool for 2 hours

Follow the instructions for removing the cake from the pan, given in the introduction to the chapter on cakes

Sprinkle powdered sugar over the cracks on top of the cake just before serving

4. Put a check next to each item below that is a peripheral device.
   - _____ a. Disk drive
   - _____ b. Arithmetic/logic unit
   - _____ c. Magnetic tape drive
   - _____ d. Printer
   - _____ e. Card reader
   - _____ f. Memory
   - _____ g. Auxiliary storage device
   - _____ h. Control unit
   - _____ i. Terminal

5. Next to each item below, indicate whether it is hardware (H) or software (S).
   - _____ a. Disk drive
   - _____ b. Memory
   - _____ c. Compiler
   - _____ d. Arithmetic/logic unit
   - _____ e. Editor
   - _____ f. Operating system
   - _____ g. Object program
   - _____ h. Terminal
   - _____ i. Central processing unit

6. Means-ends analysis is a problem-solving strategy.
   a. What are three things you must know in order to apply means-ends analysis to a problem?
   b. What is one way of combining this technique with the divide-and-conquer strategy?

7. Show how you would use the divide-and-conquer approach to solve the problem of finding a job.

▪ Programming Warm-Up Exercises

1. Write an algorithm for driving from where you live to the nearest airport that has regularly scheduled flights. Restrict yourself to a vocabulary of 36 words plus numbers and place names. You must select the appropriate set of words for this task. An example of a vocabulary is given in Appendix A, the list of reserved words in the Pascal programming language. Notice that there are just 36 words in that list. The purpose of this exercise is to give you practice writing simple, exact instructions in an equally small vocabulary.

2. Write an algorithm for making a peanut butter and jelly sandwich, using a vocabulary of just 36 words (you choose the words). Assume that all of the ingredients are in the refrigerator and that the necessary tools are in a drawer under the kitchen counter. The instructions must be very simple and exact because the person making the sandwich has no knowledge of food preparation and takes every word literally.

3. Use the following data set to test the payroll algorithm presented on page 30. Follow each step of the algorithm just as it is written, as if you were a computer. Then check your results by hand to be sure that the algorithm is correct.

ID Number	Pay Rate	Hours Worked
327	8.30	48
201	6.60	40
29	12.50	40
166	9.25	51
254	7.00	32
0		

Handwritten annotations:
332+99.60 = 431.60
264
500 370 +152.65 = 522.63

*T*heoretical Foundations

Metalanguages

Metalanguage is the word *language* with the prefix *meta*, which means "beyond" or "more comprehensive." A metalanguage is a language that goes beyond a normal language by allowing us to speak precisely about that language. It is a language for talking about languages.

One of the oldest computer-oriented metalanguages is the *Backus-Naur Form (BNF)*, which is named for John Backus and Peter Naur, who developed it in 1960. BNF syntax definitions are written out using letters, numbers, and special symbols. For example, an integer number in Pascal must be at least one digit, may or may not be more than one digit, and may or may not have a sign in front of it. The BNF definition of an integer number in Pascal is

<integer> ::= <unsigned-integer> | <sign> <unsigned-integer>
<sign> ::= + | –
<unsigned-integer> ::= <digit> | <digit> <unsigned-integer>
<digit> ::= 0 | 1 | 2 | 3 | 4 | 5 | 6 | 7 | 8 | 9

where the symbol ::= is read "is defined as," the symbol | means "or," the symbols < and > are used to enclose words called *nonterminal symbols* (symbols that still need to be defined), and everything else is called a *terminal symbol*.

The first line of the definition reads: "An integer is defined as an unsigned integer or a sign followed by an unsigned integer." This line contains nonterminal symbols that must be defined. In the second line, the nonterminal symbol <sign> is defined as a plus sign or a minus sign, both of which are terminal symbols. The third line defines the nonterminal symbol <unsigned-integer> as either a <digit> or a <digit> followed by another <unsigned integer>. The self-reference in the definition is a roundabout way of saying that an unsigned integer can be a series of one or more digits. In the last line, <digit> is defined as any one of the numeric characters 0 through 9.

BNF is an extremely simple language, but that simplicity leads to syntax definitions that can be long and difficult to read. An alternative metalanguage, the *syntax diagram*, is easier to follow. It uses arrows to indicate how symbols can be combined. Appendix E shows the syntax diagrams that define Pascal. Here are the syntax diagrams that define an integer and digit in Pascal:

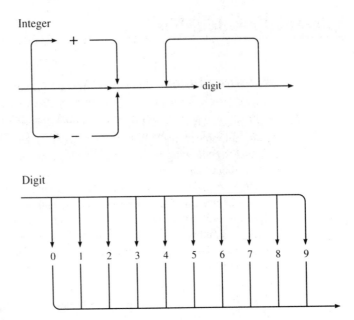

To read the diagrams, start at the left and follow the arrows. When you come to a branch, take any one of the branch paths. A lowercase word is a nonterminal symbol.

The first diagram shows that an integer can consist of an optional plus or minus sign followed by one or more digits. The second diagram defines the nonterminal symbol *digit* to be any one of the numeric characters. Using BNF, each nonterminal symbol must be defined separately. Here, the second syntax diagram can be combined with the first.

Obviously syntax diagrams are easier to interpret than BNF definitions, but they still can be difficult to read. In this text, we introduce a new metalanguage, called a *syntax template*. Syntax templates show at a glance the form a Pascal construct takes.

One final note: Metalanguages only show how to write instructions that the compiler can translate. They do not define what those instructions do (their semantics). Formal languages for defining the semantics of a programming language exist, but they are beyond the scope of this text. Throughout this book, we describe the semantics of Pascal in English.

Syntax Templates

In this book, we write the syntax rules for Pascal using a metalanguage called a *syntax template*. A syntax template is a generic example of the Pascal construct being defined. Graphic conventions show which portions are optional or can be repeated. Another template can be substituted for a word in lowercase. A **boldface** word or symbol is written in the Pascal construct just as it is in the template.

Let's look at an example. This template defines an integer in Pascal:

```
First_sixty_three_characters_of_this_identifier_are_duplicated_A

First_sixty_three_characters_of_this_identifier_are_duplicated_B
```

Program Payroll in Chapter 1 uses the user-defined identifiers listed below. (The other identifiers in the program are predefined in Pascal.) Notice that we chose the names to convey how the identifiers are used.

Identifier	*How It Is Used*
Payroll	The name of the program
Max_Hours	Maximum normal work hours
Overtime	Overtime pay rate factor
Pay_Rate	An employee's hourly pay rate
Hours	The number of hours an employee worked
Wages	An employee's weekly wages
Total	The sum of weekly wages for all employees (total company payroll)
Emp_Num	An employee's identification number
Pay_File	The output file (where the employee's number, pay rate, hours, and wages are written)

*M*atters of Style

Using Meaningful, Readable Identifiers

The names we use to refer to things in our programs are totally meaningless to the computer. The computer functions the same whether we call the value 3.14159265 Pi or Cake, as long as we always call it the same thing. However, it is much easier for somebody to figure out how a program works if the names we choose for elements actually tell something about them. Whenever you have to make up a name for something in a program, try to pick one that will be meaningful to a person reading the program.

Turbo Pascal allows you to write names with upper- and lowercase letters. It treats uppercase and lowercase letters the same. Turbo Pascal would consider the identifiers

```
PART_NUMBER        part_number        PaRt_NuMbEr        Part_Number
```

to be the same. As you can see, the last of these forms is the easiest to read. In this book we use both uppercase and lowercase letters and underscores in identifiers. We strongly urge you to do the same.

Whatever you use, be consistent throughout a program. Even though it makes no difference to the computer, a person reading the program will find inconsistent capitalization confusing.

Now that we've seen how to write identifiers, we look at some of the things that Pascal allows us to name.

Data and Data Types

A computer program operates on data (stored internally in memory, stored externally on disk or tape, or input from a keyboard, text scanner, or electrical sensor) and produces output. In Pascal each piece of data must be of a specific type. The **data type** determines how the data is represented in the computer and the kinds of processing the computer can perform on it.

Data Type   A specific class of data.

Some types of data are used so frequently that Pascal defines them for us. But most data types must be defined by the programmer. We use the standard (built-in) data types until Chapter 10, where we show you how to define your own.

Pascal defines four simple types of data. You already are familiar with three of them: integer numbers, real numbers, and characters. You'll soon be equally familiar with the fourth type, Boolean.

Integer   Integers are positive or negative whole numbers; they have no fractional part. They are made up of an optional sign and one or more digits:

+22   −16   1   −426   0   4600

When there is no sign, we assume the number is positive. Commas are not allowed.

Theoretically, integers can have any number of digits; practically, the computer limits their size. Because this limit varies among machines, Pascal has a predefined identifier, *MaxInt*, whose value is set to the largest integer number that can be represented in a given computer. In Turbo Pascal, MaxInt is equal to 32767, so the range of integers allowed is

−MaxInt−1   through   MaxInt

or

−32768   through   32767

EmpNum, the identifier for the employee number in Program Payroll, is of data type Integer.

Real   Real numbers are decimal numbers. That is, they have an integer part and a fractional part, with a decimal point in between. They also can have an exponent, as in scientific notation. (In scientific notation, a number is written as a decimal value multiplied by a power of 10 to indicate the actual position of the decimal point.) Instead of writing 3.504×10^{12}, however, we write 3.504E+12. Here are some examples of real numbers:

Background Information

Data Storage

Where does a program get the data it needs to operate? Data is stored in the computer's memory. Remember that memory is divided into a large number of separate locations or cells, each of which can hold a piece of data. Each memory location has an address we refer to when we store or retrieve data. We can visualize memory as a set of post office boxes, with the box numbers as the addresses used to designate particular locations.

Of course the actual "address" of each location in memory is a binary number in a machine language code. In Pascal we use identifiers to name memory locations, then the compiler translates them for us. This is one of the advantages of a high-level programming language: It frees us from having to keep track of the actual memory locations in which our data and instructions are stored.

$$18.0 \quad 127.54 \quad -0.57 \quad 193145.8523 \quad 1.74536E-12 \quad 3.652442E2$$

We talk more about real numbers in Chapter 8. But there is one more thing you should know about them now. When you use real numbers in a program or input them as data, always use a decimal point with at least one digit on either side. If a number doesn't have a fractional part, put a zero to the right of the decimal point. If it doesn't have an integer part, put a zero to the left of the decimal point. (So zero is written 0.0.) The only exception to this rule is when a number is written in E notation without a decimal point, as it is in the last of the valid examples below.

Valid	Not Valid
3.1415	.42
−111.011	16.
76.43	.2
0.43	.0
−1.0	0.
276E14	276.E14

In Program Payroll, the identifiers Max_Hours, Overtime, Pay_Rate, Hours, Wages, and Total are all Real because they are identifiers for data items that may have decimal points.

Char   Data type Char describes data consisting of one alphanumeric character—a letter, a digit, or a special symbol:

'A'   'a'   '8'   '2'   '+'   '−'   '$'   '?'   '*'   ' '

Each machine has a *character set,* the set of alphanumeric characters it can represent. (See Appendix J for some sample character sets.) Notice that each character is enclosed in single quotes. The Pascal compiler needs the quotes to differentiate between the character data '8' or '+' and the integer 8 or the addition sign. Notice also that the blank, ' ', is a character.

You can't add '8' and '3', but you can compare data values of type Char. Each character set is ordered in a *collating sequence.* Although this sequence varies from one machine to another, 'A' is always less than 'B', 'B' is less than 'C', and so forth. And '1' is less than '2', '2' is less than '3', and so on. None of the identifiers in Program Payroll is of type Char.

Boolean   Boolean is a type with just two values: True and False.* We use it to test conditions in a program, to help the computer make decisions. The ability to choose alternative courses of action (selection) is an important part of a programming language, as you'll see in Chapter 4.

Boolean data cannot be read in as data, as the other three types can, but it can be printed out.

Defining Terms: Declarations

Identifiers can be used to name both constants and variables. In other words, an identifier can be the name of a memory location whose contents never change or the name of a memory location whose contents do change.

How do we tell the computer what an identifier represents? With a **declaration,** a statement that associates a name (an identifier) with a description of an element in a

---

*Data type Boolean is named for George Boole (1815–1864), an English mathematician who described a system of logic using variables with just two values, True and False. (See the Background Information box on page 144.)

Pascal program (just as a dictionary definition associates a name with a description of the thing being named). In a declaration we name an identifier and what it represents; the compiler then picks a location in memory that will be associated with the identifier. We don't have to know the actual address of the memory location because the computer automatically keeps track of it for us.

Declaration   A statement that associates an identifier with a process or object so that the user can refer to that process or object by name.

Suppose that when we mail a letter, we just have to put a name on it, that the post office will look up the address. Of course everybody in the world would have to have a different name; otherwise the post office wouldn't be able to figure out whose address was whose. The same is true in Pascal. Each identifier can represent just one thing (except under special circumstances, which we talk about in Chapters 6 and 7). Every identifier you use in a program must be different from any others.

Constants and variables are collectively called *objects*. Both objects and the actual statements (instructions) in a program are stored in various memory locations. Later on, you'll see that a name also can be associated with a group of instructions, what we refer to here as a *process*.

There is a different form of declaration statement for each kind of object or process in Pascal. The forms of declaration for constants and variables are introduced here; others are covered in later chapters.

As a general rule, all identifiers in Pascal must be declared or defined before they are used. This is why all the declarations are grouped together at the beginning of a program, in the *declaration section*. Within the declaration section, the declarations appear in a standard order. Turbo Pascal does not enforce the standard order, but we will follow it in this book. The first identifiers declared are the constants.

Constants   All numbers, integer and real, are constants. So are single characters and series of characters, or *strings*.

```
16   32.3   'A'   'Howdy boys'
```

We use numeric constants as part of arithmetic expressions (as you will see later in this chapter). For example, we can write a statement that adds the constants 5 and 6 and places the result in a variable called Sum. When we use the actual value of a constant in a program, we are using a **literal value** (or *literal*).

Literal Value   Any constant value written in a program.

Notice that character literals and string literals are in single quotes. This is to differentiate between strings and identifiers. 'Amount' (in single quotes) is the character string made up of the letters *A, m, o, u, n,* and *t* in that order. Amount (without the quotes) is an identifier, the name of a place in memory.

Although character and string literals are put in quotes, literal Integers and Reals are not, because there is no chance that they will be confused with identifiers. Why? Because identifiers must start with a letter, and numbers must start with a digit or sign.

An alternative to the literal constant is the **named constant,** which is defined in the declaration section of a program. A named constant is just another way of representing a literal value. Instead of using the literal value in a statement, we give it a name in the declaration section of the program, then use that name in the statement. For example, we can write a statement that multiplies the literal values 3.14159 and 4.5. Or we can define a constant in the declaration section for each of those values, and then use the constant names in the statement. For example, we can use either

$$3.14159 \times 4.5 \quad \text{or} \quad \text{Pi} \times \text{Radius}$$

but the latter is more readable.

Named Constant   A location in memory, referenced by an identifier, where a data value that cannot be changed is stored.

It may seem easier to use the literal value of a constant than to give the constant a name and then refer to it by that name. But in fact named constants make a program easier to read because they make the meaning of literal constants clearer. And named constants also make it easier to change a program later on. In Program Payroll, the named constants Max_Hours and Overtime are defined.

This is the syntax template of the constant definition section:

```
CONST
    identifier = constant-expression;
    identifier = constant-expression;

        .
        .
        .
```

Notice that an equal sign (=) appears between the identifier and the literal value in the definition. In standard Pascal, constant-expressions are always in the form of a literal value or constant identifier. In Turbo Pascal, constant expressions can also include Pascal operators, such as + and − . The syntax of expressions will be discussed later.

This is a valid constant definition section:

```
CONST
   Stars =              '********';
   Blank =              ' ';
   Pi =                 3.14159;
   Interest_Rate =      0.12;
   Tax_Rate =           0.001;
   Effective_Rate =     Interest_Rate * (1.0 - Tax_Rate);
   Max =                20;
   Message =            'Error condition';
```

The reserved word CONST denotes the beginning of a set of constant declarations. **Reserved words** are words that have special meaning in Pascal; they cannot be used as identifiers. (Appendix A lists all of the reserved words in Pascal.) In the programs in this text, we always write reserved words in capital letters to distinguish them from identifiers.

Reserved Word   A word that has special meaning in Pascal; it cannot be used as an identifier.

---

*S*oftware Engineering Tip

Using Named Constants

It's a good idea to use named constants instead of literals. In addition to making your program more readable, it can make it easier to modify. Suppose you wrote a program last year to compute taxes. In several places you used the literal 0.05, which was the sales tax rate at the time. Now the rate has gone up to 0.06. To change your program, you have to locate every literal 0.05 and change it to 0.06. And if 0.05 is used for some other reason—to compute deductions, for example—you have to look at each place where it is used, figure out what it is used for, and then decide whether it needs to be changed.

The process is much simpler if you use a named constant. Instead of using a literal constant, suppose you had defined a named constant, Tax_Rate, with a value of 0.05. To change your program, you would simply change the definition, setting Tax_Rate equal to 0.06. This one modification changes all of the tax rate computations without affecting the other places where 0.05 is used.

Pascal allows us to declare constants with different names but the same value. If a value has different meanings in different parts of a program, it makes sense to define and use a constant with an appropriate name for each meaning.

Named constants also are reliable; they protect us from mistakes. If you mistype a name, the Pascal compiler will tell you that the name has not been defined. On the other hand, even though we recognize that the number 3.14149 is a mistyped version of pi (3.14159), the number is perfectly acceptable to the compiler. It won't warn us that anything is wrong.

Now we turn to variables, the next part of the declaration section.

Variables   A program operates on data. Data is stored in memory. While a program is executing, different values may be stored in the same memory location at different times. This kind of memory location is called a **variable,** and its contents are the *variable value*. The symbolic name that we assign to a variable memory location is the *variable name* or *variable identifier* (see Figure 2-1). In practice we simply refer to the variable name as the *variable*.

Variable   A location in memory, referenced by an identifier, in which a data value that can be changed is stored.

Declaring a variable means specifying both its name and its data type. This tells the compiler to associate a name with a memory location whose contents will be of a specific type (for example, Integer, Real, Char, or Boolean).

Pascal is a strongly typed language. This means that a variable can only contain data values of the type specified in its declaration. If the Pascal compiler comes across instructions that try to store a value of the wrong data type, it gives an error message, usually something like "TYPE MISMATCH."

Here's the syntax template of a variable declaration. Notice that a colon (:) is used between the identifier and the data type in the declaration.

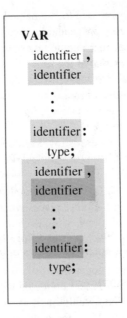

These are valid variable declarations:

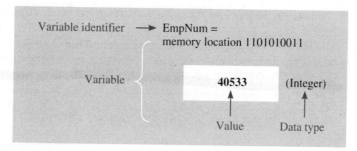

Figure 2-1
Variable

Variable identifier ⟶ EmpNum =
memory location 1101010011

Variable {
40533   (Integer)

Value   Data type

```
VAR
  ID_Num,
  Week_Num:
    Integer;
  Pay_Rate:
    Real;
  Initial,
  Letter:
    Char;
```

Now look at the VAR section of Program Payroll:

```
VAR
  Pay_Rate,      (* Employee's pay rate    *)
  Hours,         (* Hours worked           *)
  Wages,         (* Wages earned           *)
  Total:         (* Total company payroll  *)
    Real;
  Emp_Num:       (* Employee ID number     *)
    Integer;
  Pay_File:      (* Company payroll file   *)
    Text;
```

It tells the compiler to set up locations in memory for four Real variables—Pay_Rate, Hours, Wages, and Total—and to set up one location for an Integer variable called Emp_Num. (We explain type Text in Chapter 3.) Notice how we've used comments to explain to the reader what each variable represents.

Taking Action: Executable Statements

To this point we've looked only at ways of defining objects in a program. Now we'll turn our attention to ways of acting, or performing operations, on those objects.

Assignment The value of a variable is changed through an **assignment statement.** For example,

```
A := 10
```

assigns the value 10 to the variable A (puts the value 10 into the memory location called A).

Assignment Statement   A statement that gives the value of an expression to a variable.

Here's the syntax template of an assignment statement:

variable := expression

The semantics (meaning) of the assignment operator (: =) is "becomes"; the value of the variable *becomes* the value of the expression. Any previous value that the variable had is replaced by the value of the expression.

Only one variable can be on the left-hand side of an assignment statement. An assignment statement is *not* like a math equation ($x + y = z + 4$); the expression (what is on the right-hand side of the assignment operator) is evaluated, and that value is stored in the single variable on the left of the assignment operator.

The value assigned to a variable must be of the same type as the variable. Given the declarations

```
VAR
   Num,
   ID:
     Integer;
   Rate:
     Real;
   Test:
     Boolean;
   Ch:
     Char;
```

the following are valid assignments:

Variable	*Expression*
ID	:= 2856
Rate	:= 0.36
Test	:= True
Ch	:= 'B'
Num	:= ID

These are not valid assignments:

Assignment Statement	Explanation
`ID    := 2.5`	ID is Integer; 2.5 is Real.
`Ch    := 3`	Ch is Char; 3 is an Integer constant.
`Test := 'A'`	Test is Boolean; 'A' is a Char constant.
`Ch    := 'Hello'`	Ch can hold only one character.
`Test := 'True'`	Test is Boolean; 'True' is a string.
`Num   := Rate`	Num is Integer; Rate is Real.

Variables keep their assigned values until they are changed by another assignment statement.

Expressions are made up of constants, variables, and operators. These are all valid expressions:

```
ID + 2     Rate - 6.0     4 - ID     Rate     Test     ID * Num
```

The operators allowed in an expression depend on the data type of the constants and variables in the expression. The *arithmetic operators* are

`+`	Addition
`-`	Subtraction
`*`	Multiplication
`/`	Division (real result)
`DIV`	Integer division (no fractional part)
`MOD`	Modulus (remainder from integer division)

You probably are not familiar with DIV and MOD. Let's look at them more closely. Notice that they are used only with integers. When you divide one integer by another integer, you get an integer quotient and a remainder. DIV gives only the integer quotient; MOD gives only the remainder. (The operand to the right of MOD cannot be negative.)

$$
\begin{array}{rl}
3 & \leftarrow 6\,DIV\,2 \\
2\overline{)6} & \\
\underline{6} & \\
0 & \leftarrow 6\,MOD\,2
\end{array}
\qquad
\begin{array}{rl}
3 & \leftarrow 7\,DIV\,2 \\
2\overline{)7} & \\
\underline{6} & \\
1 & \leftarrow 7\,MOD\,2
\end{array}
$$

Here are some expressions using arithmetic operators and their values:

Expression	Value
3 + 6	9
3 - 6	-3
2 * 3	6
8 DIV 2	4
8 DIV 8	1
8 DIV 9	0
8 DIV 7	1
5 DIV -2	-2
8 MOD 8	0
8 MOD 9	8
8 MOD 7	1
0 MOD 7	0
-5 MOD 2	1
5 MOD -2	error
3/2	1.5

Be careful: 7.0/0.0, 7 DIV 0, and 7 MOD 0 create an error; the computer cannot divide by zero.

Because variables are allowed in expressions, the following are valid assignments:

```
ID  := Num + 6
ID  := Num DIV 2
Num := ID * 2
Num := 6 MOD ID
ID  := ID + 1
Num := Num + ID
```

Notice that the same variable can appear on both sides of the assignment operator. In the case of

```
Num := Num + ID
```

the value in Num and the value in ID are added together, then the sum of the two values is stored in Num, replacing the previous value stored there. This example shows the difference between mathematical equality and assignment. The mathematical equality

Num = Num + ID

is true only when ID equals zero. The assignment statement

```
Num := Num + ID;
```

is valid for *any* value of ID.

Real values are added, subtracted, and multiplied just like Integer values. However, DIV and MOD have no meaning when applied to Real values. To divide with Real values, use the division operator (/).

If one operand is a real number and one is an integer, the Integer value is converted into a Real value before the operation is performed. If you use the division operator (/) between two integer operands, both are converted to Real values before the division is done, and the quotient is a Real value. This conversion is only temporary, for the purpose of the particular operation; it does not affect the values that actually are stored in the Integer variables.

One of the rare exceptions to Pascal's being a strongly typed language is that it is valid to assign Integer values to Real variables. This is because any Integer value can be exactly represented in Real form. For example, the integer 2 can be exactly represented as 2.0, 342346 can be 342346.0, and so on. However, you cannot assign a Real value to an Integer variable because it is not clear what you want done with the fractional part. If the Real value is 1.7, what happens to the .7? If something is ambiguous, it is illegal.

Given the declarations

```
VAR
  A,
  B: Integer;
  X: Real;
```

the following statements are valid:

Statement	Result
A := B + 2	B + 2 gives an integer result that is stored in an Integer variable.
X := A + B	A + B gives an integer result that is automatically converted to a real number, which can be stored in a Real variable.
X := A / B	A / B gives a real result. No conversion is necessary.
X := 2 + 2.3	An integer plus a real number gives a real number, which can be stored in a Real variable.

The following statements are not valid:

Statement	Result
A := B + 2.0	An integer plus a real number gives a real number, which cannot be stored in an Integer variable.
A := A / B	An integer divided by an integer gives a real number, which cannot be stored in an Integer variable.
A := X DIV B	The variables on either side of DIV must be of data type Integer.
B := 2 / B	The division operator gives a real result, which cannot be stored in an Integer variable.

The following chart summarizes the resulting type, given the operator and the types of the operands.

	Type of Operands			
	Real	Real	Integer	Integer
Operator	Real	Integer	Real	Integer
+	Real	Real	Real	Integer
–	Real	Real	Real	Integer
*	Real	Real	Real	Integer
/	Real	Real	Real	Real
DIV	error	error	error	Integer
MOD	error	error	error	Integer

Remember that you can assign an Integer value to a Real variable, but you *cannot* assign a Real value to an Integer variable.

Output   Have you ever asked someone, "Do you know what time it is?" only to have the person smile smugly and say, "Yes, I do"? This is like the situation that currently exists between you and the computer. You now know enough Pascal syntax to tell the computer to perform simple calculations, but the computer won't give you the answers until you tell it to write them out.

In Pascal we use a Writeln statement to write out the results of calculations. *Writeln* is short for *write line,* which is how it's pronounced. The Writeln statement takes the following form:

> **Writeln** (parameter, parameter . . .)

A *parameter* can be a literal, a constant or variable identifier, or an expression. Here's an example of a Writeln statement:

```
Writeln('The answer is ', Result);
```

The Writeln statement is a standard procedure. Remember our discussion in Chapter 1 of the four basic Pascal structures: sequence, selection, loop, and procedure. There we said that a **procedure** is a subprogram. A *standard procedure* is a subprogram built into the programming language. We *call* (use) a procedure by writing its name, often followed by a list of parameters.

Procedure   A subprogram.

The **parameter list** is a way for a main program to communicate with a subprogram. In the case of Writeln, the parameter list is simply a list of what you want printed. It can contain one or more expressions, separated by commas. Writeln simply takes the data that we give it, prints it out on one line, then goes to the start of the next line. In the preceding example, there are two parameters. The first is a literal string, 'The answer is '. The second is a variable, Result, whose value is to be printed.

Parameter List   A mechanism for communicating with a subprogram.

Here's an example of a parameter list with four parameters:

```
('Rate is ', Rate, ', and tax is ', Rate * Total)
```

When you use a Writeln statement, the computer temporarily puts your program on hold, starts the Writeln subprogram running, and gives it the data from the parameter list. When Writeln has finished printing the data, the computer goes back to your program and picks up where it left off.

The parameter list makes it possible for the same subprogram to work on many different sets of data. For example, you can have Writeln print out something different each time you use it simply by changing its parameters.

The following Writeln statements produce the output shown. The variable I contains the value 2, and J contains 6. All of the items in the parameter list of a Writeln statement are printed on one line.

Statement	*What Is Printed (□ means blank)*
`Writeln(I)`	2
`Writeln('I = ', I)`	I□=□2
`Writeln('Sum = ', I + J)`	Sum□=□8
`Writeln('ERROR MESSAGE')`	ERROR□MESSAGE
`Writeln('Error= ', I)`	Error=□2
`Writeln('J:', J, 'I:', I)`	J:6I:2

Writeln prints the current value of named constants and variables; it prints string constants exactly as they appear in the parameter list. To let the computer know that you want to print a string constant—not a named constant or variable—you must use single quotes to enclose the string. If you don't put quotes around a string, you'll probably get an error message ("UNKNOWN IDENTIFIER") from the Pascal compiler. If you want to print a string that includes a single quote (an apostrophe), you must type two single quotes, with no space between them, in the string. For example, to print the word *don't,* the Writeln looks like this:

```
Writeln('don''t')
```

You also must remember to put commas between each of the expressions or string constants in a parameter list.

Beyond Minimalism: Adding Comments to a Program

All that you need to create a working program is the correct combination of declarations and executable statements. The compiler ignores comments, but they are of enormous help to anyone who must read the program. Comments can appear anywhere in a program. They are delimited by the (*   *) pair. Turbo Pascal allows the use of { and } as substitutes for (* and *). The compiler ignores anything within the pair. Here's an example:

```
(* This program computes the weight and balance of a Beechcraft
   Starship-1 airplane, given the amount of fuel, number of
   passengers, and weight of luggage in fore and aft storage.
   It assumes that there are two pilots and a standard complement
   of equipment, and that passengers weigh 170 pounds each        *)
```

Notice that a comment can run over several lines. When this happens, be sure the comment doesn't include any program statements. For example, the declaration

```
VAR
   Fuel_Load:      (* The amount of fuel, entered in pounds.
      Real;            Jet-A fuel weighs 6.7 pounds per gallon *)
```

looks reasonable, but it produces an error message because the comment encloses the data type, Real. Here's one way to write this declaration correctly:

```
VAR
   Fuel_Load:      (* The amount of fuel, entered in pounds.   *)
      Real;        (* Jet-A fuel weighs 6.7 pounds per gallon *)
```

Here's another:

```
VAR
   Fuel_Load:      (* The amount of fuel, entered in pounds.
                      Jet-A fuel weighs 6.7 pounds per gallon *)
      Real;
```

Both of these declarations place the data type outside the comment.

It is good programming style to write fully commented programs. A comment should appear at the beginning of a program to explain what the program does. Each constant definition and variable declaration should have a comment that explains how the identifier is used. In addition, comments should introduce each major step in a long program and should explain anything that is unusual or difficult to read (for example, a lengthy formula).

It's important to make your comments concise, and to arrange them in the program so that they are easy to see and it is clear what they refer to. If comments are too long or crowd the statements of the program, they make the program more difficult to read—just the opposite of what you intended!

Program Construction

Now we can collect the statements we've been discussing into a program. As you saw earlier, Pascal programs are made up of a heading, a declaration section, and a statement section. The expanded syntax template for a program looks like this:

PROGRAM program-name (filename , filename ...) ;

constant declarations

variable declarations

BEGIN

statement ;

statement

.
.
.

END.

Here's an example of a program:

```
PROGRAM Example (Input, Output);

(* This program computes the midpoint between the  *)
(* freezing and boiling points of water            *)

CONST
   Freeze = 32;        (* Freezing point of water *)
   Boil   = 212;       (* Boiling point of water  *)

VAR
   Avg_Temp:           (* Variable to hold the result  *)
      Real;            (* of averaging Freeze and Boil *)

(* The executable statements begin here *)
```

```
BEGIN (* Example *)
  Writeln('Water freezes at ', Freeze);
  Writeln(' and boils at ', Boil, ' degrees.');
  Avg_Temp := Freeze + Boil;
  Avg_Temp := Avg_Temp / 2;
  Writeln('Halfway between is ', Avg_Temp, ' degrees.')
END. (* Example *)
```

The first line of the program is the heading: the reserved word PROGRAM, our name for the program, and a list of the files used by the program. These files allow the program to communicate with the outside world. (We talk about files in Chapter 3.) Input and Output are special "files" that usually refer to a keyboard and screen, respectively. The program heading is followed by a comment that explains what the program does.

The declaration section defines the constants Freeze and Boil and the variable Avg_Temp. Comments explain how each identifier is used.

The statement section is the executable part of the program. It is set off with a BEGIN-END pair. You will see later that BEGIN and END are used in many places in a typical Pascal program, so it is a good idea to add comments after them to indicate what is beginning and what is ending (in this case, Program Example). The statement section is the part of the program that is translated into machine language instructions. During the execution phase, these instructions are executed.

Notice the semicolons between the statements. Semicolons are separators; they are not part of a statement. If you look at the template for a program, you can see that the semicolon at the end of the first statement is contained in the same shaded block as the second (optional) statement. This is because a semicolon is required at the end of one Pascal statement only when that statement is followed by another statement. Because END is not a statement (it is a *delimiter*), there is no semicolon at the end of the statement that precedes it. The period after the END indicates that this is the last line of the program.

Compound Statements

The statement section of a program is called a *compound statement*. This is the syntax template for a compound statement.

The compound statement is just a series of one or more statements enclosed (delimited) by a BEGIN-END pair and separated by semicolons. Here is the syntax template for a statement:

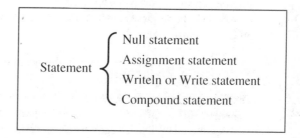

A statement can be empty (the *null statement*), any individual Pascal statement, or even another compound statement. This means that wherever a statement can be used, a compound statement also can be used. In later chapters, where we introduce the syntax for branching and looping structures, you'll see that this is very important.

We use the compound statement often, especially as part of other statements. Leaving out a BEGIN-END pair can dramatically change the meaning as well as the execution of a program. This is why we always indent the statements inside a compound statement—the indentation makes a compound statement easy to spot in a long, complicated program.

Blocks

The declaration and statement sections of a program make up a *block*. This is the syntax template for a block:

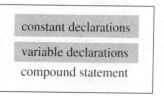

Declarations are optional. If they are used, they must appear before the compound statement.

Now we can redefine a program as a heading and a block, followed by a period:

```
heading;
block.
```

We encounter blocks again when we discuss user-defined subprograms, which are syntactically similar to programs.

Program Entry, Correction, and Execution

Once we have the program on paper, how do we get it into the machine? The most common way is to enter it on the keyboard of a computer or terminal. In this section, we examine the program entry process in general, and the Turbo Pascal program entry process in particular.

Entering a Program

The first step in entering a program is to get the computer's attention. With a personal computer, this usually means turning it on and possibly inserting a disk.

Once the computer is ready to accept your commands, you tell it that you want to enter a program by typing a command that tells it to run the editor. As we discussed in Chapter 1, the editor allows you to create and modify programs by entering information into an area of the computer's secondary memory called a **file.**

File A named area in secondary storage that is used to hold a collection of data; the collection of data itself.

A file in the computer's memory is like a file folder in a filing cabinet. It is a collection of information that has a name associated with it. You usually choose the name for the file when you create it with the editor. From that point on, you refer to the file by the name you've given it.

Each of the many different types of editors has unique features. For example, Turbo Pascal comes with an editor especially suited to entering Pascal programs; other editors have special features that make it easier to write reports.

To use the Turbo Pascal editor, you first must get into the Turbo Pascal environment. To do this, type the command TURBO and press the Enter key. If the environment appears with the Turbo Pascal version number and a copyright notice, press any key and the notice will disappear (see Figure 2-2). The screen is divided into three sections: the line of words at the top is the *main menu,* the *desktop* area is the blank section in the middle, and at the bottom is a line that lists the meanings of some of the function keys.

To use the environment's capabilities you need to activate menu items and windows. There are two ways to select an item from the main menu: with a mouse or with the keyboard. If you are using Turbo Pascal version 6.0 or higher, the environment supports use of a mouse. Earlier versions of Turbo Pascal use only the keyboard. If you are using one of these older versions, or if your computer is not equipped with a mouse, then you need only read the directions for using Turbo with the keyboard.

A mouse is a *pointing device* that allows you to point to items on the screen more quickly than by moving the cursor with the arrow keys. As the mouse is moved on a table top (or sometimes on a special mouse pad) you will see the *pointer* make corresponding motions on the screen. The pointer typically appears as a small square or an

Figure 2-2
The Turbo Pascal
Environment (ver-
sion 6.0) Initial
Display

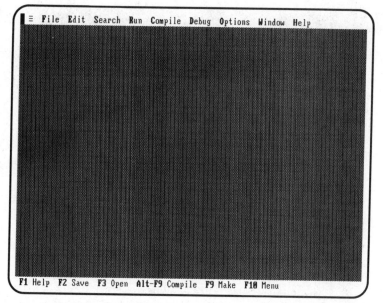

arrow. When the pointer is positioned over an item on the screen, you can press (or *click*) one of the buttons on the mouse to indicate some action that you wish to perform on the item. Most mice have two buttons: left and right. For example, in the Turbo environment, you can select an item from the main menu by moving the mouse until the pointer is on the desired item and then click the left button.

To select a menu item using the keyboard, first press the F10 key to activate the main menu, then select an item by pressing the left and right arrow keys (see Figure 2-3) to move the cursor to the item of your choice, then press Enter.

Selecting an item from the main menu causes a *submenu* to appear below it. You then can select an item from the submenu either by pointing and clicking with the mouse or by using the up and down arrow keys and pressing Enter when the cursor is on the desired item. For example, to leave the Turbo Pascal environment, you first select the File item from the main menu and then the Exit (Quit, for Turbo versions prior to 6.0) item from the file submenu. If you select a menu item by mistake, you can leave the submenu (or the main menu) by pressing the escape key (Esc) or by clicking with the pointer in the desktop area.

In addition to menus and submenus, Turbo Pascal will occasionally display *dialog boxes,* which require you to take some action or respond to a question. Five types of items appear in dialog boxes: lists, input areas, action buttons, radio buttons, and check boxes.

- *List*—choose one item from a list of values, such as a list of file names.
- *Input area*—enter a value (such as a file name).
- *Action button*—click on an action button to perform the indicated action. OK, Cancel, and Help are common action buttons.

Figure 2-3
A PC Keyboard

Cursor
movement
keys

- *Radio button*—activate (by clicking) one of the radio buttons. Each choice is accompanied by a radio button. Like the station selector buttons on a car radio, only one button may be activated at a time.
- *Check box*—check (by clicking on a box) as many boxes as you like. Each choice is accompanied by a check box.

The desktop can contain multiple *windows* (working areas) that allow us to view and interact with programs. Initially we will use only the Edit window, but Turbo Pascal provides several others. For example, the Output window is used to display output from a program. There is also a Watch window that is helpful in tracking down errors in a program. In Turbo 6.0 you can change the size of windows and move them around the screen.

A Turbo 6.0 window also has several mouse-oriented features. In the upper-left corner is a box enclosed by brackets that closes the window if you click on it. In the upper-right corner are the *window number* and an arrow in brackets. Clicking on the arrow (called the *zoom box*) causes the window to shrink or enlarge. Along the right edge of the window is a *scroll bar.* Clicking in the scroll bar causes different parts of a file to be displayed. A mark in the scroll bar indicates approximately what part of the file is on the screen. You can *drag* the mark to different places in the scroll bar to move quickly through a file. Dragging is accomplished by positioning the pointer on the mark, then holding the left mouse button down while sliding the mouse up or down. The mark will follow the pointer up or down on the screen. When it is positioned where you wish, release the button. A second scroll bar stretches across the bottom edge of the window and is used to view lines that are too wide to fit on the screen. The lower-right corner of the window is called the *resize corner.* To change a window's size, drag the resize corner to the point that makes the window the desired size. To move a window, drag the title of the window (top center) to the new position and the window will follow.

The following list summarizes actions that can be performed on Turbo 6.0 dialog boxes and windows. Both the mouse action and the corresponding keyboard action are shown. Many of the keyboard actions also work with earlier versions of Turbo.

Action	Mouse Technique	Keyboard Technique
Open a window	Click mouse on File or Window menu and appropriate submenu items	Alt-W to get window menu or F3 to open an edit window
Close a window	Click mouse on bracketed square in upper-left corner	Alt-F3
Zoom a window (fill screen)	Click mouse on bracketed arrow in upper-right corner	F5
Resize a window	Click mouse on lower-right corner and drag it to size the window	Ctrl-F5 enables Shift-arrow keys to move the lower-right corner; carriage-return sets
Move a window	Click mouse on window title and drag it as desired	Ctrl-F5 enables arrow keys to move the window; carriage-return sets
Scrolling a window or a dialog box list or input area history	Click mouse on right edge or bottom edge scroll bar and drag it in the desired direction	Use the Page Up, Page Down, and right/left/up/down arrow keys.
Move hightlight between areas of a dialog box	Move mouse	Tab and Shift-Tab keys
Check a check box	Move mouse to value and click	Select value with arrow keys and press space bar
Select a radio button	Move mouse to value and click	Select value with arrow keys
Select an item from a list	Move mouse to value and click	Select value with arrow keys and press Return
Press an action button	Move mouse to value and click	Select value with arrow keys

Now that we have covered the basics of the Turbo environment, let's return to the program entry process. The first step in entering a program is to name the file in which it will be stored. Select Open from the File submenu (called Load in earlier versions of Turbo). A dialog box appears on the screen, as shown in Figure 2-4, with the cursor at the end of *.PAS. Use the Backspace (Bksp) key to delete the *.PAS. Next, type the name of your file followed by .PAS. The .PAS indicates that this is a Pascal source program. The file name must be one to eight characters in length and should consist only of letters and digits. The first character must be a letter. For example, FILENAME.PAS would be a valid name. Press enter when you are done typing the filename.

If you have entered the name of a new program file, the box and submenu will disappear and the desktop area will be empty as shown in Figure 2-5. The screen also

Figure 2-4
A Dialog Box

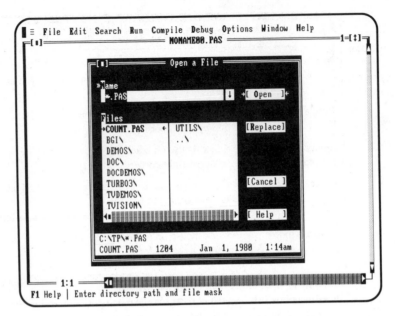

shows the name of your file and the column and line number of the current cursor position (1:1 initially). You may then type your program in the empty space. If you make a typing mistake, use the Backspace key to erase it and then type your correction. If you notice a mistake after you've typed beyond it, use the mouse or arrow keys to move to that place and make your correction, then move the cursor back to where you left off and continue typing. The Home key can be used to move to the left end of a line and the End key to move to the right end.

When you reach the bottom of the screen, some of the text automatically moves up off the top to give you more room. To go back to lines that have gone off the top, press the Page Up (PgUp) key (see Figure 2-3). To view lines that are below the bottom of the screen, press the Page Down (PgDn) key. You can accomplish the same thing with the mouse by clicking on the vertical scroll bar either above or below the mark.

There are two typing modes in the Turbo Pascal editor: Insert and Overwrite. In Insert mode, if you move the cursor into the middle of some text and begin typing, what you type will be inserted at that point. In other words, as you enter text, the letters to the right of the cursor will shift right to make room. In Overwrite mode, what you type replaces existing text—the letters to the right will not move over and are replaced by the new text. The editor is normally in Insert mode, but you can switch between the two modes by pressing the Insert (Ins) key.

The editor automatically indents each new line to match the indentation of the line before it. This feature saves having to type spaces at the beginning of each line. If you wish to indent the new line by a different amount, use the Backspace key and space bar as necessary.

There are keys for all of the frequently used commands in the Turbo editor, but you may have to press several keys at once for less frequently used commands. These *extended commands* involve the use of the key labeled Ctrl, which is used like a shift

Figure 2-5
The Display Screen
with the Editor
Ready to Accept
Entry of a Program

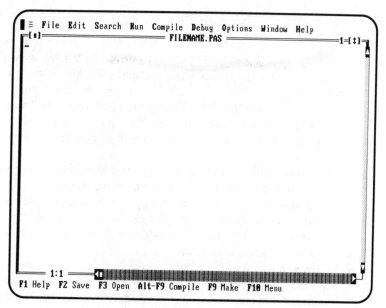

key on a typewriter: while holding down Ctrl you strike another key. For example, to issue the Ctrl-A command, you hold the Ctrl key down and at the same time press the A key once. Ctrl-Q and Ctrl-K are special in the Turbo editor: after pressing Ctrl-Q or Ctrl-K you press yet another letter to issue a command. The following table summarizes the most commonly used editor commands.

	Standard keyboard	IBM PC-compatible keyboard
Move the cursor one word to the left	Ctrl-A	Ctrl-←
Move the cursor one word to the right	Ctrl-F	Ctrl-→
Move the screen up one line	Ctrl-W	
Move the screen down one line	Ctrl-Z	
Move the cursor to the top of the screen	Ctrl-Q-E	Ctrl-Home
Move the cursor to the bottom of the screen	Ctrl-Q-X	Ctrl-End
Move the cursor to the top of the file	Ctrl-Q-R	Ctrl-PgUp
Move the cursor to the bottom of the file	Ctrl-Q-C	Ctrl-PgDn
Delete the word to the right of the cursor	Ctrl-T	
Remove the current line entirely	Ctrl-Y	
Delete the current line, leaving a blank line	Ctrl-Q-Y	
Tab	Ctrl-I	→
Undo any changes just made to the current line	Ctrl-Q-L	

There are many other Turbo Pascal editor commands, but this subset should be sufficient for most of the things you'll need to do.

Compiling and Running a Program

Once your program is stored on a file, you can compile it by selecting Compile from the Compile submenu or by pressing Alt-F9 (the Alt key is used like the Ctrl key—in this case, press the F9 key while holding down Alt). If the compiler detects an error in the program, it will automatically bring up the editor with the cursor positioned at the point it found the error. If you do not understand the Pascal syntax that appeared to cause the error, it may help to place the cursor on the keyword that you don't understand and press Ctrl-F1, which will display an overview of the syntax of that construct.

If there are errors in your program, you have to determine their cause, go back to the editor and fix them, and then compile the program again. This process is called *debugging*. Once your program compiles without errors you can run it.

After your program has compiled successfully, you run it by selecting Run from the Run submenu or by pressing Ctrl-F9. The Run command also can be used to compile and run a program in one step.

Even though a program runs, it may still have errors in its design. The computer does exactly what you tell it to do, even if that's not what you want it to do. If your program doesn't do what it should, you have to go back to the algorithm and fix it, and then go to the editor and fix the program. Finally, you compile and run the program again. The debugging process is repeated until the program does what it is supposed to do (see Figure 2-6).

Figure 2-6
Debugging
Procedure

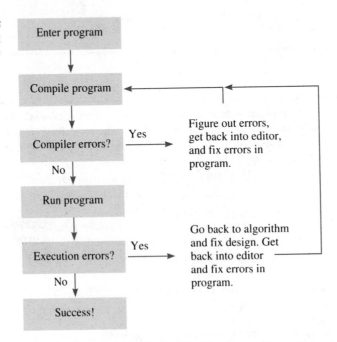

Software Engineering Tip

Understanding Before Changing

When you are in the middle of getting a program to run and you come across an error, it's tempting to start changing parts of the program to see if it will work. *Don't!* You'll nearly always make things worse. It's essential that you understand what is causing the error and that you carefully think through the solution. The only thing you should try is running the program with different input data to determine the pattern of the unexpected behavior. The Turbo Pascal debugger can help with this experimentation or testing process and will be covered briefly in later chapters.

There is no magic trick—inserting an extra semicolon or END, for example—that can automatically fix a program. If the compiler tells you that a semicolon or an END is missing, you have to examine the program in light of the syntax rules and determine precisely what the problem is. Perhaps you accidentally typed a colon instead of a semicolon. Or maybe there's an extra BEGIN.

A good rule of thumb is that if the source of a problem isn't immediately obvious, leave the computer and go somewhere where you can quietly look over a printed copy of the program. Studies show that people who do all of their debugging away from the computer actually get their programs to work in less time *and in the end produce better programs* than those who continue to work on the machine—more proof that there is still no mechanical substitute for human thought.*

*Basili, V. R., Selby, R. W., "Comparing the Effectiveness of Software Testing Strategies," IEEE Trans. on Software Engineering, Vol. SE-13, No. 12, pp. 1278–1296, Dec. 1987.

Finishing Up

When you're done working, save your files by selecting Save from the File submenu. If you have not saved a file before issuing the Exit command, the Turbo Pascal system will ask you if you want to do so. Next, remove any disks that you've inserted. Turning off the power wipes out the computer's memory, but your files are safely stored on the disks. The next time you use the computer, you simply reinsert the disks and the computer will be able to recall the files from them. (If the PC is in a lab where it gets frequent use by many people, you'll probably be asked to leave the computer on in order to save wear and tear on the machine.)

Be sure to read the manual for your particular system and editor before you enter your first program. Don't panic if you have trouble at first—almost everyone does. It becomes much easier with practice.

More About Expressions

The expressions we've used so far have contained at most a single arithmetic operator. Now let's look at more complicated expressions.

Precedence Rules

Expressions can be made up of many constants, variables, and operators. In what order are the operations performed? For example, in the assignment statement

```
AvgTemp := Freeze + Boil / 2
```

is Freeze + Boil calculated first or is Boil / 2 calculated first?

Pascal operators are ordered the same way mathematical operators are, left to right according to *precedence rules:*

```
Highest precedence: * / DIV MOD
```

```
Lowest precedence: + -
```

In the example above, we divide Boil by 2 first, then add Freeze to the result.

You can change the order of evaluation by using parentheses. In the statement

```
AvgTemp := (Freeze + Boil) / 2
```

Freeze and Boil are added first, and then their sum is divided by 2. We evaluate subexpressions in parentheses first and then follow the precedence of the operators.

When there are multiple operators with the same precedence, we evaluate them from left to right. Given the statement

```
A := (A + B) / A * 2
```

where A and B are Real variables, we evaluate the expression in the parentheses first, then divide the sum of A and B by A, and multiply the result by 2.

Expression	Value
10 DIV 2 * 3	15
10 MOD 3 - 4 DIV 2	-1
5 * 2 / 4 * 2	5.0
5 * 2 / (4 * 2)	1.25
5 + 2 / (4 * 2)	5.25

Functions

The only type of subprogram that we have looked at so far is the procedure. Pascal provides another type of subprogram called a **function.** For example, Round, Trunc, Sqr, and Sqrt are all functions.

Function   A subprogram that is used within an expression.

Functions are used in expressions in much the same way that arithmetic operators are. The name of the function usually is followed by a parameter list. The value computed by a function simply takes its place in the expression. For example, the expression

```
Sqrt(16) * 10
```

has the value 40. First the Sqrt function is executed to compute the square root of 16, which is 4. The value 4—now available for use in the rest of the expression—is multiplied by 10. Note that evaluation of the function has higher precedence than multiplication, which makes sense if you consider that the parameter is enclosed by parentheses.

Several features distinguish a function from a procedure:

- The function name is used within an expression; it does not appear as a separate statement.
- A function computes a value *(result)* that is then available for use in the expression.
- A function always returns exactly one result—no more, no less.

The Sqrt function can be given (or *passed*) either a Real value or an Integer value as a parameter; the result is always a Real. On the other hand, when the functions Trunc and Round are passed a Real parameter, they return an Integer value:

```
Round(3.7) = 4      Rounds to the nearest integer
Trunc(3.7) = 3      Truncates (cuts off) the decimal part
```

You cannot assign a Real value to an Integer variable, but you can use Round or Trunc to achieve an approximation. If Temp is an Integer variable, then

```
Temp := 16.3
```

is invalid, but

```
Temp := Round(16.3)
```

is valid (Temp is set equal to 16).

The parameter to Round could just as easily have been a Real variable or named constant instead of a literal constant. In fact, a function's parameter can be any expression that results in a value of the correct type.

In the statement

```
Hypotenuse := Sqrt(X * X + Y * Y)
```

the expression is evaluated first and only its result is passed to the function. An expression in a function's parameter list can even include calls to functions. For example, we can use Sqr to rewrite this assignment statement as follows: (Sqr computes the square of its parameter).

```
Hypotenuse := Sqrt(Sqr(X) + Sqr(Y))
```

Appendix B lists standard identifiers, including all of the functions and procedures that Pascal automatically provides.

More About Output

The Write Statement

In addition to the Writeln statement, Pascal has a second output procedure, *Write*. Write is like Writeln, except that when it finishes printing its parameter list, it does not go to the next line. So, the output from a series of Write statements appears on one line. For example, this sequence of statements

```
I := 2;
J := 6;
Write(I);
Write('I = ', I);
Write('Sum = ', I + J);
Write('Error Message');
Write('Error# ', I);
```

produces this output

```
2I□=□2Sum□=□8Error□MessageError#□2
```

The Write statement is useful when you want different parts of a program to print their results on a single line, as though the results were all computed at the same point in the program.

Write and Writeln statements can be combined within a single program to produce output. Here are some examples:

Statements	Output Produced

`Write('Hi there, ');`
`Writeln('Lois Lane. ');`
`Write('Have you seen ');`
`Writeln('Clark Kent?')`
	Hi there, Lois Lane.
	
	Have you seen Clark Kent?

`Writeln('Hi there, ');`
`Writeln('Lois Lane. ');`
`Writeln('Have you seen ');`
`Writeln('Clark Kent?')`
	Hi there,
	Lois Lane.
	Have you seen
	Clark Kent?

`Writeln('Hi there, ');`
`Write('Lois Lane. ');`
`Writeln('Have you seen ');`
`Writeln('Clark Kent?')`
	Hi there,
	
	Lois Lane. Have you seen
	Clark Kent?

What do you think these statements will output?

```
Writeln('Hi there,');
Writeln;
Writeln('Lois Lane.');
```

Although it wouldn't make sense to construct a Write statement without any parameters (because it won't do anything), a Writeln without parameters still performs a function: It causes the screen (or printer) to go to the start of the next line. The output from our example would be

```
Hi there,

Lois Lane.
```

Whenever a Writeln with no parameters follows another Writeln, a blank line is produced.
What if a Writeln with no parameters follows a Write?

```
Write('Hi there,');
Writeln;
Writeln('Clark Kent.')
```

The first Write statement causes the words *Hi there,* to be printed. The Writeln then causes the screen (or printer) to go to the next line, where the words *Clark Kent.* are printed by the last Writeln statement:

```
Hi there,
Clark Kent.
```

In fact, we could rewrite these three statements with just two statements:

```
Writeln('Hi there,');
Writeln('Clark Kent.')
```

In other words,

```
Write(parameter list);
Writeln
```

is equivalent to

```
Writeln(parameter list)
```

Formatting Output

Line Spaces and Blanks   There are two basic techniques for formatting output: To insert blank lines, use successive Writeln statements with no parameters. To insert blank space within lines, use spaces enclosed in quotes in the parameter lists of your Write and Writeln statements.

For example, to produce this output:

```
*   *   *   *   *   *   *   *   *

*   *   *   *   *   *   *   *   *   *

  *   *   *   *   *   *   *   *   *
```

you would use these statements:

```
Writeln('  *   *   *   *   *   *   *   *     *');
Writeln;
Writeln('*   *   *   *   *   *   *   *     *');
Writeln;
Writeln('  *   *   *   *   *   *   *   *   *');
```

All of the blanks and asterisks are enclosed in single quotes, so they will print just as they are written in the program. The extra Writeln statements give you the blank lines between the rows of asterisks.

If you want blanks to be printed, they must be enclosed in quotes. For example:

```
Writeln('*',                        '*')
```

produces

```
**
```

Despite all of the blank space between the two asterisks in the Writeln statement, they print side by side because the space is not enclosed by quotes.

Integers and Characters   The programmer must add space between items or lines. The items themselves can be formatted automatically. Automatic formatting varies from compiler to compiler. In this book we follow the Turbo Pascal automatic formatting in which integer numbers are automatically formatted to be right-justified in a field that is one character position wide (the field is expanded for multidigit integers).

Pascal does not confine us to automatic formatting. We can control the format of each item to be output by indicating how many columns we want a variable or constant to occupy.

This syntax template describes a formatted parameter in a Write or Writeln statement:

parameter :integer-expression

It tells us that a parameter can be followed by a colon and an integer expression that specifies the number of columns the parameter should occupy when it is output. The integer expression is called the *fieldwidth specification;* the number of columns is called the *field*. The value of the parameter is printed right justified; blanks are automatically inserted to the left to fill up the field.

Let's look at an example:

```
Ans = 33      Integer
Num = 7132    Integer
Ch  = 'Z'     Char
```

Write Statement Parameters	*Output (□ means blank)*
1. (Ans:4, Num:5, Ch:3)	□□33□7132□□Z 4 5 3
2. (Ans:2, Num:4, Ch:1)	337132Z 2 4 1
3. (Ans:6, Ch:2, Num:5)	□□□□33□Z□7132 6 2 5
4. (Ch:6, Num:4)	□□□□□Z7132 6 4
5. (Ans:1, Num:5)	33□7132 ↑ 5 1 automatically extended to fit the two-digit value

In (1) each of the values is specified to occupy enough columns so that there is at least one space separating them. In (2) the values all run together because the fieldwidth specified for each value is just large enough to hold the value. This output obviously is not very readable. It's better to make the fieldwidth larger than the minimum size required so that some space is left between values. In (3) there are extra blanks for readability; in (4) there are not. In (5) the fieldwidth is not large enough for the value in Ans, so it is automatically extended to make room for all of the digits.

This automatic extension is useful when you want a variable value to print in as few columns as possible. If the fieldwidth is specified as :1, the field is always extended to just the number of places required to print the value. For example, if the variable Total has the value 149573,

```
Write('Total inventory is ', Total:1, ' widgets. ')
```

will print

```
Total inventory is 149573 widgets.
```

If the value of Total is 6, the output is

```
Total inventory is 6 widgets.
```

If the value of Total is −1, the output is

```
Total inventory is -1 widgets.
```

You can also use fieldwidths with strings:

Write Statement Parameters	Output (□ means blank)
1. ('The answer is ':16)	□□□The answer is 16
2. (' ':5, 'X':4)	□□□□□□□□X 5 4

In (1) three blanks are inserted at the left to make up the 16 character positions. In (2) the first five blanks come from ' ':5; the next three are filled in to make 'X':4 cover 4 positions.

Real Numbers   If you do not indicate how many columns a Real value should take up in the output, the value will be printed in scientific (E) notation with one digit before the decimal point and the system's default (assumed) value for the number of columns. For Turbo Pascal the default width is 17 columns.

You can specify a fieldwidth for Real values just as for Integer values. There are two differences, however. A blank (for a positive value) or a minus sign is always put before a real number and is included in the column count, and the decimal point is included in the count.

Here are some examples:

Value of I	Write Statement	Output (□ means blank)
310.0	(I:10)	□3.100E+02
310.0	(I:9)	□3.10E+02
310.0	(I:12)	□3.10000E+02
310.0	(I:1)	□3.1E+02 (uses 8 columns)
0.0112	(I:10)	□1.120E−02
0.0112	(I:12)	□1.12000E−02
0.0112	(I:2)	□1.1E−02 (uses 8 columns)

With Reals, Pascal gives you a second option. If you specify a second colon followed by an integer, the output is in decimal form rather than scientific notation. The first number still specifies the total number of columns to be used; the second specifies the number of digits that should print after the decimal point.

Value of I	Write Statement	Output (□ means blank)
310.0	(I:10:2)	□□□□310.00
310.0	(I:10:5)	□310.00000
310.0	(I:9:5)	310.00000
32.76	(I:8:3)	□□32.760
0.012	(I:8:3)	□□□0.012
0.012	(I:8:2)	□□□□0.01 (last digit not printed)

Here too, the total number of columns is expanded if necessary, so that no significant digits (digits to the left of the decimal point) are lost. However, the number of columns for fractional digits is limited by the second field specification. This can be useful, for example, if you want your output in dollars and cents. Notice that the space for the sign is automatically inserted and that the decimal point still uses one column.

*M*atters of Style

Program Formatting

As far as the compiler is concerned, Pascal statements are free format: They can appear anywhere on a line, and more than one can appear on a single line. The compiler only needs blanks to separate symbols, and semicolons to separate statements. However, it is extremely important that your programs be readable, both for your sake and for the sake of anyone else who has to use them.

When you write an outline for an English paper, you follow certain rules of indentation to make it readable. These same kinds of rules can make your programs easier to read.

Take a look at the following program for computing the cost per square foot of a house. Although it compiles and runs correctly, it does not conform to any formatting standards.

```
PROGRAM HouseCost(Output); (* This program computes the
cost per square foot of living space for a house, given
the dimensions of the house, the number of stories, the
size of the nonliving space, and the total cost less land *)
CONST Width = 30.0: (* Width of the house *)
Length = 40.0; (* Length of the house *)
Stories = 2.5; (* Number of full stories *)

   NonLivingSpace = 825.0; (* Garage, closets, etc.*)
Price = 150000.0; (* Selling price less land *)
VAR GrossFootage, (* Total square footage *)
   LivingFootage, (* Living area *)
CostPerFoot: (* Cost/foot of living area *) Real;

BEGIN (* HouseCost *)
GrossFootage := Length * Width * Stories; LivingFootage :=
GrossFootage - NonLivingSpace; CostPerFoot := Price /
LivingFootage; Writeln('Cost per square foot is ',
CostPerFoot:6:2) END. (* HouseCost *)
```

Now look at the same program with proper formatting:

```
PROGRAM House_Cost(Output);

(* This program computes the cost per square foot of     *)
(* living space for a house, given the dimensions of     *)
(* the house, the number of stories, the size of the     *)
(* nonliving space, and the total cost less land         *)
```

```
CONST
   Width = 30.0;              (* Width of the house        *)
   Length = 40.0;            (* Length of the house       *)
   Stories = 2.5;           (* Number of full stories    *)
   Non_Living_Space = 825.0;  (* Garage, closets, etc.     *)
   Price = 150000.0;        (* Selling price less land   *)

VAR
   Gross_Footage,           (* Total square footage      *)
   Living_Footage,          (* Living area               *)
   Cost_Per_Foot:           (* Cost/foot of living area  *)
     Real;

BEGIN (* House_Cost *)
   Gross_Footage := Length * Width * Stories;
   Living_Footage := Gross_Footage - Non_Living_Space;
   Cost_Per_Foot := Price / Living_Footage;
   Writeln('Cost per square foot is ', Cost_Per_Foot:6:2)
END.   (* House_Cost *)
```

Need we say more?

Appendix G talks about programming style. Use it as a guide when you are writing programs.

PROBLEM-SOLVING CASE STUDY

Mileage

Problem: Write a program to calculate the miles per gallon a car gets on a trip, given the amounts in gallons of the fillups and the starting and ending mileage. The starting mileage was 67308.0; the ending mileage, 68750.7. During the trip, the car was filled up four times. The four amounts were 11.7, 14.3, 12.2, and 8.5 gallons. Assume that the tank was full initially and that the last fillup was at the end of the trip.

Output: The quantities on which the calculations are based and the computed miles per gallon rounded off to the nearest whole number, all appropriately labeled.

Discussion: If you calculated this by hand, you would add up the gallon amounts, then divide the sum into the mileage traveled, and round the result off to the nearest whole number. The mileage traveled is, of course, just the ending mileage minus the starting mileage. This is essentially the algorithm we use in the program. Let's make all of the quantities named constants, so that it will be easier to change the program later. Here is the algorithmic solution:

Amt1 = 11.7
Amt2 = 14.3
Amt3 = 12.2
Amt4 = 8.5
Start Miles = 67308.0
End Miles = 68750.7
Set MPG to Round((End Miles − Start Miles) / (Amt1 + Amt2 + Amt3 + Amt4))
Write the fillup amounts
Write a blank line
Write the starting mileage
Write the ending mileage
Write a blank line
Write the mileage per gallon

From the algorithm we can create tables of quantities and variables that will help us write the declaration section of the program.

Quantities

Name	Value	Function
Amt1	11.7	Number of gallons for fillup 1
Amt2	14.3	Number of gallons for fillup 2
Amt3	12.2	Number of gallons for fillup 3
Amt4	8.5	Number of gallons for fillup 4
Start_Miles	67308.0	Starting mileage
End_Miles	68750.7	Ending mileage

Variables

Name	Data Type	Function
MPG	Integer	Computed miles per gallon

Now we're ready to write the program. Let's call it Mileage. The only file that we need to list in the heading is Output. We can take the declarations from the tables and create the program statements from the algorithm. We must add comments and be sure to label the output and format it with fieldwidth specifications.

Here is the program:

```
PROGRAM Mileage (Output);

(* This program computes miles per gallon given four amounts *)
(* for gallons used, and starting and ending mileages        *)

CONST
  Amt1 = 11.7;             (* Number of gallons for fillup 1 *)
  Amt2 = 14.3;             (* Number of gallons for fillup 2 *)
  Amt3 = 12.2;             (* Number of gallons for fillup 3 *)
  Amt4 = 8.5;              (* Number of gallons for fillup 4 *)
  Start_Miles = 67308.0;   (* Starting mileage               *)
  End_Miles = 68750.7;     (* Ending mileage                 *)

VAR
  MPG:                     (* Computed miles per gallon      *)
    Integer;

BEGIN (* Mileage *)
  MPG := Round((End_Miles - Start_Miles) / (Amt1 + Amt2 + Amt3 + Amt4));
  Writeln('For the gallon amounts: ');
  Writeln(Amt1:6:1, ',', Amt2:6:1, ',', Amt3:6:1, ',', Amt4:6:1);
  Writeln;
  Writeln('a starting mileage of ', Start_Miles:8:1);
  Writeln('and an ending mileage of ', End_Miles:8:1);
  Writeln;
  Writeln('the mileage per gallon is ', MPG:3)
END.  (* Mileage *)
```

The output from this program is

```
For the gallon amounts:
  11.7,  14.3,  12.2,   8.5

a starting mileage of  67308.0
and an ending mileage of  68750.7

the mileage per gallon is  31
```

PROBLEM-SOLVING CASE STUDY

Painting Traffic Cones

Problem: The Hexagrammum Mysticum Company manufactures a line of traffic cones. The company is preparing to bid on a project that will require it to paint its cones in different colors. The paint is applied with a constant thickness. From experience, the firm finds it easier to estimate the total cost from the area to be painted. The company has hired you to write a program that will compute the surface area of a cone and the cost of painting it, given its radius, height, and the cost per square foot of three different colors of paint.

Output: The surface area of the cone in square feet, and the costs of painting the cone in the three different colors.

Discussion: From interviewing the company's engineers, you learn that the cones are measured in inches. A typical cone is 30 inches high and 8 inches in diameter. The red paint costs 10 cents per square foot; the blue costs 15 cents; the green costs 18 cents. In a math text, you find that the area of a cone (not including its base, which won't be painted) equals

$$\pi r \sqrt{r^2 + h^2}$$

where *r* is the radius of the cone and *h* is its height.

The first thing the program must do is convert the cone measurements into feet and divide the diameter in half to get the radius. Then it can apply the formula to get the surface area of the cone. To determine the painting costs, it must multiply the surface area by the cost of each of the three paints. Here's the algorithm:

Height in Feet is set equal to Height in Inches / 12
Diameter in Feet is set equal to Diameter in Inches / 12
Radius is set equal to Diameter in Feet / 2
Surface Area is set equal to Pi * Radius * Sqrt(Sqr(Radius in Feet) + Sqr(Height in Feet))
Red Cost is set equal to Surface Area * 0.10
Blue Cost is set equal to Surface Area * 0.15
Green Cost is set equal to Surface Area * 0.18
Print the Surface Area
Print Red Cost
Print Blue Cost
Print Green Cost

From the algorithm we can create tables of quantities and variables to help us write the declaration section.

PROBLEM-SOLVING CASE STUDY *cont'd*

Quantities

Name	Value	Function
Inch_Height	30.0	Height of a typical cone
Inch_Diameter	8.0	Diameter of the base of the cone
Red_Price	0.10	Price per square foot of red paint
Blue_Price	0.15	Price per square foot of blue paint
Green_Price	0.18	Price per square foot of green paint
Inches_Per_Foot	12.0	Inches in 1 foot
Pi	3.14159265	Ratio of circumference to diameter

Variables

Name	Data Type	Function
Height_In_Feet	Real	Height of the cone in feet
Diameter_In_Feet	Real	Diameter of the cone in feet
Radius	Real	Radius of the cone in feet
Surface_Area	Real	Surface area in square feet
Red_Cost	Real	Cost to paint a cone red
Blue_Cost	Real	Cost to paint a cone blue
Green_Cost	Real	Cost to paint a cone green

Now we're ready to write the program, which we'll call Cone_Paint. The only file that we need in the heading is Output. We can take the declarations from the tables and the program statements from the algorithm. We have labeled the output with explanatory messages and formatted it with fieldwidth specifications. We've also added comments where needed.

Here's the program:

```
PROGRAM Cone_Paint (Output);

(* This program computes the cost of painting traffic cones in each   *)
(* of three different colors, given the height and diameter of a cone *)
(* in inches, and the cost per square foot of each of the paints      *)

CONST
   Inch_Height = 30.0;        (* Height of a typical cone         *)
   Inch_Diameter = 8.0;       (* Diameter of the base of the cone *)
   Red_Price = 0.10;          (* Price per square foot of red paint   *)
   Blue_Price = 0.15;         (* Price per square foot of blue paint  *)
   Green_Price = 0.18;        (* Price per square foot of green paint *)
   Inches_Per_Foot = 12.0;    (* Inches in 1 foot                 *)
   Pi = 3.14159265;           (* Ratio of circumference to diameter   *)
```

PROBLEM-SOLVING CASE STUDY cont'd.

```
VAR
  Height_In_Feet,            (* Height of the cone in feet   *)
  Diameter_In_Feet,          (* Diameter of the cone in feet *)
  Radius,                    (* Radius of the cone in feet   *)
  Surface_Area,              (* Surface area in square feet  *)
  Red_Cost,                  (* Cost to paint a cone red     *)
  Blue_Cost,                 (* Cost to paint a cone blue    *)
  Green_Cost:                (* Cost to paint a cone green   *)
    Real;

BEGIN (* Cone_Paint *)

  (* Convert dimensions to feet *)

  Height_In_Feet := Inch_Height / Inches_Per_Foot;
  Diameter_In_Feet := Inch_Diameter / Inches_Per_Foot;
  Radius := Diameter_In_Feet / 2;

  (* Compute surface area of the cone *)

  Surface_Area := Pi * Radius * Sqrt(Sqr(Radius) + Sqr(Height_In_Feet));

  (* Compute cost for each color *)

  Red_Cost := Surface_Area * Red_Price;
  Blue_Cost := Surface_Area * Blue_Price;
  Green_Cost := Surface_Area * Green_Price;

  (* Print results *)

  Writeln('The surface area is ', Surface_Area:7:3, ' sq. ft.');
  Writeln('The painting cost for');
  Writeln('   Red is   ', Red_Cost:7:3, ' dollars');
  Writeln('   Blue is  ', Blue_Cost:7:3, ' dollars');
  Writeln('   Green is ', Green_Cost:7:3, ' dollars')

END. (* Cone_Paint *)
```

The output from the program is

```
The surface area is   2.641 sq. ft.
The painting cost for
      Red is     0.264 dollars
      Blue is    0.396 dollars
      Green is   0.475 dollars
```

Testing and Debugging Hints

1. Three symbols in Pascal often are confused— :, = , and : = . The colon separates a variable name and its type in a variable declaration. The equal sign separates a constant name and its value in a constant definition. The : = is used in an assignment statement.
2. Remember that a program ends with END followed by a period.
3. Every identifier that isn't predefined by Pascal must be declared. If you use a name that hasn't been declared, you will get an error message.
4. Double check every expression according to the precedence rules to be sure that the operations are performed in the desired order.
5. Avoid mixing Real and Integer values in expressions.
6. For each assignment statement, check that the expression result has the same data type as the variable to the left of the : = .
7. Remember that DIV is used for integer division and / is used for real division.
8. The semicolon is used to separate statements. It is not required between the last statement and END.
9. If the cause of an error in a program is not obvious, leave the computer and study a printed listing. Change your program only after you understand the source of the error.

Summary

The syntax (grammar) of the Pascal language is defined by a metalanguage. In this text we use a form of metalanguage called *syntax templates*. We describe the semantics (meaning) of Pascal statements in English.

Identifiers are used in Pascal to name things. Some identifiers are predefined; others are defined by the programmer. Pascal includes predefined identifiers called *reserved words* and *standard identifiers*. The identifiers you may use are restricted to those *not* reserved by the Pascal language. You will not want to define identifiers with the same names as standard identifiers, even though Pascal allows you to do so. Reserved words are listed in Appendix A, and standard identifiers in Appendix B.

Identifiers are associated with memory locations by declarations. A declaration may give a name to a location whose value does not change (a constant) or to one whose value does change (a variable). Every constant or variable has an associated data type. The basic predefined data types in Pascal are Integer, Real, Char, and Boolean.

The assignment operator is used to change the value of a variable by assigning it the value of an expression. Expressions can contain more than one operator. The order in which the operations are performed is determined by precedence rules. Multiplication and division are performed first, then addition and subtraction. Multiple operations of the same type are performed from left to right. Parentheses can be used to override the precedence rules.

Pascal provides two types of subprograms that differ primarily in the way they are called. A procedure is called by writing its name (with its parameter list) as a Pascal statement. A function is called by writing its name (with its parameter list) as part of an expression.

Writeln is a standard procedure subprogram used to display output. A Writeln statement prints the value of an expression in its parameter list, and then goes to the next line. A Writeln statement without a parameter list can be used to generate a blank line in output. The Write statement, another standard procedure, may be used to produce output without advancing to the next line.

Output should be clear, understandable, and neatly arranged. Messages in the output should describe the significance of values. Blank lines and blank spaces within lines help to organize output and improve its appearance.

Fieldwidth specifications can be used in Write and Writeln statements to control the appearance of values in the output. Fieldwidth specifications do *not* affect the values actually stored in memory, only their appearance in the output from a particular Write or Writeln statement.

A program is a heading followed by a block. The heading lists the program name and any files that are used in the program. A block is a program unit consisting of constant and variable declarations and a compound statement. A compound statement is a series of statements, separated by semicolons, and enclosed by a BEGIN–END pair.

■ *Quick Check*

1. Use the following syntax template to decide whether your last name is a valid Pascal identifier. (pp. 40–41)

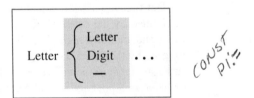

2. Define a Pascal constant that gives the name Pi to the value 3.14159. (pp. 48–49)

3. Which of the following words are reserved words in Pascal? (*Hint:* Look in Appendix A.)

    BEGIN   PI   PROGRAM   INTEGER   MAXINT

    (p. 49)

4. Declare an Integer variable called Count, a Real variable called Sum, and a Char variable called Letter. (pp. 49–51)

5. Assign the value 10 to the Integer variable Toes. (pp. 51–53)

6. You want to divide 9 by 5. a. How would you write the expression if you want the quotient to be a real number? b. How would you write it if you want the quotient to be an integer number? (pp. 54–56)

7. What is the value of the following Pascal expression?

```
5 MOD 2
```

(pp. 54–56)

8. Write a Writeln statement to print out the title of this book (Introduction to Pascal and Structured Design). (pp. 56–57)

9. Which parts of the following Writeln statement are its parameters?

```
Writeln('For radius ', Radius,
        ' the diameter is ', Pi * 2 * Radius)
```

(pp. 56–57)

10. What will the following Writeln statement print out?

```
Writeln('The answer is ', 2 + 2)
```

(pp. 56–57)

11. The following declaration is incorrect. Rewrite it, formatting the comment correctly.

```
VAR
  Annual_Receipts_MA:        (* Total of monthly cash
    Real;                       receipts in the
                                Massachusetts store   *)
```

(pp. 58–59)

12. Fill in the blanks in this program.

```
_____Circle (Output);


_____
  Pi = 3.14159;            (* Ratio of circumference
                              to diameter            *)

_____

  Circumference:          (* Computed circumference
                             of the circle           *)
    Real;

_____(* Circle *)

  Circumference __ 2 * Pi * 7;
  Writeln __'The circumference of a circle of ',
            'radius 7 is ' __

  Writeln __Circumference __
```

```
_____    (* Circle *)
```

(pp. 59–61)

13. What should you do if a program fails to run correctly and the reason for the error is not immediately obvious? (pp. 62–69)

14. How would you write the following formula as a Pascal expression that produces a Real value as a result?

$$\frac{9}{5}C + 32$$

(pp. 69–70)

15. Which Pascal functions can be used to convert a real number into an integer approximation of the number? (pp. 70–72)

16. What is the result of evaluating the expression

```
(1 + 2 * 2) DIV 1 + 1
```

(pp. 69–70)

17. Write a Write statement to print out the title of this chapter (Pascal Syntax and Semantics, and the Program Development Process). (pp. 72–74)

18. How many Writeln statements without parameters would you have to insert after a Write statement to make a blank line appear in the output? (pp. 72–74)

19. Assume the Real variable Pay contains the amount 327.66101. What fieldwidth specification would you use with the variable to print it in dollars and cents with three leading blanks? (pp. 75–77)

Answers

1. Unless your last name is hyphenated, it probably is a valid Pascal identifier.

2. CONST
       Pi = 3.14159;

3. BEGIN, PROGRAM

4.   VAR
          Count:
            Integer;
          Sum:
            Real;
          Letter:
            Char;

5. Toes := 10;   6. a. 9 / 5   b. 9 DIV 5   7. 1

8. Writeln('Introduction to Pascal and Structured Design');

9.   'For radius'
      Radius
      ' the diameter is '
      Pi * 2 * Radius

10.   The answer is   4

11. VAR
       Annual_Receipts_MA: (* Total of monthly cash *)
           Real;   (* receipts in the   *)
                              (* Massachusetts store *)

     or

     VAR
       Annual_Receipts_MA: (* Total of monthly cash
                                 receipts in the
                                 Massachusetts store *)

           Real;

12. PROGRAM Circle (Output);

       CONST
         Pi = 3.14159;   (* Ratio of circumference
                                    to diameter   *)

       VAR
         Circumference: (* Computed circumference
                                    of the circle   *)

           Real;

     BEGIN (* Circle *)
       Circumference := 2 * Pi * 7;
       Writeln('The circumference of a circle of ',
               'radius 7 is ');
       Writeln (Circumference)
     END. (* Circle *)

13. Get a fresh printout of the program, leave the computer, and study the program until you understand the cause of the problem. Then correct the algorithm and the program as necessary before you go back to the computer and make any changes in the program file.   14. 9 / 5 * C + 32   15. Trunc and Round   16. The result is 6.

17. Write('Pascal Syntax and Semantics, and the Program Development Process')

18. Two Writeln statements are necessary after a Write statement to produce a blank line in the output.

19. Pay:9:2

▪ *Exam Preparation Exercises*

1. Mark the following identifiers either valid or invalid.

	Valid	Invalid
a. Item#1	___	___
b. Data	___	___
c. Y	___	___
d. 1Set	___	___
e. Investment	___	___
f. Bin−2	___	___
g. Num_5	___	___
h. Sq Ft		

2. Given these syntax templates:

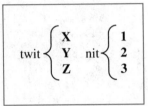

mark the following "dwits" either valid or invalid.

	Valid	Invalid
a. XYZ	_____	_____
b. 123	_____	_____
c. X1	_____	_____
d. 23Y	_____	_____
e. XY12	_____	_____
f. Y2Y	_____	_____
g. ZY2	_____	_____
h. XY23X1	_____	_____

3. Formatting a program incorrectly causes an error. True or false?

4. Mark the following constructs either valid or invalid. Assume all variables are of type Integer.

	Valid	Invalid
a. X * Y := C	_____	_____
b. Y := Con	_____	_____
c. CONST X : 10	_____	_____
d. VAR X : Integer	_____	_____
e. A := B MOD C	_____	_____

5. Match each of the following terms with the correct definition. There is only one correct definition for each term.

_____ a. program
_____ b. algorithm
_____ c. compiler
_____ d. identifier
_____ e. translation phase
_____ f. execution phase

_____ g. variable
_____ h. constant
_____ i. memory
_____ j. syntax
_____ k. semantics
_____ l. block

(1) A symbolic name made up of letters and digits but beginning with a letter
(2) A place in memory where a data value that cannot be changed is stored
(3) A program that takes a program written in a high-level language and translates it into machine code
(4) An input device
(5) The time spent planning a program
(6) Grammar rules
(7) The declaration and statement sections of a program

(8) Meaning
(9) A program that translates assembly language instructions into machine code
(10) When the machine code version of a program is being run
(11) A place in memory where a data value that can be changed is stored
(12) When a program in a high-level language is converted into machine code
(13) The part of the computer that holds both program and data
(14) A step-by-step outline for solving a problem
(15) A sequence of instructions that enables a computer to perform a particular task

6. Compute the value of each legal expression. Indicate whether the value is Real or Integer. If the expression is not legal, explain why.
   a. 10 / 3 + 5 * 2
   b. 10 MOD 3 + 5 MOD 2
   c. 10 DIV 3 + 5 DIV 2
   d. 12.5 + (2.5 / (6.2 / 3.1))
   e. - 4 * (-5 + 6)
   f. 13 MOD 5 / 3
   g. (10 / 3 MOD 2) / 3

7. What is the value of Result in each of the following statements?
   a. Result := 15 MOD 4
   b. Result := 7 DIV 3 + 2
   c. Result := 2 + 7 * 5
   d. Result := 45 DIV 8 * 4 + 2
   e. Result := 17 + (21 MOD 6) * 2
   f. Result := Sqr(4 * 2 + 2)

8. Which of the following are reserved words and which are user-defined identifiers?

	Reserved	User-Defined
a. END	___	___
b. SORT	___	___
c. WRITEHI	___	___
d. MOD	___	___
e. THEEND	___	___

9. Reserved words can be used as variable names. True or false?

10. A block consists of an optional declarations section and a compound statement. True or false?

11. If A = 5 and B = 2, what does each of the following statements produce?
    a. Writeln('A = ', A, 'B = ', B);
    b. Writeln('Sum = ', A + B);
    c. Writeln(A DIV B);
    d. Writeln(B - A);

12. Name two things that contribute to the readability of a program.

13. What does the following program print?

```
PROGRAM Exercise (Output);

CONST
    Lbs = 10;
```

```
VAR
  Price,
  Cost:
    Integer;
  Ch:
    Char;

BEGIN (* Exercise *)
  Price := 30;
  Cost := Price * Lbs;
  Ch := 'A';
  Writeln('Cost is ');
  Writeln(Cost);
  Writeln('Price is ', Price, 'Cost is ', Cost);
  Writeln('Grade ', Ch, ' costs ');
  Writeln(Cost)
END.  (* Exercise *)
```

14. Translate the following Pascal code into algebraic notation.

```
R1 := (-B + Sqrt(B - 4 * A * C)) / (2 * A)
```

15. Given the following program fragment, determine the value of each of the expressions below. If the result is Real, include the decimal point in your answer.

```
VAR
  X,
  Y:
    Integer;
  Z:
    Real;
```

For X = 4, Y = 17, and Z = 2.6:

```
a. X / Y
b. 1 / X + 2
c. Z * Y
d. X + Y MOD X
e. 14 DIV 15 * 2
f. 2 * X + Y - X
g. X DIV 2
h. 2 * 3 - 1 MOD 3
i. X MOD Y DIV X
```

16. What is the output of the following Pascal program? Be sure to use a □ to indicate each blank.

```
PROGRAM Assignment (Output);
```

DIV-division of int
MOD-remainder

```
VAR
  Ch:
   Char;
  X:
   Integer;
  Y:
   Real;


BEGIN (* Assignment *)
  Ch := 'A';
  Write(Ch);
  Ch := 'B';
  Writeln(Ch);
  X := 413;
  Y := 21.8;
  Writeln(X:6, ' is the value of X');
  Writeln(Y:6, ' is the value of Y');
END.  (* Assignment *)
```

17. Evaluate the following expressions. If the result is a real number, include a decimal point in your answer. You may have to look up some of the functions in Appendix B.
    a. Abs(-9.1)
    b. Sqrt(49)
    c. 3 * Round(7.8) + 3
    d. Trunc(6.7)
    e. Sqrt(Sqr(3) + Sqr(4))

■ *Programming Warm-Up Exercises*

1. Change Program Exercise (pages 91–92) so that it prints the cost for 15 pounds.

2. Write Pascal expressions to compute both solutions for the quadratic formula. The formula is

$$x = (-b \pm \sqrt{b^2 - 4ac})/2a$$

3. Input and run the following program. Supply the information within parentheses in the comments.

```
PROGRAM One (Output);

(* Programming Assignment One         *)
(* (your name)                        *)
(* (date copied and run)              *)
(* (description of the problem)       *)

CONST
  Debt = 300.0; (* Original value owed  *)
  Paymt = 22.4; (* Payment              *)
  Intr = 0.02;  (* Interest rate        *)
```

```
VAR
  Charg,           (* Interest times debt     *)
  Reduc,           (* Amount debt is reduced   *)
  Remain:          (* Remaining balance        *)
    Real;


BEGIN (* One *)
  Charg := Intr * Debt;
  Reduc := Paymt - Charg;
  Remain := Debt - Reduc;
  Writeln('Payment ', Paymt, 'Charge ',
          Charg, ' Balance owed ', Remain)
END.  (* One *)
```

4. Copy and run the following program. Fill in the comments, using the pattern shown in Exercise 3 above.

```
PROGRAM Two (Output);


CONST
  T_Cost = 600;
  Pounds = 10;
  Ounces = 11;


VAR
  Tot_Oz,
  U_Cost:
    Real;


BEGIN
  Tot_Oz := 16 * Pounds;
  Tot_Oz := Tot_Oz + Ounces;
  U_Cost := T_Cost / Tot_Oz;
  Writeln('Cost per unit ', U_Cost)
END.
```

Notice how hard it is to tell what the program does without the comments.

5. Complete the following Pascal program. The program should find and output the perimeter and area of a rectangle given the length and the width. Be sure to label the output. And don't forget to use comments.

```
PROGRAM Rectangle (Output);

(* This program finds the perimeter and the area of a rectangle *)
(* given the length and width                                   *)


VAR
  Length,          (* Length of the rectangle    *)
  Width,           (* Width of the rectangle      *)
  Perimeter,       (* Perimeter of the rectangle *)
  Area:            (* Area of the rectangle       *)
    Real;
```

```
BEGIN (* Rectangle *)
   Length := 10;      (* Assigns a value to Length *)
   Width := 5;        (* Assigns a value to Width  *)
```

6. Write an assignment statement to calculate the sum of the numbers from 1 to N using Gauss's formula:

Sum $= [N(N + 1)] /2$

Store the result in the Integer variable Sum.

▪ *Programming Problems*

1. Write a Pascal program that will print your initials in large block letters, each letter made up of the same character it represents. The letters should be a minimum of seven printed lines high and should appear all in a row. For example, if your initials are DOW, your program should print out

```
DDDDDDD         00000        W      W
D      D        0    0       W      W
D      D        0    0       W      W
D      D        0    0       W   W  W
D      D        0    0       W  W W  W
D      D        0    0       W W   W W
DDDDDDD         00000        WW     WW
```

Be sure to include appropriate comments in your program, choose meaningful identifiers, and use indentation as we do in the programs in this chapter.

2. Write a program to print out the value of the predefined Pascal constant MaxInt and the value −MaxInt. The output should identify which value is MaxInt and which value is −MaxInt. Be sure to include appropriate comments in your program, choose meaningful identifiers, and use indentation.

3. Write a Pascal program that converts a centigrade temperature to its Fahrenheit equivalent. The formula is

Fahrenheit $= \dfrac{9}{5}$ centigrade $+ 32$

Make the centigrade temperature a named constant, so that its value can be changed easily. The program should print both the value of the centigrade temperature and its Fahrenheit equivalent, with appropriate identifying messages. Use comments, meaningful identifiers, and indentation.

4. Write a program to calculate the diameter, the circumference, and the area of a circle given a radius of 6.75. Assign the radius to a Real variable, and then output the radius with an appropriate message. Define a named constant Pi with the value 3.14159. The program should output the diameter, the circumference, and the area, each on a separate line, with identifying labels. Use a fieldwidth specification so that the fraction part extends to five places and the total fieldwidth is ten.

5. Write a program that outputs the results of all three types of division (/, DIV, and MOD) given the Integer values 7 and 4. Output the two Integer values and each result on a separate line with appropriate messages. Use fieldwidth specifications to format the output.

Input and Design Methodology

GOALS

- To be able to construct Read and Readln statements to read values into a program.
- To be able to determine the contents of variables assigned values in Read and Readln statements.
- To be able to write appropriate prompting messages for interactive programs.
- To know when batch input/output is appropriate and how it differs from interactive input/output.
- To be able to write programs that use Text files other than Input and Output.
- To be able to apply top-down design methodology to solve a simple problem.
- To be able to take a top-down design and code it in Pascal, using self-documenting code.

Input and Design Methodology

A program needs data on which to operate. We have been writing all of the data values into the program itself, in literal and named constants. If this was the only way we could enter data, we would have to rewrite a program each time we wanted to apply it to a different set of values. In this chapter we look at ways of entering data into a program while it is running.

We have talked about general problem-solving strategies and writing simple programs. For a simple problem, it's easy to choose a strategy, write the algorithm, and code the program. But as problems become more complex, we have to use a more organized approach. In the second part of this chapter we look at a general methodology for developing algorithms—top-down design.

Getting Data into Programs

One of the biggest advantages of computers is that a program can be used with many different sets of data. To do this, the data must be kept separate from the program until it is executed. Then instructions in the program copy values from the data set into

Figure 3-1
Separating the Data from the Program

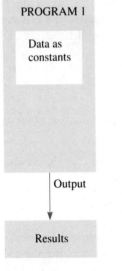

This program must be changed to work with different data values.

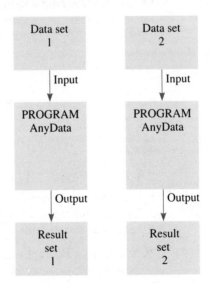

This program inputs its data from outside, so it can work with different data sets without being changed.

variables in the program. After storing these values in the variables, the program can perform calculations with them (see Figure 3-1).

The process of placing values from an outside data set into variables in a program is called *input*. The data for the program can come from an input device or from a file on an auxiliary storage device. We look at file input later in this chapter; here we consider the standard input device, the keyboard.

Read

Pascal gives us a standard procedure for inputting data called the *Read statement*. Its name is descriptive of its function: The computer "reads" what we type into it. Here is the syntax template for a Read statement:

Read (parameter , parameter ...)

From the template, you can see that Read is a subprogram. The telltale sign is the parameter list, a common characteristic of subprograms. Unlike the parameter list for a Write or Writeln statement, which can contain constants, variables, and expressions, the parameter list for a Read statement can contain only variables. Why? Because the Read parameter list specifies where input data values should be placed, and only variables can have their values changed while a program is running.

If there are multiple variables in a parameter list, they must be separated by commas. For example:

```
Read(Length, Width, Price)
```

When the parameters are Real or Integer variables, the Read statement is executed this way:

For each variable in the parameter list, starting with the first one:

1. Get a number from the keyboard.
2. Store the number in the variable.
3. Go to the next variable in the list.

When a value has been placed in the last variable in the parameter list, Read is finished.

How do you separate numbers when you are entering them? By putting blanks between them.

Just as with the assignment statement, you have to be careful that you don't try to input a Real value into an Integer variable. You can, however, read an Integer value into a Real variable.

Statement*	Data	Contents After Read
1. Read(X)	32	X = 32
2. Read(A, B, C)	3 4 60	A = 3, B = 4, C = 60
3. Read(D, E)	24	
	76	D = 24, E = 76
4. Read(Y, Z)	46 32.4 15	Y = 46, Z = 32.4
		(15 is held for later input)

*A, B, C, D, E, X, and Y are Integer variables; Z is a Real variable.

If there are not enough values entered on one line to fill all of the parameters, the computer automatically continues reading from the next line of input, as shown in example (3). If more numbers are entered than there are variables in the parameter list, the computer holds the extra numbers until it comes to the next Read statement, as shown in (4). If there are extra values left when the program ends, the computer disregards them.

There is no difference between the statements

```
Read(A);
Read(B);
```

and the statement

```
Read(A, B);
```

Using a list of variable identifiers is a convenience for the programmer.

Readln

Pascal has a second input statement called *Readln* (pronounced *read line*). Readln functions like Writeln: It goes to the next line when it is finished, but it goes to the next line of *input*, not output. After the variables in its parameter list have had values placed in them, Readln skips over any extra values on the line of input and goes to the start of the next line. The extra numbers are discarded; they are not read.

Suppose there are two Integer values on each line of input:

```
10 20
15 16
22 21
```

The table shows the contents of the variables after the Readln statements have been executed.

Statement	Contents After Readln

1. `Readln(A);`
`Readln(B);`
`Readln(C);`
	A = 10
	B = 15
	C = 22

2. `Readln(A, B, C);` `Readln(D, E);`	A = 10, B = 20, C = 15 D = 22, E = 21

3. `Readln(A, B);`
`Readln(C, D);`
`Readln(E);`
	A = 10, B = 20
	C = 15, D = 16
	E = 22

4. `Readln(A);`
`Readln(B);`
`Readln(C, D, E);`
	A = 10
	B = 15
	C = 22, D = 21, and an error occurs because there is no value to place in E

5. `Readln(A, B);`
`Readln;`
`Readln(C);`
	A = 10, B = 20
	
	C = 22

If you are entering data at the keyboard, the error in (4) would cause the computer to wait until you enter more data. If data is being read from a file, the program would stop executing and an error message would be output. Example (5) shows that a Readln with no parameters causes a line of input data to be skipped.

The Reading Marker and <eoln>

Before we explore the effects of mixing Read and Readln statements, we introduce the concept of the *reading marker*. The reading marker works like a bookmark, but instead of marking a place in a book, it keeps track of the point in the input data where the computer should continue reading. The reading marker indicates the next character to be read. Read leaves the reading marker on the character following the last piece of data that was input; Readln leaves the reading marker at the beginning of the next line.

Each input line has an end-of-line mark (<eoln>) that tells the computer where one line ends and the next begins. Read and Readln cross line boundaries (<eoln>s) to find as many values as there are variables in their parameter lists.

Where does the <eoln> come from? What is it? The first question is easy. When you are working at a keyboard, you generate an <eoln> yourself each time you hit the return or Enter key. You also can generate an <eoln> with a Writeln statement. Writeln outputs an <eoln> when it tells the screen or printer to go to the next line.

The answer to the second question varies from computer system to computer system. In Turbo Pascal, <eoln> is a sequence of two nonprintable control characters: Return and New Line. When your program is reading Char values, the Read statement will input these two characters, one at a time, when it encounters <eoln> (standard Pascal inputs a blank in place of <eoln>).

Let's look at an example that uses the reading marker and <eoln>. Given these three lines of input data:

datafile:

```
123 456 789<eoln>
987 654 321<eoln>
888 777 666<eoln>
```

and given that A, B, C, and D are Integer variables, the statements in the table produce the results shown. The part of the input list printed in color is what has been read after the Read or Readln is executed. The reading marker, denoted by the shaded gray block, indicates the next character to be read.

Statements	Values Read	Marker Position After Read/Readln
1. Read(A, B);	A = 123, B = 456	123 456 789<eoln> 987 654 321<eoln> 888 777 666<eoln>
Read(C, D);	C = 789, D = 987	123 456 789<eoln> 987 654 321<eoln> 888 777 666<eoln>
2. Readln(A, B);	A = 123, B = 456	123 456 789<eoln> 987 654 321<eoln> 888 777 666<eoln>
Readln(C, D);	C = 987, D = 654	123 456 789<eoln> 987 654 321<eoln> 888 777 666<eoln>
3. Read(A, B);	A = 123, B = 456	123 456 789<eoln> 987 654 321<eoln> 888 777 666<eoln>
Readln(C, D);	C = 789, D = 987	123 456 789<eoln> 987 654 321<eoln> 888 777 666<eoln>
4. Readln(A, B);	A = 123, B = 456	123 456 789<eoln> 987 654 321<eoln> 888 777 666<eoln>
Readln(C);	C = 987	123 456 789<eoln> 987 654 321<eoln> 888 777 666<eoln>
Readln(D);	D = 888	123 456 789<eoln> 987 654 321<eoln> 888 777 666<eoln>

Although we've used Integer values in the table, Real data values are read into Real variables in exactly the same way.

Look back at the Readln statements in Program Payroll (page 31). Emp_Num, Pay_Rate, and Hours are each read in with a separate Readln. So each data item is on a separate line.

Reading Character Data

Character data is treated differently from numeric data. Remember that a Char variable holds just *one* character. So when the program is reading values into variables declared to be of type Char, only one character is read at a time. For example, given the data

```
A10<eoln>
BBB<eoln>
999<eoln>
```

and given that X, Y, and Z are Char variables, the Read and Readln statements in the table produce the results shown.

Statements	Values Read	Marker Position After Read/Readln
1. Read(X, Y, Z);	X = 'A', Y = '1', Z = '0'	A10<eoln> BBB<eoln> 999<eoln>
2. Readln(X);	X = 'A'	A10<eoln> BBB<eoln> 999<eoln>
Readln(Y);	Y = 'B'	A10<eoln> BBB<eoln> 999<eoln>
Read(Z);	Z = '9'	A10<eoln> BBB<eoln> 999<eoln>
3. Readln(X, Y);	X = 'A', Y = '1'	A10<eoln> BBB<eoln> 999<eoln>
Readln(Z);	Z = 'B'	A10<eoln> BBB<eoln> 999<eoln>

Notice that you do not have to use quotation marks around character data values when they are input. When you write character constants in programs, you have to put single quotes around them to distinguish them from identifiers. But when a data value is read in, the type of the variable in which the value is stored determines whether the value is interpreted as a number or a character.

Before the first Read or Readln in a program and after every Readln, the reading marker points to the first character on a line. After a Read, the marker points to the character following what was just read in. This can be a problem when you want to read character data immediately following a number. Remember that we use space to separate numbers. Because a space is a character, the space is read into the Char variable instead of the character following the space (which is probably what you want).

The table below shows what happens when character data and numeric data are mixed (Ch1 and Ch2 are Char variables, and P and Q are Integer variables). Remember that a Read involving a Char variable reads only the one character that the reading marker is on. The data is

```
24 36 AB<eoln>
```

Statements	Values Read	Marker Position After Read/Readln
Read(P, Q);	P = 24, Q = 36	24 36 AB<eoln>
Read(Ch1);	Ch1 = ' '	24 36 AB<eoln>
Read(Ch2);	Ch2 = 'A'	24 36 AB<eoln>

After the second Integer value is read, the reading marker is left at the space between the 6 and the A. When the computer looks for a character to put into Ch1, it takes the blank. This leaves the marker on the letter A, which is read into Ch2.

If we want to read the A into Ch1 and the B into Ch2, we have to tell the computer to skip over the blank between the 6 and the A. There are a couple of ways to do this. We can declare an extra variable of type Char, Ch0, to hold the blank, and rewrite the statements like this:

Statements	Values Read	Marker Position After Read/Readln
Read(P, Q);	P = 24, Q = 36	24 36 AB<eoln>
Read(Ch0);	Ch0 = ' '	24 36 AB<eoln>
Read(Ch1);	Ch1 = 'A'	24 36 AB<eoln>
Read(Ch2);	Ch2 = 'B'	24 36 AB<eoln>

Or we can read into Ch1 twice. The first Read stores the blank in Ch1; the second Read puts the A into Ch1, replacing the blank.

Statements	Values Read	Marker Position After Read/Readln
Read(P, Q);	P = 24, Q = 36	24 36 AB<eoln>
Read(Ch1);	Ch1 = ' '	24 36 AB<eoln>
Read(Ch1);	Ch1 = 'A'	24 36 AB<eoln>
Read(Ch2);	Ch2 = 'B'	24 36 AB<eoln>

Let's look at a few other examples in which numeric and character input are mixed. We use the same data we used before:

```
24 36 AB<eoln>
```

Statements	Values Read	Marker Position After Read/Readln
1. `Read(Ch1, Ch2);`	Ch1 = '2', Ch2 = '4'	24 36 AB<eoln>
2. `Read(P, Q);`	P = 24, Q = 36	24 36 AB<eoln>
`Read(Ch1, Ch1);`	Ch1 = ' ', Ch1 = 'A'	24 36 AB<eoln>
`Read(Ch2, Ch2)`	Ch2 = 'B', Ch2 = '↵'	24 36 AB<eoln>

In (1), Ch1 holds '2' and Ch2 holds '4'. These are the characters '2' and '4', not the integers 2 and 4. Compare this with (2). The Read statement interprets the same data in different ways, depending on the data type of the variable that's being filled. Notice in (2) that reading the <eoln> into a Char variable causes a Return character to be stored in that variable. (The ↵ symbol is used to represent the nonprinting control character Return.) In Standard Pascal, a blank would have been stored in Ch2. The reading marker has advanced beyond the data we've shown and thus does not appear on the last line. (It is actually positioned on the New Line character that follows Return. In Standard Pascal it would have moved to the next line.)

*T*heoretical Foundations

More About Procedures and Parameters

We've defined a procedure as a type of subprogram. When your program tells the computer to go off and follow the instructions in a subprogram, the program is *calling* the subprogram. When the program calls the subprogram, the parameters in the parameter list are *passed* to the subprogram. When the subprogram finishes, the computer *returns* to the main program.

With Write and Writeln, we can pass constants, variables, and expressions to the subprogram. Read and Readln, however, accept only variables as parameters. Read and Readln store values in their parameters when they return, and only variables can have values stored in them while a program is running. Read and Readln *return* or *pass back* values through their parameters. The point to remember is that parameters can be used both to get data into a procedure and to get results back out.

Interactive Input/Output

Remember in Chapter 1 that we defined an interactive program as one in which the user communicates directly with the computer. Many of the programs that you write will be interactive. There is a certain "etiquette" involved in writing interactive programs that has to do with instructions for the user.

To get data into an interactive program, we use *input prompts*, printed messages that explain what the user should enter. Without these messages, the user has no idea what to type into a program. A program also should print out all of the data values typed in so that the user can verify that they were entered correctly. Printing the input values is called *echo printing*. Here's a sample of a program segment showing the proper use of prompts:

```
Writeln('Enter the part number:');                (* Prompt      *)
Readln(Part_Number);
Writeln('Enter the quantity of this part ordered:');   (* Prompt      *)
Readln(Quantity);
Writeln('Enter the unit price for this part:');    (* Prompt      *)
Readln(Unit_Price);
Total_Price := Quantity * Unit_Price;
Writeln('Part ', Part_Number:6, ', quantity ',     (* Echo print *)
        Quantity:6, ', at $', Unit_Price:7:2);
Writeln('each, totals $', Total_Price:7:2);
```

And here's the output, with the user's input shown in color:

```
Enter the part number:
4671
Enter the quantity of this part ordered:
10
Enter the unit price for this part:
27.25
Part   4671,   quantity     10, at $    27.25
each,  totals $ 272.50
```

The amount of information you put into your prompts depends on who is going to be using a program. If you are writing a program for people who are not familiar with computers, your messages should be more detailed. For example, "Type a four-digit part number, then press the key marked RETURN." If the program is going to be used frequently by the same people, you could shorten the prompts: "Enter PN." and "Enter Qty." If the program is for very experienced users, you can prompt for several values at once and have them type all of the values on one input line:

```
Enter PN, Qty, Unit Price:
4176 10 27.25
```

In programs that use large amounts of data, this method saves the user keystrokes and time. However, it also makes it easier for the user to enter values in the wrong order.

Prompts are not the only way programs interact with users. It can be helpful to have a program print out some general instructions at the beginning ("Press RETURN after typing each data value. Enter a negative number when done."). When data is not entered in the correct form, a message that indicates the problem should be printed. For users who haven't worked much with computers, it's important that these messages be informative and "friendly." For example:

```
ILLEGAL DATA VALUES!!!!!!!
```

is likely to upset an inexperienced user. Moreover, it doesn't offer any constructive information. A much better message would be

```
That is not a valid part number.
Part numbers must be no more than four digits long.
Please reenter the number in its proper form:
```

In Chapter 4, we introduce the statements that allow us to test for erroneous data.

Batch Input/Output

Although we tend to use examples of interactive I/O in this text, many programs are written using batch I/O. Remember that in batch processing, the user and the computer do not interact during the actual processing. This method is most effective when a program is going to input or output large amounts of data.

When a program must read in many data values, the usual practice is to prepare them ahead of time, storing them in a file. This allows the user to go back and make changes or corrections to the data as necessary before running the program. When a program is designed to print lots of data, the output can be sent directly to a high-speed printer or another disk file. This allows the user to examine the data at leisure, after the program has been run. Turbo Pascal does not support true batch processing, but we can achieve a similar effect through the use of files other than Input and Output. In the next section we discuss input and output with disk files.

Programs that are designed for file processing do not need to print prompting messages for input. It is still a good idea, however, to echo-print each data value that is read. Echo printing allows the person reading the output to verify that the input values were prepared correctly. Because file-oriented programs tend to print large amounts of data, their output often is in the form of a table, columns with descriptive headings.

Files Other Than Input and Output

In everything we've done so far, we've assumed that the input to our programs comes from the keyboard and that the output from our programs goes to the screen or printer. We've referred to the keyboard and screen as "files" called Input and Output. Strictly

Figure 3-2
3.5-inch and 5.25-
inch Floppy Disks

speaking, the keyboard and screen aren't files—at least not in the same sense as the files in which we enter our programs. A true *file* is a named area in secondary memory that holds a collection of information (for example, the program code we have entered). The information in a file usually is stored on an auxiliary storage device, such as a disk (see Figure 3-2).

The reason we sometimes call Input and Output *files* is because we treat them the same way we treat disk files. Our programs read data from the keyboard in the same way they read data from a file. And they write output to the screen in the same way they write output onto a disk file.

Why would we want a program to read data from a file instead of the keyboard? If a program is going to read a large quantity of data, it is easier to enter the data into a file with an editor than to enter it while the program is running. With the editor we can go back and correct mistakes. Also we do not have to enter the data all at once; we can take a break and come back later. And if we want to rerun the program, having the data stored on a file allows us to do so without reentering the data.

Why would we want the output from a program to be written on a disk file? The contents of a file can be displayed on a screen or printed. This gives us the option of looking at the output over and over again without having to rerun the program. Also the output stored on a file can be read into another program as input. For example, Program Payroll writes its output to File Pay_File. We can take Pay_File and read it into another program, which prints out paychecks.

Using Files

If we want a program in Turbo Pascal to use files other than Input and Output, we have to do six things:

1. Put the names of the files in the program heading.
2. Declare the files in the VAR section of the program.
3. Prepare each file for reading or writing with Reset or Rewrite statements.

4. Specify the name of the file to be used as the first parameter of each Read, Readln, Write, or Writeln statement.
5. Assign a system file name to each file that is declared, using an Assign statement as discussed later in this chapter.*
6. Close each file at the end of the program.*

Listing File Names in the Program Heading   Suppose we want Program Mileage (page 81) to read data from a file and to write its output to a file. Let's call the files InMPG and OutMPG. The program heading would look like this:

```
PROGRAM Mileage (Output, InMPG, OutMPG);
```

Why do we need to list Output in the heading if all of the output is going to be written on File OutMPG? Pascal requires that Output be in the list in case errors crop up when the program is running. Error messages must be sent to the screen; otherwise there is no way to notify the programmer directly of problems. Input, however, does not have to be listed in the program heading when all data values are going to be input from a file.

File names must be identifiers—that is, their syntax is identical to variable names. But some computer systems do not use this format for file names. For example, many systems include a period in file names; Pascal uses just letters and digits. The problem is reconciling the two formats. In Turbo Pascal, we use the nonstandard procedure Assign, discussed below, to associate a Pascal file name with the DOS system file name. (Standard Pascal merely assumes that the two names are identical.)

Declaring Files in the VAR Section   Because file names are identifiers, we have to declare them in the VAR section of the program. (Input and Output do not have to be declared in the VAR section of a program because, like MaxInt, they are predefined in Pascal.) We declare files the same way that we declare any variable: We specify the name, followed by a colon and the data type of the name. Pascal allows us to define files to be of many different data types, but here we use the standard type *Text,* which in fact is the data type of Input and Output. In our example, we would declare files InMPG and OutMPG like this:

```
VAR
  InMPG,      (* Holds gallon amounts and mileages *)
  OutMPG:     (* Holds miles per gallon output      *)
    Text;
```

Preparing Files with Reset or Rewrite   The third thing we have to do is prepare the files we've declared for either reading or writing. We prepare files for reading with the *Reset statement;* for writing with the *Rewrite statement*. In our example we are reading in from File InMPG, so we prepare it with a Reset statement:

```
Reset(InMPG)
```

*Standard Pascal does not require this operation; it is unique to Turbo Pascal.

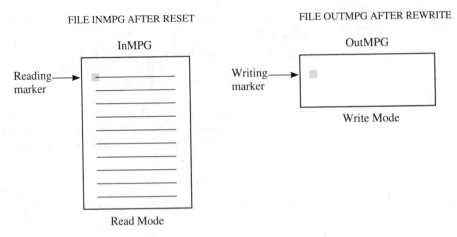

Figure 3-3
The Effect of Reset and Rewrite

FILE INMPG AFTER RESET

FILE OUTMPG AFTER REWRITE

InMPG

OutMPG

Reading marker

Writing marker

Read Mode

Write Mode

Because we are writing to File OutMPG, we prepare it with a Rewrite statement:

```
Rewrite(OutMPG)
```

Exactly what do Reset and Rewrite do? Reset sets the file reading marker to the first piece of data in the file. (Each input file has its own reading marker.) Reset also puts the file into *read mode*. A file that is in read mode cannot be written to—that is, it can be used only to input data. If you try to use a read-mode file with Write or Writeln, you'll get an error message when you run the program.

Rewrite sets the writing marker at the beginning of the file and puts the file into *write mode*. It erases any information the file previously contained (see Figure 3-3). A file that is in write mode cannot be used with Read or Readln.

At any point in a program, you can change the mode of a file using a Reset or Rewrite statement. For example, if you want to read File OutMPG after you write it, you use a Reset statement:

```
Reset(OutMPG)
```

This moves the reading marker to the beginning of the file and puts OutMPG in the read mode (see Figure 3-4). But remember that Rewrite erases the old contents of a file and that Reset always returns the reading marker to the start of the file. So you *cannot* insert a new data value into a file by reading partway through the file, switching it to write mode with a Rewrite statement, and then writing the new data value at that point. The result would be a file with just the one new value in it. The Rewrite statement erases the old contents of the file (see Figure 3-5).

In Standard Pascal you cannot use Rewrite with Input. If you try it, you'll get an error message. On many systems Reset(Input), Reset(Output), and Rewrite(Output) also produce error messages. In Turbo Pascal, however, none of these operations will give an error. If a program executes Reset(Output), succeeding Read and Readln statements may specify Output and will take data from the keyboard. Rewrite(Input) allows data to be written to the screen by specifying Input in a Write or Writeln statement.

Figure 3-4
The Effect of Reset
on an Output File

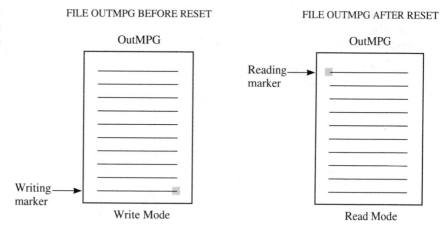

FILE OUTMPG BEFORE RESET

FILE OUTMPG AFTER RESET

Obviously, such a confusing use of Input and Output is extremely poor programming practice.

Both Reset and Rewrite are predefined procedures (notice the telltale parameters—the mark of a subprogram). Because these statements *prepare* files for reading or writing, they must appear in the program before any Read, Readln, Write, or Writeln statements that refer to the files. It's a good idea to put them right after the first BEGIN, so that the files are prepared before the program does anything else.

```
          .
          .
          .
BEGIN  (* Program *)

  (* Prepare files *)

  Reset(InMPG);
  Rewrite(OutMPG);
          .
          .
          .
END.   (* Program *)
```

Specifying Files in Read, Readln, Write, and Writeln Statements Each Read, Readln, Write, or Writeln statement that uses a particular file must have the name of that file as its first parameter. In our example, we would need a statement like

```
Read(InMPG, Amt1, Amt2, Amt3, Amt4, Start_Miles, End_Miles);
```

to instruct the computer to read data from File InMPG. And all of the Writeln statements that output to File OutMPG must list OutMPG as their first parameter:

Figure 3-5
The Effect of
Rewrite on an
Input File

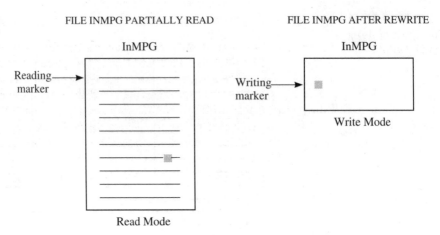

```
Writeln(OutMPG, 'the mileage per gallon is ', MPG:7:2);
```

What happens if you forget to specify the name of a file in a particular I/O statement? Read and Readln statements obtain values from Input (the keyboard); but in Standard Pascal if the identifier Input is not listed in the program heading, you'll get a syntax error. Write and Writeln statements work just as they always do: They write to Output (the screen).

Assigning a System File Name to Each File Identifier

For each file identifier in a program, Turbo Pascal requires that we call the nonstandard procedure Assign. The Assign procedure allows us to specify a file name in DOS format that will correspond to the file identifier in the program. The reason we must use Assign is that DOS file names are not in the same format as Pascal identifiers (for example, DOS file names may include a period).

Assign has two parameters. The first is the identifier that refers to the file within the program—the name that appears in the program heading, file declaration, and so on. The second parameter is a string that is a DOS-format name for a file. Suppose we have on disk a file called WEEKSPAY.DAT. We choose another name that *is* a valid Pascal identifier, such as Pay_File. We can then use the following Assign statement to link the two names together:

```
Assign(Pay_File, 'WEEKSPAY.DAT');
```

From then on, whenever we use the name Pay_File in the program, we will actually be referring to the disk file called WEEKSPAY.DAT. That is, if we write

```
Readln(Pay_File, Emp_Num);
```

the program will get an employee number from the disk file named WEEKSPAY.DAT.

The Assign statement must come before any other statement that tries to access the file. Thus the Assign statement must precede the Reset or Rewrite statement for a file.

Closing Files

At the end of a program, Turbo Pascal requires that the nonstandard procedure Close be called for files other than Input or Output. The Close procedure essentially undoes what was done by the Assign statement. That is, it breaks the association between the file identifier and its corresponding DOS file name. If this is not done for a file on which data is being written, a portion of the data at the end of the file may be lost.

A file may be closed before the end of the program if, for example, it has been entirely processed and is no longer needed. Once a file has been closed, it can have another DOS file name assigned to it. If you try to assign a new system file name to a file that hasn't been closed, an error will result.

Writing Output to a Printer

In addition to the standard predefined files Input and Output, Turbo Pascal has several other nonstandard predefined files. The only one that is of interest here is called Lst. Lst is treated just like Output, except that data which is written to Lst is printed on the printer rather than on the screen. You must include Lst as the first parameter of any Write or Writeln statement that you want to print on the printer. For example,

```
Writeln(Lst, 'This gets printed.');
```

will cause the message 'This gets printed.' to be typed on the printer, rather than on the screen. Of course, if the PC you are using does not have a printer, Lst won't work.

Because Lst is predefined, you don't have to declare it to be of Type Text, you don't have to assign a DOS file name to it, and you don't have to Rewrite or Close it. You do, however, have to add a special "USES" statement in your program. The following statement must appear directly after your program heading:

```
USES Printer;
```

The USES statement is a nonstandard feature of Turbo Pascal which will be discussed in more detail later.

When output is written on the printer, it does not automatically get printed on the screen as well. If you want information to be displayed on both the screen and the printer, you have to use two Writeln (or Write) statements. For example, the statements

```
Writeln(       'Employee number: ', Emp_Num:6); (* On screen  *)
Writeln(Lst,   'Employee number: ', Emp_Num:6); (* On printer *)
```

will display the same information on the screen and the printer, respectively.

Here's Program Mileage reworked. Now it reads its input from File InMPG, computes a real result, and writes its output to File OutMPG. Compare this program with the original version on page 81 and notice that the constants have disappeared because the data is now input at runtime.

```
PROGRAM Mileage (Output, InMPG, OutMPG);

(* This program computes miles per gallon given four amounts *)
(* for gallons used, and starting and ending mileages        *)

VAR
  Amt1,              (* Number of gallons for fillup 1    *)
  Amt2,              (* Number of gallons for fillup 2    *)
  Amt3,              (* Number of gallons for fillup 3    *)
  Amt4,              (* Number of gallons for fillup 4    *)
  Start_Miles,       (* Starting mileage                  *)
  End_Miles,         (* Ending mileage                    *)
  MPG:               (* Computed miles per gallon         *)
    Real;
  InMPG,             (* Holds gallon amounts and mileages *)
  OutMPG:            (* Holds miles per gallon output     *)
    Text;

BEGIN (* Mileage *)
  (* Prepare files *)
  Assign(InMPG, 'MILEAGE.DAT');
  Assign(OutMPG, 'RESULTS.DAT');
  Reset(InMPG);
  Rewrite(OutMPG);
  (* Get data *)
  Read(InMPG, Amt1, Amt2, Amt3, Amt4, Start_Miles, End_Miles);
  (* Compute miles per gallon *)
  MPG := Round((End_Miles - Start_Miles) / (Amt1 + Amt2 + Amt3 + Amt4));
  (* Output results *)
  Writeln(OutMPG, 'For the gallon amounts:');
  Writeln(OutMPG, Amt1:6:1, ',', Amt2:6:1, ',', Amt3:6:1, ',', Amt4:6:1);
  Writeln(OutMPG);
  Writeln(OutMPG, 'a starting mileage of ', Start_Miles:8:1);
  Writeln(OutMPG, 'and an ending mileage of ', End_Miles:8:1);
  Writeln(OutMPG);
  Writeln(OutMPG, 'the mileage per gallon is ', MPG:7:2);
  Close(InMPG);
  Close(OutMPG)
END. (* Mileage *)
```

In this program, the statement

```
Writeln(OutMPG);
```

has the same effect on OutMPG as

```
Writeln;
```

has on Output. It generates a blank line in the output file.

Programming Methodology

The programming process consists of a problem-solving phase and an implementation phase. In Chapter 1 we discussed some strategies for solving problems, and in Chapter 2 we saw how some simple programs are implemented. Here we describe a methodology for developing algorithmic solutions to more complex problems. This methodology will help you write algorithms that are easy to implement as Pascal programs and, consequently, programs that are readable, understandable, and easy to debug and modify.

Top-Down Design

The technique we use is known as **top-down design** (it's also called *stepwise refinement* and *modular programming*). It allows us to use the divide-and-conquer approach that we talked about in Chapter 1.

Top-Down Design   A technique for developing a program in which the problem is divided into more easily handled subproblems, the solutions of which create a solution to the overall problem.

In top-down design, we work from the abstract (a list of the major steps in our solution) to the particular (algorithmic steps that can be translated directly into Pascal code). You can also think of this as working from a high-level solution that leaves the details of implementation unspecified down to a fully detailed solution.

The easiest way to solve a problem is to give it to someone else and say "Solve this problem." This is the most abstract level of a problem solution: a single-statement solution that encompasses the entire problem without specifying any of the details of implementation. It's at this point that programmers are called in. Our job is to turn this abstract solution into a concrete solution, a program.

We start by breaking the solution into a series of major steps. In the process, we move to a lower level of abstraction—some of the implementation details are now specified. Each of the major steps becomes an independent subproblem that we can work on separately. In a very large project, one person (the *chief architect* or *team leader*) would formulate the subproblems and then give them to other members of the programming team, saying "Solve this problem." In the case of a small project, we just give the subproblems to ourselves. Then we choose one subproblem at a time and break it into another series of steps that in turn become smaller subproblems. The process continues until each subproblem cannot be divided further or has an obvious solution.

Why do we work this way? Why not simply write out all of the details? Because it is much easier to focus on one problem at a time. For example, suppose you are working on a program to print out certain values and discover that you need a complex formula to calculate an appropriate fieldwidth for one of them. Calculating fieldwidths is not the purpose of the program. If you shift your focus to the calculation, you are more likely to forget some detail of the printing process. What you do is write down an

*B*ackground Information

Blaise Pascal

The programming language Pascal is named for the inventor of one of the earliest known mechanical calculators, the French mathematician and religious philosopher, Blaise Pascal (1623–1662).

Pascal's father, Etienne, was a noble in the French court, a tax collector, and a mathematician. Pascal's mother died when he was three years old. Five years later, the family moved to Paris and Etienne took over the education of the children. Pascal quickly showed a talent for mathematics. When he was only 17, he published a mathematical essay that earned the jealous envy of René Descartes, one of the founders of modern geometry. (Pascal's work actually had been completed before he was 16.) It was based on a theorem, which he called the *hexagrammum mysticum,* or mystic hexagram, that described the inscription of hexagons in conic sections (parabolas, hyperbolas, and ellipses). In addition to the theorem (now called Pascal's theorem), his essay included over 400 corollaries.

When Pascal was about 20, he constructed a mechanical calculator that performed addition and subtraction of 8-digit numbers. That calculator required the user to dial in the numbers to be added or subtracted; then the sum or difference appeared in a set of windows. It is believed that his motivation for building this machine was to aid his father in his tax collecting work; the earliest version of the machine does indeed split the numbers into six decimal digits and two fractional digits, as would be used for calculating sums of money. The machine was hailed by his contemporaries as a great advance in mathematics, and Pascal built several more in different forms. It achieved such popularity that many fake, nonfunctional copies were built by others and displayed as novelties. Several of Pascal's calculators still exist in various museums.

Pascal's box, as it is called, was long believed to be the first mechanical calculator. However, in 1950, a letter from Wilhelm Shickard to Johannes Kepler written in 1624

abstract step—"Calculate the fieldwidth required"—and go on with the problem at hand. Once you've completed the general solution, you can go back to solving the step that does the calculation.

By subdividing the problem, you create a hierarchical structure called a *tree structure*. Each level of the tree is a complete solution to the problem that is less abstract than the level above it. Figure 3-6 shows a generic solution tree for a problem. Steps that are shaded have enough implementation details specified to be translated directly into Pascal statements. These are **concrete steps.** Those that are not shaded are **abstract steps;** they reappear as subproblems in the next level down. Each box in the figure represents a **module.** Modules are the basic building blocks of programs. The diagram in Figure 3-6 is also called a *module structure chart*.

was discovered. This letter described an even more sophisticated calculator built by Shickard 20 years prior to Pascal's box. Unfortunately, the machine was destroyed in a fire and never rebuilt.

During his twenties, Pascal solved several difficult problems related to the cycloid curve, indirectly contributing to the development of differential calculus. Working with Pierre de Fermat, he laid the foundation of the calculus of probabilities and combinatorial analysis. One of the results of this work came to be known as Pascal's triangle— which simplifies the calculation of the coefficients of the expansion of $(X + Y)^N$, where N is a positive integer.

Pascal also published a treatise on air pressure and conducted experiments that showed that barometric pressure decreases with altitude, helping to confirm theories that had been proposed by Galileo and Torricelli. His work on fluid dynamics forms a significant part of the foundation of that field. Among the most famous of his contributions is Pascal's law, which states that pressure applied to a fluid in a closed vessel is transmitted uniformly throughout the fluid.

When Pascal was 23, his father became ill, and the family was visited by two disciples of Jansenism, a reform movement in the Catholic Church that had begun six years earlier. The family converted, and five years later one of his sisters entered a convent. Pascal initially was not so taken with the new movement, but by the time he was 31, his sister had persuaded him to abandon the world and devote himself to religion.

His religious works are considered no less brilliant than his mathematical and scientific writings. His *Provincial Letters,* a series of 18 essays on various aspects of religion, are considered by some to mark the beginning of modern French prose.

Pascal returned briefly to mathematics when he was 35, but a year later his health, which had always been poor, took a turn for the worse. Unable to perform regular work, he devoted himself to helping the less fortunate. Three years after that, he died while staying with his sister, having given his own house to a poor family.

Concrete Step   A step for which the implementation details are fully specified.

Abstract Step   A step for which some implementation details remain unspecified.

Module   A self-contained collection of steps that solves a problem or subproblem; can contain both concrete and abstract steps.

Modules

A module begins life as an abstract step in the next higher level of the solution tree. It is completed when it solves a given subproblem, when it specifies a series of steps that does the same thing as the higher-level abstract step. At this stage a module is **functionally equivalent** to the abstract step. Don't confuse our use of *function* with Pascal

Figure 3-6   Hierarchical Solution Tree

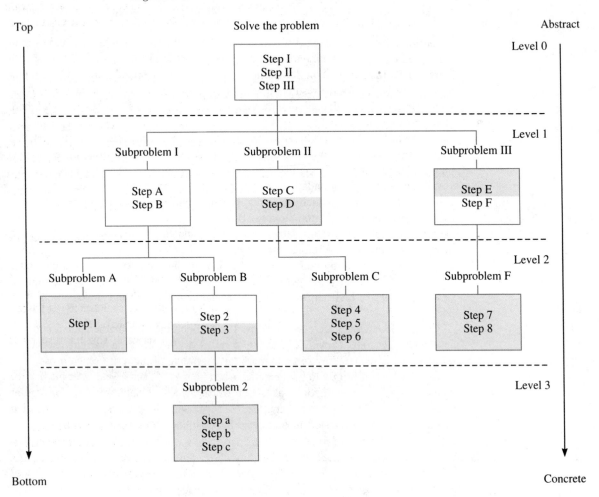

functions. Here we use the term to refer to the specific role that the module or step plays in an algorithmic solution.

Functional Equivalence   A property of a module that performs exactly the same operation as the abstract step it defines. A pair of modules are also functionally equivalent to each other when they perform exactly the same operation.

A properly written module contains only concrete steps that directly address the given subproblem and abstract steps for significant new subproblems. This is called **functional cohesion.**

Functional Cohesion   A property of a module in which all concrete steps are directed toward solving just one problem, and any significant subproblems are written as abstract steps.

The idea behind functional cohesion is that each module should do just one thing and do it well. Functional cohesion is not a well-defined property; there is no quantitative measure of cohesion. It is a product of the human need to organize things into neat chunks that are easy to understand and remember. Knowing which details to make concrete and which details to leave abstract is a matter of experience, circumstance, and personal style. For example, you might decide to include a fieldwidth calculation in a printing module if there isn't so much detail in the rest of the module that it becomes confusing. On the other hand, if the calculation is performed several times, it makes sense to write it as a separate module and just refer to it each time you need it.

Writing Cohesive Modules   Here's one approach to writing modules that are cohesive:

1. Think about how you would solve the subproblem by hand.
2. Begin writing down the major steps.
3. If a step is simple enough so that you can see how to implement it directly in Pascal, it is at the concrete level; it doesn't need any further refinement.
4. If you have to think about implementing a step as a series of smaller steps or as several Pascal statements, it is still at an abstract level.
5. If you are trying to write a series of steps and start to feel overwhelmed by details, you are probably bypassing one or more levels of abstraction. Stand back and look for pieces that you can write as more abstract steps.

We could call this the "procrastinator's technique." If a step is cumbersome or difficult, put it off to a lower level; don't think about it today, think about it tomorrow. Of course tomorrow does come, but the whole process can then be applied to the subproblem. A trouble spot often seems much simpler when you can focus on it. And eventually the whole problem is broken up into manageable units.

As you work your way down the solution tree, you make a series of design decisions. If a decision proves awkward or wrong (and many times it will!), it's easy to backtrack (go back up the tree to a higher-level module) and try something else. You don't have to scrap your whole design—only the small part you are working on. There may be many intermediate steps and trial solutions before you reach a final design.

Pseudocode   You'll find it easier to implement a design if you write the steps in pseudocode. *Pseudocode* is a mixture of English statements and Pascal-like control structures that can easily be translated into Pascal. (We've been using pseudocode in the algorithms in the Problem-Solving Case Studies.) When a concrete step is written in pseudocode, it should be possible to directly rewrite it as a statement in a program.

Remember that the problem-solving phase of the programming process takes time. If you spend the bulk of your time analyzing and designing a solution, coding and implementing the program will take very little time.

Implementing a Design

The product of top-down design is a hierarchical solution to a problem with multiple levels of abstraction. Figure 3-7 shows the top-down design we developed for Program Cone_Paint (page 83). This kind of solution forms the basis for the implementation phase of programming.

How do we translate a top-down design into a Pascal program? If you look closely at Figure 3-7, you can see that the concrete steps (those that are shaded) can be assembled into a complete algorithm for solving the problem. The order in which they are assembled is determined by their position in the tree. We start at the top of the tree, at level 0, with the first step, "Convert dimensions to feet." Because it is abstract, we must go to the next level, level 1. There we find a series of concrete steps that correspond to this step; this series of steps becomes the first part of our algorithm. Because the conversion process is now concrete, we can go back to level 0 and go on to the next step, finding the radius of the cone. This step is concrete; we can copy it directly into the algorithm. The last three steps at level 0 are abstract, so we work with each of them in order at level 1, making them concrete. Here's the algorithm:

Height in Feet is set equal to Height in Inches / 12
Diameter in Feet is set equal to Diameter in Inches / 12
Radius is set equal to Diameter in Feet / 2
Surface Area is set equal to Pi * Radius * Sqrt(Sqr(Radius in Feet) + Sqr(Height in Feet))
Red Cost is set equal to Surface Area * 0.10
Blue Cost is set equal to Surface Area * 0.15
Green Cost is set equal to Surface Area * 0.18
Print Surface Area
Print Red Cost
Print Blue Cost
Print Green Cost

From this algorithm we can construct a table of the constants and variables required, and then write the declaration and executable sections of the program.

In practice, you will not write your design as a tree diagram, but as a series of modules grouped by levels of abstraction, as we've done here:

Main Module   *Level 0*

> Convert dimensions to feet
> Radius is set equal to Diameter / 2
> Compute Surface Area
> Compute costs
> Print results

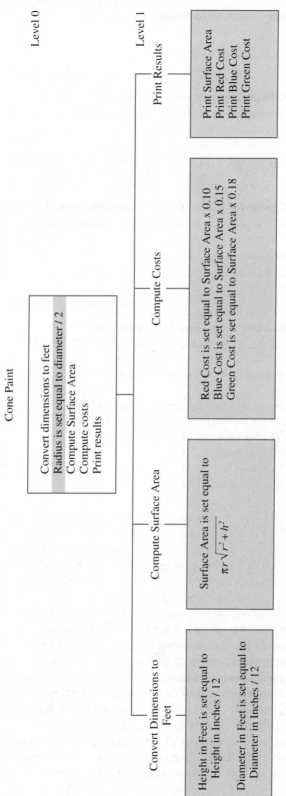

Figure 3-7 Design Tree for Program Cone_Paint

Convert Dimensions to Feet   *Level 1*

Height in Feet is set equal to Height in Inches / 12
Diameter in Feet is set equal to Diameter in Inches / 12

Compute Surface Area

Surface Area = Pi * Radius * Sqrt(Sqr(Radius) + Sqr(Height))

Compute Costs

Red Cost is set equal to Surface Area * 0.10
Blue Cost is set equal to Surface Area * 0.15
Green Cost is set equal to Surface Area * 0.18

Print Results

Print Surface Area
Print Red Cost
Print Blue Cost
Print Green Cost

If you look at Program Cone_Paint, you can see that it closely resembles this solution. The main difference is that the one concrete step at level 0 has been inserted at the proper point among the other concrete steps. You also can see that the names of the modules have been paraphrased as comments in the code.

The type of implementation that we've introduced here is called *flat* or *inline implementation*. We are flattening the hierarchical structure of the solution by writing all of the steps as one long sequence. This kind of implementation is adequate when a solution is short and has only a few levels of abstraction and when the programs it produces are clear and easy to understand, assuming appropriate comments and good style.

Longer programs, with more levels of abstraction, are difficult to work with as flat implementations. In Chapter 6 you'll see that it is possible to implement a solution directly in a *hierarchical implementation*. Here many of the modules are implemented as separate procedures and functions, and the abstract steps in the design are replaced with calls to those subprograms.

One of the advantages of implementing modules as subprograms is that they can be called from different places in a program. For example, if a problem requires that the volume of a cylinder be computed in several places, we could write a single function to perform the calculation and simply call it in each place. This gives us a *semihier-archical implementation*. The implementation does not preserve a pure hierarchy because abstract steps at various levels of the solution tree share one implementation of a module (see Figure 3-8). A shared module actually falls outside the hierarchy because it doesn't really belong at any one level.

Another advantage of implementing modules as subprograms is that you can pick them up and use them in other programs. Over time you will build a library of your own subprograms to complement those that are predefined in Pascal.

We postpone a detailed discussion of hierarchical implementations until Chapter 6. For now, our programs remain short enough for flat implementations to suffice. In the meantime, we examine flow of control, preconditions and postconditions, interface design, side effects, and other important concepts you'll need to develop hierarchical implementations.

Figure 3-8   *A Semihierarchical Module Structure Chart with a Shared Module*

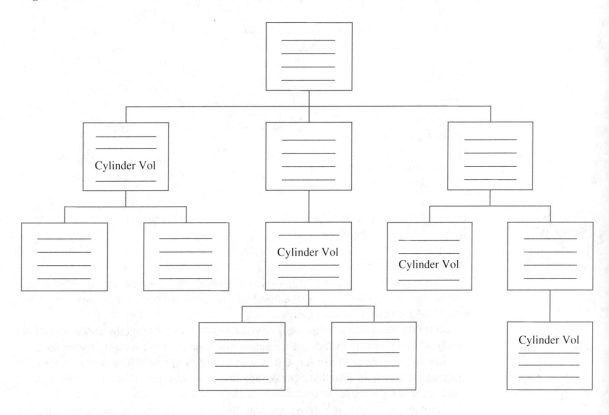

We use this outline for the top-down designs in our case studies:

Problem statement
Input description
Output description
Discussion
Assumptions (if any)
Main module
Remaining modules by levels
Module structure chart

"This was your first effort at TOP-DOWN design, wasn't it?"

Cartoon by M. LAD. TOPOLSKY

*S*oftware Engineering Tip

Documentation

As you create your top-down design, you are developing documentation for your program. *Documentation* is the written problem specifications, design, development history, and actual code of a program.

Good documentation helps users read and understand a program and is invaluable when software is being modified (maintained). If you haven't looked at your program for six months and need to change it, you'll be happy that you documented it well. Of course, if someone else has to use and modify your program, documentation is indispensable.

Documentation is both external and internal to the program. External documentation includes specifications, the development history, and the top-down design. Internal documentation includes the program format and *self-documenting code*—meaningful identifiers and comments. You can use the pseudocode from your top-down designs as comments in your programs.

This kind of documentation may be sufficient for someone reading or maintaining your programs. However, if a program is going to be used by people who are not programmers, you must provide a user's manual as well.

Be sure to keep documentation up to date. Indicate any changes you make in a program in all of the pertinent documentation. Use **self-documenting code** to make your programs more readable.

Self-Documenting Code   A program containing meaningful identifiers as well as judiciously used clarifying comments.

Now let's look at a couple of case studies that demonstrate top-down design.

PROBLEM-SOLVING CASE STUDY

Pythagorean Theorem Applied to Right Triangles

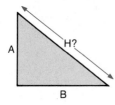

Problem: Determine the length of the hypotenuse of a right triangle given the lengths of the other two sides.

Input: Two real numbers, one for each known side of the triangle.

Output: Print the input data with a message that identifies each number (echo printing). Print the length of the hypotenuse with an identifying message.

Discussion: The Pythagorean theorem states that the square of the hypotenuse of a right triangle is equal to the sum of the squares of the other two sides. To compute the length of the hypotenuse, then, you square the lengths of the other two sides, add the squares, and then find the square root of the sum. We use the same method in our programming solution.

Assumptions: The two lengths are positive real numbers (checking for erroneous data is not done).

Main Module   *Level 0*

Get Data
Print Data
Find Length of Hypotenuse
Print Length of Hypotenuse

PROBLEM-SOLVING CASE STUDY *cont'd.*

Get Data   *Level 1*

> Print 'Enter the lengths of the two sides.'
> Read Length of A, Length of B

Print Data

> Print 'The Length of side A is ', Length of A
> Print 'The Length of side B is ', Length of B

Find Length of Hypotenuse

> Compute Sum of Squares
> Hypotenuse is set equal to Sqrt(Sum of Squares)

Print Length of Hypotenuse

> Print 'The length of the hypotenuse is ', Hypotenuse

Compute Sum of Squares   *Level 2*

> Sum of Squares is set equal to Sqr(Length of A) + Sqr(Length of B)

Module Structure Chart:

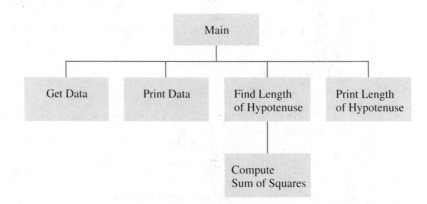

Variables

Name	Data Type	Function
LengthOfA	Real	Length of one of the known sides
LengthOfB	Real	Length of the other known side
SumOfSquares	Real	Sum of the squares of the two known sides
Hypotenuse	Real	Length of the hypotenuse

Here is the complete program. Notice how we've used the module names as comments to help distinguish the modules from one another in our flat implementation.

```
PROGRAM Triangle (Input, Output);

(* This program finds the length of the hypotenuse of a right *)
(* triangle, given the lengths of the other two sides         *)

VAR
   Length_Of_A,      (* Length of one of the known sides     *)
   Length_Of_B,      (* Length of the other known side       *)
   Sum_Of_Squares,   (* Sum of the squares of the known sides *)
   Hypotenuse:       (* Length of the hypotenuse             *)
     Real;

BEGIN (* Triangle *)
   (* Get data *)
   Writeln('Enter the lengths of the two sides.');
   Readln(Length_Of_A, Length_Of_B);
   (* Print data *)
   Writeln;
   Writeln('The length of side A is ', Length_Of_A:7:4);
   Writeln('The length of side B is ', Length_Of_B:7:4);
   (* Compute sum of squares *)
   Sum_Of_Squares := Sqr(Length_Of_A) + Sqr(Length_Of_B);
   (* Find length of hypotenuse *)
   Hypotenuse := Sqrt(Sum_Of_Squares);
   (* Print length of hypotenuse *)
   Writeln('The length of the hypotenuse is ', Hypotenuse:8:4)
END. (* Triangle *)
```

This is an interactive program. The data is input while the program is executing. If the user enters this data:

```
95.019 42.91
```

the dialogue with the user looks like this:

PROBLEM-SOLVING CASE STUDY cont'd.

```
Enter the lengths of the two sides.
95.019 42.91

The length of side A is 95.0190
The length of side B is 42.9100
The length of the hypotenuse is 104.2587
```

PROBLEM-SOLVING CASE STUDY

Weighted Average of Test Scores

Problem: Find the weighted average of three test scores. The data for each test is a score (an integer number) followed by its associated weight (a real number); each pair of numbers is on a separate line. The data is stored on File SCORES.DAT.

Input: Three lines of data, each listing a test score (integer) and weight (real number).

Output: Print input data with headings (echo printing). Print the weighted average with an explanation.

Discussion: It is common to give different weights to tests in order to arrive at a student's grade in a course. For example, if two tests are worth 30 percent each and a final exam is worth 40 percent, we multiply the first test grade by 0.30, the second test grade by 0.30, and the final grade by 0.40. We then add these three values to get a weighted average. We use this by-hand algorithm to solve the problem.

Because the data is going to be read from a file, we have to list the file name in the program heading, declare it, prepare it for reading, and remember to include the name in the parameter lists of the Readln statements.

Assumptions: The three weights add up to 1.00, and the input data is correct (checking for erroneous input data is not done).

Main Module   *Level 0*

```
Prepare File for Reading
Get Data
Print Data
Find Weighted Average
Print Weighted Average
Close File
```

PROBLEM-SOLVING CASE STUDY cont'd.

Prepare File for Reading   *Level 1*

> Reset Scores
> Assign DOS file SCORES.DAT to Scores

Get Data

> Read from Scores, Test1, Weight1
> Read from Scores, Test2, Weight2
> Read from Scores, Test3, Weight3

Print Data

> Print Heading
> Print Test1, Weight1
> Print Test2, Weight2
> Print Test3, Weight3

Find Weighted Average

> Ave is set equal to Test1 * Weight1
>   + Test2 * Weight2 + Test3 * Weight3

Print Weighted Average

> Print 'Weighted average = ', Ave

Print Heading   *Level 2*

> Print 'Test Score   Weight'

PROBLEM-SOLVING CASE STUDY *cont'd.*

Module Structure Chart:

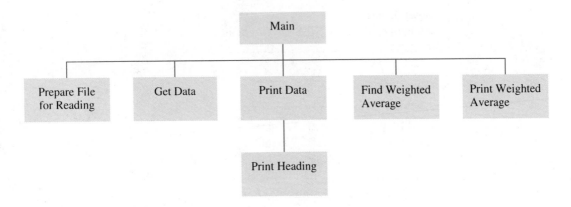

Variables

Name	Data Type	Function
Test1	Integer	Score for first test
Test2	Integer	Score for second test
Test3	Integer	Score for third test
Weight1	Real	Weight for first test
Weight2	Real	Weight for second test
Weight3	Real	Weight for third test
Ave	Real	Weighted average of the tests
Scores	Text	Input data file

Here is the complete program. There are no prompting messages because the input is taken from a file.

```
PROGRAM Test_Average (Output, Scores);

(* This program finds the weighted average of three test scores *)
```

```
VAR
  Test1,        (* Score for first test         *)
  Test2,        (* Score for second test        *)
  Test3:        (* Score for third test         *)
    Integer;
  Weight1,      (* Weight for first test         *)
  Weight2,      (* Weight for second test        *)
  Weight3,      (* Weight for third test         *)
  Ave:          (* Weighted average of the tests *)
    Real;
  Scores:       (* Input data file               *)
    Text;

BEGIN (* Test_Average *)
  (* Prepare file for reading *)
  Assign(Scores, 'SCORES.DAT');
  Reset(Scores);
  (* Get data *)
  Readln(Scores, Test1, Weight1);
  Readln(Scores, Test2, Weight2);
  Readln(Scores, Test3, Weight3);
  (* Print heading *)
  Writeln('Test Score   Weight');
  Writeln;
  (* Print data *)
  Writeln(Test1:7, Weight1:11:2);
  Writeln(Test2:7, Weight2:11:2);
  Writeln(Test3:7, Weight3:11:2);
  Writeln;
  (* Find weighted average *)
  Ave : = Test1 * Weight1 + Test2 * Weight2 + Test3 * Weight3;
  (* Print weighted average *)
  Writeln('Weighted average = ', Ave:6:2);
  (* Return file to system *)
  Close(Scores)
END.  (* Test_Average *)
```

If **File Scores** contains this data:

```
90      0.30
85      0.25
78      0.45
```

the output from the program looks like this:

```
Test Score    Weight

    90         0.30
    85         0.25
    78         0.45

Weighted average =   83.35
```

Testing and Debugging

An important part of implementing a program is testing it (checking the results). By now you should realize that there is nothing magical about the computer. It is no more infallible than whoever is writing the instructions and entering the data. Don't trust it to give you the correct answers until you've verified enough of them by hand to convince yourself that the program is working.

From here on in these Testing and Debugging sections, we offer tips on how to test your programs and what to do if a program doesn't work the way you expect. But don't wait until you've found a bug to read the Testing and Debugging sections. It's much easier to prevent bugs than it is to fix them.

The two most common error messages in testing programs that input data values from a file are "DISK READ ERROR" and "INVALID NUMERIC FORMAT." (The messages may be worded somewhat differently on your system.)

The "DISK READ ERROR" message indicates that the program has read all of the input data available on the file and that more data is needed to fill the variables in the parameter list of a Read or Readln statement. This simply may mean that the data file was not prepared properly. If a program uses Readln statements to input values and the file has a greater number of values per line than the Readln statement does parameters, then the values that are skipped by the Readln statements may account for the program's running out of data.

For example, look what happens with this data:

```
123   456   789
987   654   321
```

and this code:

```
Readln(A, B);
Readln(C, D);
Readln(E, F);
```

The first two Readlns use up the data in the file, leaving the third Readln with no data to read. There are two ways to fix the problem here: The data file can be changed so that each line holds the correct number of values, or the Readlns can be changed to read all of the values on each line.

You can also get a "DISK READ ERROR" error when a Readln statement should really be a Read statement. This can cause values to be inadvertently skipped when the program reads a data file that was prepared correctly.

The "INVALID NUMERIC FORMAT" error message tells you that numeric and character data are mixed in the input. This error message indicates that a Read or Readln statement is supposed to read a numeric value, but the reading marker is positioned at a character. (You can cause this error by entering a letter when a Pascal program prompts you to enter a number. Try it; it's useful to know how your system responds to the error, and it makes the experience a lot less startling the first time you do it accidentally.)

There are several possible sources of an "INVALID NUMERIC FORMAT" error message. The most common is an error in the preparation or entry of the data. Using the wrong variable name (which happens to be of the wrong data type) in a parameter list also can produce this message. Declaring a variable to be of the wrong data type is a variation on the problem. Last, leaving out a variable (or including an extra one) in a parameter list can cause the marker to end up positioned on the wrong type of data.

You also get error messages if your program tries to input data from a file that is in write mode, or to output data to a file that is in read mode. This usually means either that the file was Reset when it should have been prepared with Rewrite (or vice versa), or that the wrong file name was used in a Read, Readln, Write, or Writeln statement.

When you are using files other than Input and Output, remember to list a file name as the first parameter in Read, Readln, Write, and Writeln statements. If you forget to list an input file, the program stops and waits for input from the keyboard. If you forget to list an output file, you get unexpected output on the screen.

By giving you a framework that can help you organize and keep track of all of the details in designing and implementing a program, top-down design should help you avoid these errors in the first place.

In later chapters you'll see that you can test modules separately. If you make sure that each module works by itself, your program should work when you put all the modules together. Testing modules separately is less work than trying to test an entire program. In a smaller section of code it's less likely that multiple errors will combine to produce behavior that's difficult to analyze.

Testing and Debugging Hints

1. Use the top-down design methodology to avoid making mistakes.
2. Be sure that a file is in the proper mode (read or write) and that it has been assigned a DOS file name before you try to perform I/O operations on it.
3. When a program inputs from or outputs to a file, be sure each I/O statement from or to a file includes the file name as its first parameter.

4. Be sure that each Read or Readln statement has the correct number of parameters and that each of those parameters is of the correct data type.

5. If your data is mixed (character and numeric values), be sure to deal with intervening blanks.

6. Echo-print input data to verify that each value is where it belongs and in the proper format. (Remember that a Real value must have at least one digit on both sides of the decimal point.)

Summary

Programs operate on data. If data and programs are kept separate, the data is available to use with other programs, and the same program can be run with other sets of input data.

Read and Readln statements input data from the keyboard or a file, storing the data in the variables specified by their parameter lists. The Read statement leaves the reading marker on the next character to be read. The Readln statement leaves the marker on the first character of the next line. Both Read and Readln begin reading at the point indicated by the marker.

The end-of-line character (<eoln>) marks the end of a data line. You create an <eoln> each time you press the return key. Your program generates an <eoln> each time a Writeln statement is executed. In Turbo Pascal, <eoln> is represented by two control characters called Return and New Line.

Interactive programs prompt the user for each data entry and directly inform the user of errors. Designing interactive dialogue is an exercise in the art of communication.

Batch input/output allows data to be prepared before a program is run, and allows the program to run again with the same data in the event a problem crops up during processing.

Files other than Input and Output permit the output from one program to be used as input to another program. There are six things you have to do to use these files: (1) Put the file names in the program heading; (2) declare the files in the VAR section; (3) prepare the files for reading or writing with Reset or Rewrite; and (4) include the name of the file as the first parameter in each Read, Readln, Write, or Writeln that uses it; (5) assign a system file name to each file identifier before it is used; and (6) close each file after processing of it is complete.

Top-down design is a method for tackling large programming problems. It begins with an abstract solution that is then divided into major steps. Each step becomes a subproblem that is analyzed and subdivided further. A concrete step is one that can be translated directly into Pascal; those that need more refining are abstract steps. A module is a collection of concrete and abstract steps that solves a subproblem. Programs can be built out of modules using a flat implementation, a hierarchical implementation, or a semihierarchical implementation.

Careful attention to top-down design, program formatting, and documentation produces highly structured and readable programs.

■ *Quick Check*

1. Write a Pascal statement that inputs values into two variables, X and Y. (pp. 99–100)

2. Your program contains three Readln statements, each with three variables in its parameter list. The data that is fed into the program consists of three lines of four values each. Which of the data values will the program skip? (pp. 100–101)

3. Input prompts should acknowledge the user's experience.
   a. What sort of message would you have a program print to prompt a novice user to input a social security number?
   b. How would you change the wording of the prompting message for an experienced user? (pp. 106–107)

4. If a program is going to input 1000 numbers, is interactive input appropriate? (pp. 106–107)

5. What are the six things that you have to remember to do in Turbo Pascal in order to use files other than Input and Output? (pp. 107–113)

6. How many levels of abstraction are there in a top-down design before you reach the point at which you can begin coding a program? (pp. 115–124)

7. When is a flat implementation of a top-down design appropriate? (pp. 115–124)

Answers

1. Read (X, Y) or Readln (X, Y)   2. The program will skip the last value on each line.
3. a. Please type a nine-digit social security number, then press the key marked RETURN.   b. Enter SSN.   4. No. Batch input is more appropriate for programs that input large amounts of data.   5. (1) Put the file names in the program heading. (2) Declare the files in the VAR section of the program. (3) Use Reset or Rewrite to prepare each file for reading or writing. (4) Make sure that each I/O statement that uses a file has the name of the file as its first parameter. (5) Assign a system file name to each file identifier before it is used. (6) Close each file after processing of it is complete.
6. There is no fixed number of levels of abstraction. You keep refining the solution through as many levels as necessary until the steps are all concrete.   7. A flat implementation is appropriate when a design is short and has just one or two levels of abstraction.

■ *Exam Preparation Exercises*

1. What is the main advantage of having a program input its data rather than writing all the data values as constants in the program?

2. Given this line of data:

   17 13 7 3

   and this Readln statement:

   Readln(E, F);

   a. What is the value of each variable after the Readln is executed?
   b. What happens to any leftover data values in the input?

3. The <eoln> character signals the end of a line.
   a. How do you generate an <eoln> character from the keyboard?
   b. How do you generate an <eoln> character in a program's output?

4. What characters are input to variables of type Char when a Read statement encounters <eoln>?

5. Real values can be read into Integer variables. True or false?

6. Spaces may be used to separate numeric data values being entered into a Pascal program. True or false?

7. Given this data

```
14 21 64
19 67 91
73 89 27
23 96 47
```

   What are the values of variables A, B, C, and D after the following program segment is executed?

```
VAR
   A,
   B,
   C,
   D:
     Integer;

BEGIN (* Segment *)
   Readln(A);
   Readln(B, C);
   Readln(D)
END.  (* Segment *)
```

8. Put a check next to the code segments below that would always cause at least one line of input data to be skipped, whatever the initial position of the reading marker.

   _____ a. Read(A, B);   _____ d. Readln(A, B);
              Read(C, D);   Readln;
   _____ b. Readln;   _____ e. Read(A, B);
              Readln;   Readln;
   _____ c. Read;   Readln(C, D);
              Readln;   _____ f. Readln(A, B);
                                             Readln(A, B);

9. Given the data

```
11 12.35 ABC<eoln>
```

   what is the value of each variable after the following statements are executed? R is of type Integer, S is of type Real, and Chl is of type Char.
   a. Readln(R, S, Chl, Chl);
   b. Readln(Chl, R, S);

10. Define the following terms as they apply to interactive input/output.
    a. Input prompt
    b. Echo printing

11. Correct the following program so that it reads a value from File InData (DOS file name IN.DAT) and writes it to a File OutData (DOS file name OUT.DAT).

```pascal
PROGRAM Copy (OutData, Output);

VAR
  InData:
    Text;
  A:
    Integer;

BEGIN (* Copy *)
  Assign(InData, 'IN.DAT');
  Assign(OutData,'OUT.DAT');
  Rewrite(InData);
  Rewrite(OutData);
  Read(A);
  Write(OutData, A);
  Close(InData);
  Close(OutData)
END.  (* Copy *)
```

12. Use your corrected version of Program Copy to answer the following questions.
    a. If File InData initially contains the value 144, what does it contain after the program is executed?
    b. If File OutData is initially empty, what are its contents after the program is executed?

13. List three benefits of using top-down design in programming.

▪ *Programming Warm-Up Exercises*

1. Write a single Read statement that inputs the following data values into the Real variables Length, Height, and Width.

   ```
   10.25   7.625   4.5<eoln>
   ```

2. If you changed your answer to exercise 1 from a Read statement to a Readln statement (without changing the parameter list), would the statement have the same effect? If not, what would it do differently?

3. Write a pair of Readln statements that input the first two data values on each of the following lines into the Real variables Length1, Height1, Length2, and Height2.

   ```
   10.25   7.625   4.5<eoln>
   8.5   1.0   0.0<eoln>
   ```

4. Write a series of statements that input the first letter of each of the following names into the Char variables Chr1, Chr2, and Chr3.

```
Peter<eoln>
Kitty<eoln>
Kathy<eoln>
```

5. Write a set of variable declarations and a series of Readln statements to read the following lines of data into variables of the appropriate type. You can make up the variable names. Notice that the values are separated from one another by a single blank and that there are no blanks to the left of the first character on each line.

```
A 100 2.78 g 14<eoln>
207.98 w q 23.4 92<eoln>
R 42 L 27 R 63<eoln>
```

6. Write a program segment that reads three names from a file and then writes them to the screen one by one. The file is organized one name to a line, last name first, then the first name, then the middle initial (if any). There are exactly 15 characters on each file line, plus the <eoln> marker.

7. Write a code segment for an interactive program to input values for a person's age, height, weight, and the initials of their first and last names. Assume that the person using the program is a novice user. How would you rewrite the code for an experienced user?

8. Fill in the blanks in the following program, which should read four values from File DataIn and output them to File ResultsOut.

```
PROGRAM CopyFour (_____,  _____,  _____);

VAR
   Value1,
   Value2,
   Value3,
   Value4:
     Integer;
     _____,
   ResultsOut:
     _____;
 BEGIN (* CopyFour *)
       _____ (DataIn, 'DATAFILE.DAT');
       _____ (ResultsOut, 'RESULT.DAT');
       _____ (DataIn);
       _____ (ResultsOut);
       Read(_____, Value1, Value2, Value3, Value4);
       Writeln(_____, Value1, Value2, Value3, Value4);
       _____ (DataIn);
       _____ (ResultsOut)
   END.  (* CopyFour *)
```

9. Use top-down design to write an algorithm for starting an automobile with a manual transmission.

10. Use top-down design to write an algorithm for starting your computer system, and entering and running a program. The algorithm should be simple enough for a novice user to follow.

11. The quadratic formula is

$$X = \frac{-b \pm \sqrt{b^2 - 4ac}}{2a}$$

Use top-down design to write an algorithm to read the three coefficients of a quadratic polynomial from a file (InQuad) and write the two Real solutions to another file (OutQuad). Assume that the discriminant (the portion of the formula inside of the square root) is non-negative. You may use the standard functions Sqr and Sqrt.

■ *Programming Problems*

1. Write a top-down design and Pascal program to read an invoice number, quantity ordered, and unit price (all integers), and compute the total price. The program should write out the invoice number, quantity, unit price, and total price with identifying phrases. Format with indentation, and use appropriate comments and meaningful identifiers. If you are using an interactive system, write the program to be run interactively, with informative prompts for each data value.

2. How tall is a rainbow? Because of the way light is refracted by water droplets, the angle between the level of your eye and the top of a rainbow is always the same. If you know the distance to the rainbow, you can multiply it by the tangent of that angle to find the height of the rainbow. The magic angle is 42.3333333 degrees. Pascal works in radians, however, so you have to convert the angle to radians with this formula:

$$\text{Radians} = \text{degrees} \times \frac{\text{pi}}{180}$$

(Pi equals 3.14159265.)

Pascal does not provide a tangent function. But it's easy to compute the tangent with the sine and cosine functions that Pascal does provide. Here's the formula:

$$\text{Tangent} = \frac{\text{Sin(radians)}}{\text{Cos(radians)}}$$

If you multiply the tangent by the distance to the rainbow, you get the height of the rainbow.

Write a top-down design and a Pascal program to read a single Real value—the distance to the rainbow—and compute the height of the rainbow. The program should print the distance to the rainbow and its height with phrases that identify which number is which. Format with indentation, and use appropriate comments and meaningful identifiers. If you are using an interactive system, write the program so that it prompts the user for the input value.

3. You sometimes can see a second, fainter rainbow outside a bright rainbow. This second rainbow has a magic angle of 52.25 degrees. Modify the program in exercise 2 so that it prints the height of the main rainbow, the height of the secondary rainbow, and the distance to the main rainbow, with a phrase identifying each of the numbers.

Conditions, Boolean Expressions, and Selection Control Structures

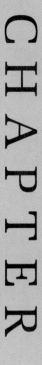

GOALS

- To be able to construct a simple Boolean expression to evaluate a given condition.
- To be able to construct a complex Boolean expression to evaluate a given condition.
- To be able to construct an IF-THEN-ELSE statement to perform a specific task.
- To be able to construct an IF-THEN statement to perform a specific task.
- To be able to construct a set of nested IF statements to perform a specific task.
- To be able to determine the preconditions and postconditions for a module, and use them to perform an algorithm walk-through.
- To be able to trace the execution of a Pascal program.
- To be able to test and debug a Pascal program.

So far, the statements in our programs have been executed in their physical order. The first statement is executed, then the second, and so on until all of the statements have been executed. But what if we want the computer to execute the statements in some other order? Suppose we want to check the validity of input data and then perform a calculation *or* print an error message, not both. To do this we must be able to ask a question and then, based on the answer, choose one or another course of action.

The IF statement allows us to execute statements in a logical order, an order that is different from their physical order. With it we can ask a question and do one thing if the answer is yes (True) or another if the answer is no (False). In the first part of this chapter, we deal with asking questions; in the second part, we deal with the IF statement itself.

Conditions and Boolean Expressions

To ask a question in Pascal, we make an assertion. If the assertion we make is true, the answer to the question is yes. If the statement is not true, the answer to the question is no. For example, if we want to ask, "Are we having spinach for dinner tonight?" we would say, "We are having spinach for dinner tonight." If the assertion is true, the answer to the question is yes. If not, the answer is no.

So asking questions in Pascal means making an assertion that is either true or false. The computer *evaluates* the assertion, checking it against some internal condition (the values stored in certain variables, for instance) and seeing whether it is true or false.

Boolean Expressions

In Pascal, assertions take the form of Boolean expressions. Just as an arithmetic expression is made up of numeric values and operations, a **Boolean expression** is made up of Boolean values and operations.

A Boolean expression can be

- a Boolean variable or constant.
- an expression followed by a relational operator followed by an expression.
- a Boolean expression followed by a Boolean operator followed by a Boolean expression.

Let's look at each of these in detail.

    Boolean Variables and Constants   Data type Boolean has just two literal constants: True and False. A Boolean variable is a variable declared to be of type Boolean, which means that its contents can be either True or False. For example, if DataOK is a Boolean variable, then

```
DataOK := True
```

is a valid assignment.

Relational Operators   We also can assign values to Boolean variables by setting them equal to the result of comparing two expressions with a relational operator. **Relational operators** test a relationship between two values.

Let's look at an example. In this program fragment, Test is a Boolean variable and A and B are Integer variables:

```
BEGIN
  Read(A, B);
  Test := A < B; (* Compares A and B with the "less than"  relational *)
                 (* operator and assigns the Boolean result to  Test  *)
```

By comparing two values, we assert that a relationship (like "less than") exists between them. If the relationship does exist, the assertion is True; if not, it is False. These are the relationships that we can test for in Pascal:

=	Equal to
<>	Not equal to
>	Greater than
<	Less than
>=	Greater than or equal to
<=	Less than or equal to

For example, if X is 5 and Y is 10, the following expressions are all True:

```
X <> Y
Y > X
X < Y
Y >= X
X <= Y
```

If X is 'M' and Y is 'P', the expressions are still True because the relational operator <, used with letters, means "comes before in the alphabet," or, more properly, "comes before in the collating sequence of the character set." For example, in the ASCII character set, all of the uppercase letters are in alphabetical order, as are the lowercase letters, but all of the uppercase letters come before the lowercase letters. So

```
'M' < 'P' and 'm' < 'p'
```

is True, but

```
'm' < 'P'
```

is False.

Of course we have to be careful to compare things that are of the same type—that is, numbers with numbers (Real or Integer) and characters with characters (Char). Comparing a value of type Char to a value of type Integer, for instance, makes no

Background Information

George Boole

Boolean algebra is named for its inventor, English mathematician George Boole. Boole was born in 1815. His father, a tradesman, began teaching him mathematics at an early age. But Boole initially was more interested in classical literature, languages, and religion, interests he maintained throughout his life. By the time he was 20, he had taught himself French, German, and Italian. He was well versed in the writings of Aristotle, Spinoza, Cicero, and Dante, and he wrote several philosophical papers himself.

At 16, to help support his family, Boole took a position as a teaching assistant in a private school. His work there and a second teaching job left him little time to study. A few years later, he opened a school and began to learn higher mathematics on his own. In spite of his lack of formal training, his first scholarly paper was published in the *Cambridge Mathematical Journal* when he was just 24. Boole went on to publish over 50 papers and several major works before he died in 1864, at the peak of his career.

Boole's *The Mathematical Analysis of Logic* was published in 1847. It would eventually form the basis for the development of digital computers. In the book, Boole set forth the formal axioms of logic (much like the axioms of geometry) on which the field of symbolic logic is built.

Boole drew on the symbols and operations of algebra in creating his system of logic. He associated the value 1 with the universal set (the set representing everything in the universe) and the value 0 with the empty set, and restricted his system to these two quantities. He then defined operations that are analogous to subtraction, addition, and

sense and produces an error message (even if the Char value is one of the digits '0' through '9'). For example, the comparisons

```
'0' < '9'
```

and

```
0 < 9
```

are valid, but

```
'0' < 9
```

generates a "TYPE MISMATCH" error message.

We can use relational operators, not only to compare variables or constants, but also to compare the results of arithmetic expressions. In the table we compare the results of adding 3 to X and multiplying Y by 10 for different values of X and Y:

multiplication. Variables in the system have symbolic values. For example, if a Boolean variable P represents the set of all plants, then the expression $1 - P$ refers to the set of all things that are not plants. We can simplify the expression, using $-P$ to mean "*not* plants." ($0 - P$ is simply 0 because we can't remove elements from the empty set.) The subtraction operator in Boole's system corresponds to the NOT operator in Pascal. In a Pascal program, we might set the value of the Boolean variable Plant to True when the name of a plant is entered, and NOT Plant is True when the name of anything else is input.

The expression $0 + P$ is the same as P. However, $0 + P + F$, where F is the set of all foods, is the set of all things that are either plants *or* foods. So the addition operator in Boole's algebra is the same as the Pascal OR operator.

The analogy can be carried to multiplication: $0 \times P$ is 0, and $1 \times P$ is P. But what is $P \times F$? It is the set of things that are both plants *and* foods. In Boole's system, the multiplication operator is the same as the AND operator.

In 1854, Boole published *An Investigation of the Laws of Thought, on Which Are Founded the Mathematical Theories of Logic and Probabilities*. In the book he described theorems built on his axioms of logic and extended the algebra to show how probabilities could be computed in a logical system. Five years later, Boole published *Treatise on Differential Equations*, then *Treatise on the Calculus of Finite Differences*. The latter is one of the cornerstones of numerical analysis, which deals with the accuracy of computations. (In Chapter 8, you'll see the important role numerical analysis plays in computer programming.)

Boole received little recognition and few honors for his work. Given the importance of Boolean algebra in modern technology, it is hard to believe that his system of logic was not taken seriously until the early twentieth century. George Boole was truly one of the founders of computer science.

Value of X	Value of Y	Expression	Result
12	2	X + 3 <= Y * 10	True
20	2	X + 3 <= Y * 10	False
7	1	X + 3 <> Y * 10	False
17	2	X + 3 = Y * 10	True
100	5	X + 3 > Y * 10	True

Boolean Operators   *Boolean operators* are the symbols AND, OR, XOR, and NOT. These symbols are reserved for Boolean expressions.

In Turbo Pascal, NOT, AND, OR, and XOR are also logical operators on integers. For example, if the variable I is declared as Integer, the following statement would produce an error message in standard Pascal but is an accepted and meaningful statement in Turbo Pascal:

```
I := I AND 15;
```

This feature is of little use in normal programming practice and you are not expected to learn how to use it. The point is that Turbo Pascal may allow expressions that appear unacceptable to be compiled successfully.

We can make more complex assertions by combining relational operators with Boolean operators. For example, suppose we want to determine whether a final score is greater than 90 *and* a midterm score is greater than 70. In Pascal, we would write the expression this way:

```
(Final_Score > 90) AND (Midterm_Score > 70)
```

The AND requires both relationships to be True in order for the overall result to be True. If either or both of the relationships are False, AND makes the entire result False.

Look at the example again. The computer first evaluates the first relational operation (because it is enclosed in parentheses), giving a temporary Boolean result. If it is True, the second expression is evaluated and the two are then combined by the AND operation to give another Boolean result. If the first expression is False, then the result of the AND must be False, so Turbo Pascal does not evaluate the second expression. This is called *short-circuit evaluation* and is not part of the ISO standard. Most Pascal compilers will evaluate both expressions first (because they are in parentheses) and then combine the resulting Boolean values with AND. Because of this it is poor practice to write a condition that depends upon short-circuit evaluation. For example,

```
(Scores > 0) AND (Total/Scores > 50)
```

would always be valid in Turbo Pascal but would produce an error in Standard Pascal if Scores is zero. In Turbo, if Scores is zero, the first expression is false and thus evaluation of the second expression is skipped, Standard Pascal, however, would try to first evaluate both expressions, causing an attempt to divide by zero in the second expression.

The OR operation takes two Boolean values and combines them. If *either* or *both* are True, the result is True. Both values must be False for the result to be False. Now we can determine whether the midterm grade is an A *or* the final grade is an A. If either the midterm grade or the final grade equals A, the assertion is True. In Pascal, we write the expression like this:

```
(Midterm_Grade = 'A') OR (Final_Grade = 'A')
```

Turbo Pascal provides the XOR (eXclusive OR) operation which takes two Boolean values and combines them such that if one is True and the other is False, the result is True. When applied to Boolean values, XOR gives the same result as the <> operator. The Turbo Pascal expression

```
(Midterm_Grade = 'A') XOR (Final_Grade = 'A')
```

is equivalent to the Standard Pascal expression

```
(Midterm_Grade = 'A') <> (Final_Grade = 'A')
```

and is True when either Midterm_Grade or Final_Grade is 'A', but not both. It is recommended that only the standard form of the expression be used.

The AND, OR, and XOR operators always appear between two expressions; the NOT operation precedes an expression. NOT takes one Boolean value and gives its opposite as the result. If (Grade = 'A') is False, then NOT (Grade = 'A') is True. NOT gives us a convenient way of reversing the meaning of an assertion. For example,

```
NOT (Hours > 40)
```

is the equivalent of

```
Hours <= 40
```

In some contexts the first form is clearer; in others, the second makes more sense.

The following pairs of expressions are equivalent:

```
NOT (A = B)                    A <> B
NOT ((A = B) OR (A = C))       (A <> B) AND (A <> C)
NOT ((A = B) AND (C > D))      (A <> B) OR (C <= D)
```

Take a close look at these expressions to be sure you understand why they are equivalent. It may help to try evaluating them with some values for A, B, C, and D. Notice the pattern here: The expression on the left is just the one to its right with NOT added and the relational and Boolean operators reversed (for example, = instead of <> and OR instead of AND). Remember this pattern. It allows you to rewrite expressions in the simplest form.*

Boolean operators can be applied to the results of comparisons; they also can be applied directly to variables of type Boolean. For example, instead of writing

```
Elector := (Age >= 18) AND (District = 23)
```

to assign a value to Boolean variable Elector, we could use two intermediate Boolean variables, Voter and Constituent:

```
Voter := Age >= 18;
Constituent := District = 23;
Elector := Voter AND Constituent;
```

The tables below summarize the results of applying AND and OR to a pair of Boolean values (represented here by Boolean variables X and Y).

*In Boolean algebra, the pattern is formalized by a theorem called *DeMorgan's Law.*

Value of X	Value of Y	Value of X AND Y
True	True	True
True	False	False
False	True	False
False	False	False

Value of X	Value of Y	Value of X OR Y
True	True	True
True	False	True
False	True	True
False	False	False

And this table summarizes the results of applying the NOT operator to a Boolean value (represented by Boolean variable X).

Value of X	Value of NOT X
True	False
False	True

Precedence of Operators

In Chapter 2 we discussed the rules of precedence, the rules that govern the evaluation of complex arithmetic expressions. Pascal's rules of precedence also govern relational and Boolean operators. Relational operators have lower precedence than all other operators, including arithmetic and Boolean operators. The OR operator has the same precedence as addition and subtraction; AND has the same precedence as multiplication and division; NOT has higher precedence than any other operator.

Here's a list showing the order of precedence for all of the operators we've talked about:

```
NOT                    Highest precedence
* / DIV MOD AND              ↓
+ - OR XOR             Lowest precedence
= <> > < >= <=
```

Operators on the same line in the list have the same precedence. If there is more than one operator with the same precedence in an expression, the operators are evaluated left to right. Appendix D, Precedence of Operators, lists the order of precedence for all operators in Pascal.

Parentheses are used to override the order of evaluation in an expression. If you're not sure whether parentheses are necessary, use them anyway. The compiler disregards unnecessary parentheses. So if they clarify an expression, use them.

One final comment about parentheses: Pascal, like other programming languages, requires that parentheses always be used in pairs. Whenever you write a complicated expression, take a minute to go through and pair up all of the opening parentheses with their closing counterparts.

*S*oftware Engineering Tip

Changing English Statements into Boolean Expressions

In most cases you can write a Boolean expression directly from an English statement or mathematical term in an algorithm. But there are some tricky situations you have to watch out for. Remember our sample Boolean expression:

```
(Midterm_Grade = 'A') OR (Final_Grade = 'A')
```

In English you would be tempted to write this expression "Midterm grade or final grade equals A." In Pascal, you can't write the expression as you would in English. That is,

```
Midterm_Grade OR Final_Grade = 'A'
```

won't work because Midterm_Grade and Final_Grade are both of type Char, and OR works only with Boolean or Integer values. You can't form the OR of two characters.

A more subtle error occurs if an expression such as

```
(Final_Score > 80) AND (Midterm_Score > 80)
```

is written to be more like English. The expression

```
Final_Score AND Midterm_Score > 80
```

is syntactically correct. In Turbo Pascal you can perform AND on two Integer values, so the compiler accepts this meaningless expression as valid. Standard Pascal would produce an error message in this case.

Returning to the example of

```
(Midterm_Grade = 'A') OR (Final_Grade = 'A')
```

You also might be tempted to write the expression without parentheses, which won't work either. Because OR has higher precedence than the relational operators, the expression

```
Midterm_Grade = 'A' OR Final_Grade = 'A'
```

is interpreted as

```
Midterm_Grade = ('A' OR Final_Grade) = 'A'
```

which tells the computer to try to form the OR of 'A' and FinalGrade. Because OR only works on Boolean or Integer values, the expression generates an error message ("TYPE MISMATCH"). If the operands are Integer instead of Char, a syntax error will not occur in Turbo Pascal; the program simply won't work properly.

In math books you might see a notation like this:

$$12 < Y < 24$$

which means "Y is between 12 and 24." This expression is illegal in Pascal because of the way it is evaluated. First the relation $12 < Y$ is evaluated, giving a temporary Boolean result. The computer would then try to compare this Boolean value with the number 24, creating another opportunity for the "TYPE MISMATCH" error message to put in an appearance. To write this expression in Pascal, you must use the AND operator:

```
(12 < Y) AND (Y < 24)
```

Relational Operators with Real and Boolean Data Types

The relational operators can be applied to any of the four basic data types: Integer, Real, Char, and Boolean. We've talked about comparing Integer and Char variables. Here we look at Real and Boolean variables.

Do not compare real numbers for equality. Because small errors are likely to arise when calculations are performed on real numbers, two Real values rarely are exactly equal. Instead we test real numbers for *near* equality. To do this, we compute the difference between the two numbers and test to see if the result is less than some maximum allowable difference.

For example:

```
Abs(R - S) < 0.00001
```

The formula Abs(R − S) computes the difference between the two real variables R and S (Abs is the absolute value function). In this example, if the difference is less than 0.00001, the two numbers are close enough to call them equal. (We discuss this problem in more detail in Chapter 8.)

Only rarely do we apply the relational operators to Boolean values. However, there are some situations where it is handy to be able to test whether two Boolean variables are equal (or different). Pascal defines False to be less than True.

The Boolean Function Odd

Pascal gives us a single predefined Boolean function, Odd, that takes an Integer operand and evaluates it as True if the operand is odd (not evenly divisible by 2). For example:

```
Odd(3) = True      (* 3 is an odd number     *)
Odd(4) = False     (* 4 is not an odd number *)
```

To test if a value is even, apply the NOT operator to the result of the Odd function. For example,

```
NOT Odd(3) = False    (* 3 is not an even number *)
NOT Odd(4) = True     (* 4 is an even number     *)
```

Flow of Control

The order in which statements are executed in a program is called the **flow of control.** In a sense, the computer is under the control of one statement at a time. When a statement has been executed, control is turned over to the next statement (like a baton being passed in a relay race).

Flow of Control   The order in which the computer executes statements in a program.

Flow of control is normally sequential (see Figure 4-1). That is, when one statement is finished executing, control passes to the next statement in the program. Where we want the flow of control to be nonsequential, we use **control structures,** special statements that transfer control to a statement other than the one that physically comes next. Control structures are so important that we focus on them in the remainder of this chapter and in the next five chapters.

Control Structure   A statement used to alter the normally sequential flow of control.

Figure 4-1
Sequential Control

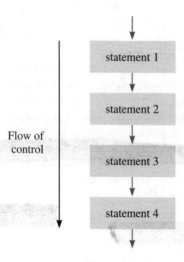

Selection

We use a selection (or branching) control structure when we want the computer to choose between two or more actions. We make an assertion. If it is True, the computer executes one statement. If it is False, it executes another (see Figure 4-2). The computer's ability to solve practical problems is a product of its ability to make decisions and execute different sequences of instructions.

Program Payroll (page 31) shows the selection process at work. The computer must decide whether or not a worker has earned overtime pay. It does this by testing the assertion that the person has worked more than 40 hours: If the assertion is True, the computer follows the instructions for computing overtime pay. If the assertion is False, the computer simply computes the regular pay.

Figure 4-2
Selection
(Branching)
Control Structure

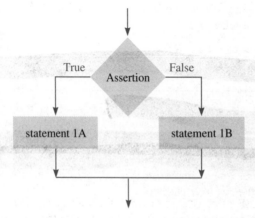

The IF Statement

The control structure that allows branches in the flow of control is called an *IF statement*. With it, we can ask a question and choose a course of action: *If* a certain condition exists, *then* perform one action, *else* perform a different action.

The computer actually performs just one of the two actions under any given set of circumstances. Yet we have to write *both* actions into the program. Why? Because depending on the circumstances, the computer can choose to execute *either* of them. The IF statement gives us a way of including both actions in a program and gives the computer a way of deciding which action to take.

The IF-THEN-ELSE Form

The IF-THEN-ELSE statement is a form of the IF statement. Here is its syntax template:

> **IF** Boolean expression
>   **THEN**
>   statement 1A
>   **ELSE**
>   statement 1B

Figure 4-3 illustrates the flow of control of the IF-THEN-ELSE statement.

The code fragment below shows how to write an IF statement in a program. Notice the indentation, which makes the statement easier to read. And notice the placement of the statement following the IF.

```
IF Hours <= 40.0
   THEN
     Pay := Rate * Hours
   ELSE
     Pay := Rate * (40.0 + (Hours - 40.0) * 1.5);
Writeln(Pay:8:2)
```

In terms of instructions to the computer, the above code fragment "if Hours is less than or equal to 40.0, compute the regular pay and then go on to execute the Writeln. But if Hours is greater than 40, compute the regular pay and the overtime pay, and then go on to execute the Writeln." Figure 4-4 shows the flow of control of this IF-THEN-ELSE statement.

IF-THEN-ELSE often is used to check the validity of input. For example, before the computer divides with a data value, it should check that the value is not zero. (Even computers can't divide something by zero.) If the divisor is zero, the computer should print out an error message. Here's the code:

Figure 4-3
IF-THEN-ELSE
Flow of Control

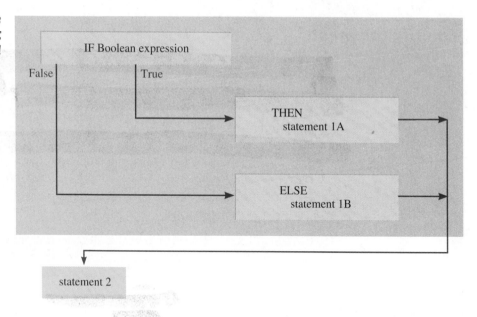

```
IF Divisor <> 0
  THEN
    Result := Dividend DIV Divisor
  ELSE
    Writeln('Division by zero is not allowed.')
```

Compound Statements

Suppose the divisor is equal to zero and we want to set the result of the division to MaxInt in addition to printing the error message? (MaxInt is as close to an infinite integer result as the computer can get.) We would need two statements in the same branch, but the syntax we've been using limits us to one.

What we really want to do is choose to execute one or another *sequence* of statements. This is easy. Remember that the compiler treats the compound statement

```
BEGIN
  Sequence of statements
END
```

like a single statement. If you put a BEGIN-END pair around the sequence of statements you want in a branch of the IF statement, the sequence of statements becomes a single compound statement. For example:

Figure 4-4   *Flow of Control for Calculating Pay*

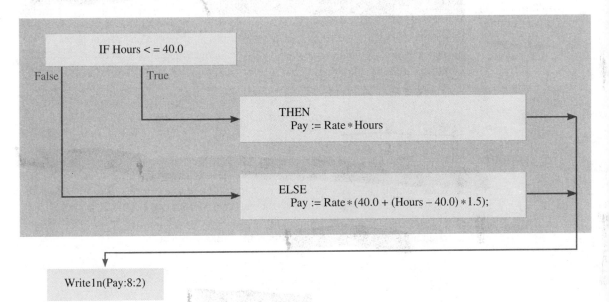

```
IF Divisor <> 0
  THEN
    Result := Dividend DIV Divisor
  ELSE
    BEGIN
      Writeln('Division by zero is not allowed.');
      Result := MaxInt
    END
```

If the value of Divisor is zero, the computer both prints the error message and sets the value of Result to MaxInt before continuing with whatever statement follows the END.

Compound statements can be used in both branches of an IF-THEN-ELSE. For example:

```
IF Divisor <> 0
  THEN
    BEGIN
      Result := Dividend DIV Divisor;
      Writeln('Division performed.')
    END
  ELSE
    BEGIN
      Writeln('Division by zero is not allowed.');
      Result := MaxInt
    END
```

There's one additional rule of Pascal syntax to remember here: Never use a semicolon before the ELSE in an IF-THEN-ELSE statement. The semicolon is used to separate statements from other statements. But the ELSE is not a statement; it is simply a part of a single IF-THEN-ELSE statement. If you put in a semicolon, Pascal looks for the start of a new statement, but immediately encounters the ELSE. Because there is no statement in Pascal that begins with an ELSE, you get an error message ("ERROR IN STATEMENT").

The IF-THEN Form

You occasionally will run into a situation where you want to say, "*If* a certain condition exists, *then* perform some action; otherwise, don't do anything." In other words, you want the computer to skip a sequence of instructions if a certain condition isn't met. You could do this by leaving the ELSE branch empty (placing a semicolon immediately after the ELSE). Or, even easier, simply leave off the ELSE. The resulting statement is called an IF-THEN statement. This is its syntax template:

> **IF** Boolean expression
> **THEN**
>   statement

Here's an example of an IF-THEN statement. Notice the indentation and the placement of the statement that follows the IF-THEN.

```
IF Age < 18
   THEN
     Write('Not an eligible ');
Writeln('voter.')
```

This statement means that if Age is less than 18, first print 'Not an eligible ' and then print 'voter.' If Age is not less than 18, skip the Write statement and go directly to the Writeln. Figure 4-5 shows the flow of control for an IF-THEN statement.

Like the statement in an IF-THEN-ELSE, the statement in an IF-THEN can be a compound statement. For example, let's say you are writing a program to compute income taxes. One of the lines on the tax form says, "Subtract line 23 from line 17 and enter result on line 24; if result is less than zero, enter zero and check box 24A." You can use an IF-THEN statement to do this in Pascal:

Figure 4-5
IF-THEN Flow
of Control

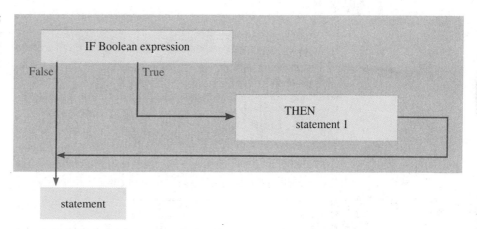

```
Result := Line17 - Line23;
IF Result < 0.0
   THEN
     BEGIN
       Writeln('Check box 24A');
       Result := 0.0
     END;
Line24 := Result
```

This code does exactly what the tax form says it should. It computes the result of subtracting line 23 from line 17. Then it looks to see if Result is less than zero. If it is, the fragment prints a message telling the user to check box 24A and then sets Result to zero. Finally, the calculated result (or zero, if the result is less than zero) is stored in a variable called Line24.

Nested IF Statements

There are no restrictions on what the statements in an IF can be. Therefore an IF within an IF is okay. In fact an IF within an IF within an IF is legal. The only limitation here is that people cannot follow a structure that is too involved. And readability is one of the marks of a good program.

When we place an IF within an IF, we are creating a **nested control structure.** Control structures nest much like mixing bowls do, smaller ones tucked inside larger ones. Here's an example:

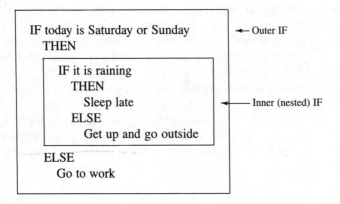

In general, any problem that involves more than two alternative courses of action can be coded using nested IF statements. For example, to print out the name of a month given its number, we could use a series of IF statements:

```
IF Month = 1
   THEN
      Writeln('January');
IF Month = 2
   THEN
      Writeln('February');
IF Month = 3
   THEN
      Writeln('March');
         .
         .
IF Month = 12
   THEN
      Writeln('December')
```

But the equivalent nested IF structure,

```
IF Month = 1
   THEN
      Writeln('January')
   ELSE IF Month = 2            (* Nested IF *)
      THEN
         Writeln('February')
   ELSE IF Month = 3            (* Nested IF *)
      THEN
         Writeln('March')
   ELSE IF Month = 4            (* Nested IF *)
         .
         .
   ELSE
      Writeln('December')
```

is more efficient because it makes fewer comparisons. The series of IF statements always tests every condition, even if the first one is satisfied. In contrast, the nested IF skips all remaining comparisons after one alternative has been selected.

We use a special indentation style with deeply nested IF-THEN-ELSE statements in order to indicate that the complex structure is really just taking one of a set of alternatives. This general multi-way branch is known as an IF-THEN-ELSE-IF control structure.

It's important to note one difference between the series of IF statements and the nested IF: More than one alternative can be taken by the series of IFs, but the nested IF can select only one. To see why this is important, consider the analogy of filling out a questionnaire. Some questions are like a series of IF statements, asking you to circle all the items in a list that apply to you (such as all your hobbies). Other questions ask you to circle only one item in a list (your age group, for example) and are thus like a nested IF structure. Both kinds of questions occur in programming problems. Being able to recognize which type of question is being asked will permit you to immediately select the appropriate control structure.

Another particularly helpful use of the nested IF is when one condition is dependent on another condition. For example, suppose we are to print 'Failing' if a student's average exam score is below 50. However, some students are auditing the class and not taking exams, so we must also check that students do have exam scores. We might write the test as,

```
IF (Scores > 0) AND (Total/Scores > 50)
  THEN
    Writeln('Failing')
```

As we saw earlier, this expression is valid in Turbo Pascal for all values of Scores, but in Standard Pascal this will cause the program to crash on the first auditor because the computer can't divide Total by zero. Good programming practice dictates that we test for nonzero scores before we test the second condition:

```
IF Scores > 0
  THEN
    IF Total/Scores > 50     (* Nested IF *)
      THEN
        Writeln('Failing')
```

This code fragment implements what is called a sequential AND, or an IF-AND-THEN-IF control structure.

Whenever you come across a problem in which some condition must be tested before another condition is tested, a nested IF structure is appropriate.

The nested IF is also effective when you want to compare a series of consecutive ranges of values. For example, the Problem-Solving Case Study on page 161 involves printing different messages for different ranges of temperatures. We present two solutions for one of the modules: one using a sequence of IF statements, the other using a nested IF structure. As you'll see, the nested IF version uses fewer comparisons, so it's more efficient.

As fast as modern computers are, many applications require so much computation that inefficient algorithms can waste hours of computer time. Always be on the lookout for ways to make your programs more efficient, as long as doing so doesn't make them difficult for the user to understand. It's usually better to sacrifice a little efficiency for the sake of readability.

The Dangling ELSE

When IF statements are nested, you may find yourself confused about the IF-ELSE pairings: To which IF does an ELSE belong? For example, suppose that if a student's average is below 60, we want to print 'Failing'; if it is 60 to 70, we want to print 'Passing but marginal'; and if it is 70 or greater, we don't want to print anything.

We code this information with an IF-THEN-ELSE nested within an IF-THEN:

```
IF Average < 70.0
   THEN
      IF Average < 60.0
         THEN
            Writeln('Failing')
         ELSE
            Writeln('Passing but marginal')
```

How do we know to which IF the ELSE belongs? An ELSE is always paired with the closest preceding IF-THEN that doesn't already have an ELSE paired with it. We indented the code to reflect this pairing, but indentation does not affect the execution of the code. Even if the ELSE aligns with the first THEN, it still belongs to the second IF.

Suppose we write the fragment like this:

```
IF Average >= 60.0
   THEN
      BEGIN
         IF Average < 70.0
            THEN
               Writeln('Passing but marginal')
      END
   ELSE
      Writeln('Failing')
```

Here we want the ELSE branch attached to the first IF statement, not the second, so we use a compound statement in the outer THEN branch. The BEGIN-END pair indicates that the nested IF is complete, so the ELSE must belong to the outer IF. An ELSE that follows a nested IF-THEN is called a **dangling ELSE.** It doesn't belong with the nested IF but will be attached to it unless we enclose the nested IF in a BEGIN-END pair.

You might be tempted to solve the dangling ELSE problem by ending the nested IF with a semicolon. For example:

```
IF Average >= 60.0
   THEN
      IF Average < 70.0
         THEN
            Writeln('Passing but marginal');
      ELSE
         Writeln('Failing')
```

But this creates an "ERROR IN STATEMENT" error message because the semicolon actually ends *both* IF statements. Remember, never use a semicolon before an ELSE.

*P*ROBLEM-SOLVING CASE STUDY

An Electronic Activity Director

Problem: You've taken a job at a year-round resort where the owner has just installed a computerized sign. She wants you to program the sign to show the current temperature and a recommended activity. Your program should read the temperature and print out the activity appropriate for that temperature using the following guidelines:

Activity	Temperature
Swimming	Temperature > 85
Tennis	70 < temperature <= 85
Golf	32 < temperature <= 70
Skiing	0 < temperature <= 32
Dancing	Temperature <= 0

Input: Temperature, an Integer value.

Output:

Input prompt message
Temperature (echo print)
Appropriate activity

Discussion: The temperature must be compared with the limits of each activity. Once the correct range is found, the corresponding activity is printed. This comparison can be made using IF statements.

PROBLEM-SOLVING CASE STUDY cont'd.

Main Module   *Level 0*

```
Get Temperature
Print activity
```

Get Temperature   *Level 1*

```
Prompt for temperature value input
Read Temperature
Echo-print Temperature
```

Print Activity

```
Print 'The recommended activity is'
IF Temperature > 85
   THEN
      Write 'swimming.'
IF Temperature <= 85 and > 70
   THEN
      Write 'tennis.'
IF Temperature <= 70 and > 32
   THEN
      Write 'golf.'
IF Temperature <= 32 and > 0
   THEN
      Write 'skiing.'
IF Temperature <= 0
   THEN
      Write 'dancing.'
```

Module Print Activity has five IF statements and a total of eight comparisons. We could code this module as a set of nested IF statements. The middle IFs seem to require compound Boolean conditions; however, the IF-THEN-ELSE structure makes this unnecessary because we wouldn't be executing the ELSE branch unless one of the conditions was already satisfied. Here's the rewritten module:

Print Activity

> Print 'The recommended activity is'
> IF Temperature > 85
>   THEN
>   Write 'swimming.'
>   ELSE IF Temperature > 70
>   THEN
>   Write 'tennis.'
>   ELSE IF Temperature > 32
>   THEN
>   Write 'golf.'
>   ELSE IF Temperature > 0
>   THEN
>   Write 'skiing.'
>   ELSE
>   Write 'dancing.'

Module Structure Chart:

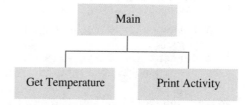

Because this algorithm has just one variable, Temperature, we won't bother with the list of variables.

```
Program Activity (Input, Output);

(* This program outputs an appropriate activity *)
(* for a given  temperature                     *)

VAR
   Temperature:        (* The outside temperature *)
      Integer;
```

```
BEGIN (* Activity *)
  (* Get Temperature *)
  Writeln('Enter the outside temperature:');
  Readln(Temperature);
  Writeln('The current temperature is ', Temperature:1, '.');
  (* Print activity *)
  Write('The recommended activity is ');
  IF Temperature > 85
    THEN
      Writeln('swimming.')
    ELSE IF Temperature > 70
      THEN
        Writeln('tennis.')
    ELSE IF Temperature > 32
      THEN
        Writeln('golf.')
    ELSE IF Temperature  > 0
      THEN
        Writeln('skiing.')
    ELSE
      Writeln('dancing.')
END.  (* Activity *)
```

Here are two sample runs of Program Activity. The user's input is in color.

```
Enter the outside temperature:
-20
The current temperature is -20.
The recommended activity is dancing.

Enter the outside temperature:
52
The current temperature is 52.
The recommended activity is golf.
```

Figure 4-6 shows how the flow of control works in Module Print Activity.

In this problem the nested IF version of the solution has just four relational operators; the other solution had eight. Because it uses fewer operations to accomplish the same function, the nested IFs are more efficient.

Notice the indentation we use for the nested IF statements. When a deeply nested selection structure represents a series of alternate choices, in which each choice depends on the previous one being False, we format the code as a series of branches. Each of the nested IF statements begins with ELSE IF. The ELSE indicates that the IF is executed only if the preceding conditions are FALSE. Besides making the code look more like a series of IF statements, this style avoids deep indentations that leave no room for writing a statement.

PROBLEM-SOLVING CASE STUDY *cont'd.*

Figure 4-6
Flow of Control for
Module Print
Activity

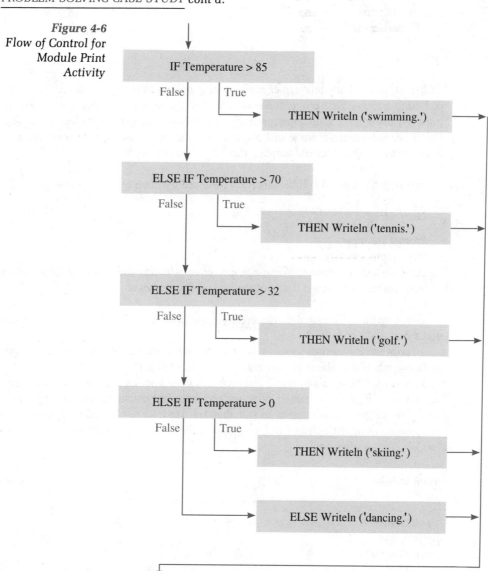

PROBLEM-SOLVING CASE STUDY

Warning Notices

Problem: Many universities send warning notices to freshmen who are in danger of failing a class. Your program should calculate the average of three test grades and print out a student's ID number, average, and whether or not the student is passing. Passing is a 60-point average or better. If the student is passing with less than a 70 average, the program should indicate that he or she is marginal.

Input: Student ID number (Integer) followed by three test grades (Integer).

Output:

Prompt for input
Input (echo print)
Print student ID number, average grade, passing/failing message, marginal indication, and error message if any of the test scores are negative

Discussion: To calculate the average, we have to read in the three test scores, add them, and divide by 3.

To print the appropriate message, we have to determine whether the average is above or below 60. If it is above 60, we have to determine if it is between 60 and 70.

If you were doing this by hand, you probably would notice if a test grade is negative and question it. If the semantics of your data imply that the values should be positive, then your program should test to be sure they are. Here we test to make sure each grade is positive, using a Boolean variable to report the result of the test. Here is the main module for our algorithm.

Main Module   *Level 0*

```
Get data
Test data
IF data OK
    THEN
        Calculate Average
        Print message indicating status
    ELSE
        Print invalid data: Score(s) less than zero.
```

Which of these steps require expansion? 'Get data', 'Test data', and 'Print message indicating status' all require multiple statements in order to solve their particular subproblem. On the other hand 'Print Invalid data: . . .' can be directly translated into a Pascal Writeln statement. What about 'Calculate Average'? It can be written as a single Pascal statement, but there's another level of detail that must be filled in: the actual formula to be used. Because the formula is at a lower level of detail than the rest of the main module, we chose to expand 'Calculate Average' as a Level 1 module.

Get Data   *Level 1*

```
Write prompt
Read Student_ID, Test1, Test2, Test3
Write Student_ID, Test1, Test2, Test3
```

Test Data

```
IF (Test1 < 0) OR (Test2 < 0) OR (Test3 < 0)
    THEN
        Data_OK is False
    ELSE
        Data_OK is True
```

Calculate Average

```
Average is set equal to (Test1 + Test2 + Test3) / 3.0
```

Print Message Indicating Status

```
Write Average
IF Average > = 60.0
  THEN
    Write 'Passing'
    IF Average < 70.0
      THEN
        Write ' but marginal.'
      ELSE
        Writeln('.')
  ELSE
    Write 'Failing.'
```

PROBLEM-SOLVING CASE STUDY cont'd.

Module Structure Chart:

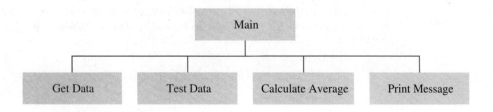

Variables

Name	Data Type	Function
Average	Real	Average of three test scores
Student ID	Integer	Student's identification number
Test1	Integer	Score for first test
Test2	Integer	Score for second test
Test3	Integer	Score for third test
Data_OK	Boolean	True if data is correct

```
PROGRAM Notices (Input, Output);

(* This program determines a student's average based on three *)
(* test scores, and the student's passing/failing status      *)

VAR
  Average:            (* Average of three test scores     *)
    Real;
  Student_ID,         (* Student's identification number  *)
  Test1,              (* Score for first test             *)
  Test2,              (* Score for second test            *)
  Test3:              (* Score for third test             *)
    Integer;
  Data_OK:            (* True if data is correct           *)
    Boolean;
```

```
BEGIN (* Notices *)
  (* Get data *)
  Writeln('Enter a Student ID number and three test scores:');
  Readln(Student_ID, Testl, Test2, Test3);
  Writeln('Student Number: ', Student_ID:1, '  Test Scores: ',
          Testl:1, ', ', Test2:1, ', ', Test3:1);
  (* Test data *)
  IF (Testl < 0) OR (Test2 < 0) OR (Test3 < 0)
    THEN
      Data_OK := False
    ELSE
      Data_OK := True;
  IF Data_OK
    THEN
      BEGIN
        (* Calculate Average *)
        Average := (Testl + Test2 + Test3) / 3.0;
        (* Print message *)
        Write('Average score is ', Average:4:2, '--');
        IF Average >= 60.0
          THEN                              (* Student is passing *)
            BEGIN
              Write('Passing');
              IF Average < 70.0
                THEN                              (* But marginal *)
                  Writeln(' but marginal.')
                ELSE
                  Writeln('.')
            END
          ELSE                              (* Student is failing *)
            Writeln('Failing.')
      END
    ELSE                              (* Invalid data *)
      Writeln('Invalid Data:  Score(s) less than zero.')
END.  (* Notices *)
```

Here's a sample run of the program. Again, the input is in color.

```
Enter a Student ID number and three test scores:
9483 73  62  68
Student Number: 9483  Test Scores: 73, 62, 68
Average score is 67.67--Passing but marginal.
```

And here's a sample run with invalid data:

```
Enter a Student ID number and three test scores:
9483 73 -10  62
Student Number: 9483  Test Scores: 73, -10, 62
Invalid Data:  Score(s) less than zero.
```

In this program we use a nested IF structure that's easy to understand although somewhat inefficient. We assign a value to Data_OK in one statement before testing it in the next. We could reduce the code by saying

```
Data_OK := NOT ((Test1 < 0) OR (Test2 < 0) OR (Test3 < 0))
```

In fact, we could reduce the code even more, using

```
IF (Test1 >= 0) AND (Test2 >= 0) AND (Test3 >= 0)
```

in place of IF Data_OK. (To convince yourself that these two variations work, try them by hand with some test data.) If these statements do the same thing, why do we use the longer form in the program? Because the longer form expresses more clearly what we are doing, even if it is a little less efficient.

*P*ROBLEM-SOLVING CASE STUDY

The Lumberyard

Problem: You've been hired by a local lumberyard to help computerize its operations. Your first assignment is to write a program that computes the total amount of an item ordered in standard units, given its type, dimensions, and the number of pieces ordered. The yard sells two kinds of items: dimensioned lumber and plywood panels. The program should first read a letter—either 'L' for lumber or 'P' for plywood—to determine the type. Next it should read four numbers. For lumber, the first two numbers are the width and depth in inches; the third number is the length in feet; and the fourth number is the number of pieces ordered. So

```
L 2 4 8 14
```

means 14 pieces of 2- by 4-inch lumber, each 8 feet long. To compute the quantity ordered, you have to calculate the total volume ordered. The unit for lumber volume is the board foot, which is equivalent to 1 square foot of lumber, 1 inch thick, or 144 cubic inches. The quantity ordered in the sample input is 74.67 board feet. To determine the board feet, we use this equation:

(2 in. × 4 in. × (8 ft. × 12 in./ft.) × 14 pieces)/144 cubic in. per board foot

For plywood, the first two numbers are the thickness of the sheet, expressed as a fraction; the third number is the length of the sheet in feet; and the last number is the number of sheets ordered. The lumberyard only stocks plywood sheets in 4-foot widths, so there's no need to enter the width. The entry

P 3 4 8 6

means 6 sheets of 3/4-inch-thick plywood, 8 feet long (and 4 feet wide). Again, to compute the quantity ordered, you have to calculate the total volume ordered. At this lumberyard, the unit for plywood volume is a full sheet. A full sheet is 4 feet (48 inches) wide, 8 feet (96 inches) long, and 1 inch thick, or 4,608 cubic inches. For the sample input, the quantity ordered is 4.5 full sheets. We use this equation:

(6 sheets × 3/4 in. × (8 ft. × 12 in./ft.) × 48 in.))/4608 cubic in. per sheet

Input: A letter (Code) and four Real numbers (Size1, Size2, Size3, Num_Ordered)

Output:

Input prompt message
Input (echo print)
Result of calculating the quantity

Discussion: To do this by hand, you would read the letter and four numbers and examine the letter to decide what to do. If the letter is 'L', you would first change all the units to inches, then multiply the four numbers together to get the total volume. Then you would divide the result by one board foot (144 cubic inches). If the letter is a 'P', you would again change all the units to inches, divide the first number by the second to get the thickness, then multiply the dimensions (don't forget the width) by the number of pieces to get the volume in cubic inches. You would divide this quantity by the volume of one full sheet (4,608 cubic inches) to get the number of sheets.

The process can be translated directly into a program. "Read the letter and four numbers" becomes a Read statement. We use an IF-THEN-ELSE statement to "examine the letter" and decide which formula to use. Each branch of the IF-THEN-ELSE has two steps. In the first, we calculate the appropriate result. In the second, we print the result and say whether it is in board feet or full sheets.

Main Module   *Level 0*

```
Get data
IF Code is set equal to 'L'
   THEN calculate lumber
   ELSE calculate plywood
```

PROBLEM-SOLVING CASE STUDY *cont'd.*

Get Data   *Level 1*

> Prompt for input
> Read Code, Size1, Size2, Size3, Num_Ordered
> Echo-print input data

Calculate Lumber

> Board_Feet is set equal to Size1 * Size2 * Size3 * 12 * Num_Ordered /
>   Board_Ft_Inches
> Write Board_Feet

Calculate Plywood

> Full_Sheets is set equal to Size1 / Size2 * Size3 * 12 * Width_Inches *
>   Num_Ordered / Plywood_Inches
> Write Full_Sheets

Module Structure Chart:

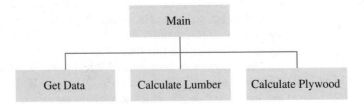

Quantities

Name	Value	Function
Board_Ft_Inches	144.0	Cubic inches in 1 board foot
Plywood_Inches	4608.0	Cubic inches in 1 full sheet of plywood
Width_Inches	48.0	Width in inches of every sheet of plywood

Variables

Name	Data Type	Function
Code	Char	Indicates lumber or plywood item
Size1	Real	First dimension
Size2	Real	Second dimension
Size3	Real	Third dimension
Num_Ordered	Real	Number ordered
Board_Feet	Real	Result for lumber item
Full_Sheets	Real	Result for plywood item

To save space, from here on we omit the list of constants and variables from the Problem-Solving Case Studies. But we recommend that you continue writing those lists as you design your own algorithms. The lists will save you a lot of work when you are writing the declarations for your programs. Here is the program that implements our design.

```
PROGRAM Lumber_Yard (Input, Output);

(* This program reads a letter and four real numbers. If      *)
(* the letter is 'L', the four numbers are interpreted as the *)
(* dimensions and quantity ordered of a lumber item, and the  *)
(* board-foot equivalent is output. If the letter is 'P', the *)
(* four numbers are the dimensions and quantity ordered of a  *)
(* plywood item, and the full-sheet equivalent is output      *)

CONST
   Board_Ft_Inches = 144.0;  (* Cubic inches in 1 board foot         *)
   Plywood_Inches = 4608.0;  (* Cubic inches in 1 full sheet of  plywood  *)
   Width_Inches = 48.0;      (* Width in inches of every sheet of  plywood *)

VAR
   Code:                     (* Indicates lumber or plywood item    *)
     Char;
   Size1,                    (* First dimension                     *)
   Size2,                    (* Second dimension                    *)
   Size3,                    (* Third dimension                     *)
   Num_Ordered,              (* Number ordered                      *)
   Board_Feet,               (* Result for lumber item              *)
   Full_Sheets:              (* Result for plywood item             *)
     Real;
```

```
BEGIN (* Lumber_Yard *)
  (* Get data *)
  Writeln('Enter letter code, three integer ',
          'dimensions, and quantity ordered:');           (* Prompt   *)
  Readln(Code, Sizel, Size2, Size3, Num_Ordered);
  Writeln('For the order data:');
  Writeln(Code, ' ', Sizel:1:0, ' ', Size2:1:0, ' ',
          Size3:1:0, ' ', Num_Ordered:1);                 (* Echo print  *)
  IF Code = 'L'
    THEN
      BEGIN
        (* Calculate lumber *)
        Board_Feet := Sizel * Size2 * Size3 * 12.0 *
                        Num_Ordered / Board_Ft_Inches;
        Writeln('the board-foot equivalent is ', Board_Feet:8:2)
      END
    ELSE
      BEGIN
        (* Calculate plywood *)
        FullSheets := Sizel / Size2 * Size3 * 12.0 *
                        Width_Inches * Num_Ordered / Plywood_Inches;
        Writeln('the full-sheet equivalent is ', Full_Sheets:8:2)
      END
END.  (* Lumber_Yard *)
```

This is a sample run of the program:

```
Enter letter code, three integer dimensions, and quantity ordered:
L 2 6 10 45
For the order data:
L 2 6 10 45
the board-foot equivalent is 450.00
```

This sample shows what happens when Code is 'P':

```
Enter letter code, three integer dimensions, and quantity ordered:
P 1 2 9 7
For the order data:
P 1 2 9 7
the full-sheet equivalent is 3.94
```

We examine this program in more detail in the next section.

Testing and Debugging

In Chapter 1 we discussed the problem-solving and implementation phases of computer programming. Testing is an integral part of both phases. Here we test both phases of the process used to develop Program Lumber_Yard. Testing in the problem-solving phase is done after the solution is developed. In the implementation phase we test after the algorithm is translated into a program, and again after the program has successfully compiled. The compilation itself constitutes another stage of testing that is performed automatically.

The Problem-Solving Phase: The Algorithm Walk-Through

To test at the problem-solving phase we do a **walk-through** of the algorithm. For each module in the top-down design, we establish a set of assertions, statements that must be true, called preconditions and a set of postconditions. **Preconditions** are assertions that must be true before a module is executed in order for the module to execute correctly. **Postconditions** are assertions that should be true after the module is executed, if it's done its job correctly. To test a module, we "walk through" the algorithmic steps to confirm that they produce the required postconditions given the stated preconditions.

Preconditions   Assertions that must be true before a module begins executing.

Postconditions   Assertions that should be true after a module is executed.

Our lumberyard algorithm has four modules: the main module, Get Data, Calculate Lumber, and Calculate Plywood. The preconditions for the main module usually are undefined except for any declared constants. In this case, Board_Ft_Inches equals 144.0, Plywood_Inches equals 4608.0, and Width_Inches equals 48.0. The main module's postconditions are that it outputs the correct result given the correct input. More specifically, the postconditions for the main module are

- the computer has read five input values (a letter and four Reals).
- the number of board feet ordered or
- the number of full sheets of plywood ordered has been calculated and displayed.

Because Get Data is the first module executed in the algorithm and because it does not rely on any predefined constants, it has no preconditions. Its postconditions are that it has input a letter into Code, and Real values into Size1, Size2, Size3, and Num_Ordered.

The preconditions for module Calculate Lumber are that Code equals 'L', and that Size1, Size2, Size3, and Num_Ordered contain Real values. Its postcondition is that the number of board feet ordered has been computed from those values and printed out.

The preconditions for module Calculate Plywood are that Code equals 'P', and that Size1, Size2, Size3, and Num_Ordered contain Real values. Its postcondition is that the number of full sheets ordered has been computed and printed out.

Now that we've established the preconditions and postconditions, we walk through the main program. At this point, we are concerned only with the steps in the main program, so for now we assume that each lower-level module executes correctly. At each step, we must determine the current conditions. If the step is a reference to another module, we have to verify that the preconditions of that module are met by the current conditions.

First we verify that the correct values have been assigned to the constants. Then, assuming Get Data correctly inputs a letter and four Integer values, the IF statement checks to see if the letter is an 'L'. If it is, the computer takes the Calculate Lumber branch. Assuming Calculate Lumber correctly calculates and prints the quantity ordered (remember, we're assuming that the lower-level modules are correct for now), that branch of the IF statement is correct.

If the letter in Code is not an 'L', the computer takes the Calculate Plywood branch. Here we have a problem. A precondition of Calculate Plywood asserts that the value of Code is 'P', but the only condition that has been established is that Code does not contain an 'L'. The program calculates the quantity of full sheets ordered if anything other than an 'L' is entered for Code. So the algorithm works as long as the data is entered correctly, but it does not catch incorrect data. This is poor design, and we return to the problem later. But let's finish up the walk-through first.

The next step is to examine each module at level 1 and answer this question: If the level-2 modules are assumed to be correct, will this module do what it is supposed to do? We simply repeat the walk-through process for each module, starting with its particular preconditions. In this example there are no level-2 modules, so the level-1 modules must be complete.

Get Data correctly reads in five values—Code, Size1, Size2, Size3, and Num_Ordered—which satisfies its postconditions. (The next refinement is actually coding this instruction. Whether or not it is coded correctly is *not* the problem at this phase; we deal with the code in testing the implementation phase.)

Calculate Lumber assigns to variable Board_Feet the result of multiplying the contents of Size1, Size2, Size3 (itself multiplied by the literal 12.0), and Num_Ordered, and dividing by the contents of Board_Ft_Inches. That's the correct formula for computing board feet, so the step is correct and the calculated value is printed. Calculate Lumber meets its required postconditions.

Calculate Plywood assigns to the variable Full_Sheets the result of dividing Size1 by Size2, multiplying by Size3 (itself multiplied by the literal 12.0), the contents of Width_Inches, and Num_Ordered, and dividing by the contents of Plywood_Inches. This is the correct formula for computing full sheets of plywood, so this step is correct and the calculated value is printed. Calculate Plywood also meets its required postconditions.

Once we've completed the algorithm walk-through, we have to correct any discrepancies and repeat the process. When we know that the modules do what they are supposed to do, we start translating the top-down design into our programming language.

We need to fix the problem we discovered in the algorithm, that the main module does not generate the proper preconditions for Calculate Plywood. We have to change the main module so that Code = 'P' is True before Calculate Plywood is entered. Here's the revised main module:

Main Module   *Level 0*

```
Get data
IF Code = 'L'
    THEN calculate lumber
IF Code = 'P'
    THEN calculate plywood
```

The main module now sees to it that data has been input to the five variables, and that Code contains the letter 'P' before Calculate Plywood is executed. This change corrects the problem we found in the walk-through, but we should also output an error message when a letter other than 'L' or 'P' is entered.

A standard postcondition for any program is that the user has been notified of invalid data. You should *validate* every input value for which any restrictions apply. A data validation IF statement tests an input value and outputs an error message if the value is not acceptable. (We are validating the data when we test for negative scores in Program Notices.) The best place to validate data is immediately after it is input. In the lumberyard algorithm, we would add a data validation test to the Get Data module.

Get Data   *Level 1*

```
Prompt for input
Read Code, Size1, Size2, Size3, Num_Ordered
Echo-print input data
IF Code is not 'L' or 'P'
    THEN
        Output an error message
```

In order to satisfy the data validation postcondition, the Lumberyard algorithm also should test the other input values. For example, a negative size or order quantity would be invalid. More elaborate checks might test for invalid combinations of dimensions. We leave you the task of other data validation as an exercise (see page 192).

The Implementation Phase

Now that we've talked about testing in the problem-solving phase, we can turn to testing in the implementation phase. Testing is done here at several points.

Code Walk-Through   After the code is written, you should go over it line by line, to be sure that you've faithfully reproduced the top-down design, a process known as a **code walk-through.** In a team programming situation, you would ask other team members to walk through the algorithm and code with you, to double-check the design and code.

Execution Trace   You also should take some actual values and hand-calculate what the output should be by doing an **execution trace.** When the program is executed, you can use these same values as input and check the results.

The computer is a very literal device—it does exactly what we tell it to do, which may or may not be what we want it to do. We try to make sure that a program does what we want by tracing the execution of the statements.

We use a nonsense program below to demonstrate the technique. We keep track of the values of the program variables on the right-hand side. Variables with undefined values are indicated with a dash. When a variable is assigned a value, that value is listed in the appropriate column.

		Value of	
Statement	*A*	*B*	*C*
PROGRAM Trace (Output);			
CONST			
X = 5;			
VAR			
A, B, C: Integer;	—	—	—
BEGIN (* Trace *)	—	—	—
B : = 1;	—	1	—
C : = X + B;	—	1	6
A : = X + 4;	9	1	6
A : = C;	6	1	6
B : = C;	6	6	6
A : = A + B + C;	18	6	6
C : = C MOD X;	18	6	1
C : = C * A;	18	6	18
A : = A MOD B;	0	6	18
Writeln(A, B, C)	0	6	18
END. (* Trace *)			

Turbo Pascal can perform this tracing for you automatically. While editing the program, place the cursor on the variable you want to trace and press Ctrl-F7. An "Add Watch" dialog box will appear with the variable name as the default entry. Press Enter and a *Watches window* will be created containing the variable name. (If you have not compiled the program before doing this, you may be told that Turbo does not recognize the variable; however, the trace will still work.) Note that the function key list at the bottom of the screen shows F8 as the "Step" key. Press F8 repeatedly to step through your program one statement at a time. As each statement is executed, the value of the watched variable will be displayed in the Watches window. You can watch several variables at once simply by repeating the Ctrl-F7 (Add Watch) procedure for each one before you start tracing the program.

Now that you've seen how the technique works, let's apply it to Program Lumber_Yard. We just list the statement section here, modified to reflect the results of our algorithm walk-through.

	Value of						
	C o d e	S i z e 1	S i z e 2	S i z e 3	N u m O r d e r e d	B o a r d F e e t	F u l l S h e e t s
Statement							
Writeln('Enter letter code, three integer ', 'dimensions, and quantity ordered:');	—	—	—	—	—	—	—
Readln(Code, Size1, Size2, Size3, Num_Ordered);	P	1.0	2.0	8.0	20.0	—	—
Writeln('For the order data:');	P	1.0	2.0	8.0	20.0	—	—
Writeln(Code, ' ', Size1:1, ' ', Size2:1, ' ', Size3:1, ' ', Num_Ordered:1);	P	1.0	2.0	8.0	20.0	—	—
IF NOT((Code = 'L') OR (Code = 'P'))	P	1.0	2.0	8.0	20.0	—	—
THEN							
Writeln('The item code is invalid.');	—	—	—	—	—	—	—
IF Code = 'L'	P	1.0	2.0	8.0	20.0	—	—
THEN							
BEGIN							
(* Calculate lumber *)							
Board_Feet := Size1 * Size2 * Size3 * 12.0 * Num_Ordered / Board_Ft_Inches;	—	—	—	—	—	—	—
Writeln('the board—foot equivalent is ', Board_Feet:8:2)	—	—	—	—	—	—	—
END							
IF Code = 'P'	P	1.0	2.0	8.0	20.0	—	—
THEN							
BEGIN							
(* Calculate plywood *)							
Full_Sheets := Size1 / Size2 * Size3 * 12.0 * Width_Inches * Num_Ordered / Plywood_Inches;	P	1.0	2.0	8.0	20.0	—	10.0
Writeln('the full—sheet equivalent is ', Full_Sheets:8:2)	P	1.0	2.0	8.0	20.0	—	10.0
END							

Figure 4-7
Branching
Structure for
Program Notices

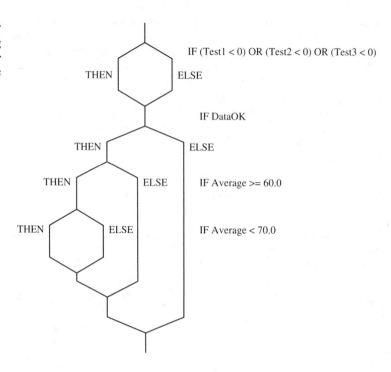

None of the parts of the THEN branch of the first two IF statements are executed for this input data, so we do not fill in any of the variable columns to their right. We always create columns for all of the variables, even though we know that some will stay empty. Why? Because it's possible that we'll encounter an error that refers to an empty variable; having a column for the variable reminds us to check for just such an error.

When a program contains branches, it's a good idea to retrace its execution with different input data so that each branch is traced at least once. In the next section we describe how to develop data sets that test each of a program's branches.

Testing Selection Control Structures   To test a program with branches, we have to execute each branch at least once and verify the results. For example, in Program Notices there are four IF-THEN-ELSE statements (see Figure 4-7). We need a series of data sets to test the different branches. For example, we could use the following sets of values for the input values of Test1, Test2, and Test3:

	Test1	Test2	Test3
Set 1	100	100	100
Set 2	60	60	63
Set 3	50	50	50
Set 4	− 50	50	50

Figure 4-8 shows the flow of control through the branching structure of Program Notices for each of these data sets. Set 1 is valid and gives an average of 100, which

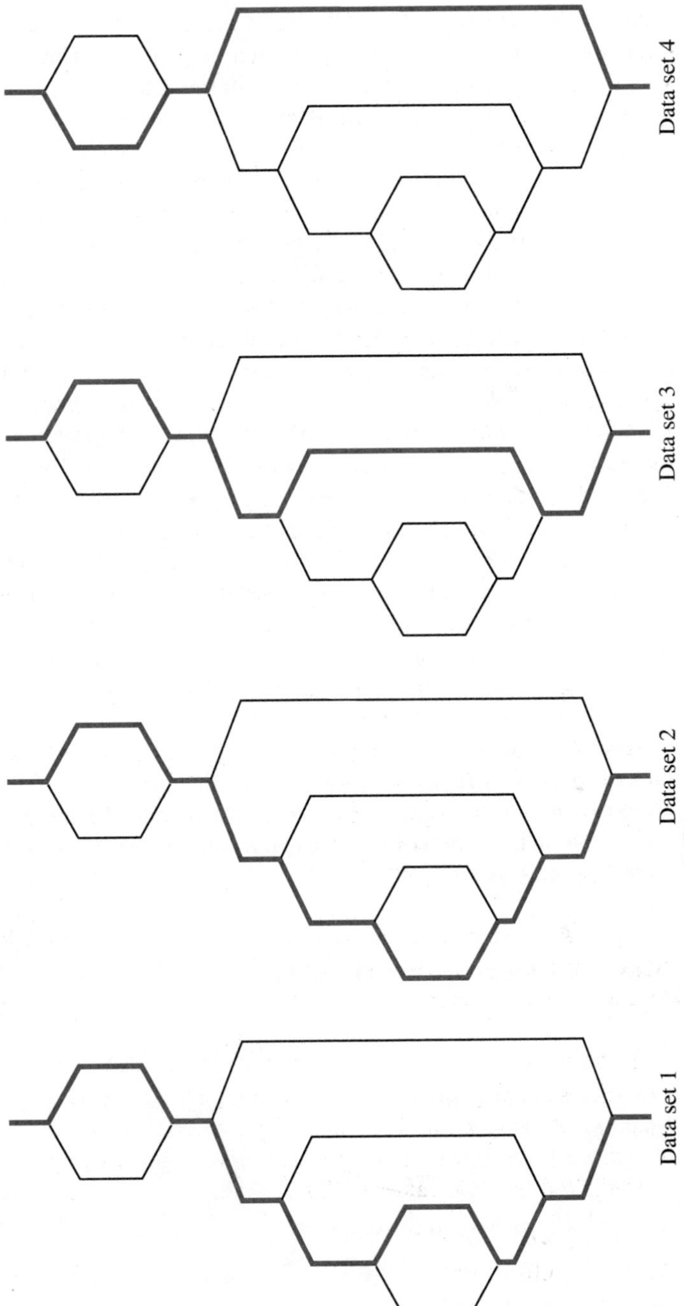

Figure 4-8   Flow of Control Through Program Notices for Each of Four Data Sets

is passing and not marginal. Set 2 is valid and gives an average of 61, which is passing but marginal. Set 3 is valid and gives an average of 50, which is failing. Set 4 has an invalid test grade, which generates an error message.

Every branch in the program is executed at least once through this series of test runs; eliminating any of the test data sets would leave at least one branch untested. This series of data sets provides **minimum complete coverage** of the program's branching structure. Whenever you test a program with branches in it, you should design a series of tests that covers all of the branches. It may help to draw diagrams like those in Figure 4-8 so that you can see which branches are being executed.

Because an action in one branch of a program often affects processing in a later branch, it is critical to test as many **combinations of branches,** or paths, through a program as possible; this way we can be sure that there are no interdependencies that could cause problems. Of course some combinations of branches may be impossible to follow. For example, if the ELSE is taken in the first branch of Program Notices, the ELSE in the second branch cannot be taken. Shouldn't we try all possible paths? Yes, in theory we should; however, the number of paths in even a small program is quite large. For example, there are sixteen possible paths in Program Lumber_Yard.

The approach to testing that we've used here is called *code coverage* because the test data is designed by looking at the code of the program. Another approach to testing, *data coverage*, attempts to test as many allowable data values as possible without regard to the program code. Complete data coverage is as impractical as complete code coverage for many programs. For example, Program Notices reads four integer values, and thus has $(2 * \text{MaxInt})^4$ possible inputs.

Often, testing is a combination of these two strategies. Instead of trying every possible data value (data coverage), we examine the code (code coverage) and look for ranges of values for which processing is identical. Then we test the values at the boundaries and, sometimes, a value in the middle of each range. For example, a simple condition, such as

Test < 0

divides the integers into two ranges:

$-\text{MaxInt} - 1$ to -1
0 to MaxInt

Thus, we should test the four values $-\text{MaxInt} - 1$, -1, 0, and MaxInt. A compound condition, such as

(Test $>= 0$) AND (Test $<= 100$)

divides the integers into three ranges:

$-\text{MaxInt} - 1$ to -1
0 to 100
101 to MaxInt

Thus, we have six values to test. In addition, to verify that the compound relational operators are correct, we should test for values of 1 (> 0) and 99 (< 100).

Conditional branches are only one factor in developing a testing strategy. We'll consider more of these factors in later chapters.

Tests Performed Automatically During Compilation and Execution

Once a program is coded and test data has been prepared, it is ready for compiling. The compiler produces two distinct outputs: a report of any errors and the translated version of the program.

Errors can be syntactic or semantic. The compiler finds syntactic errors. For example, the compiler warns you when reserved words are misspelled, identifiers are undefined, semicolons are missing, and operand types are mismatched. But it won't find all of your typing errors. If you type > instead of < , you won't get an error message. It's up to you to design test data and carefully check the code to detect semantic errors.

Semantic errors are mistakes that give you the wrong answer. They are more difficult to locate than syntactic errors and usually surface when a program is executing. Pascal detects only the most obvious semantic errors—those that result in an invalid operation (dividing by zero, for example). Although semantic errors sometimes are caused by typing errors, they more often are a product of faulty design. The mistake we found in the algorithm walk-through for the lumberyard problem is a typical semantic error.

By walking through the algorithm and the code, tracing the execution of the program, and developing a thorough test strategy, you should be able to avoid, or at least quickly locate, semantic errors in your programs.

Figure 4-9 illustrates the testing process we've been discussing. The figure shows where syntax and semantic errors occur and in which phase they can be corrected.

Figure 4-9   *Testing Process*

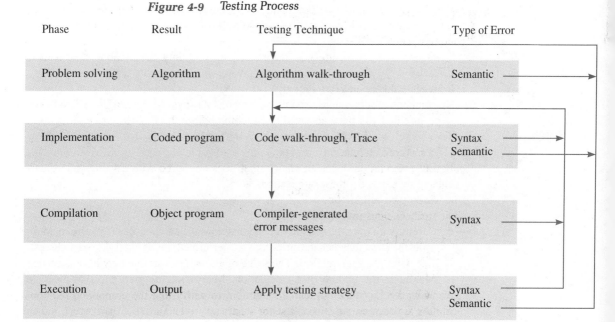

Phase	Result	Testing Technique	Type of Error
Problem solving	Algorithm	Algorithm walk-through	Semantic
Implementation	Coded program	Code walk-through, Trace	Syntax Semantic
Compilation	Object program	Compiler-generated error messages	Syntax
Execution	Output	Apply testing strategy	Syntax Semantic

Testing and Debugging Hints

1. Echo-print all input data. This way you know your input data is what it is supposed to be.
2. Test for bad data. If a data value must be positive, use an IF statement to test the value. If the value is negative, an error message should be printed; otherwise processing should continue. For example, Program Activity should have the following statement inserted after the first Writeln (the echo print):

```
IF (Temperature > 120) OR (Temperature < -25)
   THEN
      Writeln('Temperature data is in error.')
   ELSE
      BEGIN
         .
         .
```

This IF statement tests the limits of reasonable temperatures and executes the rest of the program only if the data is reasonable.
3. Use parentheses to make your Boolean expressions clear and correct. Remember that Boolean operators (AND, OR, XOR, NOT) take precedence over relational operators (= , <>, >, <, >= , <=). Enclose relational expressions in parentheses if you're combining them with Boolean operators.
4. Be sure that the opening and closing parentheses match up. To verify that parentheses are properly paired, start with the innermost pair and draw a line connecting them. Do the same for the others, working your way out to the outermost pair. For example,

(((Total/Scores) > 50) AND ((Total/(Scores − 1)) < 100))

5. Don't use =< to mean "less than or equal to"; only the symbol <= works. Likewise, => is invalid as a form of "greater than or equal to"; you must use >= to indicate this operation.
6. Remember that semicolons separate statements. Always check each IF-THEN-ELSE to be sure that you have not used a semicolon before the ELSE.
7. Take some sample values and try them by hand as we did for Program Notices. (There's more on this in Chapter 5.)
8. If your program produces an answer that does not agree with a value you've calculated by hand, try these suggestions:
   a. Redo your arithmetic.
   b. Recheck your input data.
   c. Carefully go over the section of code that does the calculation. If you're in doubt about the order in which the operations are performed, insert clarifying parentheses.
   d. Check for integer overflow. The value of an Integer variable may have exceeded MaxInt in the middle of a calculation. Many systems give an error message when this happens, but some do not.
   e. Check the conditions in branching statements to be sure that the correct branch is taken under all circumstances.
   f. Use the Turbo Pascal Watches window to trace execution of the program.

Summary

Using Boolean expressions is a way of asking questions while a program is running. The program evaluates each Boolean expression, assigning it the value True if the expression is true or False if the expression is not true.

The IF statement allows you to take different paths through a program based on the value of a Boolean expression. The IF-THEN-ELSE is used to choose between two courses of action; the IF-THEN is used to choose whether or not to take a particular course of action. The branches of an IF-THEN or IF-THEN-ELSE can be any statement, simple or compound. They can even be another IF statement.

The algorithm walk-through forces us to define preconditions and postconditions for each module in an algorithm. Then we have to verify that those assertions exist at the beginning and end of each module. By testing our design in the problem-solving phase, we can eliminate errors that can be more difficult to detect in the implementation phase.

An execution trace is a way of finding program errors once we've entered the implementation phase. It's a good idea to trace a program before you run it, so that you have some sample results to check the program's output against.

■ *Quick Check*

1. Write a Pascal expression that compares the variable Letter to the constant 'Z' and returns True if Letter is less than 'Z'. (pp. 142–145)

2. Write a Pascal expression that returns True if Letter is between 'A' and 'Z' inclusive. (pp. 142–149)

3. What kind of statement would you use to make a Pascal program print out "Is a letter" if the value in Letter is between 'A' and 'Z' inclusive, and print out "Is not a letter" if the value in Letter is outside that range? (pp. 151–156)

4. What kind of statement would you use to make a Pascal program print out "Is a letter" only if the value in Letter is between 'A' and 'Z' inclusive? (pp. 156–157)

5. On a telephone each of the digits 2 through 9 has a segment of the alphabet associated with it. What kind of control structure would you use to decide which segment a given letter falls into and to print out the corresponding digit? (pp. 157–160)

6. What is one postcondition that every program should have? (pp. 175–177)

7. In what phase of the program development process should you carry out an execution trace? (pp. 177–180)

8. You've written a program that prints out the corresponding digit on a phone given a letter of the alphabet. Everything seems to work right except that you can't get the digit '5' to print out; you keep getting the digit '6'. What steps would you take to find and fix this bug? (pp. 180–184)

Answers

1. Letter < 'Z'   2. (Letter >= 'A') AND (Letter <= 'Z')   3. An IF-THEN-ELSE statement.   4. An IF-THEN statement   5. A nested IF statement   6. That the user has been notified of invalid data values   7. The implementation phase   8. Carefully review the section of code that should print out '5'. Check the branching condition and the output statement there. Try some sample values by hand.

■ Exam Preparation Exercises

1. Given these values for Boolean variables X, Y, and Z:

   X = True, Y = False, Z = True

   evaluate the following Boolean expressions. In the blank next to each expression, write a T if the result is True or an F if the result is False.

   ___ a. (X AND Y) OR (X AND Z)
   ___ b. (X OR NOT Y) AND (NOT X OR Z)
   ___ c. X OR Y AND Z
   ___ d. NOT (X OR Y) AND Z

2. Given these values for variables I, J, K, and L:

   I = 10, J = 19, K = True, L = False

   add parentheses as necessary to the expressions below so that they evaluate to True.

   a. I = J OR K
   b. I >= J OR I <= J AND K
   c. NOT K OR K
   d. NOT L AND L

3. Given these values for Integer variables I, J, K, and L:

   I := 6, J := 7, K := 11, L := 11

   what is the output of the following code?

   ```
   Writeln('Madam');
   IF I < J
      THEN
         IF K <> L
           THEN
              Writeln('How')
           ELSE
              Writeln('Now');
              Writeln('I''m');
   IF I >= J
      THEN
         Writeln('Brown');
         Writeln('Cow')
      ELSE
         Writeln('Adam')
   ```

4. Given the Integer variables X, Y, and Z, where X is 3, Y is 7, and Z is 6, what is the output from each of the following code fragments?

```
a. IF X <= 3
      THEN
         Writeln(X + Y);
   Writeln(X + Y)
b. IF X <> -1
      THEN
         Writeln('The value of X is ', X)
      ELSE
         Writeln('The value of Y is ', Y)
c. IF X <> -1
      THEN
         BEGIN
            Writeln(X);
            Writeln(Y);
            Writeln(Z)
         END
      ELSE
         Writeln('Y');
   Writeln('Z')
```

5. Given this code fragment:

```
IF Height >= Min_Height
   THEN
      IF Weight >= Min_Weight
         THEN
            Writeln('Eligible to serve.')
         ELSE
            Writeln('Too light to serve.')
      ELSE
         IF Weight >= Min_Weight
            THEN
               Writeln('Too short to serve.')
            ELSE
               Writeln('Too short and too light to serve.')
```

H >= MH

   a. What is the output when Height exceeds Min_Height and Weight exceeds Min_Weight?
   b. What is the output when Height is less than Min_Height and Weight is less than Min_Weight?

6. Match each Boolean expression in the left column with the Boolean expression in the right column that tests for the same condition.

```
_____ a. (X < Y) AND (Y < Z)        (1) NOT (X <> Y) AND (Y = Z)
_____ b. (X > Y) AND (Y >= Z)       (2) NOT ((X <= Y) OR (Y < Z))
_____ c. (X <> Y) OR (Y = Z)        (3) ((Y < Z) OR (Y = Z)) OR (X = Y)
_____ d. (X = Y) OR (Y <= Z)        (4) NOT (X >= Y) AND NOT (Y >= Z)
_____ e. (X = Y) AND (Y = Z)        (5) NOT ((X = Y) AND (Y <> Z))
```

7. The following expressions make sense but are invalid according to Pascal's rules of syntax. Rewrite them so that they are valid Boolean expressions.

    a. $X < Y <= Z$
    b. X, Y, and Z are greater than 0
    c. X is equal to neither Y nor Z
    d. $X = Y$ and Z

8. Given these values for Boolean variables X, Y, and Z:

```
X := True, Y := True, Z := False
```

   indicate whether each expression is True (T) or False (F).

    ____ a. `NOT (Y OR Z) OR X`
    ____ b. `Z AND X AND Y`
    ____ c. `NOT Y OR (Z OR NOT X)`
    ____ d. `Z OR (X AND (Y OR Z))`
    ____ e. `X OR X AND Z`

9. For each of the following problems, decide which of the branching statements (IF-THEN-ELSE or IF-THEN) is more appropriate. Explain your answers.
    a. Students who are candidates for admission to a college submit their SAT scores. If a student's score is equal to or above a certain value, print a letter of acceptance for the student. Otherwise print a rejection notice.
    b. For employees who work more than 40 hours a week, calculate overtime pay and add it to their regular pay.
    c. In solving a quadratic equation, whenever the value of the discriminant (the quantity under the square root sign) is negative, print out a message noting that the roots are imaginary.
    d. In a computer-controlled sawmill, if a cross section of a log is greater than certain dimensions, adjust the saw to cut 4-inch by 8-inch beams; otherwise, adjust the saw to cut 2-inch by 4-inch studs.

10. What causes the error message "ERROR IN STATEMENT" when this code fragment is run?

```
IF Mileage < 24.0
   THEN
      Writeln('Gas guzzler.');
   ELSE
      Writeln('Fuel efficient.')
```

11. The following code fragment is supposed to print "Type AB" when Boolean variables TypeA and TypeB are both True, and print "Type O" when both variables are False. Instead it prints "Type O" whenever just one of the variables is False. Insert a BEGIN-END pair to make the code segment work the way it should.

```
IF TypeA OR TypeB
   THEN
      IF TypeA AND TypeB
         THEN
            Writeln('Type AB')
   ELSE
      Writeln('Type O')
```

12. The nested IF structure below has five possible branches depending on the values read into Char variables A, B, and C. To test the structure, you need five sets of data, each set using a different branch. Create the five test data sets.

```
Read(A, B, C);
IF A = B
  THEN
    IF B = C
      THEN
        Writeln('All initials are the same.')
      ELSE
        Writeln('First two are the same.')
  ELSE IF B = C
    THEN
      Writeln('Last two are the same.')
    ELSE IF A = C
      THEN
        Writeln('First and last are the same.')
      ELSE
        Writeln('All initials are different.')
```

    a. Test data set 1:   A = ____   B = ____   C = ____
    b. Test data set 2:   A = ____   B = ____   C = ____
    c. Test data set 3:   A = ____   B = ____   C = ____
    d. Test data set 4:   A = ____   B = ____   C = ____
    e. Test data set 5:   A = ____   B = ____   C = ____

13. If X and Y are Boolean variables, do the following two expressions test the same condition?

```
X <> Y
(X OR Y) AND NOT (X AND Y)
```

▪ *Programming Warm-Up Exercises*

1. Write a statement that sets the Boolean variable Available to True if Number_Ordered is less than or equal to Number_On_Hand minus Number_Reserved.

2. Declare Eligible to be a Boolean variable, and assign it the value True.

3. Write a statement containing a Boolean expression that assigns True to the Boolean variable Candidate if SAT_Score is greater than or equal to 1100, GPA is not less than 2.5, and Age is greater than 15. Otherwise Candidate should be False.

4. Given the declarations

```
VAR
  Left_Page:
    Boolean;
  Page_Number:
    Integer;
```

write a statement that sets Left_Page to True if Page_Number is even.

5. Write an IF statement (or series of IF statements) that assigns to the variable Biggest the greatest value contained in variables I, J, and K. Assume the three values are distinct.

6. Rewrite the following IF-THEN-ELSE statement using two IF-THEN statements.

```
IF Year MOD 4 = 0
  THEN
    Writeln(Year, ' is a leap year.')
  ELSE
    BEGIN
      Year := Year + 4 - Year MOD 4;
      Writeln(Year, ' is the next leap year.')
    END
```

7. Write the preconditions and postconditions for the modules in Program Notices (page 168).

8. Simplify the following program segment, taking out unnecessary comparisons.

```
IF Age > 64
  THEN
    Write('Senior voter');
IF Age < 18
  THEN
    Write('Under age');
IF (Age >= 18) AND (Age < 65)
  THEN
    Write('Regular voter')
```

9. Correct the syntax errors in the following program.

```
PROGRAM Exercise (Input, Output)

CONST
  A = 10
  B = 5
  C = 6

VAR
  D;
  E;
  F:
    Integer

BEGIN
  Read(D, E  F)
  IF (D > A)
    THEN
      D = A + D;
    ELSE
      D = A
  E := D + F
  Write('This program does not make sense,
        E, F  D)
END;
```

10. Cross out any unnecessary semicolons in the following Pascal program segment.

```
BEGIN;
  (* This is a nonsense program. *)
  A := 10;
  IF A > 0;
    THEN;
      IF A < 20;
        THEN;
          Writeln('A is in range');
        ELSE;
          BEGIN;
            Writeln('A is too high');
            A := 10;
          END;
    ELSE;
      IF A = 0;
        THEN;
          Writeln('A is null');
        ELSE;
          BEGIN;
            Writeln('A is too low');
            A := 10;
          END;
END.
```

11. Given the real variables X1, X2, Y1, Y2, and M, write a program segment to find the slope of a line through points X1 and Y1, and X2 and Y2. Use the formula

$$M = \frac{(Y1 - Y2)}{(X1 - X2)}$$

to determine the slope of the line. If X1 equals X2, the line is vertical and the slope is undefined. The segment should write the slope with an appropriate label. If the slope is undefined, it should write the message 'Slope undefined'.

12. Given the Real variables A, B, C, Root1, Root2, and Discriminant, write a program segment to determine whether the roots of a quadratic polynomial are real or imaginary. If the roots are real, find them and assign them to Root1 and Root2. If they are imaginary, write the message 'No real roots.'

    The formula for the solution to the quadratic equation is

$$\frac{-B \pm \sqrt{B^2 - 4AC}}{2A}$$

The ± means "plus or minus" and indicates that there are two solutions to the equation: one in which the result of the square root is added to −B and one in which the result is subtracted from −B. The roots are real if the discriminant (the quantity under the square root sign) is not negative.

13. Using a nested IF, write a program segment to find the smallest of three distinct integers, A, B, and C. Assign the result to variable SmallestInteger.

14. Continue to validate the data in the lumberyard case study. Test for negative numeric values. Also check for invalid plywood thicknesses. Valid thicknesses are ¼, ⅜, ½, ⅝, ¾, ⅞, ⁴⁄₄, ⁹⁄₈, and ⁵⁄₄.

▪ *Programming Problems*

1. Using a top-down design, write a Pascal program that inputs a single letter and prints out the corresponding digit on the telephone. The letters and digits on a telephone are grouped this way:

2 = ABC   4 = GHI   6 = MNO   8 = TUV
3 = DEF   5 = JKL   7 = PRS   9 = WXY

No digit corresponds to either Q or Z. For these letters your program should print a message indicating that they are not used on a telephone.

The program might operate like this:

```
Enter a single letter, and I will tell you what the corresponding
digit is on the telephone.
R
The digit 7 corresponds to the letter R on the telephone.
```

Here's another example:

```
Enter a single letter, and I will tell you what the corresponding
digit is on the telephone.
Q
There is no digit on the telephone that corresponds to Q.
```

Your program should print a message indicating that there is no matching digit for any nonalphabetic character the user enters.

On systems that use both uppercase and lowercase letters, the program should recognize only uppercase letters. Include the lowercase letters with the invalid characters.

If you are using an interactive system, prompt the user with an informative message for the input value.

The program should echo-print the input letter as part of the output. Use proper indentation, appropriate comments, and meaningful identifiers throughout the program.

2. People who deal with historical dates use a number called the Julian day in calculating the number of days between two events. The Julian day is the number of days that have elapsed since January 1, 4713 B.C. For example, the Julian day for October 16, 1956, is 2435763. There are formulas for computing the Julian Day from a given date and vice versa.

One very simple formula computes the day of the week from a given Julian day:

Day of the week = (Julian day + 1) MOD 7

This formula gives a result of 0 for Sunday, 1 for Monday, and so on up to 6 for Saturday. For Julian day 2435763, the result is 2 (a Tuesday). Your job is to write a Pascal program that inputs a Julian day, computes the day of the week using the formula, and then prints out the name of the day that corresponds to that number. Be sure to echo-print the input data and to use proper indentation and comments.

Your output might look like this:

```
Enter a Julian day number:
2451545
Julian day number 2451545 is a Saturday.
```

3. You can compute the date for any Easter Sunday from 1982 to 2048 as follows (all variables are of type Integer):

A is Year MOD 19
B is Year MOD 4
C is Year MOD 7
D is (19 * A + 24) MOD 30
E is (2 * B + 4 * C + 6 * D + 5) MOD 7
Easter Sunday is March (22 + D + E)*

Write a program that inputs the year and outputs the date (month and day) of Easter Sunday for that year. Echo-print the input as part of the output. For example:

```
Enter the year (for example, 1991):
1985
Easter is Sunday, April 7, in 1985.
```

4. The algorithm for computing the date of Easter can be easily extended to work with any year from 1900 to 2099. There are four years, 1954, 1981, 2049, and 2076, for which the algorithm gives a date that is 7 days later than it should be. Modify the program for Problem 3 to check for these years and subtract 7 from the day of the month. This correction does not cause the month to change. Be sure to change the documentation for the program to reflect its broadened capabilities.

5. Write a Pascal program that calculates and prints the diameter, the circumference, or the area of a circle, given the radius. Store the data for each calculation on a separate line in File CircleData. The first character on each line should be a 'D' (for diameter), 'C' (for circumference), or 'A' (for area) to indicate the calculation needed. The next value on the line of data should be a real number with two digits after the decimal point indicating the radius of the particular circle.

   The program should echo-print the input data. The output should be appropriately labeled and formatted to two decimal places. For example, if the input is

A 6.75

your program should print something like this:

```
The area for a circle with a radius of 6.75 is 143.14.
```

Here are the formulas you'll need:

Diameter $= 2r$

Circumference $= 2\pi r$

Area of a circle $= \pi r^2$

Use 3.14159 for pi (π). r is the radius.

---

*Notice that this formula can give a date in April.

6. The factorial of a number N is $N * (N - 1) * (N - 2) * \ldots * 2 * 1$. Stirling's formula approximates the factorial for large values of N ($\pi = 3.14159$ and $e = 2.1718282$):

$$\frac{N^N \sqrt{2\pi N}}{e^N}$$

Write a Pascal program that calculates the factorial of a number N using Stirling's formula, assigns the result to an Integer variable using the standard Pascal function Round, and then print the result appropriately labeled.

Depending on the value of N, you should obtain one of these results:

- A numerical result.
- If N equals 0, the factorial is defined to be 1.
- If N is less than 0, the factorial is undefined.
- If N is too large, the result exceeds MaxInt.

Because Stirling's formula is used to calculate the factorial of very large numbers, the factorial will approach MaxInt quickly. If the factorial exceeds MaxInt, it will cause an arithmetic overflow in the computer, in which case the program will stop running. Before you write the program, then, you first must write a small program that lets you determine, by trial and error, the largest value of N for which your computer system can compute a factorial using Stirling's formula. After you've determined this value, you can write the program using nested IFs that print different messages depending on the value of N. If N is within the acceptable range for your computer system, write the number and the result with an appropriate message. If N is 0, write the message, 'The number is 0. The factorial is 1.'. If the number is below 0, write 'The number is below 0. The factorial is undefined.'. If the number is above the largest value of N for which your computer system can compute a factorial, write 'The number is too large.'.

You may need to use the standard Pascal functions Exp (exponentiation) and Ln (natural logarithm).

Looping

GOALS

- To be able to construct syntactically correct WHILE loops.
- To be able to construct count-controlled loops with a WHILE statement.
- To be able to construct event-controlled loops with a WHILE statement.
- To be able to use EOF to control the input of data.
- To be able to use EOLN to control the input of character data.
- To be able to use flags to control the execution of a WHILE statement.
- To be able to construct counting loops with a WHILE statement.
- To be able to construct summing loops with a WHILE statement.
- To be able to choose the correct type of loop for a given problem.
- To be able to construct a nested WHILE loop.
- To be able to write the invariant conditions for a loop and use them to verify the loop.
- To be able to choose data sets that test a looping program comprehensively.

In Chapter 4 we said that the flow of control in a program can differ from the physical order of the statements. The physical order is the order in which the statements appear in a program; the order in which we want the statements to be executed is called the *logical order.*

The IF statement is one way of making the logical order different from the physical order. Looping control structures are another. A **loop** executes the same statement (simple or compound) over and over, as long as a condition or set of conditions is met.

Loop   A control structure that causes a set of statements to be reiterated.

In this chapter we discuss different types of loops and how they are constructed using the WHILE statement. We also discuss *nested loops,* loops that contain other loops, and introduce a notation for comparing the amount of work done by different algorithms.

WHILE Statement

The WHILE statement, like the IF statement, tests a condition. Here is the syntax template for the WHILE statement:

WHILE Boolean expression **DO**
    statement1

This means "If the expression is True, execute statement 1 and then go back and test the Boolean expression again. If the expression is False, skip statement 1." So statement 1 is executed over and over as long as the Boolean expression is True when it is tested. When the expression is False, the program skips statement 1 and begins executing the first statement following the loop. Of course if the expression is False to begin with, then statement 1 is not even executed. Figure 5-1 shows the flow of control of the WHILE statement.

Statement 1 can be a compound statement, which allows us to execute any group of statements repeatedly. You'll almost always use WHILE loops in the following form:

```
WHILE Boolean expression DO
  BEGIN
    series of statements
  END;
```

In this structure, if the Boolean expression is True, the entire series of statements is executed, and then the expression is checked again. If it is still True, the statements are executed again. The cycle continues until the expression becomes False.

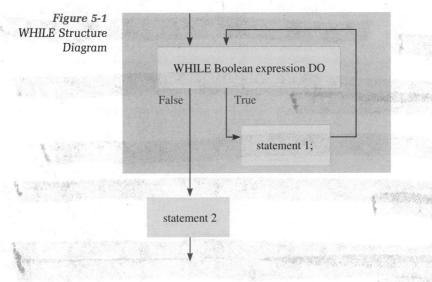

Figure 5-1
WHILE Structure
Diagram

Figure 5-2 *A Comparison of IF and WHILE*

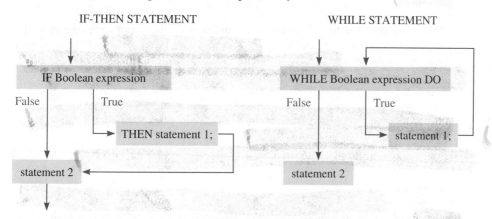

Although in some ways IF and WHILE are alike, there are fundamental differences between them (see Figure 5-2). In the IF structure, statement 1 is either skipped or executed exactly once. In the WHILE structure, statement 1 can be skipped, executed once, or executed over and over. The IF is used to *choose* a course of action; the WHILE is used to *repeat* a course of action.

Phases of Loop Execution

The statement in a loop is called the **body** of the loop. The loop body is executed in several phases:

- The moment that the flow of control first passes to a statement inside the loop is the **loop entry.**

Loop Entry   The point at which the flow of control first passes to a statement inside a loop.

■ Each time the body of a loop is executed, a pass is made through the loop. This pass is called an **iteration.**

Iteration   An individual pass through, or repetition of, the body of a loop.

■ Before each iteration, control is transferred to the **conditional test** at the beginning of the loop.

Conditional Test   The point at which the Boolean expression is evaluated and the decision is made to either begin a new iteration or skip to the first statement following the loop.

■ When the last iteration is complete and the flow of the control has passed to the first statement following the loop, the program has **exited the loop.** The condition that causes a loop to be exited is the **termination condition.** In the case of a WHILE loop, the termination condition is that the Boolean expression becomes False.

Loop Exit   That point when the repetition of the loop body ends and control passes to the first statement following the loop.

Termination Condition   The condition that causes a loop to be exited.

Notice that the loop exit occurs only at one point: when the conditional test is performed. Even though the termination condition may occur in the middle of the loop, the current iteration is completed before the computer checks the Boolean expression again.

The concept of looping is fundamental to programming. We spend some time looking at typical types of loops and ways to implement them with the WHILE statement. These looping situations come up again and again when you are analyzing problems and doing top-down design.

Loops Using the WHILE Statement

In solving problems, you will come across two major types of loops: A **count-controlled loop** repeats a specified number of times; an **event-controlled loop** repeats until something happens within the loop.

Count-Controlled Loop   A loop that executes a specified number of times.

Event-Controlled Loop   A loop that terminates when something happens inside the loop body to signal that the loop should be exited.

If you are making an angel food cake and the recipe reads, "Beat the mixture 300 strokes," you are executing a count-controlled loop. If you are making a piecrust and the recipe reads, "Cut with a pastry blender until the mixture resembles coarse meal," you are executing an event-controlled loop.

Count-Controlled Loops

A count-controlled loop uses a variable we call the **loop control variable** in the conditional test. Before we enter a count-controlled loop, we have to *initialize* (set the initial value of) the loop control variable and then test it. Then, as part of each iteration of the loop, we must *increment* (increase by 1) the loop control variable. Here's an example:

```
Count := 1;                (* Initialization  *)
WHILE Count <= 10 DO       (* Test            *)
  BEGIN
                           (* Repeated actions *)
    .
    .
    Count := Count + 1     (* Incrementation  *)
  END
```

Here Count is the loop control variable. It is set to 1 before loop entry. The WHILE statement tests the expression

```
Count <= 10
```

and executes the compound statement as long as the expression is True. The dots inside the compound statement represent a series of statements to be repeated. The last statement in the loop body increments Count by adding 1 to it.

Look at the statement in which we increment the loop control variable. Notice its form:

```
variable := variable + 1
```

This statement adds 1 to the value of the variable, and the result replaces the old value. Variables that are used this way are called **counters**. In our example, Count is incremented with each iteration of the loop—we use it to count the iterations. The loop control variable of a count-controlled loop is always a counter.

It is the programmer's responsibility to see that the condition to be tested is set correctly (initialized) before the WHILE statement begins. The programmer also must make sure the condition changes within the loop so that it becomes False at some point; otherwise the loop is never exited.

```
Count := 1;        ←——————————————  Variable count must be initialized
WHILE Count <= 10 DO
  BEGIN
     .
     .
     Count := Count + 1    ←—————  Count must be incremented (changed)

END
```

A loop that does not exit is called an **infinite loop** because in theory the loop will execute forever. If your program goes on running for much longer than you expect it to, chances are that you've created an infinite loop. You may have to issue an operating system command to stop the program. If the program is being run in the Turbo environment, you can then press Ctrl-Break to stop it. If the program had been compiled to disk and is being run from the operating system, you will have to press the Ctrl-Alt-Del key combination to reboot the operating system. Occasionally, a program will get so wrapped up in itself that even pressing Ctrl-Alt-Del will fail to stop it. You must then turn the PC off, wait about 5 seconds, and turn the machine back on. If you reboot the operating system while in the Turbo environment, any changes you've made to your program will be lost; thus it's always a good idea to save your program before running it.

How many times will the loop in our example be executed—9 or 10? To determine this, we have to look at the initial value of the loop control variable and then at the test to see what its final value will be. Here we've initialized Count to 1, and the test indicates that the loop body will be executed for each value of Count up through 10. If Count starts out at 1 and runs up to 10, the loop body will be executed 10 times. If we want the loop to execute 11 times, we have to either initialize Count to 0 or change the test to

```
Count <= 11
```

Event-Controlled Loops

There are several kinds of event-controlled loops: sentinel controlled, EOF controlled, EOLN controlled, and flag controlled. In all of these loops the termination condition depends on some event occurring while the loop body is executing.

Sentinel-Controlled Loops   Loops often are used to read in and process long lists of data. Each time the loop body is executed, a new piece of data is read and processed. Often a special data value, called a **sentinel,** is used to signal the program that there is no more data to be processed. Looping continues as long as the data value read is *not* the sentinel; it stops when the program recognizes the sentinel. In other words, reading the sentinel value is the event that controls the looping process.

A sentinel value must be something that never shows up in the normal input to a program. For example, if a program reads calendar dates, we could use February 31 as a sentinel value:

```
WHILE NOT (Month = 2) AND (Day = 31) DO
   BEGIN
      Read(Month, Day);                              (* Get a date *)
         .
         .                                           (* Process it *)
   END
```

There is a problem in the loop in the example above. The values of Month and Day are not defined before the first pass through the loop. Somehow we have to initialize these variables. We could assign them arbitrary values, but then we run the risk of those values being processed as data. Also it's not efficient to initialize variables with values that are never used.

We can solve the problem by reading the first set of data values *before* entering the loop. This is called a **priming Read.** (The idea is similar to priming a pump by pouring a bucket of water into the mechanism before starting it.) Let's add the priming Read to the loop:

```
Read(Month, Day);                          (* Get a date -- priming Read *)
WHILE NOT (Month = 2) AND (Day = 31) DO
   BEGIN
      Read(Month, Day);                            (* Get a date *)
         .
         .                                          (* Process it *)
   END
```

There is still a problem here. Notice that the first thing the program does inside the loop is to get a date. The values read for Month and Day will cause their initial values to be overwritten. The first date in the data list is never processed.

The *first* thing that the loop body should do is immediately process the data that's already been read. But then at what point do we read the next data set? We do this *last*. In this way the termination condition is applied to the next data set before it gets processed.

Here's how it looks:

```
Read(Month, Day);                          (* Get a date -- priming Read *)
WHILE NOT (Month = 2) AND (Day = 31) DO
   BEGIN
      .
      .                                            (* Process it *)
      .
      Read(Month, Day)                             (* Get the next date *)
   END
```

This segment works fine. The first data set is read in; if it is not the sentinel, it gets processed. At the end of the loop, the next data set is read in, and we go back to the beginning of the loop. If the new data set is not the sentinel, it gets processed just like the first. When the sentinel value is read, the WHILE expression becomes False, and the loop exits without processing the sentinel.

Many times the problem dictates the value of the sentinel. For example, if the problem does not allow data values of zero, then the sentinel value should be zero. Sometimes a combination of values is invalid. The combination of February and 31 as a date is such a case. Sometimes a range of values (negative numbers, for example) is the sentinel.

What happens when there aren't any invalid data values? Then you may have to input an extra value in each iteration, a value whose only purpose is to signal the end of the data. For example, look at this code segment:

```
Readln(Data_Value, Sentinel);          (* Get a date -- priming Read *)
WHILE Sentinel = 1 DO
   BEGIN
      .                                 (* Process it *)
      .
   Readln(Data_Value, Sentinel)         (* Get the next date *)
   END
```

The second value on each line of the following data set is used to indicate whether or not there is more data. In the data set below, when the sentinel value is 0, there is no more data; when it is 1, there is more data.

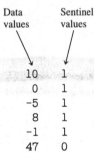

Data values	Sentinel values
10	1
0	1
-5	1
8	1
-1	1
47	0

What happens if you forget to enter the sentinel value? In an interactive program, the loop executes again, prompting for input. At that point you can enter the sentinel value, but you may get wrong results. If the input to the program is from a file, once all the data has been read from the file, the loop body is executed again. Because there isn't any data left—because the computer has reached the end of the file (EOF)—Standard Pascal will produce an error message like "TRIED TO READ PAST EOF." In the next section we describe a way to use EOF as a sentinel value. In Turbo Pascal, however, the Read statement sets the Integer variables to zero when there isn't any data left. Because the termination condition for this loop is Sentinel = 1, the loop body will not be executed again. If the condition had been Sentinel = 0, the loop would have executed forever. In Turbo Pascal, Sentinel-Controlled loops must be written with some care to avoid an infinite loop.

EOF-Controlled Loops   In Chapter 3 we said that <eoln> is a special sequence of characters that signals the end of a line of data, and that <eof> is a special character (or sequence of characters) that signals the end of a file. EOF is a built-in Boolean function that becomes True when the reading marker is at <eof>. You don't have to insert the <eof> character after your data; the system does it automatically.

```
<value> <value> <value> . . . <eoln>
<value> <value> <value> . . . <eoln>
<value> <value> <value> . . . <eoln>
<value> <value> <value> . . . <eoln>
<eof>
```

We use the EOF function to control the reading in loops in which the number of data sets is not known in advance. Here's an example:

```
WHILE NOT EOF DO
  BEGIN
    Readln(Value1, Value2, Value3,...);
     .
     .
  END
```

Because EOF is False when there is data remaining, you must use NOT EOF to control the loop. The Readln leaves the marker ready to read the character at the beginning of each new line. When all the data has been read in, the marker is at <eof>.

As we discussed in Chapter 3, in order to use a Readln we must know how the data is organized on each line. When we don't know how the data is organized, we have to use a Read statement. But look what happens if we simply replace the Readln with a Read:

```
WHILE NOT EOF DO
  BEGIN
    Read(Value);
     .
     .
  END
```

Given the sample data:

```
24  36  37<eoln>
<eof>
```

Operation	Value	Marker Position After Indicated Operation
Before the loop	Value = ?	24 36 37<eoln> <eof>
After the first pass through the loop	Value = 24	24 36 37<eoln> <eof>
After the second pass through the loop	Value = 36	24 36 37<eoln> <eof>
After the third pass through the loop	Value = 37	24 36 37<eoln> <eof>

After the third pass the reading marker is on the <eoln>. EOF returns False because the file is not empty (the <eoln> character still has to be read), and the loop is executed again. Because there is no more data, we get an error message. Notice the subtle difference between a file that is empty and a file that is out of data. Until the marker is at <eof>, the file is not really empty.

There are several ways to get around this problem. The simplest is to avoid using Read with numeric data in EOF-controlled loops. Use Readln instead. If you must use Read with numeric data, use a sentinel-controlled loop instead of an EOF-controlled loop. If neither of these alternatives works, you have to write the program to read all of the data as characters and convert them into numeric values. You'll be able to do this by the time you read Chapter 10.

Turbo Pascal imposes some additional steps in writing a program that tests for <eof> when reading data from the keyboard. The operating system does not automatically add the <eof> character at the end of data input from the keyboard: you must remember to press Ctrl-Z to signal end-of-file. Nor does the Turbo Pascal EOF function normally detect <eof> (Ctrl-Z) when it is entered. To get Turbo Pascal to recognize Ctrl-Z as <eof>, a USES statement must be added to the program. Recall from Chapter 2 that we had to insert

```
USES Printer;
```

after the PROGRAM heading to use the file Lst to print output on the printer. In a similar fashion we must insert

```
USES CRT;
```

at the same place to have Turbo Pascal detect an <eof> in keyboard input. CRT stands for Cathode Ray Tube, which is an electronics term that sometimes is used to refer to a computer screen. Just as USES Printer creates the special file Lst, USES CRT creates some special variables that are used in I/O with the screen and keyboard. One of these is the Boolean variable CheckEOF. As you might expect, you must also set CheckEOF to True to have Turbo Pascal check for <eof> in keyboard input.

To summarize, in Turbo Pascal if you want to use an EOF-controlled loop with keyboard input, you must do three things:

1. Place a USES CRT statement after the program heading.
2. Set CheckEOF to True with an assignment statement at the start of your program.
3. Remember to press Ctrl-Z when you are done entering data.

Without these first two steps, an EOF-controlled loop will behave strangely when reading from the keyboard. After Ctrl-Z is entered, the loop will continue to execute endlessly, and all of the input variables will be given unusual values: numeric variables are set to zero, and Char variables are all set to Ctrl-Z.

*T*heoretical Foundations

Separate Compilation Units

CRT and Printer are examples of *units,* a nonstandard feature of Turbo Pascal. A unit is a code segment similar to a program. Like a program, a unit can be compiled and the machine language version can be saved in a file. When a USES statement in a program specifies the name of a separately compiled unit, it is as if the source code for the unit were inserted directly into the program. However, because the unit has already been compiled, the compiler does not have to do the compilation again.

Thus, the main purpose of the UNIT construct is to allow us to write some declarations that are used in many programs, compile them, and then simply refer to them with a USES statement in those programs. One of the advantages that this has over simply copying the source code for the declarations directly into a program is that we don't have to wait for the compiler to recompile them each time we compile the program.

For example, the CRT unit declares 32 constants, 16 procedures, and 4 functions. Having to include their source code would clutter up your program with a lot of declarations, many of which you might never use, and would slow down compilation. Not to mention that we don't really care how the screen interface works, we just want to use it.

This last point brings up another advantage of units: *information hiding*. We don't have to see the code for CRT in order to use it. In fact, it's better that we don't know how it is implemented; otherwise we might be tempted to take advantage of some special aspect of its internal workings. Then, if the next version of Turbo Pascal changes how CRT works, our code would have to be rewritten. Because its implementation is hidden from us, the makers of Turbo Pascal can freely make internal improvements to it and we won't have to change our code.

Information hiding results directly from the ability to separately compile units. If you create a new unit and give someone just the machine language file and a set of instructions for using it, then they are unlikely to figure out how the unit works. However, Turbo Pascal units provide additional flexibility for hiding information. The declarations in a unit are divided into two parts: the interface and the implementation. Only the declarations in the interface section can be accessed by a program that uses the unit.

The combination of interface and implementation parts in a unit makes it possible to selectively hide certain declarations. For example, a unit might declare some constants that are needed by programs that use the unit, and others that are only used inside of the unit. The latter could then be hidden from the program in the implementation section.

Our purpose here is not to show you how to write your own units but to give you an idea of what units are and why they are useful. Additional units will be introduced later in the text. In each case we will list some of the declarations that are provided by the unit, and how to use them. The important point to remember is that you don't have to include the unit's identifiers in your own declarations; the USES statement does this for you automatically. In fact, it's a bad idea to declare an identifier with the same name as an identifier in a unit because you will no longer be able to access the one declared in the unit.

There is one other point we should mention. If a program needs to use more than one unit, you list all of the unit names in a single USES statement. For example,

```
USES CRT, Printer;
```

would cause the compiler to include the declarations from both the CRT unit and the Printer unit in a program.

EOLN-Controlled Loops   EOLN is a Boolean function that determines if the last character in a line of input has been read. EOLN becomes True when the next character to be read is the <eoln> character (Return or New Line). We use this function to control loops that process character data.

This EOLN loop reads and prints all of the characters on a line:

```
WHILE NOT EOLN DO
   BEGIN
      Read(Character);
      Write(Character)
   END
```

The loop continues until the next character to be read is the <eoln> character. At this point EOLN becomes True, NOT EOLN becomes False, and the loop stops executing. Because the program reads characters one at a time, a priming Read is not necessary. In fact if you rearrange the loop this way, to use a priming Read,

```
Read(Character);
WHILE NOT EOLN DO
   BEGIN
      Write(Character);
      Read(Character)
   END
```

the last character of input data would not get processed. After the last character is read, EOLN becomes True, and the loop exits.

EOF and EOLN can be used with files other than Input. If a file has been set to read mode using Reset, you can test for EOF or EOLN on the file by specifying the name of the file as a parameter:

```
EOF(Filename)
EOLN(Filename)
```

Flag-Controlled Loops   A **flag** is a Boolean variable that is used to control the logical flow of a program. We can set a Boolean variable to True before a WHILE; then, when we want to stop executing the loop, we reset it to False. That is, we can use the Boolean variable to record whether or not the event that controls the process has occurred. For example, the following code segment reads and sums values until the input value is negative. (Positive is the Boolean flag; all of the other variables are of type Integer.)

```
Sum := 0;
Positive := True;                          (* Initialize flag *)
WHILE Positive DO
  BEGIN
    Read(Number);
    IF Number < 0                          (* Test input value *)
      THEN
        Positive := False        (* Set flag if event occurred *)
      ELSE
        Sum := Sum + Number
  END
```

Notice that sentinel-controlled loops can be coded with flags. In fact this code uses a negative value as a sentinel.

You do not have to initialize flags to True; you can initialize them to False. If you do, you must use the NOT operator in the WHILE expression and reset the flag to True when the event occurs. Compare the code segment above with the one below (both perform the same task):

```
Sum := 0;
Negative := False;                         (* Initialize flag *)
WHILE NOT Negative DO
  BEGIN
    Read(Number);
    IF Number < 0                          (* Test input value *)
      THEN
        Negative := True         (* Set flag if event occurred *)
      ELSE
        Sum := Sum + Number
  END
```

As one more example, look at the WHILE in Program Payroll (page 31). This is a sentinel-controlled loop: An employee number (Emp_Num) with a value of 0 is used to stop the loop. We could have used a flag instead as follows. (More_Data is a Boolean variable; the other variables are of type Integer):

```
Readln(Emp_Num);
More_Data := Emp_Num <> 0;              (* More_Data is True if Emp_Num <> 0 *)
WHILE More_Data DO
  BEGIN


    Readln(Emp_Num);                    (* Get the next employee number *)
    More_Data := Emp_Num <> 0           (* And update the flag accordingly *)
  END
```

Looping Subtasks

We have been looking at ways to use loops to affect the flow of control in programs. But looping by itself does nothing. The loop body must perform a task in order for the loop to function. In this section we look at three tasks—counting, summing, and keeping track of a previous value—that often are used in loops.

Counting   A common task in a loop is to keep track of the number of times the loop has been executed. For example, the program fragment below reads, counts, and prints characters until it comes to a period. (Character is of type Char; Count is of type Integer.) The loop in this example has a counter variable; but the loop is not a count-controlled loop because the variable is not being used as a loop control variable.

```
Count : = 0;                          (* Initialize counter *)
Read(Character);                      (* Read the first character *)
WHILE Character <> '.' DO   Sentinel
  BEGIN
    Write(Character);
    Count := Count + 1; value = # of loops    (* Increment counter *)
    Read(Character)                   (* Get the next character *)
  END
```

The loop continues until a period is read. Count contains the number of characters written, one less than the number read. Notice that if a period is the first character, nothing is printed and Count contains a zero, as it should. We use a priming Read here because the loop is sentinel controlled. Even though it is reading single characters, it is not an EOLN-controlled loop.

The counter variable in this example is called an **iteration counter** because its value equals the number of iterations through the loop. *is # a thing goes thru loop*

Iteration Counter   A counter variable that is incremented with each iteration of a loop.

According to our definition, the loop control variable of a count-controlled loop is an iteration counter. However, as you've just seen, not all iteration counters are loop control variables.

Summing   Another common looping task is to sum a set of data values. Notice in the example here that the summing operation is written the same way regardless of how the loop is controlled.

```
Sum := 0;                                    (* Initialize the sum *)
Count := 1;
WHILE Count <= 10 DO
  BEGIN
    Read(Number);                            (* Input a value *)
    Sum := Sum + Number;           (* Add the value to sum *)
    Count := Count + 1
  END
```

When this fragment has been executed, Sum contains the total of the values read, Count contains 11, and Number contains the last value read.

Here Count is being incremented in each iteration. For each new value of Count, there is a new value for Number. Does this mean we can decrement Count by 1 and get the previous value of Number? No. Because Count is a counter being incremented by 1, its previous value is known. Once a new value has been read into Number, the previous value is gone forever unless we've saved it in another variable. You'll see how to do that in the next section.

Let's look at another example. We want to count and sum the first 10 odd numbers in a set of data. We need to test each number to see if it is even or odd. If it is even, we do nothing. If it is odd, we increment the counter and add the value to our sum. We use a flag to control the loop because this is not a normal count-controlled loop. In the following code segment, all of the variables are of type Integer except the Boolean flag, Less_Than_Ten.

```
Count := 0;                                 (* Initialize event counter *)
Sum := 0;                                          (* Initialize sum *)
Less_Than_Ten := True;                 (* Initialize loop control flag *)
WHILE Less_Than_Ten DO
  BEGIN
    Read(Number);                              (* Get the next value *)
    IF Odd(Number)                        (* Test to see if value is odd *)
      THEN
        BEGIN
          Count := Count + 1;                    (* Increment counter *)
          Sum := Sum + Number;                (* Add value to sum *)
          Less_Than_Ten := Count < 10     (* Update loop control flag *)
        END
  END
END
```

In this example there is no relationship between the value of the counter variable and the number of times that the loop is executed. We could have written the expression in the WHILE statement this way:

```
WHILE Count < 10 DO
```

But this might mislead a reader into thinking that the loop is count controlled in the normal way. So instead we chose to control the loop with the flag Less_Than_Ten, to emphasize that Count is incremented only when an odd number is read. The counter in this example is an **event counter;** it is initialized to zero and incremented only when a certain event occurs. The counter in the previous example was an *iteration counter;* it was initialized to one and incremented during each iteration of the loop.

Event Counter   A variable that is incremented each time a particular event occurs.

Keeping Track of a Previous Value   Sometimes we want to remember the previous value of a variable. Suppose we want to write a program that counts the number of assignment operators in a Pascal program. We can do this by simply counting the number of times a colon (:) followed by an equal sign (=) appears in the input. One way to do this is to read the input file one character at a time, keeping track of the two most recent characters, the current value and the previous one. In each iteration of the loop, a new current value is read and the old current value becomes the previous value. When EOF is encountered, the loop is finished. Here's a program that counts assignment operators this way:

```
PROGRAM Assignment_Count (InFile, Output);

(* This program counts the occurrences of := in a data file *)
```

```
VAR
  Count:                 (* Number of assignment statements  *)
    Integer;
  Previous,              (* Last character read               *)
  Current:               (* Character read in this iteration *)
    Char;
  InFile:                (* Data file                         *)
    Text;

BEGIN (* Assignment_Count *)
  Assign(InFile, 'IN.FILE.DAT');
  Reset(InFile);
  Count := 0;                                            (* Initialize counter *)
  Read(InFile, Previous);       (* Initialize previous value (priming Read) *)
  WHILE NOT EOF(InFile) DO
    BEGIN
      Read(Infile, Current);                             (* Get next value *)
      IF (Current = '=') AND (Previous = ':')            (* Test for event *)
        THEN
          Count := Count + 1;                            (* Increment counter *)
      Previous := Current        (* Replace previous value with current value *)
    END;
  Writeln(Count:1, ' assignment operators were found.');
  Close(InFile)
END.  (* Assignment_Count *)
```

Study this loop carefully. It's going to come in handy. There will be many times when you must keep track of the last value read in addition to the current value.

Theoretical Foundations

Finite State Machines

Our program for counting assignment operators is only one way to accomplish the task. Another is to design the program using a finite state machine. A *finite state machine* is an idealized model of a very simple computer. It consists of a set of *states* and a set of *transition rules* for changing from one state to another.

For example, a thermostat is a finite state machine with two states: on and off. And it has just two transition rules:

- If the measured temperature is less than the set temperature, switch from off to on.
- If the measured temperature is more than a degree warmer than the set temperature, switch from on to off.

Only one transition rule can be valid at a time.

THERMOSTAT STATE DIAGRAM

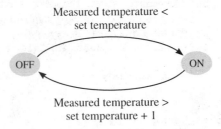

All around us are devices that can be modeled as finite state machines—traffic lights, automatic transmissions, washing machines, and elevators, for example. Each has specific states of operation and a set of rules for switching among them. In the following traffic light state diagram notice that the lights are set to blinking red from 1:00 A.M. to 6:00 A.M.

TRAFFIC LIGHT STATE DIAGRAM

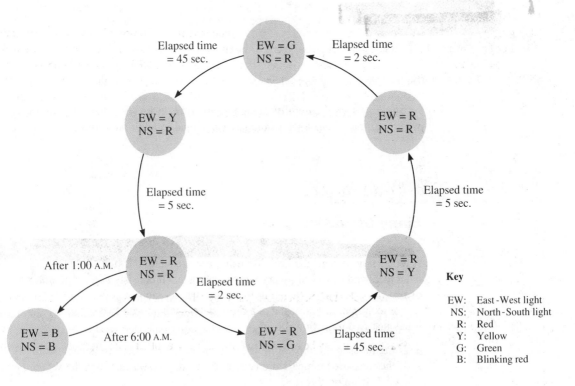

Finite state machines are not general-purpose computers. There are many problems that they cannot solve. But when a problem can be modeled as a set of states and transition rules, we can use a standard approach to writing an algorithm that solves it. You'll find that many of these problems are most easily solved with means-end analysis.

Let's rework Program Assignment_Count as a finite state machine. Here's the state diagram of the problem:

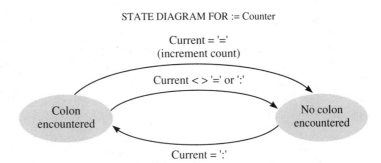

STATE DIAGRAM FOR := Counter

The first part of defining a finite state machine is to provide a way to keep track of the current state. Because there are only two states in this problem, we can use a single Boolean *state variable*, called Colon_Encountered. When the variable is True, the machine is in one state; when the variable is False, it is in the other. (In our traffic light example, we would define two Char variables EW and NS to be the state variables.)

Next, we have to determine which state the machine is in. For this, we use a nested IF-THEN-ELSE structure with one branch for each possible state.

```
IF Colon_Encountered
    THEN
    .     (* Test for each transition rule from this state. *)
    .
    ELSE
    .     (* Test for each transition rule from this state. *)
    .
```

Within each state branch, we test for each transition rule that starts from that particular state. There are two rules that start from the colon-encountered state and one that starts from the no-colon-encountered state. Associated with each transition rule is some action that may be as simple as switching to another state, or much more complex.

```
IF Colon_Encountered                        (* State = colon encountered *)
   THEN
     BEGIN
       IF Current = '='                      (* Rule:  If Current is '=' *)
          THEN
            BEGIN
              Count := Count + 1;             (* increment count     *)
              Colon_Encountered := False      (* and switch states *)
            END
          ELSE IF Current <> ':'        (* Rule:  If Current <> '=' or ':' *)
            THEN
              Colon_Encountered := False            (* switch states *)
     END
   ELSE                                 (* State = no colon encountered *)
     IF Current = ':'                      (* Rule:  If Current is ':'  *)
       THEN
         Colon_Encountered := True                  (* switch states *)
```

Next, we wrap these state tests and transition rules in a loop that inputs each character and applies them. In addition, we must specify a starting state for the finite state machine by initializing all of the state variables. In this case, we just have to assign False to Colon_Encountered. Here's the new program:

```
PROGRAM Finite_State (InFile, Output);

(* This program counts the occurrences of := in a data file by *)
(* simulating a finite state machine                           *)


VAR
  Count:                        (* Number of assignment statements *)
    Integer;
  Current:                      (* Current character               *)
    Char;
  Colon_Encountered:            (* State variable                  *)
    Boolean;
  InFile:                       (* Data file                       *)
    Text;
```

```
BEGIN (* Finite_State *)
  Assign(InFile, 'INFILE.DAT');
  Reset(InFile);
  Count := 0;
  Colon_Encountered := False;                    (* Initialize starting state *)
  WHILE NOT EOF(InFile) DO
    BEGIN
      Read(InFile, Current);
      IF Colon_Encountered                       (* State = colon encountered *)
        THEN
          BEGIN
            IF Current = '='                      (* Rule:  If Current is '='  *)
              THEN
                BEGIN
                  Count := Count + 1;                 (* increment count   *)
                  Colon_Encountered := False          (* and switch states *)
                END
            ELSE IF Current <> ':'     (* Rule:  If Current <> '=' or ':' *)
              THEN
                Colon_Encountered := False              (* switch states *)
          END
        ELSE                                   (* State = no colon encountered *)
          IF Current = ':'                        (* Rule:  If Current is ':' *)
            THEN
              Colon_Encountered := True                 (* switch states *)
    END;
  Writeln(Count:1, ' assignment operators were found.');
  Close(InFile)
END.    (* Finite_State *)
```

The thing to notice about this program is that it keeps track of the previous input value without actually storing it in a variable. Instead, it simply remembers the one aspect of the value that pertains to the problem: whether it was a colon or something else.

Program Finite_State is longer than Program Assignment_Count. For such a simple problem, it's clearly less efficient to use a finite state machine approach than to store the previous value. However, for problems that are more complex—that involve many different states—finite state machines give us a way to organize the states so that we don't leave out any combinations.

Finite state machine models are used extensively in the development of compilers and operating systems. They also are an important tool in research into theoretical issues of computing.

How to Design Loops

It's one thing to understand how a loop works when you look at it and something else again to design a loop that solves a given problem. In this section we look at how to design loops. We can divide the design process into two tasks: designing the control flow and designing the processing that takes place in the loop. And we can break each task into three phases: the task itself, initialization, and update. It's also important to specify the state of the program when it exits the loop: A loop that leaves variables and files in a mess is not well designed.

So there are seven different points to consider in designing a loop:

1. What is the condition that ends the loop?
2. How should the condition be initialized?
3. How should the condition be updated?
4. What is the process being repeated?
5. How should the process be initialized?
6. How should the process be updated?
7. What is the state of the program on exiting the loop?

We use these questions as a checklist. The first three help us design the parts of the loop that control its execution. The next three help us design the processing within the loop. The last question reminds us to make sure that the loop exits in an appropriate manner.

Designing the Flow of Control

The most important step in loop design is deciding what should make the loop stop. If the termination condition isn't well thought out, there's the potential for infinite loops and other mistakes. So here is our first question:

- What is the condition that ends the loop?

This question usually can be answered through a close examination of the problem statement. For example:

Key Phrase in Problem Statement	Termination Condition
"Sum 365 temperatures"	The loop ends when a counter reaches 365 (count-controlled loop).
"Process all the data on the file"	The loop ends when EOF is encountered (EOF-controlled loop).
"Process until 10 odd integers have been read"	The loop ends when 10 odd numbers have been input (event counter).
"The end of the data is indicated by a negative test score"	The loop ends when a negative input value is encountered (sentinel-controlled loop).

Now we need statements that make sure the loop gets started correctly and statements that allow the loop to reach the termination condition. So we have to ask the next two questions:

- How should the condition be initialized?
- How should the condition be updated?

The answers to these questions depend on the type of termination condition.

Count-Controlled Loops   If the loop is count controlled, we initialize the condition by giving the loop control variable an initial value. For count-controlled loops that use an iteration counter, the initial value is usually 1. If the process requires the counter to run through a specific range of values, the initial value should be the lowest value in that range.

The condition is updated by increasing the value of the counter by 1 for each iteration. (Occasionally you will come across a problem that requires a counter to count from some value *down* to a lower value. In this case the initial value is the greater value, and the counter is decremented by 1 for each iteration.) So for count-controlled loops that use an iteration counter, these are the answers to the questions:

- Initialize the iteration counter to 1.
- Increment the iteration counter at the end of each iteration.

If the loop is controlled by a variable that is counting an event within the loop, the control variable usually is initialized to 0, and is incremented each time the event occurs. For count-controlled loops that use an event counter, these are the answers to the questions:

- Initialize the event counter to 0.
- Increment the event counter each time the event occurs.

Sentinel-Controlled Loops   In sentinel-controlled loops, a priming Read may be the only initialization necessary. If the source of input is a file other than Input, a Reset also may be necessary to prepare the file for reading. To update the condition, a new value is read at the end of each iteration. So, for sentinel-controlled loops, we answer our questions this way:

- Reset the file if necessary, and input a value before entering the loop (priming Read).
- Input a new value for processing at the end of each iteration.

EOF- or EOLN-Controlled Loops   EOF- and EOLN-controlled loops usually do not require initialization (except to Reset a file other than Input). The status of the EOF and EOLN functions is updated every time a value is input. However, if the loop doesn't read any data, it will never reach EOF or EOLN, so updating the loop condition means the loop must keep reading data.

Flag-Controlled Loops   In flag-controlled loops, the Boolean flag variable must be initialized to True or False and then updated when the condition changes.

- Initialize the flag variable to True or False as appropriate.
- Update the flag variable as soon as the condition changes.

In a flag-controlled loop, the flag variable essentially remains unchanged until it is time for the loop to end. Then the code detects some condition within the process being repeated and changes the value of the flag (through an assignment statement). Because the update depends on the process, at times we have to design the process before we can decide how to update the condition.

Designing the Process Within the Loop

Once we've determined the looping structure itself, we can fill in the details of the process. In designing the process we first must decide what we want a single iteration to do. Assume for a moment that the process is only going to execute once. What tasks must the process perform?

- What is the process being repeated?

To answer this question, we have to take another look at the problem statement. The definition of the problem may require the process to sum up data values or to keep a count of data values that satisfy some test. For example:

Count the number of integers on File HowMany.

This statement tells us that the process to be repeated is a counting operation.
Here's another example:

Read a stock price for each business day in a week, and compute the average price.

In this case part of the process involves reading a data value. We have to conclude from our knowledge of how an average is computed that the process also involves summing the data values.

In addition to counting and summing, another common loop process is reading data, performing a calculation, and writing out the result. There are many other operations that can appear in looping processes. (We've mentioned only the simplest here; we'll look at some other processes later on.)

After we've determined the operations to be performed if the process is executed only once, we design the parts of the process that are necessary for it to be repeated correctly. We often have to add some steps to take into account the fact that the loop executes more than once. This part of the design typically involves initializing certain variables before the loop and then reinitializing or updating them before each subsequent iteration.

- How should the process be initialized?
- How should the process be updated?

For example, if the process within a loop requires that several different counts and sums be performed, each must have its own statements to initialize variables, increment counting variables, or add values to sums. Just deal with each counting or summing operation by itself: First write the initialization statement, and then write the incrementing or summing statement. After you've done this for one operation, you go on to the next.

The Loop Exit

When the termination condition occurs and the flow of control passes to the statement following the loop, the variables used in the loop still contain values. And if File Input has been used, the reading marker has been left at some point in the file. Or File Output may have new contents. If these variables or files are used elsewhere in the program, the loop must leave them ready to be used. So, the final step in designing a loop is answering this question:

■ What is the state of the program on exiting the loop?

Now we have to consider the consequences of our design and to double-check its validity. For example, suppose we've used an event counter and later processing depends on the number of events. It's important to be sure (with an algorithm walk-through) that the value left in the counter is exactly the number of events; that it is not off by 1.

Look at this code segment:

```
Comma_Count := 1;
WHILE NOT EOLN DO
  BEGIN
    Read(Character);
    IF Character = ','
      THEN
        Comma_Count := Comma_Count + 1
  END;
Writeln(Comma_Count);
```

This loop reads characters from an input line and counts the number of commas on the line. However, when the loop terminates, Comma_Count equals the actual number of commas plus 1 because the loop initializes the event counter to 1 before any events take place. By determining the state of Comma_Count at loop exit, we've detected a flaw in the initialization. Comma_Count should be initialized to zero.

Designing correct loops depends as much on experience as it does on the application of design methodology. At this point you may want to read through the first two problem-solving case studies at the end of the chapter to see how the loop design process is applied to some real problems.

Nested Logic

In Chapter 4 we described nested IF statements. WHILE statements also can be nested. Both WHILE and IF statements contain statements and are themselves statements. So the body of a WHILE statement or the branch of an IF statement can contain other WHILE and IF statements. By nesting, we can create complex control structures.

Suppose we want to extend our code for counting commas on one line, repeating it for all the lines in a file. We simply put an EOF-controlled loop around it:

```
WHILE NOT EOF DO                                        (* Outer loop test *)
  BEGIN
    Comma_Count := 0;                         (* Initialize inner loop *)
    WHILE NOT EOLN DO                              (* Inner loop test *)
      BEGIN
        Read(Character);        (* Update inner termination condition *)
        IF Character = ','
          THEN
            Comma_Count := Comma_Count + 1
      END;
    Writeln(Comma_Count);
    Readln                      (* Update outer termination condition *)
END
```

Let's examine the general pattern of a simple nested loop:

```
Initialize outer loop
Outer loop test (WHILE)
  BEGIN

        .

      Initialize inner loop
      Inner loop test (WHILE)
        BEGIN
          Inner loop processing and update
        END          .

        .

      Outer loop update
  END
```

Notice that each loop has its own initialization, test, and update. The dots represent places where processing may take place in the outer loop. It's possible for an outer loop to do no processing other than repeatedly execute the inner loop. On the other hand, the inner loop might be just a small part of the processing done by the outer loop; there could be many statements preceding or following the inner loop.

Let's look at another example. For nested count-controlled loops, the pattern looks like this (where Out_Count is the counter for the outer loop, In_Count is the counter for the inner loop, and Limit1 and Limit2 are the number of times each loop should be executed):

```
Out_Count := 1;                      (* Initialize outer loop counter *)
WHILE Out_Count <= Limit1 DO
  BEGIN
    .
    .
    In_Count := 1;                   (* Initialize inner loop counter *)
    WHILE In_Count <= Limit2 DO
      BEGIN
        .
        .
        In_Count := In_Count + 1     (* Increment inner loop counter *)
      END
    .
    .
    Out_Count := Out_Count + 1       (* Increment outer loop counter *)
  END
```

Here both the inner and outer loops are count-controlled loops, but the pattern can be used with any combination of loops. The following program fragment shows an EOLN-controlled loop nested within an EOF-controlled loop that reads and prints characters. (We use the numbers to the right of the code to trace the execution of the program below.)

```
Line_Count := 0;                                   1
WHILE NOT EOF DO                                    2
  BEGIN
    WHILE NOT EOLN DO                               3
      BEGIN
        Read(Character);                            4
        Write(Character)                            5
      END;
    Line_Count := Line_Count + 1;                   6
    Writeln;                                        7
    Readln                                          8
  END;
Writeln(Line_Count:1, ' lines read.')               9
```

To see how this code works, let's trace its execution with these data values (there are two characters on the first line: a 'T' and a blank):

```
T□<eoln>
D2<eoln>
<eof>
```

We'll keep track of the variables Line_Count and Character, as well as the Boolean expressions. To do this, we've numbered each line (except the BEGINs and ENDs). As we trace the program, we indicate the first execution of line 3 by 3.1, the second by 3.2, and so on. A box stands for a blank, and each loop iteration is enclosed by a brace (see Table 5-1).

Table 5-1   Code Trace

Statement	Variables		Expressions		
	Line_Count (Integer)	Character (Char)	EOLN	EOF	Output
1.1	0	—	—	—	—
2.1	0	—	—	F	—
3.1	0	—	F	—	—
4.1	0	T	—	—	—
5.1	0	T	—	—	T
3.2	0	T	F	—	—
4.2	0	□	—	—	—
5.2	0	□	—	—	□
3.3	0	□	T	—	—
6.1	1	□	—	—	—
7.1	1	□	—	—	<eoln>
8.1	1	□	—	—	—
2.2	1	□	—	F	—
3.4	1	□	F	—	—
4.3	1	D	—	—	—
5.3	1	D	—	—	D
3.5	1	D	F	—	—
4.4	1	2	—	—	—
5.4	1	2	—	—	2
3.6	1	2	T	—	—
6.2	2	2	—	—	—
7.2	2	2	—	—	<eoln>
8.2	2	2	—	—	—
2.3	2	2	—	T	—
9.1	2	2	—	—	2 lines read.

Here's the output:

```
T□<eoln>
D2<eoln>
2 lines read.
```

Because Line_Count and Character are variables, their values remain the same until they are explicitly changed, as indicated by the repeating values. The values of the Boolean expressions EOLN and EOF exist only when the test is made. We've indicated this with dashes in those columns at all other times.

Designing Nested Loops

To design a nested loop, we begin with the outer loop. The process being repeated includes the nested loop as one of its steps. Because that step is more complex than a single statement, our top-down design methodology tells us to make it a separate module. We then can come back to it later and design the nested loop just as we would any other loop.

For example, here's the design process for the code segment above:

1. *What is the condition that ends the loop?* EOF is reached in the input.
2. *How should the condition be initialized?* No initialization is needed.
3. *How should the condition be updated?* A Readln should be performed at the end of each iteration.
4. *What is the process being repeated?* The code should read and print all the characters on each line and count the lines.
5. *How should the process be initialized?* The line counter is set to zero.
6. *How should the process be updated?* A line is read and printed, an <eoln> character is output, and the line counter is incremented.
7. *What is the state of the program on exiting the loop?* File Input is at <eof>, Line_Count contains the number of lines input, Character contains the last input character on the file (excluding <eoln> and <eof>), and the input has been printed along with a message indicating the number of input lines.

From the answers to these questions, we can write this much of the algorithm:

Initialize Line_Count to zero
WHILE NOT EOF DO
    Read and print a line of characters
    Increment Line_Count
    Output <eoln> (Writeln)
    Go to the start of the next input line (Readln)

After designing the outer loop, it's obvious that the process (reading and printing a line of characters) is a complex step that requires us to design an inner loop. So we repeat the methodology for the corresponding lower-level module:

1. *What is the condition that ends the loop?* <eoln> is reached on a line of input.
2. *How should the condition be initialized?* The reading marker should be at the start of a line.
3. *How should the condition be updated?* A character is read during each iteration.
4. *What is the process being repeated?* The code should read a character and print it out.
5. *How should the process be initialized?* No initialization is needed.
6. *How should the process be updated?* No update is needed (the reading marker automatically moves to the next character).
7. *What is the state of the program on exiting the loop?* The reading marker is at <eoln>, and Character contains the last input character before <eoln>. (Line_Count is unchanged by the loop.)

Now we can write the algorithm:

Initialize Line_Count to zero
WHILE NOT EOF DO
   WHILE NOT EOLN DO
      Read a Character
      Write a Character
   Increment Line_Count
   Output <eoln> (Writeln)
   Go to the start of the next input line (Readln)

Of course, nested loops themselves can contain nested loops (called *doubly nested loops*), which can contain nested loops (triply nested loops), and so on. Our design process can be used for any number of levels of nesting. The trick is simply to defer details using the top-down methodology: Focus on the outermost loop first, and treat each new level of nested loop as a module within the loop that contains it.

It's also possible for the process within a loop to include more than one loop. For example, here's an algorithm that reads and prints names from a file, omitting the middle name in the output:

WHILE NOT EOF DO
   Read and print first name (ends with a comma)
   Read and discard characters from middle name (ends with a comma)
   Read and print last name (ends at <eoln>)
   Output <eoln>
   Go to the start of the next input line

Each of the first three steps in the processing requires us to design a separate loop. The first two are sentinel controlled; the last one is EOLN controlled.

This kind of complex control structure would be difficult to read if written out in full. There are simply too many variables, conditions, and steps to remember at one time. In the next three chapters we examine the Pascal control structures that allow us to break programs down into more manageable chunks—procedures and functions.

*T*heoretical Foundations

The Magnitude of Work

There is usually more than one way to solve a problem. This may leave the programmer trying to choose the most efficient algorithm by deciding how much **work** is necessary to execute it.

Work   A measure of the effort expended by the computer in performing a computation.

How do we measure the amount of work required to execute an algorithm? We use the total number of *steps* executed as a measure of work. One statement, such as an assignment, may require only one step; another, such as a loop, may require many steps. A step is defined as any operation roughly equivalent in complexity to a comparison or an assignment.

Given an algorithm with just a sequence of statements (no branches or loops), the number of steps performed is directly related to the number of statements. When we introduce branches, however, we make it possible to skip some statements in the algorithm. Branches allow us to subtract steps without physically removing them from the algorithm because only one branch is executed at a time. But because we always want to express work in terms of the worst-case scenario, we use the number of steps in the longest branch.

Now consider the effect of a loop. If a loop repeats a sequence of 15 simple statements 10 times, it performs 150 steps. Loops allow us to multiply the work done in an algorithm without physically adding statements.

Now that we have a measure for the work done in an algorithm, we can compare algorithms. For example, if Algorithm A always executes 3,124 steps and Algorithm B always does the same task in 1,321 steps, then we can say that Algorithm B is more efficient: It takes fewer steps to accomplish the same task.

If an algorithm always takes the same number of steps, we say that it executes in *constant time*. Be careful: Constant time doesn't mean small; it means that the amount of work done does not change from one run to another.

If a loop executes a fixed number of times, the work done is greater than the number of statements but still is constant. But what happens if the number of loop iterations can change from one run to the next? Suppose a data file contains N data values to be processed in a loop. If the loop reads and processes one value during each iteration, then the loop executes N iterations. The amount of work done thus depends on a variable, the number of data values. Algorithms that perform work directly proportional to the number of data values are said to execute in *linear time*. If we have a loop that executes N times, the number of steps to be executed is linearly dependent on N.

Specifically, the work done by an algorithm with a data-dependent loop is

Steps performed
by the loop
$$\overbrace{S_1 * N} + \underbrace{S_0}$$
Steps performed
outside the loop

where S_1 is the number of steps in the loop body (a constant for a given loop), N is the number of iterations (a variable), and S_0 is the number of steps outside the loop. (We can use this same formula for constant-time loops, but N would be a constant.) Notice that if N grows very large, it dominates the execution time. That is, S_0 becomes an insignificant part of the total execution time.

What about a data-dependent loop that contains a nested loop? The number of steps in the inner loop, S_2, and the number of iterations performed by the inner loop, L, must be multiplied by the number of iterations in the outer loop:

Steps performed   Steps performed   Steps performed outside
by the nested loop   by the outer loop   the outer loop

$$\overbrace{(S_2 * L * N)} +   \overbrace{(S_1 * N)} +   \overbrace{S_0}$$

By itself, the inner loop performs $S_2 * L$ steps, but because it is repeated N times by the outer loop, it accounts for a total of $S_2 * L * N$ steps. If L is a constant, then the algorithm still executes in linear time.

Now, suppose that for each of the N outer loop iterations, the inner loop performs N steps ($L = N$). Here the formula for the total steps is

$$(S_2 * N * N) + (S_1 * N) + S_0$$

or

$$(S_2 * N^2) + (S_1 * N) + S_0$$

Because N^2 grows much faster than N (for large values of N), the inner loop term (N^2) accounts for the majority of steps executed and the work done. So the corresponding execution time is essentially proportional to N^2. If we have a doubly nested loop, where each loop depends on N, then the expression is

$$(S_3 * N^3) + (S_2 * N^2) + (S_1 * N) + S_0$$

and the work and time are proportional to N^3 whenever N is reasonably large.

The table below shows the number of steps required for each increase in the exponent of N.

N	N^0 (Constant)	N^1 (Linear)	N^2 (Quadratic)	N^3 (Cubic)
1	1	1	1	1
10	1	10	100	1,000
100	1	100	10,000	1,000,000
1,000	1	1,000	1,000,000	1,000,000,000
10,000	1	10,000	100,000,000	1,000,000,000,000

As you can see, each time the exponent increases by 1, the number of steps is multiplied by an additional order of magnitude (factor of 10). That is, if N is made 10 times greater, the work involved in an N^2 algorithm increases by a factor of 100, and the work involved in an N^3 algorithm increases by a factor of 1,000. To put this in more concrete terms, an algorithm with a triply nested loop, in which each loop depends on the number of data values, takes 1,000 steps for 10 input values and 1 trillion steps for 10,000 values. On a computer that executes 1 million instructions per second, the latter case would take over eleven days to run.

The table also shows that the steps outside of the innermost loop account for an insignificant portion of the total number of steps as N gets bigger. Because the innermost loop dominates the total time, we classify an algorithm according to the highest order of N that appears in its work expression, called the *order of magnitude,* or simply the *order* of that expression. So we talk about algorithms being "order N squared" (or cubed or so on) or we describe them with what is called "Big-O notation." We express this order by putting the highest order term in parentheses with a capital O in front. For example O(1) is constant time; O(N) is linear time; O(N^2) is quadratic time; and O(N^3) is cubic time.

Determining the orders of different algorithms allows us to compare the work they require without having to program and execute them. For example, if you have an O(N^2) algorithm and a linear algorithm that perform the same task, you probably would choose the linear algorithm. We say *probably* because an O(N^2) algorithm actually may execute fewer steps than an O(N) algorithm for small values of N. Remember that if N is small, the constants and lower order terms in the work expression must be considered.

While we generally ignore the lower order terms, they do exist, giving us a polynomial expression when all the terms are written out. Such algorithms are thus said to execute in **polynomial time** and form a broad class of algorithms that encompasses everything we've discussed so far.

In addition to polynomial-time algorithms, we encounter a logarithmic-time algorithm in Chapter 12. There are also factorial (O($N!$)), exponential (O(N^N)), and hyper-exponential (O(N^{N^N})) class algorithms, which can require vast amounts of time to execute and are beyond the scope of this course. For now, the important point to remember is that the looping control structure allows an algorithm to perform more work than the number of statements it contains.

*P*ROBLEM-SOLVING CASE STUDY

Average Income by Gender

Problem: You've been hired by a law firm that is working on a sex discrimination case. Your firm has obtained File Income, which contains the salaries for every employee in the company. Each salary amount is preceded by 'F' for female or 'M' for male. As a first pass in the analysis of this data, you've been asked to compute the average income for females and the average income for males.

Input: A file, Income, of salary amounts, with one amount per line. Each amount is preceded by a character ('F' for female, 'M' for male). This code is the first character on each input line and is followed by a blank, which separates the code from the amount.

Output: The number of females and their average income, and the number of males and their average income.

Suitable

Discussion: The problem breaks down into three main steps. First we have to process the data, counting and summing the salary amounts for each sex. Next we compute the averages. Finally, we have to print the results.

The first step is the most difficult. It involves a loop with several subtasks. We'll use our checklist of questions to develop these subtasks in detail.

1. *What is the condition that ends the loop?* The termination condition is EOF on File Income. It leads to the WHILE statement

   WHILE NOT EOF on File Income DO

2. *How should the condition be initialized?* The file must be prepared for reading.
3. *How should the condition be updated?* A new data line with a gender code and amount must be input during each iteration. Here's the resulting algorithm:

   Prepare File Income for reading
   WHILE NOT EOF on File Income DO
     Readln Sex and Amount from Income
       .
       .   (Process being repeated)

4. *What is the process being repeated?* From our knowledge of how to compute an average, we know that we have to count the number of amounts and divide this number into the sum of the amounts. Because we have to do this separately for females and males, the process consists of four parts: counting the females and summing their incomes, and then counting the males and summing their incomes. We develop each of these in turn.
5. *How should the process be initialized?* Female_Count and Female_Sum should be set to zero. Male_Count and Male_Sum also should be set to zero.
6. *How should the process be updated?* When a female income is input, Female_Count is incremented, and the income is added to Female_Sum. Otherwise an income is assumed to be for a male, so Male_Count is incremented, and the amount is added to Male_Sum.
7. *What is the state of the program on exiting the loop?* File Income is at EOF. Female_Count contains the number of input values preceded by 'F'; Female_Sum contains the sum of the values preceded by 'F'; Male_Count contains the number of values not preceded by 'F'; and Male_Sum holds the sum of those values.

From the description of how the process is updated, we can see that the loop must contain an IF-THEN-ELSE statement, with one branch for female incomes and the other for male incomes. Each branch must increment the correct event counter and add the income amount to the correct total. After the loop has exited, we have enough information to compute and print the averages, dividing each total by the corresponding count.

Assumptions: There is at least one male and one female among all the data sets. The only gender codes on the file are 'M' and 'F'—any other codes are counted as 'M'. (This last assumption invalidates the results if there are any illegal codes in the data. Programming Warm-Up Exercise 11 asks you to change the program as necessary to address this problem.)

Now we're ready to write the complete algorithm:

Main Module   *Level 0*

> Separately count females and males, and sum incomes
> Compute average incomes
> Output results

Separately Count Females and Males, and Sum Incomes   *Level 1*

> Initialize ending condition
> Initialize process
> WHILE NOT EOF on File Income DO
>   Update ending condition
>   Update process

Compute Average Incomes

> Set Female_Average to Female_Sum / Female_Count
> Set Male_Average to Male_Sum / Male_Count

PROBLEM-SOLVING CASE STUDY *cont'd.*

Output Results

> Write Female_Count and Female_Average
> Write Male_Count and Male_Average

Initialize Ending Condition   *Level 2*

> Reset Income

Initialize Process

> Initialize Female_Count to 0
> Initialize Female_Sum to 0
> Initialize Male_Count to 0
> Initialize Male_Sum to 0

Female_Count := 0
Fe_Sum := 0
Ma_count := 0
Ma_Sum := 0

Update Ending Condition

> Readln Sex and Amount from Income

Readln(Infile, Sex, Amt_of_In
IF Sex = t then
Fe Sum := Fe_Sum + Amof
Fe Count := Fe_Count + 1

Else if
Ma_Sum : Ma_Sum + Amlof
Ma_Coun : Ma_Count + 1

Update Process

> IF Sex is Female
>   THEN
>   Increment Female_Count
>   Add Amount to Female_Sum
>   ELSE
>   Increment Male_Count
>   Add Amount to Male_Sum

PROBLEM-SOLVING CASE STUDY cont'd.

Module Structure Chart:

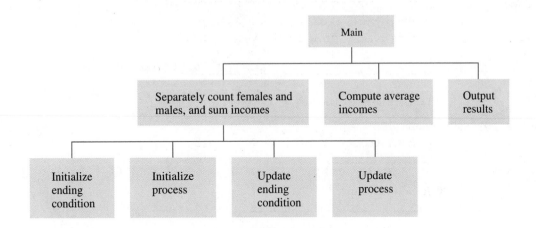

Now we can write the program:

```
PROGRAM Incomes (Income, Output);

(* This program reads a file of income amounts that are      *)
(* classified by gender, and computes the average income     *)
(* for each gender                                           *)

VAR
   Income:              (* File of income amounts           *)
      Text;
   Sex:                 (* Coded 'F' = female, 'M' = male   *)
      Char;
   Female_Count,        (* Number of female income amounts  *)
   Male_Count:          (* Number of male income amounts    *)
      Integer;
   Amount,              (* Amount of income for a person    *)
   Female_Sum,          (* Total of female income amounts   *)
   Male_Sum,            (* Total of male income amounts     *)
   Female_Average,      (* Average female income            *)
   Male_Average:        (* Average male income              *)
      Real;
```

PROBLEM-SOLVING CASE STUDY cont'd.

```
BEGIN (* Incomes *)
  (* Separately count females and males, and sum incomes *)
  (* Initialize ending condition *)
  Assign(Income, 'INCOME.DAT');
  Reset(Income);                       (* Prepare file for reading *)
  (* Initialize process *)
  Female_Count := 0;                  (* Initialize Female_Count *)
  Female_Sum := 0.0;                   (* Initialize Female_Sum *)
  Male_Count := 0;                     (* Initialize Male_Count *)
  Male_Sum := 0.0;                      (* Initialize Male_Sum *)
  WHILE NOT EOF(Income) DO
    BEGIN
      (* Update ending condition *)
      Readln(Income, Sex, Amount);               (* Get next amount *)
      (* Update process *)
      IF Sex = 'F'
        THEN
          BEGIN
            Female_Count := Female_Count + 1;  (* Increment Female_Count *)
            Female_Sum := Female_Sum + Amount     (* Sum Female Amount *)
          END
        ELSE
          BEGIN
            Male_Count := Male_Count + 1;       (* Increment Male_Count *)
            Male_Sum := Male_Sum + Amount         (* Sum Male Amount *)
          END
    END;
  (* Compute average incomes *)
  Female_Average := Female_Sum / Female_Count;
  Male_Average := Male_Sum / Male_Count;
  (* Output results *)
  Writeln('For ', Female_Count:1, ' females, the average income is ',
          Female_Average:9:2);
  Writeln('For ', Male_Count:1, ' males, the average income is ',
          Male_Average:9:2)
  Close(Income)
END.  (* Incomes *)
```

Testing: With an EOF-controlled loop, the obvious test cases are a file with data and an empty file. We also should look carefully to see if there is a case that could cause the computer to read all of the data without reaching the <eof> mark.

Then we should test input values of both 'F' and 'M' for the gender, and try some typical data (so we can compare the results with our hand-calculated values) and some atypical data (to see how the process behaves). An atypical data set for testing a counting operation is an empty file, which should result in a count of zero. Any other result for the count indicates an error. For a summing operation, atypical data might include negative or zero values.

PROBLEM-SOLVING CASE STUDY cont'd.

Program Incomes is not designed to handle empty files or negative income values. An empty file will cause both Female_Count and Male_Count to equal zero at the end of the loop. Although this is correct, the statements that compute average income will cause the program to crash because they will be dividing by zero. A negative income would simply be treated like any other value, even though it is probably a mistake.

To correct these problems we should insert IF-THEN-ELSE statements to test for the error conditions at the appropriate points in the program. When an error is detected, the program should print an error message instead of carrying out the usual computation. This prevents a crash and allows the program to keep running. We call a program that can recover from erroneous input and keep running a *robust program*.

PROBLEM-SOLVING CASE STUDY

High and Low Temperatures

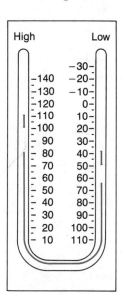

Here's another problem in loop design. In this case we design a count-controlled loop that finds the minimum and maximum values in a data set.

Problem: A heating oil company uses the temperature range for each day to determine its customers' typical oil use and to schedule deliveries. The firm has hired you to take hourly outdoor temperature readings for each 24-hour period and find the day's high and low temperatures from this data. Because you won't be getting much sleep on this job, you decide that it would be a good idea to have the computer keep track of the maximum and minimum values.

Input: Twenty-four integer numbers representing hourly temperatures.

Output:

The temperatures (echo-print)
The day's high temperature
The day's low temperature

Discussion: This is easy to do by hand. We simply scan the list, looking for the highest and lowest values. How do we simulate this process in an algorithm? Well, let's look carefully at what we actually are doing.

To find the largest number in a list of numbers, we compare the first with the second and remember which one is larger. Then we compare that number with the third one, remembering the larger number. We repeat the process until we run out of numbers. The one we remember is the largest. We use the same process to find the smallest number, only we remember the smaller number instead of the larger one.

Now that we understand the process, we can design an algorithm for it:

1. *What is the condition that ends the loop?* Because there will be exactly 24 values on the list, we can use a counter to control the loop. When it exceeds 24, the loop exits.
2. *How should the condition be initialized?* The counter should be set to 1.
3. *How should the condition be updated?* The counter should be incremented at the end of each iteration.
4. *What is the process being repeated?* The process reads a value, echo-prints it, and checks to if it should replace the current high or low value.
5. *How should the process be initialized?* In other words, what values should the first number be compared to? We have to give the variables High and Low starting values that will change immediately. So we set High to the lowest number possible ($-$MaxInt-1), and we set Low to the highest number possible (MaxInt). In this way, the first temperature read will be lower than Low and higher than High and will replace the values in each.
6. *How should the process be updated?* In each iteration, a new temperature is input and compared with High and Low. If it exceeds High, it replaces the old value of High. If it is less than Low, it replaces the old value of Low. Otherwise High and Low are unchanged. This tells us that the loop contains two IF-THEN statements, one each for comparing the input value against High and Low.
7. *What is the state of the program on exiting the loop?* Twenty-four temperature values have been input and echo-printed. The loop control variable equals 25. High contains the largest of the input values, and Low contains the smallest.

Assumptions: At least 24 integer numbers will be input before EOF is reached. None of the data values is equal to MaxInt or $-$MaxInt-1.

Main Module   *Level 0*

```
Initialize process
Initialize loop ending condition
WHILE Hours <= number of hours in time period DO
    Update process
    Update loop ending condition
Print high and low temperatures
```

PROBLEM-SOLVING CASE STUDY *cont'd.*

Initialize Process   *Level 1*

> Set High to lowest integer
> Set Low to highest integer

[handwritten:] High :=
Low :=

Initialize Loop Ending Condition

> Set Hour to 1

[handwritten:] Counter := 1

Update Process

> Get a temperature
> Echo-print the temperature
> Lowest temperature so far?
> Highest temperature so far?

[handwritten:]
Read (Temp)
Writeln (Temp)
IF temp < Low_Temp
Low_temp := Low_Temp
IF temp > High_temp
to_temp := temp
Counter : Count : 1

Update Loop Ending Condition

> Increment Hour

Print High and Low Temperatures

> Print 'High temperature is ', High
> Print 'Low temperature is ', Low

[handwritten:]
Writeln (Outfile)
Writeln (Outfile)

Lowest Temperature So Far?   *Level 2*

> IF Temperature < Low
>   THEN set Low to Temperature

PROBLEM-SOLVING CASE STUDY *cont'd.*

Highest Temperature So Far?

> IF Temperature > High
>   THEN set High to Temperature

Module Structure Chart:

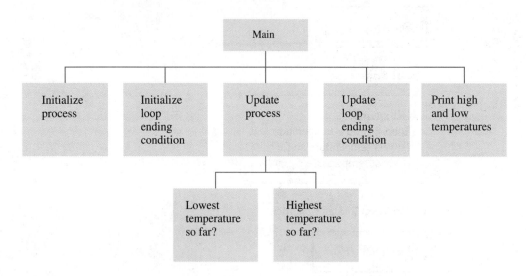

```
PROGRAM Temp_Stat (Input, Output);

(* This program calculates the high and low temperatures *)
(* from 24 hourly temperature readings                   *)

CONST
  Num_Hrs = 24;      (* Number of hours in time period        *)

VAR
  Temperature,       (* An hourly temperature reading         *)
  High,              (* Highest temperature so far            *)
  Low,               (* Lowest temperature so far             *)
  Hour:              (* Loop control variable for hours in a day *)
    Integer;
```

PROBLEM-SOLVING CASE STUDY cont'd.

```
BEGIN (* Temp_Stat *)
  (* Initialize process *)
  High := -MaxInt-1;          (* Initialize High to impossibly low value *)
  Low := MaxInt;              (* Initialize Low to impossibly high value *)
  (* Initialize loop ending condition *)
  Hour := 1;
  WHILE Hour <= Num_Hrs DO
    BEGIN
      (* Update process *)
      Read(Temperature);       (* Get an hourly temperature *)
      Writeln(Temperature);    (* Echo print the temperature *)
      (* Lowest temperature so far? *)
      IF Temperature < Low
        THEN
          Low := Temperature;
      (* Highest temperature so far? *)
      IF Temperature > High
        THEN
          High := Temperature;
      (* Update loop ending condition *)
      Hour := Hour + 1
    END;
  (* Print high and low temperature *)
  Writeln;
  Writeln('High temperature is ', High:1);
  Writeln('Low temperature is ', Low:1)
END.  (* Temp_Stat *)
```

Testing: Program Temp_Stat reads 24 Integer values. We can test the WHILE statement by entering data values until the program outputs the high and low temperatures. If the program doesn't input exactly 24 numbers, there must be an error in the control of the loop.

We should try data sets that present the high and low temperatures in different orders. For example, we should try one set with the highest temperature as the first value and another set with it as the last. We should do the same for the lowest temperature. We also should try a data set in which the temperature goes up and down several times, and another in which the temperatures are all the same. Finally, we should test the program on some typical sets of data and check the output with results we've determined by hand. For example, given this data:

```
45  47  47  47  50  50  55  60  70  70  72  75
75  75  75  74  74  73  70  70  69  67  65  50
```

The output would look like this:

```
45
47
47
47
50
50
55
60
70
70
72
75
75
75
75
74
74
73
70
70
69
67
65
50


High temperature is 75
Low temperature is 45
```

What happens if we combine the two IF-THEN statements in one IF-THEN-ELSE statement, as shown below?

```
IF Temperature < Low
   THEN
     Low := Temperature
   ELSE IF Temperature > High
     THEN
       High := Temperature
```

At first glance the single statement looks more efficient. Why should you ask if Temperature is larger than High if you know it is lower than Low? But this code segment gives the wrong answer if the highest temperature is the first value read in because of the way High and Low are initialized.

In Programming Warm-Up Exercise 8 you are asked to redo Program Temp_Stat using an initialization scheme that removes this data dependency. (HINT: Use a priming Read and set High and Low to that first value.)

PROBLEM-SOLVING CASE STUDY

Shipping Invoices

Problem: The Mill Hollow Boring and Bearing Company occasionally has to ship products outside its delivery area. The company has asked you to write an interactive program that prints shipping invoices. Only one invoice is printed at a time, but each invoice may have several items on it.

The input is a series of data sets, one set per item, each on a separate line. Each data set contains the quantity of an item shipped, a description of the item, and the unit price of the item. The end of the data is indicated by an item quantity of zero or less. After the last data set is processed, the total number of items and the total amount should be output.

Input: Each line of input contains the quantity shipped of an item (Integer), followed by a blank, followed by a 30-character description of the item, followed by another blank and then the unit price of the item (Real). The end of the data is indicated by an item quantity of zero or less.

Output: An invoice with four columns of information: the quantity of each item shipped, a description of each item, the unit price of each item, and the billing amount for the given number of items. Each column should have an appropriate heading, as should the overall invoice. After the last item has been printed, the total number of units shipped and the total amount of the invoice should be printed. Note that in this case study, when we say printed, we mean printed on paper from a printer attached to your computer. This will be accomplished with the file "Lst".

Discussion: This program simply reads each line of data and prints out the quantity, description, price, and amount for the given number of units. Running sums of the quantity and amount values must be kept. There are two loops in this program: a sentinel-controlled loop to control the reading of the data sets and a nested count-controlled loop to read and print the string of 30 characters in the item description.

Outer Loop Design: The loop exits when a sentinel value of zero or less is input for an item quantity. The termination condition is initialized with a priming Read of the quantity. The condition is updated by reading a new quantity at the end of each iteration. The process is to read and print the data for an item, and to add the quantity and dollar amount for the item to running totals. The process is initialized by setting the totals to zero. It is updated by reading the data for an item, printing a line of the invoice, and adding the appropriate values to the totals.

When the loop ends, the following is true: The reading marker is positioned just beyond the sentinel value in the input; an invoice line has been printed for each item; Quantity contains the last quantity input; Price contains the last price input; Character contains the last character in the final description; Blank contains the character separating the last quantity and description; Amount contains the price times the quantity of the last item ordered; Counter equals 31; and the quantity of items ordered and their costs have been summed in Total_Units and Total_Amount, respectively.

Inner Loop Design: The locp exits when the loop control variable exceeds 30. The loop control variable is initialized to 1 and incremented at the end of each iteration. The process is to read and print one character. No initialization or update is necessary because the reading and writing markers advance automatically. At loop exit, the reading marker should be on the character following the item description; the item description should be printed on the current line; and the loop control variable should be equal to 31.

In addition to printing an invoice line for each item, we must print **headings** at the top of the page and above each column. Programs that use loops often produce large amounts of output, and it is common to organize that output in columns with headings.

The first step in designing columnar output is to determine what is going to be printed. The next step is to make a sketch on graph paper of how the output should look. Line up the headings and put in some actual values. Once you have an acceptable design, count the number of character positions associated with each heading or data value.

Figure 5-3 shows a sample design for the output here. From it we can determine the appropriate fieldwidths for aligning headings with columns of values.

We now have enough information to write the algorithm:

Main Module   *Level 0*

> Print headings
> Print body of invoice
> Print totals

Print Headings   *Level 1*

> Print centered 'Mill Hollow Boring and Bearing Company'
> Print centered '128 East Southwest Street'
> Print centered 'North Old Newgate, New Hampshire   01010'
> Blank line
> Print centered 'Shipping Invoice'
> Blank line
> Print 'Quantity', 'Description', 'Price', 'Amount' to
>   align with columns
> Blank line

PROBLEM-SOLVING CASE STUDY *cont'd.*

Figure 5-3 Formatting Output

```
          Mill Hollow Boring and Bearing Company
                128 East Southwest Street
          North Old Newgate, New Hampshire   01010

                    Shipping Invoice

Quantity              Description                 Price      Amount

   9999    XXXXXXXXXXXXXXXXXXXXXXXXXXXXXX     99999.99     9999999.99
   9999    XXXXXXXXXXXXXXXXXXXXXXXXXXXXXX     99999.99     9999999.99

Total Units Ordered:  99999999                  Total:    9999999.99
```

Print Body of Invoice

```
Initialize process
Initialize ending condition
WHILE Quantity > 0 DO
    Update process
    Update ending condition
```

[handwritten: Counter: 1]

[handwritten: ReadLn(infile, Quantity, Descri Price, Amt);]

[handwritten: Writeln(]

Print Totals

```
Blank line
Print 'Total Units Ordered:', Total_Units,
'Total:', Total_Amount
```

[handwritten: writeLn]

Initialize Process   *Level 2*

```
Initialize Total_Units to 0
Initialize Total_Amount to 0.0
```

*[handwritten: Tot_Units := 0
Tot_Amt := 0]*

PROBLEM-SOLVING CASE STUDY *cont'd.*

Initialize Ending Condition

```
Read Quantity
```

Update Process

```
Print Quantity (aligned with heading)
Read and print description (aligned with heading)
Input Price
Print Price (aligned with heading)
Set Amount to Quantity * Price
Print Amount (aligned with heading)
Add Quantity to Total_Units
Add Amount to Total_Amount
```

Update Ending Condition

```
Read Quantity
```

Read and Print Description   *Level 3*

```
Read Blank
Print four spaces
Set Counter to 1
WHILE Counter < = Description Length DO
    Read a character
    Print the character
    Increment Counter
```

Module Structure Chart:

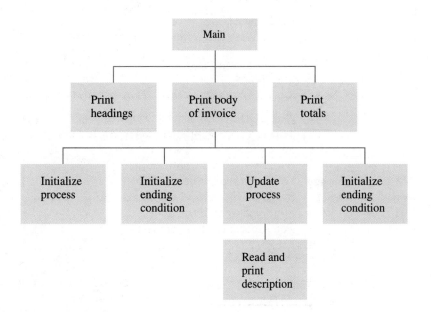

Here is the program:

```pascal
PROGRAM Invoice (Input, Output);

(* This program prints a shipping invoice given quantities, *)
(* item descriptions, and unit prices                       *)

USES Printer;

CONST
  Descr_Length = 30;       (* Characters in an item description            *)

VAR
  Quantity,                (* Number of items ordered                     *)
  Total_Units,             (* Total items in invoice                      *)
  Counter:                 (* Loop control variable for printing description *)
    Integer;
  Price,                   (* Unit price for an item                      *)
  Amount,                  (* Amount for quantity of items                *)
  Total_Amount:            (* Total amount of invoice                     *)
    Real;
  Blank,                   (* Dummy variable to hold blanks               *)
  Character:               (* Holds one character of description          *)
    Char;
```

```
BEGIN (* Invoice *)
  (* Print headings *)
  Writeln(LST, 'Mill Hollow Boring and Bearing Company':50);
  Writeln(LST, '128 East Southwest Street':43);
  Writeln(LST, 'North Old Newgate, New Hampshire  01010':50);
  Writeln(LST);
  Writeln(LST, 'Shipping Invoice':38);
  Writeln(LST);
  Writeln(LST, 'Quantity', 'Description':22, 'Price':19, 'Amount':11);
  Writeln(LST);
  (* Print body of invoice *)
  (* Initialize process *)
  Total_Units := 0;
  Total_Amount := 0.0;
  (* Initialize ending condition *)
  Read(Quantity);
  WHILE Quantity > 0 DO
    BEGIN
      (* Update process *)
      Write(LST, Quantity:6);
      (* Read and print description *)
      Read(Blank);                       (* Discard extra blank in input *)
      Write(LST, ' ':4);
      Counter := 1;                 (* Initialize loop control variable *)
      WHILE Counter <= Descr_Length DO
        BEGIN
          Read(Character);                              (* Process *)
          Write(LST, Character);
          Counter := Counter + 1        (* Update loop control variable *)
        END;
      Readln(Price);
      Write(LST, Price:10:2);
      Amount := Quantity * Price;
      Writeln(LST, Amount:12:2);
      Total_Units := Total_Units + Quantity;
      Total_Amount := Total_Amount + Amount;
      (* Update ending condition *)
      Read(Quantity)
    END;
  (* Print totals *)
  Writeln(LST);
  Writeln(LST, 'Total Units Ordered: ', Total_Units:8, 'Total:':21,
               Total_Amount:12:2)
END.  (* Invoice *)
```

Testing: Because Program Invoice is so complex, we discuss testing for it both here and in the next section. Here we look at the important points to watch for in testing data sets with typical values.

The output from this program, given valid test data, is an invoice consisting of three sections. The first section is the company name and address and the column headings. Carefully examine this section of the output for spelling mistakes, proper centering of the name and address, and correct spacing of the column headings.

The second section is the list of items being shipped. There should be one line in this section for each line of input. Check that the first and last lines of data have been processed correctly—it's in these lines that errors in loop control most often appear. Make sure that the columns of numbers are aligned under the appropriate headings. Compare the output in the Amount column with your hand-calculated results.

The third section of the output consists of the totals. Look for spelling and spacing errors, and compare the printed values against your hand-calculated results.

Testing and Debugging

The Loop Invariant

In Chapter 4, we saw that an algorithm walk-through can be used to test a design before it is implemented. Loops present some special problems in performing a walk-through because each iteration can behave differently. To test a data-dependent loop design, we would have to try every possible combination of input. In many cases this is not practical because the possibilities are too numerous, if not infinite.

What we would like to do is treat a loop as a separate module, so we can use our standard walk-through technique. But in order to establish a fixed set of preconditions and postconditions for a loop, we must determine those characteristics that do not vary from one iteration to the next. The collection of all these characteristics is called the **loop invariant,** and is expressed as a set of assertions that must always be true in order for the loop to execute correctly.

Loop Invariant   Assertions about the characteristics of a loop that must always be true for a loop to execute properly. The assertions are true on loop entry, at the start of each loop iteration, and on exit from the loop. They are not necessarily true at each point in the body of the loop.

At first, you might think that the invariant is just the Boolean expression that controls the loop. But an invariant must be true when the loop exits; and the Boolean expression is false when the loop exits. Here are some examples:

Boolean Expression	Related Invariant Condition
Loop_Control_Variable < 365. (Loop_Control_Variable is initialized before the loop.)	The loop control variable can range from 1 to 365.
Odd_Count < 10. (Odd_Count is initialized before the loop.)	The event counter is equal to the number of odd numbers input; it can range from 0 to 10.
Data >= 0. (Data is initialized before the loop.)	Only nonnegative data values are processed; the loop exits with a negative value in the input variable.

You can see that an invariant condition is related to each Boolean expression, but that they are not identical. The loop invariant and the Boolean expression must be true for the loop to execute; the loop invariant and the termination condition (the negation of the Boolean expression) must be true after the loop exits. Also the loop invariant usually consists of other conditions as well as those related to the Boolean expression. For example, it typically includes the ranges of all the variables used in the loop and the status of any files.

To create the invariant, we begin with our answer to the last question on the loop design checklist (*What is the state of the program on exiting the loop?*) because it forces us to determine the final condition of the variables and files. Then we work backward, answering the other questions on the checklist.

Let's write the invariant for the outer loop in Program Invoice. We begin with the part of the invariant associated with Total_Amount. We know that on loop exit, Total_Amount contains the sum of all the individual item amounts. Then we look at how the process is initialized and updated. Here's the related invariant condition:

- Total_Amount can range from zero upward; at the start of each iteration it must equal the total of all the values of Amount that have been computed.

In the same way, we look at the termination condition, initialization, and update of Total_Units to determine the portion of the invariant that relates to it:

- Total_Units can range from zero upward; at the start of each iteration it contains the sum of all the values of Quantity that have been input so far.

Here are the invariant conditions for the other variables and the input file:

- Price either is undefined or contains a Real value. Price contains the item price input in the most recently completed iteration.
- Amount either is undefined or contains a Real value. Amount contains the Quantity times the Price calculated in the most recently completed iteration.
- Quantity contains an Integer value, the most recently input quantity ordered of an item.
- Counter either is undefined or contains the value 31.
- Character either is undefined or contains the last character of the item description input in the previous iteration.
- Blank either is undefined or contains the character between the Quantity and the item description input in the previous iteration.

■ The reading marker is positioned in File Input just after the most recent quantity input. *While not EOF(infile)do*

In addition to the status of variables and files, most programs contain some general invariant conditions. For example:

■ One invoice line should be printed for each loop iteration, and the number of lines output should be 1 less than the number input.

Loop Testing Strategy

Even if a loop has been properly designed and verified, it is still important to test it rigorously, because there is always the chance of an error creeping in during the implementation phase. Because loops allow us to input many data sets in one run, and because there is the potential for each iteration to be affected by preceding ones, the test data for a looping program is usually more extensive than for a program with just sequential or branching statements. In order to thoroughly test a loop, we have to check for the proper execution of both a single iteration and multiple iterations.

Remember that a loop has seven parts (corresponding to the seven questions in our checklist). A test strategy must test each part. Although all seven parts aren't implemented separately in every loop, the checklist reminds us that some loop operations may serve multiple purposes, each of which should be tested. For example, the incrementing statement in a count-controlled loop may be updating both the process and the ending condition. So it's important to verify that it performs both actions properly with respect to the rest of the loop.

The loop invariant is a good place to start in designing test data. The invariant tells us what the acceptable ranges of variables are and what sorts of I/O operations we should see. To test a loop, we try to devise data sets that could cause the variables to go out of range or leave the files in improper states that violate the postconditions of the module containing the loop.

In addition to tests based on the invariant, it's good practice to test a loop for four special cases: (1) when the loop is skipped entirely, (2) when the loop body is executed just once, (3) when the loop executes some normal number of times, and (4) when the loop fails to exit.

Statements following a loop often depend on its processing. If a loop can be skipped, those statements may not execute correctly. If it's possible to execute a single iteration of a loop, the results can show whether the body performs correctly in the absence of the effects of previous iterations, which can be very helpful when you're trying to isolate the source of an error. Obviously it's important to test a loop under normal conditions, with a wide variety of inputs. If possible, the loop should be tested with real data in addition to mock data sets. Count-controlled loops should be tested to be sure they execute exactly the right number of times. And finally, if there is any chance that a loop might never exit, your test data should try to make that happen.

Testing a program can be as challenging as writing it. To test a program, you have to step back, take a fresh look at what you've written, and then attack it in every way possible to make it fail. This isn't always easy to do, but it's necessary if your programs are going to be reliable. (A *reliable program* is one that works consistently and without errors regardless of whether the input data is valid or invalid.)

To verify an algorithm, we use the loop invariant as a bridge between the statements that precede and follow the loop. We have to show that the invariant conditions are true before entering the loop. If the loop is designed correctly, they should still be true when the termination condition is reached.

To show that the invariant is true before loop entry, we compare the current set of conditions (the postconditions from the preceding statements) with the invariant. If the invariant is a subset of the current conditions, then the loop is ready to start. If the invariant contains an assertion that has not been established, then something is missing in our preparations for executing the loop.

Once we know that the invariant is true at loop entry, we must show that the invariant is true at the start of each iteration. We do this by walking through the body of the loop and determining the postconditions of each statement. Then we compare the postconditions of the last statement in the loop to the invariant. If any part of the invariant is not satisfied by these conditions, there is something wrong with the loop. Otherwise we know that the invariant will be true at the beginning of the next iteration.

When the loop exits, its termination condition is true. The postcondition of the loop is the combination of the termination condition and the invariant. The postcondition also includes any conditions that existed before the loop that have not changed.

Let's tie all this together with an example: summing the integers 1 through 10.

```
PROGRAM Sum_Up (Output);

VAR
   Sum,
   Number:
      Integer;

BEGIN (* Sum_Up *)
   Sum := 0;
   Number := 1;
   WHILE Number <= 10 DO
      BEGIN
         Sum := Sum + Number;
         Number := Number + 1
      END
END.    (* Sum_Up *)
```

To verify this program, we have to do the following:

1. Define the loop invariant.
2. Show that the invariant is true before loop entry.
3. Show that the invariant is true at the start of each iteration.
4. Show that at loop exit the invariant is still true and the termination condition is true.

This is the loop invariant:

Sum contains the sum of the integers from 0 to Number $-$ 1; Number is in the range 1 through 11 and is equal to the number of loop iterations executed plus 1.

The last part of the invariant can be stated more concisely:

Iterations = Number − 1

At loop entry, the following conditions have been established: Sum is equal to 0, and Number is equal to 1. Comparing these conditions to the invariant we see that Sum is equal to Number − 1; Number is in the range 1 through 11; and the number of iterations executed is 0, which equals Number − 1.

Next we walk through the loop body. The first statement adds the value of Number to Sum, so Sum now contains the sum of the integers from 0 to Number. The next statement increments Number, which means that Sum now contains the sum of the integers from 0 to Number − 1. At the end of this iteration, Number − 1 also equals the number of iterations. Because Number cannot be greater than 10 at the start of an iteration, we also know that Number cannot be greater than 11 at this point. So the invariant is true for the start of the next iteration.

We can tell that the loop terminates correctly from the fact that Number is initially less than 10 and is incremented in each loop iteration. So Number eventually will become greater than 10, and the loop will terminate.

This may seem like an awful lot of work to show something that's obvious anyway: The code *is* correct. But what is obvious in simple code may not be obvious in more complicated code. That's where verification methods are critically important.

Using the Debugger with Loops

The Turbo Pascal Debugger is an especially useful tool in debugging loops. Recall in Chapter 4 that the debugger allows us to create a Watch window that shows us the values of variables as we step through a program. Watching how variables change during execution of a loop often helps to identify the source of an error. In this section we introduce some features of the debugger that make it easier to trace the execution of loops.

Suppose that you suspect a loop is not reaching its complex termination condition correctly. You could add the name of every variable in the WHILE loop's expression to the Watch window and then evaluate the condition by hand, but that would be a tedious and error-prone process.

What you'd like to do is simply watch the value of the expression as the loop is executed. The Turbo Debugger allows us to do just that: when you select Add Watch, instead of entering the name of a variable, type the expression that appears in the WHILE loop. Then, as you step through the program with F8, the value of the expression will be displayed in the Watch window. Variables and expressions can be added to the Watch window at any time, even while you are tracing a program. Note that the debugger may give you an error message when you add the expression to the Watch window (Cannot access this symbol), but just ignore this.

You can enter any valid Pascal expression in an Add Watch dialog box. For example, the invariant for Program Sum_Up indicates that the number of iterations equals Number − 1. Thus, it might be useful to add a watch for Number − 1, then step through the program.

In a program with a long loop, it can also be tedious to step through every statement in the loop, especially if you are interested only in the values of some variables at one point in the loop (such as its exit). One way around this is to have the debugger run the program up to the point where the cursor is positioned.

To do this, first select Tile from the Window menu, which prevents the Edit window from covering the Watch window. Next, move the cursor to the point in the program where you want to start tracing. Then press F4 to run the program. When execution reaches the cursor position, the program stops and the Watch window shows the values of any watched variables or expressions.

For example, you could place the cursor on the statement following a loop, then press F4. The statements prior to that point will be executed automatically, then the debugger will stop the program and display any watched variables or expressions. In this case, you will see their values at loop exit. Once the debugger stops the program, you can use F8 to step through additional statements, or reposition the cursor and press F4 again to continue execution to that point.

Sometimes when you are tracing execution in a loop, you would like to see the values of variables at several places during an iteration. For example, if a loop contains a branch, you might want to look at variable values before and after the branch, and at the beginning of the loop. You could keep moving the cursor to each of these places and pressing F4, but the Turbo debugger provides a better way: setting breakpoints.

A breakpoint is a line in a program that has been marked as a place to stop execution so that the Watch window can be examined. To mark a line as a breakpoint, move the cursor there and press Ctrl-F8. Pressing Ctrl-F8 again will unmark the line. Now, when you run the program, it automatically stops at the marked line. Select Run again (or press Ctrl-F9) to continue execution. You can also use F4 to run and continue execution, but it will stop at the cursor position if that is before the next breakpoint.

For the example just described, you could mark the IF, the statement after the branch, and the WHILE, as shown in Figure 5-4. Because execution stops before a breakpoint line is executed, the breakpoints will stop execution just before and after the branch, and at the beginning of the loop. You would then press Ctrl-F9 repeatedly to step from breakpoint to breakpoint, examining the values in the Watch window each time.

In summary, we've seen three ways to trace execution in a program: stepping through one statement at a time with F8, running to the cursor position with F4, and marking breakpoint lines with Ctrl-F8, then running between them with Ctrl-F9. We've seen also that the Watch window can be used to view the values of expressions as well as variables.

The advantage of using the debugger is that it quickly and accurately traces execution of a program. It does not, however, explain the values that it displays for us. We can only make sense of the information we see in the Watch window by understanding the loop invariants prior to starting the trace.

The name "debugger" is a misnomer—it does not find and remove bugs for us but merely helps us gather more information about the execution of a program. We must then interpret that information carefully in order to identify errors.

The debugger can be a source of so much information that it is tempting to immediately use it when an error is discovered. But unless you've thought through the problem, the debugger can easily overwhelm you with information. The debugger is most helpful once you've narrowed the sources of error to a few possibilities and need only a little more information to decide which it is. Always try first to find the source of an error using the program's output, and then use the debugger as a last resort.

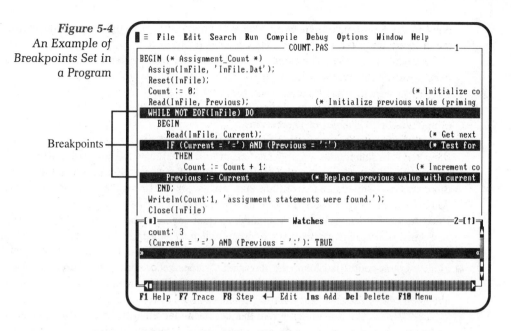

Figure 5-4
An Example of
Breakpoints Set in
a Program

Breakpoints

```
≡  File  Edit  Search  Run  Compile  Debug  Options  Window  Help
                          ──── COUNT.PAS ────                      ─1──
BEGIN (* Assignment_Count *)
  Assign(InFile, 'InFile.Dat');
  Reset(InFile);
  Count := 0;                                        (* Initialize co
  Read(InFile, Previous);            (* Initialize previous value (priming
  WHILE NOT EOF(InFile) DO
    BEGIN
      Read(InFile, Current);                         (* Get next
      IF (Current = '=') AND (Previous = ':')        (* Test for
      THEN
        Count := Count + 1;                          (* Increment co
      Previous := Current       (* Replace previous value with current
    END;
  Writeln(Count:1, 'assignment statements were found.');
  Close(InFile)
─[■]───────────────────── Watches ──────────────────2=[↑]─
 count: 3
 (Current = '=') AND (Previous = ':'): TRUE
»                                                                «

─◄□████████████████████████████████████████████████████████████□►
F1 Help  F7 Trace  F8 Step  ◄┘ Edit  Ins Add  Del Delete  F10 Menu
```

Testing and Debugging Hints

1. Plan your test data carefully to test all sections of a program.
2. Beware of infinite loops, where the expression in the WHILE statement never becomes False. The symptom: The program doesn't stop.

   If you have created an infinite loop, check your logic and the syntax of your loops. Be sure there's no semicolon immediately after the DO in the WHILE loop, which causes an infinite loop in most cases. In a count-controlled loop, make sure the loop control variable is incremented within the loop. In a flag-controlled loop, make sure the flag eventually changes.
3. If an EOF loop takes input from the keyboard, be sure that you use the CRT unit and set CheckEOF to True.
4. Avoid using Read with numeric data and EOF-controlled loops; use Readln instead. If you must use Read with numeric data, use a sentinel-controlled loop instead of an EOF-controlled loop.
5. Check the loop termination conditions carefully, and be sure that something in the loop causes them to be met. Watch closely for values that go one iteration too long or too short.
6. Write out the loop invariant—the consistent, predictable part of its behavior in each iteration. Look for patterns that the invariant establishes. Are they just what you want? Perform an algorithm walk-through to verify that all of the appropriate preconditions and postconditions occur in the right places.
7. Trace the execution of the loop by hand with a code walk-through. Simulate the first few passes and the last few passes very carefully to see how the loop really behaves.
8. If all else fails, use the Turbo Debugger.

9. An ounce of prevention is worth a pound of debugging. Use the checklist questions, write the loop invariant, and design your loop correctly to begin with. It may seem like extra work, but it really pays off in the long run.

Summary

The WHILE statement is a looping construct that allows the program to repeat a statement as long as an expression is True. When the expression becomes False, the statement is skipped, and execution continues with the first statement following the loop.

With the WHILE statement you can construct several types of loops that you will use again and again. These types of loops fall into two categories: count-controlled loops and event-controlled loops.

In a count-controlled loop, the loop body is repeated a specified number of times. You initialize a counter variable right before the WHILE statement. This variable is the loop control variable. The control variable is tested against the limit in the expression of the WHILE. The last statement in the loop body increments the control variable.

Event-controlled loops continue executing until something inside the body signals that the looping process should stop. Event-controlled loops include those that test for a sentinel value in the data, EOF, EOLN, or a change in a flag variable.

Sentinel-controlled loops are input loops that use a special data value as a signal to stop reading. EOF-controlled loops are loops that continue to input (and process) data values until there is no more data. To implement them with a WHILE statement, you must use the expression NOT EOF because EOF becomes True when there are no more data values. EOLN-controlled loops are used to input (and process) character data until there are no more characters on a line. A flag is a variable that is set in one part of the program and tested in another. In a flag-controlled loop, you must set the flag before the WHILE, test it in the expression, and change it somewhere in the body of the loop.

Counting is a looping operation that keeps track of how many times a loop is repeated or how many times some event occurs. This count can be used in computations or to control the loop. A counter is a variable that is used for counting. It may be the loop control variable in a count-controlled loop, an iteration counter in a counting loop, or an event counter that counts the number of times a particular condition occurs in a loop.

Summing is a looping operation that keeps a running total of certain values. It is like counting in that the variable that holds the sum is initialized outside the loop. The summing operation, however, adds up unknown values; the counting operation adds a constant (1) to the counter each time.

When you design a loop, there are seven points to consider: How the termination condition is initialized, tested, and updated; how the process in the loop is initialized, performed, and updated; and the state of the program upon loop exit. By answering the checklist questions, you can bring each of these points into focus.

To design a nested loop structure, simply begin with the outermost loop. When you get to where the inner loop must appear, make it a separate module and come back later to its design.

Looping programs often produce a large amount of output that can be easier to read in table form, with a heading for each column. Tables are easy to print using fieldwidth specifications.

A loop invariant is a set of conditions that specify what must be true on loop entry, at the beginning of each iteration, and at loop exit in order for the loop to work properly. Writing out the loop invariant is a part of the verification process for programs that contain loops.

The process of testing a loop is based on the loop invariant, the answers to the checklist questions, and the patterns it might encounter (for example, executing a single iteration, multiple iterations, an infinite number of iterations, or no iterations at all).

■ *Quick Check*

1. Write a WHILE statement that loops until the value of Boolean variable Done becomes True. (pp. 196–198)   *While NOT DONE DO*

2. What are the four parts of a count-controlled loop? (pp. 198–200) ·

3. You should avoid using Read with numeric data in EOF-controlled loops. True or false? (pp. 200–205)   *True*

4. Should you use a priming Read in an EOLN-controlled loop that is reading data of type Char? (pp. 206–207)   *No*   *Read for EOF*

5. How is a flag variable used to control a loop? (pp. 207–208)   *if it turns false ends it.*

6. What is the difference between a counting operation in a loop and a summing operation in a loop? (pp. 208–211)   *Counting counts times thru loop*   *Sum adds all variables in pig.*

7. What is the difference between a loop control variable and an event counter? (pp. 208–21]   *if count < 10 event*   *if false -ev*

8. What kind of loop would you use in a program that reads the closing price of a stock for each day of the week? (pp. 216–219)   *While not eLon Do*

9. How would you extend the loop in Question 9 to make it read 52 weeks' worth of prices? (pp. 219–224)

10. With what kind of loop is the following invariant most likely associated? (pp. 245–247)

    Day may range from 1 to 365 and must indicate the number of the iteration that is about to be executed.

11. How would you test a program that is supposed to count the number of females and the number of males in a data set? (Assume that females are coded with 'F' in the data; males, with 'M'.) (pp. 247–250)

Answers

1. WHILE NOT Done DO.   2. The process being repeated, plus initializing, testing, and incrementing the loop control variable.   3. True.   4. No.   5. The flag is set outside the loop; the WHILE checks the flag; and an IF inside the loop resets the flag when the termination condition occurs.
6. A counting operation increments with each iteration of the loop by a fixed value; a summing operation adds unknown values to the total.   7. A loop control variable controls the loop; an event counter simply counts certain events within the loop.   8. Because there are 5 days in a business week, you would use a

count-controlled loop that runs from 1 to 5.   9. Nest the original loop inside a count-controlled loop that runs from 1 to 52.   10. A count-controlled loop.   11. Run the program with data sets that have a different number of females and males, only females, only males, illegal values (other characters), and an empty input file.

■ *Exam Preparation Exercises*

1. In one or two sentences, explain the difference between loops and branches.

2. What does the following loop print out? (Number is of type Integer.)

```
Number :=  1;
WHILE Number < 11 DO
  BEGIN
    Number :=  Number + 1;
    Writeln(Number:7);
  END
```

3. By rearranging the order of the statements (don't change the way they are written), make the loop in Exercise 2 print the numbers from 1 to 10.

4. When the following code is executed, how many iterations of the loop will be performed?

```
Number := 2;
Done := False;
WHILE NOT Done DO
  BEGIN
    Number := Number * 2;
    IF Number > 64
      THEN
        Done := True
  END
```

5. What is the output of this nested loop?

```
I := 4;
WHILE I >= 1 DO
  BEGIN
    J := 1;
    WHILE J >= 1 DO
      BEGIN
        Write(J);
        J := J - 1
      END;
    Writeln(I);
    I := I - 1
  END
```

6. The following code segment is designed to write out the even numbers between 1 and 15. It has two flaws in it.

```
X := 2;
WHILE X <> 15 DO
   BEGIN
      X := X + 2;
      Write(X)
   END
```

a. What is the output of the code as written?

b. Correct the code so that it works as intended.

7. The following code segment is supposed to copy one line from Input to Output.

```
Read(Ch);
WHILE NOT EOLN DO
   BEGIN
      Write(Char);
      Read(Char)
   END
```

a. What is the output if the input line is "LINE1"?

b. Rewrite the code so that it works properly.

8. Does the following program segment need a priming Read? If not, explain why. If so, add the Read in the proper place. (Letter is of type Char.)

```
WHILE NOT EOF (TextFile) DO
   BEGIN
      WHILE NOT EOLN DO
         BEGIN
            Read(TextFile, Letter);
            Write(Letter)
         END;
      Readln(TextFile);
      Writeln
   END
```

9. Write the invariant conditions for the following loop. (Sum and Count are of type Integer.)

```
Sum := 0;
Count := 0;
WHILE Count < 22 DO
   BEGIN
      Sum := Sum + Count;
      Count := Count + 1
   END
```

10. What sentinel value would you choose for a program that reads telephone numbers as integers?

11. Given this code:

```
PROGRAM Pretest (Input, Output);
```

```
CONST
  N = 8;

VAR
  Sum,
  I,
  Number:
    Integer;
  Flag:
    Boolean;

BEGIN (* Pretest *)
  Sum := 0;
  I := 1;
  Flag := False;
  WHILE (I <= N) AND NOT Flag DO
    BEGIN
      Read(Number);
      IF Number > 0
        THEN
          Sum := Sum + Number
        ELSE
          IF Number = 0
            THEN
              Flag := True;
      I := I + 1
    END;
  Writeln('End of test. ', Sum:1, ' ', Number:1)
END.  (* Pretest *)
```

(handwritten annotations: `I <= 8 and true do`, `2 <= 8`, `(0+5)(670)`, `= 11`, `2`)

and these data values:

5   6   -3   7   -4   0   5   8   9

a. What are the contents of Sum and Number after Program Pretest has been executed?
b. Does the data fully test the program? Explain your answer.

12. Write the invariant for an EOF-controlled loop that reads numeric values, counts them, sums them, and sums the squares of the values. (Each input line contains exactly one value.)

13. Here is a simple count-controlled loop:

```
Count := 1;
WHILE Count < 20 DO
  Count := Count + 1
```

a. List three ways of changing the loop so that it executes 20 times instead of 19 times.
b. Which of those changes makes the value of Count range from 1 to 20?

14. This program segment is supposed to read and print all of the input data character by character. (Assume that the program has the USES CRT and CHECKEOF := True statements.)

```
Read(Character);
WHILE NOT EOF DO
  BEGIN
    Read(Character);
    WHILE NOT EOLN DO
      BEGIN
        Write(Character);
        Read(Character)
      END;
    Writeln
  END
```

a. Does it work?

b. If not, how would you fix it?

■ *Programming Warm-Up Exercises*

1. Write a program segment that sets a Boolean variable Danger to True and stops reading in data if Pressure (a Real variable being read in) exceeds 510.0. Use Danger as a flag to control the loop.

2. Write a program segment that counts the number of times the integer 28 occurs in a file of 100 integers.

3. Write a nested loop code segment that produces this output:

```
1
1 2
1 2 3
1 2 3 4
```

4. Write a program segment that reads a file of grades for a class (any size) and finds the class average.

5. a. Write statements that print the following headings in the format shown.

```
        Sales

Week1     Week2     Week3
```

   b. Write a statement that lines values up under each week's heading. The values are stored in the Integer variables Week1, Week2, and Week3. The last digit of each number should fall under the 1, 2, or 3 of its column heading.

6. Write a program segment that reads in integers and then counts and prints out the number of positive integers and the number of negative integers. If a value is zero, it should not be counted. The process should continue until EOF becomes True.

7. Write a program segment that adds up the even integers from 16 to 26 inclusive.

8. Rewrite Program Temp_Stat (page 236) using a different initialization scheme. One temperature should be read before the loop, and all values (except Hour) should be initialized to the first temperature. Trace your program to make sure it works.

9. Write a program segment that prints out the sequence of all the hour and minute combinations in a day, starting with 1:00 A.M. and ending with 12:59 A.M.

10. Rewrite the code segment for Exercise 9 so that it prints the times in 10-minute intervals, arranged as a table of 6 columns with 24 rows.

11. Change Program Incomes (page 231) so that it

   a. prints an error message when a negative income value is input and then goes on processing any remaining data. The erroneous data should not be included in any of the calculations. Thoroughly test the modified program with your own data sets.

   b. does not crash when the input file contains either no females or no males. However, it should print an appropriate error message. Test the revised program with your own data sets.

   c. rejects data sets that are coded with a letter other than 'F' or 'M' and prints an error message before continuing to process the remaining data.

12. Develop a thorough set of test data for Program Incomes as modified in Exercise 11.

▪ *Programming Problems*

1. Write a top-down design and a Pascal program that inputs an integer and a character. The output should be a diamond composed of the character and extending the width specified by the integer. For example, if the integer is 11 and the character is an asterisk (*), the diamond would look like this:

   If the integer entered is an even number, it should be rounded up to the next highest odd number. Use meaningful variable names, proper indentation, appropriate comments, and good prompting messages.

2. Write a top-down design and a Pascal program that inputs an integer larger than 1 and calculates the sum of the squares from 1 to that integer. For example, if the integer equals 4, the sum of the squares is 30 (1 + 4 + 9 + 16). The output should be the value of the integer and the sum, properly labeled. A negative input value signals the end of the data.

3. You are putting together some music tapes for a party. You've arranged a list of songs in the order in which you want to play them. However, you would like to minimize the empty tape left at the end of each side of a cassette (a cassette plays for 45 minutes on a side). So you want to figure out the total time for a group of songs and see how well they fit. Write a top-down design and a Pascal program to help you do this. The program should input a reference number and a time for each song, until it encounters a reference number of 0. The times

should each be entered in the form of minutes and seconds (two integer values). For example, if song number 4 takes 7 minutes and 42 seconds to play, the data entered for that song would be

```
4   7   42
```

The program should echo-print the data for each song and the current running time total. The last data (reference number 0) should not be added to the total time. After all of the data has been read, the program should print a message indicating the time remaining on the tape.

If you are writing this program to read data from a file, the output should be in the form of a table with columns and headings. For example:

Song Number	Song Time Minutes	Seconds	Total Time Minutes	Seconds
1	5	10	5	10
2	7	42	12	52
5	4	19	17	11
3	4	33	21	44
4	10	27	32	11
6	8	55	41	6
0	0	1	41	6

```
There are 3 minutes and 54 seconds of tape left.
```

If you are using interactive input, your output should have prompting messages interspersed with the results. For example:

```
Enter the song number:
1
Enter the number of minutes:
5
Enter the number of seconds:
10
Song number 1, 5 minutes and 10 seconds
Total time is 5 minutes and 10 seconds.
For the next song,
Enter the song number:
.
.
```

Use meaningful variable names, proper indentation, and appropriate comments. If you're writing an interactive program, use good prompting messages. The program should discard any invalid data sets (negative numbers, for example) and print an error message indicating that the data set has been discarded and what was wrong with it.

4. Using top-down design, write a program that prints out the approximate number of words in a file of text. For our purposes, this is the same as the number of gaps following words. A *gap* is defined as one or more spaces in a row, so a sequence of spaces counts as just one gap. The <eoln> marker also counts as a gap. Anything other than a space or <eoln> is considered to be part of a word. For example, there are 19 words in the following hint, according to our definition. (HINT: Only count a space as a gap if the previous character read is something other than a space.) The program should echo-print the data.

Thoroughly test the program with your own data sets.

Procedures

GOALS

- To be able to write a program that uses procedures to reflect the structure of your top-down design.
- To be able to write a module of your own design as a procedure.
- To be able to define correctly a procedure to do a specified task.
- To be able to invoke that procedure correctly.
- To be able to use actual and formal parameters correctly.
- To be able to define and use local variables correctly.
- To be able to write a program that uses multiple calls to a single procedure.

You have been using procedures and functions since the Write statement was introduced in Chapter 2. By now you should be quite comfortable with the idea of calling these subprograms to perform a task. So far, we have not considered how procedures and functions are created. That is the topic of this chapter and Chapters 7 and 8.

You might wonder why we waited until now to look at user-defined subprograms. The reason lies in the major purpose for using subprograms: we write our own procedures and functions to help organize and simplify large and complex programs. Until now our programs have been relatively small and simple, so we didn't need to write subprograms. Now that we've covered the basic control structures, we are ready to introduce subprograms so we can begin writing larger and more complex programs.

Top-Down Structured Design with Procedures

From the very beginning you have been designing your programs as collections of modules. Many of these modules are naturally implemented as *user-defined procedures*. You have been using procedures since Chapter 2, when you learned the Write and Writeln statements. Write and Writeln are examples of procedures that are built into the Pascal language. Now you will learn how to turn the modules in your algorithms into user-defined procedures.

When to Use Procedures

In general, any module can be coded as a procedure or function, although some are so simple that this really is unnecessary. Thus, in designing a program, we frequently need to decide which modules should be implemented as procedures. The decision should be based on whether the overall program will be easier to understand as a result. (There are other factors that can affect this decision, but for now this is the simplest heuristic [strategy] to use.)

If a module is only a single line, it is probably best to write it directly in the program. Turning it into a procedure would only complicate the overall program, which defeats the purpose of using subprograms. On the other hand, if a module is many lines long, it will be easier to understand the program if the module is turned into a procedure.

Keep in mind that whether you choose to code a module as a procedure or not will merely affect the readability of the program, and may make it more or less convenient to change the program later. However, your choice will not affect the correct functioning of the program.

Writing Modules as Procedures

Turning a module into a procedure is quite simple to do in Pascal. Basically, a procedure looks like a program except that the PROGRAM heading is replaced by a PROCEDURE heading, and the last END in the procedure has a semicolon following it instead of a period.

A PROGRAM heading names a program and lists the files from which it gets input and to which it sends output. Similarly, a PROCEDURE heading names a procedure and lists the variables (parameters) that serve as its input and output.

Let's look at a program using procedures. We use Program Activity from Chapter 4 as our example. Here is its design.

Activity   *Level 0*

```
Get temperature
Print activity
```

Get Temperature   *Level 1*

```
Prompt for temperature value input
Read Temperature
```

Print Activity

```
IF Temperature > 85
   THEN
      Write 'swimming'
   ELSE IF Temperature > 70
      THEN
         Write 'tennis'
   ELSE IF Temperature > 32
      THEN
          Write 'golf'
   ELSE IF Temperature > 0
      THEN
         Write 'skiing'
   ELSE
      Write 'dancing'
```

If we write the two Level 1 modules as procedures, the body of the main program will be

```
BEGIN (* Activity *)
  Get_Temp(Temperature);
  Print_Activity(Temperature)
END.  (* Activity *)
```

Notice that this is similar to the main module of our top-down design. It contains two **procedure calls,** one to a procedure named Get_Temp, and another to a procedure named Print_Activity. Each of these procedure calls has one parameter (Temperature).

Most of this code should look familiar to you, but look carefully at the PROCEDURE heading and the last END.

```
PROCEDURE Get_Temp (VAR Temp:                    (* Procedure *)
                        Integer);                (* heading   *)

BEGIN (* Get_Temp *)
  Writeln('Enter the outside temperature:');-Presently Temp is junk
  Readln(Temp);
  Writeln('The current temperature is ', Temp:1);
END;  (* Get_Temp *)
```

This segment is the **procedure declaration.** Notice that the last END is followed by a semicolon. Since this is a declaration, it will appear in the declaration section of the program. Even though a procedure looks a lot like a program, it is important to remember that only a program ends with a period.

Take a look at the PROCEDURE heading. Just like any other identifier in Pascal, the name of a procedure is not allowed to include blanks. After the name you'll see some code that looks like a variable declaration between parentheses. This is a **parameter declaration.** Procedure Get_Temp declares one parameter, called Temp, of type Integer. Notice that the name of the parameter in the heading does not have to be the same as the parameter in the call to the procedure. We'll see why later, but first, let's put the procedures and the program body together to form a complete program.

```
PROGRAM Activity (Input, Output);

(* This program outputs an appropriate activity for a given *)
(* temperature                                              *)

VAR
  Temperature:         (* The outside temperature *)
    Integer;

(* ********************************************************************** )

PROCEDURE Get_Temp (VAR Temp:                    (* Procedure heading *)
                        Integer);

(* This procedure prompts for a temperature to be entered, reads the  *)
(* input value, and echo-prints it before returning it to the program *)

BEGIN (* Get_Temp *)
  Writeln('Enter the outside temperature:');
  Readln(Temp);
  Writeln('The current temperature is ', Temp:1)
END;  (* Get_Temp *)

(* ********************************************************************** )

PROCEDURE Print_Activity (VAR Temp:              (* Procedure heading *)
                              Integer);
```

```
(* This procedure takes a temperature from the program and prints   *)
(* a message indicating an appropriate activity for the temperature *)

BEGIN (* Print_Activity *)
  Write('The recommended activity is ');
  IF Temp > 85
    THEN
      Writeln('swimming.')
    ELSE IF Temp > 70
      THEN
        Writeln ('tennis.')
    ELSE IF Temp > 32
      THEN
        Writeln ('golf.')
    ELSE IF Temp  > 0
      THEN
        Writeln('skiing.')
    ELSE
      Writeln('dancing.')
END;  (* Print_Activity *)

(**********************************************************************)


BEGIN (* Activity *)
  Get_Temp(Temperature);                        (* Procedure call *)
  Print_Activity(Temperature)                   (* Procedure call *)
END.  (* Activity *)
```

Since Program Activity is a simple program to begin with, it may seem more complicated with its modules written as procedures. However, it is clear that it much more closely resembles our top-down design; this is especially true of the main program. If you handed this code to someone, they could look at the main program and immediately tell you what it does—it gets a temperature and prints an activity. If you asked them to be more specific, they could then look up the declaration of each procedure. They are able to begin with a top-level view of the program, and then study the lower level modules as necessary, without having to read the entire program or look at a module structure chart. As our programs grow to include many modules nested several levels deep, the ability to read a program in the same manner as a top-down design will greatly aid in the development and debugging process.

An Overview of User-Defined Procedures

Now that we've seen an example of how a program is written with procedures, let's look briefly and informally at some of the more important points of procedure construction and use.

Procedures and Blocks

Remember that a program was defined in Chapter 2 as a PROGRAM heading and a block. We can expand the definition of a block to include procedures. This is an expanded syntax template for a block:

> constant definitions
> variable declarations
> . procedure declarations
> compound statement

By definition, a block can contain procedures. A procedure is defined as a PROCEDURE heading and a block. Therefore, we can declare a procedure within a procedure. . . . This shows that even very complicated top-down designs can be coded without losing the structure of the problem. It also shows that constants and variables can be declared locally within a procedure. We'll return to the topic of local variables later in this chapter.

Flow of Control in Procedure Calls

Notice that procedures are declared after the variable declarations for the main program, but before the main program itself. During compilation, the procedures and the program are translated in the order in which they physically appear. When the program is executed, however, control is transferred to the first statement in the main program, and the program proceeds in logical sequence. When the name of a procedure is encountered as a statement, logical control is passed to the first statement in the procedure body. The statements in the procedure are executed in logical order. After the last one is executed, control returns to the point immediately following the call. Because procedure calls alter the logical order of execution, procedures are considered to be control structures. Figure 6-1 illustrates this physical versus logical ordering of procedures.

Although the statements in the procedures appear first in the program, execution actually begins with the first statement in the main program (the call to Get_Temp). When Get_Temp is called, control passes to its first statement and subsequent statements in the procedure. After the last statement in Get_Temp is executed, control returns to the main program at the point following the call (which happens to be another call—to Print_Activity in this case).

The logical order of the Program Activity with procedures is identical to the logical order of our original version, but the structure of the top-down design is maintained in the coding of the second version.

Parameters

Parameters represent the way the main program and procedures (or procedures and other procedures) communicate. Parameters enable the main program to input (pass)

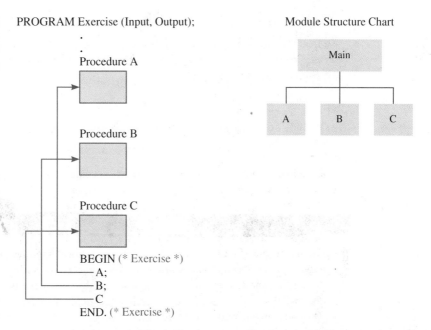

Figure 6-1
*Physical Versus
Logical Order of
Procedures*

values to a procedure to use in its processing, and the procedure to output (return) results to the program. The parameters in the program's call to a procedure are the **actual parameters.** The parameters listed in the procedure heading are the **formal parameters.**

Formal Parameter   A variable declared in a procedure heading.

Actual Parameter   A variable listed in a call to a procedure.

In Program Activity, the actual parameters are named Temperature, and the formal parameter in each procedure is named Temp. Note that all are of type Integer. The main program tells the procedure Get_Temp where to leave the temperature by giving it the location (the variable Temperature) when it turns control over to the procedure in the procedure call. When Print_Activity is called, the main program tells the procedure where to get the value to work with (from the variable Temperature).

In a sense, the formal parameter Temp is just a convenient placeholder in the procedure declaration. When the procedure is called with Temperature as its actual parameter, all the references to Temp in the procedure will *actually* be made to Temperature (hence the name actual parameter). If the procedure were to be called again with a different variable as an actual parameter, all the references to Temp would actually refer to that other variable until the procedure returned control to the main program.

Because actual and formal parameters can have different names, we can call a procedure with different actual parameters. Suppose we wanted to change Program Activity to print an activity for both the indoor and outdoor temperatures. We could define integer variables in the main program called Indoor_Temp and Outdoor_Temp, then write the body of the program as:

```
BEGIN (* Activity *)
  Get_Temp(Indoor_Temp);
  Print_Activity(Indoor_Temp);
  Get_Temp(Outdoor_Temp);
  Print_Activity(Outdoor_Temp)
END.  (* Activity *)
```

The formal parameter Temp would receive values from, or pass values to, either Indoor_Temp or Outdoor_Temp.

This brings up a second major reason for using procedures. Once a subprogram has been declared, it can be called from many places in the program (or from other subprograms). Use of multiple calls can save a great deal of effort in coding many problem solutions. If there is a task that must be done in more than one place in a program, we can avoid repetitive coding by writing it as a procedure and then calling it wherever we need it. Another example that illustrates this use of procedures appears in the Problem-Solving Case Study at the end of this chapter.

If more than one parameter is passed to a procedure, the formal and actual parameters are matched by their relative positions in the two parameter lists. For example, if you want to print the hour with the temperature, you might rewrite the heading of procedure Print_Activity as

```
PROCEDURE Print_Activity (VAR Temp,
                               Hour:
                                    Integer);
```

and the call to the procedure would then be

```
Print_Activity(Temperature, Time);
```

The main program passes the value in the first actual parameter, Temperature, to Temp because Temp is the first formal parameter. Likewise, the second actual parameter, Time, is passed to the second formal parameter, Hour.

An Analogy

Before we formally define all the terms we have been using, let's look at an analogy from daily life. You're at the local discount catalog showroom to buy a Father's Day present. To place your order, you fill out an order form. The form has places to write in the quantity of each item and its catalog number, and places where the order clerk will fill in the prices. You write down what you want and hand the form to the clerk. You wait for the clerk to check whether the items are available and calculate the cost. She returns the form, and you see that the items are in stock and the price is $48.50. You pay the clerk and go on about your business.

This illustrates how procedure calls work. The clerk is like a procedure. You, acting as the main program, have her do some work for you. You give her some information: the item numbers and quantities. These are her input parameters. You wait until she returns some information to you: the availability of the items and their prices. These are the clerk's output parameters. The clerk does this task all day long with different input values. Each order activates the same process. The shopper waits until the clerk returns information based on the specific input.

The form is analogous to the actual parameters of a procedure call. The spaces on the form represent variables in the main program. When you hand the form to the clerk, some of the places contain information and some are empty. The clerk holds the form while doing her job so she can write information in the blank spaces. (She could also change what you have written, but in this case she doesn't.)

When a program calls a procedure, it allows the procedure to access and change the variables in the actual parameter list. When the procedure finishes, the program continues, making use of whatever new information the procedure left in the variables.

The formal parameter list is the set of shorthand or slang terms the clerk uses to describe the spaces on the order form. For example, she may think in terms of "units," "codes," and "receipts." These are her terms (formal parameters) for what the order form calls "quantity," "catalog number," and "price" (the actual parameters). But she doesn't waste time reading the names on the form every time; she knows that the first item is the units (quantity), the second is the code (catalog number), and so on. In other words, she looks only at the position of each space on the form. This is how actual parameters are matched to formal parameters: by their relative positions in the two parameter lists.

Procedure Syntax and Semantics

Procedure Call (Invocation)

To call (or **invoke**) a procedure, we use its name as a statement, with the actual parameters in parentheses following the name. A **procedure call** in a program results in the execution of the body of the called procedure. This is the syntax template of a procedure call:

---

procedure name (variable identifier , variable identifier . . .)

Procedure Call   A statement that transfers control to a procedure. In Pascal, this statement is the name of the procedure, followed by a list of actual parameters.

When the last END in a procedure is encountered, control then returns to the point from which the procedure was called. This is called the **return.** There should be a return for every call that is executed in a program.

Procedure Declaration

A *procedure* is defined as a heading and a block. The heading has the following form:

> **PROCEDURE** identifier parameter list;

The optional parameter list has the form:

> (**VAR** identifier, identifier . . . : type;
>   **VAR** identifier, identifier . . . : type
>
>   ⋮
>
>)

This is a simplified version of the complete syntax template for a procedure heading. We will expand it in Chapter 7. The parameter list is a list of the formal parameters. Within the body of the procedure, these parameters are treated like any other variable. Notice that the type of each parameter is given in the parameter list.

These formal parameters are called **variable,** or **VAR, parameters** because the values of the actual parameters may be changed by the procedure. This is also why they are similar in appearance to a VAR declaration in the main program.

Variable (VAR) Parameter   A formal parameter that receives the location of a variable.

Because a procedure contains a block, other variables that are not parameters may be declared in a variable declaration section. These variables are discussed shortly.

Since Pascal requires that we define a procedure before we use it, procedures must physically appear in the program before the place where they are called. If one procedure is called by another, the procedure being called must be defined before the one that calls it. We don't have to declare Read and Write because Pascal automatically defines them for every program. Appendix B lists all the identifiers that are predefined in Pascal, including predefined procedures.

Figure 6-2   *The Temporary Nature of Parameter Matching in a Procedure Call*

When flow of control is in program Activity,
Temperature can be accessed as shown by the arrows.

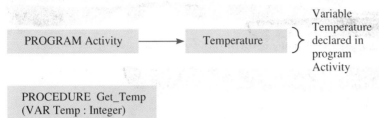

When flow of control is in procedure Get_Temp, the procedure can
access the variable indicated by the arrows.

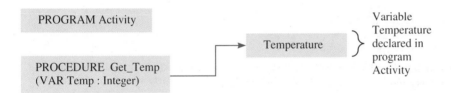

Parameters

When a procedure is executed, it uses the actual parameters given to it in the call. How is this done? Remember that a variable identifier is assigned a location in memory. When a procedure is invoked, it is a list of the *locations* of the actual parameters, not their values, that are passed to the procedure. These are passed in the order in which they appear in the actual parameter list. There is only one copy of the information—it is used by both the program and the procedure. When the procedure is called, the actual and formal parameters become synonyms for the same locations in memory. Whatever value is left by the procedure in one of those locations is the value that will be found there by the program. Therefore, you must be careful using the formal parameters since any change made to them will affect the actual parameters in the main program.

When the procedure returns control to the program, the link between the actual and formal parameters is broken. They are synonymous only during a particular call to the procedure. The only evidence that a match-up between the two parameter lists ever occurred is that some of the values in the actual parameters may have changed (see Figure 6-2).

Each actual parameter must have the same data type as the formal parameter in the same position. Also, there must be the same number of actual parameters in a call as there are formal parameters in the procedure heading. If the matched parameters are not of the same data type, a compiler error message such as TYPE MISMATCH will occur. Notice how each formal parameter in the following example is matched to the actual parameter in the same position (the data type of each of the actual parameters is what you would assume from its name):

PROCEDURE Show_Match(VAR Num1:Real; VAR Num2: Integer; VAR Letter: Char);

Show_Match(RealVariable,   Integer_Variable,   Char_Variable)

It is up to the programmer to make sure that the formal and actual parameter lists match up semantically as well as syntactically. For example, suppose we had written the Indoor/Outdoor modification to Program Activity as follows.

```
BEGIN (* Activity *)
  Get_Temp(Indoor_Temp);
  Print_Activity(Indoor_Temp);
  Get_Temp(Outdoor_Temp);
  Print_Activity(Indoor_Temp)        (* Wrong actual parameter *)
END.  (* Activity *)
```

The parameter list in the last procedure call matches the formal parameter list in its number and type of parameters, so no syntax error would be signaled. However, the output would be erroneous because the actual parameter is the wrong temperature value. Similarly, if a procedure has two formal parameters of the same data type, we must be careful that the actual parameters are in the right order. If they are in the wrong order, no syntax error will result, but the answers will be wrong.

Local Variables

Because a procedure contains a block, it can include variable declarations within the procedure itself. These variables are **local variables** because they are accessible only within the block in which they are declared. As far as the calling program is concerned, they don't exist. If you tried to print the contents of a local variable from the main program, a compile time error such as UNKNOWN IDENTIFIER would occur.

Local Variable   A variable declared within a procedure that is not accessible outside of that procedure.

In contrast, variables declared in the main program are called global variables. We will return to the topic of global variables in Chapter 7.

Local variables are destroyed when the procedure returns; therefore, every time the procedure is called, its local variables start out with their values undefined. Since every call to a procedure is independent of every other call to that same procedure, the local variables must be initialized within the procedure itself.

Because the values of local variables are destroyed when the procedure returns, they cannot be used to store values between calls to a procedure. If a procedure calculates a value that is to be used in a later call to the same procedure, the value must be passed back to the calling program through a parameter. The next time the procedure is called, the program can pass that value back to the procedure. The main program's data storage area is the only safe place to store values between procedure calls.

The following code segment illustrates each of the parts of the procedure declaration and calling mechanism that we have discussed.

```
PROGRAM Terms (Input, Output);              (* Program parameters--files *)

VAR                                             (* Global variables *)
  Global1,
  Global2:
    Integer;

  Global3:
    Real;

                                            (* Procedure declaration with *)
PROCEDURE One (VAR Position1,               (* three formal parameters    *)
                   Position2:
                       Integer;
               VAR Position3:
                   Real);

VAR                                                 (* Local variables *)
  Local1,
  Local2:
    Integer;

BEGIN    (* One *)
  .                                         (* Body of procedure One *)
  .
END;     (* One *)

BEGIN    (* Terms *)
  .                                         (* Body of Program Terms *)
  .
  One(Global1, Global2, Global3);           (* Procedure call to One with *)
  .                                         (* three actual parameters    *)
  .
END.     (* Terms *)
```

Matters of Style

Naming Procedures

When you choose a name for a procedure, keep in mind how calls to it will look. A call is written as a statement; therefore, it should sound like it is doing something. For this reason, it is a good idea to choose a name that is a verb or has a verb as part of it. For example, the statement

```
Activity(Temperature)
```

has no verb to explain its use. Adding the verb *Print* makes the name sound like an action:

```
Print_Activity(Temperature)
```

When you are picking a name for a procedure, write down sample calls with different names until you come up with one that tells someone reading the program exactly what the procedure does.

Designing Procedures

We've looked at some examples of procedures, and covered the formal definition of a procedure. But how do we design procedures? First, we need to be more specific about what procedures do. We've said that they allow us to organize our programs more like our top-down designs, but what really is the advantage of doing that?

The body of a procedure is like any other segment of code, except that it is contained in a separate block within the program. Isolating a segment of code in a separate block means that its implementation details can be "hidden" from view. As long as you know how to call a procedure and what its function is, you can use it without knowing how it actually works. For example, you don't know how the code for Readln is written (its implementation is hidden from view), yet you can still use it effectively.

The specification of what a procedure does and how it is called defines its **interface** (see Figure 6-3). By hiding a module implementation, or **encapsulating** the module, we can make changes to it without changing the main program, as long as the interface remains the same. For example, you might rewrite the body of a procedure using a more efficient algorithm.

Interface A connecting link at a shared boundary that permits independent systems to meet and act on or communicate with each other. The formal definition of the function of a subprogram and the mechanism for communicating with it.

Encapsulation Hiding a module implementation in a separate block with a formally specified interface.

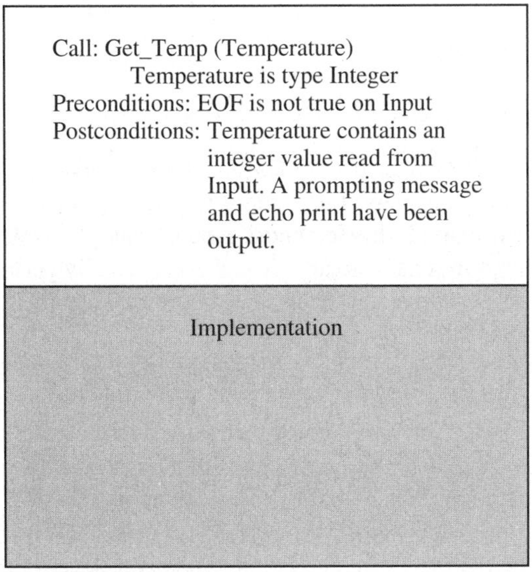

Figure 6-3
*Procedure Interface
(Visible) and Imple-
mentation (Hidden)*

Call: Get_Temp (Temperature)
    Temperature is type Integer
Preconditions: EOF is not true on Input
Postconditions: Temperature contains an
    integer value read from
    Input. A prompting message
    and echo print have been
    output.

Implementation

Encapsulation is what we do in the top-down design process when we postpone the solution of a difficult subproblem. We write down its function, what information it takes and what it returns, and then write the rest of our design as if the subproblem had already been solved. We could hand this interface specification to someone else, and they could develop a procedure for us that solves the subproblem. We needn't be concerned about how it works, as long as it conforms to the interface specification. Interfaces and encapsulation are the basis for **team programming,** in which a group of programmers work together to solve a large problem.

Thus, designing a procedure can (and should) be divided into two tasks: designing the interface and designing the implementation. We already know how to design an implementation—it is merely a segment of code that corresponds to an algorithm. To design the interface, we must define the function of the subprogram and the mechanism for communicating with it.

You already know how to specify formally the function of a subprogram. Since a procedure corresponds to a module, its function is defined by the preconditions and postconditions of the module. All that remains is to define the mechanism for communicating with the procedure. To do this, make a list of the following items:

1. Values that the procedure *receives* from the main program.
2. Values the procedure produces and *returns* to the main program.
3. Values the program has that the procedure changes (*receives* and *returns*).

Decide which identifiers inside the module reference the values in this list. These identifiers become the variables in the formal parameter list for the procedure. The formal parameters are then declared in the procedure heading. All other variables that the procedure needs are local and must be declared in the VAR section of the procedure itself. This process may be repeated for all the modules at each level.

*S*oftware Engineering Tip

Conceptual Versus Physical Hiding of a Procedure Implementation

In Pascal, the encapsulation of an implementation is purely conceptual. If you want to know how a procedure is implemented, you can always look at its definition. Some languages such as Ada and Modula-2, however, actually permit procedure implementations to be written separately from the program. Thus their implementation can be physically hidden from view.

One advantage of physical hiding is that it helps the programmer avoid the temptation to take advantage of any unusual features of a procedure's implementation. For example, suppose we were changing Program Activity to read a temperature and output an activity repeatedly. Knowing that procedure Get_Temp doesn't perform range checking on the input value, we might be tempted to use -MaxInt as a sentinel for the loop.

```
BEGIN (* Activity *)
   Get_Temp(Temperature);
   WHILE Temperature > -MaxInt DO
     BEGIN
       Print_Activity(Temperature);
       Get_Temp(Temperature)
     END
END.  (* Activity *)
```

But later, we might try to improve Get_Temp so that it checks for a valid temperature range (as it should).

```
PROCEDURE Get_Temp (VAR Temp:
                    Integer);

(* This procedure prompts for a temperature to be entered, reads the   *)
(* input value, checks to be sure it is in a valid temperature range,   *)
(* and echo-prints it before returning it to the program. It is        *)
(* assumed that the CRT unit is being used by the program and that     *)
(* CheckEOF has been set to True                                       *)
(*                                                                     *)
(* Precondition: Input is not at EOF                                   *)
(* Postconditions: Temp contains a temperature value in a valid range  *)
(*                 The reading pointer for Input has advanced          *)
(*                 If no valid data is encountered before EOF, 0 is    *)
(*                   used and an error message is printed              *)
(*                 A prompting message has been printed                *)
(*                 The temperature has been printed                    *)
(*                 Error messages and additional prompts are printed   *)
(*                   in response to invalid data                       *)
```

```
BEGIN (* Get_Temp *)
  Writeln('Enter the outside temperature:');
  Readln(Temp);                               (* Input the temperature *)
  WHILE (Temp < -40) OR (Temp > 130)          (* Check for valid range *)
    BEGIN
      IF NOT EOF
        THEN
          BEGIN
            Writeln(Temp:1, ' degrees is not in the valid ',
                    'temperature range.');
            Writeln('Enter the outside temperature:');    (* Try again *)
            Readln(Temp)
          END
        ELSE
          BEGIN
            Writeln('EOF was reached before a valid temperature ',
                    'was input: zero is substituted.');
            Temp := 0
          END
    END;
  Writeln('The current temperature is ', Temp:1)
END;  (* Get_Temp *)
```

Unfortunately, if we make this improvement, the program will be stuck in an infinite loop because Get_Temp won't let us enter the sentinel value. If the implementation of Get_Temp had been physically hidden, we would not have known about its unusual feature, and we would have changed the main program in a way that would be unaffected by the improvement to Get_Temp.

```
USES CRT;
BEGIN (* Activity *)
  CheckEOF : = True;
  WHILE NOT EOF DO
    BEGIN
      Get_Temp(Temperature);
      Print_Activity(Temperature)
    END
END.  (* Activity *)
```

In Pascal, we must compensate for the lack of physical implementation hiding by conscientiously avoiding code that depends on the internal workings of a procedure.

PROBLEM-SOLVING CASE STUDY

Comparison of Department-Store Sales

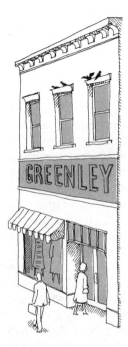

Problem: A new regional sales manager for the Greenley Department Stores has just come into town. She wants to see a monthly, department-by-department comparison in the form of bar graphs of the two Greenley stores in town. The daily sales for each department are kept on each store's accounting files. Data on each store is stored in the following form.

```
Department ID number
Number of business days for the department
Daily sales for day 1
Daily sales for day 2

   .

   .

Daily sales for last day in period
Department ID number
Number of business days for the department
Daily sales for day 1

   .

   .
```

The bar graph to be printed is of the following form.

```
Bar Graph Comparing Departments of Store#1 and Store#2

Store  Sales in 1,000s of dollars

  #    0         5        10        15        20        25
       |.........|.........|.........|.........|.........|
       Dept 1030
  1    **********************
       Dept 1030
  2    ****************************************
       
       Dept 1210
  1    ************************************************
       Dept 1210
  2    ****************************************
       
       Dept 2040
  1    **********************************************
       Dept 2040
  2    ******************************
```

As you can see from the bar graph, each star represents $500.00 in sales. No stars are printed if a department's sales are less than or equal to $250.00.

Input: Two data files (Store1, Store2), each containing

DeptID — department ID number (Integer)
NumDays — number of business days (Integer)
Sales — daily sales (Real)

repeated for each department.

Output: Bar graph showing total sales for each department.

Discussion: Reading the input data from both files is straightforward. We need to reset the files (let's call them Store1 and Store2) and read a department ID number, the number of business days, and the following daily sales for that department. After processing each department, we can read the data for the next department, continuing until we run out of departments (EOF is encountered). Since the process is the same for reading Store1 and Store2, we can use one procedure for reading both files. All we have to do is pass the file name as a parameter to the procedure. We want total sales for each department, so this procedure will have to sum the daily sales for a department as they are read. A procedure can be used to print the output heading. Another procedure can be used to print out each department's sales for the month in graphic form.

There will be three loops in this program, one in the main program, one in the procedure that gets the data, and another in the procedure that prints the bar graph. The loop for the main program tests for EOF on *both* Store1 and Store2. One graph for each store must be printed for each iteration of this loop.

The loop for the Get_Data procedure requires an iteration counter that ranges from 1 to the number of days for the department. Also, a summing operation is needed to total the sales for the period.

At first glance it might seem that the loop for the Print_Data procedure is like any other counting loop, but let's look at how we would do this process by hand. Suppose we wanted to print a bar for the value 1850. We would first make sure the number was greater than 250, then print a star and subtract 500 from the original value. We would check again to see if the new value was greater than 250, then print a star and subtract 500. This process would repeat until the resulting value was less than or equal to 250. Thus, the loop requires a counter that is decremented by 500 for each iteration, with a termination value of 250 or less. A star is printed for each iteration of the loop.

Procedure Print_Header does not receive any values from the program nor does it return any. Thus, its formal parameter list is empty.

Procedure Get_Data receives the data file from the program, and returns it after having read some values. The procedure returns the values of the department ID and its sales for the month to the program. Thus, Get_Data has three formal parameters: the data file, department ID, and department sales.

Procedure Print_Data must receive the department ID, store number, and department sales from the program to print the bar graph for an input record. Therefore, the procedure has those three values as its formal parameters.

PROBLEM-SOLVING CASE STUDY *cont'd.*

Assumptions: Each file is in order by department ID. The same departments are in each store. There is one piece of data per line of input.

Main   *Level 0*

> Print Header
> WHILE NOT EOF on file Store1 AND NOT EOF on file Store2
>   Get Data for a Store1 department
>   Print Data for the Store1 department
>   Get Data for a Store2 department
>   Print Data for the Store2 department

Print Header (No parameters)   *Level 1*

> Print chart title
> Print heading
> Print bar graph scale

Get Data (Receives/Returns: Data File; Returns: Dept ID, Dept Sales)

> Get Dept ID from Data File
> Get Num Days from Data File
> Initialize Dept Sales to 0
> Initialize Days (loop control variable) to 1
> WHILE Days is less than or equal to Num Days
>   Get Sales from Data File
>   Add Sales to Dept Sales
>   Increment Days

Print Data (Receives: Dept ID, Store Num, Dept Sales)

> Print Dept ID
> Print Store Num
> WHILE Dept Sales are greater than 250
>   Print a *
>   Subtract 500 from Dept Sales
> Go to next line (Writeln)

PROBLEM-SOLVING CASE STUDY *cont'd.*

To develop this top-down design, we had to make several passes through the design process, and several mistakes had to be fixed to arrive at the design you see here. Don't get discouraged if you don't have a perfect top-down design on the first try every time.

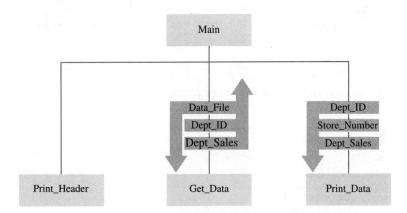

The following Pascal program parallels our design. Note that we have written the preconditions and postconditions of each procedure as comments in the program. This helps to document the interface definition of the procedures.

```pascal
PROGRAM Graph (Store1, Store2, Output);

(* This program generates bar graphs of monthly sales by department for *)
(* two Greenley department stores, permitting department-by-department  *)
(* comparison of sales *)

VAR
  Store_Num,    (* Store ID number              *)
  ID:           (* Department ID number         *)
    Integer;
  Sales1,       (* Department sales for store 1 *)
  Sales2:       (* Department sales for store 2 *)
    Real;
  Store1,       (* Accounting file for store 1  *)
  Store2:       (* Accounting file for store 2  *)
    Text;

(* ******************************************************************** *)
```

PROBLEM-SOLVING CASE STUDY cont'd.

```
PROCEDURE Print_Header;

(* This procedure prints the title for the bar chart, a heading, and  *)
(* the numeric scale for the chart.  The scale uses one mark per $500  *)
(*                                                                     *)
(* Preconditions: None                                                 *)
(* Postconditions: The heading for the bar chart has been printed      *)

BEGIN (* Print_Header *)
  Writeln('Bar Graph Comparing Departments of Store#1 and Store#2');
  Writeln;
  Writeln('Store  Sales in 1,000s of dollars');
  Writeln('  #    0         5        10        15        20        25');
  Writeln('       |.........|.........|.........|.........|.........|')
END;  (* Print_Header *)


(*********************************************************************)


PROCEDURE Get_Data (VAR Data_File:      (* Input accounting file       *)
                        Text;
                    VAR Dept_ID:         (* Department number           *)
                        Integer;
                    VAR Dept_Sales:      (* Department's monthly sales  *)
                        Real);

(* This procedure takes an input accounting file as a parameter, reads *)
(* the department ID number and number of days of sales from that      *)
(* file, then reads one sales figure for each of those days, computing *)
(* a total sales figure for the month.  This figure is returned in     *)
(* Dept_Sales  *)

(* Preconditions:  The data file contains a department ID, number of   *)
(*                 days, and one sales figure for each day             *)
(* Postconditions: The data file pointer has advanced Numdays+2 lines  *)
(*                 Dept_ID contains the department ID number           *)
(*                 Dept_Sales contains the sum of the sales values for  *)
(*                 the department, assuming correct data formatting     *)

VAR
  Num_Days,          (* Number of business days in the month         *)
  Day:               (* Loop control variable for reading daily sales *)
    Integer;
  Sale:              (* One day's sales for the department           *)
    Real;
```

PROBLEM-SOLVING CASE STUDY cont'd.

```
BEGIN  (* Get_Data *)
  Readln(Data_File, Dept_ID, Num_Days);    (* Get ID and number of days *)
  Dept_Sales := 0.0;                          (* Initialize process *)
  Day := 1;                        (* Initialize loop control variable *)
  WHILE Day <= Num_Days DO
    BEGIN
      Readln(Data_File, Sale);                   ·   (* Update process *)
      Dept_Sales := Dept_Sales + Sale;
      Day := Day + 1                (* Update loop control variable *)
    END
END;  (* Get_Data *)

(* ********************************************************************* *)

PROCEDURE Print_Data (VAR Dept_ID,          (* Department ID number      *)
                          Store_Num:        (* Store number              *)
                          Integer;
                      VAR Dept_Sales:       (* Total sales for the dept. *)
                          Real);

(* This procedure prints the department ID number, the store number,   *)
(* and a bar graph of the sales for the department.  The bar graph     *)
(* is printed at a scale of one mark per $500.                         *)
(*                                                                     *)
(* Preconditions:  Store_Num contains a valid store number            *)
(*                 Dept_Sales contains a value in the range of 0 to    *)
(*                 25000                                               *)
(*                 Dept_ID contains a valid department number          *)
(* Postconditions: A line of the bar chart is printed, with one * for  *)
(*                 each $500 in sales, with fractions over $250         *)
(*                 rounded up                                           *)
(*                 No stars are printed for sales <= $250              *)

BEGIN  (* Print_Data *)
  Writeln('     Dept ', Dept_ID:1);                        (* Print ID *)
  Write(Store_Num:3, ' ':4);                    (* Print store number *)
  WHILE Dept_Sales > 250 DO
    BEGIN
      Write('*');                        (* Print '*' for each $500 *)
      Dept_Sales := Dept_Sales - 500    (* Update loop control variable *)
    END;
  Writeln                                     (* Go to a new line *)
END;  (* Print_Data *)

(* ********************************************************************* *)
```

PROBLEM-SOLVING CASE STUDY cont'd.

```
BEGIN (* Graph *)
  Assign(Store1, 'STORE1.DAT');
  Assign(Store2, 'STORE2.DAT');
  Reset(Store1);
  Reset(Store2);
  Print_Header;
  WHILE NOT EOF(Store1) and NOT EOF(Store2) DO         (* For each dept *)
    BEGIN
      Writeln;
      Store_Num := 1;                                  (* Process Store 1 *)
      Get_Data(Store1, ID, Sales1);
      Print_Data(ID, Store_Num, Sales1);
      Store_Num := 2;                                  (* Process Store 2 *)
      Get_Data(Store2, ID, Sales2);
      Print_Data(ID, Store_Num, Sales2)
    END;
  Close(Store1);
  Close(Store2)
END.   (* Graph *)
```

Testing: This program should be tested with data files that contain the same number of data sets for both stores, and with data files that contain different numbers of data sets for both stores. The case where one or both of the files are empty should be tested. The test data should include a set that generates a monthly sales figure of $0.00 and one that generates more than $25,000 in sales. The program should also be tested to see what it does with negative days, negative sales, and mismatched department IDs. This series of tests reveals that, for this program to work correctly for the department-store employees who will be using it, we should add several checks for invalid data.

The main program of Graph reflects not only our top-down design, but calls both Get_Data and Print_Data twice. The result is a program that is shorter and more readable than one in which the code for each procedure is repeated.

Testing and Debugging

The combination of the formal parameters defined in a procedure, and the actual parameters that are passed to the procedure by the main program, constitute the interface between the procedure and the program. Errors that occur with the use of procedures are usually due to an incorrect interface between the main program and a procedure (or between two procedures, in the case of one procedure calling another).

One source of errors is mismatched actual and formal parameter lists. The Pascal compiler will ensure that the lists have the same number of parameters and that they match in type. It's the programmer's responsibility, however, to verify that each actual parameter list contains the correct variables. This is a matter of comparing the formal parameter definition to the actual parameter list in every call to the procedure. This job is much easier if you give each formal parameter a distinct name and describe its function in a comment. You can avoid mistakes in writing an actual parameter list by using descriptive variable names in the main program because they clearly state exactly what information is being passed to a procedure.

Another source of error is the failure to ensure that the preconditions for a module are met before it is called. For example, if a procedure assumes that the input file is not at EOF when it is called, then the program must ensure that this is true before making the call to the procedure. If a procedure behaves incorrectly, review its preconditions, then trace the program execution up to the point of the call to verify them. You can waste a lot of time trying to locate a bug in a correct procedure when the error is really in the part of the program prior to the call.

If the parameters match and the preconditions are correctly established, then the source of the error is most likely in the procedure itself. Trace the procedure to verify that it transforms the preconditions into the proper postconditions. Check that all local variables are initialized properly. Only the parameters that are supposed to return data to the program should be changed. (Scan the left side of assignment expressions and Read and Readln statements for parameter names that aren't supposed to change—those designated only for receiving data from the program.)

One helpful technique to use while debugging a procedure is to use the Turbo debugger Watch window to view the values of the parameters immediately before and after calls to the procedure. It is also sometimes helpful to watch the values of all local variables at the end of the procedure. Up to now, we've used F8 to trace our programs because it skips over procedure calls (including some invisible calls that the compiler inserts to initialize any units we are using). To trace into a procedure, you should use F7 instead. Then, if you set breakpoints prior to the call and at the procedure's end, and add the actual parameters and local variables to the Watch window, you will get a "snapshot" of the procedure (a picture of its status at a particular moment in time) at its two most critical points.

To test a procedure thoroughly, the input data must be arranged so that each precondition is pushed to its limits, then the postconditions must be verified. For example, if a procedure requires a parameter to be within a certain range, try calling the procedure with values within and outside that range, and at its extremes.

Testing a procedure also involves trying to arrange the data to violate its preconditions. If the preconditions can be violated, then errors that appear to be in the procedure being tested, but are really in the program or in another procedure, may crop up. For example, procedure Print_Data in Program Graph assumes that a department's sales will not exceed $25,000. If a figure of $250,000 is entered by mistake, the program will not check this before the call, and the procedure will thus try to print a row of 500 stars. When this happens, you may assume that Print_Data has gone haywire, but it's the program's fault for not checking the validity of the data. (This test should be performed in procedure Get_Data.) Thus, a side effect of one procedure can multiply and give the appearance of bugs elsewhere in a program. We take a closer look at side effects in the next chapter.

Testing and Debugging Hints

1. Follow the documentation guidelines carefully when writing procedures (see Appendix G). As your programs become more complex, it becomes increasingly important to adhere to documentation and formatting standards. Label the main BEGIN-END pair of each procedure with the procedure name. Even if the procedure name seems to define the process being done, describe that process in comments. Use comments to explain the purposes of all the formal parameters and local variables in a procedure.
2. Be sure to put a semicolon after the procedure heading. Also ensure that the last END in the procedure has a semicolon—not a period—after it.
3. Be sure the formal parameter list gives the type of each parameter.
4. Be sure the actual parameter lists of all calls to the procedure match the formal parameter list in number and order of items and types of variables.
5. Be sure to repeat the keyword VAR for each type of formal parameter (see the syntax template). In the next chapter we discuss what happens if you omit the keyword VAR in a formal parameter list.

Summary

Pascal allows programs to be written in functional modules. The structure of a program can therefore parallel its top-down design even when the program is complicated. To make your main program look exactly like Level 0 of your top-down design, simply write each functional module as a procedure. The main program then executes the procedures in logical sequence.

Communication between the calling program and the procedure is handled through the use of two lists of identifiers: the formal parameter list (which includes the type of each identifier) in the PROCEDURE heading, and the actual parameter list in the calling statement. The identifiers in these lists must agree in number, position, and type.

Part of the top-down design process involves determining what data must be received by the lower-level module and what information must be returned from it. This list of values, together with the preconditions and postconditions of a module, define its interface. The list of values becomes the formal parameter list, and the module name becomes the name of the procedure. A call to the procedure is accomplished by writing the procedure's name as a statement, with the appropriate actual parameters enclosed in parentheses.

In addition to having variables defined in its formal parameter list, a procedure may have local variables declared within it. These variables are accessible only within the block in which they are declared. Local variables must be initialized each time the procedure containing them is called because their values are destroyed when the procedure returns.

Procedures may be called from more than one place in a program and from other procedures. The positional matching mechanism allows the use of different variables as actual parameters to the same procedure. Multiple calls to a procedure, from different places and with different actual parameters, can be used to simplify greatly the coding of many complex programs.

■ *Quick Check*

1. If a design has one level 0 module and three level 1 modules, how many procedures is it likely to have? (pp. 262–265)

2. Where in a program are procedures declared? (p. 266)

3. How does the syntax of a procedure differ from the syntax of a program? (pp. 264–265, 269–270)

4. What would a call to a procedure with the heading

```
PROCEDURE Quick_Check (VAR Size:
                            Integer;
                       VAR Area:
                            Real;
                       VAR Initial:
                            Char);
```

look like if the actual parameters were the variables Radius (a Real), Number (an Integer), and Letter (a Char)? (pp. 269–272)

5. How is the match-up between the formal and actual parameters in Question 4 made? When during execution does the match-up take place, and how long does it last? What is actually passed from the program to the procedure through this mechanism? (pp. 269–272)

6. Where in a procedure are local variables defined, and what are their initial values equal to? (pp. 272–273)

7. Name one way that a procedure can be used to simplify the coding of an algorithm. (pp. 266–268)

Answers
1. Three   2. In the declaration section, just before the main program body.   3. A procedure begins with a PROCEDURE heading rather than a PROGRAM heading, and ends with an "END;" instead of an "END."   4. Quick_Check(Number, Radius, Letter)   5. The match-up is done on the basis of the parameters' positions in each list each time the procedure is called and lasts until the procedure returns. The locations of the actual parameters are passed to the procedure.   6. In the declaration section of the procedure. Their initial values are undefined.   7. The coding may be simplified if it's possible to call the procedure from more than one place in the program.

■ *Exam Preparation Exercises*

1. Define the following:

   procedure call   actual parameter
   parameter list   variable (or VAR) parameter
   positional matching   local variable
   formal parameter

2. A variable called Widgets is stored in memory location 13571. When the statements

   ```
   Widgets := 23;
   Drop(Widgets);
   ```

   are executed, what information is passed to the formal VAR parameter in procedure Drop?

3. List four advantages of using procedures and top-down design.

4. Assume that, in Exercise 2, the formal parameter for procedure Drop is called Clunkers. After the procedure performs the assignment

   ```
   Clunkers := 77;
   ```

   what is the value in Widgets? in Clunkers?

5. Identify the following items in the program fragment shown below.

   procedure heading   formal parameters
   actual parameters   procedure call
   local variables   procedure body

   ```
   PROGRAM Fragment (Input, Output);
   VAR
      Formal1,
      Formal2;
      Formal3:
         Boolean;

   PROCEDURE Test (VAR Actual1,
                       Actual2,
                       Actual3:
                          Boolean);
   VAR
      Test1,
      Test2:
         Integer;
   BEGIN
         .
         .
   END;
   ```

```
            BEGIN
               .
               .
               .
              Test(Formal1, Formal3, Formal2);
              Test(Formal2, Formal1, Formal3);
               .
               .
               .
            END.
```

6. For the program in Exercise 5, fill in the following tables to show the matching that takes place between the actual and formal parameter lists in each of the two calls to procedure Test.

<table>
<tr><td colspan="2">*First Call to Test*</td><td colspan="2">*Second Call to Test*</td></tr>
<tr><td>*Formal*</td><td>*Actual*</td><td>*Formal*</td><td>*Actual*</td></tr>
<tr><td>1. F1</td><td>A1</td><td>1. F2</td><td>A1</td></tr>
<tr><td>2. F3</td><td>A2</td><td>2. F1</td><td>A2</td></tr>
<tr><td>3. F2</td><td>A3</td><td>3. F3</td><td>A3</td></tr>
</table>

7. Show what is printed by the following program.

```
PROGRAM Pre_Exam (Input, Output);
CONST
   Ten = 10;
VAR
  A,
  B,
  C:
     Integer;

PROCEDURE Test (VAR Z,
                    X,
                    A:
                       Integer);
BEGIN (* Test *)
  Readln(Z, X, A);
  A := Z * X + A
END;  (* Test *)

BEGIN (* Pre_Exam *)
  Test(A, B, C);
  B := B + Ten;
  Writeln('The answers are ', B:6, C:6, A:6, Ten)
END.  (* Pre_Exam *)
```

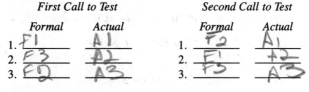

Use these data items: 3 2 4.

8. Show the output of the following program.

```
PROGRAM Example (Output);

VAR
  D,
  E:
      Integer;
PROCEDURE Test (VAR S,
                    T:
                          Integer);

BEGIN (* Test *)
  S := 3;
  S := S + 2;
  T := 4 * S;
  Writeln('In Procedure Test, the variables equal ', S:3, T:3)
END; (* Test *)

BEGIN (* Example *)
  D := 12,
  E := 14;
  Test(D, E);
  Writeln('In the main program after the first call,');
  Writeln('the variables equal ', D:3, E:3);
  D := 15;
  E := 18;
  Test(D, E);
  Writeln('In the main program after the second call ');
  Writeln('the variables equal ', D:3, E:3)
END. (* Example *)
```

9. What is the output of the following program?

```
PROGRAM Sample (Output)

VAR
  X,
  Y:
     Integer;

PROCEDURE Calculate (VAR A,
                         B,
                         C:
                             Integer);

BEGIN (* Calculate *)
  B := B + 1;
  C := A + C;
  Writeln('In Calculate, the variables equal ', A:6, B:6, C:6)
END;  (* Calculate *)
```

```
BEGIN (* Sample *)
  X := 2;
  Y := 3;
  Calculate(X, Y, Y);
  Writeln('In the main program, the variables equal ', X:6, Y:6)
END.  (* Sample *)
```

10. Number the marked statements in the following program to show the order in which they will be executed (the logical order of execution).

```
PROGRAM Execute (Input, Output)
VAR
  Number1,
  Number2:
    Integer;

PROCEDURE Logical (VAR Value1,
                       Value2:
                         Integer);
VAR
  Value3:
    Integer;
BEGIN (* Logical *)
  Readln(Value3, Value1);
  Value2 := Value1 + 10
END;  (* Logical *)

BEGIN (* Execute *)
  Writeln('Exercise');
  Logical(Number1, Number2);
  Writeln(Number1:6, Number2:6)
END.  (* Execute *)
```

11. How many of the marked statements in the preceding program are *not* procedure calls?

12. What would be the result if the last Writeln statement of the program in Exercise 10 were changed to

    `Writeln(Value1:6, Value2:6)`

13. If the program in Exercise 10 were run with the data items 10, 15, what would be the values of each of the variables just prior to the execution of the last statement in the program?

    Number1 = _____   Number2 = _____   Value3 = _____

14. The following procedure calculates the sum of the numbers from 1 to N.

```
PROCEDURE Sum_Int (VAR N,
                       Sum:
                         Integer);
```

```
BEGIN (* Sum_Int *)
  Sum := 0;
  WHILE N >= 1 DO
    BEGIN
      Sum := Sum + N;
      N := N - 1;
    END
END   (* Sum_Int *)
```

What effect will this procedure have on the values of the actual parameters?

■ Programming Warm-Up Exercises

1. Write the procedure heading for a procedure called Max that accepts a pair of integers and returns the greater of the two. Use comments to identify the parameters as receives, returns, or both.

2. Given the procedure heading

```
PROCEDURE Halve (VAR First_Number,   (* Receives/Returns *)
                     Second_Number: (* Receives/Returns *)
                         Integer);
```

   write the remainder of the procedure so that, when it returns, the original values in First_Number and Second_Number are halved.

3. Write a procedure named Increment, with one variable parameter of type Integer, that adds 15 to the value received in the parameter and returns the new value to the calling program.

4. a. Write a procedure that reads in data values of type Integer (Heart_Rate) until a normal heart rate (between 60 and 80) is read or EOF becomes True. The procedure should return a parameter, called Normal, that contains True if a normal heart rate is read, or False if <eof> is encountered.
   b. Write the invoking statement for your procedure. Use the same variable names as in the procedure.

5. Write a Pascal procedure called Calculate_Fraction that inputs a real number and returns the fractional part of that number in a parameter called Answer. For example, if the input is 16.753, the output parameter is 0.753.

6. Write a Pascal procedure called Find_Circum that finds the circumference of a circle given the radius. The formula for calculating the circumference of a circle is π multiplied by twice the radius. Use 3.14159 for π.

7. Given the procedure

```
PROCEDURE Rotate (VAR First_Value,
                      Second_Value,
                      Third_Value:
                          Integer);
VAR
  Temp:
    Integer;
```

```
BEGIN
  Temp := First_Value;
  First_Value := Second_Value;
  Second_Value := Third_Value;
  Third_Value := Temp
END;
```

    a. Add appropriate comments to the procedure that will tell a reader what the procedure does, and what is the purpose of each of the parameters and variables.

    b. Write a program that reads three values, echo-prints them, calls procedure Rotate with the three values as parameters, and then prints the parameters after the procedure returns.

8. Write a procedure called Count_Upper to count the number of uppercase letters on a line of input. The procedure should return this number to the calling program in a parameter called Up_Count.

9. Modify the procedure in Exercise 7 to perform the same sort of operation on four values. Modify the program you wrote for part b of Exercise 7 to work with the new version of this procedure.

10. Write a procedure that returns the first nonblank character it encounters on file Input. Call the procedure Skip_Blank.

11. Write a procedure that skips all characters on file Input until a blank is encountered. Call the procedure Skip_To_Blank.

12. Modify the procedure in Exercise 11 so that it returns the number of characters that were skipped.

▪ *Programming Problems*

1. This problem involves rewriting the program developed for Programming Problem 4 in Chapter 5, using procedures. If you did Programming Warm-Up Exercises 10 and 11 in this chapter, this problem should be easy.

    Develop a top-down design and write a Pascal program to determine the number of words typed in as input. For the sake of simplicity, we define a word to be any sequence of characters without blanks or <eoln>. Blanks are used to separate words. Words may be separated by any number of blanks. A word may be any length, from a single character to an entire line of characters. If you are writing the program to read data from a file, then it should echo-print the input. For an interactive implementation, you do not need to echo-print for this program.

    For example, for the following data, the program would indicate that 26 words were entered.

This isn't exactly an example of g00d english, but it
does demonstrate that a w0rd is just a se@uence of
characters   with0u+ any blank$. ##### ....

    Hint: One way of solving this problem involves using a procedure that reads seque~ of nonblank characters and another that reads sequences of blanks.

    Now that your programs are becoming more complex, it is even more importar use proper indentation and style, meaningful identifiers, and plenty of comments

2. Develop a top-down design and write a Pascal program to play the children's game Rock, Paper, Scissors. In this game, two people simultaneously choose either rock, paper, or scissors. Whether or not one wins depends not only on what one chooses, but also on what one's opponent chooses. The rules are:

Paper covers rock, paper wins.
Scissors cut paper, scissors win.
Rock breaks scissors, rock wins.
All matching combinations are ties.

   The input to the program will be on two files, Player1 and Player2. Each line of a file contains one of the letters R, P, and S (for rock, paper, and scissors, respectively). Corresponding lines in the two files represent one play by the two players. The series of plays ends when <eof> is reached on one or both of the files.

   The program should print out each play and the winner. At the end of the game, the program should print the number of plays won by each player and the number of ties, and declare an overall winner.

   As always, use plenty of comments, proper documentation and coding style, and meaningful identifiers throughout this program. You must decide which of your design modules should be coded as procedures to make the program easier to understand.

3. Write a Pascal program that accepts binary numbers from File Binary as input and translates them to decimal numbers. The decimal numbers should be output in a column with an appropriate heading. The program must read the binary numbers one digit at a time, starting from the right. As each number is read, the program should translate that number into the corresponding decimal number by multiplying it by the appropriate power of 2 (depending on where the digit was in the number). There is only one number per line, but there is an arbitrary number of blanks before each number. The program should check for bad data; if it encounters anything except a zero or a one, it should output the message "Bad integer on input." *Hint:* Use two procedures to do this; one should read the blanks before the binary number.

4. Develop a top-down design and write a Pascal program to print a calendar for one year, given the year and the day of the week that January 1 falls on. It may help to think of this task as printing 12 calendars, one for each month, given the day of the week that a month starts on and the number of days in the month. Each successive month starts on the day of the week that follows the last day of the preceding month. Days of the week should be numbered 0 through 6 for Sunday through Saturday. Years that are divisible by four are leap years. Here is a sample run for an interactive system.

```
What year do you want a calendar for?
1985
What day of the week does January 1 fall on?
(Enter 0 for Sunday, 1 for Monday, etc.)
2
```

```
                1985

             January
     S   M   T   W   T   F   S
     ─────────────────────────────
             1   2   3   4   5
     6   7   8   9  10  11  12
    13  14  15  16  17  18  19
    20  21  22  23  24  25  26
    27  28  29  30  31


             February
     S   M   T   W   T   F   S
     ─────────────────────────────
                         1   2
     3   4   5   6   7   8   9
    10  11  12  13  14  15  16
    17  18  19  20  21  22  23
    24  25  26  27  28


                     .
                     .
                     .

             December
     S   M   T   W   T   F   S
     ─────────────────────────────
     1   2   3   4   5   6   7
     8   9  10  11  12  13  14
    15  16  17  18  19  20  21
    22  23  24  25  26  27  28
    29  30  31
```

When writing your program, be sure to use proper indentation and style, meaningful identifiers, and plenty of comments.

5. Write an interactive Pascal program to calculate the volume and surface area of a cylinder, given the radius (R) and the length (L). The user must be instructed to input the radius and the length. Use one procedure to calculate the volume and another to calculate the surface area.

The formula for calculating the volume of a cylinder is $\pi R^2 L$. The formula for calculating the surface area is $2\pi R(L + R)$. Use 3.14159 for π.

Value Parameters, Nesting Procedures, and More on Interface Design

GOALS

- To be able to do the following tasks, given a Pascal program with nested procedures:

    determine whether each parameter is a VAR or value parameter.
    determine whether a variable is being referenced globally.
    determine which variables are local variables.
    determine which variables are defined in each block.

- To be able to do the following tasks, given a top-down design of a problem:

    determine what the formal and actual parameter lists should be for each module.
    determine which formal parameters should be VAR parameters and which should be value parameters.
    determine what local variables should be declared for each module.
    code the program correctly.

- To be able to determine the scope of each variable in a program.

- To be able to determine the contents of variables during execution of a program with procedures.

- To understand and be able to avoid undesirable side effects.

Chapter 6 introduced procedures and VAR parameters. We saw that care must be taken because any changes that a procedure makes to a formal VAR parameter it also makes to the corresponding actual parameter, even if that is not our intention.

This chapter introduces another kind of parameter in which *a copy of the value* of the actual parameter, rather than the location, is transmitted to the formal parameter. Formal parameters of this type are, reasonably enough, called **value parameters.** Since the procedure receives a copy of the actual parameter, changes to the formal parameter do not affect the actual parameter. Using value parameters thus helps us avoid unintentional changes to actual parameters.

This chapter also examines the Pascal rules by which a procedure may access identifiers that are declared outside its own block. We also return to the discussion of interface design that was begun in Chapter 6.

Value Parameters

When a procedure uses a VAR parameter, the *location* (the address) of an actual parameter is passed to the corresponding formal parameter. When a procedure uses a value parameter, on the other hand, a *copy* of the actual parameter is passed to the formal parameter. If a procedure contains a statement that changes a value parameter, only the copy of the actual parameter is changed, not the original.

Value Parameter   A formal parameter that receives a copy of the contents of the corresponding actual parameter.

The following table summarizes the different kinds of parameters that we've seen.

Parameter Type	Usage
Actual	Appears in a procedure *call statement*. May be passed to either a formal VAR or a formal value parameter.
Formal VAR	Appears in a procedure *heading*. Receives the *address* of the corresponding actual parameter.
Formal value	Appears in a procedure *heading*. Receives a *copy* of the value stored in the corresponding actual parameter.

A single procedure heading can contain both VAR and value parameters.

*T*heoretical Foundations

Parameter Passing Mechanisms

There are three ways of passing parameters to and from subprograms. Pascal supports only two of these mechanisms; however, it's useful to know about all three in case you have occasion to use them in another language.

Pascal VAR parameters employ a mechanism called **pass by address.** A memory address is passed to the procedure. Another name for this is **pass by reference** because the procedure can directly refer to the actual parameter.

Pascal value parameters are an example of **pass by value.** The procedure receives a copy of the value of the actual parameter. Pass by value can be less efficient than pass by address because the value of a parameter may occupy many memory locations (as we'll see in Chapter 11), but an address usually occupies only a single location. For the Integer, Char, and Boolean data types, the efficiency of either mechanism is about the same.

The third method of passing parameters is called **pass by name.** The actual parameter is passed to the procedure as a character string that must be interpreted by special run-time support software (called a **thunk**) supplied by the compiler. For example, if the name of a variable is passed to a procedure, the run-time interpreter looks up the name of the parameter in a table of declarations to find the address of the variable. Pass by name can have unexpected results. If an actual parameter has the same spelling as a local variable in the procedure, the procedure will refer to the local version of the variable instead of the variable in the calling statement.

Some versions of pass by name allow an expression or even a code segment to be passed to a procedure. Each time the procedure refers to the parameter, an **interpreter** performs the action specified by the parameter. An interpreter is similar to a compiler and nearly as complex. Thus, pass by name is the least efficient of the three parameter passing mechanisms. Pascal does not support the pass by name mechanism, although much of the same capability is provided in Standard Pascal (but not in Turbo Pascal) by **procedural parameters,** which are described in Appendix H. Pass by name is supported by the ALGOL and LISP programming languages.

There are two different ways of matching actual parameters with formal parameters, although Pascal supports only one of them. Most programming languages, Pascal among them, match actual and formal parameters by their relative positions in the two parameter lists. This is called **positional** matching, **relative** matching, or **implicit** matching. A few languages, such as Ada, also support **explicit** or **named** matching. In explicit matching, the actual parameter list specifies the name of the formal parameter to be associated with each actual parameter.

Explicit matching allows actual parameters to be written in any order in the procedure call. The real advantage is that each call documents precisely which values are being passed to which formal parameters.

Value Parameter Syntax

Value parameters are distinguished from VAR parameters by the absence of the keyword VAR in the formal parameter list. Now we can revise the syntax template for a procedure heading to the following form.

PROCEDURE identifier parameter list ;

The optional parameter list has the form (note that VAR is now optional):

(VAR identifier , identifier . . . : type ;
  VAR identifier , identifier . . . : type

⋮

)

Let's look at an example of a procedure heading with a mixture of VAR and value parameter declarations.

```
PROCEDURE Example (VAR Parameter1:      (* A VAR parameter        *)
                       Integer;
                   Parameter2,          (* Two value parameters    *)
                   Parameter3:          (* of type Real            *)
                       Real;
                   VAR Parameter4:      (* Another VAR parameter *)
                       Real;
                   Parameter5:          (* A value parameter       *)
                       Boolean;
                   Parameter6:          (* A value parameter       *)
                       Char);
```

Value parameter declarations are just like VAR parameter declarations except that the keyword VAR is omitted. Since there is no Pascal keyword to make it easy to spot value parameters, it's important to use an indentation style that will make them obvious in the code.

Matters of Style

Formatting Procedure Headings

In the example heading a specific style is followed. Comments appear next to the formal parameters to explain how each parameter is used. These comments indicate which of the three interface design categories (defined in Chapter 6) each parameter belongs to, as well as its function.

```
PROCEDURE Example (   Ch:           (* Receives a character           *)
                          Char;
                      VAR Num1,        (* Receives/returns Num1 + Ord(Ch) *)
                          Num2,        (* Receives/returns Num2 + Num1    *)
                          Sum:         (* Returns sum of Nums and Ord(Ch) *)
                          Integer);
```

Notice that the value parameter is indented the same as the VAR parameters, but the absence of VAR before it shows that it is a value parameter. At first glance, you may think that Num2 and Sum are also value parameters, but a second look shows that they are part of a list that begins with VAR.

Comments in the form of rows of asterisks before and after a procedure should be used to make the procedure stand out from the surrounding code. Each procedure also has its own block of introductory comments, just like those at the start of a program.

It's important to put as much care into documenting each procedure as you would into documenting a program.

Value Parameter Semantics

As we said earlier, a value parameter receives a copy of the actual parameter and therefore the actual parameter cannot be directly accessed or changed. When a procedure returns, the contents of any value parameters are destroyed, along with the contents of the local variables. The difference between value parameters and local variables is that the values of local variables are undefined when a procedure starts to execute, whereas value parameters are automatically set equal to the corresponding actual parameters.

Because the contents of value parameters are destroyed when the procedure returns, they cannot be used to return information to the calling procedure or program. What good are parameters that can't return information? Recall from the discussion of interface design in Chapter 6 that sometimes a procedure receives values that it doesn't change. Value parameters are the perfect choice for this situation.

A VAR parameter may be passed only a variable as an actual parameter because a procedure can assign it a new value. Since value parameters are passed copies of their actual parameters, anything that has a value may be passed to a value parameter. This includes constants, variables, and even expressions. (An expression is simply evaluated and a copy of the result is placed in the corresponding value parameter.) Also, just a an Integer value may be assigned to a Real variable, an Integer value may be passed to a value parameter of type Real. (This is not allowed with VAR parameters.)

The following table summarizes the different forms of parameters.

Formal Parameter	Syntax Example	Allowable Actual Parameters
VAR	(VAR Name: Type)	Variable of same type
Value	(Name: Type)	Variable, Constant, or Expression of same type, except that an Integer may be passed to a Real

Scope Rules and Nested Procedures

Whenever our top-down design has more than two levels of modules, there is potential for nesting procedures within other procedures. Pascal permits statements inside a procedure to access identifiers declared outside the procedure. In this section we examine the Pascal rules that control how external access takes place, both in simple cases and in cases where procedures are nested.

Local Versus Global Declarations

As we saw in Chapter 6, local variables are defined in the VAR section of a procedure (not to be confused with its VAR parameters). Recall that local variables cannot be accessed outside the block that contains them. The same access rule applies to any declarations or definitions that appear in a block: local constants and procedures may be accessed only in the block in which they are defined or declared.

So much for local declarations. What are **global** declarations? Any variable, constant, or procedure declared in the main program is global and may be referenced from any point following its declaration (including from points within procedures).

Global Any identifier declared in the main program is said to be global because it is accessible to everything that follows it.

When a procedure contains a local identifier with the same name as a global identifier, the local identifier takes precedence within the procedure. This principle is called **name precedence.**

Name Precedence A local identifier in a procedure takes precedence over a global identifier with the same spelling in any references that the procedure makes to that identifier.

Here's an example of local and global declarations.

```
PROGRAM Local_And_Global (Input, Output);

CONST
   A = 17;

VAR
   B,                (* A global variable     *)
   C:                (* Another global variable *)
      Integer;

PROCEDURE One (    C:          (* Prevents access to global C *)
                      Real);

VAR
   B:      (* Prevents access to global B *)
      Real;

BEGIN (* One *)
   B := 2.3;                   (* Assignment to local B     *)
   Writeln('A = ', A:1);       (* Output global A (= 17)    *)
   Writeln('B = ', B:3:1);     (* Output local B  (= 2.3)   *)
   Writeln('C = ', C:3:1)      (* Output local C  (= 42.0)  *)
END;   (* One *)

BEGIN (* Example *)
   B := 4;                     (* Assignment to global B *)
   C := 6;                     (* Assignment to global C *)
   One(42.0)
END.   (* Example *)
```

In this example, Procedure One accesses global constant A, but defines its own local variables B and C. Thus the output would be

```
A = 17 B = 2.3 C = 42.0
```

Local variable B takes precedence over global variable B, effectively hiding global B from the statements in Procedure One. Formal value parameter C, which receives the constant 42.0, also blocks access to global variable C from within the procedure. Formal parameters act just like local variables in this respect.

Scope Rules

If we list all the places from which an identifier could be accessed, we would describe that identifier's **scope of access,** often just called its **scope.** The rules for accessing identifiers that aren't declared locally are thus called **scope rules.**

Scope Rules   The rules that determine where in the program an identifier may be accessed, given the point where that identifier is declared.

In addition to local and global access, the Pascal scope rules must take into account what happens when procedures are nested within other procedures. Anything declared in a block that contains a nested procedure is **nonlocal** to that procedure. (Global identifiers are nonlocal with respect to all blocks other than the main program.) If a procedure accesses any identifier declared outside its own block, it is a **nonlocal access.**

Nonlocal   Any identifier declared outside a given block is said to be nonlocal with respect to that block.

The actual scope rules are as follows:

1. The scope of an identifier includes all the statements following its definition, within the block containing the definition. This includes nested blocks, except as noted in rule 2.
2. The scope of an identifier does not extend to any nested block that contains a locally defined identifier with the same spelling (local identifiers have name precedence).
3. The scope of a formal parameter is identical to the scope of a local variable in the same block.

Here is an example program to demonstrate the Pascal scope rules. To simplify the example, only the declarations and headings are spelled out. The procedure and program bodies are indicated by BEGIN and END, with dots between them. Note how Procedure Block2 is declared within Procedure Block1; it is an example of a nested procedure.

```
PROGRAM Example (Input, Output);

VAR
  A1:            (* One global variable      *)
     Integer;
  A2:            (* Another global variable *) meaningful everywhere.
     Boolean;

(******************************************************************)
                              sent as first parameter.
PROCEDURE Block3 (    A1:           (* Prevents access to global A1 *)
                         Integer;
                  VAR B2:           (* Has same scope as C1 and D2   *)
                         Boolean);

VAR
  C1,          (* A variable local to Block3        *)
  D2:          (* Another variable local to Block3 *)
     Integer;
```

```
BEGIN (* Block3 *)
  .
  .
END;  (* Block3 *)

(*********************************************************************)

PROCEDURE Block1;

VAR
  A1,        (* Prevents access to global A1               *)
  B2:        (* Local to Block1, no conflict with B2 in Block3 *)
    Integer;

  (*********************************************************************)

  PROCEDURE Block2;

  VAR
    C1,        (* Local to Block2, no conflict with C1 in Block3 *)
    B2:        (* Prevents nonlocal access to B2 in Block1, no   *)
               (* conflict with B2 in Block3 *)
      Integer;

  BEGIN (* Block2 *)
    .
    .
  END;  (* Block2 *)

  (*********************************************************************)

BEGIN (* Block1 *)
  .
  .
END;  (* Block1 *)

(*********************************************************************)

BEGIN (* Example *)
  .
  .
END.   (* Example *)
```

(handwritten annotations:) A1 B2 = Global in Block2 because in body of Block1.

(handwritten annotation:) B2 (Global) takes presidence VAR B2

Let's look at Program Example in terms of the blocks it defines and see just what these rules mean. Figure 7-1 shows the headings and declarations in Program Example with the scopes of access indicated by boxes.

Anything inside a box can refer to anything in a larger surrounding box, but outside-in references aren't allowed. Thus, a statement in procedure Block2 could access any identifier declared in Block1 or in the main program. A statement in Block2 could no

Figure 7-1
Scope Diagram for
Program Example

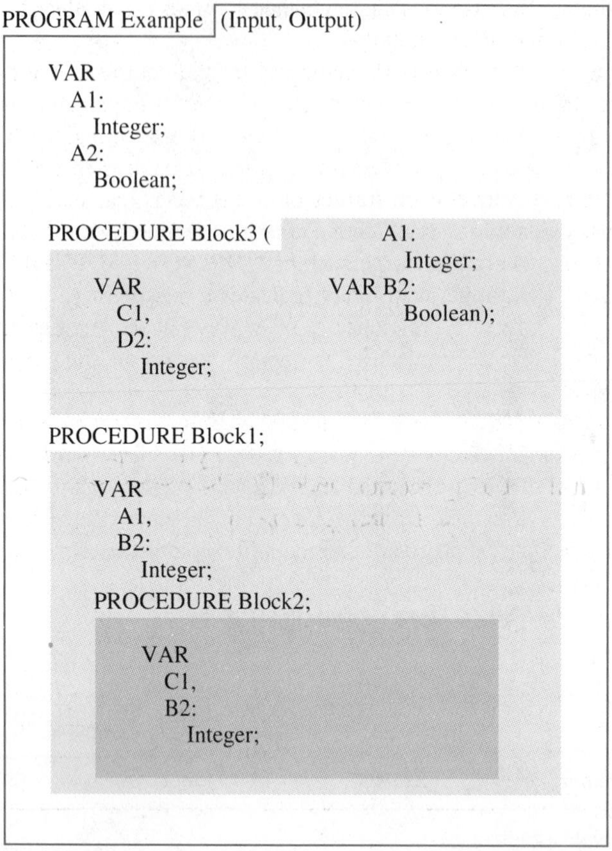

```
PROGRAM Example (Input, Output)

   VAR
     A1:
        Integer;
     A2:
        Boolean;

   PROCEDURE Block3 (          A1:
                                  Integer;
        VAR                 VAR B2:
          C1,                      Boolean);
          D2:
             Integer;


   PROCEDURE Block1;

        VAR
          A1,
          B2:
             Integer;
        PROCEDURE Block2;

             VAR
               C1,
               B2:
                  Integer;
```

access identifiers declared in Block3 because it would have to enter the Block3 box from outside. Also note that the main program can call Block3 and Block1, but it cannot call Block2.

Notice that the formal parameters for a procedure are inside the procedure's box, but the procedure name itself is outside. If the name of the procedure were inside the box, the program couldn't call the procedure. This demonstrates merely that the procedure name is an identifier declared in the block surrounding the procedure, and that it has the same scope as any other identifier declared in that block.

Imagine the boxes in Figure 7-1 as rooms whose walls are made of two-way mirrors, with the reflective side facing out and the see-through side facing in. If you stood in the room for Block2, you would be able to see out through all the surrounding rooms to the declarations of the main program (and anything between). You would not be able to see into any other rooms (such as Block3), however, because their mirrored outer surfaces would block your view. Because of this analogy, the term **visible** is often used in describing a scope of access. For example, variable A2 is visible throughout the program, meaning that it can be accessed from anywhere in the program.

Figure 7-1 does not tell the whole story: it represents only scope rules 1 and 3. We must also keep rule 2 in mind. Variable A1 is defined in two different places in Program

Example. Because of name precedence, Block1 and Block2 access the A1 defined in Block1 rather than the global A1.

Name precedence is implemented by the compiler as follows. When a statement refers to an identifier, the compiler first checks the local declarations. If the identifier isn't local, the compiler works its way outward through each level of nesting until it finds an identifier with the same spelling. If there is an identifier with the same name declared at a level even further out, it is never reached. If the compiler reaches the global declarations (including Pascal's predefined identifiers) and still can't find the identifier, an error message such as "UNKNOWN IDENTIFIER" will result.

Such a message most likely indicates a misspelling, or that the identifier was not declared before the reference to it or was not declared at all. It may also indicate, however, that the procedures are nested so that the identifier's scope doesn't include the reference.

An alternative way to document the scope of identifiers is with a table showing which identifiers may be accessed in each procedure. Across the top of the table, write the name of each procedure, including the main program. Down the side, list all the identifiers, grouped according to where they are declared. In the table, an asterisk indicates that the procedure named in the column heading can refer to the identifier to the left.

Here is a scope table for Program Example.

	Procedure			
Identifier	Example	Block3	Block1	Block2
Example				
A1	*			
A2	*	*	*	*
Block3	*	*	*	*
A1		*		
B2		*		
C1		*		
D2		*		
Block1	*		*	*
A1			*	*
B2			*	
Block2			*	*
C1				*
B2				*

You may notice from this table that a statement in a procedure can call that procedure. This process, called **recursion,** is discussed in Chapter 8 and again in Chapter 17.

Because Turbo Pascal provides the USES statement as a nonstandard extension, there are some additional considerations to keep in mind when applying the scope rules. Recall that a USES statement inserts the code for a unit into a program, and that units can define identifiers that are accessible to the program. But what if we declare an identifier that happens to have the same name as one in a unit that we're using? Normally, Pascal wouldn't allow us to have two global names that are the same. Turbo Pascal solves this problem by nesting the program inside any units that are being used. Thus, if we declare an identifier that's the same as one in a unit, rule 2 says that our identifier takes precedence over the unit's identifier.

What if we also wish to access the identifier in the unit? Turbo Pascal provides another nonstandard extension called a *qualified identifier*. To specify an identifier in a unit when there is a locally defined identifier of the same name, we write the name preceded by the name of the unit and a period. Thus, if we have the declarations

```
PROGRAM qualified (Input, Output);

USES CRT;      (* Defines CheckEOF, among other things     *)

VAR
   CheckEOF:    (* A global declaration of another CheckEOF *)
     Boolean;
```

we can access both versions of CheckEOF as in the following code segment:

```
CRT.CheckEOF := True;               (* Accesses CheckEOF in CRT unit *)
CheckEOF := NOT EOF AND NOT EOLN    (* Accesses global CheckEOF       *)
```

If we use more than one unit in a program, then the first one listed has the outermost scope and the next one is nested inside it. The program itself is nested inside the last unit listed. For example, if we write

```
PROGRAM Unit_Example (Input, Output);

USES
   CRT,        (* Defines CheckEOF *)
   Printer;    (* Defines file Lst *)

VAR
   Lst:        (* Global Lst within program       *)
     Char;
   CheckEOF:   (* Global CheckEOF within program *)
     Boolean;
```

then the CRT unit has the outermost scope; the Printer unit is nested inside of CRT, and the program's global declarations are nested inside the Printer unit. Because of name precedence, references to Lst and CheckEOF within the program will be to the variables declared in the VAR section. To access Lst in the Printer unit we must write Printer.Lst, and to access CheckEOF in the CRT unit we must write CRT.CheckEOF.

Designing Programs with Nesting

Nesting can make changing a program more difficult. For example, if we wanted procedure Block3 in Program Example to call Block2, we might have to reorganize our program because the scope rules prevent a procedure at the same level as Block1 from calling the nested Block2. One solution is to move Block2 out of Block1 and insert it above Block3 in the program so it is no longer nested.

Another solution is to nest a second copy of Block2 inside Block3. This approach follows the strict nesting of a top-down design. It also wastes program memory space, since Block2 now appears twice in the program.

Whether or not you nest procedures is a matter of style and the constraints of your top-down design. It is acceptable to list the procedures sequentially without nesting as long as you declare each one before you call it. On the other hand, strict nesting makes a procedure completely self-contained and thus easy to reuse in other programs.

We can compromise between strict nesting and straight-line declarations of procedures by nesting those procedures that are called by only one procedure, and globally declaring those that are widely used. The documentation for each globally declared procedure should include a list of all the procedures that make use of it. The documentation for procedures that make nonlocal calls should note which procedures are needed for proper execution.

Interface Design

We return now to the issue of interface design, which was first discussed in Chapter 6. Recall that the information transmitted through a procedure interface can take three forms: receives, returns, and receives/returns. Any item that can be classified purely as *receives* should be coded as a formal value parameter. Items in the remaining two classes (returns and receives/returns) will be the formal VAR parameters.

There are exceptions to this rule. Pascal requires that files be passed as VAR parameters because of the way parameters and files are implemented, and the fact that the values in a file are not stored in main memory. One more exception is described in Chapter 11.

It is sometimes tempting to skip the interface design step when writing a procedure and just use references to nonlocal variables. Don't! In addition to its parameters, a procedure's interface automatically includes any references to nonlocal identifiers. Thus, without the interface design step, you would actually be creating a poorly structured and undocumented interface. The use of nonlocal variable references is a poor programming practice that can lead to program bugs. These bugs are extremely hard to locate and usually take the form of unwanted side effects.

Side Effects

Suppose you included the following statement in a Pascal program:

```
Writeln(Variable);
```

You expect that the call to Writeln will print the value of the variable. You would be surprised if Writeln also changed the value of the variable because Writeln, by definition, does not make such changes. This would be an example of an unexpected and unwanted **side effect.**

Side Effect Any effect of one module on another module that is not a part of the explicitly defined interface between them. (A module is a procedure, a function, or the main program.)

Side effects are sometimes caused by a combination of VAR parameters and careless coding in a procedure. An assignment statement in the procedure stores a temporary result in one of the VAR parameters, accidentally changing the value of an actual parameter back in the program. As we mentioned before, using value parameters avoids this type of side effect by preventing the change from reaching the actual parameter.

Side effects can also occur when a procedure accesses a nonlocal variable. An error in the procedure might cause the value of a global variable to be changed in an unexpected way, causing an error in the main program.

The symptoms of a side effect error are misleading because the trouble appears in one part of the program when it is really caused by something in another part. To avoid such errors, the only external effect that a procedure should have is to transfer information through the well-structured interface of the parameter list (see Figure 7-2). If procedures access nonlocal variables only through their parameter lists, and if all receives-only parameters are value parameters, then each procedure is essentially isolated from other parts of the program and there won't be any side effects.

Figure 7-2
Side Effects

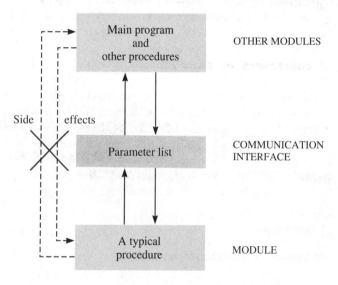

Main program
and
other procedures

OTHER MODULES

Side effects

Parameter list

COMMUNICATION
INTERFACE

A typical
procedure

MODULE

When a procedure is free of side effects, it can be treated as an independent module and reused in other programs. Procedures with side effects cannot be reused.

Here is a short example of a program that runs but produces incorrect results because of side effects.

```pascal
PROGRAM Trouble (Input, Output);

(* This is an example of poor programming style, which   *)
(* causes an error when the program is executed          *)

USES
  CRT;
VAR
  Count:              (* Supposed to count input lines, but does it? *)
    Integer;
  Ch:                 (* Holds one input character                 *)
    Char;

(* ********************************************************************** *)

PROCEDURE Char_Count;

(* Counts the number of characters in a line on file *)
(* Input and prints the count on file Output         *)

BEGIN (* Char_Count *)
  Count := 0;                                          (* Side effect *)
  WHILE NOT EOLN DO
    BEGIN
      Read(Ch);                              (* Global variable access *)
      Count := Count + 1                             (* Side effect *)
    END;
  Readln;
  Writeln(Count:1, ' characters on this line.')       (* Global access *)
END;  (* Char_Count *)

(* ********************************************************************** *)

BEGIN (* Trouble *)
  CheckEOF := True;
  Count := 0;
  WHILE NOT EOF DO
    BEGIN
      Count := Count + 1;
      Char_Count
    END;
  Writeln(Count:1, ' lines of input processed.')
END.  (* Trouble *)
```

Program Trouble is supposed to count and print the number of characters on each line of input. After the last line has been processed, it should print the number of lines. Strangely enough, each time the program is run, it reports that the number of lines of input is the same as the number of characters in the last line of input. This is because Procedure Char_Count accesses the global variable Count and uses it to store the number of characters on each line of input.

If a local variable Count is declared in procedure Char_Count, the program will work correctly. There will be no conflict between the local Count and the global Count because they are separate variables visible only to their own blocks. Ch should be declared locally in the procedure, of course, since that is the only place it is used.

Program Trouble also demonstrates one common exception to the rule of not accessing global variables. Technically, Input and Output are global variables of type Text, and procedure Char_Count directly reads and writes to them. To be absolutely correct, Input and Output should be passed as VAR parameters to the procedure. Because Input and Output are predefined in Pascal, however, it is not unusual for procedures to access them directly. To atone for this minor sin, the programmer should always document the access to Input and Output in a comment at the beginning of the procedure.

Global Constants

Contrary to what you might think, it is acceptable to reference named constants globally. Because the values of global constants cannot be changed while the program is running, no side effects will occur.

There are two advantages to globally referencing constants: 1) ease of change and 2) consistency. If we have to change the value of a constant, it's easier to change just one global definition than to change a local definition in every procedure. By defining a constant in only one place, we also ensure that all parts of the program will use exactly the same value.

This is not to say that you should define *all* constants globally. If a constant is needed in only one procedure, then it should be defined locally within that procedure.

Here is the best rule for knowing where to define constants: A constant should be declared in the lowest-level block that contains all the references to the constant. Quite often this is the program declaration block.

The following case study illustrates the interface design process, nesting, and the use of value and VAR parameters.

PROBLEM-SOLVING CASE STUDY

Reformat Names

Problem: Write a program that reads names in the form

```
Mary     Brown
  Sam    Green
```

and prints them out in the form

```
Brown, M.
Green, S.
```

The input may contain any number of blanks preceding the first name and between the first and last names. Each person's name is on a separate line of input.

Input: A series of names, with one person's name (first and last) on each line of input in the form

```
First Last
```

where there may be any number of blanks preceding the first name and one or more blanks between the two names.

Output: A corresponding series of lines of the form

```
Last, F.
```

Discussion: This would be an easy task to do by hand. We would read the two names; write down the last, followed by a comma; and write down the first letter of the first name, followed by a period. This is basically how we will program the problem. The hard part is trying to simulate "reading the two names." The program will have to read one character at a time, examine it, and decide what to do with it.

Let's analyze this process by hand, going character by character through the input. The first character will be either a blank or a letter. If it is a letter, we need to save it since it is the first initial.

Once we have the first initial, we are not interested in the rest of the first name. So we must continue to read until we reach the last name. How do we recognize the beginning of the last name? It is the first letter after the blanks following the first name. Once we find the last name, we continue reading and printing each character until we find a blank. Then we print a comma, followed by a blank, and the first initial, which we saved, followed by a period.

PROBLEM-SOLVING CASE STUDY *cont'd.*

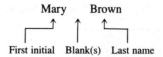

First initial   Blank(s)   Last name

Now that we have analyzed the problem, we can do our top-down design.

Assumptions: Middle names are not present in the input.

Main Module   *Level 0*

```
WHILE NOT EOF DO
   Get_Initial
   Print_Last
   Print_Initial
```

Get_Initial (Returns: Initial)   *Level 1*

```
Skip_Blanks
Save_Initial
```

Print_Last (No parameters)

```
Find_Last
Print
```

Print_Initial (Receives: Initial)

```
Writeln', ',Initial,'.'
```

Skip_Blanks (Returns: First nonblank letter)   *Level 2*

```
Get_Ch
WHILE Ch = blank
   Get_Ch
```

Save_Initial (Receives: Ch, Returns: Initial)

> Initial : = Ch

Find_Last (Returns: First character of last name)

> Skip_First
> Skip_Blanks

Print (Receives: First character of last name)

> WHILE Ch <> blank DO
>   Write(Ch)
>   Get_Ch

Skip_First (No parameters)   *Level 3*

> WHILE Ch <> blank
>   Get_Ch

Get_Ch (Returns: Ch)

> Read(Ch)

This design goes to four levels. From the design we can see that Save_Initial, Print_Initial, and Get_Ch are only one line of code each. Let's not make them procedures but, instead, put each line of code in the level above. Here is the module structure chart for Program Transpose. The chart emphasizes the importance of interface design. The shaded arrows indicate which identifiers are received or returned by each module.

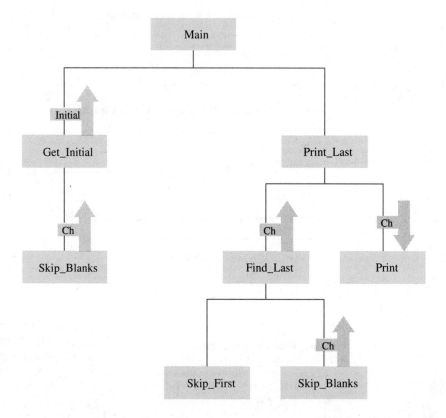

It should be noted that the module structure chart for a design specifies only how modules are called by other modules. The chart does not indicate whether the called modules are nested or declared globally. It would appear from studying this chart that Skip_Blanks will be declared twice in the program; however, we know that this isn't the case. There is another style of chart, called a **module nesting chart,** that depicts the nesting structure of modules and calls between them. Figure 7-3 shows a module nesting chart for Program Transpose.

Before coding this problem, we need to spell out clearly the module or procedure interfaces.

Main Module: Calls Get_Initial and Print_Last. Get_Initial must return the first letter of the first name (actual parameter). No parameters are passed between Main and Print_Last.

Get_Initial: Is called by Main. Calls Skip_Blanks (which reads from Input). Must return the first letter of the first name (formal VAR parameter) to Main. Skip_Blanks must return the first nonblank character (actual parameter).

Figure 7-3
Module Nesting
Chart for Program
Transpose

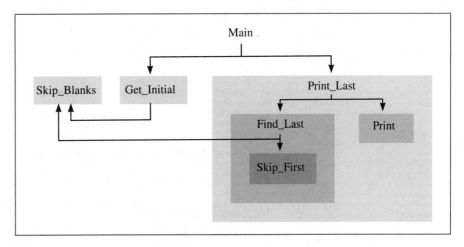

Print_Last: Is called by Main. Calls Find_Last (which reads from Input) and Print (which reads from Input and writes to Output). Returns nothing to main (no formal parameters). Must receive the first character of the last name from Find_Last (actual parameter). Must pass the first character of the last name to Print (actual parameter).

Find_Last: Is called by Print_Last. Returns the first character of the last name to Print_Last (formal VAR parameter). Calls Skip_First and Skip_Blanks (both of which read from Input). No parameters are passed between Find_Last and Skip_First. Receives the first character of the last name from Skip_Blanks (actual parameter).

Skip_First: Is called by Find_Last. Reads from Input until a blank is found, so needs nothing and returns nothing (no formal parameters).

Skip_Blanks: Is called by Get_Initial and Find_Last. Returns the first nonblank character from Input to the calling procedure (formal VAR parameter).

Print: Is called by Print_Last. Needs the first character of the last name from Print_Last (formal value parameter). Reads from Input and writes to Output until a blank or EOLN is encountered. Returns nothing.

Now we can begin to code our program. Does the physical order of the procedures matter? Yes, a procedure must be declared before it is used or referenced by another procedure. Therefore, the lowest-level modules should be declared first. Within this constraint, however, it improves readability to put the modules in logical order. For example, a lower-level module that is called by only one higher-level module may be nested within the module. An effective ordering would be:

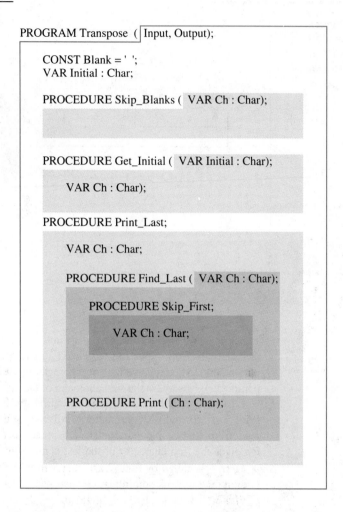

The following Pascal program parallels our design. To save space, we have omitted the preconditions and postconditions from the comments at the beginning of each procedure. Programming Warm-Up Exercise 13 asks you to fill them in.

```
PROGRAM Transpose (Input, Output);

(* This program reformats names to be in the form of last name, comma, *)
(* blank, first initial, period. The input is in the form of first     *)
(* name, blanks, last name with one person's name per input line       *)

USES
  CRT;
CONST
  Blank = ' ';      (* Name separator character *)
```

PROBLEM-SOLVING CASE STUDY cont'd.

```
VAR
  Initial:            (* Holds first initial      *)
    Char;

(**********************************************************************)

PROCEDURE Skip_Blanks (VAR Ch:          (* Returns first nonblank input *)
                            Char);

(* Reads characters from Input until a nonblank is found *)

BEGIN (* Skip_Blanks *)
  Read(Ch);
  WHILE Ch = Blank DO
    Read(Ch)
END;   (* Skip_Blanks *)

(**********************************************************************)

PROCEDURE Get_Initial (VAR Initial:     (* Returns first initial *)
                            Char);

(* Returns the first letter in the first name.
   Calls Skip_Blanks, which reads from Input *)

VAR
  Ch:      (* Holds letter returned by Skip_Blanks *)
    Char;

BEGIN (* Get_Initial *)
  Skip_Blanks(Ch);
  Initial := Ch
END;   (* Get_Initial *)

(**********************************************************************)

PROCEDURE Print_Last;

(* Skips the rest of the first name on Input,
   then prints the person's last name on Output  *)

VAR
  Ch:      (* Holds first letter of last name *)
    Char;

  (**********************************************************************)

  PROCEDURE Find_Last (VAR Ch:        (* Returns first char of last name *)
                            Char);
```

Uses in 2 places

In begining & before Main.

PROBLEM-SOLVING CASE STUDY cont'd.

```
(* Scans Input for the first letter of a person's last name by *)
(* skipping the nonblank characters in the first name, then    *)
(* skipping the blanks between the first and last names        *)

  (*******************************************************************)

  PROCEDURE Skip_First;

  (* Skips over characters remaining in a person's first name *)
  (* by reading characters from Input until a blank is found  *)

  VAR
    Ch:          (* Holds a character from the first name *)
      Char;

  BEGIN (* Skip_First *)
    Read(Ch);
    WHILE Ch <> Blank DO
      Read(Ch)
  END;   (* Skip_First *)

  (*******************************************************************)

BEGIN (* Find_Last *)
  Skip_First;
  Skip_Blanks(Ch)
END;   (* Find_Last *)

(*********************************************************************)

PROCEDURE Print (Ch:          (* Receives first character of last name *)
                   Char);

(* Prints a person's last name by printing the input parameter *)
(* and then reading and printing from Input to Output until     *)
(* a blank is read                                              *)

BEGIN (* Print *)
  WHILE Ch <> Blank DO
    BEGIN
      Write(Ch);
      IF NOT EOLN
        THEN
          Read(Ch)
        ELSE
          Ch := Blank
    END
END;   (* Print *)
```

PROBLEM-SOLVING CASE STUDY *cont'd.*

```
(*************************************************************)

BEGIN (* Print_Last *)
  Find_Last(Ch);
  Print(Ch)
END;  (* Print_Last *)

(*************************************************************)

BEGIN (* Transpose *)
  CheckEOF := True;
  WHILE NOT EOF DO
    BEGIN
      Get_Initial(Initial);
      Print_Last;
      Writeln(', ', Initial, '.');                    (* Print Initial *)
      Readln
    END
END.  (* Transpose *)
```

Testing: The test data for Program Transpose should include names of different lengths, ranging from a single character to many characters. Some of the names should be preceded by one or more blanks, and the number of blanks separating the two names should be varied. It would also be instructive to try the program with some invalid data, such as a line with no names, one name, more than two names, and so on.

Notice that Program Transpose has several procedures nested within procedures: Skip_First is nested in Find_Last, and Print and Find_Last are nested in Print_Last. Nesting is a matter of style in this program. Note how the pattern of a block is repeated at each level of nesting.

This problem is actually too simple to need such an involved structure. For example, some of the procedures have only two lines of code between BEGIN and END. We could just as easily have written these statements directly in place of the call to those procedures. However, the problem does illustrate such concepts as interface design, nesting of procedures, and multiple calls to a procedure (Skip_Blanks).

We don't mean to imply that you should never write a procedure with as few as two statements. In some cases decomposition of a problem will make a two-line procedure quite appropriate. When deciding whether to code a module directly in the next higher level or as a procedure, simply ask yourself the following question: Which way will make the overall program easier to read, understand, and modify later? With experience, you will develop your own set of guidelines for making this decision. For example, if a two-line module is to be called from several places in the program, it should be coded as a procedure.

Software Engineering Tip

Control Abstraction, Functional Cohesion, and Communication Complexity

Program Transpose contains four different WHILE loops. The control structure for this program is fairly complex. Yet, if you look at the individual modules, the most complicated control structure is an IF-THEN-ELSE within a WHILE loop.

The complexity of the program is hidden by reducing each of the major control structures to an abstract action performed by a procedure call. For example, skipping a series of blanks is an abstract action that appears as a call to Skip_Blanks. The logical properties of the action are separated from its implementation (a WHILE loop). This aspect of a design is called **control abstraction.**

Control Abstraction   The separation of the logical properties of an action from its implementation.

Control abstraction can serve as a guideline for deciding which modules to code as procedures and which to code directly. If a module contains a control structure, it should almost certainly be a procedure. For example, procedure Get_Initial lacks control abstraction. In fact, we could substitute a call to Skip_Blanks for the call to Get_Initial. If a module does not contain a control structure, you must consider other factors. Is it lengthy, or called from more than one place?

Somewhat related to control abstraction is the concept of **functional cohesion:** a module should perform exactly one abstract action.

Functional Cohesion   The principle that a module should perform exactly one abstract action.

If you can state the function that a module performs in one sentence with no conjunctions, then it is highly cohesive. A module that has more than one primary purpose is lacking in cohesion. For example, procedure Print_Last skips the remainder of the first name *and* prints the last name; a more cohesive design would do away with Print_Last, and simply call Find_Last and Print. Note that Print_Last is also lacking in control abstraction.

A module that only partially fulfills a purpose also lacks cohesion. Such a module should be combined with whatever other modules are directly related to it. For example, it would make no sense to have a separate procedure for printing the first letter of the last name because printing the last name is one abstract action.

A third and related aspect of a module's design is its **communication complexity,** the amount of information that passes through a module's interface. A module's communication complexity is often an indicator of its cohesiveness. Usually, if a module requires a large number of parameters, it is either trying to accomplish too much or it is only partially fulfilling a purpose. You should step back and see if there is an alternative way to divide the problem so that a minimal amount of information is communicated between modules.

PROBLEM-SOLVING CASE STUDY

Comparison of Department-Store Sales, Part 2

Problem: In Chapter 6 we wrote Program Graph using only VAR parameters. We also made several assumptions: each file is in order by department IDs, the same departments are in each store, and there is one piece of data per input line. What if there is an error in the data files? We have not paid too much attention to data error checking (also called **data validation**) in our programs, yet errors do occur. Let's redo the design for Program Graph to make use of value parameters where appropriate, and add some data validation. There are no changes to the Input and Output specifications of the program, so we won't repeat them here.

Discussion: We'll begin by reviewing our old design for Program Graph.

Main   *Level 0*

```
Print Header
WHILE NOT EOF on file Store1 AND NOT EOF on file Store2
    Get Data for a Store1 department
    Print Data for the Store1 department
    Get Data for a Store2 department
    Print Data for the Store2 department
```

PROBLEM-SOLVING CASE STUDY cont'd.

Print Header (No parameters)   *Level 1*

```
Print chart title
Print heading
Print bar graph scale
```

**Get Data (Receives/Returns: Data File;
              Returns: Dept ID, Dept Sales)**

```
Get Dept ID from Data File
Get Num Days from Data File
Initialize Dept Sales to 0
Initialize Days (loop control variable) to 1
WHILE Days is less than or equal to Num Days
    Get Sales from Data File
    Add Sales to Dept Sales
    Increment Days
```

Print Data (Receives: Dept ID, Store Num, Dept Sales)

```
Print Dept ID
Print Store Num
WHILE Dept Sales are greater than 250
    Print a *
    Subtract $500 from Dept Sales
Go to next line (Writeln)
```

We can check for mismatched department IDs in the main program by calling
Get_Data for both stores before we call Print_Data. We will have to keep the returned
IDs in separate variables, and compare their values after the second call to Get_Data.
We can check for too few data values by inserting tests for EOF in procedure
Get_Data. We can also add a test to the main program that will tell us if the two files
do not have the same number of data sets.

It's easy to see from the old design that all the parameters for procedure Print_Data
can be value parameters. The use of value parameters will allow us to pass the store

number as a literal constant in the calls to that procedure. It would also appear that the first parameter for procedure Get_Data could be a value parameter, but Data_File is a parameter of type Text, and files must be passed as VAR parameters.

. ***Assumptions:***   There is one piece of data per line. Sales do not exceed $25,000 for one department.

Here is our new design.

Main   *Level 0*

```
Print Header
WHILE NOT EOF on file Store1 AND NOT EOF on file Store2
   Get Data for a Store1 department
   Get Data for a Store2 department
   IF ID1 <> ID2
     THEN
        Print error message indicating mismatched IDs
     ELSE
        Print Data for the Store1 department
        Print Data for the Store2 department
IF EOF on file Store1 <> EOF on file Store2
   THEN
     IF EOF on Store1
        THEN
          Print 'Ran out of data for Store1 before Store2'
        ELSE
          Print 'Ran out of data for Store2 before Store1'
```

Print Header (No parameters)   *Level 1*

```
Print chart title
Print heading
Print bar graph scale
```

Get Data (Receives/Returns: Data File;
Returns: Dept ID, Dept Sales)

```
Get Dept ID from Data File
IF EOF on Data File
  THEN
    Print 'Data error: No data following dept. ID'
  ELSE
    Get Num Days from Data File
    Initialize Dept Sales to 0
    Initialize Days (loop control variable) to 1
    WHILE Days is less than or equal to Num Days
      IF EOF on Data File
        THEN
          Print 'Data error: Ran out of data in mid-set.'
          Set Days to Num Days + 1 (end condition)
        ELSE
          Get Sales from Data File
          Add Sales to Dept Sales
          Increment Days
```

Print Data (Receives: Dept ID, Store Num, Dept Sales)

```
Print Dept ID
Print Store Num
WHILE Dept Sales are greater than 250
  Print a *
  Subtract $500 from Dept Sales
Go to next line (Writeln)
```

The module structure chart for the design has not changed. The following Pascal program parallels our new design.

PROBLEM-SOLVING CASE STUDY cont'd.

```
PROGRAM Graph (Storel, Store2, Output);

(* This program generates bar graphs of monthly sales by department *)
(* for two Greenley department stores, permitting department by      *)
(* department comparison of sales                                    *)


VAR
  ID1,              (* Department ID number for store 1 *)
  ID2:              (* Department ID number for store 2 *)
    Integer;
  Sales1,           (* Department sales for store 1     *)
  Sales2:           (* Department sales for store 2     *)
    Real;
  Storel,           (* Accounting file for store 1      *)
  Store2:           (* Accounting file for store 2      *)
    Text;

(************************************************************************)


PROCEDURE Print_Header;

(* This procedure prints the title for the bar chart, a heading, and *)
(* the numeric scale for the chart                                   *)

BEGIN (* Print_Header *)
  Writeln('Bar Graph Comparing Departments of Store#1 and Store#2');
  Writeln;
  Writeln('Store  Sales in 1,000s of dollars');
  Writeln(' #     0         5        10        15        20        25');
  Writeln('       |.........|.........|.........|.........|.........|')
END;  (* Print_Header *)

(************************************************************************)


PROCEDURE Get_Data (VAR Data_File:      (* Receives/returns acct. file *)
                        Text;
                    VAR Dept_ID:         (* Returns dept. number        *)
                        Integer;
                    VAR Dept_Sales:      (* Returns monthly sales       *)
                        Real);

(* This procedure takes an input accounting file as a parameter, reads *)
(* the department ID number and number of days of sales from that file, *)
(* then reads one sales figure for each of those days, computing a      *)
(* total sales figure for the month. This figure is returned in         *)
(* Dept_Sales                                                           *)
```

Gobal

PROBLEM-SOLVING CASE STUDY cont'd.

Local

```
VAR
  Num_Days,        (* Number of business days in the month         *)
  Day:             (* The Loop Control Variable for a loop reading daily sale *)
    Integer;
  Sale:            (* One day's sales for the department           *)
    Real;

BEGIN (* Get_Data *)
  Readln(Data_File, Dept_ID);                    (* Get department ID    *)
  IF EOF(Data_File)                              (* Data validation test *)
    THEN
      Writeln('Data error: No data following dept. ID.')
    ELSE
      BEGIN
        Readln(Data_File, Num_Days);    (* Get number of days          *)
        Dept_Sales := 0.0;              (* Initialize process          *)
        Day := 1;                       (* Initialize Loop Control Variable *)
        WHILE Day <= Num_Days DO
          BEGIN
            IF EOF(Data_File)                    (* Data validation test *)
              THEN
                BEGIN
                  Writeln('Data error: Ran out of data in mid-set.');
                  Day := Num_Days + 1          (* Set loop end condition *)
                END
              ELSE
                BEGIN
                  Readln(Data_File, Sale);    (* Update process         *)
                  Dept_Sales := Dept_Sales + Sale;
                  Day := Day + 1              (* Update Loop Control Variable *)
                END
          END
      END
END;   (* Get_Data *)

(*******************************************************************)

PROCEDURE Print_Data (Dept_ID,           (* Receives dept. ID number   *)
                      Store_Num:   VAR   (* Receives store number      *)
                        Integer;
                      Dept_Sales:        (* Receives total dept. sales *)
                        Real);
```

```
(* This procedure prints the department ID number, the store number, *)
(* and a bar graph of the sales for the department. The bar graph is *)
(* printed at a scale of one mark per $500                           *)
```

PROBLEM-SOLVING CASE STUDY *cont'd.*

```
BEGIN (* Print_Data *)
  Writeln('     Dept ', Dept_ID:1);                    (* Print ID *)
  Write(Store_Num:3, ' ':4);                     (* Print store number *)
  WHILE Dept_Sales > 250 DO
    BEGIN
      Write('*');                         (* Print '*' for each $500 *)
      Dept_Sales := Dept_Sales - 500  (* Update Loop Control Variable *)
    END;
  Writeln                                         (* Go to a new line *)
END;  (* Print_Data *)

(*********************************************************************)

                              ⌊ω INITIALIZE ∼
BEGIN (* Graph *)
  Assign(Store1, 'STORE1.DAT');
  Assign(Store2, 'STORE2.DAT');
  Reset(Store1);
  Reset(Store2);
  Print_Header;
  WHILE NOT EOF(Store1) AND NOT EOF(Store2) DO       (* For each dept   *)
    BEGIN
      Writeln;
      Get_Data(Store1, ID1, Sales1);
      Get_Data(Store2, ID2, Sales2);
      IF ID1 <> ID2                           (* Data validation test *)
        THEN
          Writeln('Data error: Department IDs don''t match.')
        ELSE
          BEGIN
            Print_Data(ID1, 1, Sales1);
            Print_Data(ID2, 2, Sales2)
          END
    END;
  IF EOF(Store1) <> EOF(Store2)
    THEN
      IF EOF(Store1)
        THEN
          Writeln('Ran out of data for Store 1 before Store 2.')
        ELSE
          Writeln('Ran out of data for Store 2 before Store 1.');
  Close(Store1);
  Close(Store2)
END.  (* Graph *)
```

Testing: In addition to the testing that was recommended for Program Graph in Chapter 6, the new program should be run with data sets that verify the new data validation code. For example, a data set with mismatched department ID numbers should be tried, as well as some incomplete data sets.

We have not changed the overall design of Program Graph—it still consists of the same collection of modules—however, we have changed the functions of some of the modules to make them more robust in dealing with invalid data. For example, if either file ends prematurely or the department IDs are not the same for both stores, then an error message is printed. (More data validation could be added to this program, such as testing for negative sales.)

Each of the error messages in Program Graph describes the exact error that caused the message to be printed. This is effective programming practice because it aids the user of the program in determining what is wrong with the data. (Imagine how hard this would be if all the error messages just said "Data error.")

We took advantage of the fact that a value parameter can have an expression for an actual parameter by using a constant in the call to Print_Data. If we used a constant as the actual parameter for a VAR parameter, a compile-time error such as "VARIABLE IDENTIFIER EXPECTED" would result. A VAR parameter must have the address of a variable.

Testing and Debugging

One of the advantages of a modular design is that you can test the design long before the code has been written for all of the modules. If we test each module individually, then we can assemble the modules into a complete program with much greater confidence that the program is correct. In this section we will introduce a technique for testing a module separately.

Stubs and Drivers

Suppose you were given the code for a module and your job was to test it. How would you test a single module by itself? First of all, it must be called by something (unless it is the main program). Second, it may have calls to other modules that aren't available to you. To test the module, you must fill in these missing links.

When a module contains calls to other modules, we can write dummy procedures called **stubs** to satisfy those calls. A stub usually consists of a Writeln statement that prints a message like "Procedure such-and-such just got called." Even though the stub is a dummy, it allows us to determine whether the procedure is called at the right time by the program or calling procedure.

Stub   A dummy procedure or function that assists in testing part of a program. A stub has the same name and interface as a procedure or function that would actually be called by the part of the program being tested, but it is usually much simpler.

A stub can also be used to print the set of values that are passed to it; this tells us whether or not the module under test is supplying the proper information. Sometimes the stub will assign new values to its VAR parameters to simulate data being read or results being computed to give the module something to keep working on. Since we can choose the values that are returned by the stub, we have better control over the conditions of the test run.

Here is a stub that simulates procedure Print in Program Transpose.

```
PROCEDURE Print  (    Ch:            (* Receives first character of last name *)
                      Char);

(* Stub for procedure Print in Program Transpose *)

BEGIN (* Print *)
  Writeln('Print was called with Ch = ', Ch)
END;   (* Print *)
```

Here is a stub that simulates a call to Skip_Blanks by returning an arbitrarily chosen character.

```
PROCEDURE Skip_Blanks (VAR Ch:         (* Returns first nonblank input *)
                           Char);
(* Stub for procedure Skip_Blanks in Program Transpose *)

BEGIN (* Skip_Blanks *)
    Writeln('Skip_Blanks was called here. Returning ''X''.');
    Ch := 'X'
END;   (* Skip_Blanks *)
```

Each of these stubs is simpler than the procedure it simulates, which is typical because the object of using stubs is to provide a simple, predictable environment for testing a module.

In addition to supplying a stub for each call in the module, you must provide a dummy program—a **driver**—to call the module. A driver program contains the bare minimum of definitions required to call the module being tested.

Driver   A simple main program that is used to call a procedure or function being tested. The use of a driver permits direct control of the testing process.

By surrounding a module with a driver and stubs, you gain complete control of the conditions under which it executes. This allows you to test different situations and combinations that may reveal errors. For example, the following program is a driver for procedure Get_Initial in Program Transpose. A stub that simulates Skip_Blanks is also used in this example.

```pascal
PROGRAM Get_Initial_Driver (Output);

(* Provides an environment for testing procedure  *)
(* Get_Initial in isolation from Program Transpose *)

VAR
  Initial:        (* Parameter to Get_Initial *)
    Char;

(**************************************************************)

PROCEDURE Skip_Blanks (VAR Ch:          (* Returns first nonblank input *)
                            Char);

(* Stub for procedure Skip_Blanks in Program Transpose *)

BEGIN (* Skip_Blanks *)
  Writeln('Skip_Blanks was called here. Returning ''X''.');
  Ch := 'X'
END;   (* Skip_Blanks *)

(**************************************************************)

PROCEDURE Get_Initial (VAR Initial:      (* Returns first initial *)
                            Char);

(* Returns the first letter in the first name *)

VAR
  Ch:          (* Holds letter returned by Skip_Blanks *)
    Char;

BEGIN (* Get_Initial *)
  Skip_Blanks(Ch);
  Initial := Ch
END;   (* Get_Initial *)

(**************************************************************)

BEGIN (* Get_Initial_Driver *)
  Initial := 'Z';
  Get_Initial(Initial);
  Writeln('Get_Initial returned '. Initial)
END.   (* Get_Initial_Driver *)
```

Stubs and drivers are also used in team programming. The programmers develop the overall design and the interfaces between the modules. Each programmer then designs and codes one or more of the modules, and uses drivers and stubs to test the code. When all of the modules have been coded and tested, they are assembled into what should be a working program.

For team programming to succeed, it is essential that all of the module interfaces be explicitly defined and that the coded modules adhere strictly to the specifications for those interfaces. Obviously, global variable references must be carefully avoided in a team-programming situation, since it is impossible for each person to know how the rest of the team is using every variable.

Testing and Debugging Hints

1. Make sure that variables used as actual parameters to a procedure are declared in the block where the procedure call is made.
2. Declare each procedure before any calls are made to it. (Don't call a procedure that hasn't been previously declared.)
3. Be certain that formal and actual parameters are matched by position in the parameter list and that their types are the same. There is one exception: if the formal parameter is a value parameter of type Real, the actual parameter may be either Real or Integer.
4. Remember that a VAR parameter requires a variable as an actual parameter, whereas a value parameter can have any expression that supplies a value of the same data type (except as noted in the preceding hint) as an actual parameter.
5. Use value parameters unless a value must be returned. VAR parameters can change the value of an actual parameter; value parameters cannot.
6. Carefully define the preconditions, postconditions, and the parameter list to eliminate side effects. Variables used only in a procedure should be declared as local variables. *Do not* reference nonlocal variables directly from inside a procedure.
7. If the compiler displays a message such as "UNDECLARED IDENTIFIER," check that identifiers aren't misspelled (or that they are declared at all), identifiers are declared before they are referenced, and the scope of the identifier includes the reference to it.
8. If you intend to use a local name that is the same as a global name, a misspelling in the local declaration will wreak havoc. The Pascal compiler won't complain but instead will cause every reference to the local name to go to the global name instead.
9. Remember that the same identifier cannot be used in both the formal parameter list and the local declarations of a procedure.
10. Be sure the keyword VAR precedes each VAR parameter in the formal parameter list. A series of VAR parameters of the same data type may be separated by commas and preceded by a single VAR. When the keyword VAR is not used, the parameter is a value parameter. For example, given the parameter list

```
PROCEDURE One (     A,                (* value *)
                    B:                (* value *)
                    Integer;
              VAR C:                  (* VAR   *)
                    Boolean;
                    D:                (* value *)
                    Boolean;
                    E,                (* value *)
                    F:                (* value *)
                    Real;
              VAR G,                  (* VAR   *)
                    H:                (* VAR   *)
                    Integer);
```

C, G, and H are VAR parameters, and A, B, D, E, and F are value parameters.

11. Keep the scope rules in mind when arranging the order and nesting structure of procedures in a program. For example, given the structure

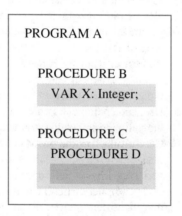

procedures B and C can be called from within program A, but procedure D cannot. Procedure B cannot call procedures C or D. Procedures B, C, and D may be called from within procedure C or procedure D.

12. If necessary, use the Debugger to see if a procedure is executing correctly when it is called (F8 skips over procedure calls, F7 steps through procedure calls). The values in the actual parameters can be displayed in the Watch window immediately before (to show the input values) and immediately after (to show the output values) the call to the procedure. You also may want to use the Watch window in the procedure itself to follow the values of local variables during its execution.

Summary

Pascal has two types of formal parameters: VAR and value. VAR parameters have the word VAR before them in the formal parameter list, while value parameters do not. Parameters that return values from a procedure should be VAR parameters. All others should be value parameters. This minimizes side effects, since only a copy of the value of an actual parameter is passed to a value parameter, and thus the original value cannot be changed.

Anything declared in the main program is visible to all procedures and is called **global.** Anything that is declared outside a procedure that is visible from within that procedure is called **nonlocal** with respect to that procedure. This may include declarations in blocks (if any) in which the procedure is nested. Do not reference nonlocal variables directly. All communication between the modules of a program should be through the formal and actual parameter lists. The use of global constants, on the other hand, is considered to be an acceptable programming practice because it adds consistency and makes a program easier to change while avoiding the pitfalls of side effects.

The scope of a declaration refers to the parts of the program from which it is visible. The scope rules say that an identifier is visible to all statements between its definition and the end of its block, except those in nested blocks that declare an identifier with the same name. The formal parameters of a procedure have the same scope as local variables declared in the procedure.

If you want to call a procedure from more than one place, don't nest it. If one procedure is an integral part of another and has no functional meaning in any other context, nest it.

Well-designed and well-documented procedures that are free of side effects can often be reused in other programs. Many programmers keep a library of procedures that they use repeatedly.

Stubs and drivers can be used to test procedures in isolation from the rest of a program. They are particularly useful in the context of team-programming projects.

■ *Quick Check*

1. a. What distinguishes a variable parameter from a value parameter in a procedure heading? (p. 300)
   b. How can you tell if a variable reference inside a procedure is local or nonlocal? (pp. 301–308)
   c. Where are local variables defined in a procedure? (pp. 301–308)
   d. When does the scope of an identifier exclude a nested block? (pp. 301–308)

2. Assume that you are designing a program and you need a procedure to read a given number of real values and return their average. The number of values is in an integer variable called Data_Points, declared in the program.
   a. How many parameters will there be in the actual and formal parameter lists, and what will their data type(s) be? (pp. 309–312)

  b. Which of the formal parameters should be VAR and which should be value? (pp. 309–319)

  c. What local variables, if any, will be required in the procedure? (pp. 309–312)

3. A program declares a variable called Framistats and a procedure called Fumble. Inside of Fumble, another procedure called Drop is declared. Inside of Drop, a variable, again called Framistats, is declared. Which version of Framistats would be accessed by the program, by Fumble, and by Drop? (pp. 301–308)

4. What is the difference between the kinds of information that are passed to VAR and value parameters? Which parameter protects the actual parameter from being changed by the procedure? (pp. 301–308)

5. Why use value parameters whenever possible? Why avoid directly accessing nonlocal variables? (pp. 309–312)

Answers

1. a. A value parameter is not preceded by VAR in a procedure heading. b. If the variable is not defined in either the VAR section of the procedure or its formal parameter list, then the reference is nonlocal. c. Local variables are declared in the VAR declaration section of the procedure. d. When the nested block declares an identifier with the same name.   2. a. There will be two parameters: an Integer containing the number of values to be read and a Real containing the average. b. The Integer should be a value parameter. The Real should be a VAR parameter. c. Local variables will be needed for an input value, the sum, and the count of the values.   3. The program and Fumble access the Framistats declared by the program. Drop accesses its own version of Framistats.   4. VAR parameters receive locations of actual parameters. Value parameters get copies of the values in the actual parameters, thus protecting the actual parameters from change.   5. Both using value parameters and not directly accessing nonlocal variables will minimize side effects. Value parameters can also be passed expressions.

■ *Exam Preparation Exercises*

1. Using a VAR parameter (passing by reference), a procedure can obtain the initial value of an actual parameter as well as change the value of the actual parameter. (True or False?)

2. Using a value parameter, the value of a variable can be passed to a procedure and used for computation there, without any modification to the actual parameter. (True or False?)

3. A particular procedure can be a nested block relative to the program that contains it, and an enclosing block to any procedures declared within it. (True or False?)

4. Identifiers declared at the beginning of a block are accessible to all statements that are part of that block, including those in nested blocks (assuming the nested blocks don't have local identifiers with the same names). (True or False?)

5. If a procedure contains a locally declared variable with the same name as a variable in an enclosing block, no confusion will result because references to variables in procedures are first interpreted as references to local variables. (True or False?)

6. Define the following:

value parameter	nonlocal access
variable parameter	scope
local variable	side effects
global variable	name precedence

7. What is the output of the following Pascal program? (If any value is undefined, indicate this with a *u*. Assume that attempting to print an undefined value doesn't cause the program to crash.)

```
PROGRAM Sample_Params(Output);
VAR
  D,
  E:
    Integer;
```
Global variables

```
(********************************************************************)

PROCEDURE One (VAR S:
                    Integer;
               T:
                    Integer);
BEGIN (* One *)
  S := 3;
  S := S + 2;
  T := 4 * S;
  Writeln('S equals ', S, ' and T equals ', T, ' within procedure One.')
END;  (* One *)
```
var variables

```
(********************************************************************)

BEGIN (* Sample_Params *)
  D := 12;
  E := 14;
  One(D, E);
  Writeln('D equals ', D, ' and E equals ', E, ' after the first call to One.')
  D := 12;
  E := 14;
  One(E, D);
  Writeln('D equals ', D, ' and E equals ', E, ' after the second call to One.');
END.  (* Sample_Params *)
```

8. Given the block structure:

```
PROGRAM Scope_Rules (Input, Output);
VAR
  A,
  B:
      Integer;

PROCEDURE Block1;
VAR
  A1,
  B1:
      Integer;
```

```
      PROCEDURE Block2;
      VAR
        A,
        A2,
        B2:
          Integer;
      BEGIN (* Block2 *)
           .    A := B2
           .
      END; (* Block2 *)

    BEGIN (* Block1 *)
         .
         .
    END; (* Block1 *)

  PROCEDURE Block3;
  VAR
    A3,
    B3:
      Integer;
  BEGIN (* Block3 *)
       .
       .
  END; (* Block3 *)

  BEGIN (* Scope_Rules *)
       .
       .
  END. (* Scope_Rules *)
```

a. A and B are global variables, accessible to all parts of Program Scope_Rules, including procedure Block2. (True or False?)

b. Since Scope_Rules is the outermost block, statements in its body can reference all variables declared in inner blocks, including procedure Block2. (True or False?)

c. Since procedure Block2 is the innermost block, its local variables can be accessed by all other blocks. (True or False?)

d. Variable A1 is global with respect to procedure Block2. (True or False?)

e. Variable B2 is local to procedure Block1. (True or False?)

f. The statement A1 := A would be legal in procedure Block1 (True or False?)

g. The statement A3 := A1 would be legal in procedure Block3. (True or False?)

h. Variables A2 and B2 are not defined in any of the outer blocks. (True or False?)

i. The statement A := B2 in procedure Block2 would assign the value of B2 to the local variable A, and the global A would not be affected. (True or False?)

j. Variables A1 and B1 are global with respect to procedure Block2, local to procedure Block1, and not defined for the program outer block. (True or False?)

9. Draw a scope diagram for the block structure in exercise 8.

10. **What is the output of the following Pascal program? Note that the program is an example of poor interface design practices.**

```
PROGRAM Params (Output);
VAR
  X:              } Global
    Integer;


(******************************************************************)

PROCEDURE Refer (VAR A:        } Global
                     Integer);

BEGIN (* Refer *)
 A := 3
END;  (* Refer *)


(******************************************************************)

PROCEDURE Value (   B:
                      Integer);

BEGIN (* Value *)
  B:= 4
END;  (* Value *)


(******************************************************************)

PROCEDURE Local;
VAR
  X:
    Integer;
BEGIN (* Local *)
  X := 5
END;  (* Local *)


(******************************************************************)

PROCEDURE Global;
BEGIN (* Global *)
  X := 7
END;  (* Global *)


(******************************************************************)
```

```
BEGIN (* Params *)
  X := 15;
  Refer(X);
  Writeln('X equals ', X, ' after the call to Refer.');
  X := 16;
  Value(X);
  Writeln('X equals , X, ' after the call to Value.');
  X := 17;
  Local;
  Writeln('X equals ', X, ' after the call to Local.');
  X := 18;
  Global;
  Writeln('X equals ', X, ' after the call to Global.')
END.  (* Params *)
```

11. Read the following program containing procedure Change. Fill in the values of all variables before and after the procedure is called. Then fill in the values of all variables after the return to the main program. (Let *u* indicate an undefined value.)

```
PROGRAM Sample (Input, Output);
VAR
  A,
  B:
    Integer;
PROCEDURE Change (    X:
                         Integer;
                  VAR Y:
                         Integer);
VAR
  B:
    Integer;
BEGIN (* Change *)
  B := X;
  Y := Y + B;
  X := Y
END;  (* Change *)

BEGIN (* Sample *)
  A := 10;
  B := 7;
  Change(A, B);
  Writeln(A:6, B:6)
END. (* Sample *)
```

Variables in Sample just before Change is called.

A ___10___

B ___7___

Variables in Change when it is first called.

X ___10___

Y ___7___

B. ___Undefined___

Variables in Sample after return from Change.

A _____

B _____

12. What is the output of the following Pascal program? (If any value is undefined, indicate this with a *u*. Assume that attempting to print an undefined value doesn't cause the program to crash.)

```pascal
PROGRAM Scope_Rule(Output);
VAR
  X:
    Integer;

(********************************************************************)

PROCEDURE Sub_A;
VAR
  X:
    Integer;
BEGIN (* Sub_A *)
  X := 5
END;  (* Sub_A *)

(********************************************************************)

PROCEDURE Sub_B;
BEGIN (* Sub_B *)
  X := 14
END;  (* Sub_B *)

(********************************************************************)

PROCEDURE Sub_C;
VAR
  X:
    Integer;
BEGIN (* Sub_C *)
  X := 3;
  Sub_A;
  Writeln('X equals ', X, ' after the call to Sub_A.');
  X := 6;
  Sub_B;
  Writeln('X equals ', X, ' after the call to Sub_B.')
END;  (* Sub_C *)

(********************************************************************)

BEGIN (* Scope_Rule *)
  X := 9;
  Sub_C;
  Writeln('X equals ', X, ' after the call to Sub_C.')
END.  (* Scope_Rule *)
```

13. What is the output of the following Pascal program? (If any value is undefined, indicate this with a *u*. Assume that attempting to print an undefined value doesn't cause the program to crash.) Why is the output in this program different from the output for Program Scope_Rule in exercise 12?

```pascal
PROGRAM More_Scope_Rule(Output);
VAR
  X:
    Integer


(******************************************************************)

PROCEDURE Sub_C;
VAR
  X:
    Integer;


(******************************************************************)

  PROCEDURE Sub_A;
  VAR
    X:
      Integer;
  BEGIN (* Sub_A *)
    X := 5
  END;   (* Sub_A *)


(******************************************************************)

  PROCEDURE Sub_B;
  BEGIN (* Sub_B *)
    X := 14
  END;   (* Sub_B *)


(******************************************************************)

BEGIN (* Sub_C *)
  X := 3;
  Sub_A;
  Writeln('X equals ', X, ' after Sub_A is called.');
  X := 6;
  Sub_B;
  Writeln('X equals ', X, ' after Sub_B is called.')
END;   (* Sub_C *)


(******************************************************************)
```

```
BEGIN (* More_Scope_Rule *)
  X := 9;
  Sub_C;
  Writeln('X equals ', X, ' after Sub_C is called.')
END.  (* More_Scope_Rule *)
```

14. Write the output produced by the execution of the following program. (This program is not intended to make any sense, only to test your knowledge of scope rules and side effects.)

```
PROGRAM Scope_Out (Input, Output);
VAR
  A,
  B,
  C:
     Integer;

PROCEDURE One (    X,
                   Y:
                       Integer;
                   VAR Z:
                       Integer);
VAR
  A:
     Integer;
BEGIN (* One *)
  A := 1;
  B := 7;
  X := Y;
  Z := A + X
END;  (* One *)

BEGIN (* Scope_Out *)
  A := 4;
  B := 5;
  C := 12;
  One(A, B, C);
  Writeln(A, B, C)
END.  (* Scope_Out *)
```

▪ *Programming Warm-Up Exercises*

1. a. Write a procedure that returns the sum of the squares of three numbers (Integers) and returns a Boolean variable equal to True if all three numbers are positive (or False otherwise). Use VAR and value parameters as required.

   b. Write the calling statement for your procedure if the three numbers are stored in A, B, and C.

2. Write a procedure that will read in a specified number of Real values and return their average. A call to this procedure might look like

```
Get_Mean_Of( 5, Mean);
```

where the first parameter specifies the number of values to be read, and the second parameter receives the result.

3. Write a Pascal procedure called Max_Value that returns the largest of three integers it receives from the calling program. A call to this procedure might look like

```
Max_Value(Integer1, Integer2, Integer3, Largest);
```

4. Write a procedure that will compute the distance between two points on a plane, given their coordinates. If one of the points is located at (X1, Y1) and the other is located at (X2, Y2), the formula for the distance is

Sqrt(Sqr(X2 − X1) + Sqr(Y2 − Y1))

All of the parameters to this procedure should be of type Real.

5. Given the following procedure body, write a heading that declares VAR and value parameters as necessary. (*Hint:* Make a list of all the identifiers in the procedure and notice which ones aren't declared locally.)

```
VAR
  Sales1,
  Sales2:
    Real;
BEGIN (* Get_Average *)
  Writeln('Department ', Dept_Num:1);          (* Receives *)
  Readln(Sales1, Sales2);
  Writeln('has weekly sales of ', Sales1:5:2,
          ' and ', Sales2:5:2);
  Avg_Sales := (Sales1 + Sales2) / 2.0;        (* Returns *)
  Writeln('for an average of ', Avg_Sales:5:2)
END;  (* Get_Average *)
```

6. Write a procedure heading for the following list.

RocketSimulation

Receives	Thrust (Real)
Receives/Returns	Weight (Real)
Receives	Time_Step (Integer)
Receives	Total_Time (Integer)
Returns	Velocity (Real)
Returns	Out_of_Fuel (Boolean)

7. Write a procedure that will have three parameters—Hours, Minutes, and Elapsed_Time—passed to it. Elapsed_Time is an Integer number of minutes to be added to the starting time passed in through Hours and Minutes. The resulting new time will be returned through Hours and Minutes. For example:

Before Call *to AddTime*	*After Call* *to AddTime*
Hours = 12	Hours = 16
Minutes = 44	Minutes = 2
Elapsed_Time = 198	Elapsed_Time = 198

8. Write a program called Acronym that will read a series of words from a line of input, and print out the acronym formed by the first letters of the words. If you reuse the procedures developed for Program Transpose in this chapter, you shouldn't have to write any procedures of your own. Example I/O:

   Input:
   United Nations International Children's Emergency Fund

   Output:
   UNICEF

9. Rewrite Program Acronym in Exercise 8 as a procedure that can be called to print the acronym formed by the words in one line of input. Write a program that calls procedure Acronym for each line of input on a file until EOF is reached. (*Hint:* The primary change to Program Acronym will be replacement of its program heading with a procedure heading.)

10. The following program was written with very poor style: global variable references were used in place of parameters. Rewrite it without global references, using good programming style.

```
PROGRAM Side_Effects(Input, Output);
VAR A,B,C: Integer;
PROCEDURE Mash_Globals
VAR Temp: Integer;
BEGIN
  Temp := A + B;
  A := B + C;
  B := Temp
END;
BEGIN
  Readln(A,B,C);
  Mash_Globals;
  Writeln('A= ',A:1, ' B= ', B:1, ' C= ',C:1)
END.
```

11. The following procedure is supposed to copy the contents of one text file into another. There are three errors—one is a syntax error, the other two cause the program to give incorrect output. Explain the effect of these errors on the output, and correct the procedure.

```
PROCEDURE File_Copy(    In_File:
                            Text;
                   VAR Out_File:
                            Text);
VAR
  Ch:
    Char;
```

```
BEGIN (* File_Copy *)
  Assign(In_File, 'INFILE.DAT');
  Assign(Out_File, 'OUTFILE.DAT');
  Reset(In_File);
  Rewrite(Out_File);
  WHILE NOT EOF(In_File) DO
    BEGIN
      Read(In_File, Ch);
      WHILE NOT EOLN(In_File) DO
        BEGIN
          Write(Out_File, Ch);
          Read(In_File, Ch)
        END;
      Readln(In_File);
      Writeln(Out_File)
    END;
  Close(In_File);
  Close(Out_File)
END;  (* File_Copy *)
```

12. Rewrite Program Graph (pp. 327–329) from the second case study of this chapter, adding data validation tests for negative sales, sales greater than $25,000, and department IDs not in order.

13. Add lists of the preconditions and postconditions to the comments at the beginning of each procedure in Program Transpose (pp. 318–321), which was developed in the first case study of this chapter.

■ *Programming Problems*

1. Write a top-down design and a Pascal program with procedures that will help you balance your checking account. The program should let you enter the initial balance for the month, followed by a series of transactions. For each transaction entered, the program should echo-print the transaction data, the current balance for the account, and the total service charges. Service charges are $0.10 for a deposit and $0.15 for a check. If the balance drops below $500.00 at any point during the month, a service charge of $5.00 will be assessed for the month. If the balance drops below $50.00, the program should print a warning message. If the balance becomes negative, an additional service charge of $10.00 should be assessed for each check until the balance becomes positive again.

   A transaction will take the form of a letter, followed by a blank and a real number. If the letter is a C, then the number is the amount of a check. If the letter is a D, then the number is the amount of a deposit. The last transaction will consist of the letter E, with no number following it. A sample run might look like this:

```
Enter the beginning balance:
879.46
Enter a transaction:
C 400.00
Transaction:  Check in amount of $400.00
```

```
Current balance:  $479.46
Service charge:  Check - $0.15
Service charge:  Below $500 - $5.00
Total service charges:  $5.15
Enter a transaction:
D 100.0
Transaction:  Deposit in amount of $100.00
Current balance:  $579.46
Service charge:  Deposit - $0.10
Total service charges:  $5.25
Enter a transaction:
E
Transaction:  End
Current balance:  $579.46
Total service charges:  $5.25
Final balance:  $574.21
```

As usual, your program should use proper style and indentation, meaningful identifiers, and appropriate comments. Also, be sure to check for data errors such as invalid transaction codes or negative amounts.

2. In this problem you will design and implement a Roman numeral calculator. The subtractive Roman numeral notation commonly in use today (such as IV, meaning "4") was used only rarely during the time of the Roman Republic and Empire. For ease of calculation, the Romans most frequently used a purely additive notation in which a number was simply the sum of its digits (4 equals IIII, in this notation). Each number starts with the digit of highest value and ends with the one of smallest value. This is the notation we will use in this problem.

   Your program will input two Roman numbers and an arithmetic operator, and will print out the result of the operation, also as a Roman number. The values of the Roman digits are as follows:

I	1
V	5
X	10
L	50
C	100
D	500
M	1000

   Thus, the number MDCCCCLXXXXVI represents 1996. The arithmetic operators that your program should recognize in the input are +, −, *, and /. These should perform the Pascal operations of integer addition, subtraction, multiplication, and division.

   One way of approaching this problem is to convert the Roman numbers into integers, perform the required operation, and then convert the result back into a Roman number for printing. The following might be a sample run of the program:

```
Enter the first number:
MCCXXVI
The first number is 1226
Enter the second number:
LXVIIII
```

```
The second number is 69
Enter the desired arithmetic operation:

+

The sum of MCCXXVI and LXVIIII is MCCLXXXXV (1295)
```

Your program should use proper style and indentation, appropriate comments, and meaningful identifiers, and avoid side effects. It should also check for errors in the input, such as illegal digits or arithmetic operators, and take appropriate actions when these are found. The program may also check to ensure that the numbers are in purely additive form—digits are followed only by digits of the same or lower value.

3. Develop a top-down design and write a program to produce a bar chart of gourmet-popcorn production for a cooperative farm group on a farm-by-farm basis. The input to the program will be a series of data sets, one per line, with each set representing the production for one farm. The output will be a bar chart that identifies each farm and displays its production in pints of corn per acre.

   Each data set will consist of the name of a farm, followed by a comma and a space, a Real number representing acres planted, a space, and an Integer number representing pint jars of popcorn produced.

   The output will be a single line for each farm, with the name of the farm starting in the first column on a line and the bar chart starting in column 30. Each mark in the bar chart will represent 250 jars of popcorn per acre. The production goal for the year is 5,000 jars per acre. A vertical bar should appear in the chart for farms with lower production, or a special mark for farms with production greater than or equal to 5,000 jars per acre. For example, given the input file

Orville's Acres,	114.8	43801
Hoffman's Hills,	77.2	36229
Jiffy Quick Farm,	89.4	24812
Jolly Good Plantation,	183.2	104570
Organically Grown Inc.,	45.5	14683

the output would be

```
                      Pop Co-Op
Farm Name                       Production in
                                Thousands of
                                Pint Jars per Acre
                                 1   2   3   4   5   6
                                ---|---|---|---|---|---|
Orville's Acres                 *************************|
Hoffman's Hills                 ********************** |
Jiffy Quick Farm                ***********  |
Jolly Good Plantation           *****************************#***
Organically Grown Inc.          ************ |
```

This problem should decompose neatly into several procedures. Your program should be written in proper programming style, with plenty of comments and no global variable references. It should handle data errors (such as a farm name longer than 29 characters) without crashing.

Functions, Precision, and Recursion

CHAPTER 8

In the last two chapters we discussed procedures. In this chapter we look at the second type of subprogram: the **function.** The main difference between procedures and functions is the way they are called. A procedure call is a statement in a program; a function call is part of an expression. You already know several built-in Pascal functions: Sqr (square), Sqrt (square-root), Round, and Trunc (truncate). Often, we can simplify the coding of complex expressions by defining our own functions, which is especially helpful when the expression is used repeatedly in a program.

Because functions are often used for numerical computations, this chapter also looks at the limitations of the computer in doing calculations. We examine how these limitations can cause numerical errors and how to avoid such errors.

Functions

Functions are very similar to procedures. The difference is that functions are used when there is only one result value, and that result is to be used directly in an expression. For example, suppose we are writing a program that calculates a prorated refund of tuition for students who withdraw in the middle of a semester. The amount to be refunded is the total tuition times the remaining fraction of the semester (the number of days remaining divided by the total number of days in the semester). The people who use the program want to be able to enter the dates the semester begins and ends, and the date of withdrawal, and have the program calculate the fraction of the semester that remains.

Since each semester begins and ends within one calendar year, we can calculate the number of days in a period by determining the day number of each date and subtracting the starting day number from the ending day number. The day number is the number associated with each day of the year if you count sequentially from January 1. December 31 has the day number 365, except in leap years, when it is 366. For example, if a semester begins on 1/3/93 and ends on 5/17/93 the calculation is as follows.

The day number of 1/3/93 is 3
The day number of 5/17/93 is 137
The length of the semester is $137 - 3 + 1 = 135$

We add one to the difference of the days because we count the first day as part of the period.

The algorithm for calculating the day number for a date is complicated by leap years and by months of different lengths. We could code this algorithm as a procedure called Compute_Day. The refund could then be computed by the following code segment.

```
Compute_Day(Start_Month, Start_Day, Start_Year, Start);
Compute_Day(Last_Month, Last_Day, Last_Year, Last);
Compute_Day(Withdraw_Month, Withdraw_Day, Withdraw_Year, Withdraw);
Fraction := (Last - Withdraw + 1) / (Last - Start + 1);
Refund := Tuition * Fraction;
```

The first three parameters to Compute_Day are received by the procedure, and the last one is returned to the main program. Since Compute_Day returns only one value, it can be written as a function instead of a procedure. Let's look at how the code segment would be written if we had a function called Day that returned the day number of a date in a given year.

```
Start  := Day(Start_Month, Start_Day, Start_Year);
Last := Day(Last_Month, Last_Day, Last_Year);
Withdraw := Day(Withdraw_Month, Withdraw_Day, Withdraw_Year);
Fraction := (Last - Withdraw + 1) / (Last - Start + 1);
Refund := Tuition * Fraction;
```

The second version of the code segment is much more intuitive. Because Day is a function, you know immediately that all its parameters receive values, and that it returns just one value (the day number for a date).

Let's look at the function definition for Day. Don't worry about how Day works; for now, we are concerned mainly with its syntax and structure.

```
FUNCTION Day (Month,            (* Month number, 1 - 12    *)
             Day_Of_Month,      (* Day of month, 1 - 31     *)
             Year:              (* Year. For example, 1992 *)
                Integer):
                Integer;

(* This function computes the day number within a year, given  *)
(* the date. It accounts correctly for leap years. The         *)
(* calculation is based on the fact that months average 30 days *)
(* in length. Thus, (Month - 1) * 30 is roughly the number of  *)
(* days in the year at the start of any month. A correction    *)
(* factor is used to account for cases where the average is    *)
(* incorrect and for leap years. The day of the month is then  *)
(* added to get the specific day number                        *)

VAR
   Correction:     (* Correction factor to account for leap year and *)
      Integer;     (* months of different lengths                    *)
```

```
BEGIN (* Day *)
  IF (Year MOD 4 = 0) AND
     ((Year MOD 100 <> 0) OR
     (Year MOD 400 = 0))                      (* Test for leap year *)
    THEN
      BEGIN
        IF Month >= 3                (* If date is after February 29 *)
          THEN
            Correction := 1          (* Then add one for leap year *)
      END
    ELSE
      Correction := 0;
  IF Month = 3                   (* Correct for different length months *)
    THEN
      Correction := Correction - 1
    ELSE IF (Month = 2) OR (Month = 6) OR (Month = 7)
      THEN
        Correction := Correction + 1
    ELSE IF Month = 8
      THEN
        Correction := Correction + 2
    ELSE IF (Month = 9) OR (Month = 10)
      THEN
        Correction := Correction + 3
    ELSE IF (Month = 11) OR (Month = 12)
      THEN
        Correction := Correction + 4;
  Day := (Month - 1) * 30 + Correction + Day_Of_Month
END;  (* Day *)
```

The first thing to note about the function definition is that it looks like a procedure definition, except the heading begins with the word FUNCTION instead of PROCEDURE. If you look closely at the heading, you will notice something else: the entire parameter list is followed by a colon (:) and then a data type.

A function returns one value, not through a parameter but through the name of the function. The data type at the end of the heading defines the type of value that the function will return. This type is called the **function type**, although a more proper term is **function result type.**

Function Result Type   The data type of the result value returned by a function.

The last statement in Function Day assigns a value to the function name. Whatever value is assigned to the function name will be returned as the result (see Figure 8-1). If more than one value is assigned to the function name, only the last one is passed back.

The function name is not a variable. It only *acts* like a variable when it appears to the left of a := . If you use the function name in an expression, it is a call to the function, even if the expression is within the body of the function itself. (This means

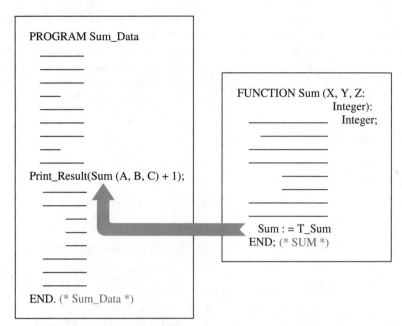

Figure 8-1
Assigning a Value
to the Function
Name Transmits the
Results Back to the
Expression That
Called the Function

you can't assign temporary values to the function name and then use them later on.) When a function is called from within itself, it is known as a **recursive call.** We return to the topic of recursion later in the chapter. For the time being, avoid using the function name in an expression within the function itself.

Keep in mind that expressions can be used in many places, in addition to assignment statements. They can appear in IF statements, in WHILE statements, as actual parameters in calls to subprograms that have value parameters, and so on.

The syntax template for the function heading is

> **FUNCTION** identifier parameter-list **:** type**;**

The parameter list is the same as for a procedure:

> (**VAR** identifier**,** identifier . . . **:** type **;**
> **VAR** identifier**,** identifier . . . **:** type
>   ⋮
>)

Let's look at a couple of example functions. Standard Pascal does not provide a power function, so we'll build one of our own. The function will be given two integers, X and N (where N $>=$ 0), and will compute X^N. We use the simple approach of multiplying repeatedly by X. Because the number of iterations is known, a count-controlled loop is appropriate. The loop will count down to 0 from the initial value of N. For each iteration of the loop, X is multiplied by the previous product.

```
FUNCTION Power (X,                (* Base number             *)
                N:                (* Power to raise base to *)
                   Integer):
                   Integer;    (* Returns X to N power    *)

(* This function computes X to the N power *)

VAR
   Result:        (* Holds intermediate powers of X *)
     Integer;

BEGIN (* Power *)
   Result := 1;
   WHILE N > 0 DO
     BEGIN
       Result := Result * X;
       N := N - 1
     END;
   Power := Result
END;   (* Power *)
```

Another function that is used frequently in calculating probabilities is the factorial. For example, 5 factorial (written 5! in mathematical notation) is $5 \times 4 \times 3 \times 2 \times 1$. Zero factorial is, by definition, equal to 1. This function has one integer parameter. As with Function Power, we use repeated multiplication, but we decrement the multiplier on each iteration.

```
FUNCTION Factorial (X:          (* The factorial to be computed *)
                      Integer):
                      Integer;

(* This function computes X! *)

VAR
   Result:        (* Holds partial products *)
     Integer;
```

```
BEGIN (* Factorial *)
   Result := 1;
   WHILE X > 0 DO
      BEGIN
         Result := Result * X;
         X := X - 1
      END;
   Factorial := Result
END;   (* Factorial *)
```

These functions are examined again when we look at recursion later in this chapter and in Chapter 17.

Boolean Functions

Functions are not restricted to returning numerical results. They can also be used to evaluate a condition and return a Boolean result. Boolean functions can be quite useful when a branch or loop depends on some complex condition. Rather than code the condition directly into the IF or WHILE statement, we can call a Boolean function to form the controlling expression.

Suppose we are writing a program that works with triangles. The program reads three angles as real numbers. Before performing any calculations on those angles, however, we should check that they really form a triangle by adding the angles to confirm that their sum is equal to 180 degrees. We can write a function that takes the three angles as parameters and returns a Boolean result. Such a function would look like this (recall that real numbers should be tested only for near equality):

```
Function Triangle (Angle1,      (* Receives first angle    *)
                   Angle2,      (* Receives second angle   *)
                   Angle3:      (* Receives third angle    *)
                   Real):
                   Boolean;     (* Returns True if a triangle *)

(* This function returns True if its three input values add up *)
(* to 180 degrees, forming a valid triangle; otherwise, False  *)

BEGIN (* Triangle *)
   (* Test for sum of angles "equal" to 180.0 *)
   Triangle := Abs(Angle1 + Angle2 + Angle3 - 180.0) < 0.00000001
END;   (* Triangle *)
```

The following program fragment shows how function Triangle might be called:

```
Readln(AngleA, AngleB, AngleC);
IF Triangle(AngleA, AngleB, AngleC)          (* function call *)
   THEN
      Writeln('The three angles form a valid triangle.')
   ELSE
      Writeln('Those angles do not form a triangle.')
```

The IF statement is much easier to understand with the function than it would be if the entire condition were coded directly. When a conditional test is at all complicated, a Boolean function is in order.

Function Interface Design and Side Effects

The interface to a function can be designed in much the same way as for a procedure. We simply write down a list of what the function needs and what it must return. Since functions return only one value, there will be only one item labeled "returns" in the list. Everything else in the list will be labeled "receives," and there won't be any "receives/returns" type of parameters.

The changing or returning of more than one value in a function call is an unwanted side effect and should be avoided. If your interface design calls for multiple values to be returned, or for the values of actual parameters to be changed, then you should use a procedure instead of a function.

A rule of thumb is never to use VAR parameters in the formal parameter list of a function—use value parameters exclusively. Let's look at an example that demonstrates the importance of this rule. Suppose we define the following function:

```
FUNCTION Side_Effect (VAR Change:
                             Integer):
                             Integer;

BEGIN (* Side_Effect *)
   Side_Effect := Change * Change;
   Change := Change + 1                     (* Side effect *)
END;   (* Side_Effect *)
```

This function returns the square of its input value, but it also increments that actual parameter before returning. Now, suppose we call this function with the following statement:

```
Y := X + Side_Effect(X)
```

If X is 2, what is the value that is stored in Y? The answer depends on the order in which your compiler evaluates the expression. If it first calls the function, then the answer is 7. If it accesses X first in preparation for adding it to the function result, the answer is 6. This is precisely why VAR parameters shouldn't be used with functions. Obviously, a function that creates such an unpredictable situation has no place in a well-written program.

An exception is the case where a file is passed to a function; remember, Pascal allows a file to be passed only to a formal VAR parameter. When a file is passed to a function, the only operations that should be performed on it are tests such as EOF and EOLN. A function should not be used to perform input or output operations. Such operations are considered to be side effects of the function.

There is an extra advantage to using only value parameters in a function definition: constants and expressions can then be used as actual parameters. For example, function Triangle can be called in the following manner using literals and an expression:

```
IF Triangle(30.0, 60.0, 30.0 + 60.0)
   THEN
      Writeln('A 30-60-90 angle combination forms a triangle.')
   ELSE
      Writeln('Something is wrong.')
```

When to Use Functions

There aren't any formal rules for determining when to use a procedure and when to use a function, but here are some guidelines:

1. If the module must return more than one value or modify any actual parameters, do not use a function.
2. If the module must perform I/O, do not use a function.
3. If there is only one value returned from the module and it is a Boolean value, a function is appropriate.
4. If there is only one value returned and that value is to be used immediately in an expression, a function is appropriate.
5. When in doubt, use a procedure. Any function can be recoded as a procedure, with the function name becoming a "returns" parameter of the procedure.
6. If both a procedure and a function are acceptable, use the one you feel more comfortable implementing.

Functions were included in Pascal to provide a way to simulate mathematical operations called functions. Pascal provides a set of built-in, commonly used mathematical functions. A list of these appears in Appendix B.

More on Real Numbers

We have used real numbers off and on since they were introduced in Chapter 2, but we have not examined them in depth. Real numbers have some special properties when used on the computer. Thus far, we've almost ignored these properties; now it's time to consider them in detail.

Representation of Real Numbers

Let's assume we have a computer where each word (location) in memory is divided into a sign plus five decimal digits. When a variable or constant is defined, the location assigned to it consists of five digits and a sign. When an Integer variable or constant is defined, the interpretation of the number stored in that place is quite straightforward.

When a Real variable or constant is defined, the number stored there has both a whole number part and a fractional part, so it must be coded to represent both parts.

Let's see what such coded numbers might look like. The range of the numbers we can represent with five digits is $-99,999$ to $+99,999$:

-99999 to +99999

| + | 9 | 9 | 9 | 9 | 9 | Largest positive number |

| + | 0 | 0 | 0 | 0 | 0 | Zero |

| − | 9 | 9 | 9 | 9 | 9 | Largest negative number |

Our precision (the number of digits we can represent) is five digits, and each number within that range can be represented exactly.

What happens if we allow one of those digits (the left-most one, for example) to represent an exponent?

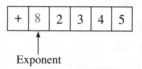

Exponent

Then $+82345$ represents the number $+2345 * 10^8$. The range of numbers we now represent is much larger:

$-9999 * 10^9$ to $9999 * 10^9$

or

$-9,999,000,000,000$ to $+9,999,000,000,000$

Our precision is now, however, only four digits; that is, any four-digit number can be represented exactly in our system. But what happens to numbers with more digits? The four left-most digits are represented correctly, and the right-most digits, or least **significant digits,** are lost (assumed to be 0). Figure 8-2 shows what happens. Note that 1,000,000 can be represented exactly, but $-4,932,416$ cannot, since this coding scheme limits us to four significant (nonzero) digits.

To extend our coding scheme to represent real numbers, we must be able to represent negative exponents. For example:

$7394 * 10^{-2} = 73.94$

or

$22 * 10^{-4} = .0022$

Figure 8-2
Coding Using Positive Exponents

NUMBER	POWER OF TEN NOTATION	CODED REPRESENTATION						VALUE
		Sign	Exp					
+99,999	$+9999 * 10^1$	+	1	9	9	9	9	+99,990
		Sign	Exp					
−999,999	$-9999 * 10^2$	−	2	9	9	9	9	−999,900
		Sign	Exp					
+1,000,000	$+1000 * 10^3$	+	3	1	0	0	0	+1,000,000
		Sign	Exp					
−4,932,416	$-4932 * 10^3$	−	3	4	9	3	2	−4,932,000

Since our scheme does not allow for a sign for the exponent, we shall change it slightly. The sign that we have will be the sign of the exponent, and a sign can be added to the far left to represent the sign of the number itself (see Figure 8-3).

All the numbers between 9999×10^{-9} and 9999×10^9 can now be represented accurately to four digits. Adding negative exponents to our scheme has allowed representation of fractional numbers.

Figure 8-4 shows how we would encode some real numbers. Note that our precision is still only four digits. The numbers 0.1032, -5.406, and $1,000,000$ can be represented exactly. The number 476.0321, however, with seven significant digits, is represented as 476.0; the "321" cannot be represented.

All computers limit the precision (number of significant digits) of a real number, although most machines use binary rather than decimal arithmetic. In our representation we used only five digits to simplify the examples, and some computers really are limited to only 4 or 5 digits of precision. A more typical system provides 7 to 15, or even 19, significant digits. We have shown only a single-digit exponent, but most systems allow two digits, and some allow up to four-digit exponents.

Figure 8-3
Coding Using Positive and Negative Exponents

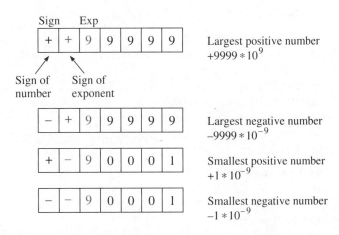

Sign   Exp

| + | + | 9 | 9 | 9 | 9 | 9 |

Sign of number   Sign of exponent

Largest positive number
$+9999 * 10^9$

| − | + | 9 | 9 | 9 | 9 | 9 |

Largest negative number
$-9999 * 10^{-9}$

| + | − | 9 | 0 | 0 | 0 | 1 |

Smallest positive number
$+1 * 10^{-9}$

| − | − | 9 | 0 | 0 | 0 | 1 |

Smallest negative number
$-1 * 10^{-9}$

	NUMBER	POWER OF TEN NOTATION	CODED REPRESENTATION						VALUE
			Sign	Exp					

Figure 8-4
Coding of Some
Real Numbers

NUMBER	POWER OF TEN NOTATION	Sign		Exp					VALUE
0.1032	$1032 * 10^{-4}$	+	−	4	1	0	3	2	0.1032
−5.4060	$-5406 * 10^{-3}$	−	−	3	5	4	0	6	−5.406
−0.003	$-3000 * 10^{-6}$	−	−	6	3	0	0	0	−0.0030
476.0321	$4760 * 10^{-1}$	+	−	1	4	7	6	0	476.0
1,000,000	$1000 * 10^{3}$	+	−	3	1	0	0	0	1,000,000

Arithmetic with Real Numbers

When we use integer arithmetic, our results are exact. Real arithmetic, however, is seldom exact. We can illustrate this by adding three real numbers X, Y, and Z, using our coding scheme.

First, we add X to Y, and then add Z to the result. Next, we add Y to Z, and then add X to that result. The associative law of arithmetic says that the two answers should be the same—but are they? Let's use the following allowable values for X, Y, and Z:

$$X = -1324 * 10^3 \qquad Y = 1325 * 10^3 \qquad Z = 5424 * 10^0$$

Here is the result of adding Z to the sum of X and Y:

$$
\begin{array}{lll}
\text{(X)} & -1324 * 10^3 & \\
\text{(Y)} & \underline{1325 * 10^3} & \\
 & 1 * 10^3 & = 1000 * 10^0 \\
\end{array}
$$

$$
\begin{array}{lll}
\text{(X + Y)} & 1000 * 10^0 & \\
\text{(Z)} & \underline{5424 * 10^0} & \\
 & 6424 * 10^0 & \leftarrow \text{(X + Y) + Z} \\
\end{array}
$$

Here is the result of adding X to the sum of Y and Z:

$$
\begin{array}{lll}
\text{(Y)} & 1325000 * 10^0 & \\
\text{(Z)} & \underline{5424 * 10^0} & \\
 & 1330424 * 10^0 & = 1330 * 10^3 \text{ (truncated to four digits)} \\
\end{array}
$$

$$
\begin{array}{lll}
\text{(Y + Z)} & 1330 * 10^3 & \\
\text{(X)} & \underline{-1324 * 10^3} & \\
 & 6 * 10^3 & = 6000 * 10^0 \leftarrow \text{X + (Y + Z)} \\
\end{array}
$$

These two answers are the same in the thousands place, but they are different thereafter. The error behind this discrepancy is called **representational error.**

Because of representational errors, it is unwise to use a real number as a loop control variable. Since precision may be lost in calculations involving real numbers, it is difficult to predict when (or even *if*) a loop control variable of type Real will become equal to the termination value. A count-controlled loop with a control variable of type Real may behave in an unpredictable fashion.

Also because of representational errors, we should never compare real numbers for exact equality. Two real numbers will rarely be exactly equal, and thus they should be compared only for near equality. If the difference between the two numbers is less than some acceptable small value, they can be considered equal for the purposes of the given problem.

Implementation of Real Numbers in the Computer

Let's formally define some of the terms we used informally in the previous section.

Real Number   A number that has a whole and a fractional part and no imaginary part.

The type Real is limited to the range and precision defined in a specific implementation of Pascal. The number of digits used to represent the exponent and the number of digits used for the number itself (called the **mantissa**) will vary from machine to machine.

Range   The interval within which values must fall, specified in terms of the largest and smallest allowable values.

Significant Digits   Those digits from the first nonzero digit on the left to the last nonzero digit on the right (plus any zero digits that are exact).

Precision   Maximum number of significant digits.

Representational Error   Arithmetic error caused by the fact that the precision of the true result of arithmetic operations is greater than the precision of the machine.

The range of allowable exponents in Turbo Pascal is -38 through $+38$, and Real numbers have 11 digits of precision in Turbo Pascal. In addition to Real, Turbo Pascal provides four other types with similar properties but different ranges and precision. These types are

Type	*Exponent Range*	*Digits of Precision*
Single	-38 to $+38$	7
Double	-308 top $+308$	15
Extended	-4932 to $+4932$	19
Comp	-63 to $+63$	19

The type Comp differs from the others in that its mantissa may contain only integer numbers; there is no fractional part.

When you declare a variable to be of type Real, the value stored in that place is interpreted as a **floating point number;** that is, part of the memory location is assumed to contain the exponent, and the number itself is assumed to be in the balance of the location. The system is called floating point representation because the number of significant digits is fixed, and the decimal point floats (is moved to different positions as necessary). In our coding scheme, every number is stored as four digits, with the left-most being nonzero, and the exponent adjusted accordingly. The number 1,000,000 was stored as

| + | + | 3 | 1 | 0 | 3 | 2 |

and 0.1032 was stored as

| + | − | 4 | 1 | 0 | 0 | 0 |

This allowed for the maximum precision possible.

There are two ways of expressing real numbers in Pascal. One way is using a decimal point; the other is by using power of 10 notation. Since many screens cannot display superscripts, an E is used before the exponent. The syntax template is shown below.

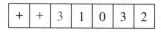

```
sign  digits . digit
sign  digits . digits E sign digits
sign  digits E sign digits
```

Sign and digits are defined as

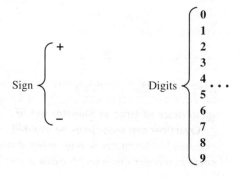

Underflow and Overflow   In addition to representational errors, there are two other problems to watch out for in real arithmetic: *underflow* and *overflow*. Underflow is the condition that arises when the value of a calculation is too small to be represented. Such values are set to 0.0.

Going back to our decimal representation, let's look at a calculation involving small numbers:

$$\begin{array}{r} 4210 * 10^{-8} \\ * \quad 2000 * 10^{-8} \\ \hline 8420000 * 10^{-16} \quad = 8420 * 10^{-13} \end{array}$$

This value cannot be represented in our scheme because an exponent of -13 is too small. Our minimum is -9. Therefore, the result of this calculation is set to 0.0. Obviously, any answer depending on this calculation will not be exact.

Overflow is a more serious problem because there is no logical recourse when it occurs. For example, the result of the calculation

$$\begin{array}{r} 9999 * 10^{9} \\ * \quad 1000 * 10^{9} \\ \hline 9999000 * 10^{18} \quad = 9999 * 10^{21} \end{array}$$

cannot be stored, so what should we do? To be consistent with our response to underflow, we could set the result to $9999 * 10^{9}$ (the maximum representable value in this case). Yet this seems intuitively wrong. The alternative is to stop with an error message, which is what Turbo Pascal does. When an overflow occurs, Turbo Pascal halts execution and displays the message FLOATING POINT OVERFLOW.

We have been discussing problems with real numbers, but integer numbers can also overflow both negatively and positively. To see how your compiler handles the situation, you should try adding 1 to MaxInt and -1 to $-$MaxInt -1.

Integers in Turbo Pascal have a range of -32768 to 32767 ($-$MaxInt -1 to MaxInt). Just as for real numbers, Turbo Pascal provides four additional nonstandard types that are similar to Integer but which have different ranges. These types are

Type	Range
ShortInt	$-128 . . 127$
LongInt	$-2147483648 . . 2147483647$
Byte	$0 . . 255$
Word	$0 . . 65535$

Types Byte and Word are special in that they do not allow negative numbers. By giving up the ability to represent the sign of a number, they allow us to store positive numbers up to twice as large as ShortInt and Integer, respectively.

Overflow can sometimes be avoided by carefully arranging computations. Suppose you would like to know how many different poker hands are possible. There are 52 cards in a poker deck, and 5 cards in one hand. What we are looking for is the number of **combinations** of 52 cards taken 5 at a time. The standard mathematical formula for the number of combinations of n things taken r at a time is

$$\frac{n!}{r!\,(n-r)!}$$

Thus, we could use the Factorial function we wrote earlier, and write this formula in an assignment statement:

Hands := Factorial(52) / (Factorial(5) * Factorial(47))

The only problem is that 52! is a very large number (approximately 8.0658×10^{67}). And 47! is also rather big (approximately 2.5862×10^{59}). Both of these numbers are well beyond the capacity of most systems to represent exactly as integers (52! requires 68 digits of precision). Even though they can be represented on many machines as real numbers, some of the precision will still be lost. By rearranging the calculations, however, we can achieve an exact result on any system with 9 or more digits of precision. How? Consider that most of the multiplications in computing 52! are cancelled when it is divided by 47!

$$\frac{52!}{5! * 47!} = \frac{52 * 51 * 50 * 49 * 48 * 47 * 46 * 45 * 44 * \ldots}{(5 * 4 * 3 * 2 * 1) * (47 * 46 * 45 * 44 * \ldots)}$$

So, we really only have to compute

Hands := 52 * 51 * 50 * 49 * 48 / Factorial(5)

which means the numerator is 311,875,200, and the denominator is 120. On a system with 9 or more digits of precision (such as Turbo Pascal's LongInt type), we thus have an exact answer of 2,598,960 poker hands.

Cancellation Error   Another type of error that can happen with real numbers is called *cancellation error*, a form of representational error that occurs when numbers of widely differing sizes are added or subtracted. Let's look at an example:

(1 + 0.00001234 − 1) = 0.00001234

The laws of arithmetic say this equation should be true, but is it, if the computer does the arithmetic?

$$
\begin{array}{r}
100000000 * 10^{-8} \\
+ \quad\quad 1234 * 10^{-8} \\
\hline
100001234 * 10^{-8}
\end{array}
$$

To four digits, the sum is $1000 * 10^{-3}$. Now the computer subtracts 1:

$$
\begin{array}{r}
1000 * 10^{-3} \\
- 1000 * 10^{-3} \\
\hline
0
\end{array}
$$

The result is 0, not .00001234.

Sometimes you can avoid adding two real numbers that are drastically different in size by carefully arranging the calculations in a program. Suppose a problem requires that many small real numbers be added to a large real number. The result will be more accurate if the program first sums the smaller numbers to obtain a larger number, and then adds the sum to the large number.

Recursion

When we introduced functions, we cautioned against using the name of the function in an expression inside the function itself. A function or any subprogram that calls itself is making a **recursive call.**

Recursive Call   A subprogram call in which the subprogram being called is the same as the one making the call.

The word **recursive** means "having the characteristic of coming up again, or repeating." In this case, a subprogram call is being repeated by the subprogram itself.

In function Power, we use the local variable Result instead of using the identifier Power to hold the intermediate powers of X. On the surface this extra variable seems redundant, but it is necessary because Power is a function name, not a variable name. If Power had been used in an expression, the logical order of execution would have caused control to be turned over to Power again. This would have been an unwanted recursive call.

Recursion is a powerful feature of Pascal and is used in more advanced work. Until you understand how to use it effectively, however, you should avoid it. If your curiosity has been piqued, we include one recursive example here. (Recursion is discussed in more depth in Chapter 17.) Let's rewrite function Power using recursion. To compute

$$X^N$$

where X and N are both nonzero, positive integers, the formula is

$$X^N = X * X * X * \ldots * X$$

Another way of writing this relationship is

$$X^N = X * (X * X * \ldots * X) \text{ or } X^N = X * (X^{N-1})$$

If we know what X^{N-1} is, we can calculate X^N, since $X^N = X * (X^{N-1})$. We can reduce X^{N-1} further:

Background Information

Practical Implications of Limited Precision

This discussion of representational, overflow, underflow, and cancellation errors may seem purely academic. In fact, these errors have serious practical implications in many problems. We close this section with three examples illustrating how limited precision can have disastrous effects.

During the Mercury space program, several of the spacecraft splashed down a considerable distance from their computed landing points. This delayed the recovery of the spacecraft and the astronaut, putting both in some danger. The problem was eventually traced to an imprecise representation of the Earth's rotation period in the program that calculated the landing point.

As part of the construction of a hydroelectric dam, a long set of high-tension cables had to be constructed to link the dam to the nearest power distribution point. The cables were to be several miles long, and each one was to be a continuous unit. (Because of the high power output from the dam, shorter cables couldn't be spliced together.) The cables were constructed at great expense and strung between the two points. It turned out that they were too short, however, so another set had to be manufactured. The problem was traced to errors of precision in calculating the length of the catenary curve (the curve that a cable forms when hanging between two points).

An audit of a bank turned up a mysterious account with a large amount of money in it. The account was traced to an unscrupulous programmer who had used limited precision to his advantage. The bank computed interest on its accounts to a precision of a tenth of a cent. The tenths of cents were not added to the customers' accounts, so the programmer had the extra tenths for all the accounts summed and deposited into an account in his name. Since the bank had thousands of accounts, these tiny amounts added up to a large amount of money. Because the rest of the bank's programs did not use as much precision in their calculations, the scheme went undetected for many months.

The moral of this discussion is twofold: 1) The results of Real calculations are often imprecise, and these errors can have serious consequences; and 2) if you are working with extremely large numbers or extremely small numbers, you need more information than this book provides and should consult a numerical methods text.

$$X^N = X * (X * (X * \ldots * X)) \text{ or } X^N = X * (X * (X^{N-2}))$$

If we know the value of X^{N-2}, we can calculate X^{N-1} and thus calculate X^N, since $X^N = X * (X * (X^{N-2}))$. We can continue this process until the innermost expression becomes X^1. We know the value of X^1; it's X.

We express this reasoning in the following recursive function Power, which has two parameters, X and N. (Compare this implementation with our earlier nonrecursive coding of Power.)

```
FUNCTION Power (X,              (* Base number              *)
                N:             (* Power to raise base to *)
                 Integer):
                  Integer;     (* Returns X to N power     *)

(* This function recursively computes X to the N power *)

BEGIN (* Power *)
  IF N = 1
    THEN
      Power := X
    ELSE
      Power := X * Power(X, N-1)
END;   (* Power *)
```

Each call to function Power in the statement Power := X * Power(X, N − 1) passes the actual parameters to a new version of the function. The value of X remains the same for each version of Power, but the value for N is decreased by 1 for each call until N − 1 becomes 1. The call to function Power where N is 1 stops the calling chain because Power can now be given a value, X. The value X is passed back to the version of function Power that made the last call. The value of Power for that version can then be calculated and passed back to the version that made that call. This process continues until the value of Power can be passed back to the original call.

Let's see what happens with a call to Power when X = 2 and N = 3. The statement

```
Num := Power(2,3)
```

in the body of the calling program assigns the value returned by the call to the variable Num. The value returned by Power and assigned to Num should be 8 (2 to the third power, or 2 * 2 * 2).

For illustrative purposes let's assume that each call to Power creates a complete new version of Power. Each box in Figure 8-5 represents the code for Power listed above, along with the values of the actual parameters for that version. The figure and the code illustrate that the Power function does what it is supposed to do. Each version of Power gets its parameters from the function call in the version above it in the diagram. There is no confusion as to which N is being used because N is a formal parameter.

If you find this example not only crystal clear but obvious, go ahead and use recursion. It is a powerful technique. If you don't feel comfortable with recursion, don't worry. Understanding recursion is not one of the goals of this chapter. We have covered it here so that you can avoid accidentally using it and can recognize the effects of unwanted recursion.

The accidental use of recursion usually results in a syntax error, such as "(EXPECTED" or "TYPE MISMATCH". Most functions have a parameter list, and if you mistakenly use the function name as a variable in an expression, the compiler spots the absence of parameters. If no syntax error is present, however, the likely result is a condition called **infinite recursion,** which is the recursive equivalent of an infinite loop.

Figure 8-5
Recursion in
Power (2,3)

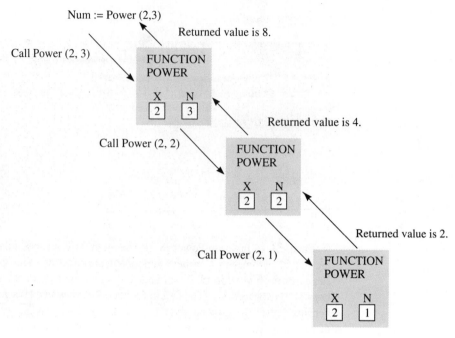

Infinite Recursion   The situation in which a subprogram calls itself over and over continuously.

In actuality, recursive calls can't go on forever. Each time a subprogram calls itself, a little more of the computer's memory space is used to store the old values of the variables. Eventually, all the memory space will be used and an error message such as "STACK OVERFLOW ERROR" will be printed.

*P*ROBLEM-SOLVING CASE STUDY

Starship Weight and Balance

Problem: The company you work for has just upgraded its fleet of corporate aircraft by adding the ultramodern Beechcraft Starship-1. As with any airplane, it is essential that the pilot know the total weight of the loaded plane at takeoff and its center of gravity. If the plane weighs too much, it won't be able to lift off. If its center of gravity is outside the limits established for the plane, it might be impossible to control. Either situation can lead to a crash. You have been asked to write a program that will determine the weight and center of gravity of this new plane.

PROBLEM-SOLVING CASE STUDY cont'd.

*The Beechcraft
Starship-1*

Input: Number of crew members, number of passengers, weight of closet contents, baggage weight, fuel in gallons.

Output: Total weight, center of gravity.

Discussion: As with most real-world problems, the basic solution is simple, but it is complicated by special cases. We use functions to hide the complexity so that the main program remains simple.

The total weight is basically the sum of the empty weight of the airplane plus the weight of each of the following: crew members, passengers, baggage, contents of the storage closet, and fuel. We use the standard average weight of a person, 170 pounds, to compute the total weight of the people. The weight of the baggage and the contents of the closet are given. Fuel weighs 6.7 pounds per gallon. Thus, total weight is equal to

TotalWeight = Empty_Weight + (Crew + Passengers) * 170 +
Baggage + Closet + Fuel * 6.7

To compute the center of gravity, each weight is multiplied by its distance from the front of the airplane and the products, called *moment arms* or simply *moments*, are then summed and divided by the total weight (see Figure 8-6). The formula is thus

Center_Of_Gravity = (Empty_Moment + Crew_Moment + Passenger_Moment +
Cargo_Moment + Fuel_Moment) / Total_Weight

The Starship-1 manual gives the distance from the front of the plane to the crew's seats, closet, baggage compartment, and fuel tanks. There are four rows of passenger seats,

PROBLEM-SOLVING CASE STUDY cont'd.

Figure 8-6
A Passenger
Moment Arm

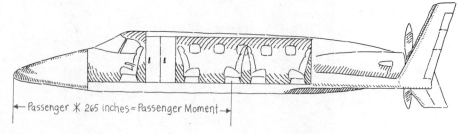

so this calculation depends on where the individual passengers sit. We have to make some assumptions about how passengers will arrange themselves. Each row has two seats. The most popular seats are in row 2 because they are near the entrance and face forward. Once row 2 is filled, passengers usually take seats in row 1, facing their traveling companions. Row 3 is usually the next to fill up, even though it faces backward, because row 4 is a fold-down bench seat that is less comfortable than the armchairs in the forward rows. The following table gives the distance from the nose of the plane to each of the "loading stations."

Loading Station	Distance from Nose (inches)
Crew seats	143
Row 1 seats	219
Row 2 seats	265
Row 3 seats	295
Row 4 seats	341
Closet	182
Baggage	386

The distance for the fuel varies because there are several tanks, and the tanks are in different places. As fuel is added to the plane, it automatically flows into the different tanks so that the center of gravity changes as they are filled. There are four formulas for computing the distance from the nose to the "center" of the fuel tanks, depending on how much fuel is being loaded into the plane. The following table lists these distance formulas.

PROBLEM-SOLVING CASE STUDY *cont'd.*

Gallons of Fuel (G)	Distance (D) Formula
0 – 59	D = 314.6
60 – 360	D = 305.8 + (−0.01233 * (G − 60))
361 – 520	D = 303.0 + (0.12500 * (G − 361))
521 – 565	D = 323.0 + (−0.04444 * (G − 521))

We can define one function for each of the different moments, and we'll call these functions CrewMoment, PassengerMoment, CargoMoment, and FuelMoment. The center of gravity is then computed with the formula we gave earlier and the following parameters:

Center_Of_Gravity = (Crew_Moment(Crew) + Passenger_Moment(Passengers) +
                Cargo_Moment(Closet, Baggage) + Fuel_Moment(Fuel) +
                Empty_Moment) / Total_Weight

The empty weight of the Starship is 9,887 pounds, and its empty center of gravity is 319 inches from the front of the airplane. Thus the empty moment is 3,153,953 inch-pounds.

We now have enough information to write the algorithm to solve this problem. In addition to printing the results, we'll also print a warning message that states the assumptions of the program, and tells the pilot to double check the results by hand if the weight or center of gravity is near the allowable limits.

Starship Weight   *Level 0*

```
Get Data
Set Total Weight to
      Empty Weight + (Passengers + Crew) * 170 +
      Baggage + Closet + Fuel * 6.7
Set Center Of Gravity to
      (Crew Moment(Crew) + Passenger Moment(Passengers) +
      Cargo Moment(Closet, Baggage) + Fuel Moment(Fuel) +
      Empty Moment) / Total Weight
Print Total Weight and Center of Gravity
Print Warning
```

<u>PROBLEM-SOLVING CASE STUDY</u> cont'd.

Get Data (Returns Crew, Passengers,
Closet, Baggage,
Fuel: Integer)   *Level 1*

Prompt for Number of Crew, Number of Passengers,
        Weight in Closet and Baggage Compartment,
        and Gallons of Fuel
Get Crew, Passengers, Closet, Baggage, Fuel
Echo-print input

Crew Moment (Receives Crew: Integer
Returns Crew Moment: Real)

Set Crew Moment to Crew * 170 * 143

Passenger Moment (Receives Passengers: Integer
Returns Passenger Moment: Real)

Initialize Moment to 0.0
IF Passengers > 6
  THEN
    Add (Passengers − 6) * 170 * 341 to Moment
    Set Passengers to 6
IF Passengers > 4
  THEN
    Add (Passengers − 4) * 170 * 295 to Moment
    Set Passengers to 4
IF Passengers > 2
  THEN
    Add (Passengers − 2) * 170 * 219 to Moment
    Set Passengers to 2
IF Passengers > 0
  THEN
    Add Passengers * 170 * 265 to Moment
Set Passenger Moment to Moment

PROBLEM-SOLVING CASE STUDY cont'd.

Cargo Moment (Receives Closet, Baggage: Integer
Returns Cargo Moment: Real)

> Set Cargo Moment to Closet $*$ 182 $+$ Baggage $*$ 386

Fuel Moment (Receives Fuel : Integer
Returns Fuel Moment : Real)

> Set Fuel Weight to Fuel $*$ 6.7
> IF Fuel $<$ 60
>   THEN
>   Set Fuel Distance to Fuel $*$ 314.6
>   ELSE IF Fuel $<$ 361
>   THEN
>   Set Fuel Distance to 305.8 $+$ ($-$0.01233 $*$ (Fuel $-$ 60))
>   ELSE IF Fuel $<$ 521
>   THEN
>   Set Fuel Distance to 303.0 $+$ (0.12500 $*$ (Fuel $-$ 361))
>   ELSE IF Fuel $<$ 565
>   THEN
>   Set Fuel Distance to 323.0 $+$ ($-$0.04444 $*$ (Fuel $-$ 521))
> Set Fuel Moment to Fuel Distance $*$ Fuel Weight

Print Warning (No parameters)

> Print a warning message about the assumptions of the program
>   and when to double check the results

Because the precision of Turbo Pascal's Integer type is not great enough to represent some of the values that must be computed in this program, we will use the nonstandard type LongInt instead.

PROBLEM-SOLVING CASE STUDY cont'd.

Module Structure Chart:

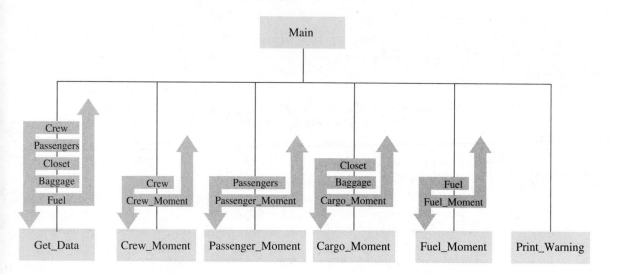

Here is the program that implements our algorithm.

```
PROGRAM Starship_Weight (Input, Output);

(* This program computes the total weight and center of gravity  *)
(* of a Beechcraft Starship-1, given the number of crew members  *)
(* and passengers, weight of closet and baggage compartment      *)
(* cargo, and gallons of fuel loaded. It assumes that each       *)
(* person weighs 170 pounds, and that the fuel weighs 6.7 pounds *)
(* per gallon. Thus, the output is approximate and should be     *)
(* hand checked if the Starship is loaded near its limits        *)

CONST
  Person       = 170;          (* Average person weighs 170 lbs. *)
  Lbs_Per_Gal  = 6.7;          (* Jet-A weighs 6.7 lbs. per gal. *)
  Empty_Weight = 9887.0;       (* Standard empty weight          *)
  Empty_Moment = 3153953.0;    (* Standard empty moment          *)
```

```
VAR
   Crew,                    (* Number of crew on board (1 or 2)      *)
   Passengers,              (* Number of passengers (0 to 8)         *)
   Closet,                  (* Weight in closet (160 pounds maximum) *)
   Baggage,                 (* Weight of baggage (525 lbs. max.)     *)
   Fuel:                    (* Gallons of fuel (10 to 565 gallons)   *)
     LongInt;
   Total_Weight,            (* Total weight of the loaded Starship   *)
   Center_Of_Gravity:       (* Center of gravity of loaded Starship  *)
     Real;


(* ******************************************************************** *)


PROCEDURE Get_Data (VAR Crew,          (* Number of crew            *)
                        Passengers,     (* Number of passengers      *)
                        Closet,         (* Weight of closet cargo    *)
                        Baggage,        (* Weight of baggage         *)
                        Fuel:           (* Gallons of fuel           *)
                          LongInt);

(* This procedure prompts for input of Crew, Passengers, Closet,  *)
(* Baggage, and Fuel values and returns the five values to the    *)
(* program after echo printing them                               *)

BEGIN (* Get_Data *)
  Writeln('Enter the number of crew.');
  Readln(Crew);
  Writeln('Enter the number of passengers.');
  Readln(Passengers);
  Writeln('Enter the weight, in pounds, of cargo in the closet');
  Writeln(' rounded up to the nearest whole number.');
  Readln(Closet);
  Writeln('Enter the weight, in pounds, of cargo in the aft baggage');
  Writeln(' compartment rounded up to the nearest whole number.');
  Readln(Baggage);
  Writeln('Enter the number of U.S. gallons of fuel loaded rounded up');
  Writeln(' to the nearest whole number.');
  Readln(Fuel);
  Writeln;
  Writeln('Starship loading data as entered:');
  Writeln('   Crew:            ', Crew:5);
  Writeln('   Passengers:      ', Passengers:5);
  Writeln('   Closet weight: ', Closet:5, ' pounds');
  Writeln('   Baggage weight: ', Baggage:5, ' pounds');
  Writeln('   Fuel:            ', Fuel:5, ' gallons');
  Writeln
END;
```

PROBLEM-SOLVING CASE STUDY cont'd.

```
FUNCTION Crew_Moment (Crew:              (* Receives number of crew members *)
                         LongInt):
                         Real;          (* Returns crew moment arm           *)

(* This function computes the crew moment arm in inch-pounds      *)
(* from the number of crew members. Global constant Person is used *)
(* as the weight of each crew member                              *)

CONST
  Crew_Distance = 143;       (* Distance of crew seats from front *)

BEGIN (* Crew_Moment *)
  Crew_Moment := Crew * Person * Crew_Distance
END;   (* Crew_Moment *)

(****************************************************************)

FUNCTION Passenger_Moment (Passengers:  (* Number of passengers  *)
                              LongInt):
                              Real;      (* Passenger moment arm  *)

(* This function computes the passenger moment arm in inch-pounds *)
(* from the number of passengers. Global constant Person is used  *)
(* as the weight of each passenger. It is assumed that the        *)
(* first two passengers sit in row 2, the second two in row 1,    *)
(* the next two in row 3, and remaining passengers in row 4       *)

CONST
  Row1 = 219;    (* Distance of row 1 seats from front *)
  Row2 = 265;    (* Distance of row 2 seats from front *)
  Row3 = 295;    (* Distance of row 3 seats from front *)
  Row4 = 341;    (* Distance of row 4 seats from front *)

VAR
  Moment:               (* Running total of moment as rows are added *)
    Real;
```

```
BEGIN   (* Passenger_Moment *)
  Moment := 0.0;
  IF Passengers > 6
    THEN                           (* Calculate for passengers 7 and 8 *)
      BEGIN
        Moment := Moment + (Passengers - 6) * Person * Row4;
        Passengers := 6                         (* 6 remain *)
      END;
  IF Passengers > 4
    THEN                           (* Calculate for passengers 5 and 6 *)
      BEGIN
        Moment := Moment + (Passengers - 4) * Person * Row3;
        Passengers := 4                         (* 4 remain *)
      END;
  IF Passengers > 2
    THEN                           (* Calculate for passengers 3 and 4 *)
      BEGIN
        Moment := Moment + (Passengers - 2) * Person * Row1;
        Passengers := 2                         (* 2 remain *)
      END;
  IF Passengers > 0
    THEN                           (* Calculate for passengers 1 and 2 *)
      Moment := Moment + Passengers * Person * Row2;
  Passenger_Moment := Moment
END;  (* Passenger_Moment *)

(**************************************************************)


FUNCTION Cargo_Moment (Closet,         (* Receives weight in closet *)
                       Baggage:        (* Receives baggage weight   *)
                         LongInt):
                           Real;       (* Returns cargo moment arm  *)

(* This function computes the total moment arm for cargo loaded *)
(* into the front closet and aft baggage compartment            *)

CONST
  Closet_Distance = 182;    (* Distance from front to closet      *)
  Baggage_Distance = 386;   (* Distance from front to bag. comp.  *)

BEGIN (* Cargo_Moment *)
  Cargo_Moment := Closet * Closet_Distance +
                  Baggage * Baggage_Distance
END;  (* Cargo_Moment *)


(**************************************************************)
```

```
FUNCTION Fuel_Moment (Fuel:          (* Receives fuel in gallons *)
                        LongInt):
                          Real;      (* Returns fuel moment arm  *)

(* This function computes the moment arm for fuel on board.  *)
(* There are four different formulas for this calculation,   *)
(* depending on the amount of fuel, due to fuel tank layout. *)
(* This function uses the global constant Lbs_Per_Gal to     *)
(* compute the weight of the fuel                            *)

VAR
  Fuel_Weight,          (* Weight of fuel in pounds     *)
  Fuel_Distance:        (* Distance from front of plane *)
    Real;

BEGIN (* Fuel_Moment *)
  Fuel_Weight := Fuel * Lbs_Per_Gal;
  IF Fuel < 60
    THEN
      Fuel_Distance := Fuel * 314.6
    ELSE IF Fuel < 361
      THEN
        Fuel_Distance := 305.8 + (-0.01233 * (Fuel -  60))
    ELSE IF Fuel < 521
      THEN
        Fuel_Distance := 303.0 + ( 0.12500 * (Fuel - 361))
    ELSE IF Fuel < 565
      THEN
        Fuel_Distance := 323.0 + (-0.04444 * (Fuel - 521));
  Fuel_Moment := Fuel_Distance * Fuel_Weight
END;  (* Fuel_Moment *)

(******************************************************************)


PROCEDURE Print_Warning;

(* This procedure warns the user of assumptions made by the *)
(* program and when to double check the program's results   *)
```

PROBLEM-SOLVING CASE STUDY cont'd.

```
BEGIN (* Print_Warning *)
  Writeln;
  Writeln('Notice:  This program assumes that passengers fill');
  Writeln('  the seat rows in order 2, 1, 3, 4, and that each');
  Writeln('  passenger and crew member weighs 170 pounds.  It');
  Writeln('  also assumes that Jet-A fuel weighs 6.7 pounds per');
  Writeln('  U.S. gallon.  The center of gravity calculations');
  Writeln('  for fuel are approximate.  If the aircraft is');
  Writeln('  loaded near its limits, the pilot''s operating');
  Writeln('  handbook should be used to compute weight and');
  Writeln('  center of gravity with more accuracy.')
END;  (* Print_Warning *)


(*****************************************************************)


BEGIN (* Starship_Weight *)
  Get_Data(Crew, Passengers, Closet, Baggage, Fuel);
  Total_Weight :=
    Empty_Weight + (Passengers + Crew) * Person +
    Baggage + Closet + Fuel * Lbs_Per_Gal;
  Center_Of_Gravity :=
    (Crew_Moment(Crew) + Passenger_Moment(Passengers) +
    Cargo_Moment(Closet, Baggage) + Fuel_Moment(Fuel) +
    Empty_Moment) / Total_Weight;
  Writeln('Total weight is ', Total_Weight:6:2, ' pounds.');
  Writeln('Center of gravity is ', Center_Of_Gravity:3:2, ' inches',
          ' from the front of the plane.');
  Print_Warning
END.  (* Starship_Weight *)
```

Testing: Because the output of this program can be used to make decisions that could result in property damage, injury, or death, it is essential that the program be tested thoroughly. It should be checked especially for overflow and representational errors by trying maximum and minimum input values in different combinations. In addition, a wide range of test cases should be tried and verified against results calculated by hand. If possible, the program's output should be checked against sample calculations done by experienced pilots for actual flights. If this program were actually to be used by pilots, it should have data validation checks added in procedure Get_Data.

PROBLEM-SOLVING CASE STUDY

Integrating a Function

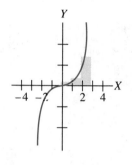

Problem: Numerically integrate (find the area under the curve) the function X^3 over an interval specified by the user. In other words, given a pair of real numbers, find the area under the graph of X^3 between those two numbers (see Figure 8-7).

Input: Two real numbers specifying the interval over which to integrate the function, and an integer number of intervals to use in approximating the integral.

Output: The input data (echo print) and the value calculated for the integral over the given interval.

Discussion: We will compute an approximation to this area. If the area under the curve is divided into equal, narrow, rectangular strips, the sum of the areas of these rectangles (Divisions) will be close to the actual area under the curve (see Figure 8-8). The narrower the rectangles, the more accurate the approximation should be.

We can use a function to compute the area of each rectangle. The user will enter the low and high values for the function, as well as the number of rectangles into which the area will be subdivided. The width of a rectangle will then be

(High − Low) / Divisions

Figure 8-7
Integral of X^3
Between 0 and 3

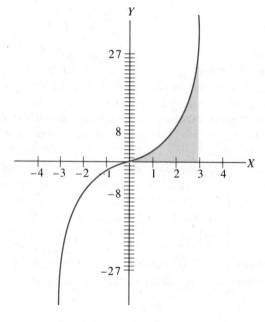

PROBLEM-SOLVING CASE STUDY cont'd.

Figure 8-8
Approximation of
Area Under a Curve

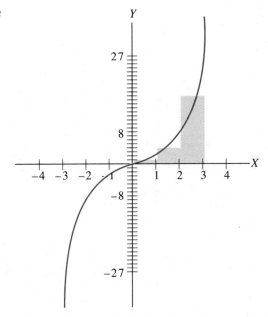

The height of a rectangle will be equal to the value of X^3 when X is at the horizontal midpoint of the rectangle. The area of a rectangle is equal to its height times its width. Since the left-most rectangle will have its midpoint at

(Low + Width/2.0)

its area will be equal to the following (see Figure 8-9):

$(Low + Width/2.0)^3 * Width$

The second rectangle will have its left edge at the point where X equals

Low + Width

and its area will be equal to the following (see Figure 8-10):

$(Low + Width + Width/2.0)^3 * Width$

The left edge of each rectangle is at a point that is Width greater than the left edge of the rectangle to its right. Thus, we can step through the rectangles by having a loop controlled by a counter starting at Divisions and counting down to zero. This loop will contain a second counter (not the loop control variable) starting at Low and counting by steps of Width up to (High − Width). Having two counters is necessary because the second counter must be a Real, and it is poor programming technique to have a loop control variable be a Real variable. For each iteration of this loop, we compute the area of the corresponding rectangle, and add this value to the total area under the curve.

PROBLEM-SOLVING CASE STUDY cont'd.

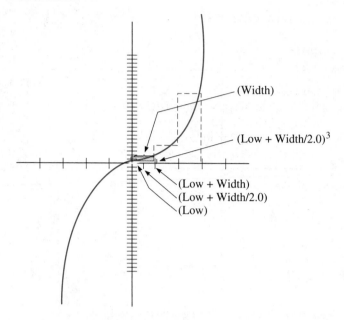

Figure 8-9
Area of the Left-
Most Rectangle

(Width)

$(Low + Width/2.0)^3$

(Low + Width)
(Low + Width/2.0)
(Low)

We want a function to compute the area of a rectangle, given the position of its left edge and its width. Let's also make X^3 a separate function called Funct, so we can substitute other functions in its place without changing the rest of the design. Our program can then be converted quickly to integrate numerically any single variable function.

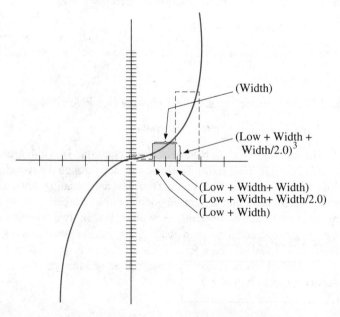

Figure 8-10
Area of the Second
Rectangle

(Width)

$(Low + Width + Width/2.0)^3$

(Low + Width+ Width)
(Low + Width+ Width/2.0)
(Low + Width)

Here is our design:

Integrate   *Level 0*

```
Get Data
Set Width to (High − Low)/Divisions
Initialize Area to 0.0
Initialize Left_Edge to Low
WHILE Divisions are greater than 0
    Set Area to Area + Rect_Area(Left_Edge, Width)
    Set Left_Edge to Left_Edge + Width
    Decrement Divisions
Print Result
```

Rect_Area (Receives Left_Edge, Width: Real;
Returns Rect_Area: Real)   *Level 1*

```
Set Rect_Area to Funct(Left_Edge + Width/2.0) * Width
```

Get_Data (Returns Low, High: Real; Divisions: Integer)

```
Prompt for Low and High
Get Low and High
Prompt for Divisions
Get Divisions
Echo-print input data
```

Funct (Receives X: Real; Returns Funct: Real)

```
Set Funct to X * X * X
```

Module Structure Chart:

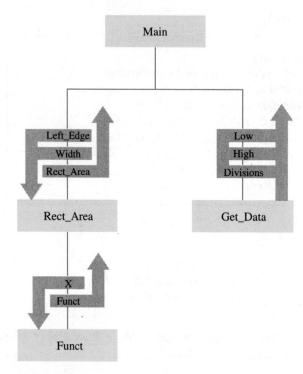

Program Integrate implements our design.

```
PROGRAM Integrate (Input, Output);

(* This program takes as input two Real values and one Integer.  *)
(* These are the Low, High values for the interval of a function *)
(* to be integrated numerically and the number of slices to be   *)
(* used in approximating the integral of the function. As        *)
(* written, this program integrates the function X cubed;        *)
(* however, any single variable function may be substituted for  *)
(* the function named Funct *)

VAR
  Low,          (* Lowest value in interval to be integrated  *)
  High,         (* Highest value in interval to be integrated *)
  Width,        (* Computed width of a rectangular slice       *)
  Left_Edge,    (* Left edge point in a rectangular slice      *)
  Area:         (* Total area under the curve                  *)
    Real;
  Divisions:    (* Number of slices to divide the interval by *)
    Integer;

(*****************************************************************)
```

PROBLEM-SOLVING CASE STUDY *cont'd.*

```
FUNCTION Rect_Area (Left_Edge,      (* Left edge point of rectangle *)
                    Width:          (* Width of rectangle          *)
                    Real):
                    Real;           (* Returns area of rectangle    *)

(* This function computes the area of a rectangle that is Width *)
(* wide, and whose height is given by the value computed by     *)
(* Funct on the midpoint of the rectangle's interval            *)

  (***************************************************************)

  FUNCTION Funct (X:                (* Receives value to be cubed *)
                  Real):
                  Real;             (* Returns X cubed            *)

  (* This function computes X cubed. You may replace this  *)
  (* function with any single variable function that is to *)
  (* be integrated by the rest of this program             *)

  BEGIN (* Funct *)
    Funct := X * X * X
  END;  (* Funct *)

  (***************************************************************)

BEGIN (* Rect_Area *)
  Rect_Area := Funct(Left_Edge + Width / 2.0) * Width
END;  (* Rect_Area *)

(***************************************************************)

PROCEDURE Get_Data (VAR Low,        (* Returns bottom of interval *)
                        High:       (* Returns top of interval    *)
                        Real;
                    VAR Divisions:  (* Returns division factor     *)
                        Integer);

(* This procedure prompts for input of Low, High, and Divisions *)
(* values, and returns the three values input to the program    *)

BEGIN (* Get_Data *)
  Writeln('Enter Low and High values of integration interval (Real).');
  Readln(Low, High);
  Writeln('Enter the number of divisions to be used (Integer).');
  Readln(Divisions);
  Writeln('The integral is computed over the interval ', Low:10:7);
  Writeln('to ', High:10:7, ' with ', Divisions:1,
          ' subdivisions of the interval. ')
END;  (* Get_Data *)

(***************************************************************)
```

PROBLEM-SOLVING CASE STUDY *cont'd.*

```
BEGIN (* Integrate *)
  Get_Data(Low, High, Divisions);                      (* Get Data *)
  Width := (High - Low) / Divisions;        (* Compute slice width *)
  Area := 0.0;
  Left_Edge := Low;
  (* Calculate and sum area of each slice *)
  WHILE Divisions > 0 DO
    BEGIN
      Area := Area + Rect_Area(Left_Edge, Width);
      Left_Edge := Left_Edge + Width;
      Divisions := Divisions - 1
    END;
  (* Print Result *)
  Writeln('The result is equal to ', Area:10:7)
END.  (* Integrate *)
```

Testing: This program should be tested with sets of data that include positive, negative, and zero values. It is especially important to try to input values of 0 and 1 for the number of divisions. The results from the program should be compared against values calculated by hand using the same algorithm, and against the true value of the integral of X^3, which is given by the formula

$$1/4 * (\text{High}^4 - \text{Low}^4)$$

Let's consider for a moment the effects of representational error on this program. The user specifies the low and high values of the interval to be integrated, as well as the number of subdivisions to be used in computing the result. The more subdivisions that are used, the more accurate the result should be, since the rectangles will be narrower and thus will approximate more closely the shape of the area under the curve. It seems that we can obtain precise results by using a large number of subdivisions. In fact, however, there is a point beyond which an increase in the number of subdivisions will *decrease* the precision of the results. If we specify too many subdivisions, the area of an individual rectangle will become so small that the computer can no longer represent its value accurately. Adding all those inaccurate values will produce a total area that has an even greater error.

Testing and Debugging

Because functions are simply another form of subprogram, the same testing and debugging techniques that are used for procedures may be applied to functions. For example, we can use stubs and drivers to test a function in isolation from the rest of the program.

The only difference is that an expression, rather than a procedure call, must be used in a driver to call the function.

The driver establishes the preconditions for calling the function and prints out the values associated with its postconditions. If the function calls any subprograms, then stubs are used to print out values showing that the function set up the necessary preconditions for the call, and to supply any postconditions from the subprogram required by the function.

When a problem requires the use of real numbers that are extremely large, extremely small, or extremely precise, it is important to keep in mind the limitations of the particular system you are using. When testing a program that performs Real calculations, determine the acceptable margin of error beforehand, and then design your test data to try to push the program beyond those limits. Carefully check the accuracy of the computed results. (Remember that when you "hand calculate" the correct results, a pocket calculator may have *less* precision than your computer system.) If the program produces acceptable results when given worst-case data, it will probably perform correctly on typical data.

Testing and Debugging Hints

1. Be sure the function heading includes the data type that will be assigned to the function name.
2. Don't forget to assign a value to the function name before the function returns. Make sure that the value assigned is of the correct type.
3. Unless you are deliberately writing a recursive function, don't use the function name in an expression within the function declaration. If you do this by mistake, a syntax error will probably occur; however, a run-time error such as "STACK OVERFLOW ERROR" may occur.
4. Remember that a function call must be part of the expression. Functions cannot be called like procedures.
5. In general, don't use VAR parameters in the formal parameter list of a function declaration. A VAR parameter must be used, however, when a file is to be passed to a formal parameter.
6. Don't directly compare Real values for equality. Instead, check them for near equality. The tolerance for near equality will depend on the particular problem you are solving.
7. Use integers if you are dealing with whole numbers only. Any integer can be represented exactly by the computer, as long as it is within the range $-\text{MaxInt} - 1$ to MaxInt. Also, integer arithmetic is faster on most machines.
8. Be aware of representational, cancellation, overflow, and underflow errors. If possible, try to arrange calculations in your program to keep real numbers from becoming too large or too small.
9. Be aware of the precision limit of the system you are using. Avoid calculations in which numbers of widely different magnitudes are added or subtracted.

Summary

Pascal provides two kinds of subprograms, procedures and functions, for us to use. A function is called from within an expression, and returns a single result value that is used in the evaluation of the expression. For the result value to be returned, it must be assigned to the function name within the function definition.

The function heading differs from a procedure heading because it begins with the keyword FUNCTION, and ends with a colon (:) and a data type. The data type specifies the type of the function result.

All the scope rules, as well as the rules about VAR and value parameters, apply to both procedures and functions. It is considered poor programming practice, however, to use VAR parameters in a function declaration. Doing so increases the potential for side effects.

Real numbers are represented in the computer by a mantissa and an exponent. This permits the use of numbers that are much larger or smaller than those that can be represented with the type Integer. The type Real also allows us to perform calculations on numbers with fractional parts.

Representational errors can affect the accuracy of a program's computations. When using real numbers, keep in mind that if two numbers are vastly different from each other in size, adding or subtracting them may give inaccurate results.

Keep in mind that the computer has a limited range of numbers that it can represent. If a program tries to compute a value that is too large or too small, an error message will probably result when the program executes.

Recursion provides an alternative to looping as a way to have statements repeated. Unless you fully understand how to use recursion, however, you may prefer to avoid it for now. We return to the topic of recursion in Chapter 17.

■ *Quick Check*

1. For each of the following, decide whether a function or a procedure is the most appropriate implementation. (pp. 350–357)
   a. Selecting the larger of two values for further processing in an expression.
   b. Printing a paycheck.
   c. Computing the area of a hexagon.
   d. Testing whether an input value is valid and returning True if it is.
   e. Computing the two roots of a quadratic equation.

2. What would the heading for a function called Min look like if it has two Integer parameters called Num1 and Num2, and returns an Integer result? (pp. 350–357)

3. What would a call to Min look like if the actual parameters are a variable called Deductions and the literal 2000? (pp. 350–357)

4. Why is it inappropriate to use a variable of type Real as a loop control variable? (pp. 357–365)

5. If a computer has four digits of precision, what would be the result of the following addition operation? (pp. 357–365)

    400400.000 + 199.9

6. What is a recursive call? (pp. 365–368)

Answers

1. a. function b. procedure c. function d. function e. procedure
2. FUNCTION Min (Num1,
                Num2:
                   Integer):
                      Integer;
3. Result := Min(Deductions, 2000)   4. Because representational errors can cause the loop termination condition to be evaluated with unpredictable results.   5. 400500.000 (Actually, 4.005E+5)   6. A subprogram call to itself.

■ *Exam Preparation Exercises*

1. A function call is always a component of an expression, but a procedure call is always a statement in itself. (True or False?)

2. Both procedures and functions must have a result type. (True or False?)

3. VAR parameters in the formal parameter list of a function are considered poor style. (True or False?)

4. Given the function heading

    ```
    FUNCTION High_Tax_Bracket  (Inc,
                                Ded:
                                   Integer):
                                      Boolean;
    ```

    is the following statement a legal call to the function if Income and Deductions are of type Integer?

    ```
    IF High_Tax_Bracket(Income, Deductions)
       THEN
          Writeln('Upper Class');
    ```

5. If a system supports 10 digits of precision for real numbers, what will be the results of the following computations?
    a. 1.4E+12 + 100.0
    b. 4.2E−8 + 100.0
    c. 3.2E−5 + 3.2E+5

6. Given the code segment

```
Sum := 0;     (* Sum is of type Integer *)
WHILE NOT EOF(Data_File) DO
  BEGIN
    Readln(Data_File, Amount);
    Sum := Sum + Round(Amount)
  END;
Writeln(Sum:6);
```

and the input data

```
0.5  0.5  0.5  0.5  0.5  0.5  0.5  (EOF)
```

what will the output be? Note that each data value is actually on a separate line. Is this value much different from the sum of the input values?

7. Rewrite the code segment in Exercise 6 so that the value printed is the integer value closest to the actual sum of the input data.

8. Rewrite the following Pascal procedure as a function, then write a function call that assigns the result of the function to the variable M. The procedure call is

```
Power (K, L, M);
```

```
PROCEDURE Power (     Base,
                      Exponent:
                        Integer;
                  VAR Answer:
                        Integer);
VAR
  I:
   Integer;
BEGIN (* Power *)
  Answer := 1;
  I := 1;
  WHILE I <= Exponent DO
    BEGIN
      Answer := Answer * Base;
      I := I + 1
    END
END; (* Power *)
```

9. You are given the following function Test and a Pascal program in which the variables A, B, C, D, and Result are declared to be of type Real. In the calling program, A := −5.0, B := −6.2, C := 0.1, and D := 16.2. What is the value of Result when each of the following calls return?

```
FUNCTION Test (    X,
                   Y,
                   Z:
                    Real):
                      Real;
BEGIN (* Test *)
  IF (X > Y) OR (Y > Z)
    THEN
       TEST := 0.5
    ELSE
       TEST := -0.5
END;  (* Test *)

a. Result := TEST (5.2, 5.3, 5.6);
b. Result := TEST (ABS(A), C, D);
```

10. Define the following terms:

recursion   mantissa
result type   exponent
representational error significant digits
overflow

11. Identify all the syntax errors in the following function declaration.

```
FUNCTION Errors:  Boolean;
                 (A:  Boolean,
                 (B:  Integer)
BEGIN (* Errors *)
  Errors := A AND NOT B
END;  (* Errors *)
```

12. Explain why it is poor programming practice to use formal VAR parameters in a function declaration.

■ *Programming Warm-Up Exercises*

1. Given two Real parameters called High and Low, write the heading for a function called Epsilon that returns a Real result.

2. Given three Real parameters called Num1, Num2, and Difference, write the heading for a function called Equal that returns a Boolean result.

3. Using the heading you wrote for Exercise 2, write a function that returns True if the absolute difference between Num1 and Num2 is less than the value in Difference, and returns False otherwise.

4. Write a heading for a function called EOForEOLN that has no parameters and returns a Boolean result.

5. Given the function heading

```
FUNCTION Hypotenuse (Side1,
                     Side2:
                        Real):
                           Real;
```

write the body of the function to return the length of the hypotenuse of a right triangle. The lengths of the other two sides are passed to the function through the formal parameters. The formula for the hypotenuse is

Sqrt(Sqr(Side1) + Sqr(Side2))

6. Write the complete function heading for the following function body, which compares EOF on two files that are passed as parameters and returns True if both files have the same status.

```
BEGIN (* Same_Status *)
  Same_Status := EOF(File1) = EOF(File2)
END;   (* Same_Status *)
```

7. Write a function called Compass_Heading that returns the sum of its four Real parameters: True_Course, Wind_Corr_Angle, Variance, and Deviation.

8. Write a function called P5 that returns the fifth power of its Real parameter.

9. Write a function called Min that returns the smallest of its three Integer parameters.

10. Write a Boolean function Test_For_Prime that receives an integer number N, tests it to see if it is a prime number, and returns True if it is. (A prime number is a positive integer whose only divisors are 1 and the number itself. The number 1 is not considered to be prime.) A call to this function might look like this:

Is_Prime := Test_For_Prime(N)

11. Given the weight of a package in pounds and ounces, and cost per ounce, write a function called Postage that returns the cost of mailing the package.

12. The recursive definition of function Power will not work if the exponent is zero, yet X^0 is simply 1. Change the definition of the function to return 1 if the parameter N is 0.

■ *Programming Problems*

1. If a principal amount (P), for which the interest is compounded Q times per year, is placed in a savings account, then the amount of interest earned after N years will be given by the following formula (I is the decimal interest rate):

Amount $= P * (1 + I/Q)^{N*Q}$

Write a Pascal program that will input the values for P, I, Q, and N, and output the interest earned for each year up through year N. You should use a function to compute the amount of interest. Your program should appropriately prompt the user, label output values, and have good style.

2. Euclid's algorithm is a method for finding the greatest common divisor (GCD) of two positive integers. It states that, for any two positive integers M and N such that M <= N, the GCD is calculated by doing the following:

   a. Divide N by M.

   b. If the remainder R = 0, then the GCD = M.

   c. If R > 0, then M becomes N, and R becomes M, and repeat step 1 until R = 0.

   Write a program that uses a function to find the GCD of two numbers. The numbers should be read in the main program from a file called Data, and the two numbers and the GCD should be properly labeled and written to a file called GCDList.

3. The distance to the landing point of a projectile, launched at an angle Angle (in radians) with an initial velocity of Velocity (in feet per second), ignoring air resistance, is given by the formula

   Distance = (Sqr(Velocity) * Sin(2 * Angle)) / 32.2

   Write a Pascal program that implements a game in which the user first enters the distance to a target. The user then enters the angle and velocity for launching a projectile. If the projectile comes within a tenth of one percent of the distance to the target, the user wins the game. If the projectile doesn't come close enough, the user is told how far off the projectile is, and is allowed to try again. If after five tries there isn't a winning input, then the user loses the game.

   To simplify input for the user, your program should allow the angle to be input in degrees. The formula for converting degrees to radians is

   Radians = Degrees * 3.14159265 / 180.0

   Each of the formulas in this problem should be implemented as a Pascal function in your program. Your program should appropriately prompt the user for input and label output values, and have proper programming style.

4. Write a program that computes the number of days between two dates. One way of doing this is to have the program compute the Julian day number for each of the dates and subtract one from the other. The Julian day number is the number of days that have elapsed since noon on January 1, 4713 B.C. The following algorithm may be used to calculate the Julian day number.

   Given Year (an integer, such as 1987), Month (an integer between 1 and 12 inclusive), and Day (an integer in the range of 1 through 31), and if Month is 1 or 2, then subtract 1 from Year and add 12 to Month.

   If the date comes from the Gregorian calendar (later than October 15, 1582), then compute an intermediate result with the following formula (otherwise let Int_Res1 equal 0):

   Int_Res1 = 2 − Year DIV 100 + Year DIV 400

   Compute a second intermediate result with the formula

   Int_Res2 = Trunc(365.25 * Year)

   Compute a third intermediate result with the formula

   Int_Res3 = Trunc(30.6001 * (Month + 1))

   Finally, the Julian day number is computed with the formula

   Julian_Day = Int_Res1 + Int_Res2 + Int_Res3 + Day + 1720994.5

Your program should make appropriate use of functions in solving this problem. These formulas require nine significant digits, and thus you will have to use Turbo Pascal's LongInt type. As usual, your program should prompt for input (the two dates) if it is to be run interactively. You should use proper style with plenty of comments.

5. Write a program that determines the precision limit of your computer system. To do this, the program begins with a single-digit value. Repeatedly add significant digits to it until a low-order digit fails to register. For example, if we have the sequence

9   99   999   9999   99999   999999   9999999   99999990

then we know that the computer is limited to seven digits of precision. The program should detect automatically when the limit has been reached. (*Hint:* If $X * 10 = X * 10 + 9$, something has been lost.) Your program should determine the precision limit for Real values, and print out the sequence of trial values.

Sets and Additional Control Structures

GOALS

- To understand the difference between atomic and composite data types.
- To be able to declare a variable of type SET.
- To be able to write set expressions.
- To be able to write relational expressions with sets.
- To be able to write a CASE statement to solve a given problem.
- To be able to write an IF-THEN-ELSE statement, using a set and the IN operator, that will prevent execution of a CASE statement with an invalid selector value.
- To be able to write a REPEAT statement to solve a given problem.
- To be able to write a FOR statement to solve a given problem.

In the preceding chapters, we introduced Pascal statements for sequence, selection, loop, and subprogram. In some cases, we introduced more than one way of implementing these structures. For example, selection may be implemented by an IF-THEN statement or an IF-THEN-ELSE statement. The IF-THEN is sufficient to implement any selection structure, but Pascal provides the IF-THEN-ELSE for convenience because the two-way branch is frequently used in programming.

This chapter introduces three new statements that are also nonessential to, but nonetheless convenient for, programming. One, the CASE statement, makes it easier to write selection structures with many branches. The other two, FOR and REPEAT, make it easier to program certain types of looping structures.

First, however, we will introduce a new data type called a set, which is sometimes used with the CASE statement. This is the first of many **user-defined** data types that we will see. In fact, the remainder of this book will be largely devoted to introducing additional user-defined data types.

Sets

A declaration associates an identifier with a process or object. The processes are procedures and functions. The objects have primarily been variables and constants of type Char, Integer, Real, or Boolean. Since each of these objects has a single value, it is logical to think of an identifier as a synonym for its value. Objects, however, may contain many values. A Text file, for example, is an object that contains any number of values.

In this chapter we introduce a new data type, the set, that allows us to associate an identifier with a collection of values. Because a set is composed of multiple values, it is called a **composite data type.** Integer, Real, Char, and Boolean are referred to as **atomic data types.** (We introduce additional atomic data types in Chapter 10.)

Composite Data Type   A data type that allows a collection of values to be associated with an identifier of that type.

Atomic Data Type   A data type that allows only a single value to be associated with an identifier of that type.

In mathematics, a set is a collection, group, or class of items. Pascal sets are the same, except that 1) the items or values must all be of the same atomic data type, and 2) they must not be real numbers because of the problems associated with representational errors.

The atomic data type that is represented by the elements of a set is called the component or base type. The fact that we can choose the base type of a set makes the set a user-defined data type. Each time we define a set variable with a different base type, we are defining a new type.

In mathematics, a set may be of any size; however, Pascal compilers impose a limit on the number of values in a **set.** In Turbo Pascal a set may contain up to 256 elements.

Set   An unordered collection of distinct values (components), chosen from the possible values of a single atomic data type (other than Real), called the component or base type.

There are three special types of sets that are important: the **subset,** a set contained within another set; the **universal set,** a set that contains all the values of the base type; and the **empty set,** which contains no values.

Subset   A set X is a subset of Y if each element of X is an element of Y. If at least one element of Y is not in X, then X is called a *proper subset* of Y.

Universal Set   The set containing all the values of the component type.

Empty Set   The set with no members.

The following syntax template illustrates how to define a variable of a set data type.

```
VAR  identifier list : SET OF data type
```

For example,

```
VAR
  Set_One,
  Set_Two:
    SET OF 'A'..'Z';
  Set_Three:
    SET OF 1..12;
```

creates set variables called Set_One, Set_Two, and Set_Three, where the first two sets may contain no, one, or any combination of capital letters, and the third set may contain no, one, or any combination of the integers in the range 1 through 12. 'A'..'Z' and 1..12 is shorthand: "A through Z, inclusive" and "1 through 12, inclusive," respectively. We look at this shorthand in detail in the next chapter. The capital letters constitute the base type of Set_One and Set_Two, and the integers 1 through 12 constitute the base type of Set_Three.

Like all variables, Set_One and Set_Two are undefined until values are put into them. An undefined set is not the same as an empty set. An empty set is one that has been defined to contain no members. We can look at an empty set and say that it is empty, but we can't make any statements about an undefined set.

To put values into a set, we use the assignment statement. We can assign the value of one set variable to another if the two variables have the same base type; we can also assign a set value to a set variable. A *set value* is a list of expressions of the base type, enclosed in square brackets. For example,

```
Set_One := ['A', 'E', 'I', 'O', 'U']
```

assigns the set value containing the letters A, E, I, O, and U to variable Set_One. A set value may also include the shorthand for a range of values. For example,

```
Set_One := ['A'..'D']
```

would assign the letters A, B, C, and D to Set_One.

In Turbo Pascal, a set value may also include expressions of the base type (Standard Pascal doesn't allow expressions). For example, if NextCh is a function returning a Char value and Current_Ch is a Char variable, the following would assign the values of NextCh and Current_Ch to Set_One.

```
Set_One := [NextCh(Data_File), Current_Ch]
```

The shorthand and expressions may be combined with lists of literal values. For example,

```
Set_One := ['E'..'M', 'A', NextCh(Data_File), 'S'..'V', 'Z',
            Current_Ch]
```

assigns the letters E through M, A, S through V, and Z and the values of NextCh and Current_Ch to variable Set_One. The following statement creates a set containing only the letter P.

```
Set_Two := ['P']
```

To define an empty set, we use

```
Set_One := []
```

Note that after this assignment, Set_One is *not* undefined; it is the empty set. To create the universal set, we use a literal containing all the values in the base type. For example,

```
Set_Two := ['A'..'Z']
```

In all these cases, we assign one set to another. We use brackets when we assign set literals to indicate that the components listed inside are members of a set.

We may also assign the results of set expressions to set variables. There are three operations defined on sets: union, intersection, and difference.

+ (Union): The union of two sets is a set made up of those components that are in either or both of the sets.

* (Intersection): The intersection of two sets is made up of those components occurring in both sets.
— (Difference): The difference between two sets is the set of components in the first set that are not in the second.

To add a value to a set, use the union operator:

```
Set_One := Set_One + ['Q']
```

To delete a value from a set, use the difference operator:

```
Set_One := Set_One - ['Q']
```

Adding a value that is already in a set has no effect; deleting a value that is not in a set has no effect.

The following code segment trace illustrates the three set operations.

Statement	*Set_One*	*Set_Two*
`Set_One := ['P'..'R'];`	`['P', 'Q', 'R']`	`Undefined`
`Set_Two := Set_One + ['S'];`	`['P', 'Q', 'R']`	`['P', 'Q', 'R', 'S']`
`Set_One := Set_One - Set_Two;`	`[]`	`['P', 'Q', 'R', 'S']`
`Set_Two := Set_Two - ['P']`	`[]`	`['Q', 'R', 'S']`
`Set_One := Set_One + ['A', 'B'];`	`['A', 'B']`	`['Q', 'R', 'S']`
`Set_One := Set_One + ['A', 'S'];`	`['A', 'B', 'S']`	`['Q', 'R', 'S']`
`Set_Two := Set_One * Set_Two;`	`['A', 'B', 'S']`	`['S']`

Notice that brackets are used to denote set literals, but they are not used in the declaration of set variables.

Using set operations can make set assignments easier. We can assign Set_One to be vowels and Set_Two to be consonants using the following code fragment.

```
Set_Two := ['A'..'Z'];               (* Universal Set *)
Set_One := ['A', 'E', 'I', 'O', 'U'];  (* Vowels        *)
Set_Two := Set_Two - Set_One;        (* Consonants    *)
```

This is certainly easier than listing every consonant.

We can also perform conditional tests on sets. The relational operators have the following meaning when applied to sets.

Expression	*Returns True* If
`Set_One = Set_Two`	Set_One and Set_Two are identical.
`Set_One <> Set_Two`	Set_One and Set_Two are not identical.
`Set_One <= Set_Two`	Set_One is a subset of Set_Two.
`Set_One < Set_Two`	Set_One is a proper subset of Set_Two—there is at least one value in Set_Two not in Set_One.
`Set_One >= Set_Two`	Set_Two is a subset of Set_One.
`Set_One > Set_Two`	Set_Two is a proper subset of Set_One—there is at least one value in Set_One not in Set_Two.

Given the assignments

```
Set_One := ['A', 'B', 'C', 'D'];
Set_Two := ['C', 'D']
```

the following expressions will be evaluated as shown.

Expression	*Result*
`Set_One = Set_Two`	False
`Set_One >= Set_Two`	True
`Set_One > Set_Two`	True
`Set_Two >= Set_One`	False
`Set_Two > Set_One`	False
`Set_Two <= Set_One`	True
`Set_Two < Set_One`	True

There is one more conditional operator specifically for use with sets. The IN operator tests whether a component is a member of a set. For example,

```
value IN Set_One
```

returns True if the value is in Set_One, and False if it is not.

The IN operator makes it convenient to write certain conditional tests. Suppose we are writing a program that counts the vowels in a file. One way of testing a letter to see if it's a vowel would be

```
IF (Letter = 'A') OR (Letter = 'E') OR (Letter = 'I') OR
   (Letter = 'O') OR (Letter = 'U')
   THEN
     (* Vowel *)
```

With the IN operator, this test can be reduced to

```
IF Letter IN ['A', 'E', 'I', 'O', 'U']
   THEN
     (* Vowel *)
```

The IN operator has the same precedence as the other relational operators; that is, it is lower in precedence than other operators. When used with sets, +, *, and − have the same precedence as when used with integers or reals.

Let's look at an example program using sets. A small airline needs a program to keep track of which seats are sold on a plane. The plane has eighteen seats, which we represent as a set. Each seat has a number designation, so we define the set as

```
Plane:
  SET OF 1..18
```

When each passenger boards the plane, a clerk enters the seat number from the passenger's ticket. After the last passenger is aboard, the clerk enters a 0 to end the program. At the end of the program, a list of the occupied seats is printed. To do this, we loop through the members of the set, printing each one that is IN the set.

```
PROGRAM Airline(Input, Output);

(* Keeps track of which seats are filled on a plane *)

VAR
  Seat:
    Integer;
  Plane:
    SET OF 1..18;

BEGIN (* Airline *)
  Plane := [];                              (* Initializes Plane to empty *)
  (* Get each passenger's seat number *)
  Writeln('Enter seat number:  ');
  Readln(Seat);
  WHILE (Seat >= 1) AND (Seat <= 18) DO (* Ends if Seat is out of range *)
    BEGIN
      Plane := Plane + [Seat];        (* Insert seat number in set Plane *)
      Writeln('Enter seat number:  ');
      Readln(Seat)
    END;
  (* Output list of occupied seats *)
  Writeln('Occupied Seats:  ');
  Seat := 1;
  WHILE Seat <= 18 DO
    BEGIN
      IF Seat IN Plane                        (* Test for Seat occupied *)
        THEN
          Writeln(Seat:2);
      Seat := Seat + 1
    END
END.  (* Airline *)
```

We now turn to the remaining control structures provided by Pascal. The first of these, the CASE statement, will demonstrate another use for sets.

Additional Control Structures

CASE Statement

The CASE statement is a selection control structure that allows us to list any number of branches. It is similar to a nested IF statement. The value of the **case selector,** an expression whose result must match a label attached to a branch, determines which one of the branches is executed. For example, look at the following statement:

```
CASE Letter OF
  'X'       : statement1;
  'L', 'M' : statement2;
  'S'       : statement3
END;    (* Case *)
statement4
```

In this example, Letter is the case selector. The statement means "If Letter is X, execute statement1 and continue with statement4. If Letter is L or M, execute statement2 and continue with statement4. If Letter is S, execute statement3 and continue with statement4." The syntax template for the CASE statement is

CASE expression **OF**

    case label **,** case label **. . . :** statement **;**

    case label **,** case label **. . . :** statement

      ⋮

    ELSE statement

END

where a case label is a literal or named constant of any atomic type except Real. (We expand the definition of *case label* in the next chapter.) The expression is the case selector, and the list of labels is the **case label list.**

Case Selector   The expression whose value determines which case label is selected. It cannot be a Real.

Case Label List   A list of values, of the same type as the case selector, appearing in the body of the CASE statement.

In the example above,

```
'X'
'L', 'M'
'S'
```

are case label lists. Each case label value may appear only once in a given CASE statement. If a value appears more than once, a compiler error will result.

The following program fragment would print an appropriate comment based on a student's grade (Grade is of type Char).

```
CASE Grade OF
  'A', 'B' : Write('Good Work');
  'C'      : Write('Average Work');
  'D', 'F' : Write('Poor Work')
END (* Case *)
```

What if we want more than one statement in a branch? Recall that we may use a compound statement anywhere a single statement may be used. The following code fragment contains a compound statement to write a message and increment a count.

```
CASE Grade OF
  'A', 'B' : Write('Good Work');
  'C'      : Write('Average Work');
  'D', 'F' :
    BEGIN
      Write('Poor Work');
      Number_In_Trouble := Number_In_Trouble + 1
    END
END (* Case *)
```

If Grade does not contain one of these letters, the definition of Pascal states that this is an error, but does not say what should happen if it occurs. Many Pascal implementations print a run-time error message, while others, such as Turbo Pascal, skip the entire statement. Turbo Pascal also handles this problem by extending the language definition and adding an ELSE branch to the CASE statement.

There is a way to make the result of an invalid case selector predictable without resorting to a nonstandard language extension. We can use the IN operator first to check the validity of the case selector. For example, the following code fragment ensures that Grade is an allowed value.

```
IF Grade IN ['A', 'B', 'C', 'D', 'F']
  THEN
    CASE Grade OF
        .
        .
        .
    END (* Case *)
  ELSE
    Writeln('Grade is not a legal letter grade. ')
```

The technique we have just described will work in any Pascal system. Turbo Pascal, however, provides a nonstandard extension to the CASE statement that simplifies dealing with invalid case selector values. In Turbo Pascal you can insert an ELSE branch just before the END of the CASE statement. The statement(s) associated with the ELSE will be executed if the case selector does not equal any of the values in the case label lists. For example,

```
CASE Grade OF
  'A', 'B' : Write('Good Work');
  'C'      : Write('Average Work');
  'D', 'F' :
    BEGIN
      Write('Poor Work');
      Number_In_Trouble := Number_In_Trouble + 1
    END
  ELSE        Write('Grade is not a legal letter grade')
END; (* Case *)
```

Note that there is no colon (:) between the reserved word ELSE and the statement associated with it. Although the ELSE clause is a convenient addition to the CASE statement, keep in mind that it is nonstandard and will not work in most other Pascal systems.

The CASE statement itself can be replaced with nested IF-THEN-ELSE statements; IF statements may always be used in place of a CASE statement. IF statements *must* be used when you can't write the selector as an expression with an atomic result. They must also be used when the branch depends on a real value.

Keep in mind that Pascal provides the CASE statement as a matter of convenience. Don't feel obligated to use a CASE statement for every multiway branch.

REPEAT Statement

The REPEAT statement is a looping control structure in which the loop condition is tested at the end of the loop. This format guarantees that the loop body is executed at least once. The syntax template for the REPEAT-UNTIL is:

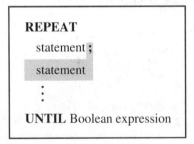

For example, the REPEAT statement

```
REPEAT
  statement1;
  statement2;
    .
    .
  statementN
UNTIL Boolean expression
```

means "Execute the statements between REPEAT and UNTIL as long as the Boolean expression is False at the end of the loop." Because UNTIL delimits the statement, a BEGIN-END pair is not necessary for the body of the loop.

Let's compare a WHILE loop and a REPEAT loop that do the same task: finding the first period in a file of data. Assume that there is at least one period in the file.

WHILE Solution

```
Read(Data, Character);
WHILE Character <> '.' DO
  Read(Data, Character);
```

REPEAT Solution

```
REPEAT
  Read(Data, Character)
UNTIL Character = '.'
```

The WHILE solution requires a priming Read so that Character will have a value before the loop is entered. This isn't required for the REPEAT solution because the Read within the loop is executed before the Boolean expression is evaluated.

Let's look at another example. Suppose a program is intended to read test scores interactively. A score must be in the range of 0 to 100. The following loops will then ensure that the input value is in the acceptable range.

WHILE Solution

```
Writeln('Enter a test score.');
Readln (Score);
WHILE (Score < 0) OR (Score > 100) DO
  BEGIN
    Writeln('Invalid score. Scores must be ',
            'in the range of 0 through 100.');
    Writeln('Enter a test score, ');
    Readln(Score)
  END
```

REPEAT Solution

```
REPEAT
  Writeln('Enter a test score.');
  Readln(Score);
  IF (Score < 0) OR (Score > 100)
    THEN
      Writeln('Invalid score. Scores must be ',
              'in the range of 0 through 100.')
UNTIL (Score >= 0) AND (Score <= 100)
```

Note that the REPEAT solution does not require the prompt and input steps to be duplicated before the loop, but it does test the input value twice.

The REPEAT can also be used to implement a count-controlled loop if we know in advance that the loop will always be executed at least once. Use of the WHILE and REPEAT statements to implement a count-controlled loop is shown below.

```
Counter := 1;
WHILE Counter <= N DO
  BEGIN
     .
     .
   Counter := Counter + 1
  END;

Counter := 1;
REPEAT
   .
   .
   Counter := Counter + 1
UNTIL Counter > N
```

The expressions controlling the two kinds of loops are *complements* (opposites) of each other. The WHILE continues looping as long as the expression is True; the REPEAT continues looping as long as the expression is False. Because the WHILE statement tests the condition before executing the body of the loop, it is called a **pretest loop.** The REPEAT statement does the opposite, and is thus known as a **posttest loop.** Figure 9-1 compares the flow of control in the WHILE and REPEAT loops.

It is important to keep in mind that WHILE uses the expression to decide when to keep looping, and REPEAT uses it to decide when to stop. To transform a WHILE into a REPEAT or vice versa, the expression must be complemented. The following list shows some common looping conditions with their complements.

Figure 9-1
Flow of Control:
WHILE and
REPEAT

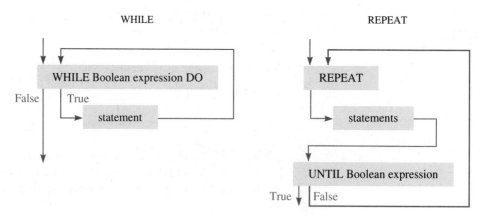

Expression	*Complement*
NOT EOF	EOF
(Ch >= 'A') AND (Ch <= 'Z')	(Ch < 'A') OR (Ch > 'Z')
I >= N	I < N
(I < N) AND NOT FOUND	(I >= N) OR FOUND

After we look at the last looping construct, the FOR statement, we will consider some guidelines for determining when to use each type of loop.

FOR Statement

The FOR statement is designed to simplify the writing of count-controlled loops. The statement

```
FOR Count := 1 TO N DO
  statement;
```

means "Set the loop control variable Count to 1. If N is less than 1, do not enter the loop. Otherwise, execute the statement and increment Count by 1. Stop the loop after it has been executed with Count equal to N." This statement is essentially the same as the following WHILE loop.

```
Count := 1;
WHILE Count <= N DO
  BEGIN
    statement;
    Count := Count + 1
  END;
```

The syntax diagram for the FOR statement is

FOR variable identifier **:=** expression $\left\{ \begin{array}{l} \textbf{TO} \\ \textbf{DOWNTO} \end{array} \right.$ expression **DO**
statement

The statement in the FOR loop may be a compound statement.

If DOWNTO is used, the loop control variable is decremented by 1 for each iteration, instead of being incremented by 1. The following two loops will execute the same number of times.

```
FOR Count := Lower_Limit TO Upper_Limit DO
  statement;

FOR Count := Upper_Limit DOWNTO Lower_Limit DO
  statement;
```

The initial and final values of the FOR loop may be expressions of any atomic data type except Real (because of the representational errors associated with Reals). Thus, in addition to Integer values, a FOR loop can be used with Char or Boolean values. For example, the following loop prints the alphabet.

```
FOR Letter := 'A' TO 'Z' DO
  Write(Letter);
Writeln;
```

Just like WHILE loops, REPEAT and FOR loops may be nested. For example, the nested FOR structure

```
FOR End_Letter := 'A' TO 'G' DO
  BEGIN
    FOR Printed_Letter := 'A' TO End_Letter DO
      Write(Printed_Letter);
    Writeln
  END;
```

prints the following triangle of letters.

```
A
AB
ABC
ABCD
ABCDE
ABCDEF
ABCDEFG
```

FOR statements are convenient, and many programmers tend to overuse them. Be warned: FOR loops are not general-purpose loops. They are designed exclusively for count-controlled loops. To use them intelligently, you should know the following facts about FOR loops.

1. The loop control variable may be used, but not changed, within the loop; that is, the loop control variable may appear in an expression, but not on the left-hand side of an assignment statement.
2. The loop control variable always steps by 1 or -1. If you need to increment or decrement by another value, you should use a WHILE or REPEAT loop.

3. In Standard Pascal, the loop control variable is undefined at the end of the loop. You might expect the control variable to be the final value plus 1, but it is not. In Turbo Pascal, it is the final value, but it is best to treat it as undefined. If, in a statement following the FOR loop, you try to use the control variable in an expression, the effects will vary from compiler to compiler. You may get an error message or erroneous results. For example,

```
FOR Count := 0 TO 10 DO
  BEGIN
    Cube := Count * Count * Count;
    Writeln(Count:1, ' ', Cube:1)
  END;
Writeln(Count:1)
```

would first print a table of the cubes of the numbers 0 through 10, then the number 10. However, in Standard Pascal, either an error message or some unpredictable value would be printed. By chance the number might be 11, but Pascal does not guarantee it.

4. When you use a FOR statement in a procedure or function, the loop control variable must be a local variable. Why? Suppose a procedure contains a FOR loop that is controlled by a global variable, and within that FOR loop, another procedure, which also contains a FOR loop controlled by the same global variable, is called. When the second procedure returns, the value of the control variable has changed, which may make it impossible for the first FOR loop to continue. To prevent situations like this from occurring, Pascal requires us to use a local variable as the loop control variable.

5. The loop is executed with the loop control variable at the initial value, the final value, and all values in between. If the initial value is equal to the final value, the FOR statement is executed once. In the TO version, if the initial value is greater than the final value, the FOR statement is not executed. In the DOWNTO version, the final value must be less than or equal to the initial value, or the statement is skipped.

6. You cannot put an additional termination condition in the loop, and the heading must be exactly like the following:

```
FOR name := initial value TO final value DO
```

or

```
FOR name := initial value DOWNTO final value DO
```

where name must be variable, and initial value and final value can be any valid expressions (variables and/or constants and operators).

Guidelines for Choosing a Looping Statement

Here are some guidelines to help you decide when to use each of the three looping statements.

1. If the loop is a simple count-controlled loop, use a FOR statement. If the loop is controlled by a counter and an event, or if the loop must count by a value other than 1 or −1, use a WHILE or REPEAT loop instead.
2. If the loop is an event-controlled loop whose body will always be executed at least once, a REPEAT statement is appropriate.
3. If the loop is an event-controlled loop and nothing is known about the first execution, use a WHILE statement.
4. If both a WHILE and a REPEAT are appropriate, use the one that better reflects the semantics of the loop—that is, if the problem is stated in terms of when to continue looping, use a WHILE statement; if the problem is stated in terms of when to stop looping, use a REPEAT statement.
5. When in doubt, use a WHILE statement.

*P*ROBLEM-SOLVING CASE STUDY

The Rich Uncle

Problem: Your rich uncle has just died, and in his desk you find two wills. One of them, dated several months ago, leaves you and your relatives a substantial part of his fortune; the other, dated last week, gives it all to his next-door neighbor. Being suspicious that the second will is a forgery, you decide to write a program to analyze writing style and thus compare the wills. The program will read and print alphanumeric characters from file Data. When the entire file has been read, it will print a summary table showing the percentage of uppercase letters, lowercase letters, decimal digits, blanks, and end-of-sentence punctuation marks in the data file ('?', '!', '.').

Input: Text on file Data.

Output: A copy of the text on file Data, and a table giving the name of each category and what percentage of the total the category represents.

Discussion: Doing this task by hand would be tedious but quite straightforward. You would set up five places to make hash marks, one for each of the categories of symbols to be counted. You would then read the text character by character, determine which category to put each character in, and make a hash mark in the appropriate place.

You can look at a character and tell immediately which category to mark. This will be simulated by using the CASE statement with branches for the uppercase letters, the lowercase letters, the digits, a blank, and punctuation marks.

Assumptions: None.

Main   *Level 0*

```
WHILE NOT EOF
    WHILE NOT EOLN
        Read a character
        Write a character
        Increment proper counter
    Readln
    Writeln
Calculate and print percentages
```

Note that we have to skip over the end-of-line markers; otherwise they would be counted as blanks.

Increment Proper Counter
(Receives/returns: Uppercase_Counter, Lowercase_Counter,   *Level 1*
    Digit_Counter, Blank_Counter, Punctuation_Counter,
    Left_Over_Counter : Integer,
    Receives: Character : Char)

```
CASE Character of
    Uppercase letters: Increment Uppercase Counter
    Lowercase letters: Increment Lowercase Counter
    Digits: Increment Digit Counter
    Blank: Increment Blank Counter
    Punctuation: Increment Punctuation Counter
```

At this point we realize that the instructions do not indicate whether the percentages are to be taken of the total number of characters read, including those that do not fit any of the categories, or of the total number of characters that fall into the five categories. We assume that all characters should be counted. We thus add to this module an IF-THEN-ELSE statement that increments a counter (called Left_Over_Counter) for all characters that do not fall into the five categories.

Calculate and Print Percentages
(Receives/returns Uppercase_Counter, Lowercase_Counter,
**   Digit_Counter, Blank_Counter, Punctuation_Counter,**
**   Left_Over_Counter : Integer,**
**   Receives: Character : Char)**

Set Total to sum of 6 counters
Print 'Percentage of uppercase letters:',
    Uppercase Counter / Total * 100
Print 'Percentage of lowercase letters:',
    Lowercase Counter / Total * 100
Print 'Percentage of decimal digits:',
    Digit Counter / Total * 100
Print 'Percentage of blanks:',
    Blank Counter / Total * 100
Print 'Percentage of end-of-sentence punctuation:',
    Punctuation Counter / Total * 100

Module Structure Chart:

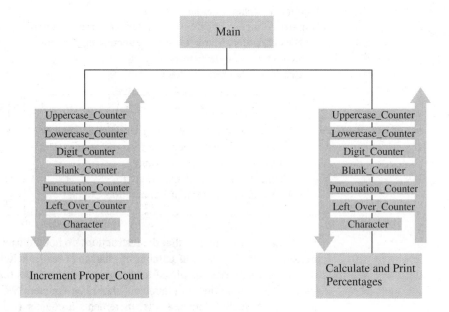

PROBLEM-SOLVING CASE STUDY cont'd.

```
PROGRAM Category_Count (Output, Data);

(* File Data is echo-printed on Output. A table is printed to    *)
(* show the percentage of characters in the file that belong     *)
(* to the five categories: uppercase letters, lowercase letters, *)
(* decimal digits, blanks, and end-of-sentence punctuation marks. *)
(* ASSUMPTION:  Percentages are based on total number of         *)
(* characters in the file                                         *)

VAR
   Uppercase_Counter,         (* Number of uppercase letters *)
   Lowercase_Counter,         (* Number of lowercase letters *)
   Digit_Counter,             (* Number of digits           *)
   Blank_Counter,             (* Number of blanks           *)
   Punctuation_Counter,       (* Number of punctuation marks *)
   Left_Over_Counter :        (* Number of other characters  *)
      Integer;
   Data:                      (* Input text file            *)
      Text;
   Character:                 (* Current input character     *)
      Char;


(*********************************************************************)


PROCEDURE Increment_Proper_Count
   (VAR Uppercase_Counter,          (* Receives/returns count    *)
        Lowercase_Counter,          (* Receives/returns count    *)
        Digit_Counter,              (* Receives/returns count    *)
        Blank_Counter,              (* Receives/returns count    *)
        Punctuation_Counter,        (* Receives/returns count    *)
        Left_Over_Counter :         (* Receives/returns count    *)
           Integer;
        Character:                  (* Receives current character *)
           Char);

(* The proper counter is incremented for each character *)
```

```
BEGIN   (* Increment_Proper_Count *)
  IF Character IN ['A'..'Z', 'a'..'z', '0'..'9', ' ', '.', '?', '!']
    THEN
      CASE Character OF
         'A', 'B', 'C', 'D',
         'E', 'F', 'G', 'H',
         'I', 'J', 'K', 'L',
         'M', 'N', 'O', 'P',
         'Q', 'R', 'S', 'T',
         'U', 'V', 'W', 'X',
         'Y', 'Z': Uppercase_Counter := Uppercase_Counter + 1;
         'a', 'b', 'c', 'd',
         'e', 'f', 'g', 'h',
         'i', 'j', 'k', 'l',
         'm', 'n', 'o', 'p',
         'q', 'r', 's', 't',
         'u', 'v', 'w', 'x',
         'y', 'z': Lowercase_Counter := Lowercase_Counter + 1;
         '0', '1', '2', '3',
         '4', '5', '6', '7',
         '8', '9': Digit_Counter := Digit_Counter + 1;
         ' ': Blank_Counter := Blank_Counter + 1;
         '.', '?', '!': Punctuation_Counter := Punctuation_Counter + 1
      END (* Case *)
    ELSE
      Left_Over_Counter := Left_Over_Counter  + 1
END; (* Increment_Proper_Count *)


(*****************************************************************)


PROCEDURE Calculate_Print (Uppercase_Counter,      (* Receives count *)
                           Lowercase_Counter,      (* Receives count *)
                           Digit_Counter,          (* Receives count *)
                           Blank_Counter,          (* Receives count *)
                           Punctuation_Counter,    (* Receives count *)
                           Left_Over_Counter:      (* Receives count *)
                              Integer);

(* The total number of characters is calculated and the percentage *)
(* of each category of characters is printed *)


VAR
  Total:          (* Total number of characters in file *)
     Integer;
```

```
BEGIN (* Calculate_Print *)
  Writeln;
  Total := Uppercase_Counter + Lowercase_Counter + Digit_Counter +
          Blank_Counter + Punctuation_Counter + Left_Over_Counter;
  Writeln(' Percentage of uppercase letters: ',
          Uppercase_Counter / Total * 100:5:2);
  Writeln(' Percentage of lowercase letters: ',
          Lowercase_Counter / Total * 100:5:2);
  Writeln(' Percentage of decimal digits: ',
          Digit_Counter / Total * 100:5:2);
  Writeln(' Percentage of end-of-sentence punctuation: ',
          Punctuation_Counter / Total * 100:5:2)
END; (* Calculate_Print *)

(******************************************************************)

BEGIN (* Category_Count *)
  Assign(Data, 'DATAFILE.DAT');
  Reset (Data);
  (* Initialize counters to zero *)
  Uppercase_Counter := 0;
  Lowercase_Counter := 0;
  Digit_Counter := 0;
  Blank_Counter := 0;
  Punctuation_Counter := 0;
  Left_Over_Counter := 0;

  WHILE NOT EOF(Data) DO
    BEGIN
      WHILE NOT EOLN(Data) DO
        BEGIN
          Read(Data, Character);
          Write(Character);
          Increment_Proper_Count(Uppercase_Counter, Lowercase_Counter,
                                 Digit_Counter, Blank_Counter,
                                 Punctuation_Counter, Left_Over_Counter,
                                 Character)
        END;
      Readln(Data);
      Writeln
    END;
  Calculate_Print(Uppercase_Counter, Lowercase_Counter, Digit_Counter,
                  Blank_Counter, Punctuation_Counter, Left_Over_Counter);
  Close(Data)
END.  (* Category_Count *)
```

PROBLEM-SOLVING CASE STUDY *cont'd.*

Testing: To be tested thoroughly, Program Category_Count must be run with all possible combinations of the categories of characters being counted. Listed below is the minimum set of cases that must be tested.

1. All the categories of characters are present.
2. Four of the categories are present; one is not. (This alone will require five test runs.)
3. Only characters that fall into one of the five categories are present.
4. Other characters are present.

The percentages listed below came from a sample run of the program on a large text file. For obvious reasons, we are showing only the percentages, not the echo print of the input.

Output from Program Category_Count

Percentage of uppercase letters: 2.05
Percentage of lowercase letters: 82.32
Percentage of decimal digits: 0.05
Percentage of blanks: 7.03
Percentage of end-of-sentence punctuation: 1.27

Program Category_Count used only a set literal. A set variable is used in the following case study, together with FOR and REPEAT.

*P*ROBLEM-SOLVING CASE STUDY

Final Grades

F   D   C   B   A

Problem: It is time to assign final letter grades in a history class. At the moment, the grades are in the form of numeric averages, ranging from 0 to 100. Every grade below 60 is an automatic F. However, the exact cutoff for the other grades may vary slightly. To determine these cutoff points, it's useful to see if there are any gaps in the range of numeric grades earned by the students. We thus print a list of numeric grades from 60 to 100, marking those that occur with an asterisk.

Input: Integer grades, one per line, read from the terminal.

Output: The numbers from 60 to 100, listed one per line. (Asterisks will mark those numbers for which at least one student earned that grade.)

Discussion: We are not interested in how many people have a particular grade, only whether it exists in the set of grades. The clue to the solution lies in the expression "set of grades." We can create a set variable to contain numbers from 60 to 100. As we read in a grade, we can test to see if it is in the range, and if so, put it into the set.

When we have read in all the grades, we can print out the values in the set. Since there is no direct way to print a set, we have to use a loop that goes from 60 to 100 and ask if the loop control variable is IN the set.

Assumptions: None.

Main   *Level 0*

```
Initialize Set_Of_Grades
REPEAT
    Read Grade
    IF Grade is in the range 60 through 100
        THEN
            Add Grade to Set_Of_Grades
UNTIL no more grades
Print numbers
```

The REPEAT loop is appropriate for the main looping structure. We want to keep reading and processing values until we reach the end of the list of numbers. A REPEAT-UNTIL end-of-file will accomplish this.

Print Numbers (Receives Set_Of_Grades)   *Level 1*

```
FOR Counter going from 60 to 100
    Print Counter
    IF Counter is in Set_Of_Grades
        Print '*'
    Go to next line
```

We need to print the numbers 60 and 100 and all those in between. This is exactly what the FOR loop is designed to do.

Even though the program is not a long one, the printing module should be made a procedure. However, we have not yet studied the mechanism that will allow us to define the set as a formal parameter of a procedure, and we do not want to access the set globally. We must code this program without using a procedure. In the next chapter, we study the mechanism that allows the use of sets as parameters.

Module Structure Chart:

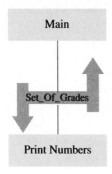

Program Grade_List implements our algorithm.

```
PROGRAM Grade_List (Input, Output);

(* The numbers between 60 and 100 are printed. Numbers that correspond *)
(* to a grade in the input file are marked with an asterisk            *)

VAR
  Set_Of_Grades:      (* Keeps track of actual grades       *)
    SET of 60..100;
  Counter,            (* Loop control variable              *)
  Grade:              (* Numeric grade between 0 and 100    *)
    Integer;
```

```
BEGIN (* Grade_List *)
  (* Turn on EOF checking for standard input *)

  CheckEOF := True;
  (* Initialize Set_Of_Grades to empty *)
  Set_Of_Grades := [];
  (* Read and add grades to Set_Of_Grades *)
  REPEAT
    Readln(Grade);                              (* Get a grade *)
    IF (Grade >= 60) AND (Grade <= 100)      (* Check if in range*)
      THEN
        Set_Of_Grades := Set_Of_Grades + [Grade]   (* Add it to set *)
  UNTIL EOF;
  (* Print Numbers *)
  FOR Counter := 60 TO 100 DO
    BEGIN
      Write(Counter:3);                        (* Print number *)
      IF Counter IN Set_Of_Grades           (* Test for set membership *)
        THEN
          Write (' *');                       (* Mark number *)
      Writeln
    END
END.  (* Grade_List *)
```

Testing: To test this program, we need to use the following types of data.

> Data that includes values less than 60,
> > values more than 100,
> > one or more values of 60,
> > one or more values of 100,
> > single values between 60 and 100,
> > duplicate values between 60 and 100.

Data that does not include some values between 60 and 100.

The following data was used to test the program. The input specification called for one value per line, but we have listed multiple values in a line to conserve space.

```
66  67  88  99  100  44  33  77  67  81  88  99  77  67  68  87  97  99  95  86
84  79  68  66   77  98  80  56  67  76  87  67  66  78  76  75  78  86  65  67
91  89  90  56   77  67  74  76  78  60
```

Here is the output produced from the input data. (Again, we have printed it in columns to save space.)

PROBLEM-SOLVING CASE STUDY cont'd.

60	*	70		80	*	90	*
61		71		81	*	91	*
62		72		82		92	
63		73		83		93	
64		74	*	84	*	94	
65	*	75	*	85		95	*
66	*	76	*	86	*	96	
67	*	77	*	87	*	97	*
68	*	78	*	88	*	98	*
69		79	*	89	*	99	*
						100	*

Testing and Debugging

The same testing techniques we used with WHILE loops apply to REPEAT and FOR loops. There are, however, a few additional considerations with these loops.

A REPEAT loop will always execute at least once. Thus, you should always try data sets that will show the result of executing a REPEAT loop the minimal number of times.

With a data-dependent FOR loop, it is important to test for proper results when the loop executes zero times. This occurs when the starting value is greater than the ending value (or less than the ending value, in the case of the DOWNTO form).

When a program contains a CASE statement, it should be tested with enough different data sets to ensure that each case branch is selected and executed correctly. The program should also be tested with a case selector containing a value that is not in any of the case labels.

If a program uses a variable of type set, you should try to find data values that will cause a value outside the base type to be assigned to the variable. For example, if a SET of 'A'..'Z' is defined in the program, try data values such as '?' and '8' to see if the program catches them before trying to perform set operations.

Testing and Debugging Hints

1. The size of a set (the number of values that can be in the set) is limited in Pascal. In Turbo Pascal, sets may contain up to 256 elements.
2. Initialize set variables before using them. Using an uninitialized set variable can result in error messages such as RANGE CHECK ERROR.
3. Do not attempt to print sets directly. Test elements for set membership and print each one that is a member.
4. Brackets are used to denote set literals, but are not used in the declaration of set variables. The set variable Letter may be defined as a SET OF 'A'..'Z', but the statement

```
Letter := Letter + 'A'
```

is not valid because 'A' is not a set. Using brackets around the 'A' makes it a set literal. Therefore

```
Letter := Letter + ['A']
```

is a valid statement.

5. All the set operators except IN have two sets as their operands. IN has a base type value as its first operand and a set as its second operand. Thus, if Letter is declared as a SET OF 'A'..'Z', the following are valid comparisons.

```
['A'] = Letter          (* Tests equality of two sets *)
'A' IN Letter      (* No brackets needed around 'A' because *)
                   (* first operand must be of base type     *)
```

6. The standard operators +, −, and * have different meanings when used with sets.
7. The REPEAT loop is a posttest loop. If there is a possibility that the loop should be skipped entirely, use a WHILE statement.
8. The FOR statement is a special-purpose loop. It is a count-controlled loop in which the initial and final values are listed in the statement itself. The increment is always 1 for the TO version and −1 for the DOWNTO version.
9. The loop control variable must be a local variable when FOR is used within a procedure or a function.
10. The case label lists are made up of values, not variables. They may, however, include named constants.
11. If there is a possibility that the case selector might not be one of the values in a case label list, test it for set membership with an IF-THEN-ELSE before executing the CASE statement. You can also use the Turbo Pascal ELSE clause which is a nonstandard extension.
12. The type of the case selector must be the same as that of the values in the case labels.
13. Double-check long CASE statements to make sure that you haven't skipped any branches.
14. Always include the comment (* Case *) after the END of a CASE statement. This helps eliminate confusion if later you must track down an error involving a mismatched BEGIN-END pair.

Summary

An identifier declared to be of an atomic data type (such as Integer, Real, Boolean, or Char) can hold only a single value. An identifier declared to be of a composite type (such as Set or Text) may represent multiple values.

A set is a collection of values and hence is a composite data type. We can create a set, put values into it with the union operator, and remove values with the difference operator. We can determine whether a value is in the set with the IN operator. These operations are useful for checking the value of a case selector prior to execution of a CASE statement. They are also useful for processing text data.

The CASE statement is a multiway selection statement. It allows the program to choose among a set of branches. The CASE is less general than a nested IF-THEN-ELSE structure, and can always be simulated by it. If CASE can be used, however, it makes the code shorter and more self-documenting. CASE cannot be used with Real values as labels.

The REPEAT is a general-purpose looping statement. It is like the WHILE loop except that its test occurs at the end of the loop, guaranteeing at least one execution of the loop. The loop continues as long as the expression is False.

Pascal also provides a special-purpose looping statement, the FOR statement, with predefined initial and final values for the loop control variable, and automatic incrementing with TO or decrementing with DOWNTO. If the ending value is smaller (TO) or greater (DOWNTO) than the initial value, the loop is not executed. The loop control variable of the FOR statement may be of any atomic data type except Real.

The FOR, REPEAT, and CASE statements are the ice cream and cake of Pascal. We can live without them, but they are very nice to have.

▪ Quick Check

1. What distinguishes an atomic data type from a composite data type? (p. 396)

2. Declare a set variable, called Digits, whose base type is the characters '0' through '9'. (pp. 396–401)

3. How would you assign the characters '0' through '4', and '6' through '9' (all of the digits except '5') to the set variable Digits? *Hint:* Use the set difference operator. (pp. 396–401)

4. How would you test whether the set variable Numbers is a proper subset of Digits? (p. 399)

5. Write a CASE statement that, given an Integer selector called Name, will print your first name if Name = 1, your middle name if Name = 2, and your last name if Name = 3. (pp. 401–404)

6. How would you change the answer to Question 5 so that it prints an error message if the value is not 1, 2, or 3? (pp. 401–404)

7. The condition in a WHILE loop is (Day < 1) OR (Day > 31). What would be the condition in an equivalent REPEAT statement? (pp. 404–407)

8. A certain problem requires a count-controlled loop that starts at 10 and counts down to 1. Which type of Pascal loop should be used? (pp. 407–410)

Answers

1. An atomic type associates one value with an identifier. A composite type may associate multiple values with an identifier.   2. VAR Digits: SET OF '0'..'9'
3. Digits := ['0'..'9'] – ['5']   4. IF Numbers < Digits

```
5. CASE Name OF
     1 : Writeln('Mary');
     2 : Writeln('Lynn');
     3 : Writeln('Smith');
   END (* Case *)
6. IF Name IN [1,2,3]
     THEN
       CASE Name OF
         1 : Writeln('Mary');
         2 : Writeln('Lynn');
         3 : Writeln('Smith')
       END (* Case *)
     ELSE
       Writeln ('Invalid name selector.')
7. (Day >= 1) AND (Day <= 31)
8.   A FOR loop: FOR Count := 10 DOWNTO 1 DO
```

■ *Exam Preparation Exercises*

1. Define the following terms:

   composite type
   case selector
   case label
   posttest loop

2. Is the following a valid declaration of a set variable?

   ```
   VAR Digits : ['0'..'9']
   ```

   Explain your answer.

3. Determine whether each of the following set expressions is valid or invalid. Assume that the variable Digits is declared as a SET OF '0'..'9'.
   ```
   a. 'A' IN Digits
   b. ['X', 'Y', 'Z'] >= ['N'..'Y']
   c. Digits / ['1']
   d. Digits * ['1']
   e. ['1'] + ['2'] + ['3'] = ['1'..'3']
   f. ['1'..'9'] > ['0'..'9'] - ['3'..'7']
   g. 4 IN Digits
   ```

4. Given the declarations and assignments
   ```
   VAR
     Digits,
     Odds,
     Evens:
       SET OF '0'..'9'
   ```

```
Digits := ['0'..'9'];
Odds := ['1', '3', '5', '7', '9'];
Evens := ['2', '4', '6', '8'];
```

evaluate these independent expressions.
a. `Digits + ['1']`
b. `Digits * ['1']`
c. `Digits - ['1']`
d. `['1'] + ['2'] + ['3'] <= Digits`
e. `['1'..'9'] > Digits - ['3'..'7']`
f. `Digits - Odds = Evens`
g. `Digits > Odds + Evens`
h. `Odds * Digits`
i. `Odds - Evens`
j. `Odds * Evens * Digits > []`

5. When a WHILE loop is converted into a REPEAT loop, the ending condition of the REPEAT loop is the complement of the ending condition of the WHILE loop. (True or False?)

6. A REPEAT loop does not require a BEGIN-END pair surrounding the loop body because REPEAT and UNTIL serve as the delimiters of the loop. (True or False?)

7. Is the following a valid FOR statement?

```
FOR Initial := 'Z' DOWNTO 'A' DO
   Write(Initial:2)
```

Assume that Initial is a variable of type Char. Explain your answer.

8. a. The value of the loop control variable may be changed within a FOR loop. (True or False?)
   b. The loop control variable of a FOR loop within a procedure must be declared locally. (True or False?)
   c. It is impossible to write an infinite loop using only the FOR statement. (True or False?)
   d. The FOR loop is a general-purpose loop because any WHILE loop can be rewritten as a FOR loop. (True or False?)

9. What will be printed by the following program fragment?

```
FOR I := 4 DOWNTO 1 DO
   BEGIN
      FOR J := I DOWNTO 1 DO
         Write(I);
      Writeln(I)
   END;
```

10. What will be printed by the following program fragment?

```
FOR Row := 1 TO 10 DO
  BEGIN
    FOR Col := 1 TO 10 - Row DO
      Write ('*');
    Write(' ':Row*2-1);
   . FOR Col := 1 TO 10 - Row DO
      Write ('*')
    Writeln;
  END
```

11. A case selector may be an expression that results in a value of type Integer, Real, or Boolean. (True or False?)

12. The values in case label lists may appear in any order, but duplicate labels are not allowed within a given CASE statement. (True or False?)

13. All possible values for the case selector must be included among the case label lists for a given CASE statement. (True or False?)

14. Rewrite the following code fragment using the CASE statement.

```
IF N = 3
  THEN
    Three := Three + 1
  ELSE IF N = 7
    THEN
      Seven := Seven + 1
  ELSE IF N = 10
    THEN
      Ten := Ten + 1;
```

■ *Programming Warm-Up Exercises*

1. Rewrite the following using set notation.
   a. (0 < I) AND (I < 25)
   b. (Ch = 'A') OR (Ch = 'J') OR (Ch = 'K')
   c. (X = 1) OR (X > 50) AND (X <= 100)

2. a. Define three set variables, called Set_A, Set_B, and Set_C, that can contain any of the uppercase alphabetic characters.
   b. Assign 'A'..'N' to Set_A.
   c. Assign 'K'..'Z' to Set_B.
   d. Show the contents of Set_C after each of the following independent operations.

   ```
   Set_C := Set_A + Set_B
   Set_C := Set_A - Set_B
   Set_C := Set_A * Set_B
   Set_C := Set_B - Set_A
   ```

e. Evaluate the following expressions.

```
Set_A <> Set_B
Set_A <= Set_B
Set_A * Set_B > Set_A
Set_A + Set_B >= Set_A
```

3. Write a program segment that reads and sums until it has summed 10 data values or until a negative value is read, whichever comes first. Use a REPEAT loop for your solution.

4. Write a procedure called Get_Yes_Or_No that returns a character equal to either 'Y' or 'N'. The procedure should read a character and test whether it is 'Y' or 'N'. If it is not, the procedure should print an appropriate error message, prompt for another input, and read a character again. The procedure should not return until it has read a valid response. Use a REPEAT loop for your solution.

5. Rewrite the following WHILE loop using a REPEAT loop.

```
Response := 'Y';
WHILE Response <> 'N' DO
   BEGIN
      Writeln('Enter Y for Yes, N for No');
      Get_Yes_Or_No(Response);
      Write('Valid response.')
   END
```

6. Rewrite the following code segment using a WHILE loop.

```
IF NOT EOF
   THEN
      REPEAT
         Read(Ch);
         Writeln(Ch)
      UNTIL EOF
```

7. Rewrite the following code segment using a FOR loop.

```
Sum := 0;
Count := 1;
WHILE Count <= 1000 DO
   BEGIN
      Sum := Sum + Count;
      Count := Count + 1
   END
```

8. Rewrite the following FOR loop as a WHILE loop.

```
FOR M := 93 DOWNTO 5 DO
   Writeln(M, Sqr(M))
```

9. Rewrite the following FOR loop using a REPEAT loop.

```
FOR K := 9 TO 21 DO
   Writeln(K, 3 * K)
```

10. Write a function that accepts two Integer parameters, called Base and Exponent, and returns Base raised to the Exponent power. Use a FOR loop in your solution.

11. Write a CASE statement that does the following:

```
If the value of Grade is
   'A', add 4 to Sum
   'B', add 3 to Sum
   'C', add 2 to Sum
   'D', add 1 to Sum
   'F', print 'Student is on probation'
```

12. Modify the code for Exercise 11 so that an error message is printed if Grade does not equal one of the five possible grades.

■ *Programming Problems*

1. Develop a top-down design and write a Pascal program that will input a two-letter abbreviation for one of the 50 states and print out the full name of the state. If the abbreviation isn't valid, the program should print an error message and ask for an abbreviation again. The names of the 50 states and their abbreviations are:

State	Abbreviation	State	Abbreviation
Alabama	AL	Montana	MT
Alaska	AK	Nebraska	NE
Arizona	AZ	Nevada	NV
Arkansas	AR	New Hampshire	NH
California	CA	New Jersey	NJ
Colorado	CO	New Mexico	NM
Connecticut	CT	New York	NY
Delaware	DE	North Carolina	NC
Florida	FL	North Dakota	ND
Georgia	GA	Ohio	OH
Hawaii	HI	Oklahoma	OK
Idaho	ID	Oregon	OR
Illinois	IL	Pennsylvania	PA
Indiana	IN	Rhode Island	RI
Iowa	IA	South Carolina	SC
Kansas	KS	South Dakota	SD
Kentucky	KY	Tennessee	TN
Louisiana	LA	Texas	TX
Maine	ME	Utah	UT
Maryland	MD	Vermont	VT
Massachusetts	MA	Virginia	VA
Michigan	MI	Washington	WA
Minnesota	MN	West Virginia	WV
Mississippi	MS	Wisconsin	WI
Missouri	MO	Wyoming	WY

Hint: Use nested CASE statements, where the outer case statement uses the first letter of the abbreviation as its selector.

2. Write a top-down design and a Pascal program that reads a date in numeric form and prints it in English. For example:

```
Enter a date in the form mm dd yy.
10   27   42
October twenty-seventh, nineteen hundred and forty-two.
```

Here is another example:

```
Enter a date in the form of mm dd yy.
12   10   10
December tenth, nineteen hundred and ten.
```

The program should work for any date in the twentieth century and should print an error message for any invalid date, such as 2 29 83 (1983 wasn't a leap year).

3. Write a Pascal program that reads full names from a file and outputs the initials for the names to a file called Initials. For example, the input

```
John James Henry
```

should produce the output

```
JJH
```

The names are stored in the file first name first, middle name, then last name, separated by an arbitrary number of blanks. There is only one name per line. The first name or the middle name could be just an initial, or there may not be a middle name.

4. Write a top-down design and a Pascal program that will convert letters of the alphabet into their corresponding digits on the telephone. The program should let the user enter letters repeatedly until a Q or a Z is entered. (Q and Z are the two letters that are not on the telephone.) An error message should be printed for any nonalphabetic character that is entered.

The letters and digits on the telephone have the following correspondence.

ABC = 2	DEF = 3	GHI = 4
JKL = 5	MNO = 6	PRS = 7
TUV = 8	WXY = 9	

Here is an example:

```
Enter a letter.
P
The letter P corresponds to 7 on the telephone.
Enter a letter.
A
The letter A corresponds to 2 on the telephone.
Enter a letter.
S
The letter S corresponds to 7 on the telephone.
Enter a letter.
C
The letter C corresponds to 2 on the telephone.
Enter a letter.
A
The letter A corresponds to 2 on the telephone.
Enter a letter.
L
The letter L corresponds to 5 on the telephone.
Enter a letter.
2
Invalid letter, enter Q or Z to quit.
Enter a letter.
Z
Quit.
```

Simple Data Types

GOALS

- To be able to use the functions Ord, Succ, and Pred with ordinal data types.
- To be able to define and use an enumerated data type.
- To be able to define and use a subrange data type.
- To be able to distinguish a named user-defined type from an anonymous user-defined type.
- To be able to tell whether two data types are compatible.
- To be able to tell whether an expression is assignment compatible with a given variable.
- To be able to use the FOR and CASE statements with user-defined enumerated data types.

In Chapter 2 we defined a data type as the general form of a class of data items. In this chapter we will give a fuller, more formal definition of data type, and the built-in data types Integer, Real, Char, and Boolean will be reviewed in terms of the expanded definition.

There are times when these built-in data types cannot adequately represent all the data in a program. Pascal has a mechanism for creating new data types; that is, we can define new data types ourselves. In this chapter we will examine this useful feature in detail.

Data Types

Data Type   A formal description of a set of values (called the *domain*) and the basic operations that can be applied to them.

Let's examine the data types Integer, Real, Boolean, and Char in light of this new definition. The formal description of Integer values and their allowable operations comes from mathematics: the integer numbers are the set of whole numbers from $-\infty$ to $+\infty$ (negative to positive infinity), and the operations are $+$, $-$, $/$, $*$, MOD, DIV, and the relational operators. Of course, Pascal limits the set of integers to $-$MaxInt to MaxInt. The formal description of Reals also comes from mathematics: real numbers are the set of all numbers from $-\infty$ to $+\infty$, and the operations are the same as those for the Integers except that DIV and MOD are excluded. Different computers place different limits on the range and precision of real numbers that can be represented. The definitions for Boolean variables come from Boolean algebra; a Boolean variable can have the value True or False, and the set of operations allowed on these values is AND, OR, and NOT.

The description of the values of type Char varies depending on the character set of the particular machine. Only the relational operations are defined for type Char. There are two widely used character sets: ASCII and EBCDIC. Turbo Pascal uses the ASCII character set. Appendix G shows the ordering of the characters in the ASCII set. The ordering is called the **collating sequence** of the set. Although the collating sequence is different for each set, the letters and digits are ordered as we would expect; that is, $'A'<'B'<'C'$ . . . and $'1'<'2'<'3'$ . . . . Numbers come before letters in the ASCII set and after letters in EBCDIC. Lowercase letters precede uppercase letters in EBCDIC, and come after uppercase letters in ASCII.

The four built-in data types have two properties in common. Each is made up of indivisible, or atomic, elements, and each is ordered. Data types with these properties are called **scalar data types.**

Scalar Data Type   A data type in which the values are ordered and each value is atomic (indivisible).

When we say that a value is atomic, we mean that it has no component parts that can be accessed independently. For example, a single character is atomic, but the string 'Good Morning' is not (it is composed of 12 values of type Char).

When we say that the values are ordered, we mean that exactly one of the relations <, >, and = is true for any pair of values. For example,

$$1 < 2 \qquad \text{'C'} > \text{'A'} \qquad 3.562 < 106.22 \qquad \text{False} = \text{False}$$

This may seem to be true for any data type, but the Set is an example of a type that is not ordered. Consider that for the two set literals

['A', 'C', 'E']   and   ['B', 'D', 'F']

the only relationship that is true is <>.

Three of the built-in data types have an additional property: each value (except the first) has a unique predecessor, and each value (except the last) has a unique successor. Types with this property are called **ordinal data types.**

Ordinal Data Types   A data type in which each value (except the first) has a unique predecessor and each value (except the last) has a unique successor.

Type Real is not ordinal because a Real value has no unique predecessor or successor. If one more digit of precision is added, the predecessor and successor change; that is, 0.52 and 0.520 are the same, but the predecessor of 0.52 is 0.51, and the predecessor of 0.520 is 0.519.

Ord, Pred, and Succ Functions

Ord, Pred, and **Succ** are three additional operations that can be performed on ordinal data types, based on the ordinal properties. Pascal provides these operations as built-in functions.

Ord   An operation that returns the position of a value in the ordering of an ordinal data type.

Pred   An operation that returns the unique predecessor of a value of an ordinal data type.

Succ   An operation that returns the unique successor of a value of an ordinal data type.

The Pascal function Ord takes an ordinal value and returns an Integer representing its place in the ordering of the data type. For example, if passed a value of type Char, Ord returns an integer representing the character's place in the collating sequence. If Ord is passed an integer, the result will be the integer itself. If passed a Boolean value, Ord returns either 0 (False) or 1 (True).

The Pascal function Pred takes an ordinal value and returns its *predecessor*, the value that precedes it in the ordering of the data type. An invalid result is returned in Turbo Pascal if Pred is passed the first value in a data type. For example, while Pred (-2147483647) returns -2147483648, Pred (-2147483648) returns $+2147483647$ (the range of the Turbo Pascal type LongInt is -2147483648 to $+2147483647$). Standard Pascal would halt with an error message in this case.

The Pascal function Succ takes an ordinal value and returns its *successor*, the value that follows it in the ordering of the data type. If Succ is passed the last element in a data type, an invalid result is returned in Turbo Pascal. In Standard Pascal, a run-time error would occur.

Here are some examples of these three operations on characters in the ASCII set,

Operation	Result
Ord('B')	66
Succ('B')	'C'
Succ('2')	'3'
Pred('A')	@

and on Integer and Boolean values.

Operation	Result
Ord(23)	23
Ord(-21)	-21
Succ(2)	3
Succ(-33)	-32
Pred(-32)	-33
Pred(0)	-1
Pred(-MaxInt-1)	MaxInt
Ord(False)	0
Ord(True)	1

Working with Characters as an Ordinal Type

Ord can be used to convert a digit that is read in character form to its numeric equivalent. Since the digits '0' to '9' are consecutive in each character set, subtracting Ord('0') from the Ord of any digit in character form gives the digit in numeric form:

```
Ord('0') - Ord('0') = 0
Ord('1') - Ord('0') = 1
Ord('2') - Ord('0') = 2
    .
    .
```

For example, in ASCII,

```
Ord('0') = 48
Ord('2') = 50
Ord('2') - Ord('0') = 50 - 48 = 2
```

Note that Ord(2) is always 2, but Ord('2') is different in each character set.

Why would you want to do this? Recall that, in Chapter 5, we showed that using Read with numeric values would not work correctly in an EOF-controlled loop. Using the Ord function allows us to read numerical data as characters and convert them to numbers, which will work with an EOF-controlled loop.

An additional operation, called **Chr,** is defined on values of type Char. The Pascal function Chr is the inverse of the Ord operation on Char values. Chr takes an integer and returns the corresponding character. In Turbo Pascal, if the integer is outside the range of the ASCII collating sequence, Chr returns some value within the character range. For example, Chr(-1) will return the same character as Chr(255).

Chr   An operation that takes an ordinal value and returns the character at that position in the collating sequence.

To convert a single-digit integer into its character representation, we use

Chr(Number + Ord('0'))

For example,

```
Chr(7 + Ord('0')) = '7'
Chr(4 + Ord('0')) = '4'
Chr(0 + Ord('0')) = '0'
```

Remember to use only single-digit integers. For example, in ASCII

```
Chr(23 + Ord('0')) = 'G'
```

not the string '23'. To get the characters '2' and '3' from 23, we would use

```
Chr(23 DIV 10 + Ord('0')) = '2'
```

and

```
Chr(23 MOD 10 + Ord('0')) = '3'
```

Theoretically, we could print the collating sequence of the characters by printing the Chr of the loop control variable in a FOR loop going from 0 to the number of characters minus 1. The counter has to run from 0 to the number of characters minus 1 because the first ordinal position is 0. The following program implements this simple algorithm.

```
PROGRAM Order (Output);

(* The character set is printed in order *)

CONST
  Num_Char = 256; (* Put in the number of characters in the set *)

VAR
  Counter:
    Integer;

BEGIN  (* Order *)
  FOR Counter := 0 TO Num_Char - 1 DO
    Writeln(Counter, Chr(Counter):3)
END.    (* Order *)
```

This simple program works well in theory, but not in practice. With the EBCDIC and ASCII sets, some characters, including those used to control the screen and the printer, are not printable and may in fact cause run-time errors or unexpected screen behavior in the output.

Another example of Chr and Ord is shown in function Lower, which converts uppercase ASCII letters to lowercase. In ASCII, each lowercase letter is exactly 32 positions beyond the corresponding uppercase letter. Notice that this function will *not* work with EBCDIC.

```
FUNCTION Lower (Ch: Char): Char;

(* Converts uppercase ASCII letters to lowercase. All other    *)
(* characters are unchanged. Uses the fact that lowercase ASCII *)
(* letters are 32 positions beyond uppercase letters *)

CONST
  Shift = 32;

BEGIN
  IF (Ch >= 'A') AND (Ch <= 'Z')
    THEN                               (* Ch is an uppercase letter *)
      Lower := Chr(Ord(Ch) + Shift)
    ELSE
      Lower := Ch
END;
```

The moral of the last two examples is that you must be familiar with the character set of the machine you are using.

User-Defined Scalar Data Types

The concept of a data type is fundamental to all programming languages. One of the strengths of the Pascal language is that it allows users to create new data types by means of a **type definition.** The declaration section of a Pascal program can include a TYPE section. In the TYPE section the user describes the domain of a new data type and gives it a name.

Type Definition   The association of a type identifier with the definition of a new data type in the TYPE declaration section of a block.

Once a new data type has been defined, its identifier can be used anywhere the standard types are used, such as in the VAR section, formal parameter lists, and later in the TYPE section. The syntax template for a TYPE declaration section is:

```
TYPE
    identifier = definition;
    identifier = definition;
        .
        .
        .
```

It is important to understand the distinction between the TYPE section and the VAR section. A definition in the TYPE section describes only the set of values in a data type. No variables of that type exist until they are declared in the VAR section. Think of a TYPE definition as creating a pattern, and a VAR declaration as making something from that pattern.

Here is an example of a type declaration section.

```
TYPE
    Days = (Sunday, Monday, Tuesday, Wednesday,
            Thursday, Friday, Saturday);
    Scores = 0..100;
    Week_Days = Monday..Friday;
    Work_Days = Week_Days;
```

Figure 10-1 shows a program outline with these TYPE definitions.

Procedures and functions can also have TYPE definition sections. The same scope rules that apply to variables also apply to type identifiers. Most types will be defined globally, although it makes sense to define a new type within a subprogram if that is

Figure 10-1   Program Outline with TYPE Section

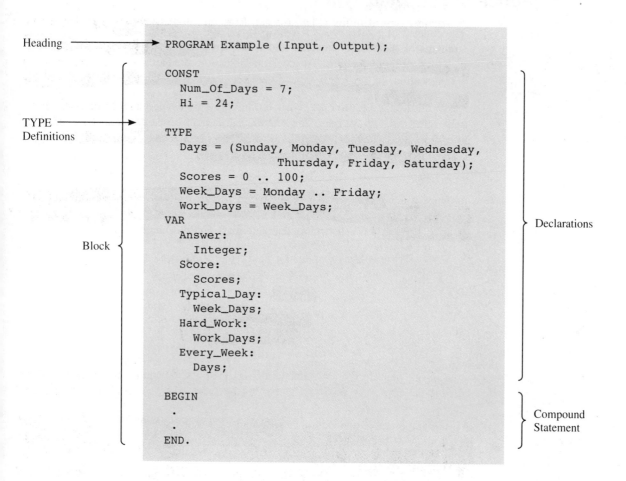

Heading

TYPE
Definitions

Block

Declarations

Compound
Statement

```
PROGRAM Example (Input, Output);

CONST
  Num_Of_Days = 7;
  Hi = 24;

TYPE
  Days = (Sunday, Monday, Tuesday, Wednesday,
               Thursday, Friday, Saturday);
  Scores = 0 .. 100;
  Week_Days = Monday .. Friday;
  Work_Days = Week_Days;
VAR
  Answer:
     Integer;
  Score:
     Scores;
  Typical_Day:
     Week_Days;
  Hard_Work:
     Work_Days;
  Every_Week:
     Days;

BEGIN
  .
  .
END.
```

the only place the type is used. The guidelines that determine where a constant should be defined also apply to data types. Note that while the CONST, TYPE, and VAR sections can be repeated and arranged in any order in Turbo Pascal, each type definition must appear after the definitions of any types or constants that it refers to and before the declaration of any variable that refers to it. Thus, it is best to simply write all type declarations between the CONST and VAR sections (standard Pascal actually requires this).

The preceding type declaration section illustrates three ways to define new scalar data types. One way is to list the literal values that are allowed in the data type (Days). Another is to define a data type to be a consecutive subset of an existing type (Scores, Week_Days). We can also create a new type that is identical to an existing type, except that it has a different name (Work_Days). More formally, a simple type can be one of the following:

1. An enumerated type
2. A subrange type
3. Another type identifier (Char, Integer, Real, and Boolean are also type identifiers)

Let's now examine in detail how to define enumerated types and subrange types.

Enumerated Data Types

Pascal allows the user to define new ordinal types by listing (enumerating) the literal values that make up the type. These literal values must be legal Pascal identifiers. The identifiers are separated by commas, and the list is enclosed in parentheses. Data types defined this way are called **enumerated data types.**

Enumerated Data Type   An ordered set of literal values (identifiers) defined as a data type.

The syntax template for an enumerated type definition is

(identifier , identifier ...)

Suppose you are writing a database program for a veterinary office. Each record must specify the type of animal. The following enumerated type might be used for this purpose.

Type identifier
↓
```
TYPE
    Animals = (Rodent, Cat, Dog, Bird, Reptile, Horse, Bovine, Sheep);
```
List of identifiers (literal values)

```
VAR
    In_Patient,
    Out_Patient:     Creation of two variables of the type Animals
        Animals;
```

Rodent is a literal in the data type Animals. Notice that Rodent is not a variable name. Instead, Rodent is one of the values that the variables In_Patient and Out_Patient can contain.

The assignment statement

```
In_Patient := Dog
```

does not assign to In_Patient the character string 'Dog', nor the contents of a variable named Dog. It assigns the value Dog, which is one of the values in data type Animals.

In Pascal, enumerated types are ordinal. They are ordered according to the way the identifiers are listed in the TYPE declaration. Applying relational operators to enumerated type values is like applying them to characters: the relation tested is "comes before" or "comes after" in the ordering of the data type.

Since enumerated types are ordinal, the Pred, Succ, and Ord operations are defined on their values. The Ord of the first identifier listed in an enumerated type is 0. Following are a few examples of these operations applied to our Animals data type.

Operation	Result
Pred(Cat)	Rodent
Pred(Horse)	Reptile
Pred(Rodent)	error (doesn't exist)
Succ(Rodent)	Cat
Succ(Cat)	Dog
Ord(Rodent)	0
Ord(Bird)	3
Ord(Sheep)	7

Turbo Pascal also provides a nonstandard mechanism for converting an ordinal value into an enumerated value. This mechanism is called the retyping facility. Each time you declare a new enumerated type, Turbo Pascal automatically creates a function with the same name as the data type. For example, if we define the type Animals as

```
TYPE
  Animals = (Rodent, Cat, Dog, Bird, Reptile, Horse, Bovine, Sheep);
```

Turbo Pascal will automatically create a function called Animals. The function Animals will take an ordinal value as its parameter and return the value of type Animals that corresponds to that number. For example,

```
Pet := Animals(2)
```

assigns the value Dog to the variable Pet. The retyping facility essentially provides us with a set of functions that act as the inverse of the Ord function. In standard Pascal, there is no way to convert an integer into its ordinal-equivalent enumerated value.

Since Rodent, Cat, and so on, are literals, they can be used in a CASE label list.

```
CASE In_Patient OF
  Rodent, Cat, Dog, Bird : Write('Cage ward');
  Reptile : Write('Terrarium ward');
  Horse, Bovine, Sheep : Write('Barn')
END;  (* CASE *)
```

The loop control variable, the initial value, and the final value in a FOR loop can be of any ordinal type, including an enumerated type. Instead of incrementing the loop control variable by 1, we can take the successor of the loop control variable, and instead of decrementing the loop control variable by 1, we can take its predecessor. For example, we can process each animal in turn with the following FOR loop.

```
FOR Out_Patient := Rodent TO Sheep DO
   (* Process Out_Patient *)
```

Here is an example using the Succ function to increment the loop counter in a WHILE loop.

```
Out_Patient := Rodent;
WHILE Out_Patient <= Bovine DO
   BEGIN
      (* Process Out_Patient *)
      Out_Patient := Succ(Out_Patient)
   END;
(* Process Out_Patient, which is now Sheep *)
```

The last value (Out_Patient = Sheep) must be processed outside the loop because trying to take the Succ of Sheep at the end of the loop would cause an error in Standard Pascal. Because of this type of error, the FOR loop is a better choice than the WHILE loop when we are working with enumerated types.

The values that make up a Set can be of any ordinal type, including an enumerated type. We could thus declare a Set type and variable as follows.

```
TYPE
   Animals = (Rodent, Cat, Dog, Bird, Reptile, Horse, Bovine, Sheep);
   Cage_Set = SET OF Rodent..Bird;

VAR
   Cage_Ward:
      Cage_Set;
```

Then we can perform operations of the following form.

```
(* Previous processing has initialized Cage_Ward *)

Cage_Ward := Cage_Ward + Dog + Cat;
IF (Rodent IN Cage_Ward) AND (Cat IN Cage_Ward)
   THEN
      Writeln('Do not place cats near rodents.');
```

Be careful not to confuse sets with enumerated types. The identifiers that make up an enumerated type must follow the rules for identifiers. For example,

```
TYPE
   Vowel = ('A', 'E', 'I', 'O', 'U');
```

is not legal because the items are not identifiers.

```
TYPE
   Places = (1st, 2nd, 3rd);
```

Type Places is not legal because identifiers must begin with a letter.

```
TYPE
   Starch = (Corn, Rice, Potato, Bean);
   Grain = (Wheat, Corn, Rye, Barley, Sorghum);
```

Type Starch and type Grain are legal by themselves, but together they are not. Identifiers must be unique. Corn cannot be defined twice.

Values for enumerated types are input indirectly by reading a number or a letter code and translating it to one of the identifiers in the enumerated type. For example, to build the database for the veterinarian, your program would read the type of animal as a series of characters, then assign one of the values of type Animals to that patient. The following program fragment reads in an animal represented by its first two letters and converts it to one of the values in type Animals.

```
Read(Ch1, Ch2);
IF Ch1 = 'R'
   THEN
      IF Ch2 = 'o'
         THEN
            In_Patient := Rodent
         ELSE
            In_Patient := Reptile
   ELSE IF Ch1 = 'C'
      THEN In_Patient := Cat
   ELSE IF Ch1 = 'D'
      THEN In_Patient := Dog
   ELSE IF Ch1 = 'B'
      THEN
         IF Ch2 = 'i'
            THEN
               In_Patient := Bird
            ELSE
               In_Patient := Bovine
   ELSE IF Ch1 = 'H'
      THEN
         In_Patient := Horse
      ELSE
         In_Patient := Sheep
```

Enumerated data type values cannot be printed directly either. Printing is done by a CASE statement, which prints the character string associated with the value.

```
CASE In_Patient OF
  Rodent : Write('Rodent');
  Cat : Write('Cat');
  Dog : Write('Dog');
  Bird: Write('Bird');
  Reptile : Write('Reptile');
  Horse : Write('Horse');
  Bovine : Write('Bovine');
  Sheep : Write('Sheep')
END;    (* CASE *)
```

Why not use just a pair of letters as a code? We use enumerated data types to make our programs more readable, and they are another way to make code self-documenting.

Subrange Types

Pascal also allows the definition of a new scalar data type to be a range of values from an existing ordinal data type. This is called a **subrange type.** The existing ordinal type, called the *host* or *base type*, can be either an enumerated type or one of the built-in ordinal types.

Subrange Type   A data type composed of a specified range of any ordinal type.

The syntax template for a subrange type definition is

> value .. value;

where each value can be a named constant or a literal. Notice that no spaces are allowed between the periods. The second value must be greater than or equal to the first.

We have seen the subrange type before. It was discussed in Chapter 9 as a shorthand notation for writing a series of literal values in the definition of a Set. The following are some examples of subrange types and the values they include.

Subrange Type	Values Included	Host Type
Num = 5..10;	5, 6, 7, 8, 9, 10	Integer
Letter = 'A'..'D';	'A', 'B', 'C', 'D'	Char
Cageable = Rodent..Dog;	Rodent, Cat, Dog, Bird	Animals
Barnyard = Horse..Sheep;	Horse, Bovine, Sheep	Animals

Using subrange types improves program readability. Stating the range of values a variable can take makes it easier to understand how the variable is used. More importantly, subrange types allow **automatic range-checking:** when a value is assigned to a variable, the system checks that it is within the specified range. If it is not, the run-time error message RANGE CHECK ERROR is displayed. This feature can be invaluable during debugging. For example, if we tried to store 'F' in a variable of type Letter (defined above to be 'A'..'D'), we would get an error message. Turbo Pascal does not normally provide automatic range-checking. If you wish to have range-checking performed, you must include a special comment, called a compiler directive, at the beginning of your program. This comment takes the following form:

```
(*$R+*)
```

You can also specify automatic range-checking using the menus in the Turbo Environment: select Options, then Compiler, and then Range-checking. If you don't use automatic range-checking, your program will run a little faster, but any errors involving out-of-range values will result in invalid output or other subtle problems that are difficult to identify and correct.

Automatic Range-Checking   The automatic detection of the assignment of an out-of-range value to a variable.

Automatic range-checking can be used whenever we know the bounds of a variable. If a counter should never get larger than 100, we create a subrange type of 1..100, and declare the counter to be of that type. If it is incremented one time too many and becomes 101, we know it immediately.

Although we could let range-checking catch invalid input values, such a tactic is poor programming practice. If an out-of-range value is input, an error message is printed and the program halts. The user is not given an opportunity to correct the input, and must re-execute the entire program. A much better practice is to do your own range-checking by putting statements in your program to check for invalid data. You can then have the program permit the user to enter corrected data.

Named and Anonymous Data Types

New data types defined in the type section are called **named types** because the definition is given a type identifier. Variables of these new data types are declared in the VAR section using the type identifier.

Named Type   A type defined in the TYPE section of a program.

Pascal also allows variables of new types to be declared directly in the VAR section. The following two examples are equivalent:

```
TYPE
  Counter_Type = 0..100;
  Coins = (Nickel, Dime, Quarter, Half_Dollar);
VAR
  Counter:
    Counter_Type;
  Change:
    Coins;
```

and

```
VAR
  Counter:
    0..100;
  Change:
    (Nickel, Dime, Quarter, Half_Dollar);
```

A type defined in the VAR section is called an **anonymous type** because it does not have a type identifier associated with it.

Anonymous Type   A type defined in the VAR section of a program.

If we can create data types in the VAR section, why bother with the TYPE section? The use of anonymous typing is considered to be poor programming practice. Named types, like named constants, make a program more readable, more understandable, and easier to modify. Also, defining a type and declaring a variable of that type are two distinct operations and should be kept separate. In addition, only named types are allowed in the formal parameter list of a function or procedure. For example,

```
PROCEDURE Example (Score: 0..100,
                   Valid: (Yes, No));
```

is an illegal procedure heading because anonymous type definitions are not allowed in the formal parameter list.

Type Compatibility

We have stated previously that, because Pascal is a strongly typed language, values of one type cannot be put into a variable of a different type. This is strictly true for the built-in ordinal types, but there is some flexibility with subranges and other user defined types. Two data types are said to be **type compatible** if they have the same type identifier, if they have the same definition, if one is a subrange of the other, or if both are subranges of the same host type.

Type Compatible   A condition where types have the same type identifier or type definition, they are subranges of the same host type, or one is a subrange of the other.

The compiler checks whether both sides of an assignment statement are type compatible. If they are not, a compile-time syntax error message is generated. The only assignment allowed between noncompatible types is the assignment of an Integer expression to a Real variable, as discussed in Chapter 2. The compiler also checks procedure and function calls to ensure that the formal and actual parameters are type compatible. VAR parameters don't have this flexibility: formal and actual VAR parameters must have the same type identifier.

At run time, each assignment statement is tested further to ensure that it is **assignment compatible.** If a variable is a subrange, a value being assigned to it must be within the range of values allowed for the variable. An assignment compatibility error causes a RANGE CHECK ERROR at run time if you have specified automatic range-checking in Turbo Pascal. Actual value parameters must also be assignment compatible with their associated formal value parameters.

Assignment Compatible   The data types are compatible and the value being assigned is within the variable's subrange.

Let's look at the declaration section of a program and some possible statements, and determine which are legal and which are not.

```
TYPE
  Colors = (Red, Yellow, Blue, Green,
            Brown, Pink, Black, Mauve);
  Primary = Red..Green;

VAR
  Paint,
  Stain:
    Colors;
  Dye:
    Primary;

PROCEDURE Mix (    Pigment1,
                   Pigment2:
                     Primary;
               VAR Result:
                     Colors);
  .
  .
```

```
BEGIN  (* Main *)
   .
   .
   Dye := Stain;
   .
   .
   Mix(Paint, Stain, Dye);                    (* Illegal *)
   .
   .
   Mix(Dye, Stain, Paint);
END.   (* Main *)
```

The heading for procedure Mix is legal. The parameters are all defined using named data types.

The assignment statement

```
Dye := Stain;
```

is legal, since the type of Dye (Primary) is a subrange of the type of Stain (Colors)— Dye is type compatible with Stain. If the value in Stain is not in the subrange Red..Green, however, a run-time assignment compatibility error will occur.

The procedure call

```
Mix(Paint, Stain, Dye);
```

is not legal. Dye (actual parameter) is of type Primary, and Result (formal parameter) is of type Colors. Actual VAR parameters must have the same type identifier as their corresponding formal VAR parameters.

The procedure call

```
Mix(Dye, Stain, Paint);
```

is legal. Dye and Pigment1 are of the same type (Primary), as are Paint and Result (type Colors). Stain and Pigment2 are of different types, but this is allowed because a value parameter is required to merely be type compatible with the actual parameter. There would be a run-time error, however, if Stain contained values outside the subrange Primary.

*T*heoretical Foundations

Type Coercion and Conversion

Pascal was one of the earliest languages to enforce type and assignment compatibility. Many prior languages allowed the programmer to assign a value of any type to a variable of any other type. Needless to say, such a lack of restrictions resulted in numerous errors and a great amount of extra debugging time.

There are times, however, when it is useful to be able to assign a value of one type to a variable of another type. For example, we might want to assign a value in a subrange of 1..100 to an Integer variable. Such an assignment is called a **type coercion.** In a sense, we coerce a value of one type into being another type. Pascal performs this coercion automatically, as long as the value and variable are assignment compatible.

Programming languages that strictly enforce strong typing by requiring the use of **conversion functions** (sometimes called **transfer functions** or **type casts**) to convert between any two types have been proposed. Conversion functions make the use of coercion explicit and thus add to the self-documenting quality of a program. They are an inconvenience, however, when they must be used in even the simplest cases.

Pascal tries to strike a balance by providing automatic coercion between types that have the same definition or are assignment compatible subranges. Pascal also provides a conversion function (Ord) that converts any ordinal type into an integer value. This conversion is simple to perform because all ordinal types are represented in the computer in a way that is similar to integers. Another conversion function that Pascal provides is Chr, which is specifically designed to convert an Integer value into a Char value. Conversion from Integer to other ordinal types is also supported by the Turbo Pascal retyping facility.

Coercion is inefficient when the binary representation of one type differs from another. For example, we saw in Chapter 8 that integer and real values are represented differently in the computer. Nonetheless, Pascal allows us to assign an integer value to a real variable. To do this, it coerces the integer representation into a real representation with a fraction and exponent. The coercion is done by an invisible function call that manipulates the bits of the integer value to form a real number; a time-consuming process.

Pascal has been criticized for making it so easy to mix integers and reals in computations. It has been argued that if programmers were required to perform each conversion explicitly, they would be more sparing in their use of **mixed mode arithmetic,** and their programs would thus be more efficient. Pascal does require explicit conversion from reals to integers by stipulating the use of the functions Trunc and Round.

We can write our own conversion functions or procedures. For example, a function that takes a character and returns a corresponding enumerated type value (as in converting 'M' to Mouse) is a conversion function. As we introduce more data types in the chapters that follow, there will be an even greater need for converting between different data types.

PROBLEM-SOLVING CASE STUDY

Rock, Paper, Scissors

Problem: Play the children's game "rock, paper, scissors." In this game, two people choose simultaneously either rock, paper, or scissors. Whether a player wins or loses depends not only on that player's choice but also on the opponent's. The rules are:

Rock breaks scissors; rock wins.
Paper covers rock; paper wins.
Scissors cut paper; scissors win.
All matching combinations are ties.
The overall winner is the player who wins the most individual games.

THE FAR SIDE   By GARY LARSON

6-28   © 1986 Universal Press Syndicate   Larson

Before paper and scissors

Input: A series of letters representing player A's plays (File_A, one letter per line) and a series of letters representing player B's plays (File_B, one letter per line), with each play indicated by 'R' (Rock), 'P' (Paper), or 'S' (Scissors).

Output: A game number, followed by which player won that game; the total number of games won by each player; and the overall winner.

Discussion: We assume that everyone has played this game and understands it. Therefore, our discussion centers on how to simulate the game in a program.

For input, we have to use alphanumeric characters to stand for rock, paper, and scissors. We can input 'R', 'P', and 'S', and convert the letters to a user-defined enumerated data type made up of the literals Rock, Paper, and Scissors.

Each player creates a file composed of a series of the letters 'R', 'P', and 'S', representing a series of individual games. The letters are read, one from each file, and converted into the appropriate literals. Let's call each literal a play. The plays are compared, and a winner is determined. The number of games won is incremented for the winning player. The game is over when there are no more plays (the files are empty).

Assumptions: The game is over when one of the files runs out of plays.

Main   *Level 0*

```
WHILE more games DO
   Get play
   IF plays are legal
      THEN
         Process play
      ELSE
         Write an error message
Print Big Winner
```

Get Plays (Returns: Player_A, Player_B, Legal)   *Level 1*

```
Read Player_A's play from File_A (Char_For_A)
Read Player_B's play from File_B (Char_For_B)
Set Legal to (Char_For_A IN ['R', 'P', 'S'])
            AND (Char_For_B IN ['R', 'P', 'S'])
IF Legal
   THEN
      Set Player_A to Convert(Char_For_A)
      Set Player_B to Convert(Char_For_B)
```

PROBLEM-SOLVING CASE STUDY *cont'd.*

Process Plays (Receives: Game_Number, Player_A, Player_B
 Receives/Returns: Wins_For_A, Wins_For_B)

```
IF Player_A = Player_B
    THEN
       Print that this Game_Number is a tie
    ELSE IF (Player_A = Paper) AND (Player_B = Rock)
    THEN
        Player_A_Wins
    ELSE IF (Player_A = Scissors) AND (Player_B = Paper)
    THEN
        Player_A_Wins
    ELSE IF (Player_A = Rock) AND (Player_B = Scissors)
    THEN
        Player_A_Wins
    ELSE
        Player_B_Wins
```

Print Big Winner (Receives: Wins_For_A, Wins_For_B)

```
Print number of games won by player A
Print number of games won by player B
IF Wins_For_A > Wins_For_B
    THEN
       Declare Player A the winner
    ELSE IF Wins_For_B > Wins_For_A
       THEN
           Declare Player B the winner
    ELSE
        Writeln 'Player A and Player B have tied'
```

Convert (Receives: Character   *Level 2*
 Returns: Play_Type)

```
CASE Character OF
   'R': Set Convert to Rock
   'P': Set Convert to Paper
   'S': Set Convert to Scissors
```

Player_A_Wins (Receives: Game_Number
　　　　　　　　　　Receives/Returns Wins_For_A)

Print message saying Player A has won this game
Set Wins_For_A to Wins_For_A + 1

Player_B_Wins (Receives: Game_Number
　　　　　　　　　　Receives/Returns Wins_For_A)

Print message saying Player B has won this game
Set Wins_For_B to Wins_For_B + 1

Now we are ready to code the simulation of the game. We must remember to initialize our counters. We assumed that we know the game number for each game, yet nowhere have we kept track of the game number. We need to add a counter in our loop in the main module.

Main

Initialize counter
Set Game_Number to 0
WHILE more games DO
　Set Game_Number to Game_Number + 1
　Get plays
　IF plays are legal
　　THEN
　　　Process plays
　　ELSE
　　　Write an error message
Print Big Winner

PROBLEM-SOLVING CASE STUDY cont'd.

Module Structure Chart:

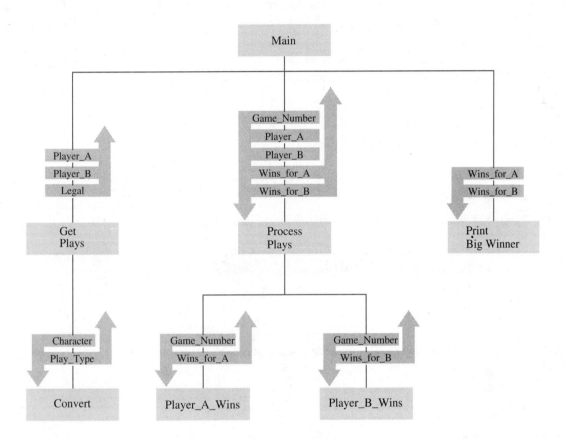

```
PROGRAM Game (File_A, File_B, Output);

(* This program simulates the children's game 'rock, paper, and   *)
(* scissors.' Each game consists of inputs from two players,       *)
(* coming from File_A and File_B. A winner is determined for each  *)
(* individual game, and for the games overall.                     *)

TYPE
  Play_Type = (Rock, Paper, Scissors);
```

```
VAR
  Player_A,           (* Player A's play        *)
  Player_B:           (* Player B's play        *)
    Play_Type;
  Wins_For_A,         (* Number of games A wins *)
  Wins_For_B,         (* Number of games B wins *)
  Game_Number:        (* Number of games played *)
    Integer;
  File_A,             (* Player A's plays        *)
  File_B:             (* Player B's plays        *)
    Text;
  Legal:              (* True if play is legal   *)
    Boolean;

(*********************************************************************)

PROCEDURE Player_A_Wins (    Game_Number:    (* Receives game number    *)
                                Integer;
                         VAR Wins_For_A:     (* Rec's/returns win count *)
                                Integer);

(* Message that Player A has won the current game is written, *)
(* and Player A's total is updated *)

BEGIN (* Player_A_Wins *)
  Writeln('Player A has won game number ', Game_Number:1, '.');
  Wins_For_A := Wins_For_A + 1
END;  (* Player_A_Wins *)

(*********************************************************************)

PROCEDURE Player_B_Wins (    Game_Number:    (* Receives game number    *)
                                Integer;
                         VAR Wins_For_B:     (* Rec's/returns win count *)
                                Integer);

(* Message that Player B has won the current game is written, *)
(* and Player B's total is updated *)

BEGIN (* Player_B_Wins *)
  Writeln('Player B has won game number ', Game_Number:1, '.');
  Wins_For_B := Wins_For_B + 1
END;  (* Player_B_Wins *)

(*********************************************************************)
```

```
PROCEDURE Process_Plays (      Game_Number:     (* Receives game number *)
                                 Integer;
                               Player_A,          (* Receives A's play *)
                               Player_B:          (* Receives B's play *)
                                 Play_Type;
                           VAR Wins_For_A,        (* Rec's/returns A's wins *)
                               Wins_For_B:        (* Rec's/returns B's wins *)
                                 Integer);

(* Process_Plays determines the winning play. If there is a tie, a *)
(* message is written. Otherwise the number of wins of the winning *)
(* player is incremented *)

BEGIN (* Process_Plays *)
  IF Player_A = Player_B
    THEN
      Writeln('Game number ', Game_Number:1, ' is a tie.')
    ELSE IF (Player_A = Paper) AND (Player_B = Rock)
      THEN
        Player_A_Wins(Game_Number, Wins_For_A)
    ELSE IF (Player_A = Scissors) AND (Player_B = Paper)
      THEN
        Player_A_Wins(Game_Number, Wins_For_A)
    ELSE IF (Player_A = Rock) AND (Player_B = Scissors)
      THEN
        Player_A_Wins(Game_Number, Wins_For_A)
    ELSE
      Player_B_Wins(Game_Number, Wins_For_B)
END;  (* Process_Plays *)


(************************************************************************)


PROCEDURE Get_Plays (VAR Player_A,      (* Returns A's plays *)
                         Player_B:      (* Returns B's plays *)
                           Play_Type;
                     VAR Legal:         (* Returns True if legal plays *)
                         Boolean);

(* Player_A's play is read from File_A, Player_B's play is read from *)
(* File_B. If both plays are legal, Legal is set to True and both    *)
(* plays are converted to corresponding values of Play_Type. Else    *)
(* Legal is False and Player_A and Player_B are undefined. File_A    *)
(* and File_B are accessed globally *)

VAR
  Char_For_A,      (* Player_A's input *)
  Char_For_B:      (* Player_B's input *)
    Char;
```

```
(*********************************************************************)

FUNCTION Convert (Character:              (* Receives play character *)
                      Char): Play_Type;   (* Returns play literal    *)

(* Converts character into associated value in Play_Type *)

BEGIN (* Convert *)
  CASE Character OF
    'R': Convert := Rock;
    'P': Convert := Paper;
    'S': Convert := Scissors
  END (* Case *)
END; (* Convert *)

(*********************************************************************)

BEGIN (* Get_Plays *)
  Readln(File_A, Char_For_A);
  Readln(File_B, Char_For_B);
  Legal := (Char_For_A IN ['R', 'P', 'S']) AND
           (Char_For_B IN ['R', 'P', 'S']);
  IF Legal
    THEN
      BEGIN
        Player_A := Convert(Char_For_A);
        Player_B := Convert(Char_For_B)
      END
END; (* Get_Plays *)

(*********************************************************************)

PROCEDURE Print_Big_Winner (Wins_For_A,    (* Receives A's win count *)
                            Wins_For_B:     (* Receives B's win count *)
                               Integer);

(* Prints number of wins for each player and the overall winner *)
```

PROBLEM-SOLVING CASE STUDY *cont'd.*

```pascal
BEGIN (* Print_Big_Winner *)
  Writeln('Player A has won ', Wins_For_A:1, ' games.');
  Writeln('Player B has won ', Wins_For_B:1, ' games.');
  (* Determine and print winner *)
  IF Wins_For_A > Wins_For_B
    THEN
      Writeln ('Player A has won the most games.')
    ELSE IF Wins_For_B > Wins_For_A
      THEN
        Writeln('Player B has won the most games.')
    ELSE
      Writeln('Player A and B have tied.')
END; (* Print_Big_Winner *)

(********************************************************************)


BEGIN (* Game *)
  Assign(File_A, 'FileA.Dat');
  Assign(File_B, 'FileB.Dat');
  Reset(File_A);
  Reset(File_B);
  Wins_For_A := 0;
  Wins_For_B := 0;
  Game_Number := 0;
  (* Play a series of games and keep track of who wins *)
  WHILE NOT EOF(File_A) AND NOT EOF(File_B) DO
    BEGIN
      Game_Number := Game_Number + 1;
      Get_Plays(Player_A, Player_B, Legal);
      IF Legal
        THEN
          Process_Plays(Game_Number, Player_A, Player_B,
                        Wins_For_A, Wins_For_B)
        ELSE
          Writeln('Game_Number ', Game_Number:1,
                  'contained an illegal play.')
    END;
  (* Print overall winner *)
  Print_Big_Winner(Wins_For_A, Wins_For_B);
  Close(File_A);
  Close(File_B)
END.  (* Game *)
```

Testing: Program Game was tested with the following files. They are listed side by side so that you can see the pairs that made up each game. Note that each combination of 'R', 'S', and 'P' is used at least once. In addition, there is an error in each file.

PROBLEM-SOLVING CASE STUDY cont'd.

File_A	File_B
R	R
S	S
S	S
R	S
R	P
P	P
P	P
R	S
S	T
A	P
P	S
P	R
S	P
R	S
R	S
P	P
S	R

Output from the Screen:

```
Game number 1 is a tie.
Game number 2 is a tie.
Game number 3 is a tie.
Player A has won game number 4.
Player B has won game number 5.
Game number 6 is a tie.
Game number 7 is a tie.
Player A has won game number 8.
Game number 9 contained an illegal play.
Game number 10 contained an illegal play.
Player B has won game number 11.
Player A has won game number 12.
Player A has won game number 13.
Player A has won game number 14.
Player A has won game number 15.
Game number 16 is a tie.
Player B has won game number 17.
Player A has won 6 games.
Player B has won 3 games.
Player A has won the most games.
```

PROBLEM-SOLVING CASE STUDY *cont'd.*

An examination of the output shows it to be correct: player A did win 6 games, player B did win 3 games, and player A won the most games. This one set of test data is not enough to test the program completely. It should be run with test data where player B wins, where player A and player B tie, where File_A is longer than File_B, and where File_B is longer than File_A.

PROBLEM-SOLVING CASE STUDY

Birthday Reminder

Problem: Everyone has at least one friend who always remembers everyone's birthday. Each year when we receive appropriate greetings on our birthday from this friend, we promise to do better about remembering the birthdays of others. Let's write a program that will print the names of those friends with a birthday in a given month.

Input: A month entered from the keyboard, with first letter capitalized.

Output: The names (and birthdays) of all friends with a birthday in that month.

Discussion: To solve this problem by hand, we would turn our calendar to the month in question and list the names written there. That is exactly what our program will do: recognize which month is being requested and call a procedure that writes out the information for that month. The information for each month will be represented as a series of Write statements.

We represent the months as an enumerated type. Thus we must convert the months as input in character form into this type. We can perform the conversion by checking just the first one, two, or three characters of the input string. February, September, October, November, and December have unique first characters. April, August, and January can be distinguished by their first two characters. June, July, March, and May require three characters to distinguish them.

Assumptions: None.

Main   *Level 0*

```
Get Month
CASE Month OF
    January   : Print_January
    February  : Print_February
    March     : Print_March
    April     : Print_April
    May       : Print_May
    June      : Print_June
    July      : Print_July
    August    : Print_August
    September : Print_September
    October   : Print_October
    November  : Print_November
    December  : Print_December
```

Get Month (Returns: Month)   *Level 1*

```
Read First_Character, Second_Character, Third_Character
CASE First_Character OF
    F : Set Month to February
    S : Set Month to September
    O : Set Month to October
    N : Set Month to November
    D : Set Month to December
    J : J_Check
    A : A_Check
    M : M_Check
```

```
PRINT JANUARY
    .
    .
    .
PRINT DECEMBER
```

J_Check (Receives: Second_Character, *Level 2*
Third_Character
Returns: Month)

```
IF Second_Character is an 'a'
    THEN
        Set Month to January
    ELSE IF Third_Character is an 'l'
        THEN
            Set Month to July
        ELSE
            Set Month to June
```

A_Check (Receives: Second_Character
Returns: Month)

```
IF Second_Character is a 'p'
    THEN
        Set Month to April
    ELSE
        Set Month to August
```

M_Check (Receives: Third_Character
Returns: Month)

```
IF Third_Character is an 'r'
    THEN
        Set Month to March
    ELSE
        Set Month to May
```

The print procedures are composed of Writeln statements that print all the information for the month. To test the program, we code all the print procedures as stubs, which print one line stating that the month has been printed.

PROBLEM-SOLVING CASE STUDY cont'd.

Module Structure Chart:

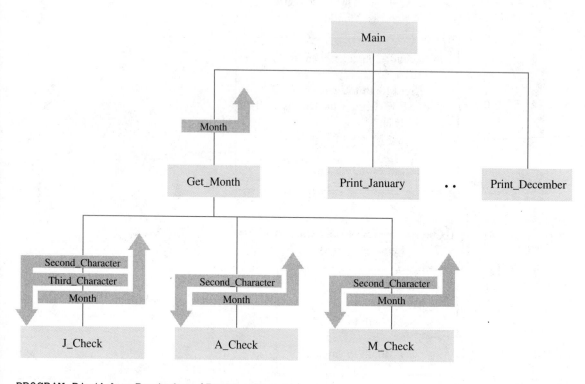

```
PROGRAM Birthday_Reminder (Input, Output);

(* This program takes a month as input and prints the *)
(* list of birthdays associated with that month       *)

TYPE
  Months = (January, February, March, April, May, June,
            July, August, September, October, November, December);

VAR
  Month:
    Months;

(***********************************************************************)

PROCEDURE Get_Month (VAR Month:
                         Months);

(* The user is prompted to enter a month. Only the    *)
(* characters needed to determine the month are read  *)
```

PROBLEM-SOLVING CASE STUDY *cont'd.*

```
VAR
  First_Character,
  Second_Character,
  Third_Character:
    Char;

(*********************************************************************)

  PROCEDURE J_Check (VAR Month:
                          Months;
                          Second_Character,
                          Third_Character:
                          Char);

  (* Determines which month beginning with J *)

  BEGIN (* J_Check *)
    IF Second_Character = 'a'
      THEN
        Month := January
      ELSE IF Third_Character = 'l'
        THEN
          Month := July
      ELSE
        Month := June
  END;  (* J_Check *)

(*********************************************************************)

PROCEDURE A_Check (VAR Month:
                        Months;
                        Second_Character:
                        Char);

(* Determines which month beginning with A *)

BEGIN (* A_Check *)
  IF Second_Character = 'p'
    THEN
      Month := April
    ELSE
      Month := August
END;  (* A_Check *)

(*********************************************************************)
```

```
   PROCEDURE M_Check (VAR Month:
                               Months;
                          Third_Character:
                          Char);

   (* Determines which month beginning with M *)

   BEGIN (* M_Check *)
     IF Third_Character = 'r'
       THEN
         Month := March
       ELSE
         Month := May
   END;   (* M_Check *)

   (********************************************************************)

BEGIN (* Get_Month *)
  Writeln('Please enter month, capitalizing first letter. ');
  Readln(First_Character, Second_Character, Third_Character);
  CASE First_Character OF
    'F' : Month := February;
    'S' : Month := September;
    'O' : Month := October;
    'N' : Month := November;
    'D' : Month := December;
    'J' : J_Check(Month, Second_Character, Third_Character);
    'A' : A_Check(Month, Second_Character);
    'M' : M_Check(Month, Third_Character)
  END (* Case *)
END;   (* Get_Month *)

(********************************************************************)

PROCEDURE Print_January;

BEGIN (* Print_January *)
  Writeln('January printed')
END;   (* Print_January *)

(********************************************************************)

PROCEDURE Print_February;

BEGIN (* Print_February *)
  Writeln('February printed')
END;   (* Print_February *)
```

PROBLEM-SOLVING CASE STUDY *cont'd.*

```
(*********************************************************************)

PROCEDURE Print_March;

BEGIN (* Print_March *)
  Writeln('March printed')
END;  (* Print_March *)

(*********************************************************************)

PROCEDURE Print_April;

BEGIN (* Print_April *)
  Writeln('April printed')
END;  (* Print_April *)

(*********************************************************************)

PROCEDURE Print_May;

BEGIN (* Print_May *)
  Writeln('May printed')
END;  (* Print_May *)

(*********************************************************************)

PROCEDURE Print_June;

BEGIN (* Print_June *)
  Writeln('June printed')
END;  (* Print_June *)

(*********************************************************************)

PROCEDURE Print_July;

BEGIN (* Print_July *)
  Writeln('July printed')
END;  (* Print_July *)

(*********************************************************************)
```

```
PROCEDURE Print_August;

BEGIN (* Print_August *)
  Writeln('August printed')
END;  (* Print_August *)

(********************************************************************)

PROCEDURE Print_September;

BEGIN (* Print_September *)
  Writeln('September printed')
END;  (* Print_September *)

(********************************************************************)

PROCEDURE Print_October;

BEGIN (* Print_October *)
  Writeln('October printed')
END;  (* Print_October *)

(********************************************************************)

PROCEDURE Print_November;

BEGIN (* Print_November *)
  Writeln('November printed')
END;  (* Print_November *)

(********************************************************************)

PROCEDURE Print_December;

BEGIN (* Print_December *)
  Writeln('December printed')
END;  (* Print_December *)

(********************************************************************)
```

PROBLEM-SOLVING CASE STUDY *cont'd.*

```
BEGIN (* Birthday_Reminder *)
  Get_Month(Month);
  CASE Month OF
    January   : Print_January;
    February  : Print_February;
    March     : Print_March;
    April     : Print_April;
    May       : Print_May;
    June      : Print_June;
    July      : Print_July;
    August    : Print_August;
    September : Print_September;
    October   : Print_October;
    November  : Print_November;
    December  : Print_December
  END (* Case *)
END.  (* Birthday_Reminder *)
```

Testing: To test this program, we run it twelve times. For each run a different month is used as input, the appropriate print procedure is called, and the corresponding message is printed. If you want to use this program, you have to create the Writeln statements to print the data for your friends. The stubs we use to test the rest of the program merely show that each print procedure is called correctly. We have more to say about testing this program in the Testing and Debugging section.

Testing and Debugging

Several times in this book we had our programs test for invalid data and write an error message. Writing an error message is certainly necessary, but it is only the first step. We must also decide what the program should do next. The problem itself and the severity of the error should determine what action is taken in any error condition. The approach taken also differs, depending on whether or not the program is being run interactively.

In a batch or file-oriented program, there is no interaction with the person entering the data. The program should therefore try to adjust for the bad data items, if at all possible.

If the invalid data is not essential, the program can skip it and continue; for example, if a program averaging test grades encounters a negative test score, it could simply skip the negative score. If an educated guess can be made about the probable value of the bad data, it can be set to that value before being processed. In either event a message should be written stating that an invalid data item was encountered and outlining the steps that were taken. Such messages form an **exception report.**

If the data is essential and no guess is possible, processing should be terminated. A message should be written to the user with as much information as possible about the invalid data item.

In an interactive environment the program can prompt the user to supply another value. The program should indicate to the user what is wrong with the original data. Another possibility is to write out a list of actions and ask the user to choose among them.

These suggestions on how to handle bad data assume that the program recognizes when bad data has been entered. There are two approaches to error detection: passive and active. Passive error detection leaves it to the system to detect errors. This may seem easier, but the programmer relinquishes control of processing when an error occurs. An example of passive error detection is automatic range checking.

Active error detection means having the program check for possible errors and determine an appropriate action if an error is encountered. An example of active error detection would be to read a value as an Integer and explicitly check it with an IF statement before assigning it to a subrange variable.

Program Birthday_Reminder uses passive error detection. If the input is typed incorrectly, the program crashes. Let's rewrite Procedure Get_Month to incorporate active error detection. The first character must be checked to see whether it is in the set of possible first letters. If not, the CASE statement must be skipped. If the first character is an 'A', 'J', or 'M', the second or third character (or both) must be checked.

The first character should be checked where it is read, in the main body of Get_Month. The second and/or third character should be checked in the procedure that uses it. Procedures J_Check, A_Check, and M_Check will need an extra parameter to let Get_Month know whether an error has occurred. If an error has occurred, Get_Month must notify the user and request another input. This implies that the CASE statement must be in a loop that continues until a month has been recognized.

This scheme will not check the spelling of each month. It will check to see only that there are enough letters to recognize a month.

```
PROCEDURE Get_Month (VAR Month:
                          Months);

(* The user is prompted to enter a month. Only the characters   *)
(* needed to determine the month are read. If the month cannot be *)
(* recognized, the user is prompted to reenter the month         *)

VAR
  First_Character,
  Second_Character,
  Third_Character:
    Char;
  Error:
    Boolean;


(* ********************************************************************* *)
```

```
PROCEDURE J_Check (VAR Month:
                         Months;
                     Second_Character,
                     Third_Character:
                         Char;
                     VAR Error:
                         Boolean);

(* If Second_Character and Third_Character are legal, Error is False *)
(* and Month is determined. ELSE Error is True and Month is         *)
(* undefined *)

BEGIN (* J_Check *)
  Error := NOT (Second_Character IN ['a', 'u'])
           OR NOT (Third_Character IN ['l', 'n']);
  IF NOT Error
    THEN
      IF Second_Character = 'a'
        THEN
          Month := January
        ELSE IF Third_Character = 'l'
          THEN
            Month := July
          ELSE
            Month := June
END; (* J_Check *)

(*********************************************************************)


PROCEDURE A_Check (VAR Month:
                         Months;
                     Second_Character:
                         Char;
                     VAR Error:
                         Boolean);

(* If Second_Character is legal, Error is False and Month   *)
(* is determined. ELSE Error is True and Month is undefined *)

BEGIN (* A_Check *)
  Error := NOT (Second_Character IN ['p', 'u']);
  IF NOT Error
    THEN
      IF Second_Character = 'p'
        THEN
          Month := April
        ELSE
          Month := August
END; (* A_Check *)
```

```
(*******************************************************************)

   PROCEDURE M_Check (VAR Month:
                              Months;
                           ThirdCharacter:
                              Char;
                         VAR Error:
                              Boolean);

   (* If Third_Character is legal, Error is False and Month      *)
   (* is determined. ELSE Error is True and Month is undefined *)

   BEGIN (* M_Check *)
      Error := NOT (Third_Character IN ['r', 'y']);
      IF NOT Error
        THEN
           IF Third_Character = 'r'
              THEN
                 Month := March
              ELSE
                 Month := May
   END; (* M_Check *)


   (*******************************************************************)

BEGIN (* Get_Month *)
   REPEAT
      Writeln('Please enter month, capitalizing first letter.');
      Readln (First_Character, Second_Character, Third_Character);
      Error := NOT (First_Character IN
                 ['F', 'S', 'O', 'N', 'D', 'J', 'A', 'M']);
      IF NOT Error
        THEN
           CASE First_Character OF
              'F' : Month := February;
              'S' : Month := September;
              'O' : Month := October;
              'N' : Month := November;
              'D' : Month := December;
              'J' : J_Check(Month, Second_Character, Third_Character, Error);
              'A' : A_Check(Month, Second_Character, Error);
              'M' : M_Check(Month, Third_Character, Error)
           END; (* Case *)
      IF Error
        THEN
           Writeln('Unable to determine which month is wanted.');
   UNTIL NOT Error
END;  (* Get_Month *)
```

Testing and Debugging Hints

1. Use a subrange type if you know the bounds on the values of a variable, and that including a value outside that range would be a fatal error.
2. Use enumerated types to make your programs more readable, understandable, and modifiable.
3. Do not use anonymous typing. Define data types in the TYPE section.
4. Enumerated type definitions are in parentheses; subrange types are not.
5. Variables cannot be used in the declaration section of a program. Information in the CONST, TYPE, and VAR sections is used by the computer at compile time. The subrange specifier 1..N makes no sense unless N is defined in the CONST section.
6. Be sure that VAR parameters have the same type identifier for both formal and actual parameters, and that value parameters have formal and actual parameters that are type compatible. Type definitions may not appear on a parameter list.
7. Be sure that Succ is not applied to the last element of a type, or that Pred is not applied to the first.
8. Enumerated type values cannot be directly input or output.
9. Routines that rely on a particular character set's collating sequence may not run on another machine.
10. Set the Options/Compiler/Range-checking menu option when compiling a program so that automatic range-checking is performed.

Summary

A data type is a set of values (domain) and the operations that can be applied to them. There are four standard scalar types in Pascal: Integer, Real, Char, and Boolean.

Types Integer, Char, and Boolean are called ordinal types: they have the property that a unique successor and a unique predecessor exist for all but the first and last items in the set of values. Ordinal data types have three additional operations defined on them: Pred, Succ, and Ord.

Pascal allows the user to define additional ordinal types. An enumerated data type is created by listing the identifiers that make up the type. A subrange type is made up of a continuous subset of an existing ordinal type. The operations defined on the subrange type are the same as those defined on the host data type. A variable of any ordinal type may be used to control a FOR loop, or as the selector in a CASE statement. User-defined ordinal types help make a program more self-documenting.

For a value to be assigned to a variable, the value must be type and assignment compatible with the variable. The same is true of actual parameters that are passed to value parameters. Actual parameters passed to VAR parameters must be of exactly the same type. Turbo Pascal will perform automatic range-checking on variables of subrange types only when the Options/Compiler/Range-checking menu option is set before a program is compiled.

User-defined data types are extremely useful in the writing of clear, self-documenting programs.

▪ *Quick Check*

1. What is the result of each of these three functions? (pp. 432–434)

   Ord(23)~~$2^?$~~   Succ('J')~~$\swarrow$~~   Pred(True)   *false*

2. Define an enumerated data type called Auto_Makes, consisting of the names of five of your favorite car manufacturers. (pp. 439–443)

3. Define a subrange type called Digits, consisting of the characters '0' through '9'. (pp. 443–444)

4. Why is the use of anonymous data types considered to be poor programming practice? (pp. 444–445)

5. Given the following two data type definitions, decide whether the types are type compatible. (pp. 445–447)

   ```
   TYPE
      Colors = (Infrared, Red, Orange, Yellow,
                Green, Blue, Indigo, Violet,
                Ultraviolet);
      Visible = Red..Violet;    subset
   ```

6. If Room_Number is a variable of type 1..500, is the following expression assignment compatible with Room_Number? (pp. 445–447)

   ```
   Pred(Room_Number DIV 500)
   ```

7. Write a FOR statement that will "count" from Red to Violet, using a control variable of type Visible, as defined in question 5. Call the control variable Rainbow. (p. 441)

   or I := Red to vient Do

Answers

1. 23, 'K', False
2. TYPE Auto_Makes = (Saab, Jaguar, Citroen, Chevrolet, Ford);
3. TYPE Digits = '0'..'9';   4. Because anonymous types cannot be passed as parameters to procedures and functions.   5. They are type compatible because one is a subrange of the other.
6. The expression is not assignment compatible because the only two values it may have (−1 and 0) are outside the subrange allowed by Room_Number.
7. FOR Rainbow := Red TO Violet DO statement;

▪ *Exam Preparation Exercises*

1. Where do the formal descriptions for the domains of the standard data types come from?

2. Distinguish between a scalar data type and an ordinal data type.

3. List the operations defined on all ordinal data types.

4. Given the type declaration,

   ```
   TYPE
         Members = (Smith, Jones, Grant, White);
   ```

   is the expression Jones > Grant equal to True or False?

Project In Lab:

- Use StackLnk Dec.; StackLnk.Pas
  back to Test 4. Pass replace Array w/ Link.

Abstract Data Type - user defined type
1. Declare it, use Dec. files to declare
2. Implementations / operations,
   a. Push, Pop, Create, Clear, Destroy, Empty, full.

Encapsulation - hide the details, provide user w/ an interface
   (don't give details).

1. Test 4.Pas.
2. RPE - Postinfix project
3. Find bottom - StackLnk. Pas } killing the stack
   a. Pop Until S.Top=NIL; } so Don't Do it.

Define new Pointer   VAR P := Ptr;
   P := S.TOP;
While P^.Next<>NIL Do   modify pointer...
   P := P^.Next
        ...Element
        ...until (bottom is equal to 'P.Element)

Print Stack (S);
to Print

While P<>Nil do
begin
Writeln (P.^.Element)
P:=P.Next.

Stack Clear (S)
At TopElement: StackElement
While not StackEmpty(S) Do
Pop(S, TopElement).

0257   pg 265
                34
                35
                36
                37
        263

While not P.Next<Nil Do
Writein (P.Next.Element
P:=Net.1

While not P.Next<Nil Do
...Its in order w/arrays

Test 4
StackLink pg

5. Scalar data types are ordered so that every variable must be less than, equal to, or greater than any other variable of that type. (True or False?)

6. Fill in the table based on the following definitions.

   ```
   TYPE
        Perfume = (Poison, Dior_Essence, Chanel_No_5, Coty);
   ```

Operation	Result
Ord(Poison)	_____
Succ(Coty)	_____
Pred(Chanel_No_5)	_____

7. The result type of function Ord must be Integer because it returns the integer representation of a character. (True or False?)

8. Pascal's functions can be divided into two categories: regular functions that do a given task (for example, Sqr squares a number) and conversion functions that translate from one type to another (for example, Round translates from Real to Integer). Classify the functions Ord, Succ, Pred, and Chr as either regular or conversion.

9. Given the following,

   ```
   TYPE
      Seasons = (Winter, Spring, Summer, Fall);
   ```

   what is the value of each of the following expressions? (If the expression is undefined, indicate this with a U.)
   a. Succ(Winter)
   b. Pred(Winter)
   c. Ord(Fall)
   d. Summer >= Fall

10. What is the value of each of the following expressions?
    a. Ord(False)
    b. Pred('C')
    c. Ord(27)
    d. Ord('4') where Ord('0') = 48

11. Automatic range checking should always be used to test input data for values that are out of range. (True or False?)

12. Only named data types can be formal VAR parameters, but anonymous data types can be actual VAR parameters. (True or False?)

13. When are two types *type compatible?*

14. Are assignment compatibility errors determined at compile time or at run time?

15. Active error detection leaves error hunting to Pascal, whereas passive error detection requires that the programmer do the error hunting. (True or False?)

16. Assigning an integer value to a real value is an example of type coercion. (True or False?)

■ *Programming Warm-Up Exercises*

1. Define an enumerated type for the local area high schools.

2. Define an enumerated type for the National Football Conference.

3. Define a subrange of the teams in Exercise 2 for the Eastern Division, Western Division, and Central Division. Did you have to redefine the order of the teams to define these subranges?

4. Define a subrange type made up of the uppercase letters.

5. Define a subrange type made up of the single-digit numbers.

6. Define a subrange type made up of the numerals '0' to '9'.

7. Define an enumerated type for the days of the week.

8. Write a procedure that converts the first two letters of a day of the week into the type defined in Exercise 7.

9. Write a procedure that prints a value of the type defined in Exercise 7.

10. Given the declarations

```
TYPE
   States = (Q1, Q2, Q3, Q4);
VAR
  S:
   States;
  Flag:
   Boolean;
```

rewrite the following FOR loop using a WHILE loop and the Succ function. Note that Succ(Q4) is not defined. Handle this possible error inside the loop.

```
BEGIN
  FOR S := Q1 TO Q4 DO
    Write(Ord(S));
END;
```

11. Given the following declaration

```
VAR
  R_Temp,
  Q_Temp,
  N:
    Integer;
  Ch1,
  Ch2:
    Char;
```

and given that N contains a two-digit number, use the Chr and Ord functions to translate N into two single characters where Ch1 holds the higher order digit, and Ch2 holds the lower order digit. For example, if N = 23, Ch1 would equal '2', and Ch2 would equal '3'. Write the two digits as characters in the same order as the original numbers.

12. Write the print procedures for Program Birthday_Reminder for your friends and family.

13. Rewrite Program Grade_List using a procedure to do the printing.

▪ *Programming Problems*

1. Read in the sides of a triangle and determine whether the triangle is an isosceles triangle (two sides are equal), an equilateral triangle (three sides are equal), or a scalene triangle (no sides are equal). Use an enumerated data type (Isosceles, Equilateral, Scalene).

    The sides of the triangle are to be entered as integer values, three per line. For each set of sides, print out the kind of triangle or an error message saying that the three sides do not make a triangle. (For a triangle to exist, any two sides together must be longer than the remaining side.) Continue analyzing triangles until <eof>.

2. Expand Program Birthday_Reminder to read in a month and a date. The date should be converted into a value in the enumerated type (First_Week, Second_Week, Third_Week, Fourth_Week) using the following formula.

    Dates 1–7:   First_Week
    Dates 8–14:   Second_Week
    Dates 15–21:   Third_Week
    Dates 22+:   Fourth_Week

    Each monthly print procedure should take the week as a parameter and print the following message heading:

    ```
    'Reminders for the ' (first, second, third, fourth) 'week
    of ' (January..) ' are: '
    ```

3. Rewrite Program Grade_List (pages 418–419) in Chapter 9 using the Succ function to increment the loop.

4. Write a Pascal program that reads a character from 'A' to 'Z' as input to produce output in the shape of a pyramid composed of the letters up to and including the letter that is input. The top letter in the pyramid should be 'A', and on each level, the next letter in the alphabet should fall between the letter that was introduced in the level above it. For example, if the input is 'E', the output will look like the following:

    ```
        A
       ABA
      ABCBA
     ABCDCBA
    ABCDEDCBA
    ```

5. Read in a real number character by character, convert the number to its numeric form, and print the result in E-notation. Your algorithm should convert the whole number part to an integer and the fractional part to an integer, and combine the two integers as follows:

    Set Result to Whole number + (Fraction/($10^{\text{number of digits in fraction}}$))

For example, 34.216 would be converted into 34 + 216/1000). You may assume that the number has at least one digit on either side of the decimal point.

6. The program that plays rock, paper, and scissors takes its input from two files. Rewrite the program using interactive input. The main module should be as follows:

```
REPEAT
    Get Command
    IF Continue
        Play Game
UNTIL Stop
```

Command should be an enumerated type (Continue, Stop). In the Get Command module the first player should be prompted to enter a C for Continue or an S for Stop. If the first player wishes to continue, ask the second player. Command should be Continue if both players enter a C and Stop otherwise. If both players wish to continue, the first player and then the second player should be prompted to enter a play.

One-Dimensional Arrays

- To be able to define a one-dimensional array for a given problem.
- To be able to choose appropriate index and component types for a one-dimensional array.
- To be able to assign a value to an array component.
- To be able to access a value stored in an array component.
- To be able to fill an array with data, and process the data in the array.
- To be able to apply subarray processing to a given problem.
- To be able to use parallel arrays.
- To be able to define and use an array with index values that have semantic content.

In the last chapter we examined the concept of a data type and looked at how to define ordinal data types. In this chapter we expand the definition of a data type to include structured types, which are organized collections of components given a single name.

Sometimes it is necessary to show relationships among different variables or to store and reference variables as a group. This is difficult to do if each variable is named individually. For example, if a set of individually named values must be printed in reverse order, all the values must be read and saved before the last one can be printed. If there are 1,000 values, we would have to define 1,000 individual variables to hold the values, and write 1,000 different Readln and Writeln statements to input and output the values—an incredibly tedious task! A one-dimensional array is a structured data type that allows us to program operations of this sort with ease.

In this chapter we discuss structured data types in general and examine the one-dimensional array data type in detail.

Unstructured Versus Structured Data Types

In Chapter 9 we introduced the set, which is one way of using an identifier to name a collection of values of a simpler type. Such a data type is called a composite type because it is composed of other types. There are two kinds of composite types: structured and unstructured. A set is an **unstructured data type.**

Unstructured Data Type   A collection of components that are not organized with respect to one another.

For example, we can ask if a specific value is in a set, but we cannot directly access an individual value: There is no way to say "assign the third value in set Paint to variable Colors." Given the following definitions

```
TYPE
  Spectrum = SET OF (Red, Orange, Yellow, Green, Blue, Indigo, Violet);

VAR
  Paint:
    Spectrum;
```

and the assignment statement

```
Paint := [Red, Green, Blue];
```

it would appear that Blue is the third element of set Paint. But we could have written the statement as

```
Paint := [Blue, Green, Red];
```

Both instances of Paint are identical. The comparison

```
[Red, Green, Blue] = [Blue, Green, Red]
```

is True. The order that we list the set elements doesn't matter. The set is the only unstructured composite type in Pascal.

A **structured data type** is made up of an *organized* collection of components of some other data type. Like the set, the collection is given a name, but each component can be accessed individually by specifying its position within the collection.

Structured Data Type   A collection of components whose organization is character-ized by the method used to access individual components. The allowable operations on a structured data type are the storage and retrieval of individual components.

Simple scalar types, both built-in and user-defined, are the building blocks for composite types. A structured composite type gathers together a set of scalar values, but unlike the unstructured composite type, imposes a specific arrangement on them (see Figure 11-1). The method used to access the individual components of a structured type depends on how the components are arranged. As we discuss other ways of structuring data, we'll look at the corresponding access mechanisms.

Figure 11-1
Atomic (Simple)
and Composite
Data Types

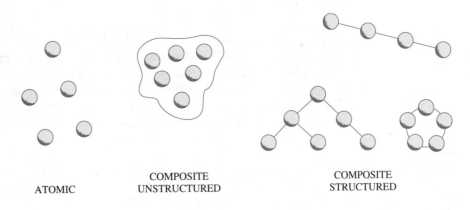

ATOMIC   COMPOSITE   COMPOSITE
                      UNSTRUCTURED   STRUCTURED

One-Dimensional Arrays

If we want to read a list of 1,000 values and print them in reverse order, we could write a program of the form:

```
PROGRAM Reverse_List (Input, Output);

VAR
  Value1,
  Value2,
  Value3,

      .
      .

  Value1000:
    Integer;

BEGIN (* Reverse_List *)
  Readln(Value1);
  Readln(Value2);
  Readln(Value3);

      .
      .

  Readln(Value1000);
  Writeln(Value1000);
  Writeln(Value999);
  Writeln(Value998);

      .
      .

  Writeln(Value1)
END.   (* Reverse_List *)
```

This program would be over 3,000 lines long! The problem is that we have to use 1,000 separate variables. Note that all the variables have the same name except for an appended number that distinguishes them. Wouldn't it be convenient if we could put the number in a counter variable and use FOR loops to go from 1 to 1000, and then from 1000 back down to 1? For example, if the counter variable is Number, we could write the body of the program as follows (we enclose Number in brackets to set it apart from Value):

```
BEGIN (* Reverse_List *)
  FOR Number := 1 to 1000 DO
    Readln(Value[Number]);
  FOR Number := 1000 DOWNTO 1 DO
    Writeln(Value[Number])
END.   (* Reverse_List *)
```

This code fragment is a correct Pascal program body *if* we define Value to be a one-dimensional array: a collection of variables, all of the same type, where the first part of each variable name is the same, and the last part is an *index value* enclosed in square brackets. In this case, the value stored in Number is the index.

A one-dimensional array is a data type, so it must be described in a TYPE definition before any variables of that type are defined.

```
TYPE
  Index_Range = 1..1000;
  Value_List = ARRAY [Index_Range] OF Integer;

VAR
  Value:
    Value_List;
```

The **TYPE** definition specifies the range of index values that are allowed: in this example, the range is a subrange of the integers starting at 1 and ending at 1000. The range of index values determines implicitly how many variables are contained in the array. The definition also indicates the data type of the variables (Integer).

The type definition describes the pattern for an array. To create an array, we must define a variable of type Value_List, such as Value. We could also define other variables of type Value_List. For example, if we defined Item and Quantity to be variables of type Value_List, each one would be an array of 1,000 integers. We could then access their individual components by writing Item[Number] and Quantity[Number].

Here is the complete Program Reverse_List, using array notation. This is certainly much shorter than our first version of the program.

```
PROGRAM Reverse_List (Input, Output);

TYPE
  Index_Range = 1..1000;
  Value_List = ARRAY [Index_Range] OF Integer;

VAR
  Value:
    Value_List;
  Number:
    Index_Range;

BEGIN (* Reverse_List *)
  FOR Number := 1 to 1000 DO
    Readln(Value[Number]);
  FOR Number := 1000 DOWNTO 1 DO
    Writeln(Value[Number])
END.   (* Reverse_List *)
```

Now that we have demonstrated how useful one-dimensional arrays can be, we define them formally and explain how individual components are accessed.

Defining Arrays

A **one-dimensional array** is a structured collection of components that can be accessed individually by specifying the position of a component with a single index value. (In Chapter 13 we introduce multi-dimensional arrays, arrays that have more than one index value.)

One-Dimensional Array   A structured collection of components, of the same type, given a single name. Each component is accessed by an index that indicates the component's position within the collection.

Here is the syntax template describing how a one-dimensional array data type is defined.

ARRAY [index-type] **OF** component-type;

The index type gives the range of index values. It is used by the compiler to determine how many components there are in this array type and how each individual component is accessed. The index type can be any ordinal type such as Char, Boolean, an enumerated type, or a subrange type. (Some compilers do not allow an index type of Integer because the resulting array would be too large to fit in memory.) The component type describes what is stored in each component of the array. Array components may be of any type, but for now we limit our discussion to atomic components.

Accessing Individual Components

To access an individual array component, we write the name of an array variable, followed by an expression enclosed in square brackets. The expression specifies which component to access. The syntax template for accessing an array component is:

array-identifier [index-expression]

The index expression may be as simple as a constant or a variable name, or as complex as a combination of variables, operators, and function calls. Whatever the form of the expression, it must result in a value that is assignment compatible with the index type.

An array component can be treated like a simple variable. We can assign it a value, read a value into it, write its contents, pass it as a parameter, and use it in an expression. Take, for example, the following two statements.

```
Value[Counter] := 0;
IF (Value[Number + 1] MOD 10) <> 0
    THEN
```

In the first statement, 0 is stored into an array component. If Counter is 1, 0 is stored in the first component of the array. If Counter is 2, 0 is stored in the second place in the array. If Counter has a value that is not within the index type, an error occurs. In our example, if Counter is 1001, trying to access Value[Counter] would cause a run-time error, assuming that the Options/Compiler/Range-checking menu option was in effect. Otherwise, in Turbo Pascal, accessing Value [1001] will return an unexpected value or possibly lead to a side-effect error.

In the second statement an array component is selected by the expression [Number + 1]. The specific array component accessed is divided by ten and checked to see if the remainder is nonzero. If [Number + 1] is 1, the value in the first place is being tested; if [Number + 1] is 2, the second place is tested; and so on. Figure 11-2 shows the indexing expression as a constant, a variable, and a more complex expression.

Accessing an Entire Array At Once

We can access an entire array at once simply by giving the array name without an index expression. For example, given the following declarations for the arrays Char_Count and Frequency,

Figure 11-2
Index as a Con-
stant, a Variable,
and an Expression

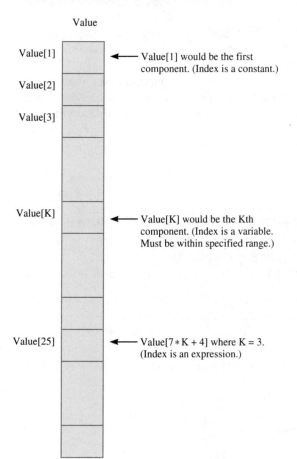

Value

Value[1] — Value[1] would be the first component. (Index is a constant.)

Value[2]

Value[3]

Value[K] — Value[K] would be the Kth component. (Index is a variable. Must be within specified range.)

Value[25] — Value[7 * K + 4] where K = 3. (Index is an expression.)

```
TYPE
  Alpha_List = ARRAY [Char] OF Integer;

VAR
  Char_Count,
  Frequency:
    Alpha_List;
```

we could write the following assignment statement

```
Char_Count := Frequency;
```

The effect is that each value in the array Frequency is copied to the corresponding component of Char_Count.

Although we can write an assignment statement containing a reference to an entire array, we cannot use entire arrays in expressions. For example, the following statement is illegal.

```
Frequency := Frequency + Char_Count;    (* Illegal statement *)
```

To add the components of one array to the corresponding components of another array, we must add each pair of components together individually using a FOR loop that runs through the array indices.

We can also pass entire arrays as parameters. This gives the procedure or function access to the entire array. For example, if we defined a procedure called Count_Line that takes a parameter of type Alpha_List, we can write

```
Count_Line(Char_Count);
```

giving Count_Line access to all the components in Char_Count. Within the procedure we can access any component of Char_Count, assign the entire array to another variable of type Alpha_List, or pass it to another procedure.

Assignment of one array to another requires that the two arrays be of *exactly* the same type. The same is true for passing arrays as parameters: the data types of the formal and actual parameters must be identical. In addition, the data type of an array variable that is used as a formal parameter must be a named data type. The procedure heading

```
PROCEDURE Pass(VAR List:
                 ARRAY [Char] OF Integer)
```

is illegal because we cannot write a type definition in a formal parameter list, whereas

```
PROCEDURE Pass(VAR List:
                 Alpha_List)
```

is legal provided Procedure Pass is within the scope of the type identifier Alpha_List. Of course, the requirement that formal parameters be named types implies that all arrays used as actual parameters must also be declared with named types.

Software Engineering Tip

Passing Large Arrays as Parameters

In Chapter 7 we said that if a variable is passed to a subprogram and it is not to be changed by the subprogram, then a formal value parameter should be used. We specifically excluded variables of type Text from this rule, and said that there would be one more exception. Large arrays are this exception.

Remember that actual parameters are copied into formal value parameters. Therefore, when an array is passed to a value parameter, the entire array is copied. Not only is extra space required to hold the copy, but the copying itself takes time. VAR parameters require only that the address of the variable be passed to the subprogram, so when an array is passed as a VAR parameter, just the address of the first component is passed. Thus, passing large arrays as VAR parameters saves both memory and time.

Of course, using a VAR parameter can lead to inadvertent errors if the values are changed within the subprogram. You must be careful to avoid this by ensuring that the documentation for the subprogram states the importance of not changing the values in the array.

The definition of what constitutes a large array is not fixed. If time and memory use are critical elements of a program, then it may be necessary to pass every array as a VAR parameter. But if program reliability is more important, even arrays with thousands of components may be passed as value parameters.

The frequency with which a subprogram is called also affects the choice. If it is called only once, then the extra time and memory are probably not important even for an array with 1,000 components. But if the subprogram is called repeatedly in a loop, the extra time will quickly add up, and you may wish to pass arrays with as few as ten components as VAR parameters.

If it's not immediately clear which approach is best, compile and run the program each way to see if the difference is significant. If the additional time and memory space required is not a problem, play it safe and use value parameters.

Examples of Defining and Accessing Arrays

We now look in detail at some specific examples of defining, declaring, and accessing arrays.

```
CONST
  Num_Students = 25;
```

```
TYPE
   Num_Grades = 1..Num_Students;                   (* Index type *)
   Grade_Type = ARRAY[Num_Grades] OF Char;         (* Array type *)

VAR
   Grades:              (* Array of 25 characters          *)
      Grade_Type;
   Counter:             (* A variable of the index type    *)
      Num_Grades;
   One_Grade:           (* A variable of the component type *)
      Char;
```

Grade_Type is a pattern for an array with 25 components, each of which can contain a character. Grades is an array variable of Grade_Type. Each component of Grades is a Char variable, just like One_Grade or any other Char variable. Figure 11-3 illustrates these relationships.

When the index type is a subrange of the integers beginning with 1, it allows us to access the components by their position in the array—that is, the first, the second, the third, and so on, until the last. This is the most common way of thinking about an array. In fact, some programming languages allow only indices of this type. Pascal, however, is much more flexible. The next example shows an array where the indices are letters.

Figure 11-3
Array Pattern,
Array Variable, and
Array Component

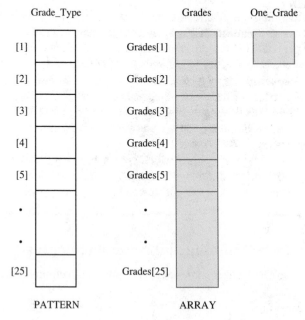

```
TYPE
  Letter_Grades = 'A'..'D';                         (* Index type *)
  Grade_Count = ARRAY[Letter_Grades] OF Integer;    (* Array type *)

VAR
  Class1_Grades,         (* Array of four integers     *)
  Class2_Grades:         (* Array of four integers     *)
    Grade_Count;
  Grade:                 (* Variable of the index type *)
    Letter_Grades;
```

Grade_Count is a pattern for an array with four components, each an integer. Class1_Grades and Class2_Grades are two array variables of this type. The first component in Class1_Grades can be accessed by Class1_Grades['A'], the second component by Class1_Grades['B'], and so on. The components in Class2_Grades can be accessed by Class2_Grades['A'], Class2_Grades['B'], Class2_Grades['C'], and Class2_Grades['D'] (see Figure 11-4).

Suppose Class1_Grades['A'] is used as a counter for the number of As in Class1, Class1_Grades['B'] is used to tally the Bs in Class1, and so on. Since the array components are variables, we must initialize the array components to 0 prior to counting, as in the following code fragment.

```
FOR Grade := 'A' to 'D' DO          (* Run through the indices *)
  BEGIN
    Class1_Grades[Grade] := 0;   (* Initialize Class1_Grades *)
    Class2_Grades[Grade] := 0    (* Initialize Class2_Grades *)
  END;
    .                             (* Process grades           *)
    .
```

The index type in the following example is an enumerated type.

```
TYPE
  Drink = (Orange, Cola, RootBeer, GingerAle, Cherry, Lemon);
  Amount_Type = ARRAY [Drink] OF Real;
```

Figure 11-4

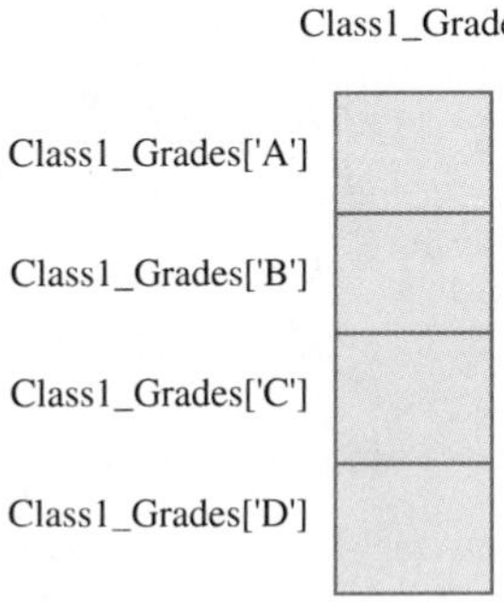

Class1_Grades

Class1_Grades['A']

Class1_Grades['B']

Class1_Grades['C']

Class1_Grades['D']

Figure 11-5

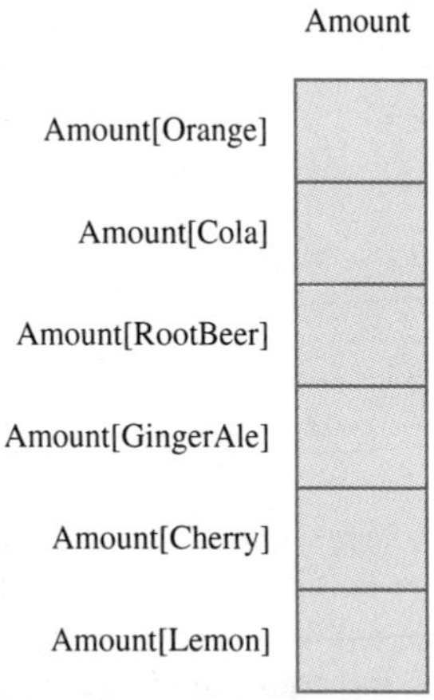

Amount

```
VAR
  Amount:                (* Array of 6 Reals, indexed by Drink *)
    Amount_Type;
  Flavor:                (* Variable of the index type          *)
    Drink;
```

Amount_Type creates a pattern for a group of six Real components representing dollar sales figures. Amount is an array of this type (see Figure 11-5). The following code will print the values in the array.

```
FOR Flavor := Orange TO Lemon DO
  Writeln(Amount[Flavor]);
```

The next example is a little more complex. It might be used to analyze occupancy rates in an apartment building. The component type is a subrange type.

```
CONST
  Building_Size = 350;        (* Number of apartments          *)
  Max_People = 5;             (* Maximum people per apartment *)

TYPE
  Occupant = 0..Max_People;          (* Component type *)
  Num_Apts = 1..Building_Size;       (* Index type     *)
  Apts = ARRAY [Num_Apts] OF Occupant;   (* Array type   *)

VAR
  Building:        (* An array of 350 subrange values, 0..5  *)
    Apts;
  Total_Number:    (* An integer for totalling the occupancy *)
    Integer;
  Counter:         (* A variable of the index type           *)
    Num_Apts;
```

Figure 11-6

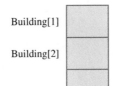

Building

Building[1]

Building[2]

•

•

Building[350]

Type Apts is a pattern for a group of 350 components. Its component type is an integer subrange type called Occupant. Building is an array of type Apts (see Figure 11-6). If values have been read into the array, then the following code will total the number of occupants in the building.

```
Total_Number := 0;
FOR Counter := 1 TO Building_Size DO
   Total_Number := Total_Number + Building[Counter];
```

Note that the named constants Building_Size and Max_People are used in defining the type Apts. If constants are used in this manner, changes can be made easily. If Building_Size changes from 350 to 400, only the CONST section needs to be changed. If the literal value 350 were used in place of Building_Size, at least two statements, and probably many more throughout the program in which the fragment is embedded, would have to be changed.

Here is one last example.

```
CONST
  Num_Students = 10;

TYPE
  Grades = 'A'..'F';                                (* Component type *)
  Range_Of_Students = 1..Num_Students;              (* Index type     *)
  Student_Type = ARRAY [Range_Of_Students] OF Grades; (* Array type    *)

VAR
  Students:
    Student_Type;        (* Array of 10 student letter grades *)
  ID_Number:
    Range_Of_Students;   (* Variable of the index type         *)
```

Array Students is pictured in Figure 11-7. Values are shown in the components, which implies that some processing of the array has already occurred. Following are some simple examples showing how the array may be used.

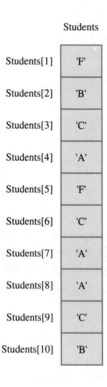

Figure 11-7
Array Variable Students with Values

Read(Students[2]);

assigns the next character in file Input to the component in Students indexed by 2;

Students[4] := 'A';

assigns the character 'A' to the component in Students indexed by 4;

ID_Number := 6;

assigns 6 to the index variable ID_Number;

Students[ID_Number] := 'C'

assigns the character 'C' to the component of Students indexed by ID_Number (that is, by 6); and

```
FOR ID_Number := 1 TO Num_Students DO
  Write(Students[IDNumber]);
```

loops through Students, printing each component. In this case, the output would be FBCAFCAACB. And, finally,

```
FOR ID_Number := 1 TO Num_Students DO
  Writeln('Student ', ID_Number:1,
          ' Grade ', Student[ID_Number]);
```

loops through Students, printing each component in a more readable form. ID_Number is used as the index, but it also has semantic content—it is the student's identification number. The output would be

```
Student 1 Grade F
Student 2 Grade B
    .

    .
Student 10 Grade B
```

Processing Arrays

There are three types of array processing that come up especially often: using part of the defined array (a subarray), using two or more arrays in parallel (parallel arrays), and using index values that have specific meaning within the problem (indices with semantic content).

Subarray Processing

The **size** of an array is established at compile time. We have to define it to be as big as it would ever need to be. Since the exact number of values to be put in the array is often dependent on the data itself, however, we may not fill all of the array components with values. The problem is that, to avoid processing empty ones, we must keep track of how many components are actually filled.

As values are put into the array, we keep a count of how many components are filled. We then use this count to process only components that have values stored in them. Any remaining places are not processed. For example, if there are 250 students in a class, a program to analyze test grades would set aside 250 locations for the grades. However, some students will surely be absent on the day of the test. So the number of test grades would be counted, and that number, rather than 250, would be used to control the processing of the array.

We often call the actual number of values in an array the **length** of the array. Procedures and functions that have array parameters should also have the length passed as a parameter. For example,

```
PROCEDURE Analyze (VAR Students:                (* An array of up to 250 students *)
                     Student_Type;
                   VAR Students_Length:  (* Number of grades actually in array *)
                     Range_Of_Students;
                   VAR Data:                     (* File grades are read from *)
                     Text);
```

Parallel Arrays

In many problems there are several pieces of information that go together. For example, we might have ID numbers and grades for a particular group of students. We can set up an Integer array for the ID number and a Char array for the grades. We can then access the components in the arrays in parallel. A particular ID number goes with a particular grade because they have the same position in their respective arrays; that is, they have the same index value. In Figure 11-8, the grade in Grade[1] is the grade for the student whose ID number is in ID_Num[1], the grade in Grade[2] is the grade for the student whose ID number is in ID_Num[2], and so on.

Indices with Semantic Content

In some problems the index has meaning beyond simple position; that is, the index has *semantic content*. For example, the employees in a company might be given identification numbers ranging from 100 to 500. If an array of salary figures were defined as

```
TYPE
    ID_Numbers = 100..500;
    Salaries = ARRAY [ID_Numbers] OF Real;

VAR
    Salary:
        Salaries;
```

the index of a specific salary would be the identification number of the person making that salary; that is, Salary[201] would be the salary for the employee whose identification number is 201.

To give you more practice with both problem solving and the use of one-dimensional arrays, we end this chapter with three case studies that involve the types of processing outlined in this section.

Figure 11-8
Parallel Arrays

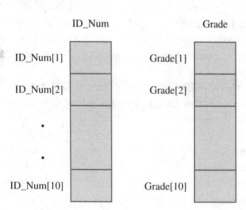

PROBLEM-SOLVING CASE STUDY

Comparison of Two Lists

Problem: You are writing a program for an application that will not tolerate erroneous input data. Therefore, the data is prepared by entering it twice onto one file. The file contains two lists of positive integer numbers, separated by a negative number. These two lists of numbers should be identical, otherwise a data entry error has occurred. You decide to write a separate program to compare the lists and print out any pairs of numbers that are not the same. The exact number of integers on each list is unknown, but each list will have no more than 500.

Input: A file (Data) containing two lists of positive integers. The lists are separated by a negative integer and are of equal length.

Output: The statement that the lists are identical, or a list of the pairs of values that do not match.

Discussion: Since the lists are on the same file, the first list will have to be read and stored until the negative number is read. Then the second list can be read and compared with the first list.

If we were checking the lists by hand, we would write the numbers from the first list on a pad of paper, one per line. The line number would correspond to the number's position in the list; that is, the first number would be on the first line, the second number on the second line, and so on. The first number in the second list would then be compared to the number on the first line, the second number to the number on the second line, and so forth.

We can use an array, called First_List, to represent the pad of paper. To define First_List, we first have to describe the form of the array in the TYPE section, then we have to declare a variable of this type in the VAR section.

```
CONST
  Max_Number = 500;        (* Maximum number *)

TYPE
  Index_Range = 1..Max_Number;
  List_Type = ARRAY[Index_Range] OF Integer;

VAR
  First_List:
    List_Type;
```

Describe structure

Create one

Now we can complete the top-down design and program for our problem.

Figure 11-9
One-Dimensional
Array Data
Structure

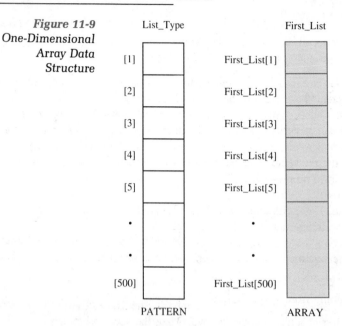

Data Structures: A one-dimensional array to hold the first list of numbers (First_List). See Figure 11-9.

Main Module   *Level 0*

> Read First List
> All_OK is set to True
> Compare Lists
> If All_OK
>   Print 'The two lists are identical.'

When procedure Read_First_List is run, the first number will be stored in First_List[1], the second in First_List[2], the third in First_List[3]. This implies that we need a counter to keep track of which number is being read. When the negative number is encountered, the counter tells us how many of the 500 places set aside were actually needed. We can use this value (call it List_Length) to control the reading and comparing loop in the Compare List module. This is another example of subarray processing.

Read First List (Receives: Data: Text   *Level 1*
                  Returns: List_Length: Index_Range
                  Receives/Returns: First_List : List_Type)

```
Initialize Counter to 0
Read a Number
WHILE Number >= zero
    Increment Counter
    Set First_List[Counter] to Number
    Read a Number
Set List_Length to Counter
```

Compare Lists (Receives: First_List: List_Type, Data: Text, List_Length: Index_Range
                  Receives/Returns: All_OK: Boolean)

```
FOR Counter going from 1 to List_Length
    Read Number from second list
    IF numbers not the same
        Set All_OK to False
        Print both numbers
```

Numbers Not the Same   *Level 2*

```
Number <> First_List[Counter]
```

Print Both Numbers

```
Writeln First_List[Counter], Number
```

Module Structure Chart:

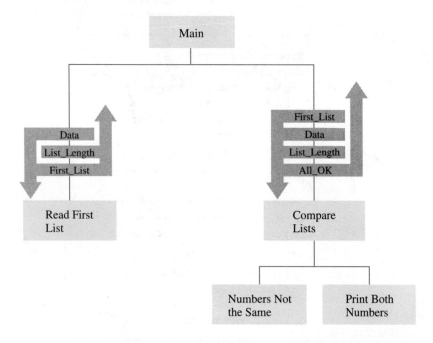

Since the last two modules are only one line each, they will be coded in module Compare Lists.

```
PROGRAM Check_Lists (Data, Output);

(* There are two lists of integers on file Data, separated by a   *)
(* negative integer. These two lists are compared. If they are    *)
(* identical, a message is printed. If not, nonmatching pairs are *)
(* printed. Assumption:  Lists are of equal length *)

CONST
  Max_Number = 500;  (* Maximum in each list *)

TYPE
  Index_Range = 1..Max_Number;
  List_Type = ARRAY[Index_Range] OF Integer;
```

```
VAR
  First_List:          (* Holds first list           *)
    List_Type;
  All_OK:              (* True if lists are identical *)
    Boolean;
  List_Length:         (* Length of first list        *)
    Index_Range;
  Data:                (* Data file                   *)
    Text;

(*******************************************************************)

PROCEDURE Read_First_List (VAR First_List:       (* Returns filled  *)
                                   List_Type;     (* First_List      *)
                               VAR List_Length:   (* Returns number  *)
                                   Index_Range;   (* of values       *)
                               VAR Data:          (* Data file       *)
                                   Text);

(* The first list is read into First_List. A count of the number of *)
(* values in the list is kept and returned in List_Length *)

VAR
  Counter:             (* Index_Variable              *)
    0..Max_Number;
  Number:              (* Variable used for reading *)
    Integer;

BEGIN (* Read_First_List *)
  Counter := 0;
  Read(Data, Number);
  WHILE Number >= 0 DO
    BEGIN
      Counter := Counter + 1;
      First_List[Counter] := Number;
      Read(Data, Number)
    END;
  List_Length := Counter
END; (* Read_First_List *)

(*******************************************************************)
```

```
PROCEDURE Compare_Lists(VAR All_OK:          (* Returns True if lists *)
                             Boolean;         (* match                 *)
                        First_List:           (* First list of numbers *)
                             List_Type;
                        List_Length:          (* Length of list        *)
                             Integer;
                        VAR Data:             (* Data file             *)
                             Text);

(* Read second list and compare to values in First_List. Lists are *)
(* assumed to be the same length *)

VAR
  Counter,     (* Loop control counter *)
  Number:
    Integer;

BEGIN (* Compare_Lists *)
  FOR Counter := 1 TO List_Length DO
    BEGIN
      Read(Data, Number);
      If Number <> First_List[Counter]
        THEN
          BEGIN
            AllOK := False;
            Writeln('Position ', Counter:1, ': ',
                    First_List[Counter]:4, ' <> ', Number:4)
          END
    END
END;  (* Compare_Lists *)

(* ***************************************************************** *)

BEGIN (* Check_Lists *)
  Assign(Data, 'DATA.DAT');
  Reset(Data);
  Read_First_List(First_List, List_Length, Data);
  All_OK := True;
  Compare_Lists(All_OK, First_List, List_Length, Data);
  IF All_OK
    THEN
      Writeln('The two lists are identical.');
  Close(Data)
END.  (* CheckLists *)
```

PROBLEM-SOLVING CASE STUDY cont'd.

Testing: The program is run with two sets of data, one in which the two lists are identical and one in which there are errors. The data and the results from each are shown below.

Data Set One	*Data Set Two*
21	21
32	32
76	76
22	22
21	21
-4	-4
21	21
32	32
76	176
22	12
21	21

Output:

The two lists are identical.

Output:

Position 3: 76 <> 176
Position 4: 22 <> 12

PROBLEM-SOLVING CASE STUDY

Frequency of Certain Characters

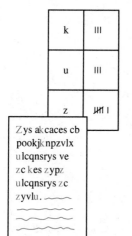

Problem: You've found a secret message, written in some sort of code. After doing some research, you decide to see if it is a simple substitution cypher—a code in which each letter is replaced by a different letter. Your research tells you that the way to break this type of code is to count the occurrences of each letter in the text and compare them to the average occurrence of letters in any English text. For example, the most common letter is probably a substitute for *e*. You decide to write a program to count the occurrences of certain characters in a text file. Rather than count every character in the message, you decide to look just at certain characters that appear to be the most common. The characters you are interested in will be input from the keyboard.

Input: A list of the characters to be counted, one per line on Input (the character # ends the list); and text to be processed character by character (on file Data).

Output: The characters to be counted and their frequency.

Discussion: To do this by hand, you would make a list of the characters you want to count. Then you would process the text by taking each character and checking to see whether it is on your list. If it is, you would make a hash mark beside it.

This algorithm can be used directly in a program. The list of characters can be read into an array of type Char. To see whether or not a character is on the list, you scan the list, comparing the character with the ones on the list. To simulate making a hash mark, you use a second, parallel array that is the same size as the character list, but whose components are of type Integer. If you find the character in the list, you add 1 to the component with the same index in the second array. For example, if the first character on our list is an A, then each time you find an A, the first slot in the integer array will be incremented.

Data Structures: A one-dimensional array of type Char to hold the characters being counted (Char_List), and a one-dimensional array of type Integer to hold the corresponding frequencies (Freq_List).

Main Module   *Level 0*

```
Reset Data
Get Char_List
Set Freq_List to 0
WHILE more characters DO
    Get a Character
    Scan list for Character
    IF Found
        Increment Freq_List
Print Char_List and Freq_List
```

Get Char_List   *Level 1*

```
Initialize Counter to 0
Read a Character
WHILE Character <> # DO
    Increment Counter
    Set Char_List[Counter] to Character
    Read a Character
Set List_Length to Counter
```

Since you don't know how many characters will be on the list, Char_List will have to be large enough to hold all the characters in the character set except one. (Since # is a signal value, it is not counted.) When Char_List has been read, Counter will hold the length of the array; that is, when the list is searched for a character, only those components between Char_List[1] and CharList[List_Length] need be examined. This is another example of subarray processing. Note that Counter is being used both as a counter and as an index.

Set Freq_List to 0

FOR Index going from 1 to List_Length
    Initialize Freq_List[Index] to 0

Get a Character

Read Character from file Data

Scan List

Initialize Found to False
Initialize Index to 0
WHILE NOT found AND more components in list
    Increment Index
    IF Character = Char_List[Index]
        Set Found to True

If Found is True, the value of Index is the position in array Char_List where the character was found.

Increment Freq_List

Set Freq_List[Index] to Freq_List[Index] + 1

Print Char_List and Freq_List

FOR Index going from 1 to List_Length
    Writeln Char_List[Index], ' occurred ', Freq_List[Index]:3,
    ' times.'

Since Get a Character and Increment Freq_List are only one simple statement each, they will be coded directly in the main module. Let's look at the interfaces of the other procedures.

Procedure	Receives	Returns	Comments
Get_Char_List		Char_List List_Length	List_Length will be last value of Index
Zero_Freq_List	Freq_List List_Length	Freq_List	
Scan_List	Char_List List_Length Character	Found Index	If Found is True, Index gives place found.
Print	Freq_List Char_List List_Length		

Remember that any variables in the Returns column must be VAR parameters. Those listed only in the Receives column, except for large arrays, should be value parameters. For large arrays, storing a copy of the array wastes memory space and execution time. Thus, in procedure Print, Freq_List is a VAR parameter.

Module Structure Chart:

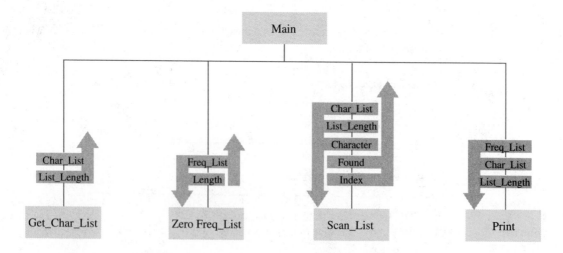

PROBLEM-SOLVING CASE STUDY *cont'd.*

```pascal
PROGRAM Char_Count (Input, Data, Output);

(* Program to count the frequency of occurrence of specified *)
(* characters in text *)

CONST
  Max_Length = 255;          (* Maximum number of different characters *)
  End_Of_List = '#';

TYPE
  Index_Range = 1..Max_Length;
  Index_Count = 0..Max_Length;
  List_Type = ARRAY[Index_Range] OF Char;
  Count_Type = ARRAY[Index_Range] OF Integer;

VAR
  Char_List:        (* Characters to be counted        *)
    List_Type;
  Freq_List:        (* Frequency counts                *)
    Count_Type;
  List_Length:      (* Number of characters to count   *)
    Index_Count;
  Found:            (* True if character found on list *)
    Boolean;
  Data:             (* Text to be counted on file Data *)
    Text;
  Character:        (* Temporary character             *)
    Char;
  Index:            (* Returns position of character   *)
    Index_Count;

(* ****************************************************************** *)


PROCEDURE Get_Char_List (VAR Char_List:      (* Returns list of *)
                             List_Type;       (* characters      *)

                         VAR List_Length:     (* Returns length of list *)
                             Index_Count);

(* Characters are read from Input and stored in Char_List until the   *)
(* End_Of_List character is read. List_Length is the number of characters *)
(* in the list. The Char constant End_Of_List is accessed globally.   *)
(* Assumption: There are no duplicate characters *)

VAR
  Counter:          (* Index_Variable  *)
    Integer;
  Character:        (* Used for reading *)
    Char;
```

```
BEGIN  (* Get_Char_List *)
  Counter := 0;
  Readln(Character);
  WHILE Character <> End_Of_List DO
    BEGIN
      Counter := Counter + 1;
      Char_List[Counter] := Character;
      Readln(Character)
    END;
  List_Length := Counter
END;  (* Get_Char_List *)

(*******************************************************************)

PROCEDURE Zero_Freq_List (VAR Freq_List:      (* Returns zeroed list *)
                               Count_Type;
                               List_Length:    (* Receives length of  *)
                                               (* list *)
                               Index_Count);

(* The first Length positions of Freq_List are set to 0 *)

VAR
  Index:          (* Loop control counter *)
    Index_Range;

BEGIN (* Zero_Freq_List *)
  FOR Index := 1 TO List_Length DO
    Freq_List[Index] := 0
END;  (* Zero_Freq_List *)

(*******************************************************************)

PROCEDURE Scan_List (    Char_List:           (* Receives list of chars  *)
                           List_Type;
                         List_Length:          (* Receives length of char *)
                           Index_Count;        (* list *)
                         Character:            (* Receives input char     *)
                           Char;
                     VAR Index:                (* Returns index of match  *)
                           Index_Count;
                     VAR Found:                (* Returns False if no     *)
                           Boolean);           (* match *)
```

```
(* Char_List is searched for Character. If Found is True, Index is *)
(* where Character is found in Char_List. If Found is False,      *)
(* Character is not in Char_List and Index is undefined *)

BEGIN (* Scan_List *)
  Found := False;
  Index := 0;
  WHILE (Index < List_Length) AND NOT Found DO
    BEGIN
      Index := Index + 1;
      IF Character = Char_List[Index]
        THEN
          Found := True
    END
END;  (* Scan_List *)

(* ***************************************************************** *)

PROCEDURE Print (VAR Freq_List:        (* Receives table of char counts  *)
                     Count_Type;
                     Char_List:        (* Receives list of chars counted *)
                     List_Type;
                     List_Length:      (* Receives length of lists       *)
                     Index_Count);

(* Character list with associated frequencies is printed *)

VAR
  Index:
    Index_Range;

BEGIN (* Print *)
  FOR Index := 1 TO List_Length DO
    Writeln(Char_List[Index], ' occurred ',
            Freq_List[Index]:3, ' times. ')
END;  (* Print *)

(* ***************************************************************** *)
```

```
BEGIN (* Char_Count *)
  Assign(Data, 'DATA.DAT');
  Reset(Data);
  Get_Char_List(Char_List, List_Length);
  Zero_Freq_List(Freq_List, List_Length);
  (* Count occurrences of desired characters in text on Data *)
  WHILE NOT EOF(Data) DO
    BEGIN
      WHILE NOT EOLN(Data) DO
        BEGIN
          Read(Data, Character);
          Scan_List(Char_List, List_Length, Character, Index, Found);
          IF Found
            THEN
              Freq_List[Index] := Freq_List[Index] + 1
        END;
      Readln(Data)
    END;
  Print(Freq_List, Char_List, List_Length);
  Close(Data)
END.  (* Char_Count *)
```

Let's do a partial code walk-through of this program with the following data. The characters to be counted are

    a   e   i   o   u

and the text is

    Roses are red,
    violets are blue.
    If I can learn Pascal,
    so can you.

Here are the contents of the arrays after procedures Get_Char_List and Zero_Freq_List are executed:

Char_List[1] is 'a'	Freq_List[1] is 0	Length is 5
Char_List[2] is 'e'	Freq_List[2] is 0	
Char_List[3] is 'i'	Freq_List[3] is 0	
Char_List[4] is 'o'	Freq_List[4] is 0	
Char_List[5] is 'u'	Freq_List[5] is 0	

We assume that the control structures of the reading loops in the main program are correct and look at the three inner statements:

```
1. Read(Data, Character)
2. Scan_List(Char_List, List_Length, Character, Index, Found)
3. IF Found
      THEN
         Freq_List[Index] := Freq_List[Index] + 1
```

The following table shows the partial walk-through. The number to the left of the period refers to one of the three statements listed above, and the number to the right of the period refers to the number of times the statement has been executed.

Statement	Character	Index	Found	Freq_List
1.1	R	?	?	
2.1	R	?	False	
3.1	R	?	False	
1.2	o	?	False	
2.2	o	4	True	
3.2	o	4	True	Freq_List[4] is 1
1.3	s	4	True	
2.3	s	?	False	
3.3	s	?	False	
1.4	e	?	False	
2.4	e	2	True	
3.4	e	2	True	Freq_List[2] is 1
.				
.				
1.9	e	?	False	
2.9	e	2	True	
3.9	e	2	True	Freq_List[2] is 2

The output from the program using this data would be as follows:

```
a occurred  7 times.
e occurred  7 times.
i occurred  1 times.
o occurred  4 times.
u occurred  2 times.
```

At first glance the output does not seem right. If you count the characters by hand, you come up with three occurrences of 'i'. Note, however, that two of these are of 'I', not 'i'. If we want to count uppercase letters and lowercase letters as the same, we have to convert one of them. (The algorithm for converting ASCII uppercase letters to lowercase letters was given in Chapter 10.)

Testing: The test data for this program should include cases in which (1) there are no characters to be counted, (2) there is no text to count, and (3) both files contain input data with a variable number of lines.

PROBLEM-SOLVING CASE STUDY

Frequency of All Characters

A	
B	
⋮	
Z	I
a	II
b	
⋮	
3	JH I
1	
2	
⋮	
8	
9	

Zys akcaces cb pookjknpzvlx ulcqnsrys ve zc kes zypz ulcqnsrys zc zyvlu. ⌇⌇⌇⌇⌇
⌇⌇⌇⌇⌇
⌇⌇⌇⌇⌇

Problem: Count the frequency of occurrence of *all* the characters in a sample of text.

Input: A file of text (Data).

Output: Each printable character in the character set, followed by the number of times it occurred.

Discussion: Program Char_Count is the implementation of an algorithm that not only uses parallel arrays and subarray processing, but parallels the way a human would do the problem. There is nothing wrong with this solution except that we are not taking advantage of all the information on hand. By slightly changing the problem statement, we can approach the solution from another angle, this time keeping in mind the features of Pascal.

Pascal already has a built-in list of all the characters—type Char. Pascal also allows us to use any ordinal type as an index type. So instead of searching a list of characters and counting them in a parallel array, we let Pascal do all that by using the characters themselves as the indices in the counting array.

In Chapter 10 we mentioned that the ASCII character set has nonprinting characters. We need to set up our array to count only those characters that are printable. Fortunately, the printing characters are all grouped together so we can define a subrange of the characters to be our index type.

We use Min_Char and Max_Char to represent the first and last values in the index range. (Min_Char and Max_Char have to be set in the CONST section; they are not built-in identifiers.)

```
CONST
  Min_Char = ' ';
  Max_Char = '~';
TYPE
  Frequency = ARRAY[Min_Char..Max_Char] OF Integer
```

Freq[Min_Char] would be the counter for blanks.

Freq[Max_Char] would be the counter for ~s.

Freq[Character] would be the counter for whatever character Character contained.

Let's look at how this problem is simplified by the fact that the index itself has meaning.

Data Structures: An array of frequencies (Freq) indexed by the characters being counted.

Main Module   *Level 0*

```
Zero Freq_Count
WHILE more characters DO
   WHILE NOT EOLN DO
      Read Character from Data
      Increment Freq_Count[Character] by 1
   Readln Data
PRINT characters and frequencies
```

Zero Freq_Count   *Level 1*

```
FOR Index from Min_Char to Max_Char DO
   Initialize Freq_Count[Index] to 0
```

Print Characters and Frequencies

```
FOR Index from Min_Char to Max_Char DO
   Writeln Index:2, 'OCCURRED', Freq_Count[Index]:3, 'TIMES'
```

Module Structure Chart:

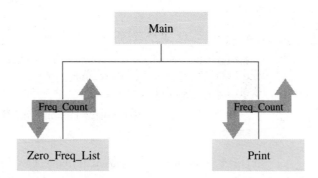

```
PROGRAM Count_All (Data, Output);

(* Program to count frequency of occurrence of all printable characters *)
(* in text.  Choose one of the two following lines, depending on the    *)
(* character set of the machine being used  *)

CONST
  Min_Char = ' ';
  Max_Char = '~';

TYPE
  Index_Range = Min_Char..Max_Char;
  Count_Type = ARRAY[Index_Range] OF Integer;

VAR
  Freq_Count:        (* Array of character counts      *)
    Count_Type;
  Character:         (* Current character              *)
    Index_Range;
  Data:              (* File with text to be analyzed *)
    Text;

(****************************************************************)

PROCEDURE Zero_Freq_Count (VAR Freq_Count:      (* Returns zeroed table *)
                                Count_Type);
(* Puts zeros in all elements of the character counting array *)

VAR
  Index:
    Index_Range;
```

PROBLEM-SOLVING CASE STUDY cont'd.

```
BEGIN (* Zero_Freq_Count *)
  FOR Index := Min_Char TO Max_Char DO
    Freq_Count[Index] := 0
END;  (* Zero_Freq_Count *)

(*******************************************************************)

PROCEDURE Print (Freq_Count:    (* Receives table of char counts *)
                   Count_Type);
(* Prints each character and the number of times it occurred *)

VAR
  Index:
    Index_Range;

BEGIN (* Print *)
  FOR Index := Min_Char TO Max_Char DO
    IF Freq_Count[Index] <> 0
      THEN
        Writeln(Index:2, ' OCCURRED ', Freq_Count[Index]:3, ' TIMES')
END;  (* Print *)

(*******************************************************************)

BEGIN (* Count_All *)
  Assign(Data, 'DATA.DAT');
  Reset(Data);
  Zero_Freq_Count(Freq_Count);                     (* Zero counters *)
  (* Keep reading and counting until no more characters *)
  WHILE NOT EOF(Data) DO
    BEGIN
      Read(Data, Character);
      Freq_Count[Character] := Freq_Count[Character] + 1;
      IF EOLN(Data)
        THEN
          Readln(Data)
    END;
  Print(Freq_Count);
  Close(Data)
END.  (* Count_All *)
```

See how much simpler the solution becomes when we take advantage of the fact that the character itself can be the index to its own frequency counter? In Programming Problem 1 at the end of this chapter, you are asked to modify this program to handle the case in which a specified subset of the characters is counted (as was done in the previous problem).

Using the same input file as was used in the previous problem,

```
Roses are red,
violets are blue.
If I can learn Pascal,
so can you.
```

we get the following output from Program Count_All:

```
  OCCURRED 10 TIMES
, OCCURRED  2 TIMES
. OCCURRED  2 TIMES
I OCCURRED  2 TIMES
P OCCURRED  1 TIMES
R OCCURRED  1 TIMES
a OCCURRED  7 TIMES
b OCCURRED  1 TIMES
c OCCURRED  3 TIMES
d OCCURRED  1 TIMES
e OCCURRED  7 TIMES
f OCCURRED  1 TIMES
i OCCURRED  1 TIMES
l OCCURRED  4 TIMES
n OCCURRED  3 TIMES
o OCCURRED  4 TIMES
r OCCURRED  4 TIMES
s OCCURRED  5 TIMES
t OCCURRED  1 TIMES
u OCCURRED  2 TIMES
v OCCURRED  1 TIMES
y OCCURRED  1 TIMES
```

Testing: Two things must be tested in this program. 1) Does it count the characters correctly, and 2) can it handle files of varying numbers of lines? To test whether this program counts characters correctly, we create a data file that contains all the printable characters at least once and some of them more than once. To make sure that the program runs correctly on files with varying numbers of lines, we test the program on an empty file, a file with one line, and a file with more than one line.

Testing and Debugging

We add a word of caution about the choice of looping structure to use when processing arrays. The most common error that you will encounter in processing arrays is the message RANGE CHECK ERROR. This means that your program attempted to access a component using an index outside the range of indexes defined for the array. For example, given the declarations

```
TYPE
  Index = 1..100;
  Table = ARRAY[Index] OF Char;

VAR
  Counter:
    Integer;
  Line:
    Table;
```

if Options/Compiler/Range-checking has been selected, then the following FOR statement would print the contents of array Line and then cause the program to crash with the RANGE CHECK ERROR error message.

```
FOR Counter := 1 TO 101 DO
  Writeln(Line[Counter]);
```

This example is trivial to debug, but you won't always use a simple FOR statement in accessing arrays. Suppose we read data into array Line in another part of the program. We use a WHILE statement that reads to EOLN:

```
Counter := 0;
WHILE NOT EOLN DO
  BEGIN
    Counter := Counter + 1;
    Read(Line[Counter])
  END
```

This seems reasonable enough, but what if the input contains a line with more than 100 characters? After the hundredth character is read, the loop continues to execute, and on the next iteration the program crashes because the array index is out of bounds.

The moral is: when processing arrays, give special attention to the design of loop termination conditions. Always ask yourself if there is any possibility that the loop could keep running after the last array component has been processed.

Whenever you see the RANGE CHECK ERROR message, the first suspicion should be a loop that fails to terminate properly. The second thing to check is any array access involving an index that is based on input data or a calculation. When an array index is input as data, then a data validation check is an absolute necessity.

Testing and Debugging Hints

1. Be consistent when using arrays. The pattern of an array is described and given a name in the TYPE section; array variables are declared in the VAR section. Values are stored in the individual components of an array variable during execution of the program. These three actions—describing, declaring, using—must all be consistent.

2. The individual components of an array are themselves variables of the component type. When values are stored into an array, they must be of the component type; otherwise, a type-conflict error occurs.

3. When an individual component in an array is accessed, the index must be within the index range. Attempting to use an index value that is not within the defined index range will cause a RANGE CHECK ERROR error, assuming that the Options/ Compiler/Range-checking menu option was in effect. Be sure to use automatic range-checking when debugging a program.

4. The size of an array must be determined at compile time, but its actual length is determined at run time. This means that an array must be declared to be as large as it could ever be for the particular problem. Subarray processing is used to process only the components that have data in them.

5. Pass the length as well as the array to procedures and functions when subarray processing is to take place within them.

Summary

In addition to being able to create user-defined atomic and unstructured composite data types, we can create structured composite data types. In a structured data type, a name is given to a group of components that have a specific arrangement. The group can be accessed as a whole, or each individual component can be accessed separately.

The one-dimensional array data type gives a name to a sequential group of components. Each component can be accessed by its relative position within the group, and each component is a variable of the component type. To access a particular component, we give the name of the array and an index that specifies which one of the group we want. The index must be of the index type, which can be any ordinal type. Therefore, the components in an array can be accessed sequentially by stepping through the values of the index type.

▪ Quick Check

1. Define an array data type called Quiz that will contain twelve components indexed by the integers 21 through 32. The component type is Boolean. (pp. 479–482)

2. If an array is to hold the number of correct answers given by students to each question on a twenty-question true/false quiz, what data types should be used for the indices and components of the array? (pp. 479–482)

3. Given the definitions

```
CONST
  Max_Length = 30;

TYPE
  Index_Range = 1..Max_Length;
  Name_String = ARRAY[Index_Range] OF Char;

VAR
  First_Name:
    Name_String;
```

write an assignment statement that will store 'A' in the first component of array First_Name. (pp. 482–483)

4. Given the declarations in Question 3, write a Writeln statement that will print the value of the fourteenth component of array First_Name. (pp. 482–483)

5. Given the declarations in Question 3, write a FOR statement that will fill array First_Name with blanks. (pp. 485–491)

6. Given the declarations in Question 3 and the following program fragment, which reads characters into array First_Name until a blank is encountered, write a FOR statement that will print out the portion of the array that is filled with input data. (pp. 491–492)

```
List_Length := 0;
REPEAT
  Read(Letter);
  IF Letter <> ' '
    THEN
      BEGIN
        List_Length := List_Length + 1;
        First_Name[List_Length] := Letter
      END
UNTIL Letter = ' ';
```

7. Define two parallel arrays indexed by the integers 1 through 100. One of the arrays will contain student numbers (type Integer); the other will consist of values of the enumerated type defined by

```
TYPE
  Gender = (Female, Male);
```

(pp. 491–492)

8. Define an array data type in which the index values represent the musical notes A through G (excluding sharps and flats), and the component type is Real. (pp. 491–492)

Answers

1. ```
   TYPE
     Quiz = ARRAY[21..32] OF Boolean;
   ```
2. The index type is 1..20; the component type is Integer.
   ```

```
3. First_Name[1] := 'A';
4. Writeln(First_Name[14]);
5. FOR Index := 1 TO Max_Length DO
      First_Name[Index] := ' ';
6. FOR Index := 1 TO List_Length DO
      Write(First_Name[Index]);
7. TYPE
     Gender = (Female, Male);
     Index = 1..100;
     Students = ARRAY[Index] OF Integer;
     Genders = ARRAY[Index] OF Gender;
   VAR
     Number:            (* Student numbers for 100 students *)
       Students;
     Sex:               (* Gender for the same 100 students *)
       Genders;
8. TYPE
     Note_Range = 'A'..'G';
     Notes = Array[Note_Range] OF Real;
```

■ *Exam Preparation Exercises*

1. Every component in an array must have the same type, which is fixed at compile time, but the type of the indices may vary during execution. (True or False?)

2. Both the indices and the components must be an ordinal type. (True or False?)

3. Write a code fragment to do the following tasks:
   a. Define a subrange data type Score_Range to be from 0 to 100.
   b. Define an array data type Student_Scores of length Max_Length. The components are of type Score_Range.
   c. Declare an array variable Quiz_One to be of the type Student_Scores.

4. Write a code fragment to do the following tasks:
   a. Define an enumerated type Bird_Type made up of bird names.
   b. Define an integer array data type Siting_Type indexed by Bird_Type.
   c. Declare an array variable Sitings of type Siting_Type.

5. Given the declarations

```
CONST
  Max_Length = 100;

TYPE
  Colors = (Blue, Green, Gold, Orange, Purple,
            Red, White, Black);
  Range = 1..Max_Length;
  Rainbow_Type = ARRAY[Range] OF Colors;
  Count_Type = ARRAY[Colors] OF Integer;
```

```
VAR
  Count:
    Count_Type;
  Rainbow:
    Rainbow_Type;
```

answer the following questions:

a. How many variables are there of type Colors?

b. How many Integer variables are there?

c. What is the index type of the array variable Count?

d. What is the index type of the array variable Rainbow?

e. How many components are there in the array variable Count?

f. How many components are there in the array variable Rainbow?

6. Using the declarations in exercise 5, write code fragments to do the following tasks:

a. Initialize Count to all zeros.

b. Initialize Rainbow to all white.

c. Count the number of times green appears in Rainbow.

d. Print the value in Count indexed by blue.

e. Total the values in Count.

7. What is the output of the following program? The data for the program is given below it.

```
PROGRAM Exercise (Input, Output);
TYPE
  List = Array [1..100] OF Integer;
VAR
  A,
  B:
    List;
  J,
  M,
  Sum_A,
  Sum_B,
  Sum_Difference:
    Integer;
BEGIN
  Sum_Difference := 0;
  Sum_A := 0;
  Sum_B := 0;
  Readln(M);
  FOR J := 1 TO M DO
    BEGIN
      Readln(A[J], B[J]);
      Sum_A := Sum_A + A[J];
      Sum_B := Sum_B + B[J];
      Sum_Difference := Sum_Difference + (A[J] - B[J])
    END;
  FOR J := 1 TO M DO
    Writeln(A[J]:6, B[J]:6, A[J] - B[J]:6);
  Writeln;
  Writeln(Sum_A:6, Sum_B:6, Sum_Difference:6);
END.
```

Data

```
    5
11   15
19   14
 4    2
17    6
 1    3
```

8. Declare array variables for each of the following situations. Be sure to use proper style.
   a. A twenty-four-component Real array for which the index goes from 1 to 24.
   b. A twenty-four-component Integer array for which the index goes from 24 to 47.
   c. A twenty-six-component Boolean array for which the index goes from 'A' to 'Z'.
   d. A ten-component Char array for which the index goes from −10 to −1.

9. Given the declarations

```
TYPE
   Arr_Type = Array [1..8] OF Integer;
VAR
   Sample:
      Arr_Type;
   I,
   K:
      Integer;
```

show the contents of the array Sample after the following code segment is executed. Use a question mark to indicate any undefined elements.

```
FOR K := 1 TO 8 DO
   Sample[K] := 10 - K
```

10. Using the same declarations given for Exercise 9, show the contents of the array Sample after the following code segment is executed.

```
FOR I := 1 TO 8 DO
   IF I <= 3
      THEN
         Sample[I] := 1
      ELSE
         Sample[I] := -1
```

▪ Programming Warm-Up Exercises

Use the following declarations in exercises 1−8. You may declare any other variables that you need.

```
CONST
   Max_Length = 100;
```

```
TYPE
  Index_Type = 1..Max_Length;
  Fail_Type = ARRAY[Index_Type] OF Boolean;
  Pass_Type = ARRAY[Index_Type] OF Boolean;
  Score_Type = ARRAY[Index_Type] OF Integer;

VAR
  Failing:
    Fail_Type;
  Passing:
    Pass_Type;
  Grade:
    Integer;
  List_Length:
    Index_Type;
  Score:
    Score_Type;
```

1. Write a Pascal procedure that will initialize Failing to False. Pass List_Length and Failing as parameters.

2. Write a Pascal procedure that has Failing, Score, and List_Length as parameters. Set Failing to True wherever the parallel value of Score is less than 60.

3. Write a Pascal procedure that has Passing, Score, and List_Length as parameters. Set Passing to True wherever the parallel value of Score is greater than or equal to 60.

4. Write a Pascal function Talley_Pass that takes Passing and List_Length as parameters, and returns the number of components in Passing that are True.

5. Write a Pascal function Error that takes Passing, Failing, and List_Length as parameters. Error is True if any parallel components are the same.

6. Write a Pascal procedure that takes Score, Passing, Grade, and List_Length as parameters. The procedure should set Passing to True wherever the parallel value of Score is greater than Grade.

7. Write a Pascal procedure that takes Grade, List_Length, and Score as parameters. The function should return the number of values in Score that are greater than or equal to Grade.

8. Write a Pascal procedure that takes Score and List_Length as parameters, and reverses the order of the components in Score; that is, Score[1] goes into Score[List_Length], Score[2] goes into Score[List_Length − 1], and so on.

▪ *Programming Problems*

1. Modify Program Count_All so that its output is the same as Program Char_Count; that is, print the frequency of occurrence of a specified list of characters.

2. The local baseball team is computerizing its records. You are to write a program that computes batting averages. There are twenty players on the team, identified by the numbers 1 through

20. Their batting records are coded on a file as follows. Each line contains four numbers: the player's identification number and the number of hits, walks, and outs he or she made in a particular game.

Example

3   2   1   1

The example above indicates that during a game, player number 3 was at bat four times and made 2 hits, 1 walk, and 1 out. For each player there are several records on the file. Each player's batting average is computed by adding the player's total number of hits and dividing by the total number of times at bat. A walk does not count as either a hit or a time at bat when the batting average is being calculated. Your program prints a table showing each player's identification number, batting average, and number of walks.

3. An advertising company wants to send a letter to all its clients announcing a new fee schedule. The clients' names are on several different lists in the company. The various lists are merged to form one file, Client_Names, but obviously, the company does not want to send a letter twice to anyone.

   Write a program that removes any names appearing on the list more than once. On each line of data, there is a four-digit code number, followed by a blank and then the client's name. For example, Amalgamated Steel is listed as

0231 Amalgamated Steel

4. Write a program that calculates the mean and standard deviation of reals stored in a file. The output should be of type Real, and should be properly labeled and formatted to two decimal places. The formula for calculating the mean of a series of reals is to add all the numbers, then divide by the number of integers. Expressed in mathematical terms, this is

$$\overline{X} = \frac{\sum_{i=1}^{N} X_i}{N}$$

   To calculate the standard deviation of a series of reals, subtract the mean from each real (you may get a negative number) and square the result, add all these squared differences, divide by the number of integers minus one, then take the square root of the result. Expressed in mathematical terms, this is

$$S = \sqrt{\frac{\sum_{i=1}^{N} (X_i - \overline{X})^2}{N - 1}}$$

5. One of the local banks is gearing up for a big advertising campaign and would like to see how long its customers are waiting for service at drive-in windows. Several employees have been asked to keep accurate records for the twenty-four-hour drive-in service. The collected information, which is read from a file, consists of the time when the customer arrived in hours, minutes, and seconds; the time when the customer was actually served; and the ID number of the teller. Write a program that does the following:
   a. Reads in the wait data.
   b. Computes the wait time in seconds.
   c. Calculates the mean, standard deviation (the square root of the sum of the squares of the differences between each value and the average divided by the number of values minus one), and range.

d. Prints a single-page summary showing the values calculated in c.

Input

The first data line contains a title.

The remaining lines each contain a teller ID, an arrival time, and a service time. The times are broken up into hours, minutes, and seconds according to a twenty-four-hour clock.

Processing

Calculate the mean and the standard deviation.

Locate the shortest wait time and the longest wait time for any number of records up to 100.

Output

The input data (echo print).

The title.

The following values, all properly labeled: number of records, mean, standard deviation, and range (minimum and maximum).

6. Your history professor has so many students in her class that she has trouble determining how well the class does on exams. She has found out that you are a computer whiz and has asked you to write a program to do some simple statistical analyses on exam scores. Your program must work for any class size up to 100 (0 < N < 100). Write and test a computer program that does the following:

a. Reads the test grades from file Data.

b. Calculates the class mean, standard deviation, and percentage of the test scores falling in the ranges <10, 10–19, 20–29, 30–39, . . . , 80–89, and >=90.

c. Prints a summary showing the mean and the standard deviation, as well as a histogram showing the percentage distribution of test scores.

Input

The first data line contains the number of exams to be analyzed and a title for the report.

The remaining lines have ten test scores on each line until the last, and one to ten scores on the last. The scores are all integers.

Output

The input data as they are read.

A report consisting of the title that was read from data, the number of scores, the mean, the standard deviation (labeled), and the histogram.

7. A small postal system ships packages within your state. Acceptance of parcels is subject to the following constraints:

a. Parcels are not to exceed a weight of 50 pounds.

b. Parcels are not to exceed 3 feet in length, width, or depth, and may not have a combined length and girth exceeding 6 feet. (The girth of a package is the circumference of the package around its two smallest sides; the mathematical formula is

$$\text{Girth} = 2 * (S1 + S2 + S3 - \text{Largest})$$

where Largest is the largest of the three parcel dimensions, S1, S2, and S3.)

Your program should process a transaction file containing one entry for each box mailed during the week. Each entry contains a transaction number, followed by the weight of the box and its dimensions (in no particular order). The program should print the transaction number, weight, and postal charge for all accepted packages, and the transaction number and weight for all rejected packages. At the end of the report, the program must print the number of packages processed and the number rejected.

Input

Parcel post table—weight and cost (contains twenty-five pairs of values). This table should be stored in two one-dimensional arrays. The postal cost of each parcel can then be determined by first searching the Weight array and then using the corresponding element in the Cost array. If a package weight falls between weight categories in the table, your program should use the cost for the higher weight.

Transaction file—transaction number, weight, and three dimensions for an arbitrary number of transactions. Assume that all weights are whole numbers, and that all dimensions are given to the nearest inch.

Output

First line—appropriate headings.

Next N records—transaction number, whether accepted or rejected; weight; and cost.

Last line—number of packages processed, number of packages rejected.

8. The final exam in your psychology class is thirty multiple-choice questions. Your instructor says that if you write the program to grade the finals, you won't have to take it.

Input

The first data line contains the key to the exam. The correct answers are the first thirty characters; they are followed by an integer number that says how many students took the exam (call it N).

The next N lines contain student answers in the first thirty character positions, followed by the student's name in the next ten character positions.

Output

For each student—the student's name; followed by the number of correct answers; followed by PASS if the number correct is 60 percent or better, or FAIL otherwise.

Applied Arrays: Lists and Strings

GOALS

- To be able to define an abstract data type.
- To be able to search a list for a component with a given value.
- To be able to sort the components of a list into ascending or descending order.
- To be able to insert a value into an ordered list.
- To be able to search an ordered list using the binary search algorithm.
- To be able to define and use character strings.

Chapter 11 introduced the concept of a one-dimensional array, a data structure that is a collection of components of the same type given a single name. In general, a one-dimensional array is the structure used to represent a list of items. In this chapter we examine some common algorithms that are applied again and again to data stored as a list in a one-dimensional array. These will be implemented as general-purpose procedures that can be modified easily to work with many types of lists.

We also consider the **character string,** a special kind of one-dimensional array that is used to process character information like words or names. We use a character string to rewrite procedure Get_Month in Program Birthday_Reminder, as promised in Chapter 10. We conclude with some case studies that make use of the procedures developed in this chapter.

The List: An Abstract Data Type

As we defined in Chapter 11, a one-dimensional array is a data structure that consists of a fixed number of homogeneous components. One use for an array is to store a list of values. We noted that a list may contain fewer values than the number of places reserved in the array. The variable List_Length keeps track of the number of values stored in the array, and subarray processing was employed in the case studies to prevent processing array components that were not part of the list of values. That is, the number of places in the array data type is fixed, but the number of values in the list stored there may vary.

In this chapter we formally define a list and develop a set of general purpose operations for creating and manipulating lists. By doing this, we are building an **abstract data type.**

Abstract Data Type   A class of data objects with a defined set of properties and a set of operations that process the data objects while maintaining the properties.

Notice that an abstract data type is not just a user-defined type; it also includes a set of operations to create and manipulate objects of the data type. To preserve the properties of the abstract data type, only these operations should be used to access it.

A list is an example of an abstract data type: It has the properties of homogeneity, order, and varying length. A list is a linear collection of components. By linear we mean that each component (except the first) has a unique component that comes before it and each component (except the last) has a unique component that comes after it. If we implement a list in an array, the components are arranged so that the predecessor and the successor of a component are physically before and after it. In Chapter 16, we introduce a way of implementing a list where the components are ordered logically rather than physically.

To complete the definition of the abstract data type list, we must add a set of operations that allow us to access and manipulate the list. The remainder of this section is devoted to developing and implementing some (but not all) of these operations.

*T*heoretical Foundations

Abstract Data Type Operator Classes

In general, the basic operations that are performed on an abstract data type fall into three categories: **constructors, observers,** and **iterators.**

Constructors   Operations that build new instances of an abstract data type (such as a list) or alter the state of an instance.

An operation that creates a new instance of an abstract data type (such as a list) is a primitive constructor. Other constructors are operations that insert an item into a list and delete an item from a list. An operation that takes two lists and merges them into a third list is a binary constructor.

Observers   Operations that allow us to observe the state of an abstract data type without changing it.

A Boolean function that returns True if a list is empty and False if it contains any components is an example of an observer. A Boolean function that tests to see if a certain value is in the list is another observer.

Iterator   Operations that allow us to process all the components in an abstract data type.

An operation that returns the first item in the list when it is called initially and returns the next one with each successive call is an iterator.

Sequential Search in an Unordered List

In Program Char_Count (Chapter 11) we used a procedure Scan_List that searched through an array of characters looking for a particular one. Scanning a list to find a particular value is part of many everyday tasks. We scan the television guide to see what time a program is aired. We scan a course syllabus to locate the current reading assignment.

We recode procedure Scan_List as a general-purpose sequential search procedure that can be used as a selector in any program that uses a list. To make it more general, we replace the problem-dependent variable names with general ones. The following definitions are assumed to be in the block that encloses this procedure (usually the main program).

```
CONST
  Max_Length = (* maximum possible number of components needed *)

TYPE
  Item_Type = (* some scalar type *)
  List_Type = ARRAY [1..Max_Length] OF Item_Type;
```

This general-purpose search procedure will need five parameters:

1. The array containing the list to be searched
2. The length of the list
3. The item being searched for
4. A flag telling whether or not the search was successful
5. The index indicating where the item was located (if found)

The array containing the list is made up of components of type Item_Type, and is itself of type List_Type.

We call the array List and the item being searched for Item. List_Length, Found, and Index serve the same purposes here as they did in procedure Scan_List; that is, Length is the number of components in the List, Found tells whether the item is in the List, and Index gives the location of Item if it is in the List.

Note that the two output parameters, Index and Found, are redundant. Index would be sufficient because the calling routine could check to see if Index was greater than List_Length. If it was, then Item was not found. We keep this redundancy, however, for clarity.

```
PROCEDURE Search (    List:               (* Array to be searched     *)
                        List_Type;
                      Item:               (* Value being searched for  *)
                        Item_Type;
                      List_Length:        (* Size of the list          *)
                        Integer;
                  VAR Index:              (* Location of value if found *)
                        Integer;
                  VAR Found:              (* True if value is found    *)
                        Boolean);

(* List is searched for Item. If Item is found, Found is True and     *)
(* Index gives the location. Otherwise, Found is False and Index is   *)
(* List_Length + 1 *)
```

```
BEGIN (* Search *)
   Found := False;
   Index := 0;
   WHILE (Index <= List_Length) AND NOT Found DO
      BEGIN
         Index := Index + 1;
         IF Item = List[Index]
            THEN
               Found := True
      END
END;  (* Search *)
```

We can use this sequential search procedure in any program requiring a list search. In this form, it will search a list of any ordinal type (Item_Type) for a value of that type (see Figure 12-1). When the procedure is used with a list of Real values, it must be modified so that the IF statement tests for near equality (for the reasons discussed in Chapter 8). In the following statement, it is assumed that Epsilon is defined as a global constant.

```
IF Abs(Item - List[Index]) < Epsilon
   THEN
      Found := True
```

This algorithm finds the first occurrence of the searched-for item. How can we modify it to find the last occurrence? We initialize Index to List_Length and decrement

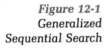

Figure 12-1
Generalized
Sequential Search

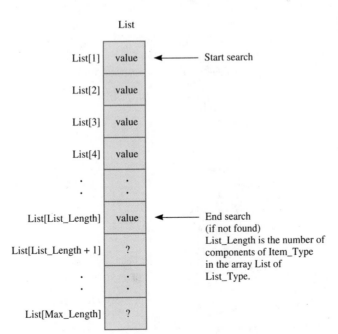

Index each time through the loop, stopping when we find the item we want or when Index becomes 0.

Before we leave this search algorithm, let's introduce a variation that makes the program more efficient, although a little more complex. The WHILE loop contains a compound condition: it stops when it either finds Item or reaches the end of List. If we insert a copy of Item into List[List_Length + 1], we guarantee that we will find Item in List. The condition that checks for the end of List (Index <= List_Length) can then be eliminated (see Figure 12-2). Eliminating a condition saves the machine time that would be required to test it. In this case, we save time during every iteration of the loop, so the savings add up quickly.

In storing a copy of Item in List[List_Length + 1], we assume that List_Length will always be less than Max_Length. This assumption must be included in the procedure documentation.

After the loop, Found can be set by checking to see if Index equals List_Length + 1. Procedure Search2 incorporates these changes.

```
PROCEDURE Search2 (    List:                 (* Array to be searched      *)
                         List_Type;
                       Item:                 (* Value being searched for   *)
                         Item_Type;
                       List_Length:          (* Size of the list           *)
                         Integer;
                   VAR Index:                (* Location of value if found *)
                         Integer;
                   VAR Found:                (* True if value is found      *)
                         Boolean);
```

Figure 12-2
Generalized
Sequential Search
with Item in Posi-
tion Length Plus
One

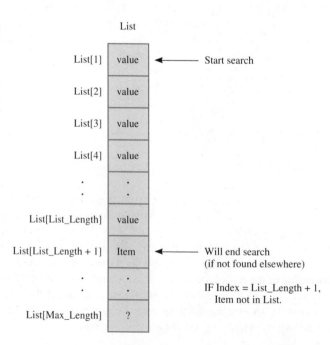

```
(* Item is inserted into List[List_Length+l]. List is searched for Item. If *)
(* Item is found somewhere other than in List[List_Length+l], Found is True *)
(* and Index says where. Otherwise, Found is False and Index is List_Length *)
(* + 1. Assumption:  List_Length is less than Max_Length *)

BEGIN (* Search2 *)
   Found := False;
   Index := 0;
   List[List_Length+l] := Item;
   (* Search List for Item *)
   WHILE NOT Found DO
      BEGIN
         Index := Index + 1;
         IF Item = List[Index]
            THEN
               Found := True
      END;
   Found := Index <> List_Length + 1
END;  (* Search2 *)
```

Sorting

Another task commonly performed on a list is ordering its components. For example, we might want to put a list of stock numbers in either ascending or descending order, or we might want to put a list of words in alphabetical order. Arranging values in order is known as **sorting** and is an example of a list constructor. In Chapter 10 we discussed the ordering inherent in any ordinal type. Because of this ordering, we can compare and sort, in ascending or descending order, values of any ordinal type.

If you were given a sheet of paper with a column of twenty numbers on it and were asked to write the numbers in ascending order, you would probably:

1. Look for the smallest number.
2. Write it on the paper in a second column.
3. Cross the number off the original list.
4. Repeat the process, always looking for the smallest number remaining on the original list.
5. Stop when all the numbers had been crossed off.

We can implement this algorithm directly in Pascal, but we need two arrays: one for the original list and a second for the ordered list. If the list is large, we might not have enough memory for two copies of it. It is also difficult to "cross off" a component. We would have to simulate this with some dummy value like MaxInt. We would set the value of the crossed-off variable to something that would not interfere with the processing of the rest of the components. A slight variation on this hand-done algorithm allows us to sort the components **in place.** This means that we do not have to use a second array because we can put a value in its proper place in the original list by having it swap places within the component that is there.

Figure 12-3
Straight Selection
Exchange Sort

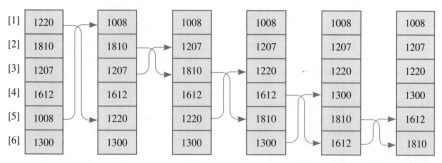

If our array is called List and contains List_Length values, we can state the algorithm as follows:

```
FOR Counter = 1 TO List_Length
   Find Minimum in List[Counter]..List[List_Length]
   Swap Minimum with List[Counter]
```

Figure 12-3 illustrates how this algorithm works.

This sort, known as straight selection, belongs to a class of sorts called exchange or interchange sorts. There are many types of sorting algorithms. Exchange sorts are characterized by exchanging pairs of components until the list is sorted. Exchanging the contents of two variables—two components in an array—requires a temporary variable so that no values are lost (see Figure 12-4).

Two parameters are needed for the exchange sorting procedure: the array containing the list to be sorted and the length of the list. As in the search procedures, we assume that a type called List_Type has been defined. The code for this sorting algorithm is:

```
PROCEDURE Ex_Sort (VAR List:  (* Array containing list to be searched     *)
                       List_Type;
                   List_Length:     (* Number of elements in the list *)
                       Integer);
```

Figure 12-4
Exchanging the
Contents of Two
Places

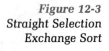

A→

1. Contents of A goes into Temp

2. Contents of
   B goes into A

B→

Temp

3. Contents of Temp
   goes into B

```
(* An unordered list with List_Length values is taken as input. The same *)
(* list with the components in ascending order is returned                *)

VAR
  Temp:                    (* Temporary variable      *)
    Item_Type;
  Pass_Count,              (* Loop control variable   *)
  Place_Count,             (* Loop control variable   *)
  Min_Index:               (* Index of minimum so far *)
    Integer;

BEGIN (* Ex_Sort *)
  FOR Pass_Count := 1 TO List_Length - 1 DO
    (* List[1]..List[Pass_Count-1] is already sorted and *)
    (* contains the Pass_Count - 1 smallest items         *)
    BEGIN
      Min_Index := Pass_Count;
      (* Find the index of the smallest component *)
      (* in List[Pass_Count]..List[List_Length]   *)
      FOR Place_Count := Pass_Count + 1 TO List_Length DO
        IF List[Place_Count] < List[Min_Index]
          THEN
            Min_Index := Place_Count;
      (* Swap List[Min_Index] and List[Pass_Count] *)
      Temp := List[Min_Index];
      List[Min_Index] := List[Pass_Count];
      List[Pass_Count] := Temp
    END
END; (* Ex_Sort *)
```

Note that the outer loop runs from 1 to List_Length − 1. Since the last value, (List [List_Length]), is in its proper place if the rest of the array is sorted, the loop does not need to be executed when Pass_Count = List_Length.

Note also that with each pass through the inner loop, we are looking for the minimum value in the rest of the array (List[Pass_Count]..List[List_Length]). Therefore Min_Index is initialized to Pass_Count and the inner loop runs from Place_Count equal to Pass_Count + 1 through List_Length.

The third point to note is that we may swap a component with itself. We can avoid such an unnecessary swap by checking to see if Min_Index is equal to Pass_Count. Since this comparison would have to be made during each iteration of the loop, it is more efficient not to check for this possibility and just to swap something with itself occasionally. If the components we are sorting are much more complex than simple numbers, we might reconsider this decision.

This algorithm sorts the components into ascending order. To sort them into descending order, we need to scan for the maximum value instead of the minimum value. Simply changing the relational operator in the inner loop from < to > will effect this change. Of course, Min_Index would no longer be a meaningful identifier and should be changed to Max_Index.

Sequential Search in a Sorted List

When we search for an item in an unordered list, we won't discover that the item is missing until we reach the end of the list. If the list is ordered, we know that an item is missing when we pass its correct place in the list. For example, if a list contains the values

```
  7
 11
 13
 76
 98
102
```

and we are looking for 12, we need only compare 12 with 7, 11, and 13 to know that 12 is not in the list.

If the item is greater than the current list component, we move on to the next component. If the item is equal to the current component, we have found what we are looking for. If the item is less than the current component, then we know that it is not in the list. In either of the last two cases, we stop looking. We can restate this algorithmically as follows.

Initialize Stop to False
WHILE NOT Stop AND more places to look
   IF Item > current component in List
     THEN increment current place
     ELSE Set Stop to True
Set Found to Item = current component

We can make this algorithm more efficient by removing the compound condition (AND more places to look), as we did in Search2. We store Item in List[List_Length + 1]. Stop is set to True if Item is less than or equal to the value in the current place in the list. On exit from the loop, we can set Found to be True if Item is equal to the current component and the current place is not List_Length + 1.

Initialize Stop to False
WHILE NOT Stop
   IF Item > current component in List
     THEN increment current place
     ELSE Set Stop to True
Set Found to (current place <= List_Length + 1)
            AND (Item = current component)

This search procedure needs the same parameters as the previous one. We must add the assumption that the list is sorted.

```
PROCEDURE Search_Ord (     List:         (* Array containing list to be searched *)
                             List_Type;
                           Item:          (* Value to be found                    *)
                             Item_Type;
                           List_Length:   (* Number of values in list             *)
                             Integer;
                       VAR Index:          (* Location of value if found           *)
                             Integer;
                       VAR Found:          (* True if value is found               *)
                             Boolean);

(* List is searched for an occurrence of Item. If Item is found, Found *)
(* is True and Index is the place in List where Item occurs. Otherwise *)
(* Found is False. Assumptions:  List is sorted in ascending order;     *)
(* List_Length is less than Max_Length *)

VAR
  Stop:              (* True when search terminates *)
    Boolean;

BEGIN  (* Search_Ord *)
  Index := 1;
  Stop := False;
  List[List_Length+1] := Item;
  (* Exit loop when value is found or not there *)
  WHILE NOT Stop DO
    (* Item is not in List[1]..List[Index-1] *)
    IF Item > List[Index]
      (* Item is not in List[1]..List[Index] *)
      THEN
        Index := Index + 1
      ELSE
        (* Item is either found or not there *)
        Stop := True;
  (* Determine whether Item was found or not there *)
  Found := (Index < List_Length + 1) AND (Item = List[Index])
END;   (* Search_Ord *)
```

On average, searching an ordered list in this way takes the same number of iterations to find an item as searching an unordered list. The advantage of this new algorithm is that we find out sooner if an item is missing. It is thus slightly more efficient; however, it works only on a sorted list.

Inserting into an Ordered List

What if we want to add a new value to an already sorted list? We can store the new value at List[List_Length + 1], increment Length, and sort the array again. However, such a solution is an inefficient way to solve the problem. Let's build another constructor, called Insert, that adds a value to a sorted list.

If we were to insert a value by hand into a sorted list, we would write the new value out to the side and draw a line showing where it belongs. We do this by scanning the list until we find a value greater than the one we are inserting. The new value goes in the list just before that point.

We can do something similar in our procedure. We can find the proper place in the list using the by-hand algorithm. Instead of writing the value to the side, we have to shift all the values larger than the new one down one place to make room for it. The main algorithm is expressed as follows, where Item is the value being inserted.

WHILE place not found AND more places to look
   IF Item > current component in List
      THEN increment current place
      ELSE place found
Shift remainder of List down
Insert Item
Increment List_Length

The algorithm for Shift List Down is

Set List[List_Length + 1] to List[List_Length]
Set List[List_Length]   to List[List_Length − 1]
    .   .
    .   .
    .   .
Set List[Index + 1]   to List[Index]

A DOWNTO version of the FOR loop can be used to shift the components in the list down one position. Insert Item and Increment List_Length can be coded directly. This algorithm is illustrated in Figure 12-5. There is something familiar about the WHILE loop in our algorithm: it is logically like the WHILE loop in Search_Ord. In Search_Ord we leave the loop either when we find Item, or when we pass the place in the list where Item belongs.

We can simply use Search_Ord to find the insertion place for us. On return from Search_Ord, if Found is False, Index is the place in List where Item should be inserted. If Found is True, we can either insert a second copy or skip the insertion, as we choose, as long as we document clearly what is done. Inserting a second copy seems more reasonable. Therefore Index is the insertion point, whether or not Item already exists in the list.

This procedure needs three parameters: the array containing the list, the number of components in the list, and the item being inserted. Again, we use the variable names List, Item, and List_Length. This time, List and List_Length must be VAR parameters because they are changed each time the procedure is invoked.

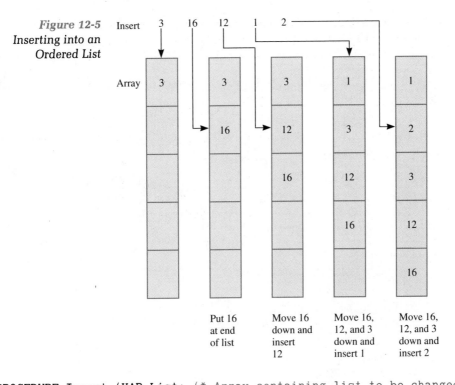

Figure 12-5
Inserting into an
Ordered List

PROCEDURE Insert (VAR List: (* Array containing list to be changed *)
                      List_Type;
                  VAR List_Length: (* Number of values in list   *)
                      Integer;
                      Item: (* Value to be inserted   *)
                      Item_Type);

(* Item is inserted into its proper place in the sorted list List.   *)
(* Assumption: List_Length is less than Max_Length. If a match occurs, *)
(* Item will be inserted before the one that is there *)

VAR
    Place_Found: (* True if value is found   *)
      Boolean;
    Index,   (* Current position in List *)
    Count: (* Loop control variable   *)
      Integer;

    (* ***)

```
PROCEDURE Search_Ord (      List:              (* Array containing list to be searched *)
                              List_Type;
                            Item:              (* Value to be found           *)
                              Item_Type;
                            List_Length:  (* Number of values in list      *)
                              Integer;
                        VAR Index:          (* Location of value if found    *)
                              Integer;
                        VAR Found:          (* True if value is found        *)
                              Boolean);

(* List is searched for an occurrence of Item. If Item is found,   *)
(* Found is True and Index is the place in List where Item occurs. *)
(* Otherwise Found is False and Index is where Item belongs.       *)
(* Assumption:  List is sorted in ascending order *)

VAR
  Stop:              (* True when search terminates *)
    Boolean;

BEGIN (* Search_Ord *)
  Index := 1;
  Stop := False;
  List[List_Length+1] := Item;
  (* Exit loop when value is found or not there *)
  WHILE NOT Stop DO        (* Item is not in List[1]..List[Index-1] *)
    IF Item > List[Index]
      THEN                         (* Item is not in List[1]..List[Index] *)
        Index := Index + 1
      ELSE                         (* Item is either found or not there *)
        Stop := True;
  (* Determine whether Item was found or not there *)
  Found := (Index <> List_Length + 1) AND (Item = List[Index])
END;  (* Search_Ord *)

(*********************************************************************)

BEGIN (* Insert *)
  Search_Ord(List, Item, List_Length, Index, Place_Found);
  (* Shift List[Index]..List[List_Length] down one *)
  FOR Count := List_Length DOWNTO Index DO
    List[Count+1] := List[Count];
  (* Insert Item *)
  List[Index] := Item;
  (* Increment List_Length *)
  List_Length := List_Length + 1
END;  (* Insert *)
```

Notice that this procedure works even if the list is empty. Search_Ord stores Item in List[1], where it is immediately found. On return from Search_Ord, Index is 1. Since Index is greater than the value of List_Length (which is 0), the FOR loop is not executed. Item is then stored in the first position in List, and List_Length is set to 1. This algorithm also works if Item is larger than any component in the list. When this happens, Index is List_Length + 1 and Item is placed at the end of the list.

This algorithm can be used as the basis for another sorting algorithm: an **insertion sort.** Values can be inserted one at a time into a list that was originally empty. An insertion sort is often used when input data must be sorted. Each value can be put into its proper place as it is read. We develop this sorting technique in the Exam Attendance case study at the end of this chapter.

Binary Search in an Ordered List

There is a second search algorithm on a sorted list that is considerably faster both for finding an item and for discovering that an item is missing. This selector algorithm is called a **binary search.** A binary search is based on the principle of successive approximation. It involves dividing the list in half (dividing by 2—that's why it's called *binary* search) and deciding which half to look in next. Division of the selected portion of the list is repeated until the item is found or it is determined that the item is not in the list.

This method is analogous to the way we look up a word in a dictionary. We open the dictionary in the middle and compare the word with one on the page that we turned to. If the word we're looking for comes before this word, we continue our search with the left-hand section of the dictionary. Otherwise, we continue with the right-hand section of the dictionary. We do this repeatedly until we find the word. If it is not there, we realize that either we have misspelled the word or our dictionary isn't complete.

The algorithm for a binary search is given below. The list of values is called List, and the value being looked for is called Item (see Figure 12-6).

1. Compare Item to List[Middle]. If Item = List[Middle], then we have found it. If Item < List[Middle], then look in the first half of List. If Item > List [Middle], then look in the second half of List.
2. Redefine List to be that half of List that we look in next, and repeat the process in step 1.

Figure 12-6
Binary Search

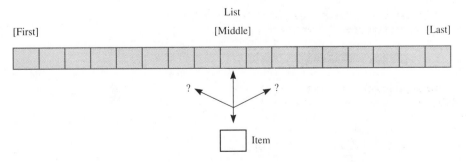

3. Stop when we have found Item or know it is missing. We know it's missing when there is nowhere else to look and we still have not found it.

This algorithm makes sense. With each comparison, at best, we find the item for which we are searching; at worst, we eliminate one half of the remaining List from consideration.

We need to keep track of the first possible place to look (First) and the last possible place to look (Last). This means that at any one time we are looking in List[First]..List[Last]. When this procedure is initialized, First is set to 1 and Last is set to the length of List.

This procedure needs the same five parameters as the previous search procedures: the array containing the list, the item, the length of the list, a Boolean flag that tells whether the item is found, and the position of the item in the list (if it is there).

```
PROCEDURE Bin_Search (      List:  (* Array containing list to be searched *)
                            List_Type;
                            Item:          (* Value to be found         *)
                            Item_Type;
                            List_Length:   (* Number of values in list  *)
                            Integer;
                       VAR Index:         (* Location of value if found *)
                            Integer;
                       VAR Found:         (* True if value is found     *)
                            Boolean);

(* List is searched for an occurrence of Item. If Item is found, Found *)
(* is True and Index gives the location of Item within List.           *)
(* Otherwise, Found is False and Index is undefined *)

VAR
  First,        (* Bound on list *)
  Last,         (* Bound on list *)
  Middle:       (* Middle index  *)
     Integer;
BEGIN (* Bin_Search *)
  First := 1;
  Last := List_Length;
  Found := False;
  WHILE (Last >= First) AND NOT Found DO
    BEGIN
      Middle := (First + Last) DIV 2;
      IF Item < List[Middle]
        (* Item is not in List[Middle]..List[Last] *)
        THEN
          Last := Middle - 1
        ELSE
          IF Item > List[Middle]
            (* Item is not in List[First]..List[Middle] *)
            THEN
              First := Middle + 1
            ELSE
              Found := True
```

```
    END;
  Index := Middle
END;  (* Bin_Search *)
```

Let's do a code walk-through of this algorithm. The value being searched for is 24. Figure 12-7a shows the values of First, Last, and Middle during the first iteration. In this iteration 24 is compared with 103, the value in List[Middle]. Since 24 is less than 103, Last becomes Middle − 1 and First stays the same. Figure 12-7b shows the situation during the second iteration. This time 24 is compared with 72, the value in List[Middle]. Since 24 is less than 72, Last becomes Middle − 1 and First again stays the same.

In the third iteration (Figure 12-7c), Middle and First are both 1. The value 24 is compared with 12, the value in List[Middle]. Since 24 is greater than 12, First becomes Middle + 1. In the fourth iteration (Figure 12-7d), First, Last, and Middle are all the same. Again 24 is compared with the value in List[Middle]. Since 24 is less than 64, Last becomes Middle − 1. This makes Last less than First, and the process stops. Found is False.

The binary search algorithm is the most complex algorithm that we have examined so far. The table below shows First, Last, Middle, and List[Middle] for searches of 106, 400, and 406, using the same data as in the previous example. Go over the results shown in this table carefully.

Item	First	Last	Middle	List[Middle]	Termination of Loop
106	1	11	6	103	
	7	11	9	200	
	7	8	7	106	Found = True
400	1	11	6	103	
	7	11	9	200	
	10	11	10	300	
	11	11	11	400	Found = True
406	1	11	6	103	
	7	11	9	200	
	10	11	10	300	
	11	11	11	400	
	12	11			Last < First
					Found = False

Notice that the loop never executed more than four times. It will never execute more than four times in a list of eleven components because the list is being cut in half each time through the loop. The table below compares a sequential search and a binary search in terms of the average number of iterations needed to find an item.

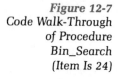

Figure 12-7
Code Walk-Through
of Procedure
Bin_Search
(Item Is 24)

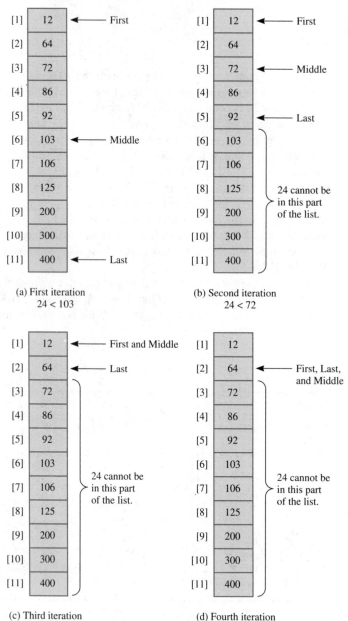

| | Average Number of Iterations | |
Length of List	Sequential Search	Binary Search
10	5.5	2.9
100	50.5	5.8
1000	500.5	9.0
10,000	5000.5	12.4

If the binary search is so much faster, why not use it all the time? It is certainly faster in terms of the number of times through the loop, but more computations are done within the binary search loop than in the other search algorithms. This means that if the number of components in the list is small (say, under twenty), the sequential search algorithms are faster because they do less work at each iteration. As the number of components in the list increases, the binary search algorithm becomes relatively more efficient. Remember, however, that the binary search requires the list to be sorted, and sorting itself takes time. Keep three factors in mind when you are deciding which search algorithm to use:

1. The length of the list to be searched
2. Whether or not the list is already ordered
3. The number of times the list is to be searched

*T*heoretical Foundations

Complexity of Searching and Sorting

We introduced Big-O notation in Chapter 5 as a way of comparing the work done by different algorithms. Let's apply it to the algorithms that we've developed in this chapter and see how they compare to each other. In each algorithm we start with a list containing some number of values. We'll refer to the number of values as N.

In the worst case, Procedure Search scans all N values to locate an item. Thus it requires N steps to execute. On average, Search takes roughly N/2 steps to find an item; however, recall that in Big-O notation, we ignore constant factors (as well as lower order terms). Thus, Procedure Search is an order N algorithm.

Search2 is also an order N algorithm because, even though we saved a comparison on each loop iteration, the same number of iterations are performed. However, making the loop more efficient without changing the number of iterations decreases the constant (the number of steps) that N is multiplied by in the algorithm's work formula. Procedure Search2 is thus said to be a constant factor faster than Search.

What about Search_Ord? The number of iterations is decreased for the case in which the item is missing from the list. However, all we have done is to take a case that would require N steps and reduce its time, on average, to N/2 steps. Thus, Search_Ord is also order N.

Now consider Bin_Search. In the worst case, it eliminates half of the remaining array components on each iteration. Thus, the worst case number of iterations is equal to the number of times N must be divided by 2 to eliminate all but one value. This number is computed by taking the logarithm, base 2, of N [written $\log_2(N)$]. Here are some examples of $\log_2(N)$ for different values of N:

N	$\log_2(N)$
2	1
4	2
8	3
16	4
32	5
1,024	10
32,768	15
1,048,576	20
33,554,432	25
1,073,741,824	30

As you can see, even for a list of over 1 billion values, Bin_Search takes only 30 iterations. It is definitely the best choice for searching large lists. Algorithms such as Bin_Search are said to be of **logarithmic order.**

Now let's turn to sorting. Procedure Ex_Sort contains a nested FOR loop. The total number of iterations is the product of the iterations performed by the two loops. The outer loop executes N − 1 times. The inner loop also starts out executing N − 1 times, but steadily decreases until it performs just one iteration: the inner loop executes N/2 iterations. The total number of iterations is thus

$$\frac{(N-1)*N}{2}$$

Ignoring the constant factors, this is N^2 iterations, and Ex_Sort is an order N^2 algorithm. Consider that, while Bin_Search takes only 30 iterations to search an ordered array of 1 billion values, putting the array into order takes Ex_Sort 1 billion times 1 billion iterations!

We mentioned that we would develop the technique of inserting values into an ordered list as they are input in a case study. In the meantime, we can consider the approach in the abstract. On average, Insert will have to shift down half of the values (N/2) in the list; thus, it is an order N algorithm. If Insert is called for each input value, we are executing an order N algorithm N times; therefore, sorting with insertion is an order N^2 algorithm.

Is every sorting algorithm order N^2? Most of the simpler ones are, but in Chapter 16, we introduce a **tree sort,** which is an order $N * \log_2(N)$ algorithm. Algorithms that are order $N * \log_2(N)$ are much closer in performance to order N algorithms than are order N^2 algorithms. For example, if N is one million, then an N^2 algorithm takes a million times a million (one trillion) iterations, but an $N\log_2(N)$ algorithm takes only twenty million iterations—it is twenty times slower than the order N algorithm but 50,000 times faster than the order N^2 algorithm.

Let's now turn our attention to a special kind of array that is useful when working with alphabetic data.

Working with Character Strings

In Standard Pascal we can specify that an array is to be **packed** by inserting the keyword PACKED before the word ARRAY in the type definition. The packed option tells the computer to put as many components as possible into each place in memory.

In Turbo Pascal, PACKED has no effect. However, packing an array of characters is useful even if no memory is saved. In Chapter 2 we introduced string constants; a packed array of characters is a **string variable.** We can assign a **string** (constant or variable) to a string variable, compare them, build a string character by character with array operations, and directly output a string variable just as we would a string constant. String variables are extremely useful in working with character information.

String   A collection of characters that is interpreted as a single data item; a packed character array.

In the declarations

```
CONST
   String_Length = 10;
TYPE
   Index_Range = 1..String_Length;
   String = PACKED ARRAY [Index_Range] OF Char;
VAR
   Word1,
   Word2,
   Word3,
   Word4:
     String;
```

Word1, Word2, Word3, and Word4 are string variables. They are still arrays, and each component character can be accessed separately using an index. For example, we can perform the following assignment,

```
Word1[10] := 'A'
```

which places the letter A in the tenth position of string Word1. In Standard Pascal, a component of a packed array may be passed to a value parameter; however, a component of a packed array *cannot* be passed to a VAR parameter. This restriction does not apply in Turbo Pascal.

Pascal allows us to assign string literals directly to string variables of the same size. The size of a string variable is the number of characters specified in the array definition of its type. If the string literal to be stored is shorter than the string variable, we must add blanks at the end of the string literal to make it the same length. Given the above declarations, the following are examples of valid and invalid assignment statements.

Statement	*Status*	*Reason*
Wordl := 'Tremendous'	Valid	Exactly 10 characters
Word2 := 'Big'	Invalid	Less than 10 characters
Word3 := 'Infinitesimal'	Invalid	More than 10 characters
Word4 := 'Small '	Valid	Exactly 10 characters (padded with blanks)

Like unpacked arrays, string variables of the same type can be assigned to one another. After the assignment

```
Wordl := Word4
```

Word1 contains 'Small   '.

The relational operators (= , <>, < = , > = , <, >) may be applied to strings of the same type. Strings are ordered according to the collating sequence of the character set. When two strings are compared, their characters are compared one by one, from left to right. The first unequal pair of characters determines the order. For example, given that Word1 and Word4 both now contain 'Small   ', the following expressions would return the results indicated:

Statement	*Result*	
Wordl <> Word4	False	(They are equal.)
Word4 <= 'Tremendous'	True	('S' comes before 'T'.)
Wordl = 'Tremendous'	False	(They are not equal.)
'Big ' < Wordl	True	('B' comes before 'S'.)
Wordl = 'SMALL '	False	('M' <> 'm')

We can print string variables directly. For example,

```
Writeln('The world is ', Word4, '.')
```

would output

```
The world is Small
```

However, we cannot read strings directly. They must be input one character at a time, in a loop.

The following program, which reads in characters and writes them out again, gives an example of declaring and using strings.

```
PROGRAM Read_Write (Input, Output);

(* This program reads in 15 characters, stores them in a string, and *)
(* prints the string *)

CONST
  Heading = 'Good morning,';              (* Define a string constant *)

TYPE
  Index_Range = 1..15;
  String15 = PACKED ARRAY [Index_Range] OF Char;    (* A string type *)

VAR
  Count:           (* Index into the string *)
    Integer;
  Message:         (* A string variable     *)
    String15;

BEGIN  (* Read_Write *)
  Writeln(Heading);                               (* String constant *)
  Writeln('Input message with exactly 15 characters.');
  (* Input message *)
  FOR Count := 1 TO 15 DO
    Read(Message[Count]);
  (* Output message *)
  Writeln(' The message is: ', Message)           (* String variable *)
END.  (* Read_Write *)
```

Note: String variable Message can
be printed directly by using
the array variable name
without subscripts.

Given the input data

```
Have a nice day
```

the output from the program would be

```
Good morning,
Input message with exactly 15 characters
 The message is: Have a nice day
```

Turbo Pascal also provides a nonstandard type called String. This type is somewhat different from the character arrays that Standard Pascal calls strings. Essentially, the Turbo Pascal string facility provides variable length character string operations as predefined procedures, functions, and operators. These are discussed here because of their great convenience. Keep in mind, however, that these capabilities are entirely nonstandard and are not likely to work under any other Pascal system.

When we define a String type in Turbo Pascal, the maximum length of a string value must be specified; which can be at most 255 characters. For example, if we wish to define a string type called Name that may contain up to 30 characters, we write

```
TYPE
  Name = String[30];
```

A string literal may then be assigned to a variable of this type. For example, if First_Name is of type Name,

```
First_Name := 'Shannon';
```

assigns the string 'Shannon' to First_Name. Notice the difference between a Turbo Pascal String variable and a packed array of characters: Turbo String variables may be assigned a string literal of any size up to whatever length has been specified, whereas a packed array of characters must always be assigned a value of its declared length. Turbo Pascal also permits us to assign a character array to a String (the character array will be truncated if it is too long); an array variable, however, cannot be assigned the value of a String variable.

Each String in Turbo Pascal always occupies as much memory as is required to hold the specified maximum number of characters. Thus, in the preceding example, the string occupies 30 character positions in memory even though its length is only seven characters. The other 23 positions are kept in reserve, in case we should ever store a 30-character string in First_Name. (Each string actually occupies one additional memory location that is used to hold its length. Thus a variable of type Name actually occupies 31 locations in memory.)

Given the declaration below

```
TYPE
  Array10 = PACKED ARRAY [1..10] OF Char;
  Array20 = PACKED ARRAY [1..20] OF Char;
  String10 = String[10];
  String20 = String[20];

VAR
  A10 : Array10;
  A20 : Array20;
  S10 : String10;
  S20 : String20;
```

the following are examples of valid and invalid statements.

Statement	Status	Reason
`A10 := 'Tremendous'`	Valid	Exactly 10 characters
`A10 := 'Big'`	Invalid	Less than 10 characters
`S10 := 'Big'`	Valid	String type variable
`A10 := 'Small     '`	Valid	Exactly 10 characters (padded with blanks)
`A10 := 'Infinitesimal'`	Invalid	More than 10 characters
`A10 := S10`	Invalid	Cannot assign string to array
`S10 := A10`	Valid	Can assign array to string
`S20 := A10`	Valid	Can assign array to string
`S10 := A20`	Valid	The array is truncated to 10 characters

The relational operators ($=$, $<>$, $<=$, $>=$, $<$, $>$) also may be applied to Turbo Pascal Strings. The only difference is that if a comparison is equal up to the end of a shorter string, the shorter string is less than the longer string. For example, given that A10 contains 'Small   ' and S10 contains 'Small', the following expressions would return the results indicated:

Statement	Result	
`S10 <> 'Small'`	False	(They are equal.)
`A10 <= 'Tremendous'`	True	('S' comes before 'T'.)
`A10 = 'Tremendous'`	False	(They are not equal.)
`'Big     ' < A10`	True	('B' comes before 'S'.)
`S10 = 'SMALL'`	False	('M' $<>$ 'm')
`A10 < S10`	False	(S10 is shorter)

Just as with character arrays, we can print String variables directly. For example,

```
Writeln('The world is ', S10, '.')
```

would output

```
The world is Small.
```

In addition, Turbo Pascal String variables can be read in directly. When read, they are filled with characters from the input file until the String variable is full or EOLN or EOF has been encountered.

Turbo Pascal includes several predefined functions, procedures, and operators for manipulating strings. Here is a list of the most useful of them.

Functions

Length(String_Var): Returns the number of characters contained in String_Var.

Pos(String1, String2): String2 is searched for an occurrence of String1. Pos returns the location of the first character that matches in String2. If no match is found, Pos returns 0.

Concat(String1, String2, ...): Returns a string consisting of the contents of its parameters, joined together in the order in which they are listed (concatenation).

Copy(String_Exp, Start_Position, Num_Chars): Returns a portion of String_Exp that is Num_Chars long, beginning at Start_Position.

Procedures

Delete(String_Var, Start_Position, Num_Chars): Deletes a portion of String_Var that is Num_Chars long, beginning at Start_Position.

Insert(String1, String2, Position): Inserts a copy of String1 into String2, beginning at Position.

Str(Value, String_Var): "Writes" the Real or Integer expression Value into String_Var. Str produces the same format as the Write statement. Fieldwidth notation may be used with the Str procedure. For example, if the variable Pi contains the Real value 3.14159265, then

```
Str(Pi:8:6, String_Var)
```

writes the string '3.141592' into String_Var.

Val(String_Exp, Num_Var, Code): "Reads" the Real or Integer expression in String_Exp into Num_Var. Val interprets the numeric characters in String_Exp like the Read statement would, according to the type of Num_Var. If an error is detected, such as nonnumeric characters in the string, Code will contain the character position of the error. If there is no error, zero is returned in Code.

Operators

Turbo Pascal also redefines the + operator to concatenate strings as in the Concat function. Thus we can have

```
'Turbo' + 'Pascal' = Concat('Turbo', 'Pascal')
```

Turbo Pascal strings may be accessed as arrays. That is a string variable may be followed by an Integer index in square brackets. The index range for a string is zero through the length specified for the string. (The Ord of the element at index zero is equal to the length of the string.) For example, we can write

```
First_Name := 'Lisa';
Write(First_Name[2]);
```

which causes the letter 'i' to be printed.

The following program gives an example of declaring and using strings.

```
PROGRAM String_Example (Input, Output);

(* This program reads a first, middle, and last name as a *)
(* single string and then outputs the name in 3 different *)
(* formats to demonstrate the use of various string       *)
(* functions and procedures. In some cases we             *)
(* have sacrificed efficiency in order to show the use of *)
(* additional procedures or functions *)

TYPE
  Long_String = String[80];

VAR
  Name,             (* The input name                *)
  First,            (* The extracted first name      *)
  Middle,           (* The extracted middle name     *)
  Last,             (* The extracted last name       *)
  Form:             (* The formatted output name     *)
    Long_String;
  Blank_Pos:        (* The position of a blank in a string *)
    Integer;

BEGIN  (* String_Example *)
  Writeln('Enter your first, middle, and last name, ',
          'each separated by a single blank:');
  Readln(Name);
  (* Find the blank between the first and middle names *)
  Blank_Pos := Pos(' ', Name);
  (* Copy the characters preceding the blank into First *)
  First := Copy(Name, 1, Blank_Pos-1);
  (* Delete the first name and blank from the input name *)
  Delete(Name, 1, Blank_Pos);
  (* Find the blank between the middle and last names *)
  Blank_Pos :=Pos(' ', Name);
  (* Copy the characters preceding the blank into Middle *)
  Middle := Copy(Name, 1, Blank_Pos-1);
  (* Copy the characters following the blank into Last *)
  Last := Copy(Name, Blank_Pos+1, Length(Name));
  (* Format the output name as Last, First *)
  Form := Last + ', ' + First;
  Writeln(Form);
  (* Append the middle initial to the output name *)
  Form := Concat(Form, ' ', Middle[1], '.');
  Writeln(Form);
  (* Delete the middle initial and insert the middle name *)
  (* between the first and last names *)
  Delete(Form, Length(Form)-2, Length(Form));
  Insert(', ' + Middle, Form, Length(Last)+1);
  Writeln(Form)
END. (* String_Example *)
```

Given the input data

```
Gabriel Daniel Fahrenheit
```

the output from the program would be

```
Fahrenheit, Gabriel
Fahrenheit, Gabriel D.
Fahrenheit, Daniel, Gabriel
```

PROBLEM-SOLVING CASE STUDY

Birthday Reminder Revisited

Problem: Rewrite procedure Get_Month, from the Birthday Reminder case study in Chapter 10, so that it uses strings to convert the input month to a value of enumerated type Month. Rerun the program without making any other changes.

Discussion: Program Birthday_Reminder inputs a month and prints a list of friends' birthdays that month. The characters in the month's name are read one at a time until the program recognizes the month, and any remaining characters in the month are ignored. Now that we know how to use strings, we can read the entire month name into a string variable and process it as a whole word rather than decoding it character by character.

We have an array of strings containing the months of the year. A month is read into a string variable. Procedure Search is used to search the array for the input string. If it is found, Index is used to access a parallel array containing the enumerated type Months. In other words, we convert the months in string form to the equivalent months in the enumerated type by using parallel arrays, one containing strings and the other containing the enumerated equivalents. If the string is not found, an error message can be issued and the user prompted to reenter the month.

Data Structures:

An array of strings containing the months of the year.
An array containing the enumerated data type made up of the months of the year.

The two arrays look like Figure 12-8. Although these two arrays look similar, they have quite different representations in the computer. One contains the months in character form; the other contains the months in the form of an enumerated data type.

Let's call the string representation of a month S_Month and the enumerated version Month, as it is called in Program Birthday_Reminder. The array of strings can be called S_Month_Ary, and the parallel array can be called Month_Ary. The algorithm for Get_Month using this structure is as follows:

PROBLEM-SOLVING CASE STUDY *cont'd.*

Figure 12-8
Data Structures for
Program Get_Month

[1]	'January '
[2]	'February '
[3]	'March '
[4]	'April '
[5]	'May '
[6]	'June '
[7]	'July '
[8]	'August '
[9]	'September '
[10]	'October '
[11]	'November '
[12]	'December '

[1]	January
[2]	February
[3]	March
[4]	April
[5]	May
[6]	June
[7]	July
[8]	August
[9]	September
[10]	October
[11]	November
[12]	December

Get Month   *Level 1*

```
REPEAT
   Get S_Month
   Search(S_Month_Ary, S_Month, 12, Index, Found)
   IF Found
      THEN
         Set Month to Month_Ary[Index]
      ELSE
         Write error message
UNTIL Found
```

Get Month   *Level 2*

```
Prompt for month
Read S_Month
```

Now we can code the new procedure Get_Month. We must remember to initialize the arrays S_Month_Ary and Month_Ary.

```
PROCEDURE Get_Month (VAR Month:     (* Returns month in enumerated form *)
                          Months);

(* The user is prompted to enter a month. If the month is valid, the  *)
(* corresponding user-defined month is returned. Otherwise the user    *)
(* is prompted to try again *)

TYPE
  String9 = String[9];
  Months_In_Char_Form = ARRAY [1..12] OF String9;
  Months_In_Enum_Form = ARRAY [1..12] OF Months;
  List_Type = Months_In_Char_Form;
  Item_Type = String9;

VAR
  S_Month:                  (* Input month in string form            *)
    String9;
  Month_Ary:                (* Table of months in enumerated form    *)
    Months_In_Enum_Form;
  S_Month_Ary:              (* Parallel table of months in string format *)

  (*******************************************************************)


  PROCEDURE Get_S_Month (VAR S_Month:        (* Input month string   *)
                             String9);

  (* Reads in a month in character form *)

  VAR
    Count:          (* Loop control variable *)
      Integer;
  BEGIN (* Get_S_Month *)
    Writeln('Please enter month, capitalizing first letter.');
    Readln(S_Month)
  END;  (* Get_S_Month *)

  (*******************************************************************)


  PROCEDURE Initialize (VAR S_Month_Ary:    (* Table of strings      *)
                            Months_In_Char_Form;
                        VAR Month_Ary:       (* Table of enum. values *)
                            Months_In_Enum_Form);
```

PROBLEM-SOLVING CASE STUDY *cont'd.*

```
BEGIN (* Initialize *)
  S_Month_Ary[1] := 'January';
  S_Month_Ary[2] := 'February';
  S_Month_Ary[3] := 'March';
  S_Month_Ary[4] := 'April';
  S_Month_Ary[5] := 'May';
  S_Month_Ary[6] := 'June';
  S_Month_Ary[7] := 'July';
  S_Month_Ary[8] := 'August';
  S_Month_Ary[9] := 'September';
  S_Month_Ary[10] := 'October';
  S_Month_Ary[11] := 'November';
  S_Month_Ary[12] := 'December';
  Month_Ary[1] := January;
  Month_Ary[2] := February;
  Month_Ary[3] := March;
  Month_Ary[4] := April;
  Month_Ary[5] := May;
  Month_Ary[6] := June;
  Month_Ary[7] := July;
  Month_Ary[8] := August;
  Month_Ary[9] := September;
  Month_Ary[10] := October;
  Month_Ary[11] := November;
  Month_Ary[12] := December;
END;  (* Initialize *)

(*****************************************************************)


BEGIN (* Get_Month *)
  Initialize(S_Month_Ary, Month_Ary);
  REPEAT
    Get_SMonth(S_Month);
    Search(S_Month_Ary, S_Month, 12, Index, Found);
    IF Found
      THEN
        Month := Month_Ary[Index]
      ELSE
        Writeln('Month is misspelled.')
  UNTIL Found
END;  (* Get_Month *)
```

Because Program Birthday_Reminder is so long, it is not repeated here. Notice that S_Month_Ary is an array of arrays—making it a **two-dimensional array.** We return to this subject in Chapter 13.

PROBLEM-SOLVING CASE STUDY

Exam Attendance

Problem: You are the grader for a U.S. government class. The teacher has asked you to prepare two lists: students taking an exam and students who have missed it. The catch is that he wants the lists before the exam is over. You decide to write a program for your portable computer that takes each student's name as the student enters the exam room, and that prints the lists of absentees and attendees for your teacher.

Input:

A list of the students in the class (file Roster)
Each student's name as he or she enters the room (Input)

Output:

A list of those students taking the exam
A list of those students who are absent

Discussion: How would you do this by hand? You would stand at the door with a class roster. As each student came in, you would check off his or her name. When all the students had entered, you would go through the roster, making a list of those present. Then you would do the same for those who are absent.

This by-hand algorithm can serve as a model for your program. As each student enters the room, you enter his or her name at the keyboard. Your program scans the list of students for that name and marks that the student is present. When the last student has entered, you can enter a special name, perhaps EndData, to signal the program to print the lists.

"Mark that the student is present" can be simulated by having a parallel array made up of the two values Present and Absent. This array is initialized to Absent; when a name is found in the list of students, the corresponding position in the second array is set to Present.

You will have to prepare the list of students in advance from the class roster, which is ordered by social security number. If you enter the names directly from the roster, they will not be in alphabetical order. Does that matter? Yes, in this case it does matter. The size of the class is 200, and the students need to enter the exam room with minimum delay (since most arrive just before the exam starts).

The size of the list and the speed required suggest that a binary search should be used. A binary search requires that the list be in sorted form. You decide to create the file with the names in order by social security number, and have the program sort them alphabetically. All the names can be input at once and sorted using procedure ExSort, or each name can be put into its proper place as it is read using procedure Insert. You decide to take the second approach.

PROBLEM-SOLVING CASE STUDY *cont'd.*

Data Structures:

A one-dimensional array of names (Student).
A one-dimensional array of "checks" (Attendance).
A temporary string to read names into (Name).

Figure 12-9 pictures the data structures used in this program.

Main   *Level 0*

> Get Class Roster
> Check in Students
> Print List(s)

Get Class Roster (Receives Students : List_Type   *Level 1*
                                    List_Length : Integer
                                    Roster : Text

> WHILE more names on roster (NOT EOF(Roster)) DO
>   Get Name
>   Insert Name into lists of students

The decision to use a signal string to end the data requires a priming Read in Check In Students. Name must have a value on entering the loop. A prompt to the student should also be included.

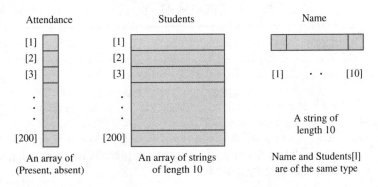

Figure 12-9
Data Structures for
Program Exam

Attendance
[1]
[2]
[3]
·
·
·
[200]
An array of
(Present, absent)

Students
[1]
[2]
[3]
·
·
·
[200]
An array of strings
of length 10

Name
[1]   · ·   [10]
A string of
length 10
Name and Students[1]
are of the same type

Check in Students (Receives Students : List_Type
List_Length : Integer
Receives/Returns Attendance : Check_Type)

```
Write 'Enter last name'
Get Name
WHILE more students (Name <> 'EndData      ') DO
  Process Name
  Write 'Enter last name'
  Get Name
```

Insert Name (Receives/Returns List : List_Type
List_Length : Integer
Receives Item : Item_Type)

For Insert Name you can use Procedure Insert, which we wrote earlier.

Process Name (Receives Students : List_Type
List_Length : Integer
Name : Name_String
Receives/Returns Attendance : Check_Type)

```
Binary Search Students for Name (use Bin_Search here)
IF Found
    THEN
        Set Attendance[Index] to Present
    ELSE
        Writeln 'Name not on list.'
```

Print (Receives Students : List_Type   *Level 1*
                    Attendance : Check_Type
                    List_Length : Integer)

> Writeln 'The following students are taking the exam.'
> Print_List(Present)
> Writeln 'The following students have missed the exam.'
> Print_List(Absent)

Print_List (Receives Students : List_Type   *Level 2*
                        List_Length : Integer
                        Attendance : Check_Type
                        Flag : Attendance_Type)

> FOR Count going from 1 to List_Length
>   IF Attendance[Count] = Flag
>   THEN Writeln Students[Count]

At this point, you need to go back over the top-down design and test it. Have you forgotten anything? Yes, you need to initialize the array Attendance to all Absent.

Initialize Attendance (Receives/Returns Attendance : Check_Type)   *Level 1*

> FOR Count going from 1 to number of students
>   Initialize Attendance[Count] to Absent

The design is now ready to be coded.

PROBLEM-SOLVING CASE STUDY *cont'd.*

Module Structure Chart:

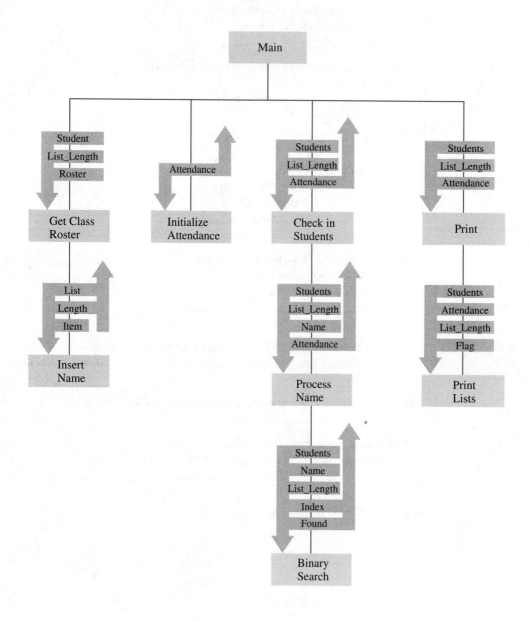

PROBLEM-SOLVING CASE STUDY *cont'd.*

```
PROGRAM Exam (Input, Output, Roster);

(* Program Exam compares students who come to take an exam against *)
(* a class roster. The list of students who took the exam and the  *)
(* list of students who missed the exam are printed *)

CONST
  Num_Students = 200;        (* Maximum number of students  *)
  Blanks = '          ';     (* Empty name string           *)
  End_Data = 'End_Data  ';   (* Sentinel value name         *)
  String_Length = 10;        (* Size of name strings        *)

TYPE
  Name_String = String[String_Length];
  Attendance_Type = (Absent, Present);
  Item_Type = Name_String;
  List_Type = ARRAY [1..Num_Students] OF Item_Type;
  Check_Type = ARRAY [1..Num_Students] OF Attendance_Type;

VAR
  Students:        (* An array of strings        *)
    List_Type;
  Attendance:      (* Array of 'check marks'     *)
    Check_Type;
  List_Length,     (* Number of students there *)
  Roster:          (* Input file                 *)
    Text;


(*******************************************************************)

PROCEDURE Insert (VAR List:        (* List to be changed          *)
                      List_Type;
                  VAR List_Length:  (* Number of elements in List *)
                      Integer;
                      Item:         (* Item to be inserted         *)
                      Item_Type);

(* Item is inserted into its proper place in the sorted list List.   *)
(* Assumption: List_Length is less than Num_Students. If a match occurs, *)
(* Item will be inserted before the one that is there *)

VAR
  Place_Found:
    Boolean;
  Index,           (* Current position in List *)
  Count:           (* Loop control variable      *)
    Integer;
```

```
(******************************************************************)

PROCEDURE Search_Ord (      List:              (* List to be searched    *)
                               List_Type;
                            Item:              (* Item to be found        *)
                               Item_Type;
                            List_Length:       (* Number of List elements *)
                               Integer;
                        VAR Index:             (* Item location if found  *)
                               Integer;
                        VAR Found:             (* True if Item is found   *)
                               Boolean);

(* List is searched for an occurrence of Item. If Item is found,  *)
(* Found is True and Index is the place in List where Item occurs. *)
(* Otherwise, Found is False and Index is where Item belongs.      *)
(* Assumption:  List is sorted in ascending order *)

VAR
  Stop:              (* True at end of search *)
    Boolean;

BEGIN (* Search_Ord *)
  Index := 1;
  Stop := False;
  List[List_Length+1] := Item;
  (* Exit loop when value is found or not there *)
  WHILE NOT Stop DO
    (* Item is not in List[1]..List[Index-1] *)
    IF Item > List[Index]
      (* Item is not in List[1]..List[Index] *)
      THEN
        Index := Index + 1
      ELSE
        (* Item is either found or not there *)
        Stop := True;
  (* Determine whether Item was found or not there *)
  Found := (Index < List_Length + 1) AND (Item = List[Index])
END;  (* Search_Ord *)

(******************************************************************)
```

PROBLEM-SOLVING CASE STUDY cont'd.

```
BEGIN   (* Insert *)
  Search_Ord(List, Item, List_Length, Index, Place_Found);
  (* Shift List[Index]..List[Length] down one *)
  FOR Count := List_Length DOWNTO Index DO
    List[Count+1] := List[Count];
  (* Insert Item *)
  List[Index] := Item;
  (* Increment List_Length *)
  List_Length := List_Length + 1
END;   (* Insert *)

(* ********************************************************************* *)

PROCEDURE Bin_Search (    List:              (* Array to be searched      *)
                          List_Type;
                          Item:              (* Item to be found          *)
                          Item_Type;
                          List_Length:       (* Number of elements in List *)
                          Integer;
                      VAR Index:             (* Location of Item if found  *)
                          Integer;
                      VAR Found:             (* True if Item is found      *)
                          Boolean);

(* List is searched for an occurrence of Item. If Item is found,    *)
(* Found is True and Index gives the location of Item within List.  *)
(* Otherwise, Found is False and Index is undefined *)

VAR
  First,         (* Bound on list *)
  Last,          (* Bound on list *)
  Middle:        (* Middle index  *)
    Integer;
```

```
BEGIN (* Bin_Search *)
  First := 1;
  Last := List_Length;
  Found := False;
  WHILE (Last >= First) AND NOT Found DO
    BEGIN
      Middle := (First + Last) DIV 2;
      IF Item < List[Middle]
        (* Item is not in List[Middle]..List[Last] *)
        THEN
          Last := Middle - 1
        ELSE
          IF Item > List[Middle]
            (* Item is not in List[First]..List[Middle] *)
            THEN
              First := Middle + 1
            ELSE
              Found := True
    END;
  Index := Middle
END;  (* Bin_Search *)


(* ********************************************************************* )


PROCEDURE Process_Name (    Students:           (* List of students       *)
                              List_Type;
                            List_Length:        (* Number of List elements *)
                              Integer;
                            Name:               (* Input student name      *)
                              Name_String;
                        VAR Attendance:         (* List of check marks     *)
                              Check_Type);

(* If Name is in Students, then corresponding position in Attendance *)
(* is set to Present. Otherwise, error message is printed. Procedure *)
(* Bin_Search is called to do the search. Procedure accesses global  *)
(* constant End_Data *)

VAR
  Index:    (* Location of student name if found *)
    Integer;
  Found:    (* True if student is on roster      *)
    Boolean;
```

PROBLEM-SOLVING CASE STUDY *cont'd.*

```
BEGIN (* Process_Name *)
  IF Name <> End_Data
    THEN
      BEGIN
        Bin_Search(Students, Name, List_Length, Index, Found);
        IF Found
          THEN
            Attendance[Index] := Present
          ELSE
            Writeln('Name not on list.')
      END
END;  (* Process_Name *)

(*********************************************************************)

PROCEDURE Print (Students:        (* List of students            *)
                   List_Type;
                 Attendance:      (* List of check marks         *)
                   Check_Type;
                 List_Length:     (* Number of elements in lists *)
                   Integer);

(* The names of those taking the exam are printed. The names of *)
(* those absent are printed *)

VAR
  Flag:                  (* Controls which list to print *)
    Attendance_Type;

  (*****************************************************************)

  PROCEDURE Print_List (Flag:              (* Type of list to print *)
                          Attendance_Type);

  (* If Flag is Absent, the students who are absent are printed.  *)
  (* If Flag is Present, the students who are present are printed *)

  VAR
    Count:        (* Loop control variable *)
      Integer;

  BEGIN (* Print_List *)
    FOR Count := 1 TO List_Length DO
      IF Attendance[Count] = Flag
        THEN
          Writeln(Students[Count])
  END;  (* Print_List *)
```

```
  (*****************************************************************)

BEGIN (* Print *)
  Writeln('The following students are taking the exam.');
  Print_List(Present);
  Writeln('The following students have missed the exam.');
  Print_List(Absent)
END;  (* Print *)

(*****************************************************************)

PROCEDURE Initialize_Attendance (VAR Attendance:  (* Check mark list *)
                                      Check_Type);

(* The array that records attendance is initialized to Absent *)

VAR
  Count:       (* Loop control variable *)
    Integer;

BEGIN (* Initialize_Attendance *)
  FOR Count := 1 TO Num_Students DO
    Attendance[Count] := Absent
END;  (* Initialize_Attendance *)

(*****************************************************************)

PROCEDURE Check_In_Students (    Students:      (* List of students    *)
                                   List_Type;
                                 List_Length:  (* Number of elements   *)
                                   Integer;
                             VAR Attendance:   (* List of check marks *)
                                   Check_Type);

(* Student names are entered at the keyboard and passed to *)
(* procedure Process_Name *)

VAR
  Name:              (* Name of student checking in *)
    Name_String;
```

PROBLEM-SOLVING CASE STUDY *cont'd.*

```
BEGIN (* Check_In_Students *)
  Write('Enter last name ');
  Readln(Name);
  Writeln;
  WHILE Name <> End_Data DO
    BEGIN
      Process_Name(Students, List_Length, Name, Attendance);
      Write('Enter last name ');
      Readln(Name);
      Writeln
    END
END;  (* Check_In_Students *)

(******************************************************************)

PROCEDURE Get_Class_Roster (VAR Students:       (* List of students    *)
                                 List_Type;
                            VAR List_Length:  (* Number of elements  *)
                                 Integer;
                            VAR Roster:        (* Roster data file    *)
                                 Text);

(* The class roster is read from file Roster *)

VAR
  Name:              (* An input student name *)
    Name_String;

BEGIN (* Get_Class_Roster *)
  (* Input names of students in the class *)
  WHILE NOT EOF(Roster) DO
    BEGIN
      Readln(Roster, Name);
      Insert(Students, List_Length, Name)
    END
END;  (* Get_Class_Roster *)

(******************************************************************)

BEGIN (* Exam *)
  Assign(Roster, 'Roster.Dat');
  Reset(Roster);
  List_Length := 0;
  Initialize_Attendance(Attendance);
  Get_Class_Roster(Students, List_Length, Roster);
  Check_In_Students(Students, List_Length, Attendance);
  Print(Students, Attendance, List_Length);
  Close(Roster)
END.  (* Exam *)
```

Testing: The program must be tested with names that are more than ten characters, exactly ten characters, and less than ten characters. Names from the terminal must be spelled incorrectly as well as correctly. The following data was used.

On Roster

```
Dale
MacDonald
Weems
Vitek
Westby
Smith
Jamison
Jones
Kirshen
NameLongerThanTenCharacters
Gleason
Thompson
Ripley
Lilly
```

Copy of the Screen During the Run

```
Enter last name    Weems
Enter last name    Dale
Enter last name    McDonald
Name not on list.
Enter last name    MacDonald
Enter last name    Vitek
Enter last name    Westby
Enter last name    NameLongerThanTenCharacters
Enter last name    Gleason
Enter last name    EndData
The following students are taking the exam.
Dale
Gleason
Jamison
NameLonger
MacDonald
Vitek
Weems
Westby
The following students have missed the exam.
Jones
Kirshen
Lilly
Ripley
Smith
Thompson
```

By assuming that all students have a unique last name, we have simplified the problem considerably. Programming Problem 2 is similar: you must account for both first and last names.

Testing and Debugging

In this chapter we have discussed and coded six general-purpose procedures: three sequential searches, a binary search, an exchange sort, and an insertion into an ordered list (which can also be used as a sort). We have used three of these procedures in programs that have been tested. We test the other three procedures by embedding them in driver programs. The drivers should read in data, call the procedure, and print out the results. Following is the algorithm for a driver to test procedure Search:

Get List of components
WHILE more items
   Get Item
   Search(List, Item, List_Length, Index, Found)
     IF Found
       THEN
         Print Item, 'found at index position', Index
       ELSE
         Print Item, 'not found in list'

The driver would have to be run with several sets of test data to test procedure Search thoroughly. The minimum set of lists of components would be:

1. A list of no components
2. A list of one component
3. A list of Max_Length components
4. A list of more than one but less than Max_Length

The minimum set of items being searched for would be

1. Item in List[1]
2. Item in List[List_Length]
3. Item between List[1] and List[List_Length]
4. Item < List[1]
5. Item > List[List_Length]
6. Item between List[1] and List[List_Length] but not there

Since Item_Type can be any data type that the relational operators can be applied to, procedure Search should be tested with components of several different types.

We leave the coding of this driver program and the creation of the test data as an exercise (see Programming Problem 5). Procedures Search2 and Ex_Sort should be tested in like manner.

At the beginning of this section, we said that three of the procedures used in this chapter had been tested in programs. However, to make sure that they stand up as general-purpose procedures, they should be subjected to the same rigorous testing proposed for Search, Search2, and Ex_Sort.

In two of the search procedures (Search2 and Search_Ord), we stored the value being searched for in List[List_Length + 1]. The assumption that List_Length would be less than Max_Length (the number of places in the array) is written into the documentation. This could lead to a potential error if the calling module doesn't check that List_Length is not equal to Max_Length.

If the assumption listed in the procedure documentation is that the condition will not occur, then the calling module must make sure that the procedure is not called with List_Length equal to Max_Length. Another way to deal with the case where List_Length equals Max_Length is to add an error flag to the procedures' formal parameter lists, and have the procedures themselves check for List_Length equal to Max_Length. If List_Length equals Max_Length, the error flag is set to True and the search is terminated. This approach changes the preconditions of the procedures so that they may be called when List_Length equals Max_Length.

Either way of handling the problem is acceptable. The important point is that it must be clearly stated whether the calling routine or the procedure is to check for the error condition.

Testing and Debugging Hints

1. Review the Testing and Debugging Hints for Chapter 11. They apply to all one-dimensional arrays, including strings.
2. Only character array strings of the same type can be compared. However, Turbo Pascal Strings of different types may be compared.
3. Don't attempt to store more characters than there are components in a packed array.
4. General-purpose procedures and functions should be tested outside the context of a particular program, using a driver.
5. Test data should be chosen carefully to test all end conditions and some in the middle. End conditions are those that reach the limits of the structure used to store them. For example, in a one-dimensional array, there should be test data items in which the number of components is 0, 1, and Max_Length (Max_Length − 1 in the case of Search2), as well as between 1 and Max_Length.

Summary

This chapter has provided practice in working with lists represented by one-dimensional arrays. Algorithms that search and sort data stored in a list have been examined, and procedures have been written to implement these algorithms. These procedures can be used again and again in different contexts because they have been written in a general fashion.

The components in the array are of type Item_Type. Item_Type can be defined as any ordinal data type or an array of characters.

Pascal provides a packed option that can be applied to data structures such as arrays. Packed arrays of Char, called strings, can be printed directly and compared. Strings are useful in working with character data. Since strings can be compared, our general-purpose procedures can be used with arrays of strings. Turbo Pascal also provides a nonstandard type called String, which is essentially an array of characters for which subarray processing is automatically performed.

■ *Quick Check*

1. In a search of an unordered array of 1,000 values, what will be the average number of loop iterations required to find a value? What is the maximum number of iterations that may be required to find a value? (pp. 541–542)

2. The following program fragment sorts a list into descending order. Change it to sort in ascending order. (pp. 529–531)

```
FOR Pass_Count := 1 TO List_Length - 1 DO
  BEGIN
    Min_Index := Pass_Count;
    FOR Place_Count := Pass_Count + 1 TO List_Length DO
      IF List[Place_Count] < List[Min_Index]
        THEN
          Min_Index := Place_Count;
    Temp := List[Min_Index];              (* Swap *)
    List[Min_Index] := List[Pass_Count];
    List[Pass_Count] := Temp
  END;
```

3. Describe how the list insertion operation could be used to build a sorted list from unordered input data. (pp. 554–556)

4. Describe the basic principle behind the binary search algorithm. (pp. 537–541)

5. Define an array data type that will hold a string of 15 characters. Define an array variable of this type, and write an assignment statement that initializes the variable to all blanks. (pp. 543–549)

Answers

1. The average number is 500 iterations. The maximum is 1,000 iterations.   2. The only required change is to replace the < symbol in the inner loop with a >. As a matter of style, MinIndex should be changed to MaxIndex.   3. The list is initialized with a length of 0. Each time a data value is read, insertion adds the value to the list in its correct position. When all the data has been read, it will be stored in order in the array.   4. The binary search takes advantage of ordered array values, looking at a component in the middle of the array and deciding whether the sought-after value precedes or follows the midpoint. The search is then repeated on the appropriate half, quarter, eighth, and so on, of the array until the value is located.

```
5. TYPE
     String15 = String[15];
   VAR
     Name:
       String15;

   Name := '               ';     (* 15 blanks *)
```

■ *Exam Preparation Exercises*

1. Design an appropriate data structure for each of the following problems.
   a. A record store sells classical records (A), jazz records (B), rock records (C), and other records (D). The owner of the store wants to total the amount of sales for each record category. Sales receipts are kept in the following format:

   Code (1 character, either A, B, C, or D)
   Amount (amount of sale)

   b. A payroll master file is made up of the following data:

   ID_Number (five-digit number)
   Rate (hourly rate of pay)
   Dependents (number of dependents)

   c. A transaction file is made up each month of the following data:

   ID_Number (five-digit number)
   Hours (number of hours worked)

   The payroll file is ordered; the transactions file is not. Payroll checks are to be issued.

2. Sketch an algorithm for processing the data structures in exercises 1a and 1b. Your answer should read like the Discussion section of a Problem-Solving Case Study. You are not being asked for a top-down design.

3. Given the declarations

```
CONST
  Name_Length = 20;
  Word_Length = 10;

TYPE
  Name_Type = String[Name_Length]
  Word_Type = PACKED ARRAY [Word_Index] OF Char;

VAR
  First_Name,
  Last_Name:
    Name_Type;
  Word:
    Word_Type;
  Flag:
    Boolean;
```

mark the following statements valid or invalid.

a. ```
FOR I := 1 TO Name_Length DO
    Write(First_Name[I])
```
b. ```
Write(Last_Name)
```
c. ```
IF First_Name = Last_Name
    THEN
       Flag := True
```
d. ```
FOR I := 1 TO Word_Length DO
    Read(Word[I])
```
e. ```
Read(Word)
```
f. ```
IF Word = First_Name
    THEN
       Flag := False
```
g. ```
IF First_Name[1] = Word[1]
    THEN
          Flag := True
```

4. a. Define a data type Name_Type to be a string of Name_Length.
   b. Define a data type Person_Type to be an array of People_Length of Name_Type.
   c. Declare an array variable People to be of type Person_Type.

5. a. Define a data type Car_Type to be an enumerated type made up of the names of cars.
   b. Define a data type Inventory to be an array of Max_Number of Car_Type.
   c. Declare an array variable Cars of type Inventory.

6. Given the declarations

```
CONST
   Name_Length = 20;
   Number_Of_Books = 200;
   Title_Length = 30;

TYPE
   Title_Index = 1..Title_Length;
   Name_Index = 1..Name_Length;
   Books_Out_Index = 1..Number_Of_Books;
   Book_Name = PACKED ARRAY [Title_Index] OF Char;
   Person_Name = PACKED ARRAY [Name_Index] OF Char;
   Book_Type = ARRAY [Books_Out_Index] OF Book_Name;
   Person_Type = ARRAY [Books_Out_Index] OF Person_Name;

VAR
   Books:
     Book_Type;
   Borrower:
     Person_Type;
   Book_In:
     Book_Name;
   Name:
     Person_Name;
```
```

mark the following statements valid or invalid.

a. `Write(Book_In)`
b. `Read(Book_In)`
c. `FOR I := 1 TO Name_Length DO`
   `Write(Book_In)`
d. `FOR I := 1 TO Number_Of_Books DO`
   `Writeln(Books[I])`
e. `FOR I := 1 TO Number_Of_Books DO`
   `IF Book_In = Books[I]`
      `THEN`
         `Writeln (Book_In, Borrower[I])`
f. `IF Book_In = Name`
   `THEN`
      `Writeln('Error')`

7. The following values are stored in an array in ascending order.

29	57	63	72	79	83	96	104	114	136

Apply procedure Bin_Search with Item = 114 to this list, and trace the values of First, Last, and Middle. Indicate any undefined values with a U.

8. The following values are stored in an array in ascending order.

28	45	97	103	107	162	196	202	257

Apply procedures Search2 and Search_Ord to this array, search for the following values, and indicate how many comparisons are required to either find the number or find that it is not in the list.

a. 28
b. 32
c. 196
d. 194

9. Write code fragments to do the following tasks, using the declarations given in exercise 6. Assume that the books listed in Books have been borrowed by the person listed in the corresponding position of Borrower.

a. Write a code fragment to print each book borrowed by Name.
b. Write a code fragment to count the number of books borrowed by Name.
c. Write a code fragment to count the number of copies of Book_In that have been borrowed.
d. Write a code fragment to count the number of copies of Book_In that have been borrowed by Name.

■ *Programming Warm-Up Exercises*

1. Write a Pascal function Index that searches an Integer array List for a value Item and returns its place in the array. There are List_Length values in List. If Item is not in the array, Index should be set to 0.

2. Write a Pascal function Count that counts the occurrences of a value Item, of type Item_Type, in an unsorted array, Num_List, of type Arr_Type. There are Last items in Num_List.

3. Write a Pascal procedure that takes as input two Integer arrays (A and B) of length List_Length. This procedure should return as output the product of all components of B for which the corresponding components of A are negative.

4. Write a Pascal function Found that searches a Real array List for a Real value greater than the value of Item. If such a value is found, the function returns True; otherwise, False is returned. The number of components in List is passed as a parameter.

5. Procedure Ex_Sort sorts the values of an array into ascending order. Rewrite it to sort the values into descending order.

6. Rewrite Search_Ord to give it an additional formal parameter Overflow. If List_Length is equal to Max_Length, Overflow is True, an appropriate error message is printed, and the search is not made. Otherwise, Overflow is False. Max_Length may be accessed globally. Change the documentation to reflect this change.

7. Rewrite procedure Search_Ord so that it searches a text file instead of an array.

8. Write a Pascal procedure that searches a list List of length List_Length for Item. If Item is found, it is deleted and the list is compacted (that is, all the components below Item are moved up one place). List_Length is adjusted appropriately. Item is of type ItemType.

9. Write a Pascal procedure that removes all occurrences of Item in a list List of length List_Length. Adjust List_Length appropriately. Item is of type Item_Type.

10. Write a Pascal procedure that initializes the Boolean array Present to False. Max_Length, the number of components in the array, may be accessed globally.

11. Write a Pascal procedure that takes two parallel arrays, Present (Boolean) and Score (Real), as parameters. This procedure should store a zero in each position of Score for which True is in the parallel position of Present. Pass List_Length as a parameter.

12. Write a Pascal function that returns the sum of the product of parallel components in two integer arrays Data and Weight. Pass List_Length as a parameter.

13. Modify procedure Bin_Search so that Index is where Item should be inserted when Found is False.

14. Modify procedure Insert so that it uses procedure Bin_Search rather than procedure Search_Ord to find the insertion point.

15. Given the following declarations for a list abstract data type:

```
CONST
  Max_Size = 200;
TYPE
  Item_Type = Integer;
  List_Type = ARRAY [1..Max_Size] OF Item_Type;
VAR
  List1,
  List2:
    List_Type;
  Length1,     (* Length of List1 *)
  Length2:     (* Length of List2 *)
    Integer;
  Item:
    Item_Type;
```

a. Write an observer function called Empty that returns True if a given list is empty. (Hint: Pass the length of the list to the function.)

b. Write an observer function called Full that returns True if no more space is left in the array containing the list.

c. Write a binary observer function called Equal that takes two lists as parameters and returns True if they are of the same length and each element in one list equals the corresponding element in the second list.

d. Write a constructor procedure called Delete that takes a list and an item, and searches the list for an instance of the item. If the item is found, it is removed from the list and succeeding items are moved up to fill the empty space.

e. Write a constructor procedure called Delete_All that removes all instances of an item from a list without leaving gaps in the array.

f. Write an observer procedure called Component that returns a component of the list if a given position number (index value) is in the range 1..LengthN. The procedure should also return a Boolean flag Valid that is False if the index is outside of this range.

■ *Programming Problems*

1. A company wants to know the percentages of total sales and total expenses attributable to each salesperson. Each has a data line giving his or her last name (maximum of twenty characters), followed by a comma, followed by his or her first name (maximum of ten characters). The next line contains his or her total sales (Integer) and expenses (Real). Write a program that produces a report with a header line containing the total sales and total expenses. Following this header should be a table with each salesperson's first name, last name, percentage of total sales, and percentage of total expenses.

2. Only authorized shareholders are allowed to attend a stockholders' meeting. Write a program to read a person's name from Input, check it against a list of shareholders, and print a message saying whether or not the person may attend the meeting. The list of shareholders is on file Data in the following format: first name (maximum ten characters), blank, last name (maximum twenty characters). Use EOF to stop reading the file. The maximum number of shareholders is 1,000.

The user should be prompted to enter his or her name in the same format as is used for the data on the file. If the name does not appear on the list, the program should repeat the instructions on how to enter the name and then tell the user to try again. A message saying that the person may not enter should be printed only after he or she has been given a second chance to enter the name. The prompt to the user should include the message that a Q should be entered to end the program.

3. Enhance the program in problem 2 as follows:
   a. Print a report showing how many stockholders there were at the time of the meeting, how many were present at the meeting, and how many people who tried to enter were denied permission to attend.
   b. Follow this summary report with a list of the names of the stockholders, with either Present or Absent after each name.

4. A life insurance company has hired you to write a program to print a list of their customers and the premium that each customer pays. Premiums are based on the age the customer was when he or she became a customer. The following table is used to determine each customer's premium, but these rates are subject to change.

Age	Premium
25	$277.00
35	287.00
45	307.00
55	327.00
65	357.00

Each age listed in this table is the upper limit for the premium; for example, if a customer signed up for a policy when she was 37, she would pay $307.00.

Write a program that reads the table into an array, then reads in the customers' names and ages when they bought the policies into another array. The table and the customers' names and ages are stored in two files. Print out a formatted, labeled list showing each customer's name, his or her age when the policy was bought, and the customer's premium.

5. The local bank in Programming Problem 5, Chapter 11, was so successful with its advertising campaign that the parent bank decided to collect data on waiting times from banks all over the state and run a contest. However, this time they decided to assign frustration levels to wait times as follows:

Wait Time	Frustration Level
Wait <= (mean − standard deviation)	'Amazed'
(Mean − standard deviation) < Wait < Mean	'Pleased'
Mean <= Wait < (mean + standard deviation)	'Calm'
(Mean + standard deviation) <= Wait < (Mean + 2 * standard deviation)	'Irritated'
(Mean + 2 * standard deviation) <= Wait	'Berserk'

where Mean is the mean waiting time and Wait is the wait time. Calculate frustration levels for each recorded wait.

Input:

Same as in Programming Problem 5, Chapter 11, except that two digits have been added to the teller ID number to indicate at which bank the teller is located.

Output:

Same as for Programming Problem 5, Chapter 11, plus 1) a bar graph (histogram) showing frustration level distribution; and 2) a table sorted by three-digit ID numbers showing (a) ID number, (b) wait time, and (c) frustration level.

6. Complete the driver program described in the Testing and Debugging section. Use it to test thoroughly procedures Search, Search2, and Ex_Sort. Choose your test data carefully, making sure that all cases are tested.

Multidimensional Arrays

GOALS

- To be able to define a two-dimensional array data type.
- To be able to access a component of a two-dimensional array variable.
- To be able to sum the rows of a two-dimensional array.
- To be able to sum the columns of a two-dimensional array.
- To be able to initialize a two-dimensional array.
- To be able to print the values in a two-dimensional array.
- To be able to define a two-dimensional array data type using the array-of-arrays form of definition.
- To be able to define a multidimensional array data type.
- To be able to process a multidimensional array variable.
- To be able to choose an appropriate array data structure for a given problem.

Data structures play an important role in the design process. The choice of data structure directly affects the design, since it determines the algorithms used to process the data. We have discussed the one-dimensional array, which gives us the ability to reference a group of data objects by one name. This simplifies the design of many algorithms.

In many problems, however, the relationships between data items are more complex than a simple list. In this chapter we begin by examining the two-dimensional array, which is useful when data is to be organized in the form of a table with rows and columns. Two-dimensional arrays are also useful for representing board games, like chess, tic-tac-toe, or Scrabble, and in computer graphics, where the screen is thought of as a two-dimensional array.

The definition of an array is then extended to allow arrays with any number of dimensions, called multidimensional arrays. Each dimension of such an array is used to represent a different feature of a component. For example, a three-dimensional array of sales figures might be indexed by (1) store number, (2) month, and (3) item number.

Two-Dimensional Arrays

A one-dimensional array is used to represent a list. A **two-dimensional array** is used to represent a table with rows and columns, provided each item in the table is of the same data type. A component in a two-dimensional array is accessed by specifying the row and column indices of the item in a table. This is a familiar task. For example, if you want to find a street on a map, you look up the street name on the back of the map to find the coordinates of the street, usually a letter and a number. The letter specifies a column to look on, and the number specifies a row. You find the street where the row and column meet.

Two-Dimensional Array   A collection of components, all of the same type, structured in two dimensions. Each component is accessed by a pair of indices that represent the component's position in each dimension.

Figure 13-1 shows a two-dimensional array that has 100 rows and 9 columns. The rows are accessed by an integer ranging from 1 to 100; the columns are accessed by an uppercase letter ranging from A to I. Each component is accessed by a row-column pair: 1,A, for example.

A two-dimensional array is defined in exactly the same way as a one-dimensional array, except that two index types must be described. The syntax template for the relevant portion of the TYPE section is shown below, along with an example.

ARRAY [index-type , index-type **. . .**] **OF** component-type;

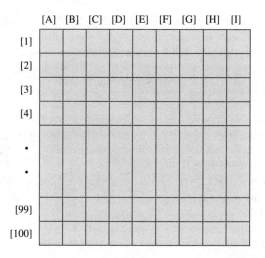

Figure 13-1
A Two-Dimensional
Array

```
TYPE
  Row_Type = 1..100;
  Column_Type = (A, B, C, D, E, F, G, H, I);
  Table_Type = ARRAY[Row_Type, Column_Type] OF Integer;
```

                             ↑   ↑

                   First   Second
                   dimension   dimension

```
VAR
  Map:
    Table_Type;
```

To access a component, two expressions (one for each dimension) are used to specify its position. There are two ways to list these expressions. One way is to put each expression in brackets beside the name of the array:

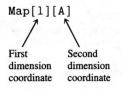

```
Map[1][A]
```

First　　　Second
dimension　dimension
coordinate　coordinate

The other way is to list the two expressions in one pair of brackets, with a comma between them:

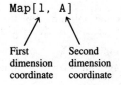

```
Map[1, A]
```

First　　　Second
dimension　dimension
coordinate　coordinate

The syntax templates for these methods are as follows.

> variable-identifier [index-expression][index-expression]...

> variable-identifier [index-expression , index-expression...]

The second form (Map[1, A]), called the abbreviated form, is more commonly used. Let's look now at some examples.

```
TYPE
  Weeks = 1..52;
  Days = 1..7;
  Year_Type = ARRAY[Weeks, Days] OF Integer;

VAR
  Year:
    Year_Type;
```

Year_Type is a two-dimensional array with 364 components. We can think of it as a table with 52 rows and 7 columns. The contents of each place in the table (each component) can be any Integer value. Year is an array variable of type Year_Type. Year[3, 7] refers to the Integer value in the third row and the seventh column. If the data represented high temperatures for each day in a year, Year[3, 7] would be the temperature for the seventh day of the third week. The code fragment shown in Figure 13-2 would print the temperature values for the third week.

Another representation of the same data might be as follows:

```
TYPE
  Days = (Monday, Tuesday, Wednesday, Thursday,
          Friday, Saturday, Sunday);
  Weeks = 1..52;
  Year_Type = ARRAY [Weeks, Days] OF Integer;

VAR
  Year:
    Year_Type;
```

Here, Year has the same number of rows and columns, but the second component is accessed by an expression of type Days. Year[3, Sunday] corresponds to the same component as Year[3, 7] in the first example. If Day_Count were of type Days and Week_Count of type Integer, the code fragment shown in Figure 13-3 would set the entire array to 0.

The order in which we define the rows and columns doesn't matter to the computer as long as we're consistent. To help visualize a two-dimensional array, we use the convention of letting the first dimension define the rows and the second dimension define the columns.

Processing Two-Dimensional Arrays

Processing data in a two-dimensional array generally means accessing the array in one of four patterns: randomly, along rows, along columns, or throughout the array. Each of these may also involve subarray processing.

The simplest way to access a component is to look in a given location. For example, a user enters map coordinates that we use as indices into an array of street names to access the sought-after name at those coordinates. This is referred to as *random access* because the user may enter any set of coordinates at random.

There are many cases where we might wish to perform an operation on all the elements of a particular row or column in a table. Consider the array Year defined previously, where the rows represent weeks of the year and the columns represent days of the week. The data represents the high temperatures for each day in a year. If we wanted the average high temperature for a given week, we would sum the values in that row and divide by 7. If we wanted the average for a given day of the week, we would sum the values in that column and divide by 52. The former case is access along rows; the latter case is access along columns.

Now, suppose that we wish to determine the average for the year. We must access every element in the array, sum them, and divide by 364. In this case, the order of access is not important. (The same is true when we initialize every element of an array to 0.) This is access throughout the array.

There are situations when we must access every element in an array in a particular order, either by rows or by columns. For example, if we wanted the average for every week, we would run through the entire array, taking each row in turn. However, if we wanted the average for each day of the week, we would run through the array a column at a time.

Let's take a closer look at these patterns of access by considering four common examples of array processing.

1. Sum the rows.
2. Sum the columns.
3. Initialize the table to all zeroes (or some special value).
4. Print the table.

First, let's define some types and variables using general identifiers, such as Row and Column, rather than problem-dependent identifiers. Then let's look at each algorithm in terms of generalized table processing.

```
CONST
  Number_Of_Rows = 4;
  Number_Of_Columns = 4;

TYPE
  Row_Range = 1..Number_Of_Rows;
  Column_Range = 1..Number_Of_Columns;
  Table_Type = ARRAY [Row_Range, Column_Range] OF Integer;

VAR
  Table:                          (* A two-dimensional array  *)
    Table_Type;
  Row_Length,                     (* Data in 1..Row_Length    *)
  Rows:                           (* A row index              *)
    Row_Range;
  Column_Length,                  (* Data in 1..Column_Length *)
  Columns:                        (* A column index           *)
    Column_Range;
  Total:                          (* A variable for summing   *)
    Integer;
```

Sum the Rows

Suppose we want to sum row number 3 in array Table and print the result. We can do this easily with a FOR loop:

```
Total := 0;
FOR Column := 1 TO Number_Of_Columns DO
  Total := Total + Table[3, Column];
Writeln('Row sum: ', Total:1);
```

This FOR loop runs through each column of Table, while keeping the row index equal to 3. Every value in row 3 is added to Total. Suppose we wanted to sum and print two rows, row 2 and row 3. We could add a duplicate of the preceding code fragment, but with the index set to 2:

```
(* Sum and print row 2 *)
Total := 0;
FOR Column := 1 TO Number_Of_Columns DO
  Total := Total + Table[2, Column];
Writeln('Row sum: ', Total:1);
(* Sum and print row 3 *)
Total := 0;
FOR Column := 1 TO Number_Of_Columns DO
  Total := Total + Table[3, Column];
Writeln('Row sum: ', Total:1);
```

or we could use a nested loop and make the row index a variable:

```
FOR Row := 2 TO 3 DO
  BEGIN
    Total := 0;
    FOR Column := 1 TO Number_Of_Columns DO
      Total := Total + Table[Row, Column];
    Writeln('Row sum: ', Total:1)
  END;
```

The second approach is shorter, but its real advantage is that we can easily modify it to process any range of rows.

The outer loop controls the rows, and the inner loop controls the columns. For each value of Row, every column is processed; then the outer loop moves to the next row. In the first iteration of the outer loop, Row is held at 2 and Column goes from 1 to Number_Of_Columns. Therefore, the array is accessed in the following order:

```
Table[2, 1] [2, 2] [2, 3] [2, 4]
```

In the second iteration of the outer loop, Row is incremented to 3, and the third row is accessed as follows:

```
Table[3, 1] [3, 2] [3, 3] [3, 4]
```

We can generalize this row processing to run through every row of the table by having the outer loop run from 1 to Number_Of_Rows. However, if we want to access only part of the array (subarray processing), we write the code fragment as follows:

```
FOR Row := 1 TO Row_Length DO
  BEGIN
    Total := 0;
    FOR Column := 1 TO Column_Length DO
      Total := Total + Table[Row, Column];
    Writeln('Row sum: ', Total:1)
  END;
```

Figure 13-6 illustrates subarray processing by row.

Sum the Columns

Suppose we want to sum and print each column. The code to perform this task is given below. Again we have generalized the code to sum only the portion of the array that contains valid data.

```
FOR Column := 1 TO Column_Length DO
  BEGIN
    Total := 0;
    FOR Row := 1 TO Row_Length DO
      Total := Total + Table[Row, Column);
    Writeln('Column sum : ', Total)
  END
```

Figure 13-6
Partial Table
Processing by Row

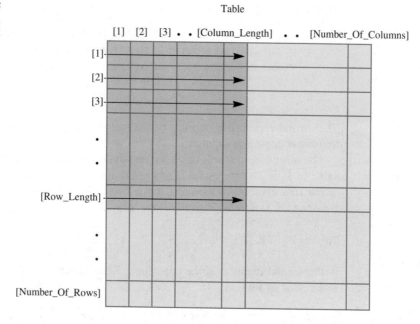

In this case, the outer loop controls the column, and the inner loop controls the row. All the components in the first column are accessed and summed before the outer loop index changes and the components in the second column are accessed. Figure 13-7 illustrates subarray processing by column.

Figure 13-7
Partial Table
Processing by
Column

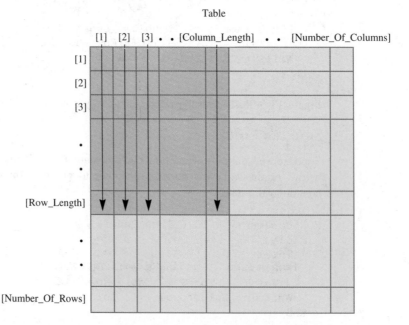

Initialize the Table

Initializing a table is the same as initializing any other array variable; each element is set to some special value, such as 0. Here is the code that implements this task.

```
FOR Row := 1 TO Number_Of_Rows DO
  FOR Column := 1 TO Number_Of_Columns DO
    Table[Row, Column] := 0;
```

In this case, we initialized the table a row at a time, but we could just as easily have run through each column instead. The order doesn't matter as long as we access every element.

This task is recoded below as a general-purpose procedure with four parameters:

```
PROCEDURE Initialize_Table  (VAR Table:           (* Array to initialize *)
                                  Table_Type;
                                  Number_Of_Rows,    (* Length of array *)
                                  Number_Of_Columns: (* Width of array  *)
                                  Integer;
                                  Item:              (* Initial value   *)
                                  Item_Type);

(* The entire array is set to Item. *)

VAR
  Row,
  Column:
    Integer:

BEGIN (* Initialize_Table *)
  FOR Row := 1 TO Number_Of_Rows DO
    FOR Column := 1 TO Number_Of_Columns DO
      Table[Row, Column] := Item
END;  (* Initialize_Table *)
```

Add procedure Initialize to your library of procedures. You can use it whenever you need to initialize a two-dimensional array with integer indices.

Print the Table

If we wish to print out a table with one row per line, then we have another case of row processing:

```
FOR Row := 1 TO Row_Length DO
  BEGIN
    FOR Column := 1 TO Column_Length DO
      Write(' ', Table[Row, Column]:14);
    Writeln
  END;
```

This code fragment prints the values of the table in columns that are 15 characters wide. As a matter of proper style, this fragment should be preceded by code that prints headings over the columns to identify their contents.

There's no rule that we have to print each row on a line. We could turn the table sideways and print each column on one line simply by exchanging the two FOR loops. When you are printing a table, you must consider which order of presentation makes the most sense and how the table fits on the page. For example, a table with 6 columns and 100 rows would be best printed as 6 columns, 100 lines long.

Almost all processing of data stored in a two-dimensional array involves either processing by row or processing by column. In our examples the index type has been Integer, but the pattern of operation of the loops is the same no matter what types the indices are.

The looping patterns for row processing and column processing are so useful that they are summarized below. To make them more general, we use the identifiers Min_Row..Max_Row for the index type of the first dimension and Min_Column..Max_Column for the index type of the second dimension. Remember that row processing has the row index in the outer loop, and column processing has the column index in the outer loop.

Row Processing

```
FOR Row := Min_Row TO Max_Row DO
  FOR Column := Min_Column TO Max_Column DO
    BEGIN
      (* Whatever processing is required *)
    END
```

Column Processing

```
FOR Column := Min_Column TO Max_Column DO
  FOR Row := Min_Row TO Max_Row DO
    BEGIN
      (* Whatever processing is required *)
    END
```

Another Way of Defining Two-Dimensional Arrays

In Pascal a two-dimensional array can also be defined as an array of arrays: the components of a one-dimensional array do not have to be atomic; they can also be structured. For example, Year could be defined as:

```
TYPE
  Weeks = 1..52;
  Days = 1..7;
  Week_Type = ARRAY[Days] OF Integer;    (* 7 integers per week *)
  Year_Type = ARRAY[Weeks] OF Week_Type; (* 52 weeks per year   *)
```

```
VAR
  Year:
    Year_Type;
```

With this definition, the components of the array type Year_Type are one-dimensional arrays of type Week_Type. In other words, Year_Type has two dimensions. We can access each row as an entity: Year[2] accesses the array of temperatures for week number 2. We can also access each individual component of Year by specifying both indices: Year[2, 1] accesses the first day of week 2.

Does it matter which way we define a two-dimensional array? In most cases it doesn't, but the features of the data are shown more clearly if the indices are specified in a single definition.

There is one situation in which it is advantageous to define a two-dimensional array as an array of arrays. If the rows have been defined first as a one-dimensional array, each can be passed to a procedure expecting as a parameter a one-dimensional array of the same type. For example, the following function returns the maximum integer value in an array of type Week_Type.

```
FUNCTION Maximum (VAR List:              (* Input list      *)
                           Week_Type;
                      List_Length:       (* Length of list *)
                      Integer):
                      Integer;

(* A maximum value is found and its value returned *)

VAR
  Max,
  I:
    Integer;

BEGIN (* Maximum *)
  Max := List[1];
  FOR I := 2 TO List_Length DO
    IF Max < List[I] THEN
      Max := List[I];
  Maximum := Max
END; (* Maximum *)
```

Using our two-part definition of Year_Type permits us to call Maximum using a component of Year as follows.

```
Max_Year := Maximum(Year[Week], 52)
```

A row from Year is passed to Maximum, which treats it like any other one-dimensional array of type Week_Type (Figure 13-8). We are able to pass the row as a parameter because both it and the formal parameter are of the same named type. The ability to

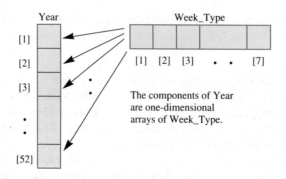

Figure 13-8
A One-Dimensional
Array

The components of Year
are one-dimensional
arrays of Week_Type.

pass a row of a two-dimensional array as a parameter to a procedure expecting a one-dimensional array can be very helpful. If we define Year_Type directly as a two-dimensional array, we cannot pass a component of Year to Maximum. The component's type is anonymous, and even though it has the same form, it is not compatible with type Week_Type.

With Year defined as an array of arrays, we can print the maximum temperature of each week of the year with the following code.

```
Writeln(' Week  Maximum');
Writeln('Number Temperature');
FOR Week := 1 TO 52 DO
   Writeln(Week:6, Maximum(Year[Week], 52):9);
```

Multidimensional Arrays

Pascal does not place a limit on the number of dimensions that an array can have. We can generalize our definition of an array to cover all cases.

Array   A collection of components, all of the same type, ordered on N dimensions (N >= 1). Each component is accessed by N indices, each of which represents the component's position within that dimension.

You should have guessed from the syntax templates that you can have as many dimensions as you want. How many should you have in a particular case? As many as there are features that describe the components in the array.

Take, for example, a chain of department stores. Monthly sales figures must be kept for each item by store. There are three important pieces of information about each item: the month in which it was sold, the store from which it was purchased, and the item number. We can define an array to summarize this data as follows:

```
CONST
    Number_Of_Items = 100;
    Number_Of_Stores = 10;

TYPE
    Item_Numbers = 1..Number_Of_Items;
    Stores = 1..Number_Of_Stores;
    Months = 1..12;
    Sales_Type = Array[Stores, Months, Item_Numbers] OF Integer;

VAR
    Sales:
        Sales_Type;
    Item:
        Item_Numbers;
    Store:
        Stores;
    Month:
        Months;
    Number_Sold:
        Integer;
    Current_Month:
        Months;
```

A graphic representation of the array variable Sales is shown in Figure 13-9. The number of components in Sales is 12,000 (10 × 12 × 100). If it is only June (Current_Month = 6), then part of the array is empty. If we want to process the

Figure 13-9
Graphical Representation of Array Variable Sales

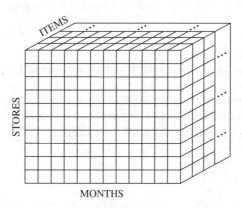

data in the array, we must use subarray processing. The following program fragment sums and prints the total number of each item sold this year to date by all stores.

```
FOR Item := 1 TO Number_Of_Items DO
  BEGIN
    Number_Sold := 0;
    FOR Store := 1 TO Number_Of_Stores DO
      FOR Month := 1 TO Current_Month DO
        Number_Sold := Number_Sold + Sales[Store, Month, Item];
    Writeln('Item #', Item:3, 'Sales to date = ', Number_Sold:6)
  END;
```

Because Item is controlled by the outer FOR loop, we are summing each item's sales by Month and Store. If we want to find the total sales for each store, we control Store in the outer FOR loop, summing its sales by Month and Item with the inner loops.

```
FOR Store := 1 TO Number_Of_Stores DO
  BEGIN
    Number_Sold := 0;
    FOR Item := 1 TO Number_Of_Items DO
      FOR Month := 1 TO Current_Month DO
        Number_Sold := Number_Sold + Sales[Store, Month, Item];
    Writeln('Store #', Store:3, 'Sales to date = ', Number_Sold:6)
  END
```

It takes two loops to access each component in a two-dimensional array; it takes three loops to access each component in a three-dimensional array. The task to be done determines which index controls the outer loop, the middle loop, and the inner loop. If we want to calculate monthly sales by store, Month controls the outer loop and Store controls the middle loop. If we want to calculate monthly sales by item, Month controls the outer loop and Item controls the middle loop.

If we want to keep track of the departments that sell each item, we can add a fourth dimension.*

```
Departments = (A, B, C, D, E, F, G);
Sales_Type = ARRAY [Stores, Months, Item_Numbers, Departments] OF Integer;
```

How would we visualize this new structure? Not very easily! Fortunately, we do not have to visualize a structure to use it. If we want the number of sales in store 1, during May, for item number 4, in department C, we simply write:

```
Sales[1, 5, 4, C]
```

*In some Turbo systems, this array may exceed the available memory space, requiring the number of items to be reduced.

*S*oftware Engineering Tip

Choosing a Data Structure

We have now seen two different data structures that can be used to represent data arranged as a table: parallel arrays and two-dimensional arrays. We can always use parallel arrays instead of a two-dimensional array. How do we decide which is most appropriate?

Recall that, in an array, all the components are of the same type; they represent the same thing. But what if we want to process information on the number of items sold, the cost of each item, and the percent tax to be charged for each item? We can define a table with the following headings to hold this information:

Item Number   Number Sold   Cost per Item   Tax Rate

If we keep the item number and number sold as real numbers, we can define a two-dimensional array of type Real with four columns, each corresponding to one of the headings; however, in this case, four parallel arrays are more appropriate. Even though the components are all of the same data type, they represent different things. The components in the Item Number column represent an identifying number, those in the Number Sold column represent the quantity sold, the Cost per Item column contains prices, and the Tax Rate column holds percentages. Defining this structure as a set of four parallel arrays also allows us to represent Item Number and Number Sold with integers, which are a better choice for this type of information.

To decide whether to use parallel arrays or a multi-dimensional array, we can ask four questions:

1. Are all the components of the same data type?
2. Do all the components represent the same kinds of values?
3. Can a set of independent features be used as indices to select a component?
4. Can each index be defined meaningfully as an ordinal data type?

If the answer to all four questions is yes, a multidimensional array is appropriate. Otherwise, parallel arrays are a better choice.

In some cases, a single data structure is more appropriate than multiple arrays. In the next chapter we look at a data structure called a *record*, a structure that allows us to group nonhomogeneous items. As we introduce more data structures, we will provide additional guidelines on how to choose among them.

PROBLEM-SOLVING CASE STUDY

City Council Election

Problem: There has just been a hotly contested city council election. Let's do an analysis of the votes for the four candidates by precinct. We want to know how many votes each candidate received in each precinct, how many total votes each candidate received, and how many total votes were cast in each precinct.

Input: Precinct number, ballot position of candidate (available on file Vote, one vote per line); and candidate names, entered from the keyboard (to be used for printing the output).

Output: A table showing how many votes each candidate received in each precinct, the total number of votes for each candidate, and the total number of votes in each precinct.

Discussion: The data is available in the form of a pair of numbers for each vote. The first number is the precinct number; the second number is the place on the ballot of the candidate for whom the vote was cast.

If we were doing the analysis by hand, our first task would be to go through the data, counting how many people in each precinct voted for each candidate. We would probably create a table with precincts down the side and candidates across the top. Each vote would be recorded as a hash mark in the appropriate column and row (see Figure 13-10).

Figure 13-10

Precinct	Smith	Jones	Adams	Smiley
1	ℍℍ //	//	ℍℍ ℍℍ //	ℍℍ
2	ℍℍ ℍℍ	//	ℍℍ	///
3	//	ℍℍ ///	ℍℍ ℍℍ ℍℍ	///
4	ℍℍ	ℍℍ ///	ℍℍ ℍℍ	//

When all of the votes had been recorded, a sum of each column would tell us how many votes each candidate received. A sum of each row would tell us how many people voted in each precinct.

As is so often the case, this by-hand algorithm can be used directly in our program. A two-dimensional array can be created where each component is a counter for the number of votes for a particular candidate in each precinct; that is, the value indexed by [2, 1] would be the counter for the votes for candidate 1 in precinct 2.

PROBLEM-SOLVING CASE STUDY *cont'd.*

Figure 13-11

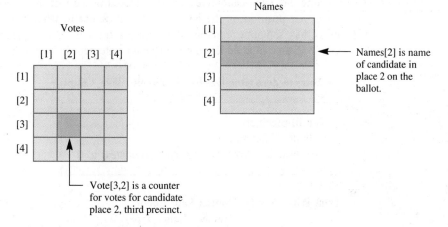

Vote[3,2] is a counter
for votes for candidate
place 2, third precinct.

Names[2] is name
of candidate in
place 2 on the
ballot.

Data Structures:

A two-dimensional array Votes, where the rows represent precincts and the columns represent candidates.

A one-dimensional array of strings containing the names of the candidates, to be used for printing (see Figure 13-11).

Main Module   *Level 0*

> Get Candidate Names
> Set Votes to Zero
> WHILE more votes
>   Read Precinct, Candidate
>   Set Votes[Precinct, Candidate] to Votes[Precinct, Candidate] + 1
> Print Totals (of votes)
> Print Totals per Candidate
> Print Totals per Precinct

Get Candidate Names (Returns Names : Name_Type)   *Level 1*

> Writeln 'Enter the names of the candidates,
>   one name per line, in the order in which
>   they appear on the ballot.'
> FOR Candidate going from 1 to the number of candidates
>   Get a Name
>   Set Names[Candidates] to Name) *what ?*

Note that each candidate's name is stored in the slot in the array corresponding to his or her position on the ballot. This will be useful when the totals are printed: the index has semantic content; it represents the candidate's place on the ballot. The Get_A_Name module is simply a Readln statement in Turbo Pascal.

Set Votes to Zero (Receives/Returns Votes : Vote_Count)

```
For all precincts
   FOR all candidates
      Initialize Votes[Precincts, Candidates] to 0
```

Print Table (Receives Votes : Vote_Count,
                      Names : Name_Type)

```
FOR all candidates
   Print Names [Candidates]:12
FOR all precincts
   FOR all candidates
      Print Votes [Precincts, Candidates]:12
   Go to next line
```

Print Totals per Candidate (Receives Votes : Vote_Count,
                                      Names : Name_Type)

```
(* Calculate column sums *)
FOR all candidates
   Initialize Total to 0
FOR all precincts
   Add Votes[Precincts, Candidates] to Total
Print 'Total votes for', Names[Candidates]:12, Total:3
```

Print Totals per Precinct (Receives Votes : Vote_Count)

```
(* Calculate row sums *)
FOR all precincts
   Initialize Total to 0
   FOR all candidates
      Add Votes[Precincts, Candidates] to Total
   Print 'Total votes for precinct', Precincts:3, ':', Total:3
```

PROBLEM-SOLVING CASE STUDY cont'd.

Module Structure Chart:

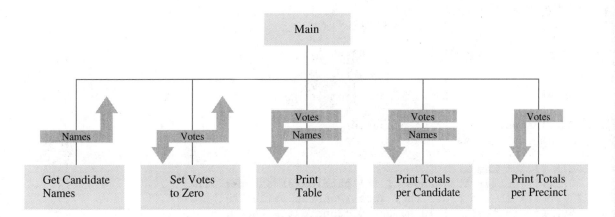

The program for this algorithm follows:

```
PROGRAM Election (Input, Output, Report, Vote);

(* Votes represented by precinct number and ballot position are *)
(* read from file Vote and tallied. Sums per precinct and per   *)
(* candidate are calculated. All totals are printed             *)

CONST
  Number_Of_Precincts = 4;
  Number_Of_Candidates = 4;

TYPE
  Precinct_Range = 1..Number_Of_Precincts;
  Candidate_Range = 1..Number_Of_Candidates;
  String10 = String[10];
  Vote_Count = ARRAY [Precinct_Range, Candidate_Range] OF Integer;
  Name_Type = ARRAY [Candidate_Range] OF String10;

VAR
  Votes:              (* Totals for precincts versus candidates *)
    Vote_Count;
  Vote,               (* Input file of precincts and candidates *)
  Report:             (* Output file receiving summaries         *)
    Text;
  Names:              (* Array of candidate names                *)
    Name_Type;
  Candidate:          (* Candidate number input from file Vote   *)
    Candidate_Range;
  Precinct:           (* Precinct number input from file Vote    *)
    Precinct_Range;
```

PROBLEM-SOLVING CASE STUDY *cont'd.*

```
(*******************************************************************)

PROCEDURE Get_Names (VAR Names:           (* Array of candidate names *)
                          Name_Type);

(* Reads in a list of candidate names *)

VAR
  Name:               (* Name read from terminal *)
    String10;
  Candidates:         (* Loop counter              *)
    Candidate_Range;

BEGIN (* Get_Names *)
  Writeln('Enter the names of the candidates one per line, ',
          'in the order they appear on the ballot.');
  FOR Candidates := 1 TO Number_Of_Candidates DO
    Readln(Names[Candidates])
END;  (* Get_Names *)


(*******************************************************************)


PROCEDURE Zero_Votes (VAR Votes:          (* Array of totals *)
                          Vote_Count);

(* Array Votes is set to all zero *)

VAR
  Precincts:          (* Loop counter *)
    Precinct_Range;
  Candidates:         (* Loop counter *)
    Candidate_Range;

BEGIN (* Zero_Votes *)
  FOR Precincts := 1 TO Number_Of_Precincts DO
    FOR Candidates := 1 TO Number_Of_Candidates DO
      Votes[Precincts, Candidates] := 0
END;  (* Zero_Votes *)


(*******************************************************************)
```

```
PROCEDURE Print_Table (Votes:              (* Array of totals            *)
                             Vote_Count;
                       Names:               (* Array of candidate names *)
                          Name_Type);

(* Votes are printed *)

VAR
  Precincts:              (* Loop counter *)
    Precinct_Range;
  Candidates:             (* Loop counter *)
    Candidate_Range;

BEGIN (* Print_Table *)
  (* Set up headings *)
  Write(Report, ' ':19);
  FOR Candidates := 1 TO Number_Of_Candidates DO
    Write(Report, Names[Candidates]:12);
  Writeln(Report);
  (* Print by row *)
  FOR Precincts := 1 TO Number_Of_Precincts DO
    BEGIN
      Write(Report, 'Precinct', Precincts:4);
      FOR Candidates := 1 TO Number_Of_Candidates DO
        Write(Report, Votes[Precincts, Candidates]:12);
      Writeln(Report)
    END;
  Writeln(Report)
END;  (* Print_Table *)

(*****************************************************************)

PROCEDURE Print_Per_Candidate (Votes:          (* Array of totals *)
                                   Vote_Count;
                               Names:           (* List of names   *)
                                  Name_Type);

(* Votes per person are summed and printed *)

VAR
  Candidates:          ——— (* Loop counter           *)
    Candidate_Range;
  Precincts:           —— (* Loop counter            *)
    Precinct_Range;
  Total:               (* Total votes for each candidate *)
    Integer;
```

```pascal
BEGIN (* Print_Per_Candidate *)
  FOR Candidates := 1 TO Number_Of_Candidates DO
    BEGIN
      Total := 0;
      (* Sum columns *)
      FOR Precincts := 1 TO Number_Of_Precincts DO
        Total := Total + Votes[Precincts, Candidates];
      Writeln(Report, 'Total votes for ', Names[Candidates]:12,
              Total:3)
    END
END;  (* Print_Per_Candidate *)


(**********************************************************************)


PROCEDURE Print_Per_Precinct (Votes:          (* Array of totals *)
                                 Vote_Count);

(* Votes per precinct are summed and printed *)

VAR
  Candidates:             (* Loop counter                    *)
    Candidate_Range;
  Precincts:              (* Loop counter                    *)
    Precinct_Range;
  Total:                  (* Total votes for each precinct *)
    Integer;

BEGIN (* Print_Per_Precinct *)
  FOR Precincts := 1 TO Number_Of_Precincts DO
    BEGIN
      Total := 0;
      (* Sum rows *)
      FOR Candidates := 1 TO Number_Of_Candidates DO
        Total := Total + Votes[Precincts, Candidates];
      Writeln(Report, 'Total votes for precinct',
              Precincts:3, ':', Total:3)
    END
END;  (* Print_Per_Precinct *)


(**********************************************************************)
```

```
BEGIN (* Election *)
  Assign(Report, 'REPORT.DAT');
  Assign(Vote, 'VOTE.DAT');
  Rewrite(Report);
  Reset(Vote);
  Get_Names(Names);              (* Get candidates names *)
  Zero_Votes(Votes);            (* Zero out counters      *)
  (* Read and tally votes *)
  WHILE NOT EOF(Vote) DO
    BEGIN
      Readln(Vote, Precinct, Candidate);
      Votes[Precinct, Candidate] := Votes[Precinct, Candidate] + 1
    END;
  Print_Table(Votes, Names);
  Print_Per_Candidate(Votes, Names);
  Print_Per_Precinct(Votes);
  Close(Report);
  Close(Vote)
END.  (* Election *)
```

Testing: This program was run with the data listed below. (We list it in three columns to save space.) The names of the candidates entered from the keyboard were Smith, Jones, Adams, and Smiley. In this data set, there is at least one vote for each candidate in each precinct. Exam Preparation Exercise 1 asks you to outline a complete testing strategy for this program.

Input Data

1 1	3 1	3 3
1 1	4 3	4 4
1 2	3 4	4 4
1 2	3 2	4 3
1 3	3 3	4 4
1 4	2 1	4 4
2 2	2 3	4 1
2 2	4 3	4 2
2 3	4 4	2 4
2 1	3 2	4 4

The output, which was written on file Report, is listed below.

PROBLEM-SOLVING CASE STUDY cont'd.

		Jones	Smith	Adams	Smiley
Precinct	1	2	2	1	1
Precinct	2	2	2	2	1
Precinct	3	1	2	2	1
Precinct	4	1	1	3	6

```
Total votes for Jones       6
Total votes for Smith       7
Total votes for Adams       8
Total votes for Smiley      9
Total votes for precinct 1:  6
Total votes for precinct 2:  7
Total votes for precinct 3:  6
Total votes for precinct 4: 11
```

PROBLEM-SOLVING CASE STUDY

Absenteeism Pattern

Problem: Management wants to see the patterns in absenteeism across each department for a week. The absentee figures are kept on file Data. Each data line contains the daily figures for departments A through F.

The figures must be in the form of a table showing the number of employees absent in each department each day and the percentage difference (+ or −) from each department's weekly average. In addition, they want a summary of absenteeism across the entire company for a week. This summary is to be in the form of a bar chart showing what percentage of the total absences occurred on each day of the week.

Input: Five lines of absentee data, each line containing the number of people out for each of six departments.

Output: Table showing absentee figures and percentage differences from the average for each day of the week, by department; and bar chart showing the percentage of total absenteeism that occurs on each day of the week.

Discussion: Each data line contains the daily absentee figures for every department. The figures must be read in and stored in a table. Once the table has been created, the average absentee rate can be calculated for each department. The table and the averages can be used to calculate the percentage difference.

The first step is to decide what the table that holds the input data should look like. The departments can be columns and the days can be rows, or vice versa. There are only six departments now, but the company is growing. It would be better to make the days of the week the columns and the departments the rows. The program can then be altered to run with more departments simply by adding a row for each. Rows can be added to a table easily; adding columns can cause a problem with printing since the width of a print line or screen is fixed.

As the data is read, it can be stored into an array having the structure shown in Figure 13-12.

Finding the average for each department requires row processing; we sum the rows and divide by 5. Comparing each day's figures to the average also requires row processing, as does printing the table. We can calculate the percentage differences while we print the table.

To compile the summary figures for the week, we must take the number of people absent on each day, divided by the total number of people absent during the entire week. A bar chart showing this information might look as follows, with each asterisk representing 10 percent:

```
                 Monday   Tuesday  Wednesday  Thursday   Friday
     Percent
        100%
         90%
         80%
         70%
         60%
         50%
         40%      *
         30%      *
         20%      *         *                               *
         10%      *         *          *          *         *
```

Figure 13-12
Absentee Data

	[Monday]	[Tuesday]	[Wednesday]	[Thursday]	[Friday]
[A]	2	1	0	1	2
[B]	1	0	0	0	0
[C]	1	1	0	1	0
[D]	3	3	2	1	2
[E]	4	0	0	2	1
[F]	1	0	0	0	2

Data line 3, etc.

Data line 2

Data line 1

This chart can be interpreted as follows: 40 percent of the total absences were on Monday, 20 percent were on Tuesday, and so on.

We can represent this chart as a two-dimensional array with ten rows and five columns. The rows represent the percentages to the nearest 10 percent. For each day the percentage of employees absent is calculated and then rounded to the nearest 10 percent to determine how many asterisks are printed in each column.

Data Structures:

Two-dimensional array for holding the input (Absentee_Data)

One-dimensional array (Averages) for holding the average daily absentee figures for each department (see Figure 13-13)

Two-dimensional array for holding the asterisks to be printed in the bar chart (see Figure 13-14).

Main Module   *Level 0*

```
Get Data
Compute the departmental averages
Print Table
Calculate Summary
Print Bar Chart
```

Get Data (Returns Absentee_Data : Table_Type   *Level 1*
Receives/Returns Data : Text)

```
FOR days Monday through Friday        column
    FOR departments A through F       rows     1-
        Read Absentee_Data[Department, Day]
```

Figure 13-13

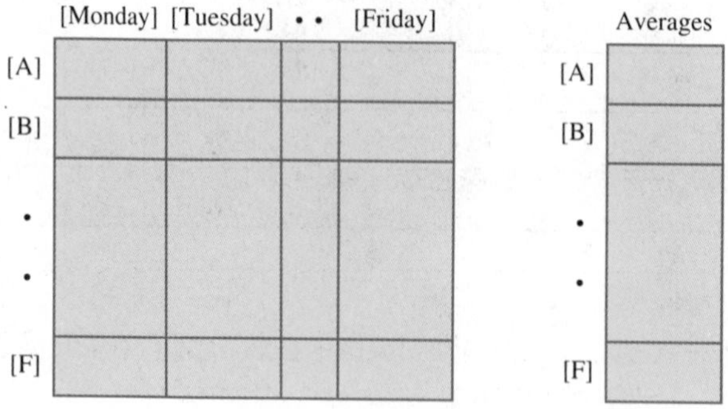

[Monday] [Tuesday] • • [Friday]   Averages

PROBLEM-SOLVING CASE STUDY *cont'd.*

Figure 13-14

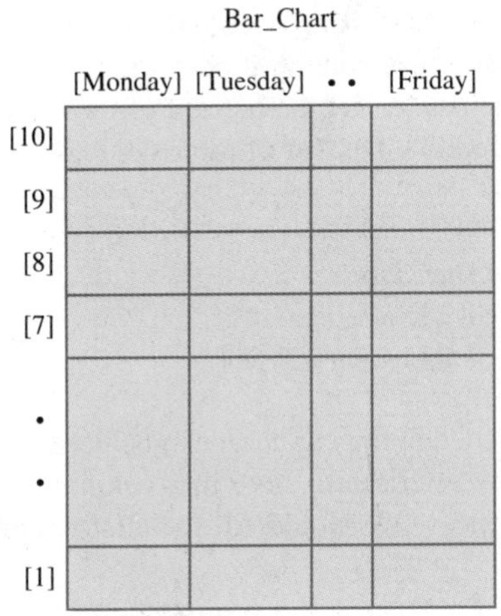

Bar_Chart

[Monday] [Tuesday] • •   [Friday]

```
[10]
 [9]
 [8]
 [7]

  •

  •

 [1]
```

Compute Averages (Receives Absentee_Data : Table_Type
                                    Returns Averages : Column_Type)

We can use the general algorithm we developed to sum the rows of the table. The average is this sum divided by 5.

Print Table (Receives Absentee_Data : Table_Type,
                          Averages : Column_Type
                Receives/Returns Report : Text)

We can use the algorithm developed in Program Election to print the table, adding instructions to calculate the percentage difference when needed.

Calculate Percentage Difference (Receives Absentee_Data : Table_Type,   *Level 2*
                                                    Averages : Column_Type
                                      Returns Percent_Dif : Integer)

Set Difference to Absentee_Data[Department, Day]
        − Averages[Department]
Set Percent_Dif to Round(Difference * 100.0
        / Averages[Department])

Calculate Summary (Receives Absentee_Data : Table_Type
                          Returns Bar_Chart : Chart_Type)

First, we can use either row processing or column processing to sum the entire table (Total Absences). We can then use column processing to sum each column, dividing the column sum by the total sum to get the percent of the total absences for each day. Next, we must put the appropriate number of asterisks into the bar chart, which we'll do in module Set Asterisks.

Set Asterisks (Receives Day : Day_Type,
Percent : Real
Returns Bar_Chart : Chart_Type)

The number of asterisks needed in the bar chart can be used as an index to tell us how many blanks and how many asterisks to store in a column. For example, if Monday had 38 percent of the absences, we would fill the first column as shown in Figure 13-15.

```
Set Index to Round(Percent / 10)
FOR Count going from 10 down to Index + 1
    Initialize Bar_Chart[Count, Day] to ' '
FOR Count going from Index down to 1
    Set Bar_Chart[Count, Day] to '*'
```

Print Barchart (Receives Bar_Chart : Chart_Type   *Level 1*
Receives/Returns Report : Text)

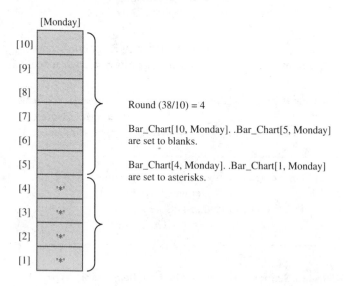

Figure 13-15

Round (38/10) = 4

Bar_Chart[10, Monday]. .Bar_Chart[5, Monday] are set to blanks.

Bar_Chart[4, Monday]. .Bar_Chart[1, Monday] are set to asterisks.

PROBLEM-SOLVING CASE STUDY cont'd.

We can use row processing to print the bar chart with appropriate headings. Note, however, that the array Bar_Chart needs to be printed upside down. We have used the index to correspond to the nearest 10 percent. Therefore, we have to print from row 10 down to row 1 to display the chart in the usual form.

```
FOR Count going from 10 down to 1
    Print Count '0%'
    FOR Days going from Monday TO Friday
        Print Bar_Chart[Count, Days]
```

Module Structure Chart:

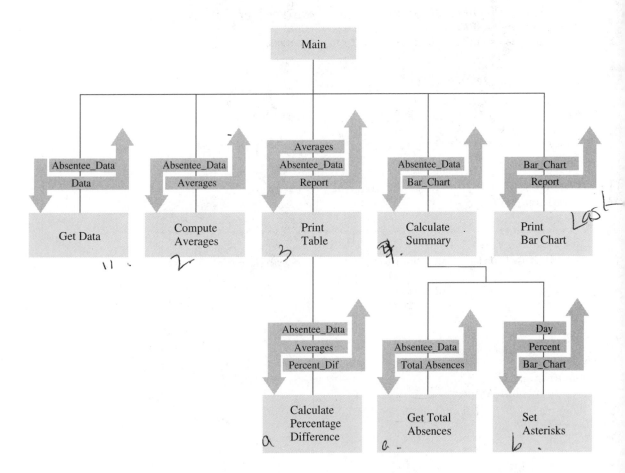

PROBLEM-SOLVING CASE STUDY cont'd.

```
PROGRAM Absent (Output, Data, Report);

(* Absentee data are examined across departments for a week.    *)
(* Percentage differences from the average per department are *)
(* printed. A summary bar chart showing percent of total        *)
(* absences on each day of the week is printed                  *)

CONST
  Number_Of_Departments = 6;

TYPE
  Day_Type = (Monday, Tuesday, Wednesday, Thursday, Friday);
  Department_Type = (A, B, C, D, E, F);
  Tens = 1..10;
  Table_Type = ARRAY [Department_Type, Day_Type] OF Integer;
  Chart_Type = ARRAY [Tens, Day_Type] OF Char;
  Column_Type = ARRAY [Department_Type] OF Real;

VAR
  Absentee_Data:     (* Absences by department and day *)
    Table_Type;
  Bar_Chart:         (* Summary charts of percentages  *)
    Chart_Type;
  Report,            (* Output file                    *)
  Data:              (* Input file                     *)
    Text;
  Averages:          (* Array of department averages   *)
    Column_Type;

(***************************************************************)

PROCEDURE Get_Data (VAR Absentee_Data:    (* Table of absences *)
                        Table_Type;
                    VAR Data:              (* Input data file   *)
                        Text);

(* Data are read from file Data *)

VAR
  Department:        (* Loop counter *)
    Department_Type;
  Day:               (* Loop counter *)
    Day_Type;
```

equivalento FI?

PROBLEM-SOLVING CASE STUDY *cont'd.*

[handwritten: Read (dept, Day)]

```
BEGIN (* Get_Data *)
  FOR Day := Monday TO Friday DO
    BEGIN
      FOR Department := A TO F DO
        Read(Data, Absentee_Data[Department, Day]);
      Readln(Data)
    END
END;  (* Get_Data *)

(*********************************************************************)

PROCEDURE Compute_Average (    Absentee_Data:  (* Table of absences *)
                               Table_Type;
                           VAR Averages:        (* Average per department *)
                               Column_Type);
```
*[handwritten: * formal because]*

```
(* Averages across the rows are calculated *)

VAR
  Department:        (* Loop counter *)
    Department_Type;
  Day:               (* Loop counter *)
    Day_Type;
  Total:             (* Total absences for each department *)
    Integer;

BEGIN (* Compute_Average *)
  FOR Department := A TO F DO
    BEGIN
      Total := 0;
      FOR Day := Monday TO Friday DO
        Total := Absentee_Data[Department, Day] + Total;
      Averages[Department] := Total / 5.0
    END
END;  (* Compute_Average *)
```
[handwritten: 1. i ← 2.]

```
(*********************************************************************)

PROCEDURE Print_Table (    Absentee_Data:  (* Table of absences      *)
                           Table_Type;
                           Averages:        (* Average per department *)
                           Column_Type;
                       VAR Report:          (* Output file for report *)
                           Text);
(* Table showing percentage differences from the averages and *)
(* original data is printed                                   *)
```

```
VAR
  Department:           (* Loop counter *)
    Department_Type;
  Day:                  (* Loop counter *)
    Day_Type;
  Percent_Dif:          (* Percent different from average *)
    Integer;

BEGIN (* Print_Table *)
  Writeln(Report, 'ABSENTEE   DATA':40);
  Writeln(Report, 'Monday':13, 'Tuesday':13, 'Wednesday':13,
          'Thursday':13, 'Friday':13);
  FOR Day := Monday TO Friday DO
    Write(Report, '   Value   %');
  Writeln(Report);
  FOR Department := A TO F DO
    BEGIN
      FOR Day := Monday TO Friday DO
        BEGIN
          Write(Report, Absentee_Data[Department, Day]:6);
          Percent_Dif := Round((Absentee_Data[Department, Day]
            - Averages[Department]) * 100.0 / Averages[Department]);
          Write(Report, Percent_Dif:7)
        END;
      Writeln(Report)
    END
END;  (* Print_Table *)

(***************************************************************)

PROCEDURE Summary (     Absentee_Data:   (* Table of absences    *)
                        Table_Type;
                    VAR Bar_Chart:        (* Charts of percentages *)
                        Chart_Type);

(* Total percentages by day are calculated *)
(* and represented in a bar chart          *)

VAR
  Department:           (* Loop counter         *)
    Department_Type;
  Day:                  (* Loop counter         *)
    Day_Type;
  Percent:              (* Percent per day       *)
    Real;
  Total,                (* Total of entire table *)
  Total_Column:         (* Total per day         *)
    Integer;
```

PROBLEM-SOLVING CASE STUDY *cont'd.*

```
(*****************************************************************)

PROCEDURE Set_Asterisks (VAR Bar_Chart:    (* Chart of percentages *)
                             Chart_Type;
                         Day:              (* Chart index          *)
                             Day_Type;
                         Percent:          (* Percentage to chart  *)
                             Real);

(* Asterisks are stored to represent each 10 percent. *)
(* Blanks are stored in balance of chart              *)

VAR
  Index:             (* Percent in integer form *)
    0..10;
  Counter:           (* Loop counter            *)
    Tens;

BEGIN (* Set_Asterisks *)
  Index := Round(Percent / 10.0);
  FOR Counter := 10 DOWNTO Index + 1 DO
    Bar_Chart[Counter, Day] := ' ';
  FOR Counter := Index DOWNTO 1 DO
    Bar_Chart[Counter, Day] := '*'
END;   (* Set_Asterisks *)

(*****************************************************************)

FUNCTION Total_Absences (Absentee_Data:    (* Table of absences *)
                            Table_Type):
                             Integer;

VAR
  Department:        (* Loop counter   *)
    Department_Type;
  Day:               (* Loop counter   *)
    Day_Type;
  Total:             (* Total absences *)
    Integer;

BEGIN (* Total_Absences *)
  Total := 0;
  FOR Department := A TO F DO
    FOR Day := Monday TO Friday DO
      Total := Total + Absentee_Data[Department, Day];
  Total_Absences := Total
END;   (* Total_Absences *)
```

PROBLEM-SOLVING CASE STUDY cont'd.

```
(***************************************************************)

BEGIN (* Summary *)
  Total := Total_Absences(Absentee_Data);
  FOR Day := Monday TO Friday DO
    BEGIN
      Total_Column := 0;
      FOR Department := A TO F DO
        Total_Column := Total_Column + Absentee_Data[Department, Day];
      Percent := (Total_Column / Total) * 100.0;
      Set_Asterisks(Bar_Chart, Day, Percent)
    END
END;  (* Summary *)

(***************************************************************)

PROCEDURE Print_Bar_Chart (    Bar_Chart:      (* Charts of percentages *)
                                  Chart_Type);
                           VAR Report:         (* Output file for report *)
                                  Text);

(* Summary data are represented in a bar chart *)

VAR
  Counter:      (* Loop control *)
    Tens;
  Day:          (* Loop control *)
    Day_Type;

BEGIN (* Print_Bar_Chart *)
  Writeln(Report);
  Writeln(Report, 'BAR CHART:  ABSENCES BY DAY':40);
  Writeln(Report, '    Monday    Tuesday   Wednesday Thursday',
          ' Friday');
  FOR Counter := 10 DOWNTO 1 DO
    BEGIN
      Write(Report, Counter:2, '0%');
      FOR Day := Monday TO Friday DO
        Write(Report, Bar_Chart[Counter, Day]:5, '      ');
      Writeln(Report)
    END
END;  (* Print_Bar_Chart *)

(***************************************************************)
```

PROBLEM-SOLVING CASE STUDY *cont'd.*

```
BEGIN (* Absent *)
  Assign(Report, 'REPORT.DAT');
  Assign(Data, 'DATA.DAT');
  Rewrite(Report);
  Reset(Data);
  Get_Data(Absentee_Data,Data);
  Compute_Average(Absentee_Data, Averages);
  Print_Table(Absentee_Data, Averages, Report);
  Summary(Absentee_Data, Bar_Chart);
  Print_Bar_Chart(Bar_Chart)
  Close(Report);
  Close(Data)
END.  (* Absent *)
```

Testing: The program is run with the following test data, which includes at least one zero in each row and column. Exam Preparation Exercise 2 asks you to outline a complete testing strategy for this program.

On File Data

```
0  6  3  3  4  1
1  0  1  3  0  3
1  1  0  2  1  1
1  0  1  0  0  1
2  3  4  2  1  0
```

Listed below are the results written on file Report.

ABSENTEE DATA

	Monday		Tuesday		Wednesday		Thursday		Friday
Value	%	Value	%	Value	%	Value	%	Value	%
0	−100	1	0	1	0	1	0	2	100
6	200	0	−100	1	−50	0	−100	3	50
3	67	1	−44	0	−100	1	−44	4	122
3	50	3	50	2	0	0	−100	2	0
4	233	0	−100	1	−17	0	−100	1	−17
1	−17	3	150	1	−17	1	−17	0	−100

```
                  BAR CHART:   ABSENCES BY DAY
        Monday      Tuesday    Wednesday Thursday   Friday
100%
 90%
 80%
 70%
 60%
 50%
 40%     *
 30%     *                                            *
 20%     *            *                                *
 10%     *            *           *          *         *
```

Something looks a little strange: the percentages in the bar chart add up to 110 percent. Remember, in Chapter 8, we mentioned that strange things can happen with real numbers. In Program Absent, each percentage figure is changed to an integer for use as an index. To do this, some of the percentages were rounded to the nearest 10 percent. When we noticed that the percentages added up to 110 percent, we put a debug Writeln statement in the program to monitor what was happening. The percentages (in decimal form) and the rounded values used as an index are shown below.

Percent	Index
0.369	4
0.173	2
0.130	1
0.065	1
0.260	3
0.997	11

This is a classic example of round-off error. Programming Warm-Up exercise 10 asks you to rewrite the procedures that create the bar chart using a smaller interval, so that an asterisk represents 5 percentage points instead of 10.

Testing and Debugging

Errors with multidimensional arrays usually fall into two major categories: index range errors and type conflict errors. In addition, an undefined-value error may result from trying to access undefined (uninitialized) components.

As the number of dimensions increases, so does the likelihood of a subtle logic error. The syntax of your nested loop structure may be valid, but what you intended to have happen may not be what you coded. Using meaningful identifiers for your loop control variables will help. If you were to use I, J, and K as the loop control variables in the department store example, it would be easy to interchange them by mistake. If you use Item, Store, and Month, you are less likely to confuse the indices. Also, if you use enumerated or other distinct types for indices, the compiler will find any interchanged index variables.

Remember that any variables with the same type identifier can be assigned to each other. The key words here are *same type identifier.* For example, given the declarations

```
TYPE
  Months = 1..12;
  Years = 1950..2000;
  Item = ARRAY [Months] OF Integer;
  Table1 = ARRAY [Years] OF Item;
  Table2 = ARRAY [Years, Months] OF Integer;

VAR
  Table_A:
    Table1;
  Table_B:
    Table2;
  Table_C:
    ARRAY [Years] OF Item;
  New_Item,
  Old_Item:
    Item;
```

the following are examples of valid and invalid assignments:

Statement	Status	Reason
`New_Item = Old_Item`	Valid	One-dimensional array assignment
`Table_A[1976] := New_Item`	Valid	First dimension (row) of two-dimensional array assigned value of a one-dimensional array
`Old_Item := Table_B[1984]`	Valid	One-dimensional array assigned value of a row of a two-dimensional array
`Table_A := Table_B`	Invalid	Different named types
`Table_C := Table_A`	Invalid	Different types—one is named, the other is not
`Table_B[1976] := New_Item`	Invalid	Different named types

Be careful when comparing arrays. Strings can be compared as units, but all other arrays must be compared component by component. For example, the following code would find whether Table_A[1992] is equal to Old_Item.

```
Equal := True;
Month := 1;
WHILE Equal AND (Month <= 12) DO
  IF Table_A[1992, Month] = Old_Item[Month]
    THEN
      Month := Month + 1
    ELSE
      Equal := False;
```

Note that, because there are two ending conditions on the loop, a WHILE loop was used in the preceding fragment. A FOR loop can be used only for a simple count-controlled loop.

Testing and Debugging Hints

1. Initialize all components of an array if there is any chance that you will attempt to access the entire array.
2. Use subrange or enumerated types for index variables, and be careful when passing parameters to avoid array index range errors.
3. Use meaningful identifiers for index variables.
4. Globally define data types that will be passed as parameters.
5. Use the proper number of indices with array names when referencing an array component.
6. Select range-checking when you compile your program so that out-of-range index values will be detected.

Summary

Two-dimensional arrays are useful for processing information that is represented naturally in table form. Processing data in two-dimensional arrays usually takes one of two forms: processing by row or processing by column. An array of arrays, which is useful if rows of the array must be passed as parameters, is an alternative way of defining a two-dimensional array.

A multidimensional array is a collection of like components, ordered on more than one dimension. Each component is accessed by a set of indices, one for each dimension, that represents the component's position on the various dimensions. Each index may be thought of as describing a feature of a given array component.

Data structures should be selected to reflect accurately the relationships inherent in the data itself. Two-dimensional arrays and parallel arrays can be used to hold the same data. An analysis of what the data means can help you to make the appropriate choice.

■ *Quick Check*

1. Define a two-dimensional array data type, called Chart, with 30 rows and 10 columns. The component type of the array is Real. (pp. 578–583)

2. Assign the value 27.3 to the component in row 13, column 7 of an array variable, called Plan, of type Chart. (pp. 578–583)

3. Nested FOR loops can be used to sum the values in each row of array Plan. What range of values would the outer FOR loop count through to do this? (pp. 583–585)

4. Nested FOR loops can be used to sum the values in each column of array Plan. What range of values would the outer FOR loop count through to do this? (pp. 585–586)

5. Write a program fragment that initializes array Plan from Question 2 to all zeros. (p. 587)

6. Write a program fragment that prints the contents of array Plan. (pp. 587–588)

7. Given the type definitions

```
TYPE
    One_Dim_Index = 'A'..'Z';
    Two_Dim_Index = 1..100;
    One_Dim = ARRAY [One_Dim_Index] OF Integer;
    Two_Dim = ARRAY [Two_Dim_Index] OF One_Dim;
```

rewrite the definition of type Two_Dim without referring to type One_Dim. (pp. 588–590)

8. How many components does the following data type contain? (pp. 590–592)

```
CONST
    Max_Index = 10;

TYPE
    Range = 1..Max_Index;
    Four_Dim = ARRAY [Range, Range, Range, Range] OF Char;
```

9. Write a program fragment that fills a variable of type Four_Dim, called Quick, with blanks. (pp. 590–592)

10. Suppose you are writing a program to process a table of employee numbers, names, and pay rates. Is a two-dimensional array an appropriate data structure for this problem? Explain. (p. 593)

Answers

1.
```
CONST
    Max_Row = 30;
    Max_Column = 10;

TYPE
    Rows = 1..Max_Row;
    Columns = 1..Max_Column;
    Chart = ARRAY[Rows, Columns] OF Real;
```

2. Plan[13, 7] := 27.3;

3. FOR Row := 1 TO 30 DO

4. FOR Column := 1 TO 10 DO

5. FOR Row := 1 TO 30 DO
     FOR Column := 1 TO 10 DO
       Plan[Row, Column] := 0.0;

6. FOR Row := 1 TO 30 DO
     BEGIN
       FOR Column := 1 TO 10 DO
         Write(Plan[Row, Column]:8:1);
       Writeln
     END

7. TYPE
     Two_Dim = ARRAY [Two_Dim_Index, One_Dim_Index] OF Integer;

8. Ten thousand (10 * 10 * 10 * 10)

9. FOR Dim1 := 1 TO Max_Index DO
     FOR Dim2 := 1 TO Max_Index DO
       FOR Dim3 := 1 TO Max_Index DO
         FOR Dim4 := 1 TO Max_Index DO
           Quick[Dim1, Dim2, Dim3, Dim4] := ' ';

10. A two-dimensional array is inappropriate because the data types of the columns are not the same. Parallel arrays are appropriate in this case.

■ *Exam Preparation Exercises*

1. Outline a testing strategy that fully tests Program Election.

2. Outline a testing strategy that fully tests Program Absent.

3. Given the declarations

```
CONST
  Number_Of_Weeks = 5;
  Number_Of_Teams = 6;

TYPE
  Week_Range = 1..Number_Of_Weeks;
  Team_Range = 1..Number_Of_Teams;
  Sold_Type = ARRAY[Team_Range, Week_Range] OF Integer;
```

```
VAR
  Weeks:
    Week_Range;
  Teams:
    Team_Range;
  Tickets:
    Sold_Type;
```

answer the following questions:

a. What is the number of rows in Tickets?

b. What is the number of columns in Tickets?

c. How many Integer variables have been declared?

d. What kind of processing (row or column) would be needed to total the ticket sales by weeks?

e. What kind of processing (row or column) would be needed to total the ticket sales by teams?

4. Given the declarations

```
CONST
  Number_Of_Schools = 10;

TYPE
  School_Index = 1..Number_Of_Schools;
  Sport_Type = (Football, Basketball, Volleyball);
  Participant_Type = ARRAY [School_Index, Sport_Type] OF Integer;
  Money_Type = ARRAY [Sport_Type, School_Index] OF Real;

VAR
  Kids_In_Sports:
    Participant_Type;
  Cost_Of_Sports:
    Money_Type;
  Schools:
    School_Index;
  Sports:
    Sport_Type;
```

answer the following questions:

a. What is the number of rows in Kids_In_Sports?

b. What is the number of columns in Kids_In_Sports?

c. What is the number of rows in Cost_Of_Sports?

d. What is the number of columns in Cost_Of_Sports?

e. How many Integer variables have been declared?

f. How many Real variables have been declared?

g. What kind of processing (row or column) would be needed to total the amount of money spent on each sport?

h. What kind of processing (row or column) would be needed to total the number of children participating in sports at a particular school?

5. Given the following code segments, draw the arrays and their contents after the code is executed. Indicate any undefined positions with a question mark.

   a.

```
TYPE
  Ex_A = ARRAY [1..4, 1..3] OF Integer;
VAR
  Example_A: Ex_A;
  I, J: Integer
    .
    .
    .
FOR I := 1 TO 4 DO
  FOR J := 1 TO 3 DO
    Example_A[I,J] := I * J
```

  b.
```
TYPE
  Ex_B = ARRAY [1..4, 1..3] OF Integer;
VAR
  Example_B: Ex_B;
  I, J: Integer;
    .
    .
    .
FOR I := 1 TO 3 DO
  FOR J := 1 TO 3 DO
    Example_B[I, J] := (I + J) MOD 3
```

  c.
```
TYPE
  Ex_C = ARRAY [1..8, 1..2] OF Integer;
VAR
  Example_C: Ex_C;
  I, J: Integer;
    .
    .
    .
Example_C[8, 1] := 4;
Example_C[8, 2] := 5;
FOR I := 1 TO 7 DO
  BEGIN
    Example_C[I, 1] := 2;
    Example_C[I, 2] := 3;
  END
```

6. a. Define an enumerated type Teams made up of the clubs on your campus.
  b. Define an Integer array type Record_Type indexed by Teams.
  c. Declare an array variable Win_Loss to be of type Record_Type.

7. Given the following declarations

```
TYPE
   Name = PACKED ARRAY [1..20] OF Char;
   T_List = ARRAY [1..50] OF Name;
VAR
   One_Name : Name;
   List : T_List;
```

indicate whether each of the following are valid or invalid.

a. `List[3] := One_Name`

b. `List[14,27] := 'z'`

c. `List[3][7] := 'y'`

d. `Readln(List[7])`

e. `Writeln(List[9])`

8. Declare the array variables described below. Use proper style.

   a. A table with five rows and six columns that contains Boolean values.

   b. A table, indexed from −5 to 0 and 'A' to 'F', that contains Real values.

   c. A Char table with rows indexed by uppercase letters and columns indexed by lowercase letters.

9. A logging operation keeps records of thirty-seven loggers' monthly production for purposes of analysis, using the following array structure:

```
CONST
   Number_Loggers = 37;

TYPE
   Logger_Index = 1..Number_Loggers;
   Month_Type = 1..12;
   Cut_Type = ARRAY [Logger_Index, Month_Type] OF Integer;

VAR
   Logs_Cut:
      Cut_Type;
   Monthly_High,
   Monthly_Total,
   Yearly_Total,
   High:
      Integer;
   Month,
   Best_Month:
      Month_Type;
   Logger,
   Best_Logger:
      Logger_Index;
```

a. The following statement would assign the January log total for logger number 7 to Monthly Total. (True or False?)

```
Monthly_Total := Logs_Cut[7, 1]
```

b. The following statements would compute the yearly total for logger number 11. (True or False?)

```
Yearly_Total := 0;
FOR Month := 1 TO Number_Loggers DO
   Yearly_Total := Yearly_Total + Logs_Cut[Month, 11]
```

c. The following statements would find the Best_Logger (most logs cut) in March. (True or False?)

```
Monthly_High := 0;
FOR Logger := 1 TO Number_Loggers DO
  IF Logs_Cut[Logger, 3] > Monthly_High
    THEN
      BEGIN
        Best_Logger := Logger;
        Monthly_High := Logs_Cut[Logger, 3]
      END;
```

d. The following statements would find the logger with the highest monthly production and the logger's best month. (True or False?)

```
High := 0;
FOR Month := 1 TO 12 DO
   FOR Logger := 1 TO Number_Loggers DO
     IF Logs_Cut[Logger, Month] > High
       THEN
         BEGIN
           High := Logs_Cut[Logger, Month];
           Best_Logger := Logger;
           Best_Month := Month
         END;
```

10. Declare the Real array variables described below. Use proper style.
    a. A three-dimensional array where the first dimension is indexed from -1 to $+3$, the second dimension is indexed from 'A' to 'Z', and the third dimension is indexed from 1 to 20.
    b. A four-dimensional array where the first two dimensions are indexed from 1 to 10, and the third and fourth are indexed from 'a' to 'f'.

■ *Programming Warm-Up Exercises*

1. Write a Pascal function that returns True if all the values in a two-dimensional array are positive and False otherwise. The array, the number of columns, and the number of rows should be passed as parameters.

2. Write a Pascal procedure to initialize the diagonals of a two-dimensional Char array to a specified character. The array (Data of type Data_Type), the dimensions of the array (Length), and the specified character (Character) should be passed as parameters.

3. Write a Pascal procedure Copy that takes an Integer array Data, defined to be Max_Rows by Max_Columns, and copies the values into a second array Data2, defined the same way. Data and Data2 are of type Data_Type. The constants Max_Rows and Max_Columns may be accessed globally.

4. Write a Pascal procedure that finds the largest value in a two-dimensional array of fifty rows and fifty columns.

5. Using the declarations in Exam Preparation Exercise 3, write procedures to do the following tasks. Use proper style. Only constants may be accessed globally.
   a. Determine the team that sold the most tickets during the first week of ticket sales.
   b. Determine the week in which the second team sold the most tickets.
   c. Determine the week in which the most tickets were sold.
   d. Determine the team that sold the most tickets.

6. Using the declarations in Exam Preparation Exercise 4, write procedures, in proper style, to do the following tasks. Only constants may be accessed globally.
   a. Determine which school spent the most money on football.
   b. Determine which sport the last school spent the most money on.
   c. Determine which school has the most students playing basketball.
   d. Determine in which sport the third school had the most students participating.
   e. Determine the total amount spent by all the schools on volleyball.
   f. Determine the total number of students playing all sports. (Assume that each student plays only one sport.)
   g. Determine which school had the most students participating in sports.
   h. Determine which was the most popular sport in terms of money spent.
   i. Determine which was the most popular sport in terms of student participation.

7. Given the following declarations
```
CONST
  Number_Of_Items = 100;
  Number_Of_Stores = 10;

TYPE
  Item_Numbers = 1..Number_Of_Items;
  Stores = 1..Number_Of_Stores;
  Months = 1..12;
  Sales_Type = Array[Stores, Months, Item_Numbers] OF Integer;
```
   write a Pascal procedure to initialize an array of type Sales_Type to 0. The constants Number_Of_Stores and Number_Of_Items may be accessed globally. The array should be passed as a parameter.

8. Sales figures are kept on items sold by store, by department, and by month. Write a Pascal procedure to calculate the total number of items sold during the year by each department in each store. The data is stored in an array of type Sales_Type as defined on page 592. (See page 591 for the definition of the first three indexes.) The array containing the data should be passed as a parameter. The constants Number_Of_Stores and Number_Of_Items may be accessed globally.

9. Write a Pascal function that returns the sum of the elements in a specified row of an array. The array, the number of columns, and which row is to be totaled should be passed as parameters.

10. Rewrite procedure Set_Asterisks from program Absent so that an asterisk represents 5 percentage points instead of 10.

■ *Programming Problems*

1. A deck of playing cards can be represented as a two-dimensional array, where the first dimension is rank and the second dimension is suit. Read in a bridge hand (thirteen cards), and determine whether the player should pass or bid. Each card should be input on a line by itself, with the suit given first and rank next.

   The decision to pass or bid is based on the number of points the hand is worth. Points are counted as follows:

   An ace is worth 4 points.
   A king is worth 3 points.
   A queen is worth 2 points.
   A jack is worth 1 point.

   Add up the points in the hand and print one of the following messages.

Below 13 points,	'Pass'
Between 13 and 16 points,	'Bid one of a suit'
Between 17 and 19 points,	'Bid one no trump'
Between 20 and 22 points,	'Bid one of a suit'
Over 22 points,	'Bid two of a suit'

2. Write an interactive program that plays tic-tac-toe. Represent the board as a three-by-three character array. Initialize the array to blanks and ask each player in turn to input a position. The first player's position will be marked on the board with an O, and the second player's position will be marked with an X. Continue the process until a player wins or the game is a draw. To win, a player must have three marks in a row, in a column, or on a diagonal. A draw occurs when the board is full and no one has won.

   Each player's position should be input in the form of an index into the tic-tac-toe board, that is, a row number, space, and column number. Make the program user friendly.

   After each game print out a diagram of the board showing the ending positions. Keep a count of the number of games each player has won and the number of draws. Before the beginning of each game, ask each player if he or she wishes to continue. If either player wishes to quit, print out the statistics and stop.

3. Write a Pascal program to read in two two-dimensional arrays, then multiply one by the other. This is called matrix multiplication. For example, if First_Array appears as

   ```
   2  7
   9  3
   ```

   and Second_Array appears as

   ```
   8
   6
   ```

then the Product_Matrix is

```
Product_Matrix[1,1] = 2 * 8 + 7 * 6
Product_Matrix[2,1] = 9 * 8 + 3 * 6
```

Matrix multiplication can be done only if the number of columns in the multiplicand (the first array) equals the number of rows in the multiplier (the second array).

The program should read in the two arrays, test to see if multiplication is possible, then multiply them if it is. The output will be a printout of the two arrays and will either output the product array or print a message saying that multiplication is not possible.

4. Photos taken in space by the Galileo spacecraft are sent back to earth as a stream of numbers. Your job is to take a matrix (two-dimensional array) of the numbers and print it as a negative picture.

If the numbers received represent levels of brightness, then one approach to generating a picture is to print a dark character (like a $) when the brightness level is low, and print a light character (like a blank or a period) when the level is high. Unfortunately, errors in transmission sometimes occur. Thus, your program should first attempt to find and correct these errors. Assume a value is in error if it differs by more than one from each of its four neighboring values. Correct the erroneous value by giving it the average of its neighboring values, rounding it to the nearest integer.

Example:

```
   5        The 2 would be regarded as an error and would be given
 4 2 5      a corrected value of 5.
   5
```

Note that values on the corners or boundaries of the matrix have to be processed differently from the values on the interior. Your new program should print a negative image of the corrected picture on a new page.

5. The following diagram represents an island surrounded by water (shaded area).

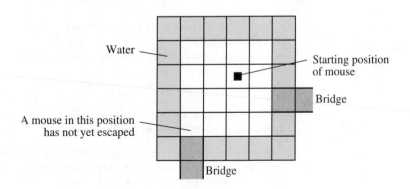

Two bridges lead out of the island. A mouse is placed on the black square. Write a program to make the mouse take a walk across the island. The mouse is allowed to travel one square at a time, either horizontally or vertically. A random number between 1 and 4 should be used to decide which direction the mouse is to take. The mouse drowns when he hits the water or escapes when he crosses a bridge. You may generate a random number up to 100 times. If the mouse does not find his way by the hundredth try, he will die of starvation. Restart the mouse in a new array and go back and repeat the whole process. Count the number of times he escapes, drowns, and starves.

Input:

First record—the size of the array, including border of water and bridges (will not be larger than 20 × 20)

Next N records—the rows of the two-dimensional array, where the positions containing negative numbers represent the water, the positions in the edge containing a 0 represent the bridges, the position containing a 1 represents the starting position of the mouse, and all other positions contain zeros

Output:

A line stating whether the mouse escaped, drowned, or starved
A line showing the mouse's starting position and the position of the two bridges
A map showing the frequency of the mouse's visits to each position

You should print the items above (double space between trips) for each trip by the mouse.

6. In competitive diving, each diver makes three dives of varying degrees of difficulty. Nine judges score the dive from 0 to 10 in steps of 0.5. The total score is obtained by discarding the lowest and highest of the judges' scores, adding the remaining scores, and then multiplying the scores by the degree of difficulty. The divers take turns, and when the competition is finished they are ranked according to score. Write a program to do the above, using the following input and output specifications.

Input:

Number of divers
Diver's name (ten characters), difficulty (Real), and judges' ratings (Real)

There will be a record like the above for each diver. All the records for Dive 1 will be grouped together, then all for Dive 2, then all for Dive 3.

Output:

Input data echo-printed in tabular form with appropriate headings, for example, Name, Difficulty, judge's number (1–9)
A table that contains the following information, sorted by final total, in descending order (highest diver first):

Name	Dive 1	Dive 2	Dive 3	Total

where name is the diver's name; Dive 1, Dive 2, and Dive 3 are the total points received for a single dive, as described above; and Total is the overall total

7. You work for the Jet Propulsion Laboratory. They want you to write a program that takes an array containing the digitized representation of a picture of the night sky and locates the stars on it. Each element of the array represents the amount of light hitting that portion of the image when the picture was taken. Intensities range from 0 to 20.

Sample Input:

0	3	4	0	0	0	6	8
5	13	6	0	0	0	2	3
2	6	2	7	3	0	10	0
0	0	4	15	4	1	6	0
0	0	7	12	6	9	10	4
5	0	6	10	6	4	8	0

A star is probably located in the area covered by the array element i,j, if the following is the case:

(A(i,j) + sum of the 4 surrounding intensities) / 5 > 6.0

Ignore possible stars along the edges of the array.

Input:

A title
An array of intensities

Output:

The desired output is a star map containing asterisks where you have found a star and blanks elsewhere, such as

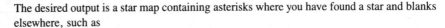

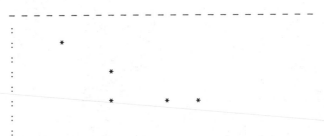

Print two blanks for the "no star" case. The presence of a star should be indicated by a blank, followed by an asterisk. The chart should have a border and be labeled with the title.

Records and Data Abstraction

GOALS

- To be able to define a record data type.
- To be able to access a field in a record variable.
- To be able to use arrays of records to solve a given problem.
- To be able to define a hierarchical record structure.
- To be able to access values stored in a hierarchical record variable.
- To be able to use the WITH statement to simplify accessing fields in records.
- To be able to choose and design an appropriate array and/or record data structure for a given problem.

In the last three chapters, we looked in depth at a homogeneous structured data type called an array. We discussed common algorithms that are applied to arrays: sorting, linear searching, and binary searching. We added a data structures section to our top-down design. Clearly, how we choose to represent our data is an important aspect of the programming process.

Although the array is an extremely useful data structure, it can be used only when the components are all the same data type. In this chapter we examine a nonhomogeneous structured data type called a **record.** The components of a record do not have to be of the same data type, and they are accessed by name rather than by relative position.

The last chapter closed with a discussion of how to choose a data structure. We continue this discussion at the end of this chapter, including the record among the possible choices.

Records

Records allow us to group related components together, regardless of their data types. Each component in a record is given a name called a **field identifier,** which is used to access the component.

Record   A structured data type with a fixed number of components that are accessed by name, not by index. The components may be different types.

Field Identifier   The name of a component in a record.

The syntax template for the record data type is given below.

> **RECORD**
> field-list
> **END;**

Here is the template for a field list.

> identifier, identifier . . . : type;
> identifier, identifier . . . : type

You probably recognize this syntax as being nearly identical to a series of variable declarations. Be careful: this is a type declaration, and we must still declare variables of this type in the VAR section for any memory locations to be associated with these identifiers. As an example, let's use a record to describe a student in a class. We want to store the first and last name, the overall grade point average prior to this class, the grade on programming assignments, the grade on quizzes, the final exam grade, and the final course grade.

```
CONST
  Name_Length = 15;

TYPE
  Grade_Type = (A, B, C, D, F);
  Name_String = String[Name_Length];
  Student_Record = RECORD
                     First_Name,
                     Last_Name : Name_String;
                     GPA : Real;
                     Program_Grade : 0..400;
                     Quiz_Grade,
                     Final_Exam : 0..300;
                     Course_Grade : Grade_Type
                   END;   (* Record *)

VAR
  First_Student,
  Student:
    Student_Record;
  Index,
  Grade:
    Integer;
```

First_Name, Last_Name, GPA, Program_Grade, Quiz_Grade, Final_Exam, and Course_Grade are field identifiers within the record type Student_Record. These field identifiers make up the field list. Note that each field identifier is given a type.

First_Name and Last_Name are of type Name_String, which is a string type. GPA is a Real field. Program_Grade is an Integer field in the subrange 0 to 400. Quiz_Grade and Final_Exam are Integer fields in the subrange 0 to 300. Course_Grade is an enumerated data type made up of the grades A through D and F.

None of these fields is associated with memory locations until we declare a variable of this record type. Student_Record is merely a pattern for a record (see Figure 14-1). First_Student and Student are variables of type Student_Record.

Figure 14-1
Pattern for a Record

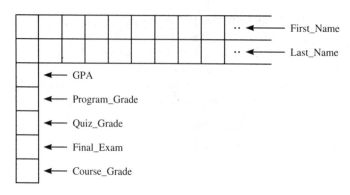

The fields of a record variable are accessed by giving the name of the variable, followed by a period, and then the field identifier. This expression is called a **field selector.** The syntax template is

record-variable.field-identifier

To access the GPA of First_Student, we would write,

```
First_Student.GPA
```

To access the final exam score of Student, we would write,

```
Student.Final_Exam
```

Field Selector   The expression used to access components of a record variable. It is formed using the record variable name and the field identifier, separated by a period.

The component of a record accessed by the field selector is treated just like any other variable of the same type. It may be used in an assignment statement, passed as a parameter, and so on. Figure 14-2 shows the record variable Student with the field selector for each field. In this example, some processing has already taken place, so values are stored in some of the components.

Let's demonstrate the use of these field selectors. Using our example record, the following code segment reads in a final exam grade; adds up the program grade, the quiz grade, and the final exam grade; and then assigns a letter grade to the result.

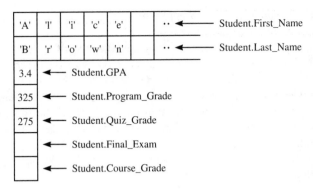

Figure 14-2
Record Variable
Student with Field
Selectors

```
Read(Student.Final_Exam);
Grade := Student.Final_Exam + Student.Program_Grade + Student.Quiz_Grade;
IF Grade >= 900
   THEN
      Student.Course_Grade := A
   ELSE
      IF Grade >= 800
         THEN
            Student.Course_Grade := B
   ELSE ...
```

Just as we can read values into specific components of an array, we can read values into fields of a record. Read(Student.Final_Exam) reads a value from Input and stores the value into the Final_Exam field of Student. As with arrays, we *cannot* read in whole records when using text files; we must read values into a record one field at a time. In the next chapter we look at a different kind of file from which whole records can be read at once.

The record component Student.Last_Name is an array. We access the individual elements in this component just as we would access the components in any other array: we give the name of the array followed by the index, which is enclosed in brackets.

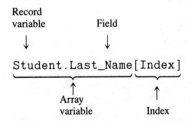

For the record structure defined earlier, Student.Last_Name[1] would access the first letter in the last name, Student.First_Name[2] would access the second position in the first name, and so on.

In addition to being able to access individual components of a record variable, we can manipulate records as a whole. This means, for example, that entire records can be formal parameters for procedures or functions. Let's define a function that takes our example record as a parameter.

The task of this function is to determine if a student's grade in a course is consistent with his or her overall grade point average (GPA). *Consistent* is defined to mean that the course grade is the same as the rounded GPA. The GPA is calculated on a 4-point scale, where A is 4, B is 3, C is 2, D is 1, and F is 0. If the rounded GPA is 4 and the course grade is A, then the function returns True. If the rounded GPA is 4 and the course grade is not A, then the function returns False. Each of the other grades is tested the same way.

Function Consistent is coded below. The formal parameter A_Student is a record of type Student_Record.

```
FUNCTION Consistent (A_Student:
                        Student_Record);
                        Boolean;

(* This function returns True if the course *)
(* grade is consistent with the overall GPA *)

TYPE
  GPA = 0..4;

VAR
  Int_GPA:
    GPA;

BEGIN (* Consistent *)
  Int_GPA := Round(A_Student.GPA);
  CASE Int_GPA OF
    0 : Consistent := (A_Student.Course_Grade = F);
    1 : Consistent := (A_Student.Course_Grade = D);
    2 : Consistent := (A_Student.Course_Grade = C);
    3 : Consistent := (A_Student.Course_Grade = B);
    4 : Consistent := (A_Student.Course_Grade = A);
  END   (* Case *)
END;    (* Consistent *)
```

Being able to manipulate records as a whole also means that one record variable can be assigned to another record variable of the same type. For example, if Another_Student is declared to be of Student_Record, the statement

```
Another_Student := Student
```

assigns the entire contents of the record variable Student to the record variable Another_Student.

Let's review the syntax and semantics of the record data type in the context of another example. A parts wholesaler wants to computerize her operation. Until now she has kept the inventory on handwritten 8 × 10 cards. A typical inventory card contains the following data:

Part number: 1A3321
Description: cotter pin
Cost: 0.012
Quantity on hand: 2100

A record is a natural choice for describing a part. Each item on the inventory card can be a field of the record. The record definition looks like this:

```
TYPE
   Part_Type = RECORD
                  Part_Number : String[6];
                  Description : String[20];
                  Cost : Real;
                  Quantity : Integer
               END;   (* Record *)

VAR
   Part:
     Part_Type;
```

The reserved words RECORD and END bracket the field declaration. Each field identifier is followed by a colon and a type, *just like the declaration of any variable*. Field identifiers must be unique within a record type, just as variable identifiers must be unique within a VAR section.

Once a record variable has been declared, the field selectors of the record variable are treated and used in the same way as any other declared variable. Field selectors can be used in expressions such as:

```
Part.Quantity := Part.Quantity + 24;
IF Part.Cost <= 5.00
   THEN
      Writeln('Cost is ', Part.Cost:4:2);
```

If the parts wholesaler supplied inventory data that looked like

```
2B3310Ring, piston            2.95    15
```

then the following statement would read and store the data in the appropriate fields.

```
Readln(Part.Part_Number, Part.Description, Part.Cost, Part.Quantity);
```

Part.Part_Number, Part.Description, Part.Cost, and Part.Quantity are the field selectors for the fields of the record variable Part.

Our examples have shown record types defined within the TYPE section—that is, as named types. You can also define record types anonymously in the VAR section; however, we do not recommend that you do so. Defining any data type in the VAR section is anonymous typing. All the arguments given in the last three chapters against anonymous typing apply to record types as well.

Arrays of Records

Although single records can be useful, many applications require a collection of records. For example, a business needs a list of parts records, and a teacher needs a list of students in a class. Arrays are ideal for these applications. We simply define an array whose components are records.

Let's define a grade book to be a list of students as follows:

```
CONST
   Name_Length = 15;
   Max_Students = 150;
   Test_Points = 300;
   Prog_Points = 400;

TYPE
   Test_Index = 0..Test_Points;
   Program_Index = 0..Prog_Points;
   Student_Index = 1..Max_Students;
   Grade_Type = (A, B, C, D, F);
   Name_String = String[Name_Length];
   Student_Record = RECORD
                       First_Name,
                       Last_Name : Name_String;
                       GPA : Real;
                       Program_Grade : Program_Index;
                       Quiz_Grade,
                       Final_Exam : Test_Index;
                       Course_Grade : Grade_Type
                    END;   (* Record *)
   Students = ARRAY [Student_Index] OF Student_Record;

VAR
   Grade:
      Integer;
   Count:
      Student_Index;
   Grade_Book:
      Students;
   List_Length:
      Integer;
```

Figure 14-3
Array Grade_Book
with Records as
Elements

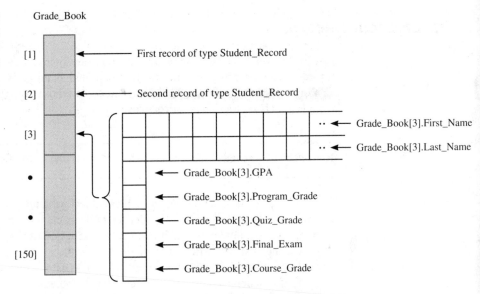

This structure can be visualized as shown in Figure 14-3.

An element of Grade_Book is selected by an index. Grade_Book[3] is the third component in the array variable Grade_Book. Each component of Grade_Book is a record of type Student_Record. To access the course grade of the third student, we use the following expression:

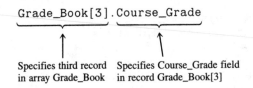

```
Grade_Book[3].Course_Grade
```

Specifies third record   Specifies Course_Grade field
in array Grade_Book   in record Grade_Book[3]

To access the first character in the last name of the third student, we use the following expression:

```
Grade_Book[3].Last_Name[1]
```

Specifies third record   Specifies Last_Name   Specifies first character
in array Grade_Book   field (an array)   in Last_Name field

The following code fragment prints the first and last name of each student in the class:

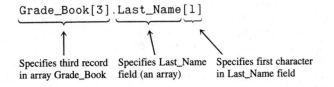

```
FOR Count := 1 TO List_Length DO
   Writeln(Grade_Book[Count].First_Name,' ', Grade_Book[Count].Last_Name)
```

Hierarchical Records

Just as the components of an array can be of any type, so can the components of a record. We have seen cases where the type of a field identifier is an array. A component of a record can also be another record. Records whose components are themselves records are called **hierarchical records.**

Hierarchical Records   Records in which at least one of the fields is itself a record.

Let's look at an example where a hierarchical structure is appropriate. A small machine shop keeps information about each of its machines. There is descriptive information, such as the identification number, a description of the machine, the purchase date, and the cost. Statistical information is also kept, such as the number of down days, the failure rate, and the date of last service. What is a reasonable way to represent all this information? First, let's look at a flat (nonhierarchical) record structure that holds this information.

```
CONST
  Number_Of_Machines = 25;
  Length_Of_Description = 50;

TYPE
  Machine_Index = 1..Number_Of_Machines;
  Description_Type = String[Length_Of_Description];
  Machine_Record = RECORD
                     ID_Number : Integer;
                     Description : Description_Type;
                     Fail_Rate : Real;
                     Last_Serviced_Month : 1..12;
                     Last_Serviced_Day : 1..31;
                     Last_Serviced_Year : 1900..2020;
                     Down_Days : Integer;
                     Purchase_Date_Month : 1..12;
                     Purchase_Date_Day : 1..31;
                     Purchase_Date_Year : 1900..2020;
                     Cost : Real
                   END;  (* Record *)
  Inventory_Type = ARRAY [Machine_Index] OF Machine_Record;
```

Type machine record has eleven fields. There is so much detailed information here that it is difficult to quickly get a feeling for what the record represents. Let's see if we can reorganize it into a hierarchical structure that makes more sense. The information can be divided into two groups: information that changes and information that does not. There are also two dates to be kept: date of purchase and date of last service.

These observations suggest use of a record describing a date, a record describing the statistical data, and an overall record containing the other two as components. The following type definition reflects this structure.

```
CONST
  Number_Of_Machines = 25;
  Length_Of_Description = 50;

TYPE
  Machine_Index = 1..Number_Of_Machines;
  Description_Type = String[Length_Of_Description];
  Date_Type = RECORD
                Month : 1..12;
                Day : 1..31;
                Year : 1900..2020
              END;  (* Record *)
  Statistics_Type = RECORD
                      Fail_Rate : Real;
                      Last_Serviced : Date_Type;
                      Down_Days : Integer
                    END;  (* Record *)
  Machine_Record = RECORD
                     ID_Number : Integer;
                     Description : Description_Type;
                     History : Statistics_Type;
                     Purchase_Date : Date_Type;
                     Cost : Real
                   END;  (* Record *)
  Inventory_Type = ARRAY [Machine_Index] OF Machine_Record;

VAR
  Inventory:
    Inventory_Type;
  Machine:
    Machine_Record;
  Counter:
    Machine_Index;
  Current_Date:
    Date_Type;
  Sum:
    Integer;
```

The contents of a machine record are now much more obvious. Two of the components of the record type Machine_Record are themselves records. Purchase_Date is of record type Date_Type, and History is of record type Statistics_Type. One of the components of record type Statistics_Type is a record of type Date_Type.

How do we access a hierarchical structure such as this one? We build the accessing expressions (field selectors) for the fields of the embedded records from left to right, beginning with the record variable name. Following are some expressions and the components they access.

Expression	Component Accessed
`Machine.Purchase_Date`	Date_Type record variable
`Machine.Purchase_Date.Month`	Month field of a Date_Type record variable
`Machine.Purchase_Date.Year`	Year field of a Date_Type record variable
`Machine.History.Last_Serviced.Year`	Year field of a Date_Type record variable contained in a record of type Statistics_Type

Figure 14-4 is a pictorial representation of Machine with values. Look carefully at how each component is accessed.

We can, of course, have an array of hierarchical records. Inventory is such an array. We can access the year that the first machine was purchased using the following expression,

```
Inventory[1].Purchase_Date.Year
```

Figure 14-4   *Hierarchical Records in Machine*

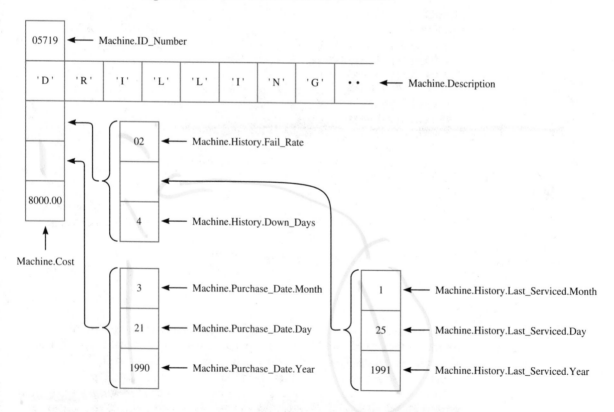

WITH Statement

In working with record variables, we often need to access one or more fields repeatedly in a small section of code. As we have seen, field selectors can get rather long and cumbersome. The WITH statement allows us to abbreviate the notation of field selectors by specifying the record name once and then using just the field identifiers to select the record components. The form of the WITH statement is:

```
WITH record variable DO
   statement
```

Let's look at how the WITH statement simplifies the code of a procedure to print out a record of type Machine_Record. First we show how we write the procedure without the WITH statement.

```
PROCEDURE Write_Machine (Machine:
                                Machine_Record);

BEGIN (* Write_Machine *)
   Writeln(Machine.ID_Number);
   Writeln(Machine.Description);
   Writeln(Machine.History.Fail_Rate);
   Writeln(Machine.History.Last_Serviced.Month:2, '/',
           Machine.History.Last_Serviced.Day:2, '/',
           Machine.History.Last_Serviced.Year:4);
   Writeln(Machine.History.Down_Days:4);
   Writeln(Machine.Purchase_Date.Month:2, '/',
           Machine.Purchase_Date.Day:2, '/',
           Machine.Purchase_Date.Year:4);
   Writeln(Machine.Cost:8:2)
END;  (* Write_Machine *)
```

Now let's see how the WITH statement can be used to simplify this procedure.

```
PROCEDURE Write_Machine (Machine:
                                Machine_Record);
```

```
BEGIN (* Write_Machine *)
  WITH Machine DO
    BEGIN
      Writeln(ID_Number);
      Writeln(Description);
      Writeln(History.Fail_Rate);
      Writeln(History.Last_Serviced.Month:2, '/',
              History.Last_Serviced.Day:2, '/',
              History.Last_Serviced.Year:4);
      Writeln(History.Down_Days:4);
      Writeln(Purchase_Date.Month:2, '/',
              Purchase_Date.Day:2, '/',
              Purchase_Date.Year:4);
      Writeln(Cost:8:2)
    END
END;  (* Write_Machine *)
```

Within the scope of the WITH statement, each field name refers to the record variable named in the WITH statement. In this case, each field name refers to the record variable Machine. Thus, within the scope of the WITH statement, each record component can be selected by the field identifier alone; the full field selector is not necessary.

This example can be simplified further by using a nested WITH statement. Let's rewrite procedure Write_Machine so that every field selector is reduced to a simple identifier. Notice that the nested WITH statements mimic the hierarchy of the record structure in this code.

```
PROCEDURE Write_Machine (Machine:
                            Machine_Record);

BEGIN (* Write_Machine *)
  WITH Machine DO
    BEGIN
      Writeln(ID_Number);
      Writeln(Description);
      WITH History DO
        BEGIN
          Writeln(Fail_Rate);
          WITH Last_Serviced DO
            Writeln(Month:2, '/', Day:2, '/', Year:4);
          Writeln(Down_Days:4)
        END;
      WITH Purchase_Date DO
        Writeln(Month:2, '/', Day:2, '/', Year:4);
      Writeln(Cost:8:2)
    END
END;  (* Write_Machine *)
```

Here is another example. The following code segment prints out the ID number and year of purchase of each machine with a failure rate of more than 8 percent:

```
FOR Counter := 1 TO Number_Of_Machines DO
  WITH Inventory[Counter] DO
    WITH History DO
      IF Failure_Rate > 0.08
        THEN
          Writeln(ID_Number:6, Purchase_Date.Year:6);
```

Pascal allows us to abbreviate nested WITH statements further by listing record and field names in a single WITH statement. For example, the preceding nested WITH statements can be abbreviated as follows:

```
FOR Counter := 1 TO Number_Of_Machines DO
  WITH Inventory[Counter], History DO
    IF Failure_Rate > 0.08
      THEN
        Writeln(ID_Number:6, Purchase_Date.Year:6);
```

Here is another example. The following code segment counts the number of machines that have not been serviced within the current year:

```
Sum := 0;
FOR Counter := 1 TO Number_Of_Machines DO
  WITH Inventory[Counter], History DO
    IF Current_Date.Year <> Last_Serviced.Year
      THEN
        Sum := Sum + 1;
```

More on Choosing Data Structures

Representing Logical Entities with Hierarchical Records

We have demonstrated how we design our algorithms and data structures in parallel. We progress from the logical or abstract data structure envisioned at the top level through the refinement process until we reach the concrete coding in Pascal. We also have shown two ways to represent the logical structure of a machine record in a shop inventory. The first used a record where all the components in an entry were defined (made concrete) at the same time. The second used a hierarchical record where the dates and statistics describing a machine's history were defined in lower-level records.

Let's look again at the two different structures we declared to represent our logical data structure.

```
CONST
  Number_Of_Machines = 25;
  Length_Of_Description = 50;
```

```
TYPE
  Machine_Index = 1..Number_Of_Machines;
  Description_Type = String[Length_Of_Description];

(* 1 *)

  Machine_Record = RECORD
                     ID_Number : Integer;
                     Description : Description_Type;
                     Fail_Rate : Real;
                     Last_Serviced_Month : 1..12;
                     Last_Serviced_Day : 1..31;
                     Last_Serviced_Year : 1900..2020;
                     Down_Days : Integer;
                     Purchase_Date_Month : 1..12;
                     Purchase_Date_Day : 1..31;
                     Purchase_Date_Year : 1900..2020;
                     Cost : Real
                   END;   (* Record *)

(* 2 *)

  Date_Type = RECORD
                Month : 1..12;
                Day : 1..31;
                Year : 1900..2020
              END;   (* Record *)
  Statistics_Type = RECORD
                      Fail_Rate : Real;
                      Last_Serviced : Date_Type;
                      Down_Days : Integer
                    END;   (* Record *)
  Machine_Record = RECORD
                     ID_Number : Integer;
                     Description : Description_Type;
                     History : Statistics_Type;
                     Purchase_Date : Date_Type;
                     Cost : Real
                   END;   (* Record *)
```

Which of these two representations is better? The second one is better for two reasons.

First, it groups elements together logically. The statistics and the dates are entities within themselves. We may want to have a date or a machine history in another record structure. If we define the dates and statistics only within Machine_Record (as in the first structure), we would have to define them again for every other data structure that needs them, giving us multiple definitions of the same logical entity.

Second, the details of the entities (statistics and dates) are pushed down to a lower level in the second structure. The principle of deferring details to as low a level as possible should be applied to designing data structures as well as to designing algorithms. How a machine history or a date is represented is not relevant to our concept of a machine record, so the details need not be specified until it is time to write the algorithms to manipulate those fields.

Pushing the implementation details of a data structure to a lower level separates the logical description from the implementation. This concept is analogous to control abstraction, which we discussed in Chapter 7. The separation of the logical properties of a data structure from its implementation details is called **data abstraction,** which is a goal of effective programming and the foundation upon which abstract data types are built (see Chapter 12).

Data Abstraction   The separation of a data structure's logical properties from its implementation.

Eventually, all the logical properties have to be defined in terms of concrete data types and routines written to manipulate them. If the implementation is properly designed, the same routines can be used to manipulate the structure in a wide variety of applications. For example, if we have a routine to compare dates, that routine can be used to compare dates representing days on which equipment was bought or maintained, or dates representing people's birthdays. The concept of designing a low-level structure and writing routines to manipulate it is the basis for the abstract data type constructed in the second case study, Manipulating Dates, at the end of this chapter.

Style Considerations in Choice of Data Structure

Just as there are style considerations in writing programs, there are also style considerations in choosing data structures. A program can produce a correct answer, but if it is difficult to debug, read, or modify, it can still be a poor program. A data structure can be used to solve a problem, and yet not reflect accurately the relationships within the problem. If the data structure does not reflect these relationships, it is not an effective structure for that program.

A data structure is a framework for holding data. This framework should be tailored to each particular problem by reflecting the relationships among data values, making it easy for users to see how the data items are related and how they should be processed to produce the required output. Since each problem is different, it is impossible to give a set of rules by which to judge an effective data structure. Instead, we examine the choices within a specific context, discuss the issues involved, and make some generalizations.

In Program Absent in Chapter 13, absentee data, made up of the number of people who were absent from each of six departments of a company during a particular week, was analyzed. The data was broken down further by day of the week. The main data structure used was a two-dimensional array Absentee_Data, where the first dimension represented departments, and the second dimension represented the days of the week. Each component was an integer value that represented the number of people who were absent. A one-dimensional array Averages held the average daily absentee figures for each department (see Figure 14-5).

Figure 14-5
Arrays
Absentee_Data
and Averages

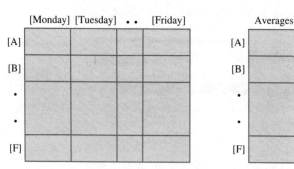

Would a record structure be a better choice to represent this information? Let's look at two possible representations of this same information as an array of records, and discuss the implications of each representation.

```
TYPE
   Day_Type = (Monday, Tuesday, Wednesday, Thursday, Friday);
   Department_Type = (A, B, C, D, E, F);
   Absences_By_Week = RECORD
                         By_Department : ARRAY [A..F] OF Integer
                      END;  (* Record *)
   Absences_By_Dept = RECORD
                         By_Week : ARRAY [Monday..Friday] OF Integer
                      END;  (* Record *)
   Table1_Type = ARRAY [Monday..Friday] OF Absences_By_Week;
   Table2_Type = ARRAY [A..F] OF Absences_By_Dept;

VAR
   Table1:
     Table1_Type;
   Table2:
     Table2_Type;
```

Table1 represents the data by day of the week, and Table2 represents the data by department. These two representations are pictured in Figures 14-6 and 14-7.

Figure 14-6
Absence Records
by Day

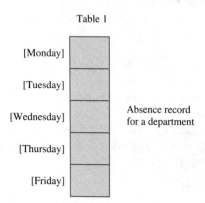

Absence record
for a department

Figure 14-7
Absence Records by
Department

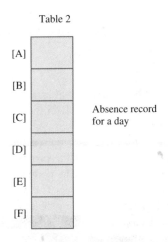

Table 2

[A]

[B]

[C]   Absence record
             for a day

[D]

[E]

[F]

Table1 and Table2 provide another example of data abstraction. In the first representation, the fact that the absences are recorded by day of the week is the important feature. The detail that the absences are further broken down by department is pushed to a lower level. Conversely, in the second representation, the fact that the absences are further broken down by day of the week is pushed to a lower level. In the two-dimensional array representation, both features—recording by department and by day of the week—are equally important (see Figure 14-8).

The best representation for a particular problem is the one that reflects the emphasis of the processing within the problem. This emphasis can be determined by looking at the questions that are being asked—that is, the results to be computed. If the primary processing involves absences by day of the week, the first structure is best. If the primary processing involves absences by department, the second representation is best. If both aspects of the processing are equally important, the two-dimensional array representation is best.

In this particular problem, management asks for absentee patterns across departments; therefore, the second record structure, Table2, is a better choice. In fact, the array Averages, which is used in the processing, can be incorporated in record type Absences_By_Dept.

Figure 14-8
Two-Dimensional
Array of
Absentee_Data

Absentee_Data

      [Monday] [Tuesday] • • [Friday]
[A]

[B]

 •

 •

[F]

```
Absences_By_Dept = RECORD
                      By_Week:  ARRAY [Monday..Friday] OF Integer;
                      Average:  Real
                   END;  (* Record *)
```

Notice that if all the processing on a two-dimensional array is either row processing *or* column processing, then an array of records may reflect the problem and the processing better than a two-dimensional array.

Data structures that accurately reflect the relationships among the data values in a problem lead to effective programs. The logic of the program is easier to understand because the data structures mirror the problem. The code of the program is easier to maintain because the logic of the program is clearer. The program is easier to modify because the data structure accurately represents the problem.

We should make one additional point here. The best structure is the *simplest* one that accurately reflects the problem and the processing. For example, don't use either an array or a record if simple variables suffice.

When you are deciding whether or not to use a structured data type, ask yourself, "Can I process as I read, or must all the data be read in before I can begin processing?" For example, if you are finding the average of a set of test grades, each test grade can be added into the sum as it is read. All you need are simple variables—no structured data types are necessary.

What if you want to compare each grade to the average? Since the average cannot be calculated until all the grades have been read, each individual grade must be kept in memory. Therefore, the test grades should be stored in an array. Of course, if the grades are on a file, the file can be reset and the grades reread, but remember that rereading the grades takes much more time than storing them in an array and retrieving them.

This discussion presupposes that you know where to begin. What if you look at a problem and don't even know what the choices are? Go back and carefully examine the problem statement. Do you understand what is being asked? Can you do by hand what is being asked? If so, what sorts of forms would you use? Would you set up a table with rows and columns on a sheet of paper? Would you set up a column and make hash marks? More than likely, the appropriate data structure resembles the forms you would create to do the job by hand.

If you cannot do the job by hand, your problem is more fundamental than the choice of a data structure—you need to clarify the problem. Try writing down everything you know about the problem. Then write down what your output must be and what you must have as input to produce that output. If necessary, refer to the problem-solving heuristics in Chapter 2.

PROBLEM-SOLVING CASE STUDY

Automated Address Book

Problem: You have a pocket address book that you have used for years, and it is now falling apart. Instead of copying all the items into a new book, you decide to automate your address book, including the following information for each entry:

Name _____

Address _____
      (street)

_____
(city)   (state)   (zip)

Telephone (_____) _____ - _____

Birth Date _____ / _____ / _____

Input: A series of entries containing a first and last name, a phone number, and a birth date. The exact form of an entry is to be determined.

Output: The entries in alphabetical order on file Friend_List.

Discussion: There are all kinds of interesting things we could do with the address book information if we had it on a computer file: print a listing, input a name and have the phone number printed, print a list of the people with birthdays each month, print names and addresses in zip-code order to facilitate sending cards, and so on. Let's not be too ambitious. We should do the program in stages. In the first stage we create the address book and save the information on a file. Since we want to enhance the program at a later time, we need to make the data structure as flexible as possible. As we do the top-down design, we pay particular attention to the development of the data structure.

As we start our design phase for this problem, we call all the information about one person an entry. We want to keep our entries in order by last name so that we can use a binary search to locate specific people. We can either enter the entries in alphabetical order, or enter them in any order and then sort them. Since some last names have changed over the years and you have not bothered to copy them on the appropriate page, it will be easier to let the program sort them rather than to enter them in alphabetical order.

Data Structure: To be determined.

Main Module *Level 0*

```
WHILE more entries DO
    Get Entry
    Insert Entry in alphabetical order
Write Entries on file
```

Before we can write the module for procedure Get_Entry, we have to decide what information we will keep on each person. Since we use this address book mainly to look up telephone numbers, we need each person's name and phone number. We skip addresses for now, but include birth dates.

Get Entry (Returns Entry: Entry_Type) *Level 1*

```
Get Name
Get Number
Get Birth Date
```

Write Entries on File (Receives Address_Book: Book_Type
List_Length: Friend_Count
Receives/Returns: Friend_List: Text)

```
Print First_Name, ' ', Last_Name
Print Area_Code, Phone_Number
Print Month, '/', Day, '/', Year
```

Get Name *Level 2*

```
Get first name
Get last name
```

Get Phone Number

```
Get area code
Get phone number
```

PROBLEM-SOLVING CASE STUDY cont'd.

Get Birth Date

```
┌─────────────────────────────┐
│                             │
│   Get Month, Day, Year      │
│                             │
└─────────────────────────────┘
```

Now we must decide what data types to use. We began with the general concept of an entry. We refined it to include the items needed in the entry. To go any further, we must decide how we will represent these items in Pascal. Up to this point, our design has been independent of any programming language, but now we must design specific algorithms for our data structure: reading in items, sorting items, and printing items.

Two of the items are names, that is, strings of alphabetic characters. These can be represented as strings. The area code and number can be integer numbers, but the phone number might be larger than MaxInt on some machines. Therefore, the area code is an integer number but the phone number is a string. We can represent birth dates as three integer numbers: Month, Day, and Year. Thus, an entry is represented by the seven components shown in Figure 14-9.

We can create a set of parallel arrays to hold all these items. First_Name, Last_Name, and Phone_Number are arrays of strings; Area_Code, Month, Day, and Year are one-dimensional arrays of integers. Each parallel row represents the information for one entry. This set of structures is shown in Figure 14-10.

This seems to be a very clumsy way of representing this logical structure: a parallel structure made up of seven different arrays. Yet this is the structure that you have to use for this type of problem if your programming language does not have the record data type—and some do not. However, in Pascal it makes more sense to define an entry using the record data type.

Let's look now at a data structure in which a record is used to represent the address book. The following declarations describe this structure.

```
CONST
  Name_Length = 15;
  Number_Of_Friends = 150;
```

Figure 14-9
Entry for
Address_Book

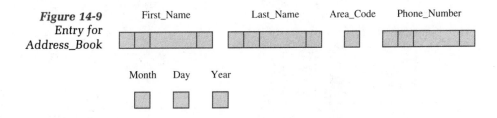

PROBLEM-SOLVING CASE STUDY *cont'd.*

```
TYPE
   Name_Index = 1..Name_Length;
   Friend_Index = 1..Number_Of_Friends;
   Name_Type = String[Name_Length];
   Entry_Type = RECORD
                    First_Name,
                    Last_Name : Name_Type;
                    Area_Code : 0..999;
                    Phone_Number : String[8];
                    Month : 1..12;
                    Day : 1..31;
                    Year : 1900..2020
                END;   (* Record *)
   Book_Type = ARRAY [Friend_Index] OF Entry_Type;

VAR
   Address_Book:
     Book_Type;
```

First_Name, Last_Name, Area_Code, Phone_Number, Month, Day, and Year are field identifiers within the record type Entry_Type. First_Name and Last_Name are strings of type Name_Type. Area_Code is an integer in the subrange 0 to 999. It could have been represented in a three-element character array, but a simple integer suffices. Phone_Number is defined as an eight-element character array. Phone numbers have only seven digits, but we decided to include the hyphen between the first three digits and the last four digits since this is how phone numbers are usually printed.

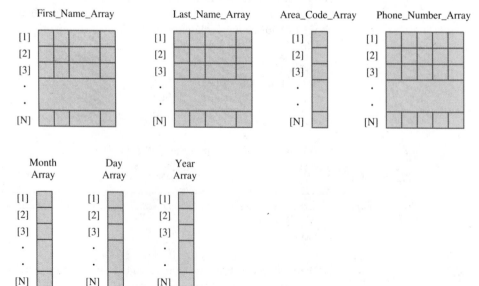

Figure 14-10
Parallel Arrays for Address_Book

PROBLEM-SOLVING CASE STUDY cont'd.

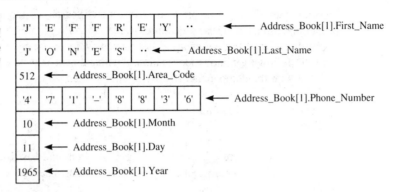

Figure 14-11
Entry for Record
Variable
Address_Book[1]

Month is an integer in the subrange 1 to 12. Day is an integer in the subrange 1 to 31. Year is an integer in the subrange 1900 to 2020. A complete entry with values stored in the record variable Address_Book[1] is shown in Figure 14-11.

We have now defined a data structure to hold the information in our address book. Before we can finish the algorithms to read the data, we have to decide how we want to enter the data. Let's enter it interactively. The user can be prompted to enter each component, and end of line (pressing Return) can be used to end the first and last name.

Since the first name and the last name are both character strings of length 15, we can use Readln to input both. The only thing that differs is the user prompt. Our design for this portion of the algorithm now looks like this:

Get Name (Returns Entry : Entry_Type)   *Level 2*

> Print 'Enter first name and press return.'
> Get first name
> Print 'Enter last name and press return.'
> Get last name

We can redo the module for getting the phone number.

Get Phone Number (Returns Entry : Entry_Type)   *Level 2*

> Prompt for Phone_Number
> Read Area_Code
> Read Phone_Number

Because the birth date can be read with a single statement, we will incorporate Get Birth Date directly into Get Entry.

In Chapter 12 we wrote procedures Insert and Search_Ord to insert an item into its proper place in a list. These procedures were used in Program Exam to insert last names as they were read into an array of last names. We can use the same procedures here with the following minor modification. The statement that compared the item being inserted with the components already in the list was:

```
IF Item > List[Index]
   THEN
```

Since our data structure is an array of records, Item and List[Index] are records, not simple variables. Therefore, the name of the field that is being compared must be added as follows:

```
IF Item.Last_Name > List[Index].Last_Name
   THEN
```

When coding the design, we need to write the prompts for the phone number and the birth date. Also, we haven't made any provision for keying errors, which is not realistic. After an entry has been read and before it is entered into the address book, let's ask the user whether the entry is correct. If the user says it is, the entry can be stored. If the user says it is not, the entry will not be saved.

We also have not determined how to end the reading process. After each entry, let's ask the user whether another entry is to be read. The main module now needs rewriting.

Main Module   *Level 0*

```
REPEAT
   Get Entry
   Print 'Is this entry correct? (Y or N)'
   Read Character
   IF Character IN ['y', 'Y']
      THEN
         Insert Entry
   Print 'Do you wish to continue? (Y or N)'
   Read Character
UNTIL Character IN ['n', 'N']

WHILE more entries
   Write Entries
```

Be suspicious of a boss who schedules
meetings instead of making decisions.

Frankes

Read Act
Request for Acting
Read Pascal Chapter 13
Read Vindication 1-35

January
19
Thursday

PROBLEM-SOLVING CASE STUDY *cont'd.*

Module Structure Chart:

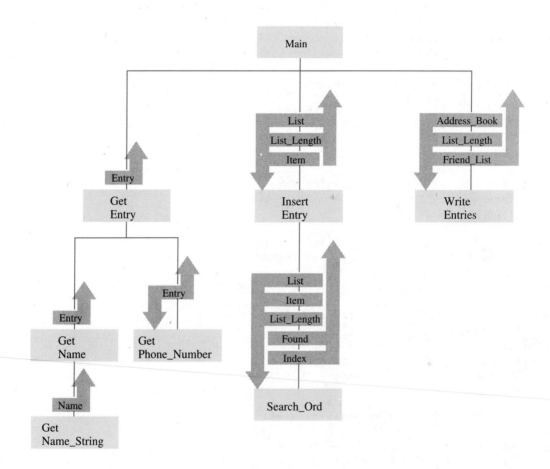

```
PROGRAM Friends (Input, Output, Friend_List);

(* First names, last names, phone numbers and birth dates are read *)
(* from the terminal.  An alphabetical listing is written on file  *)
(* Friend_List *)

CONST
  Name_Length = 15;
  Number_Of_Friends = 150;
  Blanks = '               ';
```

PROBLEM-SOLVING CASE STUDY cont'd.
_____

```
TYPE
  Friend_Index = 1..Number_Of_Friends;
  Friend_Count = 0..Number_Of_Friends;
  Name_Type = String[Name_Length];
  Entry_Type = RECORD
                   First_Name,
                   Last_Name : Name_Type;
                   Area_Code : 0..999;
                   Phone_Number : String[8];
                   Month : 1..12;
                   Day : 1..31;
                   Year : 1900..2020
                 END;  (* Record *)
  Book_Type = ARRAY [Friend_Index] OF Entry_Type;
  Item_Type = Entry_Type;
  List_Type = Book_Type;

VAR
  Address_Book:      (* Array of friend records         *)
    Book_Type;
  Character:         (* For response from keyboard       *)
    Char;
  Entry:             (* Current record being entered     *)
    Entry_Type;
  List_Length:       (* Number of entries in Address_Book *)
    Friend_Count;
  Friend_List:       (* Entries saved to use later       *)
    Text;

(*****************************************************************)

PROCEDURE Insert (VAR List:         (* List being inserted into   *)
                      List_Type;
                  VAR List_Length:   (* Number of entries in List *)
                      Integer;
                      Item:          (* Item being inserted        *)
                      Item_Type);

(* Item is inserted into its proper place in the sorted list.    *)
(* Assumption:  List_Length is less than Max_Length.  If a match *)
(* occurs, Item will be inserted before the one that is there    *)

VAR
  Place_Found:       (* Flag set if match occurs *)
    Boolean;
  Index,             (* Current position in List *)
     ·.                (* Loop control variables   *)
```

```
(****************************************************************)

PROCEDURE Search_Ord (    List:          (* List being searched    *)
                             List_Type;
                          Item:          (* Item being searched for *)
                             Item_Type;
                          List_Length:   (* Number of items in List *)
                             Integer;
                      VAR Found:         (* Match flag              *)
                             Boolean;
                      VAR Index:         (* Position to insert item *)
                             Integer);

(* List is searched for an occurrence of Item. If it is found,    *)
(* Found is True and Index is the place in the List where Item    *)
(* occurs.  Otherwise, Found is False and Index is List_Length + 1. *)
(* Assumption:  List is sorted in ascending order                 *)

VAR
  Stop:        (* Loop control flag *)
    Boolean;

BEGIN (* Search_Ord *)
  Index := 1;
  Stop := False;
  List[List_Length+1] := Item;
  (* Exit loop when value is found or not there *)
  WHILE NOT Stop DO
     (* Item is not in List[1]..List[Index-1] *)
     IF Item.Last_Name > List[Index].Last_Name
       THEN
          (* Item is not in List[1]..List[Index] *)
          Index := Index + 1
       ELSE
          (* Item is either found or not there *)
          Stop := True;
  (* Determine whether Item was found or not there *)
  Found := (Index <> List_Length + 1) AND (Item = List[Index])
END;  (* Search_Ord *)

(****************************************************************)
```

```
BEGIN (* Insert *)
  Search_Ord(List, Item, List_Length, Place_Found, Index);
  (* Shift List[Index]..List[List_Length] down one *)
  FOR Count := List_Length DOWNTO Index DO
    List[Count+1] := List[Count];
  List[Index] := Item;                    (* Insert Item         *)
  List_Length := List_Length + 1          (* Increment List_Length *)
END;   (* Insert *)


(******************************************************************)

PROCEDURE Get_Name (VAR Entry:          (* Record receiving names *)
                         Entry_Type);

(* Readln is called twice:  Once to get the first name and *)
(* once to get the last name *)

VAR
  Name:
    Name_Type;


  (******************************************************************)

BEGIN (* Get_Name *)
  Writeln('Enter first name and press return.');
  Readln(Entry.First_Name);
  Writeln('Enter last name and press return.');
  Readlin(Entry.Last_Name);
END;   (* Get_Name *)

(******************************************************************)

PROCEDURE Get_Phone_Number (VAR Entry:   (* Record receiving number *)
                                Entry_Type);

(* Area code and phone number are read and returned *)

VAR
  Index:
    1..9;
  Character:
    Char;

BEGIN (* Get_Phone_Number *)
  Writeln('Enter area code, blank, and the number. Include ''-''.');
  Read(Entry.Area_Code);
  Read(Character);                              (* Skip over blank *)
  Readln(Entry.Phone_Number)
END;   (* Get_Phone_Number *)
```

PROBLEM-SOLVING CASE STUDY *cont'd.*

```
(*********************************************************************)

PROCEDURE Get_Entry (VAR Entry:           (* Record being built *)
                         Entry_Type);

(* A complete entry is built and returned. Get_Name and *)
(* Get_Phone_Number are called *)

BEGIN (* Get_Entry *)
  Get_Name(Entry);
  Get_Phone_Number(Entry);
  Writeln('Enter birth date as three integers: Month, Day, Year');
  Readln(Entry.Month, Entry.Day, Entry.Year)
END;   (* Get_Entry *)

(*********************************************************************)

PROCEDURE Write_Entries (    AddressBook:     (* Array of friends    *)
                                Book_Type;
                             List_Length:   (* Number of entries   *)
                                Friend_Count;
                         VAR Friend_List:   (* File receiving list *)
                                Text);

(* All the entries are written on file Friend_List *)

VAR
  Counter:
    Friend_Index;

BEGIN (* Write_Entries *)
  FOR Counter := 1 TO List_Length DO
    BEGIN
      Writeln(Friend_List, Address_Book[Counter].First_Name, ' ',
              Address_Book[Counter].Last_Name);
      Writeln(Friend_List, '(', Address_Book[Counter].Area_Code:3, ') ',
              Address_Book[Counter].Phone_Number);
      Writeln(Friend_List, Address_Book[Counter].Month:2, '/',
              Address_Book[Counter].Day:2, '/',
              Address_Book[Counter].Year:4);
      Writeln(Friend_List)
    END
END;   (* Write_Entries *)

(*********************************************************************)
```

```
BEGIN  (* Friends *)
  Assign(Friend_List, 'FRIEND.DAT');
  List_Length := 0;
  Rewrite(Friend_List);
  REPEAT
    Get_Entry(Entry);
    Writeln('Is this entry correct? (Y or N)');
    Readln(Character);
    IF Character IN ['y', 'Y']
      THEN
        Insert(Address_Book, List_Length, Entry);
    Writeln('Do you wish to continue? (Y or N)');
    Readln(Character)
  UNTIL Character IN ['n', 'N'];
  Write_Entries(Address_Book, List_Length, Friend_List)
  Close(Friend_Last)
END.  (* Friends *)
```

Testing: This is an interactive program in which the user has a great deal of control. The user is prompted to enter data, then is asked if the data has been entered correctly. If the user indicates that there has been an error, the data is not saved. After the information about a person is entered, the user is asked whether he or she wishes to continue.

In testing this program, each of the options must be selected by the user at least once. When testing an interactive program, you may be tempted to sit down and just enter data randomly. However, if you don't keep a record of the data entered, the saved file will show only the correct entries. You won't know whether or not the sections of code that allow the program to ignore an incorrect entry were tested.

PROBLEM-SOLVING CASE STUDY

Manipulating Dates

Dates are often necessary pieces of information. Both the address book and machine shop examples had a date as part of the data. In fact, the machine shop example had two dates: the date of purchase and the date of last service. Each time we needed a date, we defined it again.

Often our processing of dates calls for us to compare two dates, print out a date, or determine the date a certain number of days away. Let's stop this duplication of effort and do the job once and for all—we'll write the code to support dates as an abstract data type.

The format for this case study has to be a little different. Instead of Input and Output sections, we give the formal parameter lists that define the input and output for the routines.

Problem: Create a structure to represent a date, and write a set of routines to operate on the structure. Make the structure and the routines general enough so they can be used in any program that needs to have these operations performed on dates. The operations are defined below.

Compare two dates: A test that takes two dates and determines whether the first comes before the second, is the same as the second, or comes after the second.

Print out a date: An output transformation that takes a date as input and writes it in the following form:

```
Month day ',' year (example:  January 1, 1991)
```

Determine the date a certain number of days away: Take as input a date and an integer value Days_Away. Return a date that is the input date plus Days_Away. For example, given the date January 1, 1991, and the value 20 for Days_Away, this constructor routine will return the date January 21, 1991.

Discussion: We discuss each of the routines separately after we have determined a common data structure for representing a date. Note that we are using the terms *routines* and *modules* rather than *procedures* and *functions* at this stage. One of the decisions to be made in each case is whether the routine should be coded as a procedure or a function.

To make this structure as useful as possible, we must make our representation as general as possible. Month and day can remain as subranges, as we have defined them in the previous examples. The year should not be limited, however; we make it a positive integer. We have chosen to represent only dates AD to simplify the routines.

```
TYPE
   Date_Type = RECORD
                  Month : 1..12;
                  Day : 1..31;
                  Year : 1..MaxInt
               END;  (* Record *)
```

Data Structures: All the routines operate on one or more record variables of type DateType.

Compare two dates: This operation takes two dates (Date1 and Date2) and determines whether the first one comes before the second one, they are the same, or the first one comes after the second one. We define an enumerated type with three values: Before, Same, After. The operation can then be coded as a function of the enumerated type. The interface between the operation and any module that uses it is the function heading

```
FUNCTION Compare (Date1,
                  Date2:
                     Date_Type):
                        Relation;
```

where Relation is the enumerated type (Before, Same, After).

If we were to compare dates in our head, we would first look at the years. If the years were different, we would immediately determine which date came first. If the years were the same, we would look at the months. If the months were the same, we would have to look at the days. As so often happens, this algorithm can be used directly in our function.

Compare

IF Date1.Year < Date2.Year
  Set Compare to Before
  ELSE IF Date1.Year > Date2.Year
    Set Compare to After
  ELSE IF Date1.Month < Date2.Month
    Set Compare to Before
  ELSE IF Date1.Day > Date2.Day
    Set Compare to After
  ELSE IF Date1.Day < Date2.Day
    Set Compare to Before
  ELSE IF Date1.Day > Date2.Day
    Set Compare to After
  ELSE
    Set Compare to Same

Function Compare is coded below. Note that the enumerated type Relation

```
TYPE
   Relation = (Before, Same, After);
```

must be defined in the main program.

```
FUNCTION Compare (Date1,        (* Date record to be compared *)
                  Date2:        (* Date record to be compared *)
                     Date_Type):
                        Relation;
```

PROBLEM-SOLVING CASE STUDY cont'd.

```
(* If Date1 is before Date2, Before is returned.  If Date1 is  *)
(* equal to Date2, Same is returned.  If Date1 is after Date2, *)
(* After is returned *)

BEGIN  (* Compare *)
  IF Date1.Year < Date2.Year                      (* Compare year  *)
    THEN
      Compare := Before
    ELSE IF Date1.Year > Date2.Year
      THEN
        Compare := After
    ELSE IF Date1.Month < Date2.Month             (* Compare month *)
      THEN
        Compare := Before
    ELSE IF Date1.Month > Date2.Month
      THEN
        Compare := After
    ELSE IF Date1.Day < Date2.Day                 (* Compare day   *)
      THEN
        Compare := Before
    ELSE IF Date1.Day > Date2.Day
      THEN
        Compare := After
    ELSE
      Compare := Same
END;  (* Compare *)
```

Testing: In testing this function, each path must be taken at least once. Programming Warm-Up exercise 11 asks you to design test data for this function and to write a driver that does the testing.

Print out a date: To make this routine more general, we should make the file on which the date is to be written a formal parameter. If the date is to be written on the screen, Output can be used as the actual parameter.

The date is to be printed in the form month, day, comma, and year. Since the month is represented as an integer in the subrange 1..12, we can use a CASE statement to print out the month in word form. We need a blank to separate the month and the day, and a comma followed by a blank to separate the day and the year. This is so straightforward that no further discussion is necessary. The procedure heading forms the interface between the operation and the modules that use it.

```
PROCEDURE Print_Date  (VAR Out_File:    (* File to write date on     *)
                            Text;
                            Date:        (* Date record to be written *)
                            Date_Type);
```

```
(* The date is printed out in standard form, with the month     *)
(* followed by the day, followed by the year.  The month is not  *)
(* abbreviated *)

BEGIN (* Print_Date *)
  CASE Date.Month OF
    1 : Write(Out_File, 'January');
    2 : Write(Out_File, 'February');
    3 : Write(Out_File, 'March');
    4 : Write(Out_File, 'April');
    5 : Write(Out_File, 'May');
    6 : Write(Out_File, 'June');
    7 : Write(Out_File, 'July');
    8 : Write(Out_File, 'August');
    9 : Write(Out_File, 'September');
   10 : Write(Out_File, 'October');
   11 : Write(Out_File, 'November');
   12 : Write(Out_File, 'December')
  END;  (* Case *)
  Write(Out_File, ' ', Date.Day:1, ', ', Date.Year:5)
END;  (* Print_Date *)
```

Testing: In testing this procedure, each month should be printed at least once. The year and the day each should be tested at their end points and several points between.

Determine the date a certain number of days away: The algorithm to calculate a date in the future is more complex than the previous two algorithms dealing with dates. If the current date plus Days_Away is still within the same month, there is no problem. If the current date plus Days_Away is within the next month, then the day must be calculated and the month must be changed. Days_Away could, in fact, be several months away or even in the next year (or the next . . .).

We can determine whether the given date (call it Date) plus Days_Away is within the current month by adding Days_Away to the day field of the date and comparing this value (call it New_Day) with the maximum number of days in the current month. If New_Day is greater than the number of days in the month, the month must be incremented, and New_Day must be adjusted. This process can be repeated until New_Day is within the current month. We must not forget to increment the year when the month changes from December to January, and to check for leap year when the month is February. The procedure heading can be defined as follows:

```
PROCEDURE Adjust_Date(    Date:
                          Date_Type;
                          Days_Away:
                          Integer;
                      VAR New_Date:
                          Date_Type);
```

Adjust Date

```
Set New_Day to Current.Day + Days_Away
Set New_Date to Date
REPEAT
   Set Days_In_Month to number of days in Date.Month
   IF New_Day <= Days_In_Month
      Set New_Date.Day to New_Day
      Set Finished to True
   ELSE
      Set New_Day to New_Day - Days_In_Month
      Set New_Date.Month to (New_Date.Month MOD 12) + 1
      IF New_Date.Month = 1
         Set New_Date.Year to New_Date.Year + 1
      Set Finished to False
UNTIL Finished
```

We can use the old rhyme "Thirty days hath September, April, June, and November . . . " to determine how many days are in each month.

Number of Days

```
CASE Month
   9,4,6,11 : Set Days_In_Month to 30
   1,3,5,7,8,10,12 : Set Days_In_Month to 31
   2 : IF (Date.Year MOD 4 = 0) and not (Date.Year MOD 100 = 0) or
       (Date.Year MOD 400 = 0)
       THEN Set Days_In_Month to 29
       ELSE Set Days_In_Month to 28
```

The algorithm for finding the number of days in a month can be coded as an integer function that takes New_Date as a parameter. This function can be embedded within procedure Adjust_Date.

```
PROCEDURE Adjust_Date (   Date:           (* Initial date record   *)
                            Date_Type;
                          Days_Away:      (* Number of days to add *)
                            Integer;
                      VAR New_Date:       (* Resulting date record *)
                            Date_Type);
```

```
(* New_Date is the date Days_Away from Date. Days_Away must be *)
(* nonnegative *)

VAR
  New_Day,                  (* Days_Away + Date.Day        *)
  Number_Of_Days:           (* Number of days in month     *)
    Integer;
  Finished:                 (* New_Date has been calculated *)
    Boolean;                (* When Finished is True        *)

  (*************************************************************)

FUNCTION  Days_In_Month  (Date:
                                 Date_Type):
                                 Integer;

(* Days_In_Month returns the number of days in Date.Day. *)
(* Leap year is considered *)

BEGIN (* Days_In_Month *),
  WITH Date DO
    CASE Month OF
      9,4,6,11: Days_In_Month := 30;
      1,3,5,7,8,10,12 : Days_In_Month := 31;
      2 : IF (Year MOD 4 = 0) AND NOT (Year MOD 100 = 0) OR
             (Year MOD 400 = 0)
          THEN                                      (* Leap year *)
             Days_In_Month := 29
          ELSE
             Days_In_Month := 28
    END   (* Case *)
END;   (* Days_In_Month *)

  (*************************************************************)
```

PROBLEM-SOLVING CASE STUDY *cont'd.*

```
BEGIN  (* Adjust_Date *)
  New_Day := Date.Day + Days_Away;
  (* Initialize New_Date to Date *)
  New_Date := Date;
  REPEAT
    Number_Of_Days := Days_In_Month(New_Date);
    IF New_Day <= Number_Of_Days
      (* This is the correct month *)
      THEN
        BEGIN
          New_Date.Day := New_Day;
          Finished := True
        END
      ELSE
        (* Increment month and continue *)
        BEGIN
          New_Day := New_Day - Number_Of_Days;
          New_Date.Month := (New_Date.Month MOD 12) + 1
          IF New_Date.Month = 1
            THEN
              New_Date.Year := NewDate.Year + 1;
          Finished := False
        END
  UNTIL Finished
END;  (* Adjust_Date *)
```

Testing: To test this procedure, we need to construct a driver that calls procedure Adjust_Date with different values for both Date and Days_Away. The values for Days_Away must include 28, 29, 30, and 31, as well as multiples of these values and numbers less than 28. Leap year must be tested; a year with the last two digits 00 must be tested. Values that cause the year to change must be tested, as well as values that cause the year to change more than once. Programming Warm-Up exercise 12 asks you to carry out this testing.

A date is a logical entity for which we have now developed an implementation. We have created, implemented, and tested a date data type that we can use whenever we have the date as part of our data. If a particular problem requires an additional operation on a date, it can be implemented, tested, and added to our set of date operations.

We have said that data abstraction is an important principle of proper style. What we have done here is an example of data abstraction. From now on, when a problem needs a date, we can stop our decomposition at the logical level. We do not need to worry about the implementation details each time.

PROBLEM-SOLVING CASE STUDY

Birthday Calls

Problem: In Chapter 10 we commented that everyone has at least one friend who never forgets important dates in the lives of his or her friends. Let's write a program to go through your address book and print the names and phone numbers of all the people who have birthdays within the next two weeks, so you can give them a call.

Input: A date (from the keyboard); and a list of names, phone numbers, and birth dates (file Friend_List).

Output: The names, phone numbers, and birthdays of anyone whose birthday is within the next two weeks.

Discussion: When looking for birthdays, we are interested in month and day only—the year is not important. If we were going through a conventional address book checking for birthdays by hand, we would write down the month and day of the date two weeks away and compare it to the month and day of each friend's birth date.

We can use the same algorithm in our program. Procedure Adjust_Date can be used to calculate the date two weeks (fourteen days) from the current date. Procedure Compare can be used to determine whether a friend's birthday comes before or on the date two weeks away. How do we ignore the year? We set the year of each friend's birth date to the current year for the comparison. However, if the current date plus fourteen days is in the next year, and the friend's birthday is in January, then we must set the year to the current year plus one for the comparison to work correctly.

Data Structure: Date data type.

Main Module   *Level 0*

```
Get Current Date
Adjust Date (Current_Date, 14, Target_Date)
WHILE NOT EOF (Friend_List)
    Get Entry
    Set Temp_Date to Entry.Birth_Date
    Set Temp_Date.Year to Current_Date.Year
    IF (Target_Date.Year<>Current_Date.Year) AND (Entry.Birth_Date.Month = 1)
        Set Temp_Date.Year to Target_Date.Year
    IF Compare(Temp_Date, Target_Date) <= Same
        Print Entry
```

Get Current Date (Returns Current_Date : Date_Type   *Level 1*

> Print 'Please input current date as month, day, and year.'
> Print 'Use digits for month. Separate with blanks.'
> Read Current_Date.Month, Current_Date.Day, Current_Date.Year

Print Entry (Receives Entry : Entry_Type2,
                    Temp_Date : Date_Type)

> Print First_Name, Last_Name
> Print Phone Number
> Print Birthday

Since Adjust_Date, Compare, and Print_Date already exist, no more decomposition is necessary.

Module Structure Chart:

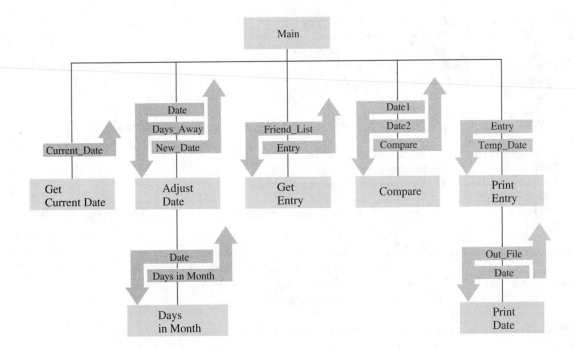

```
PROGRAM Birthday_Calls (Input, Output, Friend_List);

(* A date is read from the keyboard, and a date two weeks away is   *)
(* calculated.  Names, phone numbers, and birthdays of all those    *)
(* on file Friend_List whose birthdays come on or before the date   *)
(* two weeks away are printed *)

CONST
  Name_Length = 15;
  Days_Hence = 14;

TYPE
  Name_Type = String[Name_Length];
  Date_Type = RECORD
                  Month : 1..12;
                  Day : 1..31;
                  Year : 0..MaxInt
               END;  (* Record *)
  Phone_Type = RECORD
                   Area_Code : 0..999;
                   Number : String[8];
                END;  (* Record *)
  Entry_Type2 = RECORD
                    First_Name,
                    Last_Name : Name_Type;
                    Phone : Phone_Type;
                    Birth_Date : Date_Type
                 END;  (* Record *)
  Relation = (Before, Same, After);

VAR
  Entry:            (* Current record from Friend_List being checked *)
    Entry_Type2;
  Current_Date,     (* Month, Day and Year of current day            *)
  Temp_Date,        (* Month and Day of Birth_Date, current year     *)
  Target_Date:      (* Two weeks from current date                   *)
    Date_Type;
  Friend_List:      (* Input file of friend records                  *)
    Text;

(********************************************************************)

PROCEDURE Get_Current_Date (VAR Current_Date:   (* Today's date *)
                                  Date_Type);

(* Current date is entered from the console *)
```

PROBLEM-SOLVING CASE STUDY cont'd.

```pascal
BEGIN (* Get_Current_Date *)
  Writeln('Please input current date as month, day, and year.');
  Writeln('Use digits for month. Separate with blanks.');
  Readln(Current_Date.Month, Current_Date.Day, Current_Date.Year)
END;  (* Get_Current_Date *)

(* ************************************************************** *)

FUNCTION Compare (Date1,          (* Date record to be compared *)
                  Date2:          (* Date record to be compared *)
                    Date_Type):
                      Relation;

(* If Date1 is before Date2, Before is returned.  If Date1 is  *)
(* equal to Date2, Same is returned.  If Date1 is after Date2, *)
(* After is returned *)

BEGIN  (* Compare *)
  IF Date1.Year < Date2.Year                     (* Compare year *)
    THEN
      Compare := Before
    ELSE IF Date1.Year > Date2.Year
      THEN
        Compare := After
    ELSE IF Date1.Month < Date2.Month            (* Compare month *)
      THEN
        Compare := Before
    ELSE IF Date1.Month > Date2.Month
      THEN
        Compare := After
    ELSE IF Date1.Day < Date2.Day                (* Compare day  *)
      THEN
        Compare := Before
    ELSE IF Date1.Day > Date2.Day
      THEN
        Compare := After
    ELSE
      Compare := Same
END; (* Compare *)

(* ************************************************************** *)
```

PROBLEM-SOLVING CASE STUDY cont'd.

```
PROCEDURE Print_Date (VAR Out_File:          (* File receiving date *)
                                 Text;
                          Date:               (* Date being written  *)
                              Date_Type);

(* The date is printed out in standard form, with the month      *)
(* followed by the day, followed by the year.  The month is not *)
(* abbreviated *)

BEGIN (* Print_Date *)
  CASE Date.Month OF
     1 : Write(Out_File, 'January');
     2 : Write(Out_File, 'February');
     3 : Write(Out_File, 'March');
     4 : Write(Out_File, 'April');
     5 : Write(Out_File, 'May');
     6 : Write(Out_File, 'June');
     7 : Write(Out_File, 'July');
     8 : Write(Out_File, 'August');
     9 : Write(Out_File, 'September');
    10 : Write(Out_File, 'October');
    11 : Write(Out_File, 'November');
    12 : Write(Out_File, 'December')
  END;  (* Case *)
  Write(Out_File, ' ', Date.Day:1, ', ', Date.Year:5)
END;  (* Print_Date *)

(*******************************************************************)

PROCEDURE Adjust_Date (     Date:            (* Starting date       *)
                                Date_Type;
                            Days_Away:        (* Number of days to add *)
                                Integer;
                        VAR New_Date:         (* Calculated new date  *)
                                Date_Type);

(* New_Date is the date Days_Away from Date. Days_Away must be *)
(* nonnegative. *)

VAR
  New_Day,            (* Days_Away + Date.Day     *)
  Number_Of_Days: (* Number of days in month *)
    Integer;
  Finished:           (* True when New_Date has been calculated *)
    Boolean;

  (*******************************************************************)
```

```pascal
    FUNCTION Days_In_Month (Date:           (* Date being checked *)
                              Date_Type):
                                Integer;

  (* Days_In_Month returns the number of days in Date.Day. *)
  (* Leap year is considered *)

  BEGIN (* Days_In_Month *)
    WITH Date DO
      CASE Month OF
        9,4,6,11 : Days_In_Month := 30;
        1,3,5,7,8,10,12 : Days_In_Month := 31;
        2 : IF (Year MOD 4 = 0) AND NOT (Year MOD 100 = 0) OR
               (Year MOD 400 = 0)
            THEN
              Days_In_Month := 29
            ELSE
              Days_In_Month := 28
      END (* Case *)
  END;  (* Days_In_Month *)

  (**************************************************************)

BEGIN (* Adjust_Date *)
  New_Day := Date.Day + Days_Away;
  (* Initialize New_Date to Date *)
  New_Date := Date;
  REPEAT
    Number_Of_Days := Days_In_Month(New_Date);
    IF New_Day <= Number_Of_Days
      (* This is the correct month *)
      THEN
        BEGIN
          New_Date.Day := New_Day;
          Finished := True
        END
      ELSE
        (* Increment month and continue *)
        BEGIN
          New_Day := New_Day - Number_Of_Days;
          New_Date.Month := (New_Date.Month MOD 12) + 1;
          IF New_Date.Month = 1
            THEN
              New_Date.Year := New_Date.Year + 1;
          Finished := False
        END
  UNTIL Finished
END;  (* Adjust_Date *)
```

PROBLEM-SOLVING CASE STUDY _cont'd._

```
(*************************************************************)

PROCEDURE Print_Entry (Entry:           (* Valid friend record *)
                            Entry_Type2;
                        Temp_Date:      (* Birthday of friend  *)
                            Date_Type);

(* The name, phone number, and birthday are printed *)

BEGIN (* Print_Entry *)
  WITH Entry DO
    BEGIN
      Writeln(First_Name, ' ', Last_Name);
      Writeln(Phone.Area_Code:3, ' ', Phone.Number);
      Print_Date(Output, Temp_Date);
      Writeln;
      Writeln
    END
END; (* Print_Entry *)

(*************************************************************)

PROCEDURE Get_Entry (VAR Friend_List:   (* Input file of friends *)
                            Text;
                     VAR Entry:          (* Next friend from file *)
                            Entry_Type2);

(* An Entry is read from file Friend_List *)

VAR
  Character:          (* Input character       *)
    Char;
```

PROBLEM-SOLVING CASE STUDY *cont'd.*

```
BEGIN (* Get_Entry *)
  WITH Entry DO
    BEGIN
      Read(Friend_List, First_Name);
      (* Skip over blank *)
      Read(Friend_List, Character);
      Readln(Friend_List, Last_Name);
      (* Skip over ( *)
      Read(Friend_List, Character);
      Read(Friend_List, Phone.Area_Code);
      (* Skip over ) and blank *)
      Read(Friend_List, Character, Character);
      Readln(Friend_List, Phone_Number);
      WITH BirthDate DO
        Readln(Friend_List, Month, Character, Day, Character, Year);
      (* Skip over blank line *)
      Readln(Friend_List)
    END
END;  (* Get_Entry *)


(***********************************************************************)


BEGIN (* Birthday_Calls *)
  Assign(Friend_List, 'FRIEND.Dat');
  Reset(Friend_List);
  Get_Current_Date(Current_Date);
  Adjust_Date(Current_Date, Days_Hence, Target_Date);
  WHILE NOT EOF(Friend_List) DO
    BEGIN
      Get_Entry(Friend_List, Entry);
      Temp_Date := Entry.Birth_Date;
      Temp_Date.Year := Current_Date.Year;
      IF (Target_Date.Year <> Current_Date.Year) AND
         (Entry.Birth_Date.Month = 1)
        THEN
          Temp_Date.Year := Target_Date.Year;
      IF (Compare(Temp_Date, Target_Date) <= Same) AND
         (Compare(Temp_Date, Current_Date) >= Same)
        THEN
          Print_Entry(Entry, Temp_Date)
    END;
  Close(Friend_List)
END.  (* Birthday_Calls *)
```

Testing: The only portions of this program that need to be checked are the main program and the input and output routines. The operations on dates have already been tested thoroughly.

The input routine is the mirror image of the output routine from the program that created the address lists, which simply prints out exactly what was read in for the name and telephone number. The date is written out in a different format, but the routine that writes the date has already been tested. Therefore, only the logic of the main program needs extensive testing.

The logic in the main program is straightforward. The test data should include birthdays less than two weeks away, exactly two weeks away, and more than two weeks away. The current date should include the cases where two weeks away is within the same month, within the next month, and within the next year.

Note that *fourteen* was defined in the program as a named constant Days_Hence. The program can be run to print birthdays within any time period by changing this named constant.

Testing and Debugging

As we have demonstrated in several examples, hierarchical records simplify the logical design of a program, but they make the coding more complicated. The deeper the nesting of a structure, the longer the field selector becomes. We showed that using the WITH statement simplifies the field selector. The fields of the record variable listed in the WITH statement can be accessed by field name only within the scope of the WITH statement.

The good news is that the WITH statement is useful. The bad news is that, if you don't use the WITH statement carefully, you may wind up with unexpected errors. For example, look what happens if you accidentally put the WITH statement in the wrong place:

```
WITH Inventory[Counter] DO
  FOR Counter := 1 TO Number_Of_Machines DO
    Writeln(ID_Number);
```

You would assume that this code writes out the ID numbers of all the machines in the machine shop. However, one of two things will happen, both of which are incorrect.

The record in the WITH statement is Inventory[Counter]. If Counter is undefined, a run-time error occurs. If Counter is defined and within the bounds of the array Inventory, Inventory[Counter] refers to one of the records in the array. The FOR loop then prints out its ID_Number Number_Of_Machines times. To make this code do what you expect, you must put the WITH statement within the FOR statement. The correct version is:

```
FOR Counter := 1 TO Number_Of_Machines DO
  WITH Inventory[Counter] DO
    Writeln(ID_Number);
```

The use of the abbreviated form of the WITH for nested hierarchical records can also lead to problems if you are not careful. For example,

```
WITH Address_Book[1], Birth_Date DO
  BEGIN
     .
     .
  END;
```

allows you to access all the fields of Address_Book[1] by field identifier. In addition, the fields of Address_Book[1].Birth_Date can be accessed by field identifier. Look what happens if the comma is replaced by a period:

```
WITH Address_Book[1].Birth_Date DO
  BEGIN
     .
     .
  END;
```

This form allows you to access only the fields of Address_Book[1].Birth_Date by field identifier.

These two WITH statements look similar, but they are quite different. This subtle difference becomes clearer if we visualize the scope of the two statements. Those fields that can be accessed by field identifier only are shown in the boxes in Figure 14-12. The First_Name, Last_Name, and Phone fields of Address_Book[1] can still be accessed in the second case, but only by their full field selector, such as Address_Book[1]. First_Name.

Figure 14-12
Scope of Two WITH Statements

Address_Book[1]

WITH Address_Book[1], Birth_Date DO

Address_Book[1].Birth_Date

WITH Address_Book[1].Birth_Date DO

We said earlier that field names must be unique within a record. However, the temptation to use the same field identifier in more than one record still exists. For example, Name is such a meaningful identifier that it might be used logically in more than one record. Look at the following declarations:

```
CONST
  Name_Length = 20;
  Class_Size = 150;
  Number_Of_Cities = 1000;

TYPE
  Name_String = String[Name_Length];
  Person = RECORD
               Name : Name_String;
               Classification : (Freshman, Sophomore, Junior, Senior);
               Age : 0..100
             END;   (* Record *)
  City = RECORD
             Name,
             State : Name_String;
             Elevation : Integer
           END;   (* Record *)
  Roster = ARRAY [1..Class_Size] OF Person;
  List_Of_Cities = ARRAY [1..Number_Of_Cities] OF City;

VAR
  Name:
    Name_String;
  Student:
    Person;
  Students:
    Roster;
  Cities:
    List_Of_Cities;
```

The declarations are valid, even though the identifier Name is used in three places: as a variable, a field identifier in record Person, and a field identifier in record City. No ambiguities arise because Name, Student.Name, Students[Counter].Name, and Cities[Counter].Name are all unique. No ambiguities arise for the compiler, that is; ambiguities can arise for someone reading the program, particularly if a WITH statement is being used. For example, which Name is being referred to in the following code segment?

```
WITH Students[Counter], Student DO
   BEGIN
         .
         .
      FOR K := 1 TO Name_Length DO
         Read(Name[K]);
         .
         .
   END;
```

The Name in the above code refers to the Name field of the record variable Student. Is that what you thought? The reference is difficult to determine from the code, but the scope rules clarify it for the compiler. The Students[Counter] record overrides the variable Name, but the Student record overrides the Name field in the Students[Counter] record. Therefore, Name refers to the Name field in the Student record. If a WITH statement refers to two record variables of the same type, a compiler error message occurs because the field names within the WITH statement are ambiguous.

Using the WITH statement can help the compiler generate more efficient code. It can also save some writing, and possibly can make the program more readable. However, the WITH statement should be used with care, since it can sometimes lead to confusing results or hard-to-detect errors.

Testing and Debugging Hints

1. Be sure to specify the full field selector when referencing a component of a record variable. The only exception is using a WITH statement when the record variable is already specified.
2. When using arrays in records or arrays of records, be sure to include the index with the array name when accessing individual components.
3. Process each field of a record separately, except when assigning one record variable to another (of the same type) or passing the record as a parameter.
4. Watch out for possible confusion or ambiguity when using the WITH statement.
5. Avoid using the same field identifiers in different record types, even though this is allowed.
6. If the record variable in a WITH statement is a record from an array of records, do not change the index of the specified record variable within the WITH statement.
7. Be careful when using the abbreviated form of the WITH for hierarchical records.

Summary

The record is a useful data structure for grouping data relating to a single object. We can use a record variable to refer to the record as a whole, or we can use a field selector to access any individual field (component) of the record. Records of the same type may be assigned directly to each other. Comparison of records, however, must be done field by field. Reading and writing of records must also be done field by field. (There is an exception to this, which is discussed in the next chapter.) Since the components of arrays and records can be of any type, we can build quite complex structures made up of arrays of records, where the components of the records are themselves arrays and records.

The design of our algorithms and data structures must be done in parallel. At the top level of our design, we visualize the data structures as abstract objects, such as tables, lists, and entries. As we refine our algorithms, we get more specific about data structure. Our tables take on shape; our entries become more concrete. When we reach the point in the design where a module must apply a specific algorithm to a data structure, then—and only then—do we determine the exact form our data structure will take.

Applying the top-down, defer-details principle to data structures is an example of data abstraction. The logical description of the data structure is at a higher level. The details of how the data structure is implemented are pushed down to a lower level.

■ *Quick Check*

1. Write the type definition for a record data type called Time with three fields called Hour, Minute, and Second. The data type for the Hour field is a subrange from 0 through 23. The other two fields contain subranges from 0 through 59. (pp. 630–631)

2. Assume a variable called Now, of type Time, has been defined. Write the assignment statements necessary to store the time 8:37:28 into Now. (pp. 632–636)

3. Define a hierarchical record data type called Interval that consists of two fields of type Time. The fields are called Past and Present. (pp. 638–640)

4. Assume a variable called Channel_Crossing, of type Interval, has been defined. Write the assignment statements necessary to store the time 7:12:44 into the Past field of Channel_Crossing. Write the assignment statement that stores the value of variable Now into the Present field of Channel_Crossing. (pp. 638–640)

5. Define a data type called Boat_Times that is an array of Interval values indexed by an enumerated data type called Boat_Names. (Assume Boat_Names is already defined.) (pp. 636–637)

6. Decide what form of data structure is appropriate for the following problem. A card in a library catalog system must contain the call number, author, title, and description of a single book. (pp. 643–648)

7. What happens when a WITH statement refers to two record variables of the same type? (pp. 641–643, 676–679)

Answers

1. TYPE Time = RECORD
                Hour : 0..23;
                Minute : 0..59;
                Second : 0..59
              END; (* Record *)

2. Now.Hour := 8;
   Now.Minute := 37;
   Now.Second := 28;
3. TYPE Interval = RECORD
                     Past,
                     Present : Time
                  END; (* Record *)
4. Channel_Crossing.Past.Hour := 7;
   Channel_Crossing.Past.Minute := 12;
   Channel_Crossing.Past.Second := 44;
   Channel_Crossing.Present := Now;
5. TYPE Boat_Times = ARRAY [Boat_Names] OF Interval;
6. A simple record with four fields is sufficient.
7. A compiler error message is printed because references to the field names within the WITH statement are ambiguous.

▪ *Exam Preparation Exercises*

1. Define the following terms:

   record
   field identifier
   field selector
   hierarchical record
   data abstraction

2. Given the declarations

```
TYPE
   Code_Range = 1..25;
   Token_Range = 1..2000;
   Symbol_Range = 1..20;
   Guide_Range = 1..200;
   Code = ARRAY [Code_Range] OF Char;
   Ref = RECORD
           Token : ARRAY [Token_Range] OF Code;
           Symbol : ARRAY [Symbol_Range] OF Code
         END;  (* Record *)
   Map = RECORD
           Map_Code : Code;
           Style : (Formal, Brief);
           Chart : Ref
         END;  (* Record *)
   Guide_Type = ARRAY [Guide_Range] OF Map;
```

```
VAR
  Guide:
    Guide_Type;
  A_Map:
    Map;
  A_Ref:
    Ref;
  I,
  Count:
    Integer;
  A_Code:
    Code;
```

mark each of the following statements as valid or invalid. (Assume that all the valid variables have defined values.)

Statement	*Valid*	*Invalid*

a. `IF Map.Style = Brief`
   `THEN`
     `Count := Count + 1`
	————	————

b. `Guide[1].Chart.Token[2] := A_Map`	————	————
c. `Guide[6].Chart := A_Ref`	————	————
d. `A_Map.Map_Code[1] := A_Ref.Token[1]`	————	————
e. `Guide[100].Chart.Token[1, 2] := A_Code[2]`	————	————
f. `Guide[20].Token[1] := A_Code`	————	————

g. `IF Guide[20].Style = Formal`
   `THEN`
     `Guide[20].Chart.Token[1, 1] := 'A'`
	————	————

h. `A_Map := Guide[5]`	————	————
i. `A_Map.Chart := A_Ref`	————	————

3. Using the declarations in exercise 2, write assignment statements to do the following:
   a. Assign the value of the Chart field of the seventy-first element of Guide to the variable A_Ref.
   b. Assign the first element of the Token field of the Chart field of the eighty-eighth element of Guide to the variable A_Code.
   c. Assign the value X to the first element of the twenty-third element of the Token field of the Chart field of the ninety-fourth element of Guide.
   d. Assign the fourth element of the Map_Code field of A_Map to the ninth element of the twentieth element of the Symbol field of A_Ref.

4. What are the two basic differences between a record and an array?

5. A hierarchical record structure may not contain another hierarchical record structure as a field. (True or False?)

6. If the fields of a record are all the same data type, an array data structure could be used instead. (True or False?)

7. For each of the following descriptions of data, determine which general type of data structure (array, record, array of records, or hierarchical record) is appropriate.
   a. A payroll entry with a name, address, and pay rate.

    b. A person's address.

    c. An inventory entry for a part.

    d. A list of addresses.

    e. A list of hourly temperatures.

    f. A list of passengers on an airliner, including names, addresses, fare class, and seat assignment.

    g. A departmental telephone directory with last name and extension number.

    h. A street name.

8. Given the declarations

```
TYPE
  Date = RECORD
            Month : 1..12;
            Day : 1..31;
            Year : 0..MaxInt
         END;  (* Record *)
  Name = String[15];
  Person = RECORD
              First_Name,
              Last_Name : Name;
              Birth_Date : Date
           END;  (* Record *)

VAR
  Today;
    Date;
  A_Name:
    Name;
  Friend,
  Self:
    Person;
```

show the value of each variable after the following program segment is executed.

```
A_Name := '               ';
Friend.First_Name := A_Name;
Friend.Last_Name := A_Name;
Today.Month := 1;
Today.Day := 1;
Today.Year := 1987;
Friend.Birth_Date := Today;
Self := Friend;
```

9. Given the declarations in exercise 8, explain why the following program segment is invalid.

```
WITH Friend, Self DO
   Birth_Date := Today;
```

10. WITH Statements cannot be nested. (True or False?)

11. Declare a record type called Rec_Type to contain two integer variables and one Boolean variable.

12. Given the declarations

```
TYPE
  Complex = RECORD
              Real_Part,
              Imaginary_Part : Real
            END; (* Record *)
VAR
  C:
    Complex;
```

rewrite the following code using Pascal's WITH statement

```
C.Real_Part := 5.7;
C.Imaginary_Part := 7.2;
Writeln(C.Real_Part:7:1, C.Imaginary_Part:7:1)
```

13. Given the declarations

```
TYPE
  Name_Type = RECORD
                First,
                Last : String[12];
              END; (* Record *)
  Place_Type = RECORD
                 City : String[12];
                 State : String[2];
                 Zip_Code : String[5];
               END; (* Record *)
  T_Person = RECORD
               Name : Name_Type;
               Place : Place_Type
             END;
VAR
  Person:
    T_Person;
```

Write Pascal code that assigns information about yourself to Person.

■ Programming Warm-Up Exercises

1. a. Write a record declaration to contain the following information about a student:

   Name (string of characters)
   Social security number (string of characters)
   Class (freshman, sophomore, junior, senior)
   Grade point average
   Sex (M, F)

   b. Declare a record variable of the type in part a, and write a program segment that prints the information in each field of the variable.

   c. Declare Roll to be an array variable of 3,000 records of the type in part a.

2. Write a program segment to read in a set of part numbers and associated unit costs. Keep the data sorted by part number as you read it in. Use an array of records with two fields, Number and Price, to represent each pair of input values. Assume one pair of input values per line of data.

3. Write a hierarchical Pascal record definition to contain the following information about a student:

   Name (up to thirty characters)
   Student ID number
   Credit hours to date
   Number of courses taken
   Course grades (a list of up to fifty elements containing the course ID and the letter grade)
   Date first enrolled (month and year)
   Class (freshman, sophomore, junior, senior)
   Grade point average

   Each record and user-defined enumerated type should have a separate type definition.

4. a. Declare a record type called Apt for an apartment locator service. The following information should be included:

   Landlord (a string of up to twenty characters)
   Address (a string of up to twenty characters)
   Bedrooms (Integer)
   Price (Real)

   b. Declare Available to be an array type of up to 200 records of type Apt.
   c. Write a procedure to read values into the fields of a variable of type Apt. (The record variable should be passed as a parameter.) The order in which the data is read is the same as that of the items in the record.

5. Using the declarations given in Exam Preparation exercise 2, write statements to do the following:
   a. Assign the value in the Chart field of A_Map to A_Ref.
   b. Assign A_Map to the fourth element of Guide.
   c. Assign A_Code to the Map_Code field of the tenth element of Guide.
   d. Compare the first characters in A_Code and in the Map_Code field of the second element of Guide. If they are equal, then output the Map_Code field and the Style field of the second element of Guide.
   e. Compare A_Map.Chart and A_Ref for equality. Show which elements (if any) are not equal by outputting the indexes for the appropriate Token fields and/or Symbol fields. For example, if the second Token fields of both records were not equal, you would output "2," and so on, for the remaining nonequal elements.

6. You are designing an automated library catalog system. The library contains 50,000 books. For each book, there is a catalog entry consisting of the call number (up to ten characters), the number of copies in the library (an integer), the author (up to thirty characters), the title (up to 100 characters), and a description of the contents (up to 300 characters).
   a. Write the type definitions necessary to contain this information.
   b. Estimate how many characters of memory space are required to hold all the catalog information for the library. (Assume that an integer value occupies the equivalent of four characters in memory.)
   c. How many book records can a computer with 650,000 characters of memory hold?

7. Write a procedure that reads the information for a book into a record of the type defined in exercise 6. Write another procedure that prints the information contained in a record of the type defined in exercise 6. The record should be passed as a parameter to each of these procedures.

8. You are writing the subscription renewal system for a magazine. For each subscriber, the system is to keep the following information:

Name (first, last)
Address (street, city, state, zip code)
Expiration date (month, year)
Date renewal notice was sent (month, day, year)
Number of renewal notices sent so far
Number of years for which subscription is being renewed (0 for renewal not yet received; otherwise 1, 2, or 3 years)
Whether or not the subscriber's name may be included in a mailing list for sale to other companies

Write a hierarchical record type definition to contain this information. Each subrecord should be declared separately as a named data type.

9. You are writing a program that keeps track of the terminals connected to a company computer. The computer may have up to thirty terminals connected to it. For each terminal, the following information must be kept:

Brand and model (a string of up to fifteen characters)
Data rate (a subrange of 10 through 19,200 characters per second)
Parity (an enumerated type of Even, Odd, One, Zero, or None)
Echoplex (an enumerated type of Half or Full)
Data bits (a subrange of 7 through 8)
Stop bits (a subrange of 1 through 2)

Design a data structure for this problem, and write the type definitions for all the data types that are needed to implement your design.

10. Rewrite the following program segment using a WITH statement.

```
FOR Term := 1 TO 30 DO
  BEGIN
    Write (Term_List[Term].Model:16);
    Write (Term_List[Term].Rate:7);
    CASE Term_List[Term].Parity OF
      Odd  : Writeln(' Odd');
      Even : Writeln(' Even');
      One  : Writeln(' One');
      Zero : Writeln(' Zero');
      None : Writeln(' None')
    END (* Case *)
  END
```

11. a. Design the data sets necessary to test adequately function Compare (page 671).
    b. Write a driver and test function Compare using your test data.

12. a. Design the data sets necessary to test adequately procedure Adjust_Date (pages 665–667).
     b. Write a driver and test procedure Adjust_Date using your test data.

13. Write a record declaration to contain a string of not more than twenty characters and the length of the string. Then write a recognizer function that returns the length of a string stored in this record. The length of a string will be the number of characters actually stored in the array (less than or equal to twenty).

14. Write a procedure that concatenates (combines) two strings into a third string. Use the declaration you wrote in exercise 13. If the new string is longer than the twenty character limit, discard any excess characters (i.e. truncate the resulting string to twenty characters).

15. You are writing a program to keep track of a manufacturing company's inventory. For each part, information needs to be stored about the part number, part name, cost, and quantity.

Write a procedure and the necessary declarations to read in a variable of record type Inventory.

■ *Programming Problems*

1. The Emerging Manufacturing Company has just installed its first computer and hired you as a junior programmer. Your first program is to read employee pay data and produce two reports: 1) an error and control report, and 2) a report on pay amounts. The second report must contain a line for each employee and a line of totals at the end of the report.

Input:

Transaction File
Set of five job site number/name pairs
One line for each employee containing ID number, job site number, and number of hours worked

These data items have been presorted by ID number.

Master File
ID number
Name
Pay rate per hour
Number of dependents
Type of employee (1 is management, 0 is union)
Job site
Sex (M, F)

This file is ordered by ID number.

NOTE: 1) union members, unlike management, get time and a half for hours over 40; and 2) the tax formula for tax computation is as follows: if number of dependents is 1, tax rate is 15%. Otherwise, the tax rate is the greater of 2.5% or

$$\left[1 - \left\{ \frac{\text{No. of dep.}}{\text{No. of dep.} + 6} \right\} \right] \times 15\%$$

Output:

Error and Control Report

Lists the input lines for which there is no corresponding master record, or where the job site numbers do not agree. Continues processing with the next line of data

Gives the total number of employee records that were processed correctly during the run

Payroll Report (Labeled for Management)

Contains a line for each employee showing the name, ID number, job site name, gross pay, and net pay

Contains a total line showing the total amount of gross pay and total amount of net pay

2. The Emerging Manufacturing Company has decided to use its new computer for parts inventory control as well as payroll. You are writing a program that is to be run each night. It takes the stock tickets from the day's transactions, makes a list of the parts that need ordering, and prints an updated report that must be given to the five job site managers each morning. Note that you are not being asked to update the file.

Input:

Transaction File

Set of five job site number/name pairs

One line for each stock transaction containing part ID number, job site number, and number of parts bought or sold (a negative number indicates that it has been sold)

This data has been presorted by site number within part number.

Master File

Part ID number

Part name (no embedded blanks)

Quantity on hand

Order point

Job site

This file is also ordered by job site number within part ID number. If a part is not in the master file and the transaction is a sale, an error message should be printed. If the transaction is a purchase, the part should be listed in the proper place in the parts report. Note that there is a separate entry in the master file for parts at each job site.

Output:

Error and Control Report

Contains error messages

Lists the parts that need to be ordered (those for which quantity on hand is less than order point)

A Report for All the Parts in the Master File

Contains the part number

Contains the part name

Contains the job site name

Contains the number on hand

Remember, this report is for management. Be sure it is written so managers can read it.

3. You have taken a job with the IRS because you want to learn how to save on your income tax. They want you to write a toy tax computing program so that they can get an idea of your programming abilities. The program reads in the names of the members of families and each person's income, and computes the tax that the family owes. You may assume that people with the same last name who appear consecutively in input are in the same family. The number of deductions that a family can count is equal to the number of people listed in that family in the input data. Tax is computed as follows:

$$\text{adjusted income} = \text{income} - (5000 * \text{number of deductions})$$
$$\text{tax rate} = \text{adjusted income}/100{,}000 \text{ if income} < 60{,}000$$
$$.50, \text{ otherwise}$$
$$\text{tax} = \text{tax rate} * \text{adjusted income}$$

There will be no refunds, so you must check for people whose tax would be negative and set it to zero.

Input entries are as follows:

last name, first name. total income

Example:

Jones,	Ralph.	19,765.43
Jones,	Mary.	8,532.00
Jones,	Francis.	
Atwell,	Humphrey.	5,678.12
Murphy,	Robert.	13,432.20
Murphy,	Ellen.	
Murphy,	Paddy.	
Murphy,	Eileen.	
Murphy,	Conan.	
Murphy,	Nora.	

Input:
The data as described above, with an end-of-file indicating the end of the run.

Output:
A table containing all the families, one family per line, with each line containing the last name of the family, their total income, and their computed tax.

4. Your assignment is to write a program for a computer dating service. Clients give you their names, phone numbers, and a list of interests. Your job is to maintain lists of men and women using the service and to match up the compatible couples.

Data Structures:
The problem requires you to maintain two lists, one for men and one for women. The lists must include the following information: name (twenty characters), phone number (eight characters), number of interests (maximum number is ten), interests (ten characters each; must be in alphabetical order), and a variable that gives the position of the client's current match (0 if not matched). When a new client is added to the list, his or her name is added to the bottom of the appropriate list. (You do not keep the names of the clients in alphabetical order.)

Input:

Number of current clients

Sex (seven characters), name (twenty characters), phone number (eight characters), number of interests, list of interests (ten characters for each one; interests are separated by commas, with a period after the final interest). There is a record like this for each of the current clients.

The rest of the file includes data lines that look like one of the following (all the lines start with a ten-character word as outlined below; □ indicates a blank):

NewClient □ sex (seven characters), name (twenty characters), number of interests, interests (ten characters for each one; see above for description)

If the keyword NewClient occurs, you should add the client to the appropriate list by storing the required information. Match him or her with a member of the opposite sex. (A match occurs when three of the interests are the same. Interests are sorted, which makes the matching process easier. Use an insertion sort to sort interests.) Make sure you then designate both persons matched as described above. Print the name of the new client, his or her match, and both phone numbers. If no match is found, print an appropriate message.

OldClient□ name (twenty characters)

Unmatch this name from its current match by setting the match variables for the name and its match to 0.

PrintMatch

Print a list of all matched pairs.

PrintNot□□

Print the names and phone numbers of clients who are not currently matched.

StopProg□□

This will be the last line in the file.

Output:

Information as described above, printed with appropriate titles.

5. A sparse matrix is a matrix (two-dimensional array) in which the great majority of elements are zero. It is inefficient to store these as two-dimensional arrays since most of the elements do not contain any useful information. Instead, the elements that are not equal to zero should be stored as an array of records where the first two fields of the record contain the row and column number and the third field contains the element. For example, this matrix

0.0	0.0	7.0	0.0	0.0
0.0	0.0	0.0	0.0	8.0
0.0	0.0	0.0	0.0	0.0

would be stored as follows

1	3	7.0
2	5	8.0

Write a Pascal program that reads a sparse matrix and converts it into an array of records of this form. The program should then output the records (properly labeled).

Files and Pointers

GOALS

- To be able to define a nontext (binary) file data type.
- To be able to create and access a nontext (binary) file.
- To be able to define a pointer data type.
- To be able to create and access pointer variables.
- To be able to dynamically create and access pointer-referenced variables.
- To be able to destroy dynamic pointer-referenced variables.
- To be able to use pointers to improve program efficiency.
- To be able to merge the data in two or more files.

This chapter may seem somewhat redundant considering that you have been using files since Chapter 1. Files are so important that we had to describe how to use them from the beginning. You couldn't have run your first program if you hadn't learned to create a file. Your programs would have been trivial if you hadn't known how to read in data values from a file.

In this chapter we look at a file as a data structure. We review Text files and define another type of file called a **binary file.** A binary file is created within one program to be read by another program, or the same program at a later time. It takes less machine time to write or read a binary file than it does for a Text file, so binary files should be used when possible.

Pointers are the last of the built-in data types in Pascal. A **pointer** is a simple data type that contains the address of a variable or structure rather than a data value. Pointers have two main purposes: they can make a program more efficient and they can be used to build complex structures. We demonstrate how they make a program more efficient in this chapter. Chapter 16 explains how to build complex structures using pointers.

Files

Files are exceedingly important data structures. Programs use files to communicate with the outside world and with each other: data values are read from files, and results are written to files that can be displayed. A program can communicate with itself through the use of files: data values that must be saved from one execution of the program to the next are written to a file, and the output file from one run then becomes the input file for the next run. A program can communicate with another program in just the same way as it can communicate with itself: output from one program can become the input for another program.

A file that is used to communicate with people or programs is an **external file.** The external files used by a program are listed in the program heading. A file can also be used strictly as an internal data structure; for example, a program may use a file for temporary data storage. A file that is used but not saved is called an **internal** or **scratch file.** In Pascal the **file data type** is a collection of like components accessed sequentially.

External File   A file that is used to communicate with people or programs. It is stored externally to the program.

Internal File   A file that is created but not saved.

File Data Type   A collection of components, all of the same data type, accessed sequentially one component at a time.

What makes the file data structure different from the other data structures is that only one component is available to the program at a time. You access each component individually, beginning with the first component. Each time you access a file, you get the next component. The only way to access a component that you have accessed previously is to Reset the file and start from the beginning. (Turbo Pascal, however, offers an alternative to sequential access for binary files, which will be introduced later.)

Let's review Text files and see how the definition of the file data type relates to them.

Text Files Reviewed

The files we have used so far have all been of type Text, which can be thought of as a file of characters broken up into lines. The components of Text files are characters. The built-in operations defined on Text files are reviewed below, where In_File, IO_File, and Out_File are files of type Text.

`Assign(IO_File, Name_Str)`	Associates file IO_File with the DOS file named Name_Str. Name_Str may be a literal or variable string.
`Close(IO_File)`	Terminates processing of file IO_File.
`Reset(In_File)`	Opens file In_File and prepares to read file In_File from the beginning. If the file is empty or doesn't exist, the function EOF(In_File) is True. Otherwise, the function EOF(In_File) is False.
`Rewrite(Out_File)`	Opens file Out_File and prepares to write at the beginning. The old contents of the file (if any) are lost.
`EOF(In_File)`	Returns True if the next character to be read is the <eof> character (that is, no more characters remain in the file). Returns False otherwise.
`EOLN(In_File)`	Returns True if the next character to be read is the <eoln> character. Returns False otherwise.
`Read(In_File, . . . )`	Reads values from In_File into the variables named on the parameter list.
`Readln(In_File, . . . )`	Same as Read except that it skips to beginning of the next line before returning.
`Write(Out_File, . . . )`	Writes values of expressions and variables named in the parameter list on Out_File.
`Writeln(Out_File, . . . )`	Same as Write except that it writes the <eoln> character on Out_File before returning.

Here are some additional, nonstandard operations that Turbo Pascal provides for Text files:

Append(File_Variable)	File_Variable is a file identifier declared in the VAR section. This procedure is the same as Rewrite except that it places all newly written data at the end of the current contents of the file. The file is not cleared of data as with Rewrite.
Erase(File_Variable)	File_Variable is a file identifier declared in the VAR section. Erase deletes the external file associated with File_Variable from the disk. The file should be closed before it is erased.
Rename(IO_File, Name_Str)	Renames the DOS file associated with IO_File to Name_Str. Name_Str may be a literal or variable string.
SeekEOF(File_Variable)	File_Variable is a file identifier declared in the VAR section. SeekEOF is a function that is used much like EOF except that it changes the current file position by skipping all blank, tab, and end-of-line characters, then returns True or False depending upon whether it has encountered end-of-file. SeekEOF is useful when you are reading numeric data in an EOF-controlled loop.
SeekEOLN(File_Variable)	File_Variable is a file identifier declared in the VAR section. SeekEOLN is a function that is similar to EOLN except that it changes the current file position by skipping all blank and tab characters, then returns True or False depending on whether it has encountered end-of-line.

If we restrict our operations to character data only, these operations are consistent with our definition of a file. When character data are being input, the Read operation accesses one character at a time. When character data are output, the Write operation outputs one character at a time.

The function EOLN is consistent with the definition of the file data type because it asks if the next component (the next character) to be read is the <eoln> character. The function EOF is consistent because it asks if the next component is the <eof> character.

When numeric data are being input or output, the Read and Write operations do not seem to be consistent with the definition of the file data type. The component of a Text file is a character, and a Read or Write with numeric parameters may access more than one character. This seeming inconsistency can be explained by the fact that the Read and Write procedures themselves access the file components sequentially, one character at a time. If a parameter for a Read or Readln is of type Integer or Real, characters are accessed sequentially and converted from character form into numeric form. If a parameter for a Write or Writeln is of type Integer or Real, the number is converted from its numeric form to its character representation and then written out, character by character.

In Chapter 5 we indicated that using the Read procedure in combination with EOF to input numeric data can cause a problem. The <eoln> character always follows the last number on a Text file. Therefore, EOF will not be true after the last numeric value has been read, and the loop will attempt to execute one more time. We said then that the only way to solve this problem is to read the numbers in as characters and convert them.

Let's review Text files by writing just such a procedure. We read an unsigned integer number as a sequence of characters from a Text file and convert it to its numeric form. Turbo Pascal allows numeric data to be separated only by a series of blanks, tabs, <CR>'s, and/or Ctrl-Z's. However, we will write this procedure to recognize any nondigit as a separator. Here are the specifications for the procedure.

```
PROCEDURE Read_Int (VAR Data_File:      (* Input file of characters   *)
                         Text;
                    VAR Number:          (* Resulting converted integer *)
                         Integer;
                    VAR Error:           (* Bad input indicator flag    *)
                         Boolean);

(* Reads and converts the next unsigned integer value encountered  *)
(* on Text file Data_File. There may be leading blanks. Any         *)
(* nondigit marks the end of the number. If either EOF or a         *)
(* nondigit character is encountered before the first digit, Error  *)
(* is True and Number is undefined. Otherwise Error is False and    *)
(* Number contains the value *)
```

We read in a digit in character form, convert it to its numeric value, multiply the previous value by 10 (to shift the number a digit position to the left), and add in the new digit. This process continues until we find a character that is not a number.

Read Int (Returns Number : Integer,
Error : Boolean
Receives/Returns Data_File : Text)

```
Initialize Number to 0
Initialize Error to False
Skip Blanks
IF Character is not a digit
   THEN
      Set Error to True
   ELSE
      WHILE more digits
         Set Number to Number * 10 + (Ord(Digit) − Ord('0'))
         Get another digit
```

Skip Blanks (Returns Character : Char
Receives/Returns Data_File: Text)

> Initialize Character to ' '
> WHILE NOT EOF AND Character is a blank
>   Get another character

The code for procedure Read_Int is as follows:

```
PROCEDURE Read_Int (VAR Data_File:      (* Input file of characters   *)
                         Text;
                    VAR Number:         (* Resulting converted integer *)
                         Integer;
                    VAR Error:          (* Bad input indicator flag    *)
                         Boolean);

(* Reads and converts the next unsigned integer value encountered  *)
(* on Text file Data_File.  There may be leading blanks.  Any       *)
(* nondigit marks the end of the number.  If either EOF or a        *)
(* nondigit character is encountered before the first digit, Error *)
(* is True and Number is undefined.  Otherwise Error is False and  *)
(* Number contains the value *)

VAR
  Character:              (* Current input character being converted *)
    Char;

(* ***************************************************************** *)

PROCEDURE Skip_Blanks (VAR Data_File:
                            Text;        (* Input file of characters *)
                       VAR Character:    (* Returns first nonblank   *)
                            Char);

(* Blanks are skipped.  First nonblank is returned.  IF EOF is *)
(* encountered before a nonblank is found, character is a       *)
(* blank *)

BEGIN (* Skip_Blanks *)
   IF SeekEOF does not return True for Data_Fi!
     THEN
       Get a character from Data_File
     ELSE
       Set character to blank
END;  (* Skip_Blanks *)

(* ***************************************************************** *)
```

```
BEGIN  (* Read_Int *)
  Error := False;
  Skip_Blanks(Character);
  IF NOT (Character IN ['0'..'9'])
    THEN
      Error := True
    ELSE
      BEGIN
        Number := 0;
        WHILE Character IN ['0'..'9'] DO
          BEGIN
            Number := Number * 10 + (Ord(Digit) - Ord('0'));
            Read(Data_File, Character)
          END
      END
END;   (* Read_Int *)
```

Figure 15-1 contains diagrams describing the execution of Procedure Read_Int with four different lines of data. (Each example is independent of the others.)

Other Files

The components of a file can be of any type, simple or structured, except another file. The syntax template for defining a file in the TYPE section is

FILE OF type;

The following declarations are all valid:

```
CONST
  String_Length = 15;
  Array_Length = 20;

TYPE
  Array_Index = 1..Array_Length;
  String15 = String[String_Length];
  Words = FILE OF String15;
  Part = RECORD
           Description : String15;
           ID_Num : Integer;
           Cost : Real
         END;   (* Record *)
  Parts = FILE OF Part;
  Name = ARRAY[Array_Index] OF Char;
  Names = FILE OF Name;
  Integers = FILE OF Integer;
```

Figure 15-1
Code Walk-Through
of Procedure
Read_Int

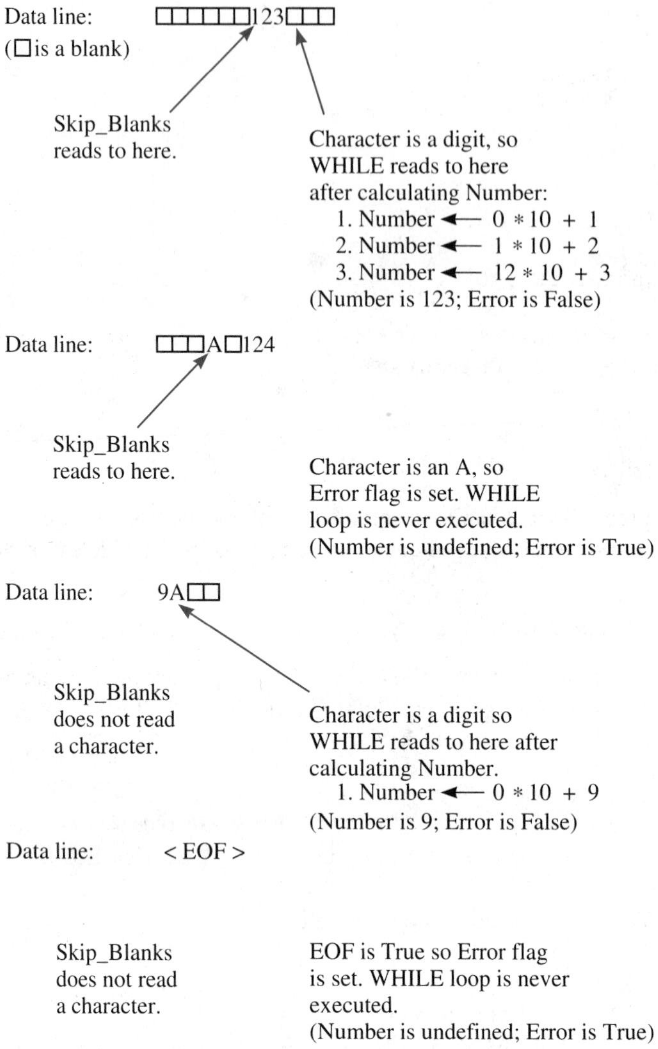

Data line: ☐☐☐☐☐123☐☐☐
(☐ is a blank)

Skip_Blanks
reads to here.

Character is a digit, so
WHILE reads to here
after calculating Number:
    1. Number ⟵ 0 ∗ 10 + 1
    2. Number ⟵ 1 ∗ 10 + 2
    3. Number ⟵ 12 ∗ 10 + 3
(Number is 123; Error is False)

Data line: ☐☐☐A☐124

Skip_Blanks
reads to here.

Character is an A, so
Error flag is set. WHILE
loop is never executed.
(Number is undefined; Error is True)

Data line: 9A☐☐

Skip_Blanks
does not read
a character.

Character is a digit so
WHILE reads to here after
calculating Number.
    1. Number ⟵ 0 ∗ 10 + 9
(Number is 9; Error is False)

Data line: < EOF >

Skip_Blanks
does not read
a character.

EOF is True so Error flag
is set. WHILE loop is never
executed.
(Number is undefined; Error is True)

```
VAR
  In_File,
  Out_File:
    Text;
  Dictionary:              (* File of Strings      *)
    Words;
  A_Word:                  (* Component of Dictionary *)
    String15;
  Inventory:               (* File of Parts        *)
    Parts;
  A_Part:                  (* Component of Inventory *)
    Part;
  Mail:                    (* File of Names        *)
    Names;
  A_Name:                  (* Component of Mail    *)
    Name;
  Data:                    (* File of Integers     *)
    Integers;
  A_Number:                (* Component of Data    *)
    Integer;
```

In_File and Out_File are files of type Text. Dictionary is a file of strings. Inventory is a file of records. Mail is a file of arrays. Data is a file of integer numbers.

The built-in operations defined on nontext files are Reset, Rewrite, Read, Write, Append, Assign, Close, Erase, Rename, Seek, and EOF. Nontext files are not broken into lines, so EOLN, Readln, and Writeln have no meaning with them. Reset, Rewrite, and EOF have the same meaning for nontext files as they do for text files. Read and Write are simplified for nontext files because they operate in a manner consistent with the definition of a file: exactly one component of the file is read or written.

Read(Mail, A_Name)	The next component in file Mail is returned in A_Name.
Write(Mail, A_Name)	A_Name is written on Mail.

The file marker operates with nontext files in exactly the same manner as it does with text files. After a call to the Read procedure for a nontext file, the file marker is at the next component to be read.

Turbo Pascal defines five additional operations that are valid only for nontext files. These are FilePos, FileSize, Seek, Flush, and Truncate.

FilePos(In_File)	Returns the current position of the reading marker. The first component on a file is number 0.
FileSize(IO_File)	Returns the integer number of components in file IO_File. The result is 0 when the file is empty.
Seek(IO_File, Pos)	Moves the marker to the component of file IO_File that is at position Pos in the file. The first component of a file is at position 0.

`Flush(IO_File)`	If IO_File is in write mode, makes sure that all data that has been written to the file is actually written on the disk. If IO_File is in Read mode, makes sure that the next Read will actually get data from the disk. (With nontext files, Turbo Pascal may keep part of a file in main memory, rather than storing it on the disk.)
`Truncate(IO_File)`	Truncates the file IO_File (deletes any data beyond the current position in the file).

Using nontext files can simplify the coding of a program considerably. An entire data structure can be read or written at once, as shown in the following examples.

`Read(Dictionary, A_Word)`	Inputs a string.
`Read(Inventory, A_Part)`	Inputs a record.
`Read(Mail, A_Name)`	Inputs an array.
`Read(Data, A_Number)`	Inputs an integer number.
`Write(Inventory, A_Part)`	Writes a record.
`Write(Mail, A_Name)`	Writes an array.

Data is stored in nontext files in internal machine representation, which is why reading and writing are so easy—there is no translation to or from text format.

Because all data entered from a keyboard is in text format, we cannot create a nontext file with an editor. Only a program can create a nontext file. A file in text format can be converted into nontext format by a simple translating program that reads the data from the text file and writes it out to a nontext file. For example, the following short program reads data in from a text file and writes it out on a nontext file.

```
PROGRAM Convert (Input, Output, Parts_File);

(* Data about parts are read from Input in character *)
(* format and written out to file Parts_File         *)

CONST
  String_Length = 10;

TYPE
  Range = 1..String_Length;
  Name_Type = String[String_Length];
  Part = RECORD
            Name : Name_Type;
            ID_Number : Integer;
            Cost : Real
         END; (* Record *)
  Parts = FILE OF Part;
```

```
VAR
  A_Part:          (* Part being entered from input *)
    Part;
  Parts_File:      (* File being constructed       *)
    Parts;
  Character:       (* Character read from input    *)
    Char;
  Counter:         (* Loop control variable        *)
    Range;

BEGIN (* Convert *)
  Assign(Parts_File, 'Parts.Dat');
  Rewrite(Parts_File);
  WHILE NOT EOF DO
    BEGIN
      (* Read a record from Input, a Text file *)
      Read(A_Part.Name);
      Read(A_Part.ID_Number);
      Read(A_Part.Cost);
      Readln;
      (* Write a record to a binary file Parts_File *)
      Write(Parts_File, A_Part)
    END;
  Close(Parts_File)
END.  (* Convert *)
```

Because nontext files are written in the internal representation of the machine, they are called **binary files.** All internal files and those external files that are used only to transfer data from one program to another should be written as binary files because they are more efficient.

Binary File   A file in which the data is written in the internal representation of a machine.

Pointers

We have only one data type left to cover: the **pointer.** Surprisingly, the word pointer isn't used in the type definition; the symbol ^ is used instead. In many ways we've saved the best till last. Pointers are the most interesting data type of all. They are what their name implies: variables that tell where to find something else; that is, pointers contain the addresses or locations of other variables, called **dynamic variables.** Dynamic variables are not declared in the declaration section of the program like other variables; they are created at execution time. The advantage of being able to create variables at execution time is that we don't need to create any more of them than we need.

Pointer   A simple data type consisting of an unbounded set of values, each of which addresses or otherwise indicates the location of a variable of a given type. The operations defined on pointer variables are assignment and test for equality.

Dynamic Variable   A variable created during execution of a program.

Let's begin this discussion by looking at pointers themselves. Then we will show how to use them to create dynamic variables. The syntax template for defining a pointer type is:

$$\boxed{\text{\textasciicircum}type;}$$

The following declaration section illustrates how pointers are defined:

```
TYPE
  Range = 1..25;
  Range_Pointer = ^Range;      (* Points to variables of type Range *)
  Color = (Red, Green, Blue);
  Color_Pointer = ^Color;      (* Points to variables of type Color *)
  Date = RECORD
            Day : 1..31;
            Month : 1..12;
            Year : 1900..2020
         END;  (* Record *)
  Date_Pointer = ^Date;           (* Points to variables of type Date *)

VAR
  Range_Ptr:          (* A variable of type Range_Pointer *)
    Range_Pointer;
  Color_Ptr:          (* A variable of type Color_Pointer *)
    Color_Pointer;
  Date_Ptr:           (* A variable of type Date_Pointer  *)
    Date_Pointer;
```

Range_Ptr, Color_Ptr, and Date_Ptr are pointer variables. Range_Ptr is a pointer to a variable of type Range, Color_Ptr is a pointer to a variable of type Color, and Date_Ptr is a pointer to a variable of type Date. These declarations cause the compiler to create three cells, Range_Ptr, Color_Ptr, and Date_Ptr, the contents of which are memory addresses. As in the case of all variables, their values are not yet defined.

Range_Ptr   Color_Ptr   Date_Ptr

This declaration looks strange. We have declared three pointer variables, but we haven't declared anything for them to point to—we haven't declared any variables of types Range, Color, or Date. The variables that Range_Ptr, Color_Ptr, and Date_Ptr point to are created dynamically; that is, we create variables of type Range, Color, and Date whenever they are needed during the execution of the program. These variables are created using a built-in procedure called New.

New(Range_Ptr)	Creates a variable of type Range for Range_Ptr to point to and leaves its address in Range_Ptr.
New(Color_Ptr)	Creates a variable of type Color for Color_Ptr to point to and leaves its address in Color_Ptr.
New(Date_Ptr)	Creates a variable of type Date for Date_Ptr to point to and leaves its address in Date_Ptr.

The call to procedure New always does two things: it creates a variable of the type to which its parameter points, and returns the address of this variable in the parameter. The variable created by procedure New is a dynamic variable.

How do we access these newly created variables if we don't know their names? The pointer variable followed by ^ accesses the variable pointed to. These are called **referenced variables** because they are not given a name, but rather are referenced through a pointer variable. Figure 15-2 pictures a pointer and the variable that it is referencing.

Referenced Variable   A variable created and accessed not by a name but by a pointer variable; a dynamic variable.

Range_Ptr^ is a referenced variable of type Range. It can contain any integer value in the range 1..25. Color_Ptr^ is a referenced variable of type Color. It can contain Red, Green, or Blue. Date_Ptr^ is a referenced record variable of type Date. Date_Ptr^.Day is the Day field of Date_Ptr^. Date_Ptr^.Month is the Month field of Date_Ptr^. Date_Ptr^.Year is the Year field of Date_Ptr^. Notice how the accessing expression is built.

Date_Ptr	A pointer variable of type Date_Pointer.
Date_Ptr^	A referenced record variable of type Date.
Date_Ptr^.Year	The Year field of a referenced record variable of type Date.

If we define an array called Dates to be an array of pointers, we can access the Day field of the third date as follows:

```
Dates[3]^.Day
```

Figure 15-2
A Pointer and Its
Referenced Variable

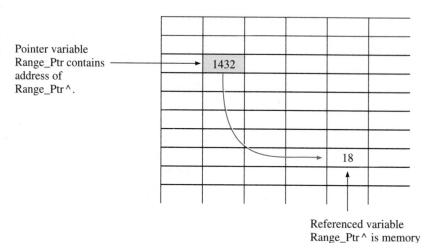

Pointer variable
Range_Ptr contains
address of
Range_Ptr^.

Referenced variable
Range_Ptr^ is memory
location 1432.

Referenced variables can be used in the same way as any other variable. The following statements are all valid:

```
Range_Ptr^ := 18;
Color_Ptr^ := Red;
Date_Ptr^.Day := 3;
Date_Ptr^.Month := 12;
Date_Ptr^.Year := 1999;
Dates[3]^.Day := 4;
Dates[3]^.Month := 1
Dates[3]^.Year := 2020
```

Figure 15-3 shows the results of these assignments.

Referenced variables can be destroyed at any time during the execution of a program when they are no longer needed. The built-in procedure Dispose is used to destroy a referenced variable.

`Dispose(Range_Ptr)`   Returns the locations for the variable of type Range to the Pascal run-time support system to be used again. Range_Ptr is then undefined.

`Dispose(Color_Ptr)`   Returns the locations used for the variable of type Color to the Pascal run-time support system to be used again. Color_Ptr is then undefined.

`Dispose(Date_Ptr)`   Returns the locations used for the variable of type Date to the Pascal run-time support system to be used again. Date_Ptr is then undefined.

Figure 15-3
Results of Assign-
ment Statements

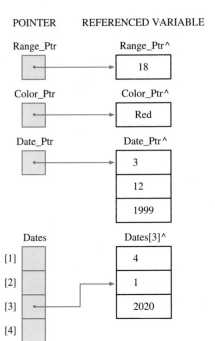

It is counterproductive to keep dynamic variables when they are no longer needed. If this is done too often, you may run out of memory.

Only two operations may be applied to pointer variables:

1. Pointer variables of the same type may be tested for equality (see Figure 15-4a).
2. Pointer variables of the same type may be assigned to one another (see Figure 15-4b).

Figure 15-4
Operations on
Pointer Variables

a. Pointer variables of the same type may be tested for equality.

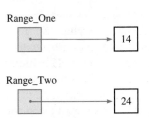

Range_One <> Range_Two is True
Range_One = Range_Two is False

b. Pointer variables of the same type may be assigned to one another.

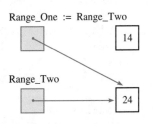

Range_One <> Range_Two is False
Range_One = Range_Two is True

We cannot assign pointers of different types to each other because they do not point to variables of the same type. If we could, it would be possible to assign a referenced variable of one type to a variable of another type, thereby violating the assignment compatibility rules of Pascal.

Referenced variables, on the other hand, may be used in any way that is legal for named variables of the same type. For example, given the declarations

```
TYPE
    Number_Range = 1..50;
    Number_Pointers = ^Number_Range;

VAR
    Number_One,
    Number_Two:
        Number_Pointers;
```

Number_One^ + Number_Two^ is legal because we are adding the contents of two variables of type Number_Range pointed to by Number_One and Number_Two. We cannot, however, add Number_One and Number_Two because they are pointer variables.

Let's look at another example.

```
New(Number_One);           (* Creates a dynamic variable          *)
New(Number_Two);           (* Creates a dynamic variable          *)
Number_Two^ := 44;         (* Assigns a value to a dynamic variable *)
Number_One^ := Number_Two^; (* Assignment of dynamic variables     *)
Number_One := Number_Two;  (* Assignment of pointers              *)
Dispose(Number_Two);       (* Destroys a dynamic variable         *)
```

`New(Number_One);` `New(Number_Two);`	Creates a pair of referenced variables of type Number_Range and stores their locations in Number_One and Number_Two. The referenced variables are undefined even though the pointer variables now have values (see Figure 15-5a).
`Number_Two^ := 44;`	The referenced variable pointed to by Number_Two is assigned the value 44 (see Figure 15-5b).
`Number_One^ := Number_Two^`	Assigns the contents of the referenced variable Number_Two^ to the referenced variable Number_One^ (see Figure 15-5c).
`Number_One := Number_Two`	Assigns the contents of the pointer variable Number_Two to the pointer variable Number_One (see Figure 15-5d).

`Dispose(Number_Two)`	Returns the referenced variable Number_Two^ back to the run-time support system to be used again. Number_Two is undefined (see Figure 15-5e).

In Figure 15-5e, notice that the variable referenced by Number_One before the assignment statement shown in Figure 15-5d is still there. It cannot be accessed, however, unless there is another pointer variable referencing it. Notice also that in Figure 15-5e Number_One is now referencing a variable that no longer exists. These situations can be avoided by disposing of Number_One before assigning Number_Two to it, and by setting Number_One to NIL after we dispose of Number_Two (see Figure 15-6).

```
New(Number_One);
New(Number_Two);
Number_Two^ := 44;
Number_One^ := Number_Two^;
Dispose(Number_One);
Number_One := Number_Two;
Dispose(Number_Two);
Number_One := NIL
```

NIL is a reserved word used to indicate that a pointer points to nothing. Now Number_One is not referencing a variable that doesn't exist—it is defined to be pointing at nothing.

Let's review the syntax and semantics of pointers and dynamic variables in another short example. In the TYPE section, we define a structure and a pointer to the structure. In the VAR section, we declare a variable of the pointer type.

```
CONST
  String_Length = 20;

TYPE
  Name_String = String[String_Length];
  Data_Type = RECORD
                Last_Name,
                First_Name : Name_String
              END;  (* Record *)
  Pointer_Type = ^Data_Type;

VAR
  Pointer:
    Pointer_Type;
```

To get a record variable of Data_Type, we invoke the procedure New with Pointer as a parameter. Thus,

```
New(Pointer)
```

Figure 15-5
Results from Sample Code Segment

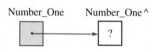

Number_One

Number_Two

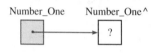

INITIAL CONDITION

a. New(Number_One);
    New(Number_Two)

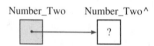

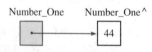

b. Number_Two^ := 44

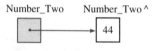

c. Number_One^ := Number_Two

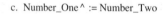

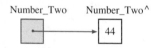

d. Number_One := Number_Two

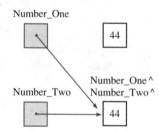

e. Dispose(Number_Two)

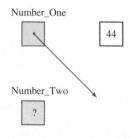

Figure 15-6
Results from Sam-
ple Code Segment
After It Was
Modified

Number_One

Number_Two

INITIAL CONDITION

a. New(Number_One);
   New(Number_Two)

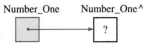

Number_One   Number_One^

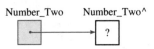

Number_Two   Number_Two^

b. Number_Two^ := 44

Number_One   Number_One^

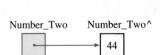

Number_Two   Number_Two^

c. Number_One^ := Number_Two^

Number_One

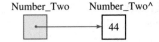

Number_Two

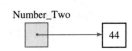

d. Dispose(Number_One);

Number_One

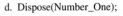

Number_Two   Number_Two^

e. Number_One := Number_Two

Number_One

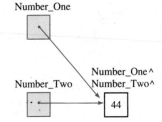

Number_One^
Number_Two   Number_Two^

f. Dispose(Number_Two)

Number_One

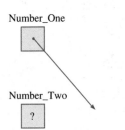

Number_Two

g. Number_One := NIL

Number_One

Number_Two

creates a record variable of Data_Type. To access the record variable, we give the pointer name followed by an up-caret.

Pointer^	Accesses the record pointed to by the pointer variable Pointer.
Pointer^.Last_Name	Accesses the Last_Name field.
Pointer^.First_Name	Accesses the First_Name field.

At the beginning of this chapter, we said that pointers are used for two reasons: to make a program more efficient and to create complex data structures called linked structures. We give an example of the use of pointers to make a program more efficient in the third case study in this chapter, Personnel Records. Linked structures are covered in Chapter 16.

PROBLEM-SOLVING CASE STUDY

Campaigning for a Candidate

Problem: A friend is running for City Council. It's down to the wire, and we want to call all those people who showed an interest in our friend and remind them to vote on election day. We have three different lists of people we should call. We don't want to annoy people by calling them twice—or worse still, three times—so we decide to merge the three lists and remove any duplicates. The three lists are each sorted in order by last name, and there are no duplicates within any of the lists. A dummy record with a last name of all Zs is appended at the end of each file.

Input: The computer files were all generated from the same Pascal program. The components of each file are records that contain a person's last name, first name, and telephone number. The declarations used in the program that created the files are as follows:

```
CONST
  Name_Length = 15;

TYPE
  Name_String = String[Name_Length];
  Phone_Type = RECORD
                 Area_Code : 0..999;
                 Number : String[8];
               END;  (* Record *)
  Data = RECORD
           Last_Name : Name_String;
           First_Name : Name_String;
           Phone : Phone_Type
         END;  (* Record *)
  Data_List = FILE OF Data;
```

A dummy record containing all Zs for the last name and blanks in the other two fields signals the end of each file.

Output: Files One, Two, and Three merged on file Master_List, which should have the same form as the three input files; and a printed copy of file Master_List.

Discussion: One of our problem-solving heuristics is to solve simpler problems first. Let's solve the problem for two lists, and then expand the solution to three lists.

How would we do this process by hand if we had two stacks of index cards? We would probably take the top card from each stack and compare the names. If they were the same, we would put one in a new stack and throw the other one away. If they weren't the same, we would put the card with the name that came first alphabetically in the new stack and take a replacement card from that stack. We would repeat this process until one of the stacks of index cards became empty. Then we would move the rest of the other stack to the new one. Of course the lists might both end at the same time with a duplicate name.

This same process can be employed to solve the problem using two computer lists. Rather than having two stacks of index cards, we have two computer files. Reading in a name is the equivalent of "take a replacement card from that stack."

Now that we have solved the problem for two files, we can expand the solution to three files. We can merge the first two files and store the result on a file, then merge that file with the third file.

Data Structures: Four external files of type Data_List, one scratch file of type Data_List.

Main Module   *Level 0*

```
Reset input files
Rewrite output files
Merge files One and Two into Temp_File
Reset Temp_File
Merge files Temp_File and Three onto Master_List
Print Master_List
```

Merge (Receives/Returns One, Two, Temp : Data_List)   *Level 1*

```
Read a component from One (Component_From_One)
Read a component from Two (Component_From_Two)
WHILE neither component is the dummy record
   Process components
Append any left
```

PROBLEM-SOLVING CASE STUDY cont'd.

Print Master List (Receives/Returns Master_List : Data_List)

```
Reset Master_List
Read component
WHILE component on Master_List not dummy
    Write component
    Read component
Write dummy record
```

Process Components (Receives/Returns Component_From_One,   *Level 2*
                    Component_From_Two : Data)

```
IF Component_From_One.Last_Name < Component_From_Two.Last_Name
    THEN
        Write Component_From_One
        Read Component_From_One
    ELSE IF Component_From_One > Component_From_Two
        THEN
            Write Component_From_Two
            Read Component_From_Two
    ELSE
        Write Component_From_Two
        Read Component_From_One
        Read Component_From_Two
```

Since Process Components is fairly simple, we have chosen to include it as part of procedure Merge in the program.

Append Any Left (Receives Component_From_One, Component_From_Two : Data
                Receives/Returns One, Two, Temp : Data_List)

```
WHILE component on One not dummy
    Write Component_From_One
    Read Component_From_One
WHILE component on Two not dummy
    Write Component_From_Two
    Read Component_From_Two
Write dummy record
```

PROBLEM-SOLVING CASE STUDY *cont'd.*

Module Structure Chart:

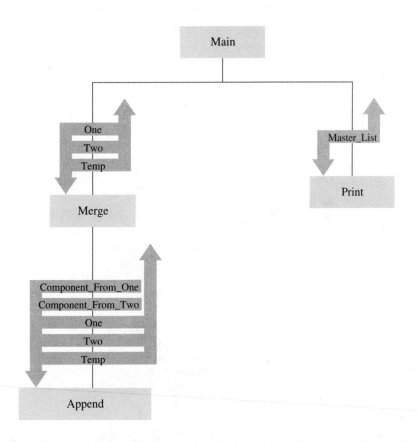

```
PROGRAM Merge_Lists (One, Two, Three, Master_List, Output);

(* Files One, Two, and Three are merged and written *)
(* on File Master_List.  Master_List is printed      *)

CONST
  Dummy = 'ZZZZZZZZZZZZZZZ';
  Name_Length = 15;
```

```
TYPE
  Name_String = String[String_Length];
  Phone_Type  = RECORD
                     Area_Code : 0..999;
                     Number : String[8]
                  END; (* Record *)
  Data = RECORD
             Last_Name : Name_String;
             First_Name : Name_String;
             Phone : Phone_Type
          END; (* Record *)
  Data_List = FILE OF Data;

VAR
  One,              (* Input file                *)
  Two,              (* Input file                *)
  Three,            (* Input file                *)
  Master_List,      (* Output file               *)
  Temp_File:        (* Temporary file (internal) *)
    Data_List;


(* ******************************************************************** *)


PROCEDURE Append (VAR One,            (* Input file, possibly empty  *)
                       Two,            (* Input file, possibly empty  *)
                       Temp:           (* Output file                 *)
                         Data_List;
                       Component_From_One,  (* Active record from One *)
                       Component_From_Two:  (* Active record from Two *)
                         Data);

(* Remainder of either One or Two is appended to Temp *)

BEGIN (* Append *)
  (* Append rest of One, if there *)
  WHILE Component_From_One.Last_Name <> Dummy DO
    BEGIN
      Write(Temp, Component_From_One);
      Read(One, Component_From_One)
    END;
  (* Append rest of Two, if there *)
  WHILE Component_From_Two.Last_Name <> Dummy DO
    BEGIN
      Write(Temp, Component_From_Two);
      Read(Two, Component_From_Two)
    END;
  (* Write dummy record *)
  Write(Temp, Component_From_Two)
END;  (* Append *)
```

PROBLEM-SOLVING CASE STUDY cont'd.

```
(* ***************************************************************** )

PROCEDURE Merge (VAR One,              (* Input file to merge *)
                     Two,              (* Input file to merge *)
                     Temp:             (* Merged output file  *)
                       Data_List);

(* Files One and Two are merged onto Temp.  Constant Dummy is *)
(* accessed globally.  Assumption: Files have been reset       *)

VAR
  Component_From_One,
  Component_From_Two:
    Data;

BEGIN (* Merge *)
  Read(One, Component_From_One);
  Read(Two, Component_From_Two);
  WHILE (Component_From_One.Last_Name <> Dummy) AND
        (Component_From_Two.Last_Name <> Dummy) DO
    IF Component_From_One.Last_Name < Component_From_Two.Last_Name
      THEN
        BEGIN
          Write(Temp, Component_From_One);
          Read(One, Component_From_One)
        END
      ELSE IF Component_From_One.Last_Name > Component_From_Two.Last_Name
        THEN
          BEGIN
            Write(Temp, Component_From_Two);
            Read(Two, Component_From_Two)
          END
      ELSE
        BEGIN
          Write(Temp, Component_From_One);
          Read(One, Component_From_One);
          Read(Two, Component_From_Two)
        END;
  Append(One, Two, Temp, Component_From_One, Component_From_Two)
END;  (* Merge *)

(* ***************************************************************** )

PROCEDURE Print (VAR Master_List:            (* File to print on output *)
                       Data_List);

(* File Master_List is printed.  Constant Dummy is accessed globally *)
```

PROBLEM-SOLVING CASE STUDY cont'd.

```pascal
VAR
  Component:
    Data;

BEGIN (* Print *)
  Reset(Master_List);
  Read(Master_List, Component);
  WHILE Component.Last_Name <> Dummy DO
    BEGIN
      WITH Component, Phone DO
        Writeln(Last_Name, ' ', First_Name, ' ',
                Area_Code:3, ' ', Number);
      Read(Master_List, Component)
    END
END;  (* Print *)


(************************************************************************)


BEGIN (* Merge_Lists *)
  Assign(One, 'ONE.DAT');
  Assign(Two, 'TWO.DAT');
  Assign(Three, 'THREE.DAT');
  Assign(Temp_File, 'TEMPFILE.DAT');
  Assign(Master_List, 'MASTLIST.DAT');
  Reset(One);
  Reset(Two);
  Reset(Three);
  Rewrite(Temp_File);
  Rewrite(Master_List);
  Merge(One, Two, Temp_File);
  Reset(Temp_File);
  Merge(Three, Temp_File, Master_List);
  Print(Master_List);
  Close(One);
  Close(Two);
  Close(Three);
  Close(Temp_File);
  Close(Master_List)
END.  (* Merge_Lists *)
```

Testing: Since we have three input files, there are several cases to test.

1. File One is empty.
2. File Two is empty.
3. File Three is empty.
4. Files Two and Three are empty.
5. Files One and Three are empty.
6. Files One and Two are empty.

7. All three files are empty.
8. All three files have values.

There are data-dependent conditions that should be tested as well:

1. The files should be tested with each one containing the name that comes first in the alphabet.
2. The files should be tested with each pair containing duplicate names in the first position, an intermediate position, and the last position.
3. The files should be tested with each one containing the name that comes last in the alphabet.

Since files One, Two, and Three are binary files, a program has to be written to create test data files. It may be more trouble than it is worth to thoroughly test this program using the procedure outlined above. If it is truly a one-shot deal, three short files with values might suffice. If this program is to be used more than once, however, it should be tested rigorously.

Before leaving this problem, we should talk about efficiency. Input/output operations take longer to execute than any other operations performed on data. Operations on binary files take less time than operations on text files, but they are still time consuming. We could have written a different merge procedure to merge the third file and temporary file onto the Master_List and print the components as they are written to the file. If we had done that, we would not have had to read Master_List back in to print it.

If this program were to be run several times, it would be worthwhile to recode it so that Master_List would not have to be reread. Programming Warm-Up exercise 9 asks you to do this. Programming Problem 1 asks you to rewrite this program using EOF instead of a dummy record to end each list.

PROBLEM-SOLVING CASE STUDY

Sports Banquet

Problem: Information on student athletes is available on a file. The names of all the students who play both soccer and track must be printed so that they can be invited to a special sports banquet. The data file is composed of records that contain the name of each student, along with a set containing the names of the sports in which the student participates. The following declarations were used to create the structure for each student record:

```
CONST
  Name_Length = 20;
```

```
TYPE
  Sport_Type = (Tennis, Soccer, Football, Baseball,
                Basketball, Volleyball, Track);
  Sport_Set_Type = SET OF Sport_Type;
  Name_String = String[String_Length];
  Student_Type = RECORD
                   Name : Name_String;
                   Sport : Sport_Set_Type
                 END;  (* Record *)
```

Input: File of student records (Student_File).

Output: The names of the students who participate in both soccer and track.

Discussion: If the information were on paper, we would scan the list, checking to see if a student plays both soccer and track. If so, we would add the student's name to our list of students to invite. This is exactly what the program does. A constant set made up of soccer and track (Foot_Sports) is compared with the set that describes each student. If the intersection of the two sets is equal to Foot_Sports, then that student plays both soccer and track.

Data Structure: A record containing a field with a string of twenty characters and a set with the component type Sport_Type.

Main Module   *Level 0*

```
Set Foot_Sports to [Soccer, Track]
WHILE more students DO
  IF Sport field of student * Foot_Sports = Foot_Sports
    THEN
        Print Name field
```

The program is so simple that it can be coded directly.

```
PROGRAM SPORT (Input, Output, Student_File);

CONST
  Name_Length = 20;
```

```
TYPE
  Sport_Type = (Tennis, Soccer, Football, Baseball,
                Basketball, Volleyball, Track);
  Sport_Set_Type = SET OF Sport_Type;
  Name_String = String[Name_Length];
  Student_Type = RECORD
                   Name  : Name_String;
                   Sport : Sport_Set_Type
                 END; (* Record *)
  File_Type = FILE OF Student_Type;

VAR
  Student_File:
    File_Type;
  Foot_Sports:
    Sport_Set_Type;
  A_Student:
    Student_Type;

BEGIN (* Sport *)
  Assign(Student_File,'STUDENT.DAT');
  Reset(Student_File);
  Foot_Sports := [Soccer, Track];
  (* Get a student record and examine the sports *)
  WHILE NOT EOF(Student_File) DO
    BEGIN
      Read(Student_File, A_Student);
      IF A_Student.Sport * Foot_Sports = Foot_Sports
        THEN
          Writeln(A_Student.Name)
    END;
  Close(Student_File)
END.  (* Sport *)
```

Testing: This is a simple program involving only one input file. There are two cases to test. The data must include students who play both track and soccer, and students who play only one of the two or neither. The following segment of code was used to generate a test file in which Athletes is an array of Student_Type records.

```
BEGIN
  Assign(Student_File, 'STUDENT.DAT');
  Rewrite(Student_File);
  Athletes[1].Name := 'Susy';                          (* Both *)
  Athletes[1].Sport := [Tennis, Soccer, Baseball, Track];
  Athletes[2].Name := 'Sarah';                      (* Neither *)
  Athletes[2].Sport := [Volleyball, Baseball];
  Athletes[3].Name := 'June';                       (* Neither *)
  Athletes[3].Sport := [];
  Athletes[4].Name := 'Bobby';                         (* Both *)
  Athletes[4].Sport := [Tennis..Track];
  Athletes[5].Name := 'Judy';                           (* One *)
  Athletes[5].Sport := [Track];
  Athletes[6].Name := 'Phil';                           (* One *)
  Athletes[6].Sport := [Soccer, Tennis];
  FOR Counter := 1 TO 6 DO
    Write(Student_File, Athletes[Counter]);
  Close(Student_File)
END.
```

Following is the output from running Program Sport with the Student_File:

```
Susy
Bobby
```

PROBLEM-SOLVING CASE STUDY

Personnel Records

Problem: We have a file of personnel records, and there is a great deal of data associated with each person. The task is to read in these records, sort them, and write them out again on the same file.

Input: A file of personnel records in binary format written using the following declarations.

```
TYPE
  String20 = String[20];
  String200 = String[200];
  String100 = String[100];
  Personnel_Data = RECORD
                    First_Name : String20;
                    Last_Name : String20;
                    Address : RECORD
                              Street,
                              City,
                              State : String20;
                        END;  (* Record *)
                    Work_History : String200;
                    Education : String100;
                    Payroll_Data : String200
                  END;  (* Record *)
```

The number of records in the file Master_List is unknown. The maximum number of employees that the company has ever had is 1,000.

Output: File Master_List with the records in alphabetical order by last name.

Discussion: In Chapter 12 we developed two general-purpose sort procedures: Ex_Sort, which sorted an array of values already in memory, and Insert, which inserted new data items in order. Although either one would work here, let's use Ex_Sort since we used Insert in the Exam Attendance case study in Chapter 12.

In Ex_Sort, the contents of two variables are swapped during each iteration. Swapping two variables is a simple operation. If large records are being sorted, however, swapping two of them can be time consuming. The Pascal code to swap two records is the same, regardless of the size of the records, but the length of time to make the swap varies greatly depending on the size of the records. For example, it may take ten times as long to swap records with twenty fields as it does to swap records with two fields.

If we are dealing with large records, we can make the sorting operation more efficient and save memory by making the records dynamic variables, and by sorting pointers to the records rather than the records themselves. This way, only simple pointer variables are swapped on each iteration, rather than whole records.

Procedure Ex_Sort has to be modified somewhat to sort large records rather than single values. The records themselves are dynamic variables, and a pointer to each is stored in an array. It is these pointers that are swapped when the algorithm calls for exchanging two values.

We have to define the array Person, which holds pointers to the personnel records, to be the maximum we might need; however, we have to create a Personnel_Data record only when we need one. Therefore, room for 1,000 pointers is set aside in memory for the Person array, but there are only as many Personnel_Data records in memory as

PROBLEM-SOLVING CASE STUDY cont'd.

Figure 15-7
Array of Pointers to Personnel Data Records

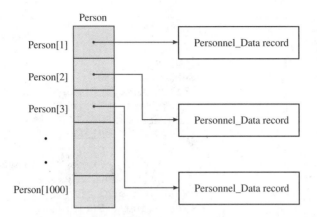

there are records on the file (see Figure 15-7). The Person array before and after sorting is shown in Figure 15-8. Note that when the algorithm says to swap the contents of two records, we swap the pointer instead.

Main Module   *Level 0*

```
WHILE more records
   Get a dynamic variable
   Read record into dynamic variable
Sort pointer (use Ex_Sort)
Write Records back on Master_File
```

Remember that the Ex_Sort procedure finds the minimum value in the list of values and swaps it with the value in the first place in the array. Then the next smallest value in the list is swapped with the value in the second place. This process continues until all the values are in order.

The place in this algorithm that has to be changed is where the minimum value is determined. Instead of comparing two components in the list, we compare the last name fields in the records to which these components point. The statement that did the comparison in Procedure Ex_Sort must be changed from

```
IF List[Place_Count] < List[Min_Index]
```

to

```
IF List[Place_Count]^.Last_Name < List[Min_Index]^.Last_Name
```

PROBLEM-SOLVING CASE STUDY *cont'd.*

Figure 15-8
*Person Array Before
and After Sorting*

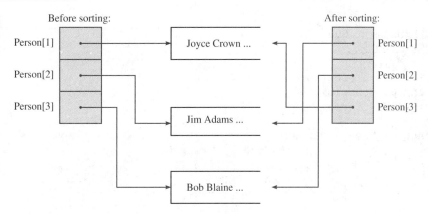

Write Records   *Level 1*

> FOR Index going from 1 to List_Length
>   Write Personnel_Data record on Master_List

This module is so simple that we code it as part of the main program.

Data Structures: An array (Person) of pointers to Personnel_Data.

Module Structure Chart:

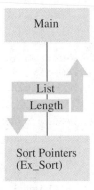

```
PROGRAM Sort_Pointers (Master_List, Output);

(* Personnel records on file Master_List are sorted by last name and *)
(* rewritten on Master_List *)
```

```
CONST
  Max_Length = 1000;

TYPE
  String20 = String[20];
  String200 = String[200];
  String100 = String[100];

  Personnel_Data = RECORD
                       First_Name : String20;
                       Last_Name : String20;
                       Address : RECORD
                                    Street,
                                    City,
                                    State : String20
                                 END; (* Record *)
                       Work_History : String200;
                       Education : String100;
                       Payroll_Data : String200
                   END; (* Record *)
  Index_Range = 1..Max_Length;
  Person_Pointer = ^Personnel_Data;
  List_Type = ARRAY[IndexRange] OF Person_Pointer;
  Person_File = FILE OF Personnel_Data;

VAR
  Person:               (* Array of pointers to personnel records  *)
    List_Type;
  List_Length:          (* Number of valid pointers in Person       *)
    Integer;
  A_Person:             (* Pointer to temporary record being built  *)
    Person_Pointer;
  Index:                (* Loop control variable                    *)
    Index_Range;
  Master_List:          (* Input file of personnel records          *)
    Person_File;

(*******************************************************************)


PROCEDURE Pointer_Ex_Sort (VAR List:          (* Array of pointers     *)
                               List_Type;
                               List_Length:  (* Total pointers in List *)
                               Integer);

(* An unordered list with List_Length pointers is taken as input.  The *)
(* same list is returned with the pointers ordered so that the records *)
(* to which the pointers point are in ascending order by last name     *)
```

PROBLEM-SOLVING CASE STUDY cont'd.

```
VAR
  Temp_Pointer:            (* Used for swapping       *)
    Person_Pointer;
  Pass_Count,              (* Loop control variable   *)
  Place_Count,            (* Loop control variable   *)
  Min_Index:              (* Index of minimum so far *)
    Index_Range;

BEGIN (* Pointer_Ex_Sort *)
  FOR Pass_Count := 1 TO (List_Length - 1) DO
    (* The records pointed to by List[1]..List[Pass_Count - 1] are *)
    (* already sorted and contain the first Pass_Count - 1          *)
    (* alphabetically last names *)
    BEGIN
      Min_Index := Pass_Count;
      (* Find the index of the pointer to the alphabetically first *)
      (* last name left in List[Pass_Count]..List[List_Length]     *)
      FOR Place_Count := Pass_Count + 1 TO List_Length DO
        IF List[Place_Count]^.Last_Name < List[Min_Index]^.Last_Name
          THEN
              Min_Index := Place_Count;
        (* Swap List[Min_Index] and List[Pass_Count] *)
        Temp_Pointer := List[Min_Index];
        List[Min_Index] := List[Pass_Count];
        List[Pass_Count] := Temp_Pointer
    END
END;  (* Pointer_Ex_Sort *)

(********************************************************************)

BEGIN (* Sort_Pointers *)
  Assign(Master_List, 'MASTLIST.DAT');
  Reset(Master_List);
  List_Length := 0;
  (* Read and store personnel records *)
  WHILE NOT EOF(Master_List) DO
    BEGIN
      List_Length := List_Length + 1;
      New(A_Person);
      Read(Master_List, A_Person^);
      Person[List_Length] := A_Person
    END;
  Pointer_Ex_Sort(Person, List_Length);
  Rewrite(Master_List);
  FOR Index := 1 TO List_Length DO
    Write(Master_List, Person[Index]^);
  Close(Master_List)
END.  (* Sort_Pointers *)
```

PROBLEM-SOLVING CASE STUDY *cont'd.*

Testing: There is only one file involved here, so testing the program completely requires only that we create a Master_File with some records. Passive error detection has been used for the case where the file has more than 1000 records; the program will crash with a range error if this case arises.

Remember that a program must be written to generate the test data because binary files must be created by another Pascal program. Output from a text editor cannot be used directly. The file can be created on a text editor, but it must be read as a text file and written out as a binary file. An editor is used to create a test file of names. Then Program Create reads this file and writes it out in binary (String20) format. The output from this program, Master_List, is then the input test file for Program Sort_Pointers with the declaration of Personnel_Data modified as shown here.

```
PROGRAM Create_Data (Data, Master_List, Output);

(* Text file Data is read in Character format and written out on    *)
(* Master_List in binary format.  Data contains names, one per line *)

TYPE
  String20 = String[20];
  Data_File = FILE OF String20;

VAR
  Name:            (* Current name being read in  *)
    String20;
  Data:            (* Input file of names         *)
    Text;
  Master_List:     (* Output file of names        *)
    Data_File;

BEGIN (* Create_Data *)
  Assign(Data, 'DATA.DAT');
  Assign(Master_List, 'MastList.Dat');
  Reset(Data);
  Rewrite(Master_List);
  WHILE NOT EOF(Data) DO
    BEGIN
      Readln(Data, Name);
      Write(Master_List, Name)
    END;
    Close(Data);
  Close(Master_List)
END.  (* Create_Data *)
```

File Data:

```
Shanklin
Gordon
Cava
Sheehan
McCorkle
Pinard
Ripley
Kirshen
Gleason
Thompson
```

In this particular case, testing is difficult because of the large size of each record, which makes the records time consuming to input. To make this task somewhat easier, you can generate test records that contain only one field, the last name field. For the test runs, put comment delimiters around the additional fields in Program Sort_Pointers. This technique is shown below as revised declarations for Program Sort_Pointers.

Program Create reads file Data and writes it out on file Master_List. File Master_List can then be used as test input for Program Sort_Pointers. For this test, Program Sort_Pointers should be modified in the following way:

```
PersonnelData = RECORD
         (*       First_Name : String20;              *)
                  Last_Name : String20;
         (*       Address : RECORD                    *)
         (*                  Street,                   *)
         (*                  City,                     *)
         (*                  State : String20          *)
                  END;  (* Record *)
         (*       Work_History : String200;           *)
         (*       Education : String100;              *)
         (*       Payroll_Data : String200            *)
              END;  (* Record *)
```

The following is a listing of file Master_List after it was processed by Program Sort_Pointers. The names are indeed in alphabetical order.

```
Cava       Gleason    Gordon    Kirshen
McCorkle   Pinard     Ripley    Shanklin
Sheehan    Thompson
```

What we have tested is that the program correctly sorts pointers to referenced variables of type String20. Because Pointer_Ex_Sort directly compares the strings that make up the last names, it is ordering the names according to the collating sequence of the character set. As we mentioned in Chapter 12, this can lead to problems when upper- and lowercase characters are mixed. For example, in the ASCII set, Macartney would come after MacDonald. Programming Warm-Up exercise 14 asks you to correct Pointer_Ex_Sort so that it orders names regardless of the case of the individual characters.

Testing and Debugging

The error programmers most commonly make when working with files is to forget to put the file name as a parameter to an input statement. If the file name is not there, the default file Input is assumed. If Input is the keyboard, the program waits for data to be entered. If Input is a file, an end-of-file error occurs.

Other common errors are to run out of data prematurely and to lose the first or last components in the file. The only advice that we can give you here is to be careful when designing the input section of your program. Always hand simulate the input before you code it. When checking your output, be sure to check whether the first and last components have been processed.

The most common error associated with the use of pointer variables is to confuse the pointer variable with the variable that it references. Again, the only general advice that we can give you is to be careful when working with pointers.

Testing and Debugging Hints

1. Declare all Text file variables, other than Input and Output, and use Assign, Close, Reset, and Rewrite on these files. Specify the file variable when using Append, Assign, Close, Reset, Rewrite, SeekEOF, SeekEOLN, Read, Readln, Write, Writeln, EOF, and EOLN for all Text files other than Input and Output.
2. Declare all nontext file variables. Specify the file variable when using Append, Assign, Close, EOF, Read, Reset, Rewrite, SeekEOF, and Write.
3. Files passed as parameters must be VAR parameters.
4. Remember that a character read when EOLN is True returns a blank.
5. Readln, Writeln, and EOLN have no meaning with nontext files.
6. Don't forget to use the Assign procedure for internal files (though they need not appear in the program heading).
7. Nontext files must be created by programs. Data from a word processor or the keyboard is in text format.
8. Internal (scratch) files can be declared in procedures, but external files must be declared in the main program.

9. Pointers cannot be printed. Pointer variables contain memory addresses so the values they contain cannot be printed. Even if they could, they might not tell us what we need to know to debug a program. Programs using pointers are therefore more difficult to debug than programs without them.

10. Pointers must point to variables of the same type to be compared or assigned one to another.

11. Do not confuse a pointer with the variable it points to (references).

P := Q	Copies the contents of Q into P.
P^ := Q^	Copies the contents of the variable to which Q points into the variable to which P points.
P^ := Q	Is illegal because one is a pointer and one is the variable being pointed to.
P := Q^	Is illegal because one is a pointer and one is the variable being pointed to.

12. Do not write pointer variables onto a file. Because memory is allocated differently for each program, the address stored in a pointer variable is valid only for a particular execution of a single program.

Summary

Programs communicate with the outside world and with each other through files, which are composed of a number of like components and reside in external storage. One component of a file is accessible at a time, in sequential order. Input is the standard Pascal input file; Output is the standard Pascal output file. If no file name is listed on Read and Write statements, these standard files are assumed. Input and Output are Text files. Text files are files of characters broken up into lines. EOLN is a function that is used to determine if a Text file marker is at the end of a line.

The components of a file can be of any type other than another file. EOF is a function that is used to determine if the last component in the file has been accessed. Turbo Pascal provides other nonstandard procedures and functions for accessing files.

Pointers are a simple data type that can contain the address of another variable. They are used to create dynamic variables. The pointer is created at compile time, but the variable to which the pointer points is created at run time. The built-in procedure New creates a variable of the type the pointer references and returns the variable's address in the pointer. Dynamic variables are called referenced variables because they are not given a name, but rather are referenced through a pointer variable.

The use of dynamic variables saves memory space because a variable is created only when it is needed. When a dynamic variable is no longer needed, it can be disposed of and those memory locations can be used again. The use of dynamic variables can also save machine time when large records are being sorted. The pointers to the large records can be sorted rather than the large records themselves.

■ Quick Check

1. Given a user-defined data type called Map_Element, how would you define binary file data type called Map in which each component is a value of type Map_Element? (pp. 692–701)

2. Given a binary file called Measures whose components are of type Integer, and an Integer variable called Width, how would you input a value from Measures into Length? (pp. 692–701)

3. How would you define a pointer type called To_Some_Number that points to a variable of type Integer? (pp. 701–710)

4. a. How would you dynamically create a referenced variable that is pointed to by a pointer variable called Number, of type To_Some_Number?
   b. How would you store the value 0 in the variable referenced by Number? (pp. 701–710)

5. How would you destroy the dynamic variable referenced by Number? (pp. 701–710)

6. What are two ways in which pointers may be used to improve program efficiency? (pp. 701–710)

7. When data in two files are being merged, what must be done if you run out of data on one file before running out of data on the other file? (pp. 710–717)

Answers

1. TYPE
       Map = FILE OF Map_Element;
2. Read(Measures, Width);
3. TYPE
       To_Some_Number = ^Integer;
4. a. New(Number)   b. Number^ := 0;   5. Dispose(Number);   6. Pointers improve memory space efficiency because we create only as many dynamic variables as are needed. It is more efficient in terms of time to move pointers than to move large data structures, as in the case of sorting large records.
7. The remainder of the nonempty file must be copied to the output file.

■ Exam Preparation Exercises

1. Given the data line

   ☐☐☐213☐

   show the file operations at the component level that must occur to execute the statement Readln(Number), where Number is an integer variable.

2. What are the differences between accessing array elements and accessing file components?

3. Which of the following can be used with any file type?
   a. Read
   b. EOLN
   c. EOF
   d. Write
   e. Writeln

4. When is it appropriate to use an internal file instead of an external file?

5. How many component types may be collected in one file?

6. Show a Read operation on a text file that is inconsistent with the definition of the file data type.

7. What Pascal procedure associates a DOS file name with a file variable?

8. What is wrong with the following type definition?

```
TYPE
  X = ARRAY[1..10] OF Char;
  Y = FILE OF X;
  Z = FILE OF Y;
```

9. What is the relationship between pointer variables and dynamic variables?

10. What Pascal procedure releases the space reserved for a dynamic variable back to the system?

11. How can the use of pointers make a program run faster?

12. What part of a Pascal program determines how much space is allocated when New(P) is executed?

13. What changes must be made in Program Sport so that the records are read into a referenced variable rather than into a named variable?

14. What changes must be made in Program Convert so that the records are read into a referenced variable rather than a named variable?

15. When should binary files be used and when should text files be used?

16. What is the output from the following Pascal program?

```
PROGRAM Pointer (Output);
VAR
  R,
  S:
    ^Integer;
  Z:
    Integer;
BEGIN (* Pointer *)
  New(R);
  R^ := 27;
  Writeln(R^, S^);
  Z := 54;
  S^ := Z;
  Writeln(R^, S^);
  New(R);
  R^ := 6;
  Writeln(R^, S^);
END.  (* Pointer *)
```

▪ *Programming Warm-Up Exercises*

1. Declare a file type Text2 that has component type Char.

2. Write the Pascal code needed to print the last character on every line of file Input.

3. Recode procedure Read_Int in this chapter to accept integers that are immediately preceded by a ' + ' or a ' − ' symbol. The output parameter Number should be negative if the integer starts with the ' − ' symbol.

4. Write a declaration for a binary file type containing real numbers.

5. Write the Pascal code to advance the file marker for file Skipped to EOF if only blanks remain in the file.

6. Write a Boolean function that takes two binary files of type Data_Type as input, and returns True if the next records on the files (type Rec_Type) are identical and False otherwise.

7. Write an integer function that returns the number of records on file Data.

8. Declare a pointer type that points to a record type named Ref_Rec.

9. Recode Program Merge_Lists in this chapter so that the master list is printed (to the file Output) as it is written to the file Master_List.

10. Write an IF statement that compares the two dynamic integer variables pointed to by variables P and Q, puts the larger into the integer variable named Biggest, and eliminates the original two dynamic variables.

11. Declare the variables used in exercise 10.

12. Write a Boolean function that takes as parameters two pointer variables Pointer1 and Pointer2. The function should return True if the two pointers reference the same variable and False otherwise.

13. Write a Boolean function that takes as parameters two pointer variables Pointer1 and Pointer2. The function should return True if their referenced variables are identical and False otherwise.

14. Rewrite procedure Pointer_Ex_Sort from program Sort_Pointers so that it correctly orders the records regardless of whether characters in the last names are uppercase or lowercase. *Hint:* Convert all the characters in both strings to uppercase before making the comparison.

15. The following code segment is supposed to copy a text file (In1) to another text file (Out1). The code does not work. Describe the output of the code as it is written, then rewrite it so that it works properly.

```
Reset(Inl);
Rewrite(Outl);
Read(Inl, Character);              (* Character is of type Char *)
WHILE NOT EOF(Inl) DO
  BEGIN
    Read(Inl, Character);
    WHILE NOT EOLN(Inl) DO
      BEGIN
        Write(Outl, Character);
        Read(Inl, Character);
      END;
    Readln(Inl);
    Writeln(Outl);
  END;
```

Inl looks like this

```
ABCDEF<eoln>
GHIJK<eoln>
LMNOP<eoln>
<eof>
```

16. Given the declarations

```
TYPE
  Bin_File = FILE OF Integer;
VAR
  Data : Bin_File
```

write a Pascal procedure that accepts input from the standard input device and writes it to the binary file Data.

17. Given the declarations

```
TYPE
  Data_Type = RECORD
                Number : Integer;
                Grade : Char
              END; (* Record *)
  Ptr_Type = ^Data_Type;
VAR
  P,
  Q:
    Ptr_Type;
```

write a Pascal procedure that exchanges the values pointed at by P and Q.

■ *Programming Problems*

1. Program Merge_Lists merges three files into one, assuming that each file ends with a dummy record. Rewrite Program Merge_Lists using EOF. Assume that there are no dummy records on any of the files.

2. Program Merge_Lists merges three files by merging two files, and then merging the third file with the result from merging the first two. Another way to solve the same problem is to merge three files at the same time, putting the result on a fourth file. Write a top-down design to solve the problem using this second strategy. Code your design in Pascal. Thoroughly test your program.

3. In Chapter 10 we introduced the problem of creating an automated address book with names, phone numbers, and birth dates. In Chapter 14 we printed the entry for each friend whose birthday was within two weeks of a given date. The data was on Text file Friend_List. Complete the creation of an automated address book by writing a program to add each person's address to the file. Your program should read an entry from file Friend_List, display the name on the screen, and prompt the user to enter the street address, city, state, and zip code. The complete entry should be written on binary file Address_Book.

   Add a field to Entry_Type2 (Program Birthday_Calls) of type Address_Type, which is a record that contains the street address, the city, the state, and the zip code. The file Address_Book should be a file of Entry_Type2. Make the module that prompts the user for the address as user-friendly as possible. Give the user a chance to read and approve the address before the entry is written to Address_Book.

4. In Chapter 12, Program Exam printed the names of those students taking an exam and the names of those students missing an exam. Parallel arrays were used because the record data type had not yet been introduced. Rewrite Program Exam combining Students and Attendance into a record (type Student_Type) with two fields: Name and Attendance. Make these records referenced variables rather than named variables; that is, Students should be an array of pointers to records of type Student_Type.

Dynamic Data Structures

GOALS

- To be able to define a linked list data structure for a given problem.
- To be able to print the contents of a linked list.
- To be able to insert new items into a linked list.
- To be able to delete items from a linked list.
- To be able to define and use a stack data structure.
- To be able to define and use a queue data structure.
- To be able to define and use a binary tree data structure.

In the last chapter we saw that Pascal has a mechanism for creating dynamic variables. This means that we can define a type at compile time, but not create any variables of that type until run time. These dynamic variables, which can be of any simple or structured type, can be created or destroyed at any time during execution of the program using the procedures New and Dispose. A dynamic variable is referenced not by a name but through a pointer that contains its address (location). Every dynamic variable has an associated pointer by which it can be accessed. We used dynamic variables to save space and machine time. In this chapter we see how to use them to build data structures that can grow and shrink as the program executes.

Static Versus Dynamic Structures

As we have already pointed out, many problems in computing involve lists of items. The structure we have used for implementing a list is the array, a static structure. The size of a static structure is fixed at compile time, and it exists as long as the part of the program (block) in which it is declared is executing. Yet when we are working with lists, many times we have no idea of the number of components we will have. The usual approach in this situation is to declare an array large enough to hold the maximum amount of data we can logically expect. Since we usually have less data than the maximum, the length of the subarray in which we have placed values is recorded and only that part of the array is accessed. This subarray can vary in length during execution, but the array itself cannot vary in size (see Figure 16-1).

There is another technique for representing a list in which the list components are dynamic variables that are created only as they are needed. Rather than being *physically* next to each other, as in an array, the components are *logically* next to each other (see Figure 16-2). Each component contains information about the location of the next component—a pointer to the next component in the list is stored with each component.

Such a list can expand or contract as the program executes. We don't have to know in advance how long it will be (see Figure 16-3). The only limitation is the amount of available memory space. Data structures built using this technique are called **dynamic data structures.** A dynamic data structure is built out of nodes. Each node is made up of a component (the data) and a pointer (the link).

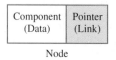

Node

Dynamic Data Structure   A data structure that can expand and contract during execution.

Let's look at how we can use Pascal pointer variables to create dynamic data structures.

Figure 16-1
Array

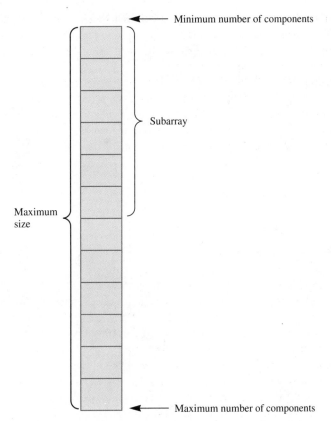

Figure 16-2
Physical Versus
Logical Ordering

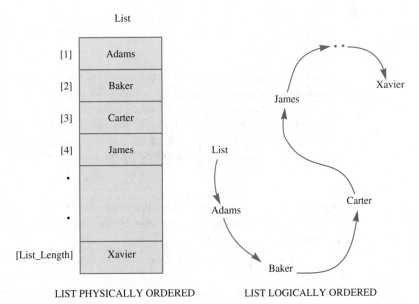

LIST PHYSICALLY ORDERED   LIST LOGICALLY ORDERED

Figure 16-3
Dynamic Data
Structure

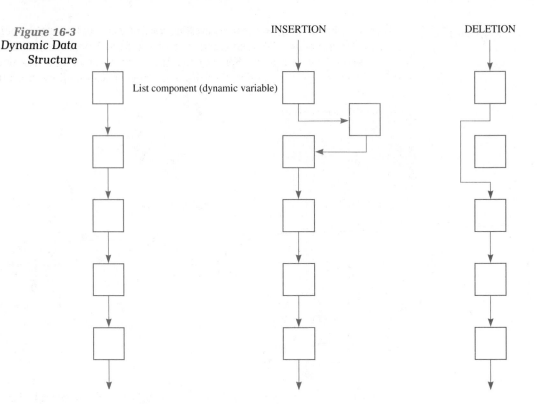

List component (dynamic variable)

INSERTION

DELETION

Linked Lists

Since each node contains a pointer that links it to the next node, a dynamic list is called a **linked list.** Accessing a linked list is a little like playing the children's game of treasure hunt—each child is given a clue to the hiding place of the next clue and the chain of clues eventually leads to the treasure. We access the list with a pointer variable that holds the address of the first node in the list. The pointer variable is called the **external pointer.** Every other node is accessed by the pointer field in the node before it.

Linked List   A list in which the order of the components is determined by an explicit link field in each node, rather than by the sequential order of the components in memory.

External Pointer   A named pointer variable that references the first node in a linked list.

To create a linked list, we begin by creating the first node and saving the pointer to it in the external pointer. We then create a second node and store the pointer to it in the link field of the first node. We continue this process—creating a new node and storing the pointer to it in the link field of the previous node—until we reach the end of the list.

Given the declarations

```
CONST
    Name_Length = 10;

TYPE
    Component_Type = String[Name_Length];
    Node_Pointer = ^Node_Type;
    Node_Type = RECORD
                    Component: Component_Type;
                    Link: Node_Pointer
                END;   (* Record *)

VAR
    List,                          (* External pointer to list *)
    Current,                       (* Moving pointer          *)
    New_Node:
        Node_Pointer;
```

the following code fragment creates a linked list with the names Adams, Baker, and Carter as the components in the list.

```
New(List);
List^.Component := 'Adams     ';
New(New_Node);
New_Node^.Component := 'Baker     ';
List^.Link := New_Node;
Current := New_Node;
New(New_Node);
New_Node^.Component := 'Carter    ';
Current^.Link := New_Node;
New_Node^.Link := NIL;
Current := New_Node
```

Let's go through each of these statements, describing in words what is happening and showing the linked list as it appears after the execution of the statement.

New(List)   A dynamic variable of Node_Type is created. The pointer to this node is left in List. List is the external pointer to the list we are building.

```
List^.Component := 'Adams        '
```
The character string 'Adams   ' is stored in the Component field of the first node.

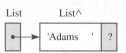

```
New(New_Node)
```
A dynamic variable of Node_Type is created. The pointer to this node is left in New_Node.

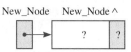

```
New_Node^.Component := 'Baker       '
```
The character string 'Baker   ' is stored in the Component field of the new node.

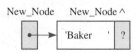

```
List^.Link := New_Node
```
The pointer to the node containing 'Baker   ' in its Component field is stored in the Link field of List. New_Node still points to this node. The node can be accessed by both New_Node^ and List^.Link^.

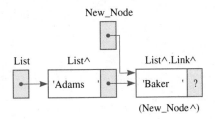

`Current := New_Node`

The pointer to the new node is copied into Current. Current, New_Node, and List^.Link all point to the node containing 'Baker   ' as its component.

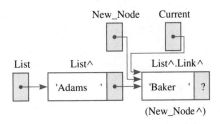

`New(New_Node)`

A dynamic variable of Node_Type is created. The pointer to this node is stored in New_Node.

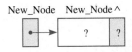

`New_Node^.Component := 'Carter    '`

The character string 'Carter   ' is stored in the Component field of the new node.

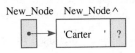

`Current^.Link := New_Node`

The pointer to the new node containing 'Carter   ' in the Component field is stored in the Link field of the node that contains 'Baker   '.

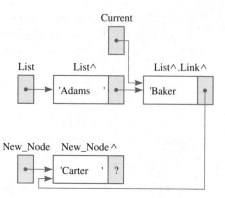

```
New_Node^.Link := NIL
```
The special pointer constant NIL is stored in the Link field of the last node in the list. When used in the Link field of a node, NIL means the end of the list. NIL is shown in the diagram as a / in the link field.

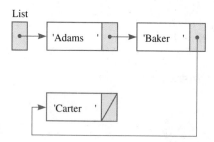

```
Current := New_Node
```
Current is updated.

Before we go on to generalize this algorithm for creating a linked list, a word should be said about the declarations. The pointer type Node_Pointer is defined to be a pointer to a record of type Node_Type, which has not yet been defined. This definition is an exception to the rule that identifiers must be defined before they are used. A pointer type may be defined to point to a type that has not yet been defined.

In the previous example, we used three pointers:

1. List, which was used to create the first node in the list and became the external pointer to the list.
2. New_Node, which was used to create a new node when it was needed.
3. Current, which was updated to always point to the last node in the linked list.

When building any linked list, we always need three pointers to perform these functions. The algorithm that we used is generalized below to apply to building a linked list of integer numbers from file Data. It is assumed that the file is not empty.

New(List)
Current is set equal to List
Readln(Data, List^.Component)
WHILE NOT EOF(Data)
  New(New_Node)
  Readln(Data, New_Node^.Component)
  Current^.Link is set equal to New_Node
  Current is set equal to New_Node
Current^.Link is set equal to NIL

The following program implements this algorithm:

```
PROGRAM Create_List (Output, Data);

(* Integers are read from file Data and stored in a Linked list.   *)
(* List is the external pointer to the list.  Assumption:  File is *)
(* not empty *)

TYPE
  Node_Pointer = ^Node_Type;
  Node_Type = RECORD
                 Component : Integer;
                 Link : Node_Pointer
              END;  (* Record *)

VAR
  List,                    (* External pointer to the list           *)
  New_Node,                (* Pointer to the newest node             *)
  Current:                 (* Pointer to the last node               *)
    Node_Pointer;
  Data:                    (* A file of integer numbers, one per line *)
    Text;
```

```
BEGIN (* Create_List *)
  New(List);
  Current := List;
  Readln(Data, List^.Component);
  WHILE NOT EOF(Data) DO
    BEGIN
      New(New_Node);
      (* Get a node *)
      Readln(Data, New_Node^.Component);
      (* Link it into list *)
      Current^.Link := New_Node;
      (* Set Current to last node *)
      Current := New_Node
    END;
  (* Set Link to end-of-list marker *)
  Current^.Link := NIL
END.  (* Create_List *)
```

Let's do a code walk-through and see just how this algorithm works.

`New(List)`	A variable of Node_Type is created. The pointer is left in List. List will remain unchanged as the pointer to the first node. List is the external pointer to the list.
`Current := List`	Current now points to the last node (the only node) in the list.
`Readln(Data, List^.Component)`	The first number is read into the Component field of the first node in the list.
`WHILE NOT EOF(Data) DO`	An event-controlled loop is used to read integer numbers from file Data until EOF.
`New(New_Node)`	Another variable of type Node_Type is created, with New Node referencing it.
`Readln(Data, New_Node^.Component)`	The next number on file Data is read into the Component field of the newly created node.
`Current^.Link := New_Node`	The pointer to the new node is stored in the Link field of the last node in the list.
`Current := New_Node`	Current is again pointing to the last node in the list.

```
Current^.Link := NIL
```
                                        The Link field of the last node is
                                        assigned the special end-of-list
                                        symbol NIL.

Following is the linked list that resulted when the program was run with the numbers
32, 78, 99, and 21 as data. The final values are shown for the auxiliary variables.

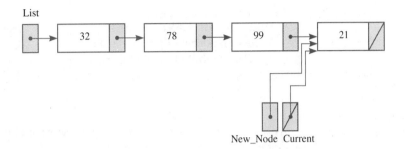

Algorithms on Linked Lists

Now that we have looked at two examples of creating a linked list, let's look at algorithms that process components in a linked list. We need to be able to insert a component into a list, delete a component from a list, and print the components in a list. For each of these operations, we make use of the fact that NIL is in the Link field of the last node. NIL can be assigned to any pointer variable. It means that the pointer points to nothing. Its importance lies in the fact that we can compare the Link field of each node to NIL to see when we have reached the end of the list.

As we develop these algorithms, we use the following declarations:

```
TYPE
  Node_Pointer = ^Node_Type;
  Node_Type = RECORD
                Component : Integer;
                Link : Node_Pointer
              END;  (* Record *)

VAR
  List:                    (* External pointer to list *)
    Node_Pointer;
```

Printing the components of a linked list is the easiest of the algorithms, so we begin there.

Printing a Linked List   To print the components of a linked list, we need to access the nodes one at a time. This requirement implies an event-controlled loop where the event that stops the loop is reaching the end of the list. The loop control variable is a pointer that is initialized to the external pointer and advanced (incremented) by setting it equal to the Link field of the current node. When the loop control pointer equals NIL, the last node has been accessed.

Print

```
Set Current to List
WHILE Current <> end of the list
    Write Component of Current node
    Set Current to Link field of Current
```

This algorithm can be coded directly as the general procedure Print. Note that the algorithm works even if List is empty (has no nodes).

```
PROCEDURE Print (List:                  (* Pointer to head of linked list *)
                 Node_Pointer);

(* The Component of the nodes in List are printed *)

VAR
  Current:                    (* Loop control pointer *)
    Node_Pointer;

BEGIN (* Print *)
  Current := List;
  WHILE Current <> NIL DO
    BEGIN
      Writeln(Current^.Component);
      Current := Current^.Link
    END
END;   (* Print *)
```

Let's do a code walk-through using the following list.

Current := List

Current and List both reference the first node in the list.

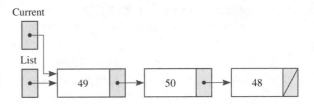

```
WHILE Current <> NIL

Writeln(Current^.Component)
Current := Current^.Link
```

The loop is entered because Current is not NIL.
The number 49 is printed.
Current now points to the second node in the list.

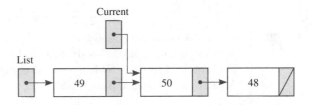

```
WHILE Current <> NIL

Writeln(Current^.Component)
Current := Current^.Link
```

The loop repeats since Current is not NIL.
The number 50 is printed.
Current now points to the third node in the list.

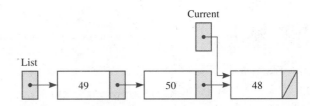

```
WHILE Current <> NIL

Writeln(Current^.Component)
Current := Current^.Link
```

The loop repeats since Current is not NIL.
The number 48 is printed.
Current is now NIL.

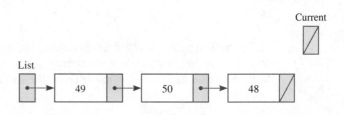

```
WHILE Current <> NIL
```
                                          The loop is not repeated because
                                          Current is NIL.

Inserting into a Linked List   A procedure for inserting a component into a linked list must have two parameters: the external pointer to the linked list and the item to be inserted. The phrase *inserting into a linked list* could mean either inserting the component at the top of the list (as the first node) or inserting the component into its proper place according to some ordering (alphabetic or numeric). Let's examine these two situations separately.

Inserting a component at the top of a list is easy because we don't have to search the list to find where the element belongs.

Insert Top

Get a new node (New_Node)
Set Component field of New_Node to Item
Set Link field of New_Node to External pointer
Set External pointer to New_Node

This algorithm is coded in procedure Insert_Top.

```
PROCEDURE Insert_Top (VAR List:    (* Pointer to head of linked list *)
                          Node_Pointer;
                      Item:    (* Number being placed in list    *)
                          Integer);

(* A node with Item in its component field is inserted as the top    *)
(* element in List.  Assumption:  List has been initialized          *)

VAR
   New_Node:               (* Temporary pointer *)
     Node_Pointer;

BEGIN (* Insert_Top *)
   New(New_Node);
   New_Node^.Component := Item;
   New_Node^.Link := List;
   List := New_Node
END;  (* Insert_Top *)
```

Before Insert_Top is called the first time, the list must be initialized by setting List to NIL. The following code walk-through shows the steps in inserting a component with the value of 20 as the first node in the linked list that was printed in the last section.

```
New(New_Node)
New_Node^.Component := Item
```

A new node is created.
The number 20 is stored in the
Component field of the new
node.

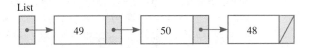

```
New_Node^.Link := List
```

The Link field of New_Node
now points to the first node in
the list.

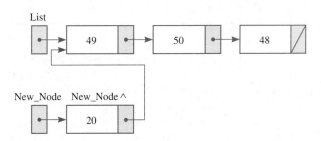

```
List := New_Node
```

The external pointer to the list
now points to the node
containing the new component.

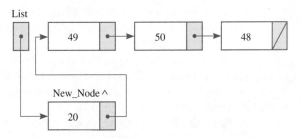

To insert a component into its proper place in a list, we have to loop through the
nodes until we find where the component belongs. If the list is kept in increasing numeric
order, we can recognize where a component belongs by finding the node in the list that
contains a value greater than the one being inserted. Our new node should be inserted

directly before the node with that value; therefore, we must keep track of the node before the current one to insert our new node. We call this node Previous. This method leads to the following algorithm:

Insert in Place

> Get a new node (New_Node)
> Set Component field of New_Node to Item
> Set Previous to List
> Set Current to Link field of List
> WHILE Item > Component field of Current
>   Set Previous to Current
>   Set Current to Link field of Current
> Insert New_Node between Previous and Current

This algorithm is correct, but there is a problem with coding it. If the new component is larger than all the other components in the list, the event that stops the loop (finding a node whose component is larger than the one being inserted) does not occur. An infinite loop does not occur, however, because the process is stopped by an error. When the end of the list is reached, the program tries to access the referenced variable of the pointer that contains NIL, which causes the program to crash. We can take care of this case by making sure that Current never equals NIL inside the loop.

We would like to use the following expression to control the WHILE loop.

Current <> NIL AND Item > Component field of Current

However, this expression cannot be coded directly. Most Pascal compilers evaluate both sides of an expression, even if the first side evaluates to False; that is, even if Current is equal to NIL, the other side of the expression is still evaluated, giving us the error we are trying to avoid. Instead, we move the comparison of Component to the body of the loop, and record the result in the Boolean variable Found. Found is used in the loop control expression.

There is one more point to consider in our algorithm—the special case when the list is empty or the new value is less than the first node in the list. Previous is NIL in this case, and NewNode must be inserted between List and Current instead of between Previous and Current.

Procedure Insert implements our algorithm with these changes incorporated.

```
PROCEDURE Insert (VAR List:      (* Pointer to head of linked list *)
                    Node_Pointer;
                  Item:      (* Number being placed into list  *)
                    Integer);
```

```
(* A node with Item in its component field is inserted into its    *)
(* proper place in List.  Assumption:  The Component fields are in *)
(* increasing order *)

VAR
  Found:                        (* True when insertion place is found *)
    Boolean;
  Current,                      (* Moving pointer                     *)
  Previous,                     (* Node before Current                *)
  NewNode:                      (* New node                           *)
    NodePointer;

BEGIN (* Insert *)
  (* Set up node to be inserted *)
  New(NewNode);
  NewNode^.Component := Item;
  (* Find previous insertion point *)
  Previous := NIL;
  Current := List;
  Found := False;
  WHILE (Current <> NIL) AND NOT Found DO
    IF Item > Current^.Component
      THEN
        BEGIN
          Previous := Current;
          Current := Current^.Link
        END
      ELSE
        Found := True;
  (* Insert NewNode *)
  NewNode^.Next := Current;
  IF Previous = NIL
    THEN
      List := NewNode
    ELSE
      Previous^.Link := NewNode
END;   (* Insert *)
```

There are two things to notice about this procedure. First, the parameter List is a VAR parameter in case the new node has to be inserted at the top. Second, this procedure can be made to work for any scalar type component by changing the type of Item in the heading.

Let's go through this code for each of the three cases: inserting at the top (Item is 20), inserting in the middle (Item is 60), and inserting at the end (Item is 100). Each insertion begins with the list below.

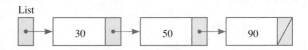

Insert(List, 20)

```
New(New_Node)
New_Node^.Component := Item
Previous := NIL
Current := List
Found := False
```
These five statements initialize the variables used in the searching process. The variables and their contents are shown below.

```
IF Item > Current^.Component
  Found := True
```
Since 20 is less than 30, Found becomes True in the first loop iteration.

```
New_Node^.Next := Current
IF Previous = NIL
  List := New_Node
```
Because Previous is NIL, the THEN branch is taken, and 20 is inserted between List and Current.

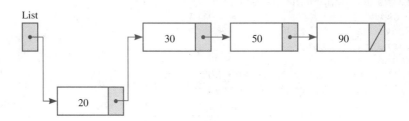

Insert(List, 60)

```
New(New_Node)
New_Node^.Component := Item
Previous := NIL
Current := List
Found := False
```
These five statements initialize the variables used in the searching process. The variables and their contents are shown below.

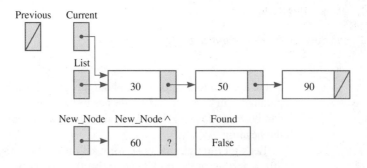

```
WHILE (Current <> NIL) AND NOT Found
```
This expression is True, so the loop is entered.

```
IF Item > Current^.Component
```
Since 60 is greater than 30, the THEN branch is taken.

```
Previous := Current                          Pointer variables are
Current := Current^.Link                          advanced.
```

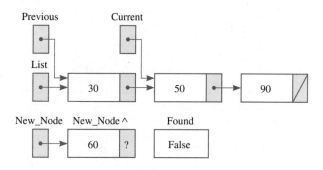

```
WHILE (Current <> NIL) AND NOT Found      This expression is True, so the
                                              loop is repeated.
IF Item > Current^.Component              Since 60 is greater than 50,
                                              the THEN branch is taken.

Previous := Current                       Pointer variables are
Current := Current^.Link                      advanced.
```

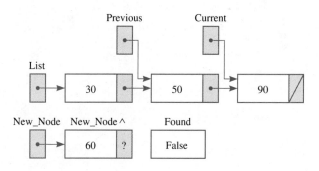

```
IF Item > Current^.Component              Since 60 is not greater than
                                              90, the ELSE branch is
                                              taken.

Found := True
WHILE (Current <> NIL) AND NOT Found      The expression is False, so the
                                              loop isn't repeated.

New_Node^.Next := Current                 Set link field if New_Node.
```

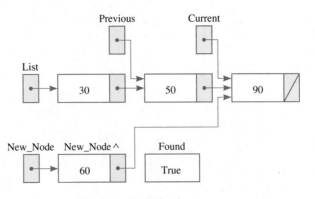

```
IF Previous = NIL
Previous^.Link := New_Node
```

Because Previous does not equal NIL, the ELSE branch is taken. The completed list is shown with the auxiliary variables removed.

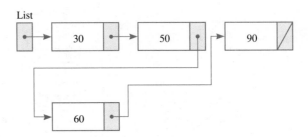

Insert(List, 100)

We do not repeat the first part of the search, but pick up the walk-through where Previous is pointing to the node whose component is 50, and Current is pointing to the node whose component is 90.

```
IF Item > Current^.Component
```

Since 100 is greater than 90, the THEN branch is taken.

```
Previous := Current
Current := Current^.Link
```

The pointer variables are advanced.

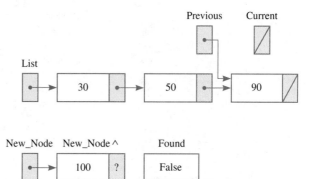

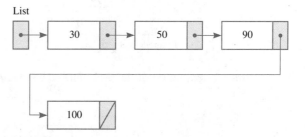

```
WHILE (Current <> NIL) AND NOT Found     Condition is False because
                                             Current is NIL.
New_Node^.Next := Current                Because Previous does not equal
IF Previous = NIL                            NIL, the ELSE branch is
  Previous^.Link := New_Node                 taken. New_Node is inserted
                                             between Previous and Current.
                                             List is shown with auxiliary
                                             variables removed.
```

Deleting from a Linked List   To delete a new node from a linked list, we have to loop through the nodes until we find the node we want to delete. We look at the mirror image of our insertions: deleting the top node and deleting a node whose component is equal to an input parameter.

To delete the first node, we just change the external pointer to point to the second node. The value in the node being deleted should be returned as an output parameter. The coding is so straightforward that it needs no further explanation.

```
PROCEDURE Remove_Top (VAR List:    (* Pointer to head of linked list *)
                           Node_Pointer;
                      VAR Item:    (* Number removed from the list   *)
                           Integer);

(* The top node is removed from List. Its Component field is     *)
(* returned in Item.  Assumption:  There is at least one node in *)
(* List *)
```

```
VAR
   Temp_Pointer:                (* Temporary pointer *)
      Node_Pointer;

BEGIN (* Remove_Top *)
   Temp_Pointer := List;
   Item := List^.Component;
   List := List^.Link;
   Dispose(Temp_Pointer)
END;   (* Remove_Top *)
```

We don't need to show a complete code walk-through since the code is so straight-forward. Instead, we show the state of the data structure in two stages: after the first two statements and at the end. We use one of our previous lists. Following is the data structure after the execution of the first two statements in the procedure.

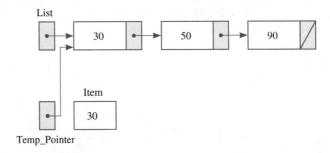

After the execution of the procedure, the structure is as follows:

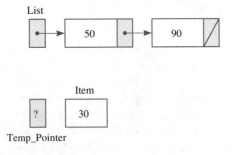

The procedure for deleting a node whose component contains a certain value is similar to the Insert procedure. The difference is that we are looking for a match, not a Component field greater than our Item. If we make the assumption that the component we are looking for is in the list, our loop control is simple. We don't have to worry about accessing a NIL pointer.

As in the Insert procedure, we need the node before the one that is to be deleted to change its Link field. In the following procedure, we demonstrate another technique for keeping track of the previous node. Instead of comparing Item with the Component field of Current, we compare it with the Component field of the node to which that Current's Link field points; that is, we compare Item with Current^.Link^.Component. When Current^.Link^.Component is equal to Item, Current is the previous node.

```
PROCEDURE Delete (VAR List:          (* Pointer to head of linked list *)
                      Node_Pointer;
                  Item:          (* Number within list to delete   *)
                      Integer;

(* The node whose Component field contains Item is deleted from     *)
(* List.  The node is Disposed.  Assumptions:  There is a Component *)
(* field that equals Item.  The Components are in ascending order   *)

VAR
   Temp_Pointer,           (* Temporary pointer     *)
   Current:                (* Loop control pointer *)
      Node_Pointer;

BEGIN (* Delete *)
  (* Check if first node *)
  IF Item = List^.Component
    THEN
      (* Delete first node *)
      BEGIN
        Temp_Pointer := List;
        List := List^.Link
      END
    ELSE
      BEGIN
        Current := List;
        (* Search for node in rest of list *)
        WHILE Current^.Link^.Component <> Item DO
          Current := Current^.Link;
        (* Delete Current^.Link *)
        Temp_Pointer := Current^.Link;
        Current^.Link := Current^.Link^.Link
      END;
  Dispose(Temp_Pointer)
END;  (* Delete *)
```

Let's delete the node whose component is 90. The structure is shown, with the nodes labeled as they would be when the WHILE loop is entered.

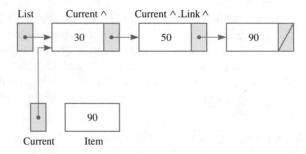

WHILE Current^.Link^.Component <> Item   Since 50 is not equal to 90,
                                           the loop is executed
                                           another time.

Current := Current^.Link   Pointer is advanced.

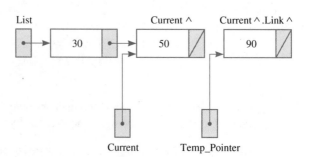

WHILE Current^.Link^.Component <> Item   Since 90 is equal to 90, the
                                           loop is exited.

Temp_Pointer := Current^.Link
Current^.Link := Current^.Link^.Link   The Link field of the node
                                           whose component is 90 is
                                           stored in the Link field of
                                           the node whose field is 50.
                                           The Link field is NIL in
                                           this case.

```
Dispose(Temp_Pointer)
```
Locations used for
Temp_Pointer^ (the node
that was deleted) are
available to be used again.
Temp_Pointer is undefined.

Note that NIL was stored in Current^.Link only because the node whose component was 90 was the last one in the list. If there had been more nodes beyond this one, a pointer to the next node would have been stored in Current^.Link.

Pointer Expressions

As you can see from the last procedure, pointer expressions can be quite complex. Let's look at some examples.

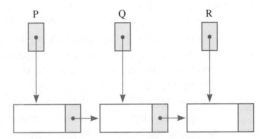

P, Q, and R point to nodes in a list. To access the fields of the nodes, we use P^, Q^, and R^. Use the preceding diagram to convince yourself that the following equivalencies are true.

```
P^.Link = Q
P^.Link^ = Q^
P^.Link^.Link = R
P^.Link^.Link^ = R^
Q^.Link = R
Q^.Link^ = R^
```

Remember the semantics of assignment statements for pointers.

```
P := Q
```
Assigns the value of pointer Q to pointer P.

```
P^ := Q^
```
Assigns the value of the variable referenced by Q to the variable referenced by P.

Choice of Data Structure

We have now looked in detail at two ways of representing lists of components: one where the components are physically next to each other (an array), and one where the components are logically next to each other (a linked list). Let's look at common operations on lists, and examine the advantages and disadvantages of each representation on each operation.

Common Operations

1. Read components sequentially into a list.
2. Access all the components in the list in sequence.
3. Insert or delete the first component in a list.
4. Insert or delete the last component in a list.
5. Insert or delete the Nth component in a list.
6. Access the Nth component in a list.
7. Sort the components in a list.
8. Search the list for a specific component.

Reading sequentially into a list is a little faster with an array representation because procedure New doesn't have to be called for each component. Accessing the components in sequence takes approximately the same time with both structures.

Inserting or deleting the first component is much faster using a linked representation. Conversely, the last component can be inserted or deleted much more efficiently in an array: there is direct access to the last component, and no shifting is required. In a linked representation, the entire list must be searched to find the last component.

On average, the time spent inserting or deleting the Nth component is about equal for the two types of lists. A linked representation would be better for small values of N, and an array representation would be better for values of N near the end of the list.

Accessing the Nth element is *much* faster in an array representation. We can access it directly by using N as the index into the array. In a linked representation, we have to access the first N − 1 components to reach the Nth one.

In sorting an existing linked list, we remove the elements one by one and insert them in their proper places in a second linked list. When the sorting is finished, we can set the external pointer of the original list to point to the first component of the new list. Thus, sorting a linked list uses no more memory space than sorting an array. However, a linked list is limited to this type of sorting algorithm. With an array representation, much faster sorting algorithms can be used.

In general, searching a list for a specific component is much faster in an array representation because a binary search can be used. When the components in the list to be searched are not ordered, the two representations are about the same.

When you are trying to decide whether to use an array representation or a linked representation, determine which of these common operations will be applied most frequently. Use your analysis to determine which structure would be better in the context of your particular problem.

There is an additional point to consider when deciding whether to use an array or a linked list. How accurately can you predict the maximum number of components in the list? Does the number of components in the list fluctuate widely? If you know the maximum and it remains fairly constant, an array representation is probably more useful. Otherwise, it would be better to choose a linked representation to use memory more efficiently.

Other Data Structures

Linked lists can be used to implement many more complicated data structures. The study of data structures forms a major topic in computer science. Entire books and courses are developed to cover the subject. Our purpose in this section is not to make you an expert in data structures, but to pique your interest for the future. We mention briefly three of the most useful structures: stacks, queues, and binary trees. A thorough treatment is left to a data structures text.

Stacks

A **stack** is a data structure that can be accessed from only one end. We can insert an element at the top (as the first) and we can remove the top (first) element. This structure models a property commonly encountered in real life. Accountants call it *LIFO,* which stands for "last in, first out." The plate holder in a cafeteria has this property. You can take only the top plate. When you do, the one below it rises to the top so the next person can take one. Cars in a noncircular driveway exhibit this property. The last car in has to be the first car out. The term *push* is used for the insertion operation, and the term *pop* is used for the deletion operation. Figure 16-4 shows what happens when you push an element on a given stack and then pop the stack.

Stack　　A data structure in which insertions and deletions can be made from only one end.

Figure 16-4
Stack

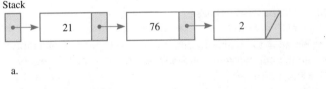

a.

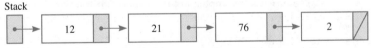

b. Push(Stack, 12) pushes a new element on the stack with a value of 12

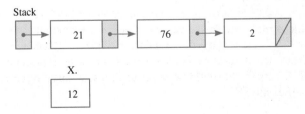

c. Pop(Stack,X) pops an element from the stack and returns its value in X

Stacks are used frequently in systems software. The Pascal run-time support system uses a stack to keep track of procedure and function parameters, and local and dynamic variables. The Pascal compiler uses a stack to translate arithmetic expressions. Stacks are used whenever we wish to remember a sequence of objects or actions in the reverse order from that in which they occurred. The algorithm and code segment to read in a line of characters and print it out in reverse order using a stack is shown here.

Reverse Line

```
Initialize Stack
WHILE NOT EOLN
    Read a character
    Push character onto a stack
WHILE More Characters on Stack
    Pop character
    Write character
```

Initialize Stack

Since we are implementing a stack as a linked list, all we have to do is set Stack to NIL to initialize the stack. There are many ways in which a stack can be implemented, however, so we create a procedure Initialize, even if it is only one line of code. Thus, the algorithm using that stack does not have to be changed if the implementation is changed.

More Characters on Stack

We need to be able to determine when the stack is empty. This operation can also be done with one line—if Stack is NIL, the stack is empty. We code this as the one-line function Empty.

The program to implement this algorithm follows.

```
PROGRAM Reverse_Line (Input, Output);

(* A line of characters is read in and printed in reverse order *)

TYPE
  Stack_Pointer = ^Stack_Type;
  Component_Type = Char;
  Stack_Type = RECORD
                 Component : Component_Type;
                 Link : Stack_Pointer
               END; (* Record *)
```

```
VAR
  Character:          (* Temporary character read in or written out *)
    Char;
  Stack:              (* Pointer to list of characters           *)
    Stack_Pointer;

(************************************************************************)

PROCEDURE Pop (VAR Stack:               (* Pointer to top of stack    *)
                   Stack_Pointer;
               VAR Component:           (* Object removed from stack *)
                   Component_Type);

(* The first component is removed from stack. *)
(* Assumption:  Stack is not NIL             *)

VAR
  Pointer:            (* Temporary pointer *)
    Stack_Pointer;

BEGIN (* Pop *)
  Pointer := Stack;
  Component := Stack^.Component;
  Stack := Stack^.Link;
  Dispose(Pointer)
END;  (* Pop *)

(************************************************************************)

PROCEDURE Push (VAR Stack:              (* Pointer to top of stack     *)
                    Stack_Pointer;
                Component:              (* Object put onto stack       *)
                    Component_Type);

(* Component is inserted as the first component in Stack. *)
(* Assumption:  Stack has been initialized to NIL         *)

VAR
  Pointer:            (* Temporary pointer *)
    Stack_Pointer;

BEGIN (* Push *)
  New(Pointer);
  Pointer^.Component := Component;
  Pointer^.Link := Stack;
  Stack := Pointer
END;  (* Push *)

(************************************************************************)
```

```
PROCEDURE Initialize (VAR Stack:              (* Stack being initialized *)
                           Stack_Pointer);

BEGIN (* Initialize *)
  Stack := NIL
END;  (* Initialize *)


(*****************************************************************)

FUNCTION Empty (Stack:                        (* Pointer to top of stack *)
                     Stack_Pointer):
                       Boolean;

BEGIN (* Empty *)
  Empty := (Stack = NIL)
END;  (* Empty *)


(*****************************************************************)

BEGIN (* Reverse_Line *)
  Initialize(Stack);
  (* Read and save characters *)
  WHILE NOT EOLN DO
    BEGIN
      Read(Character);
      Push(Stack, Character)
    END;
  (* Print characters in reverse order *)
  WHILE NOT Empty(Stack) DO
    BEGIN
      Pop(Stack, Character);
      Write(Character)
    END
END.  (* Reverse_Line *)
```

In Chapter 14 we wrote a set of procedures to operate on the date abstract data type that we had defined. We have just done the same thing for the stack data structure. We defined and coded the operations Initialize, Push, Pop, and Empty. Initialize, Push, and Pop are constructors, and Empty is an observer. We have not built any test operations for the stack abstract data type. The components on the stack can be of any data type. Component_Type can be an integer, a real, an array, a record—whatever needs to be accessed in the reverse order. We will use these operations later without further comment.

We have adhered to the principle of abstraction by writing procedure Initialize and function Empty instead of inserting the code for these operations in the program. The method of implementing a stack thus can be changed without changing the main program.

Queues

A **queue** (pronounced like the letter Q) is a data structure in which elements are entered at one end and removed from the other. Accountants call the property *FIFO* for "first in, first out." A waiting line in a bank or supermarket and a line of cars on a one-way street are types of queues. Indeed, queues are often used in computer simulations of situations like these.

Queue A data structure in which insertions are made at one end and deletions are made at the other.

Whereas the terminology for the insert and remove operations on stacks is standard (Push, Pop), no such standardization exists with queues. The operation of inserting at the rear of the queue is called many names in the literature: Insert, Enter, and Enqueue are three common ones. Correspondingly, the operation for removing from the front of the queue is variously called Delete, Remove, and Dequeue.

We have chosen to call our procedures Enqueue and Dequeue. Since we are accessing both ends, we need two external pointers: Front and Rear. Figure 16-5 shows an empty queue (a), insertion into a queue (b), and deletion from a queue (c). Since we have not coded these operations before, we develop them here using the following declarations:

```
CONST
  Name_Length = 15;

TYPE
  Node_Pointer = ^Node_Type;
  Component_Type = String [Name_Length];
  Node_Type = RECORD
                Component : Component_Type;
                Link : Node_Pointer
              END;  (* Record *)
  Queue_Type = RECORD
                 Front : Node_Pointer;
                 Rear : Node_Pointer
               END;  (* Record *)

VAR
  Queue:
    Queue_Type;
```

To insert an Item at the Rear, we must take care of two cases: the one in which the queue is empty, and the one in which it has at least one component. If the queue is empty, we must set both Rear and Front to point to the element that is entering the queue. If there is at least one component in the queue already, we have to insert the new component after Rear^ and redefine Rear to point to the new component.

Figure 16-5
Queue Operations

a. An empty queue

b. Insertion into a queue

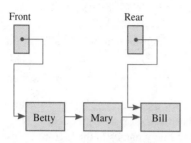

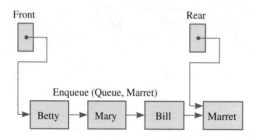

Enqueue (Queue, Marret)

c. Deletion from a queue

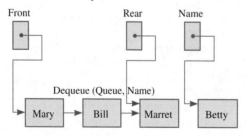

Dequeue (Queue, Name)

Enqueue

```
Get a new node (New_Node)
Set Component field of New_Node to Component
IF Empty Queue
   THEN
      Set Front field of queue to New_Node
   ELSE
      Set Link field of last component to New_Node
Set Rear field of queue to New_Node
```

Empty Queue

```
Set Empty to Rear field of queue = NIL
```

Procedure Enqueue and function Empty are coded as follows:

```
Function Empty_Q (Queue:                   (* Head of queue to examine *)
                  Queue_Type):
                     Boolean;

BEGIN (* Empty_Q *)
  Empty_Q := (Queue.Rear = NIL)
END;  (* Empty_Q *)

(********************************************************************)

PROCEDURE Enqueue (VAR Queue:          (* Head of queue          *)
                       Queue_Type;
                       Component:     (* Item to insert into queue *)
                       Component_Type);

(* Component is inserted into the rear of Queue *)

VAR
  New_Node:   (* New node *)
    Queue_Pointer;
```

```
BEGIN (* Enqueue *)
  (* Initialize a new node *)
  New(New_Node);
  New_Node^.Component := Component;
  New_Node^.Link := NIL;
  WITH Queue DO
    BEGIN
      IF Empty_Q(Queue)
        THEN
          Front := New_Node
        ELSE
          Rear^.Link := New_Node;
      Rear := New_Node
    END
END;  (* Enqueue *)
```

Removing an element from the front of the queue is just like popping a stack or removing the first node from any linked list. The only additional task that must be done is to check if the queue is empty after the node is removed. If it is, the rear pointer must be set to NIL. The name of the list in the following code is Front.

```
PROCEDURE Dequeue (VAR Queue:          (* Head of Queue            *)
                        Queue_Type;
                   VAR Component:       (* Item removed from queue *)
                        Component_Type);

(* The first node in the queue is removed.  The Component field of *)
(* the node is returned in Component.  Assumption:  There is at    *)
(* least one node *)

VAR
  Pointer:
    Queue_Pointer;

BEGIN (* Dequeue *)
  Pointer := Queue.Front;
  Component := Queue.Front^.Component;
  Queue.Front := Queue.Front^.Link;
  Dispose(Pointer);
  IF Empty_Q(Queue)
    THEN
      Queue.Rear := NIL
END;  (* Dequeue *)
```

To complete our set of queue operations, we need an operation to initialize a queue. If an empty queue is one where Rear is NIL, then all we have to do is set Rear to NIL to initialize the queue.

```
PROCEDURE Initialize_Q (VAR Queue:          (* Head of queue *)
                               Queue_Type);
BEGIN (* Initialize_Q *)
  Queue.Rear := NIL
END;  (* Initialize_Q *)
```

By defining the queue structure and the operations for manipulating it, we have added one more abstract data type to our repertoire. Initialize, Enqueue, and Dequeue are constructors, and Empty_Q is an observer for the abstract type.

Binary Trees

The concept of a linked list can be extended to structures containing nodes with more than one pointer field. One of these structures is known as a **binary tree** (Figure 16-6). The tree is referenced by an external pointer to the node, called the *root* of the tree. The root has two pointers: one to its *left child* and one to its *right child*. Each child again has two pointers: one to its left child and one to its right child. The left and right child of a node are called *siblings*.

For any node in a tree, the left child of the node is the root of the left subtree of the node. Likewise, the right child is the root of the right subtree. Nodes whose left and right children are both NIL are called *leaf nodes*.

Although Figure 16-6 shows a binary tree with only seven nodes, there is no theoretical limit on the number of nodes in a tree. It is easy to see why it is called binary—each node can have two branches. If you turn the figure upside down, you can see why it is called a tree.

There is a special kind of binary tree called a **binary search tree.** In a binary search tree, the component in any node is greater than the component in its left child and any of its children (left subtree), and it is less than the component in its right child and any

Figure 16-6
Binary Tree

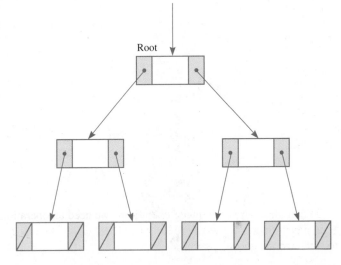

of its children (right subtree). This definition assumes no duplicates. The tree shown below is an example of a binary search tree.

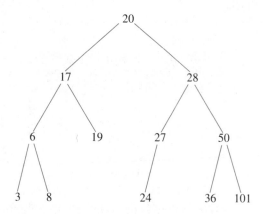

A binary search tree is useful because, if we are looking for a certain component, we can tell which half of the tree it is in by using just one comparison. We can then tell which half of that half the component is in with one more comparison. This process continues until we either find the component (a number in this case), or we determine that it is not there. The process is analogous to a binary search of an array.

Let's search for the number 50.

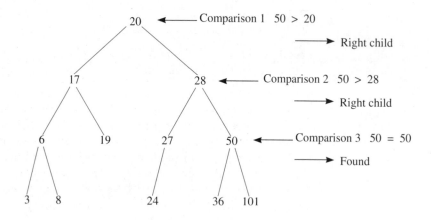

Now let's look for 18, a number that is not there.

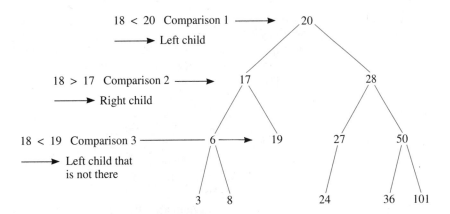

18 < 20 Comparison 1 ———————→ 20
    ———→ Left child

18 > 17 Comparison 2 ———————→ 17   28

18 < 19 Comparison 3 ———————— 6 ——→ 19   27   50
    ———→ Left child that
         is not there
                                    3   8   24   36 101

The left child of 19 is NIL, so we know that 18 isn't in the tree. Not only do we know the 18 is not there, but we are at the right place to insert 18 if we want to do so.

To summarize: We compared the item we were looking for with the component in the tree, and took the appropriate branch if the component and the item were not the same. When we started to take a branch that was NIL, we knew that the item was not in the tree.

Let's develop and code the algorithm to insert an item in a binary search tree. Up to this point, we've assumed that there are no duplicate values in the list to be searched. But what if there are duplicates? We can handle this situation by changing our definition of a node to include both the component and a frequency count that tells us how many components with that value have been inserted into the tree. If the value we want to insert is already there, we increment an associated frequency; if the value is not there, we insert a node containing it. Thus only one copy of a value is ever stored in the tree, and additional copies are represented by incrementing the count. Of course, when we initialize a node, we must set the associated frequency to 1. This method has the advantage of conserving memory by not storing the duplicate values.

The components in the binary search tree have two fields: Value and Count. The nodes in the tree have three fields: the component, Left (pointer to the left child), and Right (pointer to the right child). Tree_Ptr is a pointer that we use to keep our place in the tree. We are finished either when we find the item or when we have inserted a node containing the item. The basic algorithm is as follows:

Main Module   *Level 0*

```
Set Tree_Ptr to Tree
Set Finished to False
REPEAT
  IF Tree_Ptr^.Component.Value = Item
    THEN
        Increment Count field
        Set Finished to True
    ELSE IF Tree_Ptr^.Component.Value > Item
      THEN
      (* Check left subtree *)
        IF Tree_Ptr^.Left = NIL
          THEN
              Insert Item as Left_Leaf
          ELSE
              Set Tree_Ptr to Tree_Ptr^.Left
      ELSE
      (* Check right subtree *)
        IF Tree_Ptr^.Right = NIL
          THEN
              Insert Item as Right_Leaf
          ELSE
              Set Tree_Ptr to Tree_Ptr^.Right
UNTIL Finished
```

Right_Leaf and Left_Leaf are enumerated types that tell into which branch of Tree_Ptr the new node is to be inserted.

Insert Item as Leaf   *Level 1*

```
Initialize New_Node
CASE Leaf OF
  Left_Leaf : Set Tree_Ptr^.Left to New_Node
  Right_Leaf : Set Tree_Ptr^.Right to New_Node
Set Finished to True
```

Initialize NewNode

```
New(New_Node)
Set New_Node^.Right to NIL
Set New_Node^.Left to NIL
Set New_Node^.Component.Value to Item
Set New_Node^.Component.Count to 1
```

This algorithm is coded in three procedures, with the insertion procedure embedded within the main procedure Search_And_Count.

```
TYPE
  Tree_Pointer = ^Tree_Node;
  Value_Type = Integer;
  Component_Type = RECORD
                     Value : Value_Type;
                     Count : Integer
                   END;  (* Record *)
  Tree_Node = RECORD
                Component : Component_Type;
                Left,
                Right : Tree_Pointer
              END;  (* Record *)

(* *****************************************************************)


PROCEDURE Initialize (VAR New_Node:       (* Node being initialized *)
                          Tree_Pointer;
                      Item:            (* Value for new node     *)
                          Value_Type);

(* A Node is initialized with Item in the Value field and 1 in the *)
(* Count field.  Left and Right are set to NIL *)

BEGIN (* Initialize *)
  New(New_Node);
  New_Node^.Right := NIL;
  New_Node^.Left := NIL;
  New_Node^.Component.Value := Item;
  New_Node^.Component.Count := 1
END;  (* Initialize *)

(* *****************************************************************)
```

```
PROCEDURE Search_And_Count (VAR Tree:              (* Tree of scores      *)
                                     Tree_Pointer;
                                Item:           (* Input search value *)
                                     Value_Type;

(* Search_And_Count searches the binary search tree pointed to by *)
(* Tree looking for the component Item.  IF Item is equal to a    *)
(* Component.Value in the tree, Component.Count is incremented.    *)
(* ELSE Item is inserted into the tree with a Count field of 1.   *)
(* Assumption:  Tree contains at least one component              *)

TYPE
  Leaf_Type = (Right_Leaf, Left_Leaf);

VAR
  Tree_Ptr:              (* Advancing pointer variable *)
    Tree_Pointer;
  Finished:              (* Loop control flag          *)
    Boolean;

  (********************************************************************)

  PROCEDURE Insert (VAR Tree_Ptr:   (* Node new item is attached to *)
                           Tree_Pointer;
                        Leaf:        (* Which pointer to attach to   *)
                           Leaf_Type;
                        Item:        (* Value to put into new node   *)
                           Value_Type;
                   VAR Finished:    (* Flag to stop insertion task  *)
                           Boolean);

  (* Item is inserted into Tree_Ptr as the Leaf child *)

  VAR
    New_Node:    (* Pointer to node being linked to Tree_Ptr's node *)
      Tree_Pointer;

  BEGIN (* Insert *)
    (* Initialize node *)
    Initialize(New_Node, Item);
    (* Insert node *)
    CASE Leaf OF
      Left_Leaf : Tree_Ptr^.Left := New_Node;
      Right_Leaf : Tree_Ptr^.Right := New_Node
    END;   (* Case *)
    Finished := True
  END;   (* Insert *)

  (********************************************************************)
```

```
BEGIN (* Search_And_Count *)
  (* Initialize looping variables *)
  Tree_Ptr := Tree;
  Finished := False;
  (* Search for Item in Tree *)
  REPEAT
    WITH Tree_Ptr^ DO
      BEGIN
        IF Component.Value = Item
          THEN
            BEGIN                                    (* Match found *)
              Component.Count := Component.Count + 1;
              Finished := True
            END
          ELSE
            IF Component.Value > Item
              THEN                          (* Search left subtree *)
                IF Left = NIL
                  THEN                      (* Insertion place found *)
                    Insert(Tree_Ptr, Left_Leaf, Item, Finished)
                  ELSE
                    Tree_Ptr := Left
              ELSE                          (* Search right subtree *)
                IF Right = NIL
                  THEN                      (* Insertion place found *)
                    Insert(Tree_Ptr, Right_Leaf, Item, Finished)
                  ELSE
                    Tree_Ptr := Right
      END
  UNTIL Finished;
END;  (* Search_And_Count *)
```

P ROBLEM-SOLVING CASE STUDY

Simulated Card Deck

Problem: As an avid card player, you plan to write a program to play solitaire once you have become thoroughly comfortable with dynamic data structures. As a prelude to that program, you decide to write a procedure that creates a deck of playing cards. The playing cards are structured as a linked list.

Input: None.

Output: Deck, the external pointer to the linked list of playing cards.

Discussion: The suits can be represented using an enumerated type. Rank can be represented using the numbers 1 through 13, with the ace as a 1 and the king as a 13. The first card can be generated, and its pointer stored in the external pointer to the list. The balance of the fifty-two cards can be generated in a loop. After every thirteenth card, the suit is incremented.

Data Structures: A linked list in which the components are cards, represented as follows:

```
Card_Type = RECORD
              Suit : Suits;
              Rank : 1..13
            END; (* Record *)
```

Main Module   *Level 0*

```
New(Deck)
Set Suit of Deck to Club
Set Rank of Deck to 1
Set Current to Deck
FOR Count going from 2 to 52
  New(New_Node)
  IF Rank of Current = 13
     THEN
         Set Suit of New_Node to Succ(Suit)
         Set Rank of New_Node to 1
     ELSE
         Set Suit of New_Node to Suit of Current
         Set Rank of New_Node to Rank of Current + 1
  Set Link of Current to New_Node
  Set Current to New_Node
```

The code for the global declarations and procedures follows.

PROBLEM-SOLVING CASE STUDY *cont'd.*

```
TYPE
  Node_Pointer = ^Node_Type;
  Suits = (Club, Diamond, Heart, Spade);
  Card_Type = RECORD
                Suit : Suits;
                Rank : 1..13                (* 1 is ace;  13 is king  *)
              END;  (* Record *)
  Node_Type = RECORD
                Card : Card_Type;
                Link : Node_Pointer
              END;  (* Record *)

VAR
  Deck:                           (* External pointer to deck of cards *)
    Node_Pointer;


(*********************************************************************)

PROCEDURE Create_Deck (VAR Deck:        (* Pointer to list of cards *)
                       Node_Pointer;

(* Creates a list of fifty-two nodes.  Each node represents a       *)
(* playing card.  Deck is the external pointer to the list.  The    *)
(* cards are in order by suit and by rank *)

VAR
  New_Node,               (* Pointer to newest card   *)
  Current:                (* Pointer to previous card *)
    Node_Pointer;
  Count:                  (* Loop control variable    *)
    Integer;
```

```
BEGIN (* Create_Deck *)
  New(Deck);
  Deck^.Card.Suit := Club;
  Deck^.Card.Rank := 1;
  Current := Deck;
  (* Loop to create balance of deck *)
  FOR Count := 2 to 52 DO
    BEGIN
      New(New_Node);
      (* Test for change of suit *)
      IF Current^.Card.Rank = 13
        THEN
          (* Change suit *)
          BEGIN
            New_Node^.Card.Suit := Succ(Current^.Card.Suit);
            New_Node^.Card.Rank := 1
          END
        ELSE
          (* Increment rank *)
          BEGIN
            New_Node^.Card.Suit := Current^.Card.Suit;
            New_Node^.Card.Rank := Current^.Card.Rank + 1
          END;
      Current^.Link := New_Node;
      Current := New_Node
    END;
  (* Set end-of-list marker *)
  Current^.Link := NIL
END;  (* Create_Deck *)
```

PROBLEM-SOLVING CASE STUDY

Solitaire Simulation

There is a solitaire game that is quite simple, but seems difficult to win. Let's write a program to play the game, and then run it a number of times to see if it really is that difficult to win or if we have just been unlucky.

Although this card game is played with a regular poker or bridge deck, the rules deal with suits only; the face values (ranks) are ignored. The rules are listed below. Rules 1 and 2 are initialization.

1. Take a deck of playing cards and shuffle it.
2. Place four cards side by side, left to right, face up on the table.

3. If the four cards (or right-most four if there are more than four on the table) are of the same suit, move them to a discard pile. Otherwise, if the first one and the fourth one (of the right-most four cards) are of the same suit, move the cards between (second and third) to a discard table. Repeat until no cards can be removed.
4. Take the next card from the shuffled deck and place it face up to the right of those already there. Repeat this step if there are less than four cards face up (assuming there are more cards in the deck).
5. Repeat steps 3 and 4 until there are no more cards in the deck. You win if all the cards are on the discard pile.

Figure 16-7 walks through the beginning of a typical game to demonstrate how the rules operate. Remember the game deals with suits only. There must be at least four cards face up on the table before the rules can be applied.

Input: The number of times the simulation is to be run (Number_Of_Games), and the number of times the deck is to be shuffled between games (Number_Of_ Shuffles).

Output: Number of games played, and number of games won.

Discussion: A program that plays a game is an example of a *simulation program*. The program simulates what a human does when playing the game. Programs that simulate games or processes are common in computing.

In developing a simulation, the first step is to decide how to represent the physical items being simulated. In a card game, the basic item is, of course, a card. A deck of cards becomes a list of fifty-two cards in the program. Cards face up on the table and the discard pile must also be simulated in this program.

Putting a card face up on the table means that a card is being taken from the deck and put on the table where the player can see it. The cards on the table can be represented by another list. The rules that determine whether or not cards can be moved to the discard pile are applied to the top four cards in this list—that is, the last four cards put in the list.

The discard pile is also a list of cards. If no cards remain on the table (they are all on the discard pile) at the end of the game, then the player has won. If any cards remain on the table face up, the player has lost.

A linked list seems a logical choice for representing these three lists (the deck, the cards face up on the table, and the discard pile). The simulation requires a lot of deleting from one list and inserting into another list, and these operations are quite simple with a linked list. In fact, the procedures Insert_Top and Remove_Top that we coded in a previous section can be used.

Using dynamic variables to represent our lists instead of arrays saves memory space. If an array representation were used, three arrays of fifty-two components each would have to be used. In a linked representation, we use only fifty-two components in all, since a card can be in only one list at a time.

Now we are ready to complete the top-down design.

Figure 16-7
Solitaire Game

Initialize with the first 4 cards.

Remove the 2 inner cards.

Add 2 cards (need at least 4 cards to play).

Remove all 4 cards.

Add 4 more cards.

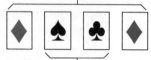

Remove the 2 inner cards.

Add 2 cards until another match.

Remove the 2 inner cards from group of last 4.

Remove the last 4 cards.

Add cards until another match.

Remove the 2 inner cards from group of last 4.

Add cards until another match.

Remove all 4 cards.

Data Structure: A linked list representing a deck of cards (Deck), a linked list representing the cards on the table (On_Table), and a linked list representing the discard pile (Discard_Pile).

Main Module   *Level 0*

```
Initialize
Create Deck of cards
WHILE more games to play
    Shuffle
    Play Game
    IF Won, increment won count
    Re-create Deck
Print number of games won
```

Initialize (Returns Number_Of_Games, Number_Of_Shuffles : Integer,
**   On_Table, Discard_Pile : Node_Pointer)**   *Level 1*

```
Prompt for number of games to be played
Read number of games
Prompt for number of shuffles
Read number of shuffles
Initialize On_Table to NIL
Initialize Discard_Pile to NIL
```

Create Deck

We can use procedure Create_Deck developed in the previous case study to create the deck. Although we don't use the rank field, we leave it there because we may want to print out the contents of the various lists during debugging. Some of the routines developed in this case study, such as the one to shuffle the cards, may be used elsewhere. They should be tested with a complete representation of a deck of cards.

Shuffle Deck

The shuffle module is a difficult one. Let's come back to it later.

Play Game (Receives/Returns Deck, On_Table, Discard_Pile : Node_Pointer)

> WHILE more cards in Deck
>   Turn up card
>   Try to Remove

Won (Receives On_Table : Node_Pointer)

> On_Table contains no cards at the end of game

Recreate Deck (Receives/Returns Deck, On_Table, Discard_Pile : Node_Pointer)

> WHILE more cards in On_Table
>   Remove card from On_Table (Remove_Top)
>   Insert into Deck (Insert_Top)
> WHILE more cards in Discard_Pile
>   Remove card from Discard_Pile (Remove_Top)
>   Insert into Deck (Insert_Top)

Turn up Card (Receives/Returns Deck, On_Table : Node_Pointer)   *Level 2*

> Remove card from Deck (Remove_Top)
> Insert into On_Table (Insert_Top)

Try Remove (Receives/Returns On_Table, Discard_Pile : Node_Pointer)

To play the game, we need to check the first card and the fourth card first. If these do not match, we can't move any cards. If they do match, we check to see how many can be moved. This process continues until there are fewer than four cards face up on the table, or until no move can be made.

```
Initialize flag Moved to True
WHILE Four on Table AND Moved
   IF First = Fourth
     THEN
        IF First, Second, and Third match
          THEN
             Move Four cards to Discard_Pile
          ELSE
             Move Two (Second and Third) to Discard_Pile
     ELSE
        Moved is set equal to False
```

Move Four (Receives/Returns On_Table, Discard_Pile : Node_Pointer)   *Level 3*

```
FOR Counter going from 1 to 4
   Remove top card from On_Table
   Insert into Discard_Pile
```

Move Two (Receives/Returns On_Table, Discard_Pile : Node_Pointer)

```
Save top card from On_Table
Move top card from On_Table to Discard_Pile
Move top card from On_Table to Discard_Pile
Replace original top card
```

Remove Card and Insert into Deck

We have already coded the procedures to remove the top element from a list (Procedure Remove_Top) and to insert an element as the first in a list (Procedure Insert_Top). We modify variable names to reflect the nature of this program. We also need to add a line of code to test whether or not there is an element to be moved.

Four on Table (Receives On_Table : Node_Pointer

Returns Four_On_Table : Boolean)

We need to know whether there are four cards on the table—that is, whether the list On_Table contains at least four cards. There are two ways to handle this problem: define a function that counts the number of cards in On_Table, or keep a record of each insertion and deletion applied to On_Table. If all of On_Table had to be counted each time, it would be better to keep track of how many insertions and deletions were made. However, the entire count is not needed. We need to know only if there are at least four cards (nodes) in the list.

Set Count to 0
Set Pointer to On_Table
WHILE Count <> 4 AND Pointer <> NIL
    Set Count to Count + 1
    Set Pointer to Link field of Pointer
Set Four_On_Table to Count = 4

In this discussion we have used First to stand for the suit of the first card on the table, Second to stand for the suit of the second card on the table, and so on. The values of these suits have to be determined. We define four one-line functions of type Suits to determine these variables, as shown below.

First (Receives On_Table : Node_Pointer

Returns First : Suits)

First is set equal to Suit field of On_Table^.Card

Second (Receives On_Table : Node_Pointer

Returns Second : Suits)

Second is set equal to Suit field of On_Table^.Link^.Card

Third (Receives On_Table : Node_Pointer
Returns Third : Suits)

Third is set equal to Suit field of On_Table^.Link^.Link^.Card

---

Fourth (Receives On_Table : Node_Pointer
Returns Fourth : Suits)

Fourth is set equal to Suit field of On_Table^.Link^.Link^.Link^.Card

---

Shuffle (Receives Number_Of_Shuffles : Integer,   *Level 1*
Receives/Returns Deck : Node_Pointer)

When a human shuffles a deck of cards, he or she divides the deck into two nearly equal parts and then merges the two parts back together. This process can be simulated directly (a simulation within a simulation). The list Deck can be divided into two lists, Half_A and Half_B. Then these two lists can be merged back into Deck. We use a random number generator to determine how many cards go into Half_A. The rest go into Half_B.

Turbo Pascal has a built-in random number generator. Function Random takes an integer parameter and returns a random integer ranging from 0 up to (but not including) the value specified in the parameter. Thus, to obtain a number in the range 1 through 52, we would use the expression:

Random(52) + 1

```
FOR counter going from 1 to Size_Of_Cut
   Remove_Top a card from Deck (Temp_Card)
   Insert_Top Temp_Card into Half_A
Set Half_B to Deck
Set Deck to NIL
IF Size_Of_Cut <= 26
   THEN
      Merge(Half_A, Half_B, Size_Of_Cut, Deck)
   ELSE
      Merge(Half_B, Half_A, 52 − Size_Of_Cut, Deck)
```

Merge (Receives Half_A, Half_B : Node_Pointer,   *Level 2*
Size_Of_Cut : Integer,
Receives/Returns Deck : Node_Pointer)

The merge algorithm is much simpler than the one developed in the last chapter because a component is taken alternately from each list without regard to the contents of the component. Also, we know the exact length of each list. We call the Merge procedure with four parameters: the shorter list, the longer list, the length of the shorter list, and the external pointer to the deck.

```
FOR counter going from 1 to Length
    Remove a card from Shorter_List (Temp_Card)
    Insert Temp_Card onto Deck
    Remove a card from Longer_List (Temp_Card)
    Insert Temp_Card onto Deck
FOR counter going from 1 to (52 − Length * 2)
    Remove a card from Longer_List (Temp_Card)
    Insert Temp_Card onto Deck
```

Because Initialize and Won are such short modules, they are written directly in the main program.

Module Structure Chart:

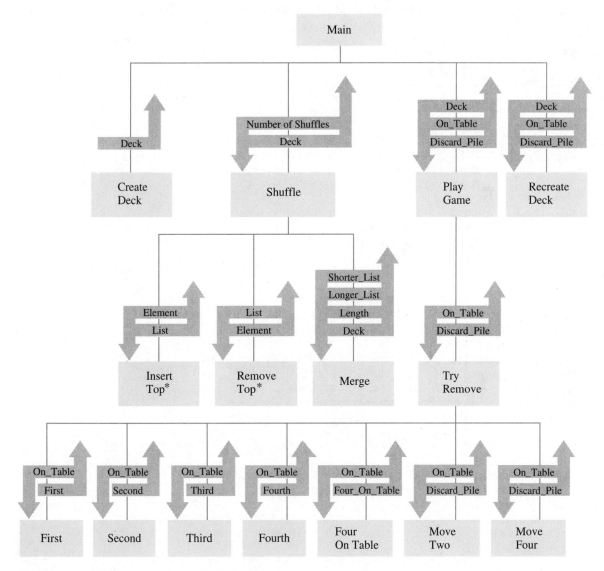

*Remove_Top and Insert_Top are also used by Recreate_Deck and Merge.

```
PROGRAM Solitaire (Input, Output);

(* This program is a simulation of a card game. *)
(* See text for rules of the game              *)

CONST
  Deck_Size = 52;
  Half_Deck = 26;

TYPE
  Node_Pointer = ^Node_Type;
  Suits = (Club, Diamond, Heart, Spade);
  Card_Type = RECORD
                Suit : Suits;
                Rank : 1..13            (* 1 is ace; 13 is king *)
              END; (* Record *)
  Node_Type = RECORD
                Card : Card_Type;
                Link : Node_Pointer
              END; (* Record *)

VAR
  Deck,                  (* External pointer to deck of cards  *)
  On_Table,              (* Node_Types face up on the table    *)
  Discard_Pile:          (* Node_Types on discard pile         *)
    Node_Pointer;
  Number_Of_Shuffles,    (* Number of shuffles per game        *)
  Number_Of_Games,       (* Number of games to play            *)
  Games_Played,          (* Number of games played             *)
  Games_Won:             (* Number of games won                *)
    Integer;


(*********************************************************************)

PROCEDURE Create_Deck (VAR Deck:        (* Pointer to list of cards *)
                            Node_Pointer);

(* Creates a list of Deck_Size nodes.  Each node represents a     *)
(* playing card.  Deck is the external pointer to the list.  The  *)
(* cards are in order by suit and by rank *)

VAR
  New_Node,            (* Pointer to newest card   *)
  Current:             (* Pointer to previous card *)
    Node_Pointer;
  Count:               (* Loop control variable    *)
    Integer;
```

```
BEGIN (* Create_Deck *)
  New(Deck);
  Deck^.Card.Suit := Club;
  Deck^.Card.Rank := 1;
  Current := Deck;
  (* Loop to create balance of deck *)
  FOR Count := 2 to Deck_Size DO
    BEGIN
      New(New_Node);
      (* Test for change of suit *)
      IF Current^.Card.Rank = 13
        THEN
          (* Change suit *)
          BEGIN
            New_Node^.Card.Suit := Succ(Current^.Card.Suit);
            New_Node^.Card.Rank := 1
          END
        ELSE
          (* Increment rank *)
          BEGIN
            New_Node^.Card.Suit := Current^.Card.Suit;
            New_Node^.Card.Rank := Current^.Card.Rank + 1
          END;
      Current^.Link := New_Node;
      Current := New_Node
    END;
  (* Set end-of-list marker *)
  Current^.Link := NIL
END;  (* Create_Deck *)

(*********************************************************************)

PROCEDURE Remove_Top (VAR List:           (* Pointer to list of cards *)
                          Node_Pointer;
                      VAR Element:         (* Top card returned        *)
                          Card_Type);

(* The first card (node) is removed from List. The entire node is *)
(* returned in Element *)

VAR
  Pointer:             (* Temporary pointer *)
    Node_Pointer;
```

```
BEGIN (* Remove_Top *)
  IF List <> NIL
    THEN
      BEGIN
        Pointer := List;
        Element := List^.Card;
        List := List^.Link;
        Dispose(Pointer)
      END
END;  (* Remove_Top *)

(* ********************************************************************* *)

PROCEDURE Insert_Top (VAR List:          (* Pointer to list of cards *)
                          Node_Pointer;
                          Element:        (* Type of card to insert   *)
                          Card_Type);

(* Element is inserted as the first card (node) in List. *)
(* Assumption:  List has been initialized to NIL         *)

VAR
  Pointer:          (* Temporary pointer *)
    Node_Pointer;

BEGIN (* Insert_Top *)
  New(Pointer);
  Pointer^.Card := Element;
  Pointer^.Link := List;
  List := Pointer
END;  (* Insert_Top *)

(* ********************************************************************* *)

PROCEDURE Shuffle (VAR Deck:             (* Pointer to list of cards  *)
                       Node_Pointer;
                       Number_Of_Shuffles: (* Times to perform shuffle *)
                       Integer);
```

```
(* Shuffle takes an input list of Deck_Size nodes and returns the *)
(* list with the nodes in a different order.  The input list is   *)
(* divided into two parts, which are then merged. The process is  *)
(* repeated Number_Of_Shuffles times *)

VAR
  Half_A,                (* Half of the list       *)
  Half_B:                (* Half of the list       *)
    Node_Pointer;
  Temp_Card:             (* Temporary card         *)
    Card_Type;
  Count1,                (* Loop control variable *)
  Count2:                (* Loop control variable *)
    Integer;
  Size_Of_Cut:           (* Size of Half_A         *)
    0..Deck_Size;

(***********************************************************************)

PROCEDURE Merge (      Shorter_List,     (* Pointer to list of cards *)
                       Longer_List:      (* Pointer to list of cards *)
                         Node_Pointer;
                       Length:           (* Length of shorter list   *)
                         Integer;
                   VAR Deck:             (* Resulting list of cards  *)
                         Node_Pointer);

(* Shorter_List and Longer_List are merged into Deck.  Length is *)
(* number of nodes in Shorter_List *)

VAR
  Count:                 (* Loop control variable *)
    Integer;
  Temp_Card:             (* Temporary card         *)
    Card_Type;
```

```
  BEGIN (* Merge *)
    (* Merge two halves back into Deck *)
    FOR Count := 1 TO Length DO
      BEGIN
        Remove_Top(Shorter_List, Temp_Card);
        Insert_Top(Deck, Temp_Card);
        Remove_Top(Longer_List, Temp_Card);
        Insert_Top(Deck, Temp_Card)
      END;
    FOR Count := 1 TO (Deck_Size - 2 * Length) DO
      BEGIN
        Remove_Top(Longer_List, Temp_Card);
        Insert_Top(Deck, Temp_Card)
      END
  END;  (* Merge *)


(***************************************************************)


BEGIN (* Shuffle *)
  FOR Count1 := 1 TO Number_Of_Shuffles DO
    BEGIN
      Size_Of_Cut := Random(52)
      Half_A := NIL;
      Half_B := NIL;
      (* Divide Deck into two parts *)
      FOR Count2 := 1 TO Size_Of_Cut DO
        BEGIN
          Remove_Top(Deck, Temp_Card);
          Insert_Top(Half_A, Temp_Card)
        END;
      FOR Count2 := Size_Of_Cut + 1 TO Deck_Size DO
        BEGIN
          Remove_Top(Deck, Temp_Card);
          Insert_Top(Half_B, Temp_Card)
        END;
      IF Size_Of_Cut <= Half_Deck
        THEN
          Merge(Half_A, Half_B, Size_Of_Cut, Deck)
        ELSE
          Merge(Half_B, Half_A, Deck_Size - Size_Of_Cut, Deck)
    END
END;  (* Shuffle *)
```

PROBLEM-SOLVING CASE STUDY *cont'd.*

```
(********************************************************************)

FUNCTION First (On_Table:                  (* Pointer to list of cards *)
                     Node_Pointer):
                        Suits;

(* First returns the suit of the first card (node) in On_Table *)

BEGIN (* First *)
  First := On_Table^.Card.Suit
END;  (* First *)

(********************************************************************)

FUNCTION Second (On_Table:                  (* Pointer to list of cards *)
                     Node_Pointer):
                        Suits;

(* Second returns the suit of the second card in On_Table *)

BEGIN (* Second *)
  Second := On_Table^.Link^.Card.Suit
END;  (* Second *)

(********************************************************************)

FUNCTION Third (On_Table:                  (* Pointer to list of cards *)
                     Node_Pointer):
                        Suits;

(* Third returns the suit of the third card in On_Table *)

BEGIN (* Third *)
  Third := On_Table^.Link^.Link^.Card.Suit
END;  (* Third *)

(********************************************************************)

FUNCTION Fourth (On_Table:                  (* Pointer to list of cards *)
                     Node_Pointer):
                        Suits;

(* Fourth returns the suit of the fourth card in On_Table *)

BEGIN (* Fourth *)
  Fourth := On_Table^.Link^.Link^.Link^.Card.Suit
END;  (* Fourth *)

(********************************************************************)
```

PROBLEM-SOLVING CASE STUDY cont'd.

```
PROCEDURE Move_Four (VAR On_Table,       (* Pointer to list of cards *)
                         Discard_Pile:    (* Pointer to list of cards *)
                           Node_Pointer);

(* The first four cards are moved from On_Table to Discard_Pile *)

VAR
  Temp_Card:        (* Temporary card       *)
    Card_Type;
  Count:            (* Loop control variable *)
    Integer;

BEGIN (* Move_Four *)
  FOR Count := 1 TO 4 DO
    BEGIN
      Remove_Top(On_Table, Temp_Card);
      Insert_Top(Discard_Pile, Temp_Card)
    END
END; (* Move_Four *)

(******************************************************************)

PROCEDURE Move_Two (VAR On_Table,        (* Pointer to list of cards *)
                        Discard_Pile:     (* Pointer to list of cards *)
                          Node_Pointer);

(* The second and third cards are moved from On_Table to Discard_Pile *)

VAR
  Temp_Card,        (* Temporary card *)
  First:            (* Temporary card *)
    Card_Type;

BEGIN (* Move_Two *)
  Remove_Top(On_Table, First);
  (* Remove second card *)
  Remove_Top(On_Table, Temp_Card);
  Insert_Top(Discard_Pile, Temp_Card);
  (* Remove third card *)
  Remove_Top(On_Table, Temp_Card);
  Insert_Top(Discard_Pile, Temp_Card);
  (* Replace first card *)
  Insert_Top(On_Table, First)
END; (* Move_Two *)
```

```
(********************************************************************)

FUNCTION Four_On_Table (On_Table:         (* Pointer to list of cards *)
                            Node_Pointer):
                               Boolean;

(* Four_On_Table is True if On_Table contains at least four cards *)

VAR
  Count:            (* Loop control variable *)
    Integer;

BEGIN (* Four_On_Table *)
  Count := 0;
  WHILE (Count <> 4) AND (On_Table <> NIL) DO
    BEGIN
      Count := Count + 1;
      On_Table := On_Table^.Link
    END;
  Four_On_Table := (Count = 4)
END;  (* Four_On_Table *)


(********************************************************************)

PROCEDURE Try_Remove (VAR On_Table,       (* Pointer to list of cards *)
                          Discard_Pile:   (* Pointer to list of cards *)
                             Node_Pointer);

(* If first (top) four cards are the same suit, they are moved from   *)
(* On_Table to Discard_Pile.  If the first card and the fourth card   *)
(* are the same suit, the second and third card are moved from        *)
(* On_Table to Discard_Pile.  Process continues until no further move *)
(* can be made *)

VAR
  Moved:            (* Flag to record whether a move has been made *)
    Boolean;
```

```
BEGIN (* Try_Remove *)
  Moved := True;
  WHILE Four_On_Table(On_Table) AND Moved DO
    IF First(On_Table) = Fourth(On_Table)
      THEN                                      (* A move will be made *)
        BEGIN
          IF (First(On_Table) = Second(On_Table)) AND
             (First(On_Table) = Third(On_Table))
            THEN
              (* Four alike *)
              Move_Four(On_Table, Discard_Pile)
            ELSE
              (* First and fourth alike *)
              Move_Two(On_Table, Discard_Pile)
        END
      ELSE
        Moved := False
END;  (* Try_Remove *)

(*****************************************************************************)


PROCEDURE Play_Game (VAR Deck,               (* Deck of playing cards  *)
                         On_Table,           (* Cards face up on table *)
                         Discard_Pile:       (* Cards on discard pile   *)
                           Node_Pointer);

(* Places the next card in the deck face up on the table *)
(* and calls Try_Remove to apply rules for moving           *)

VAR
  Count:                         (* Loop control variable *)
    Integer;
  Temp_Card:                     (* Temporary card         *)
    Card_Type;
```

```
BEGIN (* Play_Game *)
  FOR Count := l to Deck_Size DO
    BEGIN
      (* Turn up card *)
      Remove_Top(Deck, Temp_Card);
      Insert_Top(On_Table, Temp_Card);
      Try_Remove(On_Table, Discard_Pile)
    END
END;  (* Play_Game *)


(******************************************************************)


PROCEDURE Recreate (VAR Deck,          (* Deck of playing cards  *)
                        On_Table,       (* Cards face up on table *)
                        Discard_Pile:   (* Cards on discard pile  *)
                         Node_Pointer);

(* Gathers cards and puts them back into Deck *)

VAR
  Temp_Card:          (* Temporary card *)
    Card_Type;

BEGIN (* Recreate *)
  (* Move cards from On_Table to Deck *)
  WHILE On_Table <> NIL DO
    BEGIN
      Remove_Top(On_Table, Temp_Card);
      Insert_Top(Deck, Temp_Card)
    END;
  (* Move cards from Discard_Pile to Deck *)
  WHILE Discard_Pile <> NIL DO
    BEGIN
      Remove_Top(Discard_Pile, Temp_Card);
      Insert_Top(Deck, Temp_Card)
    END
END;  (* Recreate *)


(******************************************************************)
```

```
BEGIN (* Solitaire *)
  (* Initialize *)
  Games_Won := 0;
  On_Table := NIL;
  Discard_Pile := NIL;
  Writeln('Enter number of games to play.');
  Readln(Number_Of_Games);
  Writeln('Enter number of shuffles per game.');
  Readln(Number_Of_Shuffles);
  Create_Deck(Deck);
  Writeln('Returned from Create_Deck');
  FOR Games_Played := 1 TO Number_Of_Games DO
    BEGIN
      Shuffle(Deck, Number_Of_Shuffles);
      Play_Game(Deck, On_Table, Discard_Pile);
      (* Determine if game was won *)
      IF On_Table = NIL
        THEN
          (* Game won *)
          Games_Won := Games_Won + 1;
      Recreate(Deck, On_Table, Discard_Pile)
    END;
  Writeln('Number of games played: ', Number_Of_Games);
  Writeln('Number of games won:    ', Games_Won)
END.  (* Solitaire *)
```

Testing: To exhaustively test the portion of the program that plays the solitaire game, all possible configurations of a deck of fifty-two cards have to be generated. Although this is theoretically possible, it is impractical. There are 52! (52 factorial) possible arrangements of a deck of cards. 52! equals

$$52 * 51 * 50 * \ldots 2 * 1$$

This is a large number. Try multiplying it out.

Therefore, another method of testing is required. At a minimum, the questions to be examined are:

1. Does the program recognize a winning hand?
2. Does the program recognize a losing hand?

To answer these questions, we must examine at least one hand declared to be a winner and several hands declared to be losers. Rather than input specific hands, we let the program run on 100 cases to see if there were any winning hands in that number of cases. There were none.

From past experience we know this solitaire game is difficult. We let the simulation run 500 times and there is one winning hand. Intermediate prints are put in to examine the winning hand. It is correct. Several losing hands are also printed; they are indeed losing hands. Satisfied that the program is working correctly, we set up runs that varied in length, number of shuffles, and seed for the random number generator. The results are listed below. There is no strategy behind the particular choices of parameters; they are random.

Number of Games	Number of Shuffles	Games Won	Seed
100	1	0	3.00
100	2	0	4.00
500	3	1	4.00
1,000	6	4	3.00
1,000	1	6	4.00
10,000	4	41	4.00
10,000	4	48	3.00
10,000	4	44	1.37

PROBLEM-SOLVING CASE STUDY

SAT Scores

Problem: The admissions department has created a file containing the SAT scores of all the entering freshmen. They have asked you to print these scores in ascending numeric order, along with a frequency count of the number of students making each score.

Input: An unknown number of (unordered) SAT scores on file Freshmen (Freshmen is a file of integers).

Output: A numeric listing of all the SAT scores with associated frequencies.

Discussion: In Chapter 12 we described a sorting algorithm based on inserting an element into an already sorted list (procedure Insert). We can use the same principle here. We can initialize a binary search tree with the first SAT score, and then insert each new score into this binary search tree using the procedure we wrote in the last section. The only problem is how to print the values in the search tree in ascending order. We can look at the following binary search tree and read off the values in order: 2, 3, 4, 5, 7, 10, 13, 15, and 17. The question is, How did we do it?

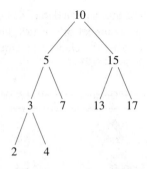

Let's make some observations about the values in this tree and see if we can generalize them into an algorithm. The smallest value is in the left-most node in the tree. The next smallest value is in the parent node of the smallest value. The third smallest value is the sibling of the node containing the smallest value. These three nodes constitute the left subtree of the node containing 5, and 5 is the next node in order.

The algorithm so far is to print the values in the left subtree of the node that contains 5 and then print the 5. What comes next? It's 7, the value in the right child of 5. (If the value 6 were in the tree, it would be the left child of 7 and would have to be printed first.) After 7 is printed, the next value is 10, the parent of 5, whose right child was just printed.

The process is to print the left subtree of a node, print the node, print the right subtree of a node, and then move back up to print the parent of the node. This process requires that we move back up the tree. Thus, the nodes passed on the way down must be saved. When the values in a subtree have been printed, we back up and print the value in the parent node. This implies that the nodes must be retrieved in the reverse order from that in which they were saved. The stack data structure does exactly this.

The top-down design for this problem can now be completed.

Data Structure: A binary search tree where each node contains an SAT score and its associated frequency of occurrence.

Main Module   *Level 0*

> Read first score
> Initialize Tree
> WHILE more scores
>   Read a score
>   Process a score
> Print scores and frequencies

"More scores" is an end-of-file loop.

Initialize Tree (Receives SAT : Value_Type,   *Level 1*
　　　　Receives/Returns New_Node : Tree_Pointer)

We can use procedure Initialize developed for procedure Search_And_Count.

Process Score (Receives Item : Value_Type,
　　　　Receives/Returns Tree: Tree_Pointer)

To process the score, we can use the procedure Search_And_Count that was developed previously.

Print (Receives Tree: Tree_Pointer)

Also, we have already developed the broad outline for the print operation. We move down the tree as far to the left as possible, remembering the nodes we pass on the way by pushing them on a stack. We recognize that we have gone as far left as possible when the pointer we are advancing is NIL. We then back up and process the previous node. We back up by popping the stack on which we have been putting the nodes as we passed them. We have printed the last value when we have printed the right subchild of a node and can't back up anymore—that is, when the stack is empty. We use a function similar to Empty_Q to check whether the stack is empty.

```
Current is set equal to Tree
REPEAT
  (* Move as far left as possible *)
  WHILE Current <> NIL
    Push Current <> NIL
    Set Current to Left child of Current
  (* Move back up the tree one node *)
  IF NOT Empty(Stack)
    Pop Current off stack
    Print SAT and Count fields of Component field of Current
    (* Move to right subtree *)
    Set Current to Right child of Current
UNTIL Current = NIL AND stack is empty
```

Because this is a complicated algorithm, an algorithm walk-through is in order. We use a portion of the tree we used before, and we refer to a node by its contents.

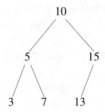

Current is set equal to Tree	Current now points to node containing 10.
WHILE Current <> NIL	Current is not NIL. Loop is executed.
Push Current on a stack	Stack now contains 10.
Current is set equal to left child of Current	Current now points to node containing 5.
WHILE Current <> NIL	Current is not NIL. Loop is executed.
Push Current on a stack	Stack now contains 5 and 10.
Current is set equal to Left child of Current	Current now points to node containing 3.
WHILE Current <> NIL	Current is not NIL. Loop is executed.
Push Current on a stack	Stack now contains 3, 5, and 10.
Current is set equal to Left child of Current	Current now contains NIL.

The situation at this point is pictured below.

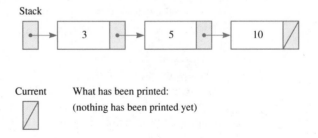

WHILE Current <> NIL	Current is NIL. Loop is skipped.
IF NOT Empty(Stack)	Stack is not empty.
Pop Current off stack	Current now contains pointer to 3.
Print..	The number 3 is printed.
Current is set equal to Right child of Current	Current is NIL.
UNTIL Current is NIL AND stack is empty	Current is NIL but stack is not empty.
WHILE Current <> NIL	Current is NIL. Loop is skipped.
IF NOT Empty(Stack)	Stack is not empty.

Pop Current off stack	Current now contains pointer to 5.
Print..	The number 5 is printed.
Current is set equal to Right child of Current	Current is pointing to node containing 7.
UNTIL Current is NIL AND stack is empty	Current is not NIL and stack is not empty.

The situation at this point is pictured below.

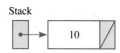

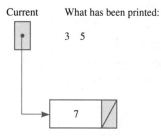

WHILE Current <> NIL	Current is not NIL. Loop is executed.
Push Current on a stack	Stack now contains 7 and 10.
Current is set equal to Left child of Current	Current is NIL.
WHILE Current <> NIL	Current is NIL. Loop is skipped.
IF NOT Empty(Stack)	Stack is not empty.
Pop Current off stack	Current points to node containing 7.
Print..	The number 7 is printed.
Current is set equal to Right child of Current	Current is NIL.
UNTIL Current is NIL AND stack is empty	Current is NIL but stack is not empty.
WHILE Current <> NIL	Current is NIL. Loop is skipped.
IF NOT Empty(Stack)	Stack is not empty.
Pop Current off stack	Current points to node containing 10.
Print..	The number 10 is printed.
Current is set equal to Right child of Current	Current now points to node containing 15.
UNTIL Current is NIL AND stack is empty	Current is not NIL but stack is empty.

The situation at this point is pictured below.

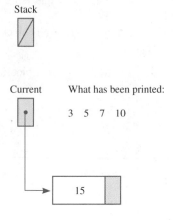

Stack

Current   What has been printed:

3   5   7   10

15

WHILE Current <> NIL	Current is not NIL. Loop is executed.
Push Current on a stack	Stack contains 15.
Current is set equal to Left child of Current	Current points to node containing 13.
WHILE Current <> NIL	Current is not NIL. Loop is executed.
Push Current on a stack	Stack now contains 13 and 15.
Current is set equal to Left child of Current	Current is NIL.
WHILE Current <> NIL	Current is NIL. Loop is skipped.
IF NOT Empty(Stack)	Stack is not empty.
Pop Current off stack	Current points to node containing 13.
Print..	The number 13 is printed.
Current is set equal to Right child of Current	Current is NIL.
UNTIL Current is NIL AND stack is empty	Current is NIL but stack is not empty.
WHILE Current <> NIL	Current is NIL. Loop is skipped.
IF NOT Empty(Stack)	Stack is not empty.
Pop Current off stack	Current points to node containing 15.
Print..	The number 15 is printed.
Current is set equal to Right child of Current	Current is NIL.
UNTIL Current is NIL AND stack is empty	Current is NIL and stack is empty. Loop exits.

The situation at the end of the print module is shown below.

PROBLEM-SOLVING CASE STUDY *cont'd.*

Stack

Current   What has been printed:

3   5   7   10   13   15

Module Structure Chart:

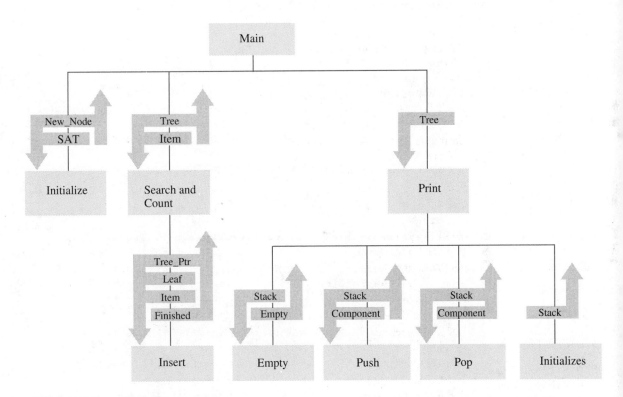

Initialized is also used by Insert.

```
PROGRAM Sort_SAT_Scores (Freshmen, Output);

(* SAT scores are read from file Freshmen and sorted using a binary *)
(* search tree.  Frequencies of each value are kept, and the sorted *)
(* SAT scores with frequencies are printed *)
```

PROBLEM-SOLVING CASE STUDY cont'd.

```
TYPE
  Tree_Pointer = ^Tree_Node;
  Value_Type = 0..1600;
  Component_Type = RECORD
                      Value : Value_Type;
                      Count : Integer
                    END; (* Record *)
  Tree_Node = RECORD
                Component : Component_Type;
                Left,
                Right : Tree_Pointer
              END; (* Record *)
  Stack_Pointer = ^Stack_Element;
  Stack_Element = RECORD
                    Element : Tree_Pointer;
                    Link : Stack_Pointer
                  END; (* Record *)
  Data_File = FILE OF Value_Type;

VAR
  Tree:                        (* Pointer to tree of SAT scores *)
    Tree_Pointer;
  SAT:                         (* Temporary input SAT scores    *)
    Value_Type;
  Freshmen:                    (* Input file of SAT scores      *)
    Data_File;

(*******************************************************************)

PROCEDURE Initialize (VAR New_Node:      (* Node being initialized *)
                          Tree_Pointer;
                          SAT:            (* Score for new node     *)
                          Value_Type);

(* Tree node is initialized to first SAT score *)

BEGIN (* Initialize *)
  New(New_Node);
  New_Node^.Component.Value := SAT;
  New_Node^.Component.Count := 1;
  New_Node^.Right := NIL;
  New_Node^.Left := NIL
END;  (* Initialize *)

(*******************************************************************)
```

```
PROCEDURE Search_And_Count (VAR Tree:              (* Tree of scores      *)
                                Tree_Pointer;
                            Item:              (* Input search value *)
                                Value_Type);

(* Search_And_Count searches the binary search tree pointed to by *)
(* Tree looking for the component Item.  IF Item is equal to a     *)
(* Component.Value in the tree, Component.Count is incremented.     *)
(* ELSE Item is inserted into the tree with a Count field of 1.     *)
(* Assumption:  Tree contains at least one component              *)

TYPE
  Leaf_Type = (Right_Leaf, Left_Leaf);

VAR
  Tree_Ptr:              (* Advancing pointer variable *)
    Tree_Pointer;
  Finished:              (* Loop control flag            *)
    Boolean;

(*********************************************************************)

  PROCEDURE Insert (VAR Tree_Ptr:   (* Node new item is attached to *)
                        Tree_Pointer;
                    Leaf:         (* Which pointer to attach to   *)
                        Leaf_Type;
                    Item:         (* Value to put into new node   *)
                        Value_Type;
                    VAR Finished:   (* Flag to stop insertion task  *)
                        Boolean);

  (* Item is inserted into Tree_Ptr as the Leaf child *)

  VAR
    New_Node:   (* Pointer to node being linked to Tree_Ptr's node *)
      Tree_Pointer;

  BEGIN (* Insert *)
    (* Initialize node *)
    Initialize(New_Node, Item);
    (* Insert node *)
    CASE Leaf OF
      Left_Leaf  : Tree_Ptr^.Left := New_Node;
      Right_Leaf : Tree_Ptr^.Right := New_Node
    END; (* Case *)
    Finished := True
  END;  (* Insert *)
```

```
(******************************************************************)

BEGIN (* Search_And_Count *)
  (* Initialize looping variables *)
  Tree_Ptr := Tree;
  Finished := False;
  (* Search for Item in Tree *)
  REPEAT
    WITH Tree_Ptr^ DO
      BEGIN
        IF Component.Value = Item
          THEN
            BEGIN                              (* Match found *)
              Component.Count := Component.Count + 1;
              Finished := True
            END
          ELSE
            IF Component.Value > Item
              THEN                      (* Search left subtree   *)
                IF Left = NIL
                  THEN                  (* Insertion place found *)
                    Insert(Tree_Ptr, Left_Leaf, Item, Finished)
                  ELSE
                    Tree_Ptr := Left
              ELSE                      (* Search right subtree  *)
                IF Right = NIL
                  THEN                  (* Insertion place found *)
                    Insert(Tree_Ptr, Right_Leaf, Item, Finished)
                  ELSE
                    Tree_Ptr := Right
      END;
  UNTIL Finished
END;  (* Search_And_Count *)


(******************************************************************)

FUNCTION Empty (Stack:                  (* Pointer to top of stack *)
                  Stack_Pointer):
                  Boolean;

(* Empty is True if there are no nodes on the stack *)

BEGIN (* Empty *)
  Empty := (Stack = NIL)
END;  (* Empty *)


(******************************************************************)
```

PROBLEM-SOLVING CASE STUDY cont'd.

```
PROCEDURE Push (VAR Stack:          (* Pointer to top of stack      *)
                      Stack_Pointer;
                Component:    (* Tree node pointer being pushed *)
                      Tree_Pointer);

(* Node containing Component is put on stack *)

VAR
  New_Node:          (* New node to put on top of stack *)
    Stack_Pointer;

BEGIN (* Push *)
  New(New_Node);
  New_Node^.Element := Component;
  New_Node^.Link := Stack;
  Stack := New_Node
END;  (* Push *)

(*******************************************************************)

PROCEDURE Pop (VAR Stack:          (* Pointer to top of stack      *)
                    Stack_Pointer;
              VAR Component:    (* Tree node pointer being popped *)
                    Tree_Pointer);

(* First node is removed from stack *)

VAR
  Temp_Pointer:          (* Pointer to node being removed from stack *)
    Stack_Pointer;

BEGIN (* Pop *)
  Temp_Pointer := Stack;
  Component := Stack^.Element;
  Stack := Stack^.Link;
  Dispose(Temp_Pointer)
END;  (* Pop *)

(*******************************************************************)

PROCEDURE Initialize_S (VAR Stack:        (* Stack being initialized *)
                              Stack_Pointer);
BEGIN (* Initialize_S *)
  Stack := NIL
END;  (* Initialize_S *)

(*******************************************************************)
```

```
PROCEDURE Print (Tree:                (* Pointer to tree of SAT scores *)
                    Tree_Pointer);

(* SAT and frequency fields of nodes in Tree *)
(* are printed in numeric order by SAT field *)

VAR
  Stack:              (* Pointer to stack being built from the tree *)
    Stack_Pointer;
  Current:            (* Temporary pointer for traversing the tree  *)
    Tree_Pointer;

BEGIN (* Print *)
  (* Initialize Stack *)
  Initialize_S(Stack);
  (* Initialize moving pointer *)
  Current := Tree;
  Writeln(' SAT ', '  Frequency');
  REPEAT
    (* Move as far left as possible *)
    WHILE Current <> NIL DO
      BEGIN
        Push(Stack, Current);
        Current := Current^.Left
      END;
    (* If there are any more nodes on the stack, pop the stack,  *)
    (* print the contents of the node, and move to right subtree *)
    IF NOT Empty(Stack)
      THEN
        BEGIN
          Pop(Stack, Current);
          Writeln(Current^.Component.Value:5,
                  Current^.Component.Count:7);
          Current := Current^.Right
        END
  UNTIL (Current = NIL) AND (Empty(Stack))
END;  (* Print *)


(*********************************************************************)
```

```
BEGIN (* Sort_SAT_Scores *)
  Assign(Freshmen, 'FRESHMEN.DAT');
  Reset(Freshmen);
  Read(Freshmen, SAT);
  Initialize(Tree, SAT);
  (* Create binary search tree *)
  WHILE NOT EOF(Freshmen) DO
    BEGIN
      Read(Freshmen, SAT);
      Search_And_Count(Tree, SAT)
    END;
  (* Print the SAT scores and frequencies *)
  Print(Tree);
  Close(Freshmen)
END.  (* Sort_SAT_Scores *)
```

Testing: A test data file for this program must include some values once, and some other values more than once. A rigorous testing requires multiple files, one to satisfy each of the following conditions:

1. The smallest SAT score is first (single value).
2. The smallest SAT score is first, with copies in other positions, including last.
3. The largest SAT score is first (single value).
4. The largest SAT score is first, with copies in other positions, including last.
5. The smallest SAT score is last (single value).
6. The largest SAT score is last (single value).

Sample input data, including single values and multiple values, are shown below. The output from Program Sort_SAT_Scores follows the sample data.

Sample Input	Sample Output	
1200	SAT	Frequency
1300	300	1
600	400	1
400	600	3
1300	900	1
600	1200	2
600	1201	1
1200	1202	1
300	1300	2
900	1304	1
1201		
1202		
1304		

*T*heoretical Foundations

Comparison of Sorting Algorithms

The sorting algorithm used in Program Sort_SAT_Scores is a binary tree sort. Items are stored in a binary search tree and then written out in order. This algorithm is certainly more complex than both the exchange sort and the insertion sort, which were discussed in Chapter 12. Is it a better sorting algorithm? This question can't be answered without first defining what is meant by "better."

If we define "better" to mean "takes less time to program," the answer is certainly no. Program Sort_SAT_Scores is considerably longer than the others and has a much more complex data structure that is more difficult to debug. If we define "better" to mean "takes less time to run," the answer would depend on how many SAT scores there were to sort. If the number of SAT scores is quite small, a simple sort like those in Chapter 12 is better. As the number of items to sort gets larger, however, the binary tree sort gets relatively more and more efficient. Although the insertion sort is somewhat faster than the exchange sort, they are both classified as $O(N^2)$ sorts.

The sort that uses a binary search tree is classified as an $O(N \log_2 N)$ sort. The number of comparisons between two values in the center of the algorithm is approximately $N * \log_2 N$. The following table compares N^2 and $N * \log_2 N$ for increasing values of N. The values in the table are the number of comparisons required to sort N values for various sizes of N.

N	N^2	$N \log_2 N$
4	16	8
8	64	24
32	1024	160
64	4096	384
128	16384	896
256	65536	2048
512	262144	4608

This table seems to indicate that an $O(N \log_2 N)$ sort should be used for any value of N. This is not true, however, because $O(N \log_2 N)$ sorts are more complex; the parts of the algorithm that surround the comparison take longer to execute. A good rule of thumb is to use a simple $O(N^2)$ sort for sorting less than forty components and an $O(N \log_2 N)$ sort for sorting more than forty components.

Space also may be a consideration in determining what sort to use. The binary tree sort uses more memory because there are two pointer variables in each node. If you are sorting a large file on a machine with a small memory, you may have to use a slower sort that takes less space.

Testing and Debugging

All the procedures that inserted a value into a linked list assumed that the list had been initialized. There is no practical way to check that the list has been initialized from within a procedure; there is no test to see if a pointer is undefined. It is therefore reasonable for the procedure to make this assumption.

All the procedures that deleted a value from a linked list assumed that an item was there to be deleted (Remove_Top, Pop, and Dequeue), or that the specific item to be deleted was in the list (Delete). The calling routines were responsible for guaranteeing this precondition.

When deleting from a linked list, the procedure or function can detect easily that the component is not there or that there is no component to remove. Should these procedures have been written to guard against trying to delete a component that is not there? It depends on the interface between the calling routine and the procedure. Either the calling routine takes responsibility for ensuring that the value is there to be deleted (guarantees the precondition), or the procedure should test for the case in which there is no value to delete or the specific value is not there. If the procedure does the testing, a flag should be returned to the calling routine showing whether or not the value was deleted.

It does not matter at which level the checking is done for this error condition, but the higher-level module should determine which way the situation is handled. Thus, when writing a top-down design, either don't call the delete module if the list is empty, or have the delete module check for the error condition and return a flag indicating whether or not the delete was executed properly.

Following is a version of the Pop procedure in which error checking is included within the procedure itself. Notice that there is an additional parameter, Underflow.

```
PROCEDURE Pop (VAR Stack:            (* Pointer to top of stack    *)
                   Stack_Pointer;
               VAR Component:         (* Object removed from stack *)
                   Component_Type;
               VAR Underflow:         (* Error flag *)
                   Boolean);

(* If the stack is empty, Underflow will be True and Item will be *)
(* undefined.  Otherwise, Underflow will be False, the first node *)
(* will be deleted, and Item will contain the component field of  *)
(* the deleted first node.  Deleted node is disposed              *)

VAR
  Temp_Pointer:        (* Temporary pointer *)
    Stack_Pointer;
```

```
BEGIN (* Pop *)
  IF Empty(Stack)
    THEN
      Underflow := True
    ELSE
      BEGIN
        Temp_Pointer := Stack;
        Item := Stack^.Component;
        Stack := Stack^.Link;
        Dispose(Temp_Pointer);
        Underflow := False
      END
END;  (* Pop *)
```

Whenever it is possible for an error condition to occur in a procedure, you must decide where to check for the condition. If your calling module is responsible for seeing that the situation does not occur, the assumption that the condition will not occur must be stated in the documentation of the procedure. If the procedure is to check for the error condition, your documentation of the procedure must state how the error will be handled if it occurs. Many times the procedure tests for the error condition and simply sets a flag to return if the error occurs, leaving the determination of what to do about the error to the upper-level routine. The key point about error detection is that the interface between a calling routine and a procedure must make it absolutely clear which level is responsible for the error checking.

Testing and Debugging Hints

1. Be sure that the pointer field in the last node in a linked list has been set to NIL.
2. When visiting the components in a linked list, be sure that you test for the end of the list in such a way that you don't try to access the component of a NIL pointer. Trying to access the referenced variable when the pointer is NIL will have unpredictable results in Turbo Pascal.
3. Be sure to initialize the external pointer to each dynamic data structure.
4. Dispose(Pointer) leaves Pointer undefined; trying to access Pointer^ will have unpredictable results in Turbo Pascal.
5. Dispose of all dynamic variables when they are no longer needed. If you don't do so in a large program, you may run out of memory space.
6. Pass the pointer, not the object being pointed to, as a parameter.
7. Keep close track of pointers. Changing pointer values prematurely may cause problems when you try to get back to the referenced variable.
8. Be sure to test for possible error conditions when working with linked lists. There are two ways to handle error checking. The calling routine can check for the error condition and not call the procedure if the error occurs, or the procedure can test for the error condition. The documentation of both the calling routine and the procedure should state clearly how error checking is done.

Summary

Dynamic data structures grow and contract during run time. They are made up of nodes that contain two kinds of fields: the component, and one or more pointers to records of the same type. The pointer to the first record is saved in a named variable called the external pointer to the structure.

A linked list is a dynamic data structure in which the components are logically ordered by their pointer fields, rather than physically ordered as they are in an array. The end of the list is indicated by the special pointer constant NIL.

A stack is a data structure in which insertions and deletions are made at the same end. Components are both inserted and removed from the beginning of the list. A stack is a last in, first out (LIFO) structure.

A queue is a data structure in which insertions and deletions are made at different ends. Components are inserted at the rear of the list and removed from the front of the list. A queue is a first in, first out (FIFO) structure.

A binary tree is a dynamic data structure in which each node has two pointers, one to the left child (left subtree) and one to the right child (right subtree). In a binary search tree, all the values in the left subtree of a node are less than the value in the node, and all the values in the right subtree of a node are greater than the value in the node.

Developing data structures and the algorithms to manipulate them is one of the most engaging aspects of problem solving and programming. We hope that this introduction to the subject of data structures stands you in good stead.

■ *Quick Check*

1. What distinguishes a linked list from an array? (pp. 736–745)

2. When printing the contents of a linked list, what operation advances the current node pointer to the next node? (pp. 745–748)

3. What is the difference between the operations of inserting a new item at the top of a linked list, and inserting the new item in place? (pp. 748–755)

4. In deleting an item from a linked list, why do we need to keep track of the previous node (the node before the one to be deleted)? (pp. 755–759)

5. What is the difference between a stack and a linked list? (pp. 761–764)

6. What is the difference between a queue and a stack? (pp. 765–769)

7. What distinguishes a binary tree from the other linked data structures (linked list, stack, queue)? (pp. 769–775)

Answers

1. Arrays are static structures whose components are ordered by their relative locations in memory. Linked lists are dynamic data structures in which the ordering is defined by an explicit link field in each node.   2. The current node pointer is set equal to the link field of the current node.   3. When inserting an item in place, the list must first be searched to find the proper place. We don't have to search the list when inserting at the top.   4. Because we must set the link field of the previous node equal to the link field of the current node as part of the deletion operation.   5. Items may be inserted or deleted anywhere in a linked list, but with a stack we may insert or delete only at the top of the structure. 6. Items are inserted and deleted at only one end of a stack, but with a queue we add items to one end and delete them from the other.   7. A binary tree has multiple link fields in each node, while the other linked structures have only one link field per node.

▪ *Exam Preparation Exercises*

1. In a linked list, elements are only logically next to each other, whereas in an array they are also physically next to each other. (True or False?)

2. Which of the following are always dynamic data structures?
   a. Linked list   c. Stack
   b. Binary tree   d. Array

3. The expression below can appear before the type name Node_Type is defined. (True or False?)

   ```
   TYPE
       Ptr_Type = ^Node_Type;
   ```

4. Use the Pascal code below to identify the values of the variable references and Boolean comparisons that follow. The value may be undefined, or the reference may be invalid.

   ```
   TYPE
       Ptr_Node = ^Node_Type;
       Node_Type = RECORD
                       Number : Integer;
                       Character : Char;
                       Link : Ptr_Node
                   END;  (* Record *)

   VAR
       Current,
       First,
       Last:
           Ptr_Type;
   ```

```
BEGIN
  First := NIL;
  Last := NIL;
  Current := NIL;
  New(Current);
  Current^.Number := 13;
  Current^.Character := 'z';
  New(Current^.Link);
  Last := Current^.Link;
  Last^.Number := 9;
  New(First);
  Last^.Link := First;
  First^.Number := 9;
  First^.Character := 'h';
  First^.Link := Current;
      .
      .
      .
```

Expression	Value
a. First^.Link^.Number	_____
b. First^.Link^.Link^.Character	_____
c. First^.Link^ = Last^	_____
d. Current.Link^.Number	_____
e. Current^.Link = Last^	_____
f. First^ = Last^.Link^	_____
g. Current < Last	_____

5. A stack is one of the abstract data structures that is often implemented with linked lists. (True or False?)

6. a. Which element of a stack is the first to be removed?
   b. Which element of a queue is the first to be removed?

7. Choose a data structure (array, linked list, or binary search tree) for each of the following situations. Assume unlimited memory but limited time.
   a. A fixed list of 1,000 elements to keep counts for particular values.
   b. A fixed list of 1,000 to 4,000 (usually 1,500) elements that has elements printed according to position requests input to the program.
   c. A list of an unknown number of elements that is read, then printed in reverse order.

8. Choose a data structure (array, linked list, or binary search tree) for each of the following situations. Assume limited memory but unlimited time.
   a. A fixed list of 1,000 elements to keep counts for particular values.
   b. A fixed list of 1,000 to 4,000 (usually 1,500) elements that has elements printed according to position requests input to the program.
   c. A list of an unknown number of elements that is read, then printed in reverse order.

9. What is the difference between inserting an item into an empty queue and into one that has elements? (Assume a linked-list implementation.)

10. Which of the following are binary search trees?

a.

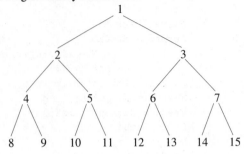

b.

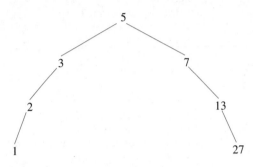

c.

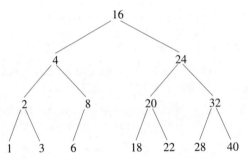

11. Referring to the binary tree in 10.c, write the values of the given items.

Item	Value
a. The root	_____
b. The largest value in the left subtree of 24	_____
c. The parent of 4	_____
d. The sibling of 8	_____
e. The leaf nodes of the right subtree of 4	_____
f. The right child of 20	_____

12. Does an O(N log$_2$N) sort most likely become more time-consuming than an O(N^2) sort as the number of elements gets larger or smaller?

13. What is the output for the following Pascal program given the input data 5, 6, 3, and 1?

```
            PROGRAM Linked (Input, Output);
            TYPE
              Ptr = ^Person;
              Person = RECORD
                           SS_Num : Integer;
                           Link : Ptr
                       END; (* RECORD *)
            VAR
              Head,
              P:
                Ptr;
              SS_Number:
                Integer;
            BEGIN (* Linked *)
              Head := NIL;
              WHILE NOT EOF DO
                BEGIN
                  Readln(SS_Number);
                  New(P);
                  P^.SS_Num := SS_Number;
                  P^.Link := Head;
                  Head := P
                END;
              P := Head;
              WHILE P <> NIL DO
                BEGIN
                  Write(P^.SS_Num);
                  P := P^.Link
                END
            END. (* Linked *)
```

14. Suppose the following list of character values is inserted into an empty binary search tree (the commas are not part of the data). Draw the tree.

    J, R, D, G, T, E

▪ *Programming Warm-Up Exercises*

1. To avoid special handling of empty linked lists for insertion and deletion routines, some programmers prefer to have a dummy node permanently in the list. (The list is considered empty if it contains only the dummy node.) Rewrite the queue subprograms Empty, Enqueue, Dequeue, and Initialize to use a dummy node whose component value is equal to a constant named Dummy. Do not keep any unnecessary code. *Hint:* The first element of the queue follows the dummy node.

2. Use an array to implement a stack data structure limited to 100 elements. Write the subprograms and declarations necessary for this implementation (the component type should be Integer). *Hint:* The last item entered into the stack is known by saving an array index position.

3. Rewrite procedure Dequeue in this chapter to immediately return a Boolean value that is True if the queue is empty.

4. Write the declarations needed to create a dynamic tree data structure whose nodes have the following information:

Name (twenty characters)
Age (integer)
Aptitude (real)

5. Write a procedure to receive a value N, pop N elements from a stack, and place them on a queue. Have the procedure check for any possible error conditions and return a Boolean True if an error is found. Determine what other parameters need to be received or returned and declare them in the procedure heading. You may assume that the basic stack and queue operations of this chapter have already been coded.

6. Write a function Count_Q that returns the number of nodes in a queue. The function should leave the queue unchanged.

7. Write a function Count_List that returns the number of nodes in a linked list pointed to by its parameter List.

8. Write a procedure Copy_List that makes a copy of a linked list. The list to be copied is List and the copy is Copy.

9. Given the following declarations

```
TYPE
  Ptr = ^Node;
  Node = RECORD
           Number : Integer;
           Link : Ptr
         END; (* Record *)
VAR
  Head:
    Ptr;
```

write a procedure that searches a linked list for an Integer variable Key and exchanges it with the number preceding it on the list. If Key is the first value on the list or if Key is not found, then no exchange occurs.

10. Using the same declarations given in exercise 9, write a procedure that reorganizes the elements in a linked list so that the last element is first, the second to last is second, etc. *Hint:* Use a temporary list.

11. Write a procedure and any necessary declarations that returns the bottom number from a stack. The procedure should leave the stack unchanged. See page 762 for an example declaration of a stack type.

■ *Programming Problems*

1. In Program Solitaire in this chapter, all insertions into a linked list were made using procedure Insert_Top, and all the deletions from a linked list were made using procedure Remove_Top. In some cases this was inefficient. For example, procedure Recreate takes the cards from

On_Table and moves them one by one to Deck. Then the cards on the Discard_Pile are moved one by one to Deck.

Rewrite Program Solitaire to make it more efficient. Instead of using Remove_Top and Insert_Top to re-create the deck, use the following algorithm:

```
Set Deck to On_Table
Set Pointer to Deck
WHILE Pointer^.Link <> NIL
    Set Pointer to Pointer^.Link
Set Pointer^.Link to Discard_Pile
```

Also use the same strategy to make procedure Merge more efficient.

2. Write a program to process file Address_Book as created in Programming Problem 4 in Chapter 15. Your program should read in the entries and store them in a linked list ordered by birth date. The output should consist of a list by month of the names and telephone numbers of the people who have birthdays each month.

3. Rewrite the program described in Problem 2 using a binary search tree rather than a linked list.

4. A *palindrome* is a string of characters that reads the same forward and backward. Write a program that reads in a string of characters and determines if the string is a palindrome. Use EOLN to end the string. Echo-print the string, followed by "Is a palindrome" if the string is a palindrome and "Is not a palindrome" if the string is not a palindrome. For example, given the following input string:

Able was I ere I saw Elba

the string would print "Is a palindrome." Consider upper- and lowercase letters to be the same. (*Hint:* Use a stack and a queue.)

Recursion

CHAPTER 17

GOALS

- To be able to identify the base case(s) and the general case in a recursive definition.
- To be able to write a recursive algorithm for a problem involving only simple variables.
- To be able to write a recursive algorithm for a problem involving structured variables.
- To be able to write a recursive algorithm for a problem involving linked lists.
- To be able to write a recursive algorithm for a problem involving binary trees.

In Chapter 8 we said that putting the name of a function in an expression within the function itself would cause the function to be called recursively, and we cautioned that inadvertent recursive calls cause errors. In this chapter we show how to use recursion correctly. Recursion is a powerful technique that can be used in place of iteration.

Recursive solutions are generally less efficient than iterative solutions to the same problem. However, some problems lend themselves to simple, elegant, recursive solutions and are exceedingly cumbersome to solve iteratively. Many of the older programming languages, like FORTRAN, BASIC, and COBOL, do not allow recursion. Some languages are especially oriented to recursive algorithms—LISP is one of these. Pascal lets us take our choice: we can implement both iterative and recursive algorithms in Pascal.

Our examples are broken into two groups: problems that use only simple variables and problems that use structured variables. If you are studying recursion before reading Chapter 11 on structured data types, then cover only the first set of examples and leave the rest until you have completed the chapters on structured data types.

What Is Recursion?

You may have seen a set of gaily painted Russian dolls that fit inside one another. Inside the first doll is a smaller doll, inside of which is an even smaller doll, inside of which is yet a smaller doll, and so on. A recursive algorithm is like such a set of Russian dolls. It reproduces itself with smaller and smaller examples of itself until a solution is found (there are no more dolls). In our example in Chapter 8 we said that the ability of a function or a procedure to invoke itself was known as *recursion*. A better explanation is: procedures and functions that invoke themselves are recursive.

Let's review the one recursion problem from Chapter 8. The problem was to calculate the result of taking a positive integer to a positive power. We noted that the formula for exponentiation could be rewritten successively as follows:

$$X^N = \underbrace{X * X * X * X * \ldots * X}_{N \text{ times}}$$

$$X^N = X * \underbrace{(X * X * \ldots * X)}_{(N - 1) \text{ times}}$$

$$X^N = X * X * \underbrace{(X * X * \ldots * X)}_{(N - 2) \text{ times}}$$

Another way of writing the formula would be:

$$X^N = X * X^{N-1}$$

This definition is a classic **recursive definition:** the definition is given in terms of a smaller version of itself.

Recursive Definition   A definition in which something is defined in terms of smaller versions of itself.

X^N is defined in terms of multiplying X times X^{N-1}. How is X^{N-1} defined? Why as $X * X^{N-2}$, of course! And X^{N-2} is $X * X^{N-3}$, X^{N-3} is $X * X^{N-4}$, and so on. In this example, "in terms of smaller versions of itself" means that the exponent is decremented each time.

When does the process stop? When we have reached a case where we know the answer without resorting to a recursive definition. In this example, it is the case where N equals 1: X^1 is X. The case (or cases) for which an answer is explicitly known is called the **base case;** the case for which the solution is expressed in terms of a smaller version of itself is called the **recursive** or **general case.** A **recursive algorithm** is an algorithm that expresses the solution in terms of a call to itself, a recursive call. A recursive algorithm must terminate; that is, it must have a base case.

Base Case   The case for which the solution can be stated nonrecursively.

General Case   The case for which the solution is expressed in terms of a smaller version of itself. Also known as *recursive case*.

Recursive Algorithm   A solution that is expressed in terms of a) smaller instances of itself and b) a base case.

Figure 17-1 shows function Power with the base case and the recursive call marked. The function is embedded in a program that reads in a number and an exponent and prints the results. Let's trace the execution of this recursive function, with Number equal to 2 and Exponent equal to 3. We use a new format to trace recursive routines: we number the calls and then discuss what is happening in paragraph form. For illustrative purposes, we assume that each call creates a new version of the function Power. You also can follow this process by running the program with the Turbo Debugger, stepping through the code with the F7 key.

Call 1: Power is called with Number equal to 2 and Exponent equal to 3. These are the formal parameters X and N, respectively. Therefore, X is equal to 2 and N is equal to 3. N is not equal to 1, so Power is called with X and N − 1 as parameters. Execution of the call to the function halts until an answer is sent back from this recursive call.

Call 2: X is equal to 2 and N is equal to 2. Since N is not equal to 1, the function Power is called again, this time with X and N − 1 as parameters. Execution of this call to the function halts until an answer is sent back from this recursive call.

Call 3: X is equal to 2 and N is equal to 1. Since N is equal to 1, the value of X is stored in Power. This call to the function has finished executing, and Power is passed back to the place in the statement from which the call was made.

Call 2: This call to the function can now complete the statement that contained the recursive call because Power now has a value. This value (which is 2) is multiplied by X, and the result is stored in Power. This call to the function has finished executing, and Power is passed back to the place in the statement from which the call was made.

Call 1: This call to the function can now complete the statement that contained the recursive call because Power now has a value. This value (which is 4) is multiplied by X, and the result is stored in Power. This call to the function has finished executing, and Power is passed back to the place in the statement from which the call was made.

Figure 17-1
Function Power

```
PROGRAM Exponentiation (Input, Output);

VAR
  Number,              (* Number that is being raised to power    *)
  Exponent,            (* Power the number is being raised to     *)
  Answer:              (* Result of raising the number to the power *)
    Integer;

(*********************************************************************)

FUNCTION Power (X,              (* Number that is being raised to power *)
                 N:             (* Power the number is being raised to  *)
               Integer):
               Integer;

(* This function computes X to the N power by multiplying X times *)
(* the result of computing X to the N - 1 power. Assumption:      *)
(* N is greater than zero *)

BEGIN (* Power *)
  IF N = 1
    THEN  ◄─────────────────────────────────────────  (* Base case *)
      Power := X
    ELSE
      Power := X * Power(X, N - 1) ◄───────────  (* Recursive call *)
END;  (* Power *)

(*********************************************************************)

BEGIN (* Exponentiation *)
  Readln(Number, Exponent);
  Answer := Power(Number, Exponent); ◄────────  (* Nonrecursive call *)
  Writeln(Answer)
END.  (* Exponentiation *)
```

Since the first call (the nonrecursive call) has now been completed, this is the final value of the function Power.

This trace is summarized in Figure 17-2. Each box represents a call to the function Power. The values for the parameters for that call are shown in each box.

What happens if there is no base case? We have infinite recursion, the equivalent of an infinite loop. For example, if the statement

IF N = 1

were omitted, Power would be called over and over again. Eventually, the program would halt with an error message such as ERROR STACK OVERFLOW. Infinite recursion will also occur if Power is called with N less than or equal to zero.

Figure 17-2
Execution of
Power(2, 3)

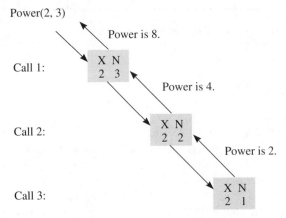

Recursive Algorithms with Simple Variables

Let's look at another example: calculating a factorial. The factorial of a number N (written N!) is N multiplied by N − 1, N − 2, N − 3, and so on. Another way of expressing factorial is

$$N! = N * (N - 1)!$$

This expression looks like a recursive definition. (N − 1)! is a smaller instance of N!—it takes one less multiplication to calculate (N − 1)! than it does to calculate N!. If we can find a base case, we can write a recursive algorithm. Fortunately, we don't have to look too far: 0! is defined to be 1.

Factorial

IF N is 0
  THEN
    Factorial is set equal to 1
  ELSE
    Factorial is set equal to N * Factorial (N − 1)

This algorithm can be coded directly.

```
FUNCTION Factorial (N:          (* Factorial number being computed *)
              Integer):
              Integer;
```

```
BEGIN (* Factorial *)
  IF N = 0
    THEN                                         (* Base case *)
      Factorial := 1
    ELSE
      Factorial := N * Factorial(N - 1)          (* General case *)
END; (* Factorial *)
```

Let's trace this function with an original N of 4.

Call 1: N is 4. Since N is not 0, the ELSE branch is taken. The assignment statement cannot be completed until the recursive call to function Factorial with N − 1 as the actual parameter has been completed.

Call 2: N is 3. Since N is not 0, the ELSE branch is taken. The assignment statement cannot be completed until the recursive call to function Factorial with N − 1 as the actual parameter has been completed.

Call 3: N is 2. Since N is not 0, the ELSE branch is taken. The assignment statement cannot be completed until the recursive call to function Factorial with N − 1 as the actual parameter has been completed.

Call 4: N is 1. Since N is not 0, the ELSE branch is taken. The assignment statement cannot be completed until the recursive call to function Factorial with N − 1 as the actual parameter has been completed.

Call 5: N is 0. Since N is equal to 0, Factorial is set to 1. This call to the function has finished executing. Factorial (which is 1) is sent back as the result.

Call 4: The assignment statement in this copy can now be completed. Factorial is Factorial times N. This call to the function has now finished executing. Factorial (which is 1) is returned as the result.

Call 3: The assignment statement in this copy can now be completed. Factorial is Factorial times N. This call to the function has now finished executing. Factorial (which is 2) is returned as the result.

Call 2: The assignment statement in this copy can now be completed. Factorial is Factorial times N. This call to the function has now finished executing. Factorial (which is 6) is returned as the result.

Call 1: The assignment statement in this copy can now be completed. Factorial is Factorial times N. This call to the function has now finished executing. Factorial (which is 24) is returned as the result. Since this is the last of the calls to Factorial, the recursive process is over. The value 24 is returned as the final value of the call to function Factorial with an actual parameter of 4. Figure 17-3 summarizes the execution of function Factorial with an actual parameter of 4.

Let's organize what we have done in these two solutions into an outline for writing recursive algorithms.

1. Understand the problem. (We threw this in for good measure: it is always the first step.)
2. Determine the base case(s).
3. Determine the recursive case(s).

Figure 17-3
Execution of
Factorial(4)

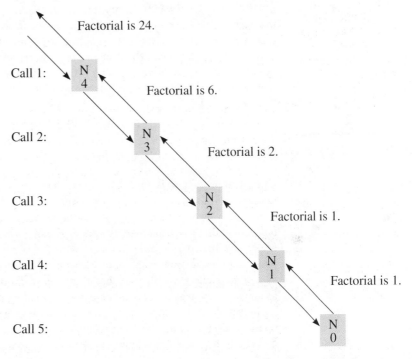

Answer := Factorial(4)

Factorial is 24.

Call 1:

Factorial is 6.

Call 2:

Factorial is 2.

Call 3:

Factorial is 1.

Call 4:

Factorial is 1.

Call 5:

We have used the factorial and the power algorithms to demonstrate recursion because they are easy to visualize. In practice, one would never want to calculate either of these functions using the recursive solution. In both cases the iterative solutions are simpler and much more efficient because starting a new iteration of a loop is a faster operation than calling a function or a procedure. Let's compare the code for the iterative and recursive versions of the factorial problem.

```
FUNCTION Factorial (    N:
                        Integer):
                         Integer;
```

```
(* Iterative solution *)
VAR
  Factor,
  Counter:
    Integer;
BEGIN (* Factorial *)
  Factor := 1;
  FOR Counter := 2 TO N DO
    Factor := Factor * Counter;
  Factorial := Factor
END; (* Factorial *)
```

```
(* Recursive solution *)



BEGIN (* Factorial *)
  IF N = 0
    THEN
      Factorial := 1
    ELSE
      Factorial := N * Factorial(N - 1)
END;   (* Factorial *)
```

The iterative version has two local variables; the recursive version has none. There are usually fewer local variables in a recursive routine than in an iterative routine. Also, the iterative version always has a loop; the recursive version always has a branch. A branching structure is the main control structure in a recursive routine. A looping structure is the main control structure in an iterative routine.

In the next section we examine a more complicated problem—one in which the recursive solution is not immediately apparent.

Towers of Hanoi

One of your first toys may have been three pegs with colored circles of different diameters. If so, you probably spent countless hours moving the circles from one peg to another. If we put some constraints on how the circles or disks can be moved, we have an adult game called the Towers of Hanoi. When the game begins, all the circles are on the first peg in order by size, with the smallest on the top. The object of the game is to move the circles, one at a time, to the third peg. The catch is that a circle cannot be placed on top of one that is smaller in diameter. The middle peg can be used as an auxiliary peg, but it must be empty at the beginning and the end of the game.

To get a feel for how this might be done, let's look at some sketches of what the configuration must be at certain points if a solution is possible. We use four circles or disks. The beginning configuration is:

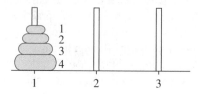

To move the largest circle (circle 4) to peg 3, we must move the three smaller circles to peg 2. Then circle 4 can be moved into its final place:

Let's assume we can do this. Now, to move the next largest circle (circle 3) into place, we must move the two circles on top of it onto an auxiliary peg (peg 1 in this case):

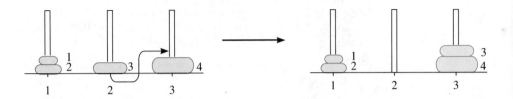

To get circle 2 into place, we must move circle 2 to another peg, freeing circle 2 to be moved to its place on peg 3.

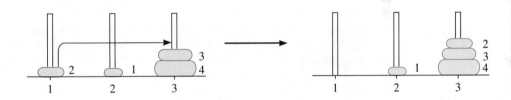

The last circle (circle 1) can now be moved into its final place, and we are finished.

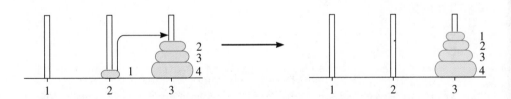

Notice that to free circle 4, we had to move three circles to another peg. To free circle 3, we had to move two circles to another peg. To free circle 2, we had to move one circle to another peg. This sounds like a recursive algorithm: to free the Nth circle, we have to move N − 1 circles. Each stage can be thought of as beginning again with three pegs, but with one fewer circle each time. Let's see if we can summarize this process, using N instead of an actual number.

To Get N Circles Moved from Peg 1 to Peg 3

Get N − 1 circles moved from peg 1 to peg 2
Move Nth circle from peg 1 to peg 3
Get N − 1 circles moved from peg 2 to peg 3

This algorithm certainly sounds simple; surely there must be more, but this is really all there is to it.

Let's write a recursive procedure that implements this algorithm. We can't actually move disks, of course, but we can print out a message to do so. Notice that the beginning peg, the ending peg, and the auxiliary peg keep changing during the algorithm. To make the algorithm easier to follow, we call the pegs Begin_Peg, End_Peg, and Aux_Peg. These three pegs, along with the number of circles on the beginning peg, are the parameters of the procedure.

We have the recursive or general case; what about a base case? How do we know when to stop the recursive process? The clue is in the expression "To get N circles moved." If we don't have any circles to move, we don't have anything to do. We are finished with that stage. Therefore, when the number of circles equals 0, we do nothing (that is, return).

```
PROCEDURE Towers (Circles,       (* Number of circles to move       *)
                  Begin_Peg,     (* Peg containing circles to move   *)
                  Aux_Peg,       (* Peg holding circles temporarily  *)
                  End_Peg:       (* Peg receiving circles being moved *)
                  Integer);

BEGIN (* Towers *)
  IF Circles > 0
    THEN
      BEGIN
        (* Move N - 1 circles from beginning peg to auxiliary peg *)
        Towers(Circles - 1, Begin_Peg, End_Peg, Aux_Peg);
        Writeln('Move circle from peg ', Begin_Peg:2, ' to peg', End_Peg:2);
        (* Move N - 1 circles from auxiliary peg to ending peg *)
        Towers(Circles - 1, Aux_Peg, Begin_Peg, End_Peg)
      END
END;  (* Towers *)
```

It's hard to believe that such a simple algorithm actually works; but we'll prove it to you. Following is a driver program that calls procedure Towers. Write statements have been added so you can see the values of the actual parameters with each recursive call. Since there are two recursive calls within the procedure, we have indicated which recursive statement issued the call.

```
PROGRAM Test_Towers (Input, Output);

(* This program reads in a value from the console and calls *)
(* procedure Towers with this value as the parameter         *)

VAR
  Circles:                      (* Number of circles on starting peg *)
    Integer;

(***********************************************************************)

PROCEDURE Towers (Circles,      (* Number of circles to move          *)
                  Begin_Peg,    (* Peg containing circles to move     *)
                  Aux_Peg,      (* Peg holding circles temporarily    *)
                  End_Peg:      (* Peg receiving circles being moved *)
                    Integer);

(* This recursive procedure moves the number of circles in Circles   *)
(* from Begin_Peg to End_Peg.  All but one of the circles are moved  *)
(* from Begin_Peg to Aux_Peg, the last circle is moved from Begin_Peg *)
(* to End_Peg, then the circles are moved from Aux_Peg to End_Peg.    *)
(* The subgoals of moving circles to and from Aux_Peg are what        *)
(* involve recursion *)

BEGIN (* Towers *)
  Writeln(Circles:7, Begin_Peg:9, Aux_Peg:7, End_Peg:7);
  IF Circles > 0
    THEN
      BEGIN
        Write('From  first:  ');
        Towers(Circles - 1, Begin_Peg, End_Peg, Aux_Peg);
        Writeln(' ':48, ' move circle ', Circles:2, ' from ',
                Begin_Peg:2, ' to ', End_Peg:2);
        Write('From second:  ');
        Towers(Circles - 1, Aux_Peg, Begin_Peg, End_Peg)
      END
END;  (* Towers *)

(***********************************************************************)

BEGIN (* Test_Towers *)
  Writeln('Input number of Circles.  ');
  Readln(Circles);
  Writeln('OUTPUT WITH ', Circles:3, ' CIRCLES');
  Writeln;
  Write('CALLED FROM    CIRCLES', 'BEGIN':8, 'AUXIL.':8, 'END':5);
  Writeln(' ':4, 'INSTRUCTIONS');
  Write('Original   :');
  Towers(Circles, 1, 2, 3)
END.  (* Test_Towers *)
```

The output from a run with three circles follows. "Original" means that the actual parameters listed beside it are from the nonrecursive call, which is the first call to procedure Towers. "From first:" means that the actual parameters listed are for a call issued from the first recursive statement. "From second:" means that the actual parameters listed are for a call issued from the second recursive statement. Notice that a call cannot be issued from the second recursive statement until the preceding call from the first recursive statement has completed execution.

OUTPUT WITH   3 CIRCLES

CALLED FROM	CIRCLES	BEGIN	AUXIL.	END	INSTRUCTIONS
Original :	3	1	2	3	
From first:	2	1	3	2	
From first:	1	1	2	3	
From first:	0	1	3	2	
					move circle 1 from 1 to 3
From second:	0	2	1	3	
					move circle 2 from 1 to 2
From second:	1	3	1	2	
From first:	0	3	2	1	
					move circle 1 from 3 to 2
From second:	0	1	3	2	
					move circle 3 from 1 to 3
From second:	2	2	1	3	
From first:	1	2	3	1	
From first:	0	2	1	3	
					move circle 1 from 2 to 1
From second:	0	3	2	1	
					move circle 2 from 2 to 3
From second:	1	1	2	3	
From first:	0	1	3	2	
					move circle 1 from 1 to 3
From second:	0	2	1	3	

Recursive Algorithms with Structured Variables

In our definition of a recursive algorithm, we said there were two cases: the recursive or general case, and the base case for which an answer can be expressed nonrecursively. In the general case for all our algorithms so far, a parameter was expressed in terms of a smaller value each time. When structured variables are used, the recursive case is often in terms of a smaller structure rather than a smaller value; the base case occurs when there are no values left to process in the structure.

We examine the recursive definition for printing the components in a one-dimensional array of N components to show what we mean.

Print Array

> IF more components
>   Write the value in the first component
>   Print array of N − 1 components

The recursive case is to print the values in an array that is one component smaller; that is, the size of the array gets smaller with each recursive call. The base case is when the size of the array becomes 0: there are no more components to print.

Our parameters must include the index of the first component (the one to be printed). How do we know when there are no more components to print (when the size of the array to be printed is 0)? We know we have printed the last component in the array when the index of the next component to be printed is beyond the length of the array. Therefore, the index of the last component in the array must be passed as a parameter. We call the indexes First and Last. When First is greater than Last, we are finished. The name of the array is List of type Ary_Type.

```
PROCEDURE Print (List:          (* Array containing numbers to print  *)
                     Ary_Type;
                 First,         (* Index first component in the array *)
                 Last:          (* Index last component in the array  *)
                     Integer);

BEGIN (* Print *)
  IF First <= Last
    THEN
      BEGIN
        Writeln(List[First]);
        Print(List, First + 1, Last)
      END
END;  (* Print *)
```

List

[1]	23
[2]	44
[3]	52
[4]	61
[5]	77

Print(List, 1, 5)

Here is a code walk-through with the array shown at the left.

Call 1: First is 1 and Last is 5. First is less than Last, so the value in List[First] (which is 23) is printed. Execution of this call halts while the array from First + 1 to Last is printed.

Call 2: First is 2 and Last is 5. First is less than Last, so the value in List[First] (which is 44) is printed. Execution of this call halts while the array from First + 1 to Last is printed.

Call 3: First is 3 and Last is 5. First is less than Last, so the value in List[First] (which is 52) is printed. Execution of this call halts while the array from First + 1 to Last is printed.

Call 4: First is 4 and Last is 5. First is less than last, so the value in List[First] (which is 61) is printed. Execution of this call halts while the array from First + 1 to Last is printed.

Call 5: First is 5 and Last is 5. First is equal to Last, so the value in List[First] (which is 77) is printed. Execution of this call halts while the array from First + 1 to Last is printed.

Call 6: First is 6 and Last is 5. First is greater than Last, so the execution of this call is completed. Control is passed back to the preceding call.

Call 5: Execution of this call is completed. Control is passed back to the preceding call.

Calls 4, 3, 2, and 1: Execution is completed in turn, and control is passed back to the preceding call.

Notice that once the deepest call (the call with the highest number) was reached, each of the calls before it returned without doing anything. When no statements are executed after the return from the recursive call to the procedure or function, the recursion is known as **tail recursion.** Tail recursion often indicates that the problem could be solved more easily using iteration. We used the array example because it made the recursive process easy to visualize; in practice, an array should be printed iteratively.

Figure 17-4 shows the execution of procedure Print with the values of the actual parameters for each call. Notice that the array gets smaller with each recursive call (List[First]..List[Last]). If we want to print the components in the array in reverse order recursively, all we have to do is interchange the two statements within the IF statement.

Recursion Using Pointer Variables

The previous recursive algorithm using a one-dimensional array could have been done much more easily using iteration. Now we look at two algorithms that cannot be done more easily with iteration: printing a linked list in reverse order and traversing a tree.

Printing a Linked List in Reverse Order

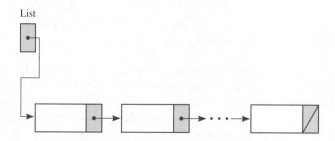

Printing a list in order from first to last is easy. We set a running pointer Pointer to List and cycle through the list until Pointer is NIL.

Print(List, 1, 5)

Figure 17-4
Execution of
Print(List, 1, 5)

Print(List, 1, 5)

List, which is the array, is not shown in the boxes.

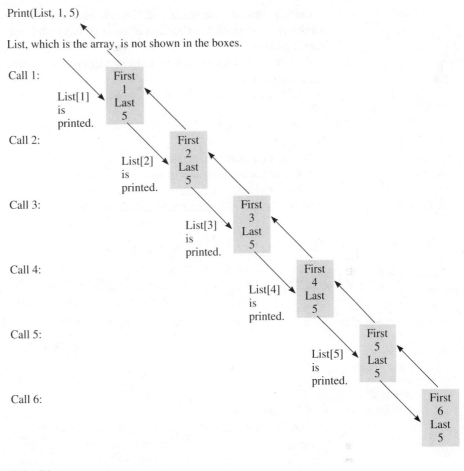

Call 1:

List[1]
is
printed.

First
1
Last
5

Call 2:

List[2]
is
printed.

First
2
Last
5

Call 3:

List[3]
is
printed.

First
3
Last
5

Call 4:

List[4]
is
printed.

First
4
Last
5

Call 5:

List[5]
is
printed.

First
5
Last
5

Call 6:

First
6
Last
5

Print List

```
Pointer is set equal to List
WHILE Pointer <> NIL
    Write Pointer^.Component
    Pointer is set equal to Pointer^.Link
```

To print the list in reverse order, we must print the value in the last node first, then the value in the next-to-last node, and so on. Another way of expressing this is to say that we can't print a value until all the values in all the nodes following it have been printed. We might visualize the process as the first node's turning to its neighbor and saying, "Tell me when you have printed your value. Then I'll print my value." The second node says to its neighbor, "Tell me when you have printed your value. Then I'll print mine." That node, in turn, says the same to its neighbor, and this continues until there is nothing to print.

Since the number of neighbors gets smaller and smaller, we seem to have the makings of a recursive solution. The end of the list is reached when the running pointer is NIL. When that happens, the last node can print its value and send the message back to the one before it. That node can then print its value and send the message back to the one before it, and so on.

Rev_Print List

> IF List is not NIL
>   Rev_Print rest of nodes in List
>   Write current node in List

This algorithm can be coded directly into the following procedure:

```
PROCEDURE Rev_Print (List:          (* Pointer to head of linked list *)
                  Node_Pointer);

(* The components of List are printed in reverse order *)

BEGIN (* Rev_Print *)
  IF List <> NIL
    THEN
      BEGIN                              (* Recursive call *)
        Rev_Print(List^.Link);
        Writeln(List^.Component)
      END
END;  (* Rev_Print *)
```

This algorithm seems complex enough to warrant a code walk-through. We use the following list:

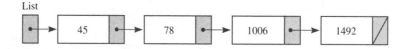

Call 1: List is a pointer pointing to the node containing 45. List is not NIL. Execution of this call halts until the recursive call with the actual parameter List^.Link has been completed.

Call 2: List is a pointer pointing to the node containing 78. List is not NIL. Execution of this call halts until the recursive call with the actual parameter List^.Link has been completed.

Call 3: List is a pointer pointing to the node containing 1066. List is not NIL. Execution of this call halts until the recursive call with the actual parameter List^.Link has been completed.

Call 4: List is a pointer pointing to the node containing 1492. List is not NIL. Execution of this call halts until the recursive call with the actual parameter List^.Link has been completed.

Call 5: List is NIL. Execution of this call is complete. Control is passed back to the preceding call.

Call 4: List^.Component (which is 1492) is printed. Execution of this call is complete. Control is passed back to the preceding call.

Call 3: List^.Component (which is 1066) is printed. Execution of this call is complete. Control is passed back to the preceding call.

Call 2: List^.Component (which is 78) is printed. Execution of this call is complete. Control is passed back to the preceding call.

Call 1: List^.Component (which is 45) is printed. Execution of this call is complete. Since this is the nonrecursive call, execution continues with the statement immediately following RevPrint(List).

Figure 17-5 shows the execution of procedure Rev_Print. The actual parameters are pointers that cannot be printed, so $\longrightarrow$ 45 means the pointer to the node whose component is 45.

Recursion with Trees

A binary tree can be defined recursively as a finite set of nodes that either is empty, or consists of a root and two disjoint binary trees called the left subtree and the right

Figure 17-5
Execution of
Rev_Print(List)

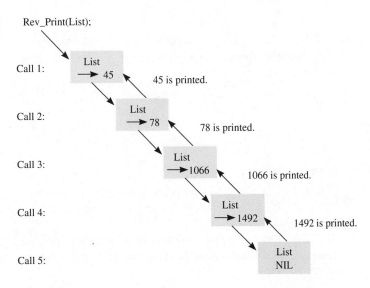

subtree. We can make use of this recursive definition to *traverse the tree,* which means visiting each of the nodes in the tree in an organized fashion. "Visiting" implies any sort of action we wish—for example, printing, counting, or summing.

In Chapter 16 we developed an algorithm to print the values in a binary search tree in numeric order. This is called an **in-order traversal,** in which a node is visited between visits to the nodes in its left subtree and the nodes in its right subtree. Let's re-examine this algorithm.

To print the values in a binary search tree, we look to see if there is a left subtree. If so, we call the procedure for printing the tree, but with a pointer to the root of the left subtree. When there is a left child, we print the current node and then call the procedure to print the subtree whose root is the right child. If there is no right child, then the procedure returns to the call that is responsible for printing the parent of the current node. We print that value, print the value in the parent of that node, and then print the values in the right child of that node. We can generalize this process as follows:

Print (In_Order)

> Print (in order) the values in the left subtree.
> Print the value in the node.
> Print (in order) the values in the right subtree.

Like the solution to the Towers of Hanoi problem, this looks too simple; yet, it is the algorithm. Also, as in Towers of Hanoi, the base case is a "do nothing" case. The end of the recursive calls is recognized when the root of the subtree is NIL—that is, the subtree is empty.

```
PROCEDURE In_Order (Tree:          (* Pointer to root of binary tree *)
                    Pointer);

(* Print the components of a binary search tree in order *)

BEGIN (* In_Order *)
  IF Tree <> NIL
    THEN
      BEGIN
        In_Order(Tree^.Left);
        Writeln(Tree^.Component);
        In_Order(Tree^.Right)
      END
END;  (* In_Order *)
```

In Chapter 16 we wrote a procedure to print a binary search tree using a stack. In fact, the Pascal compiler and the run-time support system implement recursion using a stack. Each time a procedure or function is called, its actual parameters are put on a stack. Let's do a code walk-through indicating what is happening to the stack at each recursive call. Figure 17-6 shows the contents of the stack at the beginning of each call. The components (which are pointers) are shown one on top of the other. The most recently pushed element is on the top. The notation ⟶ 10 refers to the pointer that points to the node containing 10. We use the same subtree that we used in Chapter 16. Since there are two recursive calls, we distinguish them by using L for the call with Tree^.Left and R for the call with Tree^.Right.

Figure 17-6   *Execution of In_Order(Tree)*

In_Order(Tree)

a. Call 1: ⟶ 10

b. Call 1L: ⟶ 5
            ⟶ 10

c. Call 2L: ⟶ 3
            ⟶ 5
            ⟶ 10

d. Call 3L: NIL
            ⟶ 3
            ⟶ 5
            ⟶ 10

e. Call 2L: ⟶ 3
            ⟶ 5
            ⟶ 10

f. Call 1R: NIL
            ⟶ 3
            ⟶ 5
            ⟶ 10

g. Call 2L: ⟶ 3
            ⟶ 5
            ⟶ 10

h. Call 1L: ⟶ 5
            ⟶ 10

i. Call 1R: ⟶ 7
            ⟶ 5
            ⟶ 10

j. Call 2L: NIL
            ⟶ 7
            ⟶ 5
            ⟶ 10

k. Call 1R: ⟶ 7
            ⟶ 5
            ⟶ 10

l. Call 2R: NIL
            ⟶ 7
            ⟶ 5
            ⟶ 10

m. Call 1R: ⟶ 7
            ⟶ 5
            ⟶ 10

n. Call 1L: ⟶ 5
            ⟶ 10

o. Call 1: ⟶ 10

p. Call 1R: ⟶ 15
            ⟶ 10

q. Call 2L: ⟶ 13
            ⟶ 15
            ⟶ 10

r. Call 3L: NIL
            ⟶ 13
            ⟶ 15
            ⟶ 10

s. Call 2L: ⟶ 13
            ⟶ 15
            ⟶ 10

t. Call 2R: NIL
            ⟶ 13
            ⟶ 15
            ⟶ 10

u. Call 2L: ⟶ 13
            ⟶ 15
            ⟶ 10

v. Call 1R: ⟶ 15
            ⟶ 10

w. Call 2R: NIL
            ⟶ 15
            ⟶ 10

x. Call 2R: ⟶ 15
            ⟶ 10

y. Call 1: ⟶ 10

z. Stack is empty

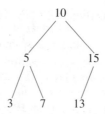

Call 1 (nonrecursive, Figure 17-6a): Tree (which is pointing to the node that contains 10) is on the stack. Tree is not NIL, so In_Order is called with Tree^.Left as the actual parameter. This pointer (Tree^.Left) is put on the stack.

Call 1L (Figure 17-6b): Tree is pointing to the node that contains 5. Tree is not NIL, so In_Order is called with Tree^.Left as the actual parameter. Tree^.Left is put on the stack.

Call 2L (Figure 17-6c): Tree is pointing to the node that contains 3. Tree is not NIL, so In_Order is called with Tree^.Left as the actual parameter. Tree^.Left is put on the stack.

Call 3L (Figure 17-6d): Tree is NIL. Execution of this call is complete. The stack is popped.

Call 2L (Figure 17-6e): Tree^.Component (which is 3) is printed. In_Order is called with Tree^.Right as the actual parameter. Tree^.Right is put on the stack.

Call 1R (Figure 17-6f): Tree is NIL. Execution of this call is now complete. Control is now passed back to the preceding call. The stack is popped.

Call 2L (Figure 17-6g): Execution of this call is now complete. Control is passed back to the preceding call. The stack is popped.

Call 1L (Figure 17-6h): Tree^.Component (which is 5) is printed. In_Order is called with Tree^.Right as the actual parameter. Tree^.Right is put on the stack.

Call 1R (Figure 17-6i): Tree is not NIL. In_Order is called with Tree.^Left as the actual parameter. Tree^.Left is put on the stack.

Call 2L (Figure 17-6j): Tree is NIL. Execution of this call is complete. The stack is popped.

Call 2L (Figure 17-6k): Tree^.Component (which is 7) is printed. In_Order is called with Tree^.Right as the actual parameter. Tree^.Right is put on the stack.

Call 1R (Figure 17-6l): Tree is NIL. Execution of this call is complete. The stack is popped.

Call 1L (Figure 17-6m): Execution of this call is complete. The stack is popped.

Call 1L (Figure 17-6n): Execution of this call is complete. The stack is popped.

Call 1 (nonrecursive, Figure 17-6o): Tree^.Component (which is 10) is printed. In_Order is called with Tree^.Right as the actual parameter. Tree^.Right is put on the stack.

Call 1R (Figure 17-6p): Tree is not NIL. In_Order is called with Tree^.Left as the actual parameter. Tree^.Left is put on the stack.

Call 2L (Figure 17-6q): Tree is not NIL. In_Order is called with Tree^.Left as the actual parameter. Tree^.Left is put on the stack.

Call 3L (Figure 17-6r): Tree is NIL. Execution of this call is complete. The stack is popped.

Call 2L (Figure 17-6s): Tree^.Component (which is 13) is printed. In_Order is called with Tree^.Right as the actual parameter. Tree^.Right is put on the stack.

Call 2R (Figure 17-6t): Tree is NIL. Execution of this call is complete. The stack is popped.

Call 2L (Figure 17-6u): Execution of this call is now complete. The stack is popped.

Call 1R (Figure 17-6v): Tree^.Component (which is 15) is printed. In_Order is called with Tree^.Right as the actual parameter. Tree^.Right is put on the stack.

Call 2R (Figure 17-6w): Tree is NIL. Execution of this call is complete. The stack is popped.

Call 1R (Figure 17-6x): Execution of this call is now complete. The stack is popped.

Call 1 (nonrecursive, Figure 17-6y): Execution of this call is now complete. The stack is popped (Figure 17-6z). Execution continues with the first statement following the original call to procedure In_Order.

Another way of looking at recursion is as an automatic stack data structure mechanism. Often we can use recursion as a substitute for writing complicated stack handling declarations and procedures. For example, the string reversal problem in the last chapter could be written more easily as a recursive procedure. The iterative algorithm was as follows:

```
Initialize stack
WHILE NOT EOLN
    Read a character
    Push character onto a stack
WHILE More Characters on Stack
    Pop character
    Write character
```

The recursive algorithm for the same task is as follows:

Reverse

```
IF NOT EOLN
    THEN
        Read a character
        Reverse
        Write character
```

The number of characters left on a line of input gets smaller with each call. The base case occurs when there are no more characters to be read. The code for the recursive procedure is shown embedded within Program Reverse_Line.

```
PROGRAM Reverse_Line (Input, Output);

(* A line is read from the keyboard and printed in reverse order *)

(*******************************************************************)

PROCEDURE Reverse;

(* A character is read from the keyboard, but before it is printed, *)
(* Reverse calls itself recursively.  When EOLN is ultimately       *)
(* encountered, the routine returns to the previous call, writes    *)
(* out the character that was read in then, and returns again.  The *)
(* process continues until all characters have been printed, with   *)
(* the first character read in being the last printed               *)

VAR
  Character:              (* The character read in during current call *)
    Char;

BEGIN (* Reverse *)
  IF NOT EOLN
    THEN                                      (* Recursive case *)
      BEGIN
        Read(Character);
        Reverse;
        Write(Character)
      END
  (* Empty ELSE is the base case *)
END;  (* Reverse *)


(*******************************************************************)

BEGIN (* Reverse_Line *)
  Reverse
END.  (* Reverse_Line *)
```

Recursion or Iteration?

Recursion is an alternative form of program control. When iterative control structures are used, processes are made to repeat by embedding code in a looping structure such as a WHILE, FOR, or REPEAT-UNTIL. In recursion, a process is made to repeat by having a procedure or function call itself. A selection statement is used to control the repeated calls.

Each time a recursive call is made, space must be assigned for all local variables. The overhead involved in any procedure or function call is time consuming. If an iterative solution is obvious, use it; it will be more efficient. There are problems for which the recursive solution is more obvious, however, such as the Towers of Hanoi problem and tree traversals. Computer science students should be aware of the power of recursion. If the definition of a problem is inherently recursive, then a recursive solution should certainly be considered.

PROBLEM-SOLVING CASE STUDY

Converting Decimal Integers to Binary Integers

Problem: Convert a decimal integer (base 10) to a binary integer (base 2).

Discussion: The algorithm for this conversion is as follows:

1. Take the decimal number and divide it by 2.
2. Make the remainder the right-most digit in the answer.
3. Replace the original dividend with the quotient.
4. Repeat, placing each new remainder to the left of the previous one.
5. Stop when the quotient is 0.

This is clearly an algorithm for a calculator and paper and pencil. Expressions such as "to the left of" certainly cannot be implemented in Pascal as yet. Let's do an example— convert 42 from base 10 to base 2—and get a feel for the algorithm before we try to write a computer solution. Remember, the quotient from one step becomes the dividend in the next.

Step 1

```
      21  ← Quotient
  2 ⟌ 42
      4
      2
      2
      0  ← Remainder
```

Step 2

```
      10  ← Quotient
  2 ⟌ 21
      2
      1
      0
      1  ← Remainder
```

Step 3

```
       5  ← Quotient
  2 ⟌ 10
      10
       0  ← Remainder
```

Step 4

```
       2  ← Quotient
  2 ⟌ 5
      4
       1  ← Remainder
```

	Step 5		*Step 6*

$$\begin{array}{r} 1 \leftarrow \text{Quotient} \\ 2\overline{)\,2} \\ 2 \\ \hline 0 \leftarrow \text{Remainder} \end{array} \qquad \begin{array}{r} 0 \leftarrow \text{Quotient} \\ 2\overline{)\,1} \\ 0 \\ \hline 1 \leftarrow \text{Remainder} \end{array}$$

It looks as though the problem can be implemented with a straightforward iterative algorithm. The remainder is, of course, the MOD operation, and the quotient is the DIV operation.

> WHILE Number > 0
>   Remainder is set equal to Number MOD 2
>   Write Remainder
>   Number is set equal to Number DIV 2

Let's do a walk-through to test this algorithm.

Number	*Remainder*
42	0
21	1
10	0
5	1
2	0
1	1

Answer:	0	1	0	1	0	1
(remainder from step	1	2	3	4	5	6)

The answer is backwards! An iterative solution (using only simple variables) doesn't work. We need to print the last remainder first. The first remainder should be printed only after the rest of the remainders have been calculated and printed.

In the case of our example, this means that we should print 42 MOD 2 after (42 DIV 2) MOD 2 has been printed. But this in turn means that we should print (42 DIV 2) MOD 2 after ((42 DIV 2) DIV 2) MOD 2 has been printed. Now this begins to look like a recursive definition. We can summarize by saying that, for any given number, we should print Number MOD 2 after (Number DIV 2) MOD 2 has been printed. This becomes the following algorithm:

PROBLEM-SOLVING CASE STUDY cont'd.

Convert Number

> .
> .
> IF Number > 0
>   Convert Number DIV 2
>   Write Number MOD 2

IF Number is 0, we have called Convert as many times as we need to and can begin printing the answer. The base case is simply when we stop making recursive calls. The recursive solution to this problem is encoded in procedure Convert.

```
PROCEDURE Convert (Number:        (* Number being converted to binary *)
                   Integer);

BEGIN (* Convert *)
  IF Number > 0
    THEN                                      (* Recursive call *)
      BEGIN
        Convert(Number DIV 2);
        Write(Number MOD 2:6)
      END
  (* Empty ELSE branch is the base case *)
END;  (* Convert *)
```

Let's do a code walk-through of Convert(10). We pick up our example at step 3, where the dividend is 10.

Call 1: Convert is called with an actual parameter of 10. Number is not equal to 0; execution of the THEN branch of this call halts until the recursive call to Convert with an actual parameter of (Number DIV 2) has been completed.

Call 2: Number is 5. Since Number is not equal to 0, execution of this call halts until the recursive call to Convert with an actual parameter of (Number DIV 2) has been completed.

Call 3: Number is 2. Since Number is not equal to 0, execution of this call halts until the recursive call to Convert with an actual parameter of (Number DIV 2) has been completed.

Call 4: Number is 1. Since Number is not equal to 0, execution of this call halts until the recursive call to Convert with an actual parameter of (Number DIV 2) has been completed.

Call 5: Number is 0. Execution of this call to Convert is completed. Control is passed back to the preceding call.

Call 4: Execution of this call resumes with the statement following the recursive call to Convert. Number MOD 2 (which is 1) is printed. Execution of this call to Convert is completed.

Call 3: Execution of this call resumes with the statement following the recursive call to Convert. Number MOD 2 (which is 0) is printed. Execution of this call to Convert is completed.

Call 2: Execution of this call resumes with the statement following the recursive call to Convert. Number MOD 2 (which is 1) is printed. Execution of this call to Convert is completed.

Call 1: Execution of this call resumes with the statement following the recursive call to Convert. Number MOD 2 (which is 0) is printed. Execution of this call to Convert is completed. Since this is the nonrecursive call, execution resumes with the statement immediately following the original call.

Figure 17-7 shows the execution of procedure Convert with the values of the actual parameters.

Figure 17-7
Execution of
Convert(10)

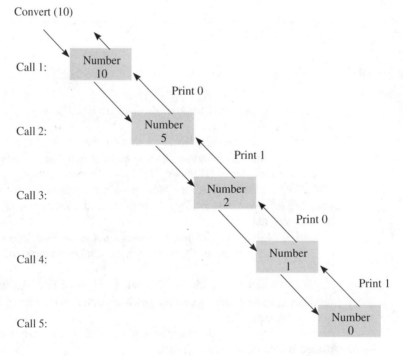

PROBLEM-SOLVING CASE STUDY

Minimum Value in an Integer Array

Problem: Find the minimum value in an integer array indexed from 1 to Size.

Discussion: This problem is easy to solve iteratively, but the objective here is to think recursively. The problem has to be stated in terms of a smaller case of itself. Since this is a problem using an array, a smaller case probably involves a smaller array. The minimum value in an array of length Size is the smaller of List[Size] and the smallest value in an array from List[1]..List[Size − 1].

Minimum(List[1]..List[Size])

> Set Min_So_Far to Minimum(List[1]..List[Size − 1])
> IF List[Size] < Min_So_Far
>   THEN Set Minimum to List[Size]
>   ELSE Set Minimum to Min_So_Far

This algorithm looks reasonable. All we need is a base case. We always know the minimum value: when there is only one value. So our base case occurs when Size is 1.

```
FUNCTION Minimum (List:          (* Array containing numbers to examine *)
                    Ary_Type;
                  Size:          (* Index of last element in array      *)
                    Integer):
                      Integer;

VAR
  Min_So_Far:                    (* Minimum returned from recursive call *)
    Integer;

BEGIN (* Minimum *)
  IF Size = 1
    THEN
      Minimum := List[Size]
    ELSE
      BEGIN
        Min_So_Far := Minimum(List, Size − 1)
        IF List[Size] < Min_So_Far
          THEN
            Minimum := List[Size]
          ELSE
      END    Minimum := Min_So_Far
END;   (* Minimum *)
```

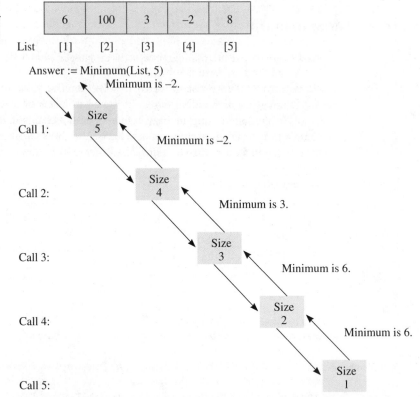

Figure 17-8
Execution of
Minimum(List, 5)

We do not provide a code walk-through for this function. A diagram showing the actual parameters for each call appears in Figure 17-8.

Testing: To test this function, we need a driver program that reads values into an array, calls the function, and prints the results. The cases to be tested are the end cases (Size equal to 1 and Size equal to Max_Length) and several cases between.

Testing and Debugging

Recursion is a powerful technique when used correctly. Improperly used, recursion can cause bugs that are difficult to diagnose. The best way to debug a recursive algorithm is to construct it correctly in the first place. To be realistic, however, we give a few hints about where to look if an error occurs.

Testing and Debugging Hints

1. Be sure there is a base case. If there is no base case, the algorithm continues to issue recursive calls until all the memory has been used. Each time the procedure or function is called, either recursively or nonrecursively, space is assigned for the parameters. If there is no base case to end the recursive calls, eventually all the memory will be assigned. A message such as STACK OVERFLOW ERROR indicates that the base case is missing.

2. Be sure you have not used a WHILE structure. The basic structure in a recursive algorithm is the IF-THEN-ELSE. There must be at least two cases: the recursive case and the base case. The base case may do nothing, and thus the ELSE branch is not present. The branching structure, however, must be there. If a WHILE statement is used in a recursive algorithm, the WHILE statement usually should not contain a recursive call.

3. Do not reference global variables directly within a recursive procedure or function.

4. Formal parameters that relate to the size of the problem must be value parameters. Actual parameters that relate to the size of the problem are usually expressions. Only value parameters can be passed expressions.

5. The Turbo Debugger can be used to trace a series of recursive calls, which often helps to locate errors in a recursive algorithm.

Summary

A recursive algorithm is expressed in terms of a smaller instance of itself. It must include a recursive case, for which the algorithm is expressed in terms of itself, and a base case, for which the algorithm is expressed in nonrecursive terms.

In many recursive problems, the smaller instance refers to a numeric parameter that is being reduced with each call. In other problems, the smaller instance refers to the size of the data structure being manipulated. The base case is the one in which the size of the problem (value or structure) reaches a point where an explicit answer is known.

In the example for finding the minimum using recursion, the size of the problem was the size of the array being searched. When the array size became 1, the solution was known. If there is only one component, it must be the minimum (as well as the maximum).

In the Towers of Hanoi game, the size of the problem was the number of disks to be moved. When there was only one left on the beginning peg, it could be moved to its final destination.

■ *Quick Check*

1. What distinguishes the base case in a recursive algorithm? (pp. 824–827)

2. What is the base case in the Towers of Hanoi algorithm? (pp. 830–834)

3. In working with simple variables, the recursive case is often in terms of a smaller value. What is typical of the recursive case in working with structured variables? (pp. 834–856)

4. In printing a linked list in reverse order recursively, what is the base case? (pp. 836–839)

5. What is the base case for the in-order binary tree traversal? (pp. 839–844)

Answers

1. The base case is the simplest case: the case where the solution can be stated nonrecursively.
2. When there are no more circles left to move.   3. It is often stated in terms of a smaller structure.
4. When the current node pointer is NIL.   5. When the subtree is empty: when an offspring pointer is NIL.

▪ *Exam Preparation Exercises*

1. Recursion is an example of:
   a. selection.
   b. a data structure.
   c. repetition.
   d. data-flow programming.

2. A procedure can be recursive and a function cannot. (True or False?)

3. When a procedure is called recursively, the actual parameters and local variables of the calling version are saved until its execution is resumed. (True or False?)

4. Given the recursive formula $F(N) = -F(N - 2)$, with base case $F(0) = 1$, what are the values of $F(4)$ and $F(6)$? What is the value of $F(5)$?

5. When can one have infinite recursion?

6. What control structure appears most commonly in a recursive procedure?

7. If you develop a recursive algorithm that employs tail recursion, what should you consider?

8. A recursive algorithm depends on making something smaller. When the algorithm works on a data structure, what may become smaller?
   a. Distance from a position in the structure.
   b. The data structure.
   c. The number of variables in the recursive procedure.

9. What is the base case of a recursive procedure that traverses a binary tree?

10. What abstract data structure does Pascal use to save information for pending recursive calls of a procedure or function?

11. Given the input data

    ABCDE<eoln>

    what is the output for the following program?

```
PROGRAM Exercise_11 (Input, Output);
PROCEDURE Reverse;
VAR
  Ch:
    Char;
BEGIN (* Reverse *)
  IF NOT EOLN
    THEN
      BEGIN
        Read(Ch);
        Reverse;
        Write(Ch)
      END
END;  (* Reverse *)
BEGIN (* Exercise 11 *)
  Reverse
END.  (* Exercise 11 *)
```

12. Given the following input

```
15
23
21
19
```

what is the output for the following code?

```
PROGRAM Exercise_12 (Input, Output);
PROCEDURE Numbers;
VAR
  N:
    Integer;
BEGIN (* Numbers *)
  IF NOT EOF
    THEN
      BEGIN
        Readln(N);
        Write(N);
        Numbers;
        Write(N)
      END
END;  (* Numbers *)
BEGIN (* Exercise 12 *)
  Numbers
END.  (* Exercise 12 *)
```

■ *Programming Warm-Up Exercises*

1. Write a Pascal function that implements the recursive formula: F(N) = F(N − 1) + F(N − 2) with base cases F(0) = 1 and F(1) = 1.

2. Add whatever is necessary to fix the function below so that F(3) = 10.

```
FUNCTION F (N:
                 Integer):
                    Integer

BEGIN
  F := F(N - 1) + 3
END;
```

3. Rewrite procedure Line_Print without using recursion.

```
PROCEDURE Line_Print (In_File:
                                 Text);

VAR
  Charact:
     Char;

BEGIN (* Line_Print *)
  IF NOT EOF(In_File)
    THEN
      BEGIN
        IF NOT EOLN(In_File)
          THEN
            BEGIN
              Read(In_File, Charact);
              Write(Charact)
            END
          ELSE
            Writeln;
          Line_Print(In_File)
      END
END;   (* Line_Print *)
```

4. Rewrite procedure Square_Print using recursion.

```
PROCEDURE Square_Print;

VAR
  Count:
     Integer;
```

```
BEGIN
  FOR Count := 1 TO 10 DO
      Writeln(Count:6, Count * Count:6)
END;
```

5. Modify function Factorial of this chapter to print its parameter and returned value indented two spaces for each level of call to the function. The call Factorial(3) should produce the output:

```
3
  2
    1
      0
      1
    1
  2
6
```

6. Write a recursive procedure to print the nodes of a binary tree so that the components are printed after their children are printed.

7. Using the stack procedures of Chapter 16, write a recursive procedure that prints the contents of a stack bottom first and reconstructs it before returning control to the calling routine.

8. Write a recursive function that sums the integers from 1 to N.

9. Rewrite the following procedure so that it is recursive.

```
PROCEDURE Square_Root (N:
                            Integer);
VAR
  I:
    Integer;
BEGIN
  FOR I := N DOWNTO 1 DO
    Writeln(I, Sqrt(I):8:4);
END;
```

10. Given the following declarations:

```
TYPE
  Pointer = Node;
  Node = RECORD
            Info : Integer;
            Link : Ptr
          END; (* Record *)
VAR
  Head,
  Position:
    Ptr;
  Key:
    Integer;
```

write a recursive function that searches a linked list for the Integer variable Key. If the value is on the list, the function should return a pointer to it. If the value is not on the list, the function should return NIL.

▪ *Programming Problems*

1. Write a recursive palindrome checker (see Programming Problem 4, Chapter 16).

2. Write a program to place eight queens on a chessboard in such a way that no queen is attacking any other queen. This is a classic problem that lends itself to a recursive solution. The chessboard should be represented by an 8 × 8 Boolean array. If a square is occupied by a queen, the value is True. Otherwise, the square is False. The status of the chessboard when all eight queens have been placed is the solution.

3. A maze is to be represented by a 10 × 10 array of an enumerated data type composed of three values: Path, Hedge, and Exit. There is one exit from the maze. Write a program to determine if it is possible to exit the maze from a given starting point. You may move vertically or horizontally in any direction that contains Path; you may not move to a square that contains Hedge. If you move into a square that contains Exit, you have exited.

   The input data consists of two parts: the maze and a series of starting points. The maze is entered as ten lines of ten characters (P, H, and E). Each succeeding line contains a pair of integers that represents a starting point (that is, row and column numbers). Continue processing entry points until EOF.

4. Rewrite Program Sort_SAT_Scores (see Chapter 16) so that the scores are printed in reverse order; that is, the largest score is printed first. (Do not change the elements in the binary search tree.)

5. A group of soldiers is overwhelmed by an enemy force. Only one person can go for help because they have only one horse. To decide which soldier should go for help, they put their names in a helmet and put one slip of paper for each soldier with a number on it in another helmet. For example, if there are five soldiers, then the second helmet has pieces of paper with the numbers 1 to 5 each written on a separate slip.

   The soldiers arrange themselves in a circle and pull a name and a number from the helmets. Starting with the person whose name was pulled, they count off in a clockwise direction until they reach the number that was pulled. When the count stops, that soldier is eliminated from the circle. This continues until there is one soldier left—that soldier rides for help.

   Implement this process in Pascal. The names are stored on a file, and the last name on the file is followed by the word STOP. Use a circular linked list to represent the soliders, and use recursive procedures to count around the circle and to eliminate the soldiers. Output the total number of soldiers in the group and the name of the soldier who will go for help.

Graphics: Another Form of Output

CHAPTER 18

GOALS

- To be able to initialize graphics mode.
- To be able to plot points and draw lines on the screen.
- To be able to draw circles and arcs on the screen.
- To be able to draw and fill a shape on the screen.
- To be able to draw pie slices and bar graphs on the screen.
- To be able to write text on the screen.

All of the output we have seen so far has been in the form of text (numbers and words). Many computers provide a second means of displaying the results of computation: graphical output. There are many situations in which a graph, chart, or picture conveys information more meaningfully than does any table of words and numbers. Figure 18-1 provides an example of such a situation.

In this chapter we will examine the means provided by the Turbo Pascal Graph unit for displaying graphical output on the screen of a PC. Standard Pascal does not include any graphics capability, so the material in this chapter is valid only for Turbo Pascal. Also, this chapter covers the initial setup details only for the most common PC display systems. Although graphics can be displayed on other computer systems, each system has its own requirements for programs using graphics, and these requirements are likely to differ from those described in this chapter.

The Graphics Screen

When we output information with Write or Writeln, the data is displayed line by line on the screen of the computer. Because each character occupies the same amount of horizontal space on a line, the characters on the various lines align vertically in columns. Thus when we discussed the formatting of output, we described fieldwidths as occupying a certain number of columns on a line. A standard display screen allows 80 characters to be displayed on each line and will show up to 25 lines at once. We say therefore that the screen is 80 columns wide by 25 lines high. To plan the format of output, we can mark off on a piece of graph paper an area that is 80 squares across and 25 squares high and then design the appearance of the output within this area.

To plan graphical output for the screen, we use much the same technique. There are two important differences, however. First, the graphics screen has many more squares, each of which is much smaller than the space occupied by a character. Second, rather than writing a character in each of the squares, we place a single point in each square. The point may be black, white, or one of a variety of colors.

A typical graphics screen is 320 squares wide and 200 squares high. On a normal display screen, each of the squares is a little less than $\frac{1}{32}$ of an inch on each side. The number of rows and columns of squares on the screen is called the **resolution** of the display. The more squares that can be displayed, the greater the resolution. Higher resolution permits us to display finer lines and features on a screen. (See Figure 18-2.) The difference between low and high resolution is like the difference between drawing with a broad felt-tip marker and drawing with a fine ballpoint pen. A fine pen allows us to draw tiny details, but requires a lot more work when we must fill in large areas of a picture.

Resolution   The number of points that may be displayed on a screen, usually measured in terms of how many points will fit within the width and height of the screen.

Figure 18-1
*Tabular Versus
Graphical Output*

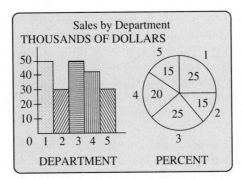

Figure 18-2
*The Difference
Between High- and
Low-Resolution
Graphics Screens*

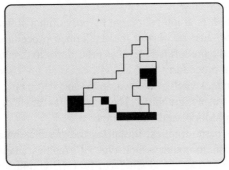

Low Resolution

High Resolution

The terms **horizontal resolution** and **vertical resolution** refer to the individual measurements of width and height, respectively. Each of the squares on the graphics screen is called a **picture element** or **pixel** for short. For example, we could describe a graphics screen as having a resolution of 320 by 200 pixels.

Pixel (picture element)   A square on a graphics screen that may contain one displayed point.

A particular graphics display will always have some maximum resolution, limiting the extent to which fine details can be displayed. It may, however, have other modes of operation in which it provides lower resolution. Usually a lower resolution display will provide some additional feature in exchange for the reduction in resolution. When Turbo Pascal is used with the IBM Color Graphics Adapter (CGA), we are allowed to choose one of five graphics modes. In the mode with the highest resolution, appropriately called CGAHi we can display black-and-white graphics with a resolution of 640 pixels across and 200 pixels up and down. If we choose one of the lower resolution modes, we gain the advantage of being able to draw in four different colors (these modes are called CGAC0, CGAC1, CGAC2, and CGAC3). Many other models of graphics adapter are supported by Turbo Pascal. While these are not covered in this chapter, all the commands to display graphics are essentially the same for every graphics adapter.

The screen can be in only one mode at a time. We cannot, therefore, use CGAHi mode in one portion of the screen and CGAC0 in another. Whenever a new graphics mode is selected, the screen is automatically wiped clear of anything that was previously displayed.

On a PC equipped with an IBM Color/Graphics Display (or an equivalent display screen), it is possible to use up to four colors in graphics mode. Graphical output is not included in Standard Pascal because of its dependence on the type of display screen attached to a computer. Unlike text output, graphics simply cannot be displayed in any standard way on every system.

Turbo Pascal supports graphical output by providing a collection of predefined procedure subprograms. Just as we use the predefined procedures Write and Writeln to output text, we use the predefined graphics procedures to display graphical output. The first set of graphics procedures that we will examine are used to initialize graphics, select a graphics mode, switch between graphics and text mode, and to tell the computer when we are done using graphics. The procedures are called InitGraph, Restore-CRTMode, SetGraphMode, and CloseGraph.

InitGraph, as its name implies, initializes the graphics hardware and software. Its function is to tell the computer which type of graphics adapter is being used, what graphics mode is to be used, and where to find the graphics software. To tell it this information, we pass three parameters to InitGraph. The first parameter is the name of the graphics adapter. Turbo Pascal predefines the names of many graphics adapters, but we will use CGA in all of our examples. If your system has another type of graphics adapter, you will have to look its name up in the system manuals and Turbo Pascal Library Reference. The second parameter is the name of a graphics mode, such as CGAHi, CGAC0, CGAC1, CGAC2, and CGAC3. These modes will be discussed below.

These first two parameters to InitGraph must be variables. Therefore, we will have to define two Integer variables and assign the adapter name and mode to them before calling InitGraph. The third parameter specifies where the graphics software is stored on disk. We use a null string (''), which selects the current disk directory. The parameter will be different if your system stores the graphics software somewhere else. Your instructor or system manuals should provide you with the correct parameter in such a case. The following is an example of how to set up a program to display graphics.

```
PROGRAM Graphics_Example (Output);
USES Graph;
VAR
   My_Adapter,
   My_Mode:
      Integer;

(* Other declarations *)
```

```
BEGIN (* Graphics_Example *)
  My_Adapter := CGA;
  My_Mode := CGACO;
  InitGraph(My_Adapter, My_Mode,");
  .
  .
  .
```

Once the graphics hardware and software have been initialized, we can switch back and forth between text and graphics modes using the procedures RestoreCRTMode and SetGraphMode. RestoreCRTMode does not take any parameters. SetGraphMode takes one parameter, which is one of the graphics mode names listed previously.

At the end of a program, or whenever the program is done displaying graphics, it is good practice to tell the computer to disable the graphics hardware and software. The procedure CloseGraph, which has no parameters, is used for this task. CloseGraph returns the screen to text mode. Once it is called, you must use InitGraph to reinitialize graphics before any additional graphical output can be displayed.

The following table summarizes these four procedures.

Procedure	Graphics/Text Mode
InitGraph	Initializes graphics
RestoreCRTMode	Selects text mode
SetGraphMode	Selects graphics mode
CloseGraph	Disables graphics

The CGA Adapter and Color Selection

When graphics are displayed on the screen in one of the CGA medium-resolution modes, it is necessary to specify the color that will be displayed. How do we specify a color? In Turbo Pascal, colors are specified by integers. Because of the way in which the PC displays colors, however, there's no simple correspondence between integers and colors. Thus, in some cases the color blue corresponds to the integer 1, but in other cases the integer 1 may represent a different color. To see why the color numbering scheme is complicated, we have to take a look at how the PC generates color graphics.

A PC may have up to 16 different colors available. Only four of those colors can be in use at any one time, however. The situation is like that of an artist who has many colors of paint to choose from but has room only for four colors on his or her palette. Just as the colors that the artist chooses make up the artist's palette of paints, the four colors that you choose from among the 16 possibilities make up the PC's palette.

There are four palettes to choose from. Each palette specifies three of the four colors, leaving the fourth color to be chosen by the user. The fourth color is the background color of the screen. The following table lists the four palettes that may be used with the CGA adapter.

One of these palettes is selected when we call the InitGraph or SetGraphMode procedure. The last digit of the mode name specifies the palette. For example, the statements

```
My_Adapter := CGA;
My_Mode := CGAC3;
InitGraph (My_Adapter, My_Mode);
```

		Color Number		
	0	1	2	3
Palette 0	Background	Light green	Light red	Yellow
Palette 1	Background	Light cyan	Light magenta	White
Palette 2	Background	Green	Red	Brown
Palette 3	Background	Cyan	Magenta	Light gray

select the palette in which color number 1 is cyan (blue-green), color number 2 is magenta (purple-red), and color number 3 is light gray. Color number 0, the background color of the screen, must be specified with a call to the predefined procedure Set-BkColor. The SetBkColor procedure has one parameter; it is the number of a background color. The following table lists the background colors that are available, along with their color numbers. Turbo Pascal provides predefined named constants whose names and values correspond to what is shown in the table. We will use these named constants in our examples to improve their readability.

Dark Colors		Light Colors	
Number	Color	Number	Color
0	Black	8	DarkGray
1	Blue	9	LightBlue
2	Green	10	LightGreen
3	Cyan	11	LightCyan
4	Red	12	LightRed
5	Magenta	13	LightMagenta
6	Brown	14	Yellow
7	LightGray	15	White

Some inexpensive display screens can display only the dark colors, listed in the left-hand column of the preceding table. On such screens, if you select one of the light colors as the background, its darker counterpart will appear; for example, DarkGray will appear as Black. In addition, on such screens Palette 2 will appear identical to Palette 0, and Palette 3 will appear the same as Palette 1. To be able to use all 16 background colors and all four palettes, you must have a display that is equivalent to the IBM Color/Graphics Display.

High Resolution Mode

The highest resolution CGA mode is called CGAHi. In this mode the resolution is 200 by 640 pixels and the screen displays only one color on a black background. The color is chosen by the SetBkColor procedure. For example, SetBkColor (Yellow) sets the display color to Yellow in CGAHi mode. If you have drawn something in Yellow and then change the drawing color to Red, all the previous drawing will become Red. There can be only one color on the screen at a given time in CGAHi mode.

Basic Graphics Operations

Creation of graphics output in Turbo Pascal involves changing the appearance of pixels on the screen. Initially all of the pixels are colored black, so nothing appears on the screen. We create a graphics display by changing some of these black pixels to another color so that dots, lines, circles, and so on appear on the screen. Turbo Pascal provides many operations for changing pixels. The most basic of these permit us to change a single pixel. Before we can discuss operations on pixels, however, we must look at the way in which we specify a point on the screen.

Screen Coordinates

Like a sheet of graph paper, the screen is divided up into many small squares, each of which is a single pixel. What we must do to change the color of pixels is to indicate to the computer which pixels are to be changed. We do this through the use of coordinates.

If we assign the rows and columns of the screen (graph paper) numbers (see Figure 18-3), we can specify the position of any pixel on the screen (square on the paper) by giving its row and column number. (The mechanism is similar to the one used in the game of Battleship, in which the players specify their shots by calling out row and column numbers.)

Coordinates in Turbo Pascal graphics are specified by integer numbers, starting with zero. The column number of a pixel is called its X coordinate, and the row number its Y coordinate. In CGAHi mode, the X coordinates range from 0 through 639. In the CGAC0, CGAC1, CGAC2, and CGAC3 modes, the X coordinates range from 0 through 319. In all CGA modes, the Y coordinates range from 0 to 199. The upper left corner of the screen has the coordinates X = 0, Y = 0. When specifying coordinates, you always give the X coordinate first. If you specify a coordinate value that is outside of the screen area, it is simply ignored.

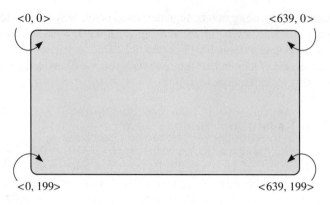

Figure 18-3
Display Screen
Coordinates in
CGAHi Mode

Plotting Individual Points on the Screen

The simplest graphics operation is to specify a new color for a single pixel on the screen. Turbo Pascal provides a predefined procedure, called PutPixel, that allows us to do this. The syntax of PutPixel requires three parameters:

```
PutPixel(X, Y, Color)
```

The first two parameters are the X and Y coordinates of a single pixel on the screen. The third parameter specifies the color to which the pixel will be changed. For now, we consider only CGAHi mode, which has just one color. In CGAHi mode, the color parameter is simply 1. (A little later in this section we will take a detailed look at how colors are specified in the other graphics modes.)

Here is an example of a call to the PutPixel procedure:

```
PutPixel(450, 76, 1);
```

This call will cause a single point to appear on the screen at a location that is 450 pixels to the right of the left edge of the screen and 76 pixels down from the top.

Selecting Drawing Colors in CGA Modes

Earlier, we described the way to initialize graphics and select a graphics mode and its corresponding palette. When we used the PutPixel procedure above, we specified what color the pixel should be with the number 1. The 1 could signify Yellow, Blue, Red, or any other CGA color, depending on the last call to the SetBkColor procedure. Generally, when a figure is placed on the screen, its color is specified in terms of the palette, not the actual color. There are two colors in the CGAHi mode palette, 0 and 1; 0 specifies the black background color and 1 specifies the color chosen with SetBkColor. In the medium resolution modes, there are four colors available, the three preset colors (1, 2, and 3) of the palette chosen with InitGraph or SetGraphMode and the background color (0) specified with SetBkColor. While PutPixel allows you to directly specify the color of the pixel, the following procedures use the "current" drawing color, which is chosen with the SetColor procedure. Like PutPixel, SetColor uses a palette color number, not the actual color, to specify a color. Because the palette color numbers are not very meaningful, you may want to declare constants to clarify what color is being used. For example,

```
CONST
  Pl_Cyan = 1;
  .
  .
  .
SetGraphMode(CGAC1);
SetColor(Pl_Cyan);
```

is more meaningful than just

```
SetGraphMode(CGAC1);
SetColor(1);
```

In the examples in this chapter we will declare constants for each of the palette colors used.

Drawing a Line on the Screen

Lines are simply collections of adjacent points, so we could draw a line on the screen by making many calls to PutPixel. This approach, however, would be very tedious. Because we frequently wish to display lines, Turbo Pascal provides another predefined procedure, called Line, that draws a line between any two specified points on the screen using the current color. The Line procedure has four parameters. The first two are the coordinates of one end point and the second two are the coordinates of the other end point. The line that is drawn will include the two end-point pixels.

Here is an example call to procedure Line that will cause a line to be drawn diagonally across the screen in CGAHi mode (see Figure 18.4).

```
Line(0, 0, 639, 199)
```

Figure 18-4
Display Screen After Execution of Sample Call Procedure Line

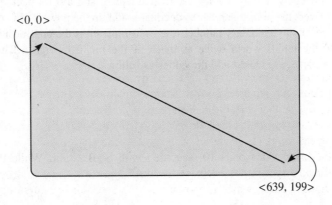

<0, 0>

<639, 199>

Line Style

Turbo Pascal also has the capability of controlling the appearance of any drawn lines by calling the SetLineStyle procedure. There are three parameters to the SetLineStyle procedure:

```
SetLineStyle(Style, Pattern, Width)
```

There are five predefined constants that can be used to specify a style; the first four are SolidLn (the default when SetLineStyle has not been called), DottedLn, CenterLn, and DashedLn. They produce the following lines.

SolidLn

————————————————————————

DottedLn

• •

CenterLn

— · — · — · — · — · — · — · — · — ·

DashedLn

— — — — — — — — — — — —

The fifth line style constant is UserBitLn. It produces a line according to the value of the Pattern parameter (when any of the other line styles are specified, the Pattern parameter is ignored). The Pattern parameter is an integer of type Word whose binary representation corresponds to a series of 16 pixels that are repeated to form a line. For example, if you specify a style of UserBitLn with a Pattern of 61839, the equivalent binary number is 1111000110001111, and the resulting line will look like this:

— · —— · — · —— · —— · —— · — —

The approach to take when using UserBitLn is to draw a pattern on graph paper that is 1 square wide and 16 squares long. Then, repeat the pattern several times to be sure that it results in the desired line style. Next, convert the pattern to a 16-bit binary number by writing a 1 for each filled square and a 0 for each empty square. Finally, convert the binary number to decimal—add up the powers of two corresponding to the one-bits in the binary number (the right-most bit is the ones position, and each position to the left is worth twice as much as the bit to its right). Thus, for the preceding example, we would add up values as follows:

Figure 18-5
Rectangle Example

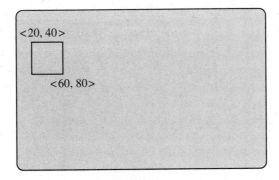

it will draw the following lines (See Figure 18-5):

```
Line(20, 40, 20, 80);
Line(20, 80, 60, 80);
Line(60, 80, 60, 40);
Line(60, 40, 20, 40);
```

Circles, Arcs, and Ellipses

Three procedures in Turbo Pascal's Graph unit produce curved figures: Circle, Arc, and Ellipse. These procedures use the current drawing color and the current line width. However, all curved figure procedures produce solid lines regardless of the current line style. The Circle procedure requires three parameters. The first two are the coordinates of the center of the circle, and the third is its radius in pixels.

If we are in CGAC3 mode and have set the drawing color to 3, then the statement

```
Circle(159, 99, 50);
```

will draw a cyan circle with a radius of 50 pixels in the center of the screen, as shown in Figure 18-6. To draw a portion of a circle instead of a whole circle, we use a procedure called Arc. There are five parameters for the Arc procedure:

```
Arc(X, Y, StartAngle, EndAngle, Radius);
```

The first two parameters are the coordinates of the center of the arc. The third and fourth parameters are the beginning and ending angles of the arc, where 0 degrees is directly to the right (along the X axis), and the angles increase in a counterclockwise fashion (90 degrees would be straight up, −90 degrees would be down, etc.) Whether the starting and ending angles are positive or negative, the sweep of the arc is always counterclockwise. The Radius parameter is the distance between the arc and its center. If we have selected CGAC3 mode and set the drawing color to 3, then the statements

```
Arc( 50, 100,  0,  90, 50);
Arc(250, 100, 90, 180, 50);
```

Figure 18-6
Output from the
Circle Procedure
Example

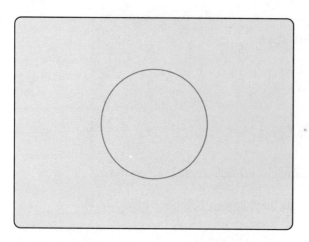

Figure 18-7
Example of Calling
the Arc Procedure

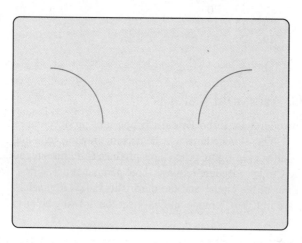

will produce the display shown in Figure 18-7. The first statement produces the left arc, the second produces the right arc.

The third curved figure that can be drawn with the Turbo Pascal Graph unit procedures is an elliptical arc. The procedure Ellipse draws an arc much like the Arc procedure, except that the arc is part of an ellipse, not a circle. There are six parameters for the Ellipse procedure:

```
Ellipse(X, Y, StartAngle, EndAngle, XRadius, YRadius);
```

As with the Arc procedure, the first two parameters are the coordinates of the center of the elliptical arc. The third and fourth parameters are the beginning and ending angles of the arc. To produce a complete ellipse, use zero for both the starting and ending angles. Unlike the Arc procedure, Ellipse has two radius parameters; XRadius and YRadius. These parameters determine the width and height of the ellipse. Because they are radii, the actual size of the ellipse will be double their values. If we are in CGAC3 mode and have set the drawing color to 3, then the statement

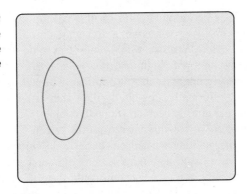

Figure 18-8
Output from the
Ellipse Procedure
Example

```
Ellipse(80, 100, 0, 0, 25, 50);
```

will produce the display shown in Figure 18-8.

Filling Shapes

So far, all of the drawing operations we have looked at have produced outlined figures, much like those in a child's coloring book. There are many instances in which we would like to fill shapes on the screen with color because filled shapes are often easier to see than outlined shapes. Turbo Pascal allows us to do this with the procedures called FloodFill and FillEllipse.

Just as in a child's coloring book, the area to be filled must first be outlined on the screen. The FloodFill procedure then acts as a command to color in an outlined area. FloodFill has three parameters:

```
FloodFill(XCoord, YCoord, BorderColor);
```

The first two parameters are the coordinates of any point within the region to be filled. When FloodFill colors an area, it begins by coloring the pixel defined by these coordinates. It then colors all of the pixels around that pixel, then all of the pixels around those, and so on, until all of the pixels within the border have been colored. The color thus appears to start at one point and grow outward from it on the screen. The third parameter is the color of the outline that is to be filled.

It is important to note that the outline must be a closed figure—there can be no gaps in the outline. Otherwise, the color will spill over and fill everything outside of the figure as well. The outline must also be entirely of the specified border color, because FloodFill will color over everything within the outline that is of another color. Thus, if part of the outline is of a color other than the specified border color, that part will be treated just like a gap in the outline. (FillEllipse is discussed later in this chapter.)

Filling the Screen with a Color

Suppose a problem requires that output be displayed in brown, cyan, and magenta against a light gray background. The palette that is closest to this combination is Palette

3. Light gray is not the background color for this palette, however—it is one of the drawing colors. Conversely, brown is not a drawing color, although we could choose it as the background color. What we would really like to do in this case is to reverse the roles of brown and light gray in the palette.

Let's consider how we might do this. Turbo Pascal allows us to draw figures using the background color. Normally, this ability is of little use except when we wish to erase something that has already been drawn on the screen. (If we draw over something using the background color, it will vanish from the screen.) So it is possible to draw in brown—it's just that nothing will appear because the screen is already filled with brown. What if we were to fill the entire screen with another color? That is, what if we set every pixel to light gray? The screen would then be entirely light gray, and if we were to draw with brown, the brown figures would appear against the light gray background. This is our solution: we have to fill the screen with one of the drawing colors from our palette, and then we can use the background color as if it were a drawing color.

How do we fill the screen with a color? We could draw 200 horizontal lines across the screen, but that would be very tedious. Instead, we write the following statements (after the palette has been selected and before any figures have been drawn):

```
SetBkColor(Brown);
SetColor(3);
FloodFill(1, 2, 2);
```

The screen then would be colored light gray, and our color selection would be brown (0), cyan (1), and magenta (2).

There are times when it is useful to fill an area with a colored pattern of pixels, rather than a solid color. For example, if you were drawing a picture of a house on the screen, you might like the wall of the house to resemble bricks. Rather than fill the wall area with solid red, you would fill it with a pattern of red pixels that resembles bricks.

Filling with Patterns

Just as the Graph unit provides procedures to choose a line style and drawing color, there are procedures to choose a fill pattern and color: SetFillStyle and SetFillPattern. SetFillStyle has two parameters. The first parameter specifies 1 of 12 predefined fill patterns or UserFill,which is discussed below. The predefined patterns are shown in the following table.

Pattern Name (predefined constant)	Pattern
EmptyFill	Fills area with background color
SolidFill	Fills area with specified color
LineFill	Fills area with horizontal lines
LtSlashFill	Fills area with / / / /
SlashFill	Fills area with ⁄⁄⁄⁄
BkSlashFill	Fills area with ＼＼＼
LtBkSlashFill	Fills area with \ \ \ \
HatchFill	Fills area with ＃＃＃
XHatchFill	Fills area with ＸＸＸＸ
InterleaveFill	Fills area with ▰▰▰▰
WideDotFill	Fills area with · : · : · :
CloseDotFill	Fills area with ⫶⫶⫶⫶⫶⫶
UserFill	Pattern defined with SetFillPattern

In the house drawing example, you might choose the InterleaveFill pattern to represent the bricks. The second parameter specifies the color of the fill (unless UserFill is selected, in which case the color is ignored). If you use any of the fill procedures (such as FloodFill) before calling SetFillStyle, the pattern is automatically SolidFill and the color is the last one in the palette (color number 3 in the CGAC0, CGAC1, CGAC2, and CGAC3 palettes). The remainder of this section requires the use of arrays. If you are studying graphics prior to reading Chapter 11, you should skip ahead to the section entitled Filled Ellipses.

The SetFillPattern procedure is used to create a user-defined pattern, which is used whenever UserFill is specified in the call to SetFillStyle. SetFillPattern has two parameters. The second parameter specifies the palette color in which the pattern will be drawn. The first parameter is of the type FillPatternType (predefined by the Graph unit), which is ARRAY [1..8] OF Byte. This array will hold an 8-by-8 block of pixels. How do we fit 64 pixels into an array with only 8 elements? Recall from Chapter 1 that computers work with binary digits, called bits. Each bit can represent either a 1 or a 0. A byte is a collection of 8 bits. Therefore an array of 8 bytes contains 64 bits. Each bit in the pattern array will represent one pixel in the 8-by-8 block. The first element of the array will contain the 8 bits that make up the top row of pixels in the pattern; the second element will contain the second row of pixels; and so on.

How do we fill this array? One way would be to convert the binary pattern of pixels into a set of eight integer values and store them into the array of eight bytes. This process is time consuming and results in a program that is full of odd-looking integer values. We will use a better, self-documenting method.

Each bit in a byte has a corresponding integer value. If we add up the values of the bits in a row of the pattern, we get a value that can be stored in an element of the pattern array. We will define constants to represent each bit in a byte.

```
CONST
  B7 = 128; (* Left-most bit in a byte *)
  B6 = 64;
  B5 = 32;
  B4 = 16;
  B3 =  8;
  B2 =  4;
  B1 =  2;
  B0 =  1; (* Right-most bit in a byte *)
```

We can now create the appropriate value simply by adding together the constants for the bits that we want to set to 1 in a row of the pattern array. For example, suppose we wish to create our own brick pattern; then given the definitions

```
VAR
  BrickPattern:            (* Holds a block of pixels *)
    FillPatternType;
```

if we wanted to create the brick-like pattern

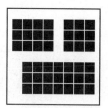

we would write the following code segment:

```
BrickPattern[1] := 0;                         (*            *)
BrickPattern[2] := B7+B6+B5+B4+  B2+B1+B0;    (* #### ### *)
BrickPattern[3] := B7+B6+B5+B4+  B2+B1+B0;    (* #### ### *)
BrickPattern[4] := B7+B6+B5+B4+  B2+B1+B0;    (* #### ### *)
BrickPattern[5] := 0                          (*            *)
BrickPattern[6] :=    B6+B5+B4+B3+B2+B1+B0;    (*  ####### *)
BrickPattern[7] :=    B6+B5+B4+B3+B2+B1+B0;    (*  ####### *)
BrickPattern[8] :=    B6+B5+B4+B3+B2+B1+B0;    (*  ####### *)
```

As you can see, once the bit constants have been defined, creating a pattern is quite easy. It is simply a matter of writing eight assignment statements that include the constants for the pixels that are to be colored and omit the ones that are to be left blank. If the expressions are formatted as shown above, then the pattern will be visible in the code. To display a 100-pixel-by-80-pixel red brick wall in the center of a white screen, we would write

```
SetFillStyle(UserFill, 0);
SetFillPattern(BrickPattern, 2);
SetColor(2);
Rectangle(110, 60, 209, 139);
FloodFill(111, 61, 2);
```

When you decide to create a pattern, you should first draw the pattern by filling in squares on a sheet of graph paper. Mark off a section of the paper that is 8 by 8 squares, and draw the pattern within this section. Keep in mind that when a fill procedure draws the pattern on the screen, it will surround this square with exact copies of it. You may want to do this yourself, on the graph paper, just to see how the pattern will appear on the screen.

Filled Ellipses

In addition to the FloodFill procedure, which fills an existing shape, the Graph unit also provides the procedure FillEllipse, which draws a filled ellipse. The FillEllipse procedure has four parameters:

```
FillEllipse(X, Y, XRadius, YRadius);
```

As with the Ellipse procedure, the first two parameters are the coordinates of the center of the ellipse. Unlike the Ellipse procedure, there is no starting angle or ending angle— a complete ellipse is always drawn. The third and fourth parameters equal half of the ellipse's diameter along the X and Y axes. FillEllipse first draws a complete ellipse according to the line style specified by the most recent call to SetLineStyle, then fills the ellipse according to the pattern selected by the most recent call to SetFillStyle.

Bar and Pie Charts

The Graph unit also provides four procedures that can be used to display numeric data graphically. These procedures, PieSlice, Sector, Bar, and Bar3D, are similar to the procedures we have seen before.

Procedure PieSlice draws a filled wedge, bounded by a circular arc with lines from the center of the arc to each end of the arc, then fills the bounded area. PieSlice can be used to draw the individual sections of a pie chart, as shown in Figure 18-9. The lines are drawn according to the current line style settings and fill pattern. As with the Arc procedure, there are five parameters for the PieSlice procedure:

```
PieSlice(X, Y, StartAngle, EndAngle, Radius);
```

The first two parameters are the arc's center coordinates. The remaining three parameters are the beginning and ending angles of the arc, and the distance from the arc to its center.

Procedure Sector is like PieSlice, except that it draws an elliptical arc. There are six parameters for the Sector procedure:

Figure 18-9
A Pie Chart Drawn
with Five Calls to
Procedure PieSlice

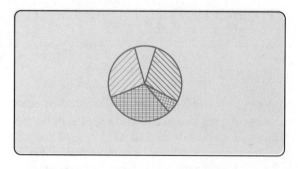

Figure 18-10
Bar Example

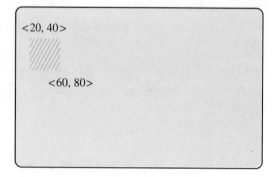

```
Sector(X, Y, StartAngle, EndAngle, XRadius, YRadius);
```

The first two parameters are the coordinates of the center of the elliptical arc. The third and fourth parameters are the beginning and ending angles of the arc, and the fifth and sixth parameters are equal to half the diameter of the ellipse along the X and Y axes.

The other two procedures for displaying numerical data are Bar and Bar3D. Procedure Bar is similar to Procedure Rectangle but instead of an empty outline of a rectangle, a filled rectangular area with no outline is produced. Procedure Bar has four parameters: the coordinates of two pixels, which define the opposite corners of the rectangle. For example, if the current fill pattern is LtSlashFill and you write a call to Bar as:

```
Bar(20, 40, 60, 80)
```

it will produce a filled area as shown in Figure 18-10.

The Bar3D procedure also fills an area but puts it within an outline and optionally adds the appearance of depth. Bar3D has six parameters:

```
Bar3D(X0, Y0, X1, Y1, Depth, Top)
```

Like the Bar procedure, X0, Y0, X1, and Y1 are the coordinates of opposite corners of the face of the bar. The Depth parameter specifies the width in pixels of the side of the bar (see Figure 18-11). The last parameter, Top, is a Boolean value that specifies

Figure 18-11   *Examples of Bar and Bar3D Output*

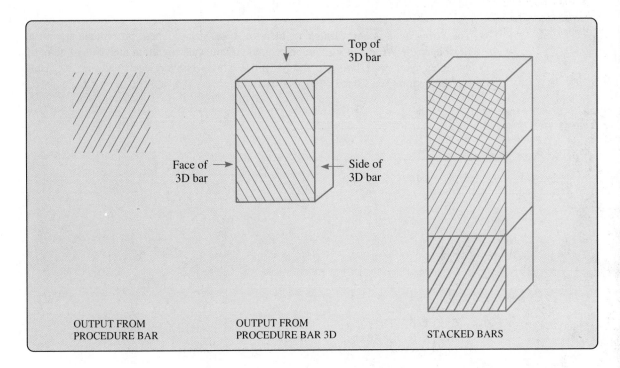

Top of
3D bar

Face of
3D bar

Side of
3D bar

OUTPUT FROM
PROCEDURE BAR

OUTPUT FROM
PROCEDURE BAR 3D

STACKED BARS

whether the 3-D (three-dimensional) bar should have a top drawn on it (See Figure 18-11). The last parameter is normally True unless you are stacking bars as shown in Figure 18-11. Note that only the fronts of the bars are filled; the sides are outlined without filling the areas they enclose.

Combining Text and Graphics

Often it is useful to be able to label some part of a graphics figure with a message. For example, if the display shows a graph of sales performance, then we might want to label the horizontal axis with month names and the vertical axis with dollar amounts. Turbo Pascal allows us to combine text output with graphics to achieve such results.

Everything we've printed so far has begun at the left edge of the screen. When printing text with graphics, we want to be able to position the text near whatever part of the figure it will label. The Graph unit provides two procedures for putting text on a graphics mode screen: OutText and OutTextXY. OutText puts text onto the screen according to the current position. OutTextXY positions text according to coordinates in its parameter list. These procedures are so similar, we will discuss them together. The parameters are shown in the following example calls:

```
OutText(StringValue)
OutTextXY(X, Y, StringValue)
```

The StringValue is any variable or literal of type String. These procedures are not as flexible as the Write and Writeln procedures; if you want to output the value of numeric variables, you must first use the Str procedure to convert each value to its string representation (See Chapter 12). For example,

```
VAR
  X:
    Real;
  I:
    Integer;
  IStr,
  XStr:
    String[10];

BEGIN
    .
    .
  I := 12;
  X := 1.555;
  Str(I:3, IStr);
  Str(X:8:1, XStr);
  OutText('I is ' + IStr + '; X is ' + XStr)
```

would print 'I is 12; X is 1.6'. The string is printed below and to the right of the specified location. If OutText is used, the specified location is the current position; OutText also changes the current position to be at the end of whatever is printed. If OutTextXY is used, then the X and Y parameters specify the graphic coordinates of the upper left corner of the first character to be displayed.

Positioning a message near a figure requires some careful planning. You must consider the height and width of the message. If you would like to center a message with respect to a point A, you must start printing at a point B that is half the height of the message above and half the width of the message to the left of point A. To aid in the placement of the string, the Graph unit provides two functions, TextHeight and TextWidth. These functions each take a string as a parameter. TextHeight returns an integer that is the height of the tallest character of the string in pixels; TextWidth returns the number of pixels from the leading edge of the first character to the trailing edge of the last character in the string.

For example, suppose we wanted to write 'Centered Triangle' centered below the base of a triangle drawn on the screen. The base of the triangle is 50 pixels below the center of the screen at absolute coordinates of <159, 149>. We will provide for some space above the message by adding five pixels to get a Y coordinate of 154. The X coordinate will be 159 minus half of the length of the message. Here is the program fragment that will accomplish the task.

```
Message := 'Centered Triangle';
OutTextXY(159 - (TextWidth(Message) DIV 2), 154, Message);
```

As another example, the following fragment will print the current position coordinates centered at the current position using OutTextXY (note that the current position is moved by this code).

```
Str(GetX:1, XStr);        (* Convert the X location to a string *)
Str(GetY:1, YStr);        (* Convert the Y location to a string *)
AllStr := '<' + XStr + ',' + YStr + '>';
MoveRel(-(TextWidth(AllStr) DIV 2), -(TextHeight(AllStr) DIV 2));
OutText(AllStr);
```

If you try to display a message outside the boundaries of the screen, it will not appear. There is one more useful procedure for outputting text in graphics mode, which we will cover very briefly. It allows you to change the font (character style), direction, and size of messages printed with OutText and OutTextXY. The procedure SetTextStyle has the following parameters:

```
SetTextStyle(Font, Direction, Size);
```

Font is either the value DefaultFont or one of the other predefined fonts: TripleXFont, SmallFont, SansSerifFont, or GothicFont. Direction is either HorizDir (left to right) or VertDir (turned counterclockwise 90 degrees, bottom to top). Size specifies a factor by which the standard character sizes are multiplied; a size of 4 is twice as large as a size of 2. The normal values for Size are 1 for DefaultFont and 4 for the other fonts.

PROBLEM-SOLVING CASE STUDY

Triangle

Problem: Write a program that will draw a triangle on the screen. The triangle should be 101 pixels tall and 121 pixels wide at the base, and it should be centered on the screen. The base of the triangle should be colored light gray, the right side should be magenta, and the left side should be cyan. The background color should be brown.

Output: A graphics screen with a triangle displayed as described in the preceding paragraph.

Algorithm: If you were to do this by hand, you would begin by taking a sheet of graph paper and marking off the center of the paper. You would then mark a spot 50 squares above the center and another 50 squares below, to establish the centered height of the triangle. For the base, you would draw a 121-square-long horizontal line, starting sixty squares to the right of the lower mark. For the sides of the triangle, you would then draw lines running from the ends of the base to the point that marks the top of the triangle.

The only way to specify a line for the computer, however, is to give the coordinates of its end points. We can use our by-hand algorithm to determine these coordinates. Because the size of the color graphics screen is 320 by 200 pixels, the center of the screen is at coordinates <159, 99>. The top of the triangle will thus be 50 pixels above this point, at the coordinates <159, 49>. The midpoint of the base of the triangle will be 50 pixels below the center of the screen, at <159, 149>. The ends of the base line will be 60 pixels on either side of this point, at <99, 149> and <219, 149>. Notice that when a horizontal line is drawn, only the X coordinate changes. The following figure shows the triangle, with the coordinates and dimensions indicated.

Figure 18-12
Drawing a Triangle

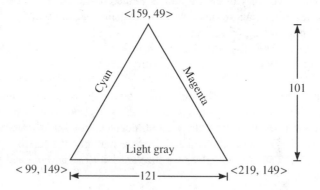

Now that we have the end points for each of the three lines, we are almost ready to write the algorithm. We have only to determine how to color the triangle. Looking at the various color palette tables, we can see that CGAC3 mode will provide the required set of colors. We are now ready to write the algorithm.

```
Initialize graphics mode
Set background color to brown
Set the drawing color to light gray (color number 3)
Draw the base (<99, 149> to <219, 149>)
Set the drawing color to magenta (color number 2)
Draw the right side (<159, 49>, to <219, 149>)
Set the drawing color to cyan (color number 1)
Draw the left side (159, 149> to <99, 149>)
Pause to allow viewing of the display
Turn off graphics mode
```

PROBLEM-SOLVING CASE STUDY *cont'd.*

We have seen how to carry out all but one of these steps. How do we make the computer pause? Turbo Pascal's Crt unit provides a procedure called Delay that can be used to pause in a program. Delay has one parameter—an Integer value specifying the length of time the machine will pause, in thousandths of a second, (milliseconds). Thus to make the machine pause for ten seconds, we would write

```
Delay(10000);
```

This program will need two Integer variables for InitGraph (My_Adapter and My_Mode). To improve readability, we will use several named constants.

Name	Value	Function
P1_Light_Gray	3	Color number
P1_Magenta	2	Color number
P1_Cyan	1	Color number
Ten_Seconds	10000	Ten-second delay time in milliseconds

Now we are ready to write the program. We'll call it TriGraph.

```
PROGRAM TriGraph(Input, Output);

(* This program draws a triangle in the center of the screen, using   *)
(* three colors in Turbo Pascal CGAC3 graphics mode.  The triangle is *)
(* 101 pixels high by 121 pixels wide.                                 *)

USES
   Graph,                    (* Contains the graphics procedures    *)
   CRT;                      (* Contains the Delay procedure        *)

CONST
   P1_Light_Gray = 3;        (* Color number                        *)
   P1_Magenta    = 2;        (* Color number                        *)
   P1_Cyan       = 1;        (* Color number                        *)
   Ten_Seconds   = 10000;    (* Ten-second delay time in milliseconds *)

VAR
   My_Adapter,
   My_Mode:
      Integer;
```

PROBLEM-SOLVING CASE STUDY cont'd.

```
BEGIN   (* TriGraph *)
  My_Adapter := CGA;
  My_Mode := CGAC3;
  InitGraph(My_Adapter, My_Mode, '');
  SetBkColor(Brown);
  SetColor(Pl_Light_Gray);
  Line(99, 149, 219, 149);
  SetColor(Pl_Magenta);
  Line(159, 49, 219, 149);
  SetColor(Pl_Cyan);
  Line(159, 49, 99, 149);
  Delay(Ten_Seconds);
  CloseGraph
END. (* TriGraph *)
```

Testing and Debugging: This program is very straightforward. The most likely place for bugs is our calculation of the coordinates for the line end points. The program should be run and the resulting display checked visually to determine whether the triangle is drawn correctly.

PROBLEM-SOLVING CASE STUDY

Triangle, the Sequel

Problem: Draw the triangle of the previous case study with the current position relative commands. Also, use SetLineStyle to draw thick, easy-to-see lines.

Algorithm: Another way to draw a triangle by hand is to begin by taking a sheet of graph paper and marking the center of the paper. You then mark a spot 50 squares above the center; this is the top of the triangle. Count 60 squares to the right and 100 squares down from the top corner of the triangle and mark a spot; then draw a line from the top to this second spot. The third corner of the triangle is 120 squares to the left of the second; so you draw a line of that length to the left. Finally, from the end of the second line you draw a line to the starting point.

A similar method can be used to draw the triangle in Turbo Pascal using the relative position drawing procedures. We do need to calculate the coordinates of the starting point. The center of the screen is <159, 99>; the top of the triangle will thus be 50 pixels above the center at coordinates <159, 49>.

Now we can draw a line from the top of the triangle to a point 60 pixels to the right and 100 pixels down. From there we draw a line 120 pixels to the left. Finally we draw a line back to <159, 49>. Again we use Palette 3 (mode CGAC3) to provide the required set of colors.

We are now ready to write the algorithm.

Initialize graphics mode
Set background color to brown
Set palette to cyan/magenta/light gray (palette number 3)
Set the current position to the top of the triangle at <159, 49>
Set the drawing color to magenta (color number 2)
Draw the right side from the current position + 60 in the X direction, + 100 in
   the Y
Set the drawing color to light gray (color number 3)
Draw the base from the current position − 120 in the X direction
Set the drawing color to cyan (color number 1)
Draw the left side from the current position to the top at <159, 49>
Pause to allow viewing of the display
Turn off graphics mode at the end of the program

Here is the program TriGraph2.

```
Program TriGraph2(Input, Output);

(* This program draws a triangle in the center of the screen, using  *)
(* three colors in Turbo Pascal CGAC3 graphics mode. The triangle is *)
(* 101 pixels high by 121 pixels wide.                               *)

USES
   Graph,                 (* Contains the graphics procedures     *)
   CRT;                   (* Contains the Delay procedure         *)

CONST
   Pl_Light_Gray = 3;     (* Color number                         *)
   Pl_Magenta    = 2;     (* Color number                         *)
   Pl_Cyan       = 1;     (* Color number                         *)
   Ten_Seconds   = 10000; (* Ten-second delay time in milliseconds *)

VAR
   My_Adapter,
   My_Mode:
      Integer;
```

```
BEGIN    (* TriGraph2 *)
  My_Adapter := CGA;
  My_Mode := CGAC3;
  InitGraph(My_Adapter, My_Mode, '');
  SetBkColor(Brown);
  MoveTo(159, 49);
  SetColor(Pl_Magenta);
  LineRel(60, 100);            (* Draw right side *)
  SetColor(Pl_Light_Gray);
  LineRel(-120, 0);            (* Draw bottom     *)
  SetColor(Pl_Cyan);
  LineTo(159, 49);             (* Draw left side  *)
  Delay(Ten_Seconds);
  CloseGraph
END. (* TriGraph2 *)
```

Summary

Graphical output is an alternative to printed text as a means of displaying the results of computation. There are situations in which graphical output is more appropriate and more meaningful than printed text. Many computer systems have the capacity to provide this second form of output, including many personal computers. By providing a set of graphics output operations, Turbo Pascal allows us to take advantage of the graphics capability of the PC.

The graphics screen may be envisioned as a sheet of graph paper, with rows and columns of empty squares. We can draw on the screen by selectively filling in these squares, which are called pixels. The number of rows and columns of pixels determines the resolution of the graphics screen. The PC Color Graphics Adapter provides two different resolutions: 320 horizontal by 200 vertical, and 640 horizontal by 200 vertical. The latter, called high resolution graphics, permits us to draw in one color against a black background. The other level of resolution, called medium resolution graphics, allows us to draw in three colors against a background that is chosen from a set of 16 colors. The group of colors used for drawing constitutes a palette. The CGAC0, CGAC1, CGAC2, and CGAC3 modes provide four palettes to choose from. If a PC is not equipped with an IBM Color/Graphics Display or its equivalent, then only eight of the background colors and two of the palettes may be displayed. Of course, if the PC has a black-and-white display screen, then no colors may be displayed.

Turbo Pascal implements some graphics operations by providing a set of predefined, nonstandard procedure subprograms in its Graph unit. These subprograms permit us to choose a graphics mode, palette, and background color. This set of procedures also allows us to draw points, lines, circles, and arcs and fill figures with color. The graphics operations are available only in Turbo Pascal, not in Standard Pascal. In other systems that provide graphics, the operations are carried out differently.

Turbo Pascal also provides a set of standard procedures that allow us to display text on the screen along with graphical output. These operations allow us to label a figure so as to make it more meaningful to the user. The FloodFill procedure is used to fill a bounded area of the screen with a pattern of pixels that is specified by an array of 8 bytes in SetPattern or SetFillStyle.

■ *Quick Check*

1. What graphics mode would be appropriate for a complicated black-and-white figure with many tiny details? (pp. 858–861)

2. Which procedures are used to draw points and lines? (pp. 863–868)

3. Where are the Circle and Arc procedures predefined? (pp. 868–871)

4. The FloodFill routine requires that a pair of coordinates and a color be given as parameters. What purpose does each of these parameters serve? (pp. 871–875)

5. How is a line drawn with LineRel? (pp. 863–868)

6. What are the differences between the LineTo and the LineRel procedures? (pp. 863–868)

7. What are the differences between the Arc and PieSlice procedures? (pp. 868–877)

Answers

1. CGAHi mode   2. PutPixel, Line, LineTo, and LineRel   3. In the Graph unit, which must be accessed by a USES statement   4. The coordinates specify a point within the figure to be filled. The color parameter is the color of the outline that is to be filled.   5. LineRel draws a line from the current position to another point. The two parameters to LineRel specify the X and Y distances from the current position to that point.   6. Both the LineTo and LineRel procedures draw a line from the current position to another point. The LineTo parameters specify the coordinates of that second point; the LineRel parameters specify the X and Y distances from the current position to that point.   7. The PieSlice procedure draws an arc just as the Arc procedure but adds lines from the center of the arc to its endpoints and then fills the bounded area.

■ *Exam Preparation Exercises*

1. Define the following terms:

   pixel
   resolution
   palette
   background color
   absolute-position graphics
   current-position relative graphics

2. What is the resolution of the screen in each of the five graphics modes supported by the CGA adapter?

3. A certain problem requires that a traffic light be drawn on the screen against a brown background. What graphics mode would you select? What palette would you choose? How would you color the background brown?

4. When the FloodFill procedure is called, what happens if the figure to be filled has a break in its outline?

5. How many colors may be displayed at one time in medium resolution using the CGA adapter? How many colors are there to choose from?

6. Current-position relative graphics, absolute-position graphics, and text may all be displayed on the screen at the same time. (True or False?)

7. All current-position relative figures are relative to what was previously drawn. There is no way to move the current position directly to a given coordinate position on the screen. (True or False?)

8. Since red appears only on one of the CGA palettes, the numeric code for red will always be the same. (True or False?)

9. Turbo Pascal offers standard procedures to switch between text mode and graphics mode without reinitializing graphics. (True or False)?

■ *Programming Warm-Up Exercises*

1. Write a series of four Line statements that will draw a square, with sides that are 100 pixels long, centered on the screen. The square should be magenta against a blue background. Assume that the screen already has been set to CGAC3 mode and the background color has been selected.

2. Write a code fragment that will set the screen to CGAHi mode and select blue as the drawing color. Draw the X and Y axes of a graph that is 150 pixels high and 500 pixels wide. Then draw lines connecting the series of points given by the coordinates <0, 50>, <100, 75>, <200, 40>, <300, 60>, <400, 90>, and <500, 120>. Center the message 'Five Year Stock Price Summary', below the graph.

3. Write a single statement that will fill the figure described in exercise 1 with cyan.

4. Rewrite program TriGraph2 to draw the left side first, then the base, then the right side.

5. Write a code fragment that will draw a blue circle of radius 75, centered on a screen with a light gray background. Your solution should use one of the four-color CGA modes.

6. Rewrite program TriGraph2 so that the background is green, the triangle is red filled with brown, and the constants are appropriately renamed.

7. Write a code fragment that draws the figures described in exercise 2 using LineRel for the axes and connected lines.

8. Modify the code segment written for exercise 7 that will fill the area below the data line with blue.

9. Write a code fragment that will draw an octagon on the screen, fill it with red, and print the word 'STOP' in white in the center of the octagon.

10. Write a code fragment that will create a checkerboard on a CGA screen. The checkerboard should be an 8 × 8 grid of alternating red- and black-filled squares that cover the entire screen. The upper left and lower right corners should be red.

■ *Programming Problems*

1. Write a program that will draw a smiling face on the screen. The face should be a yellow-filled circle with a black outline, against a light green background. The eyes should be a pair of small black circles, and the mouth should be a black arc. If your display screen does not support the light colors, you may use the corresponding darker colors.

2. Write a program that will draw a target on the screen. The target should consist of five concentric circles, each filled with a color different from the one that surrounds it. The innermost circle should be red; you may choose the other colors. The inner circle should be labeled '100', the second circle out '75', the third circle '50', the fourth circle '25', and the outer circle '10'.

3. Write a program that draws a pie graph centered in the left half of the screen and a segmented 3D bar centered in the right half of the screen. The pie graph should have a radius of 75 and be divided into 3 sections: the upper right quarter of the pie should be filled with a light hatch fill, the other two sections should divide evenly the remaining three-quarters of the pie, with the lower right section being filled with a light slash fill and a light backslash fill in the upper left. The 3D bar should be a total of 145 pixels high, 40 pixels wide, and 10 pixels deep with a base that is 25 pixels from the bottom of the screen. The top quarter segment of the 144-pixel range from top to bottom should be light-hatch filled. The next two segments should divide evenly the remaining range. The middle segment should have a light slash fill and the bottom segment should have a light backslash fill. The centered message

```
Federated Charities — Expenses
```

should appear at the top of the screen. A legend should appear at the bottom that consists of bounded 8 × 8 pixel filled squares each followed by a label. The fill styles should be light-hatch (labeled 'Fund-raising'), light slash (labeled 'Distribution'), and light backslash (labeled 'Benefits'). The background should be blue, the text brown, the outlines green, and the fill red.

Turbo Pascal Units and Abstract Data Types

- To be able to write the interface section of a Turbo Pascal Unit.
- To be able to write the implementation section of a Turbo Pascal Unit.
- To be able to write the initialization section of a Turbo Pascal Unit.
- To be able to develop an abstract data type specification.
- To be able to implement an abstract data type using Turbo Pascal's Unit facility.

CHAPTER 19

In previous chapters we have discussed data abstraction and abstract data types. An abstract data type was defined as a data type together with the set of operations defined for that type. One of the chief advantages of building an abstract data type is that it allows us to hide the implementation details from the user. It is sufficient for us to define the data type and provide the user with descriptions of the interfaces to the operations for the type. The user does not have to know how the operations work in order to use them. Because the user cannot write code that depends on how we've implemented the operations, we are free to modify or make improvements to them as long as we don't change the interface.

We also pointed out that, in Standard Pascal, there is no way to physically hide the implementation of an abstract data type. Because Standard Pascal requires that a program contain all of the code that will be used, all of the implementation details will be visible to the programmer. Turbo Pascal, however, provides a nonstandard extension that permits us to physically hide an implementation: the Unit.

Turbo Pascal Units

To physically hide a piece of code, you have to keep it out of the user's sight. You can lock it up in a desk drawer, but if they need to incorporate it into their own program, they must be allowed to see it. Of course, once they know how it is written, they can write their program to take advantage of the internal workings of your code. This is precisely what we wish to avoid, but how to do it?

Let's forget about what Standard Pascal requires, and think in the abstract for a moment. What is the minimum amount of information that the user needs in order to use a subprogram? The definition of its interface. So, if we could somehow separate the interface from the implementation, then we need only show the interface to the user and can keep the implementation locked up. This is precisely what the Turbo Pascal Unit does for us.

We've used units such as CRT and Graph since Chapter 3. Now it's time to start defining our own. A unit is similar to a program in that it contains declarations and statements. It is, however, divided up somewhat differently. Each unit has a heading and three parts: interface, implementation, and initialization. Let's look at the syntax template for a unit.

> unit heading **;**
> interface part
> implementation part
> initialization part **.**

From this you can see that a unit ends with a period. In Standard Pascal, the main program is the only module that ends with a period—the period signals the end of the program to the compiler. Just like a program, a unit can be compiled into machine language, and its object code then can be stored in a file for later use. We make use of a user-defined unit just as we do a predefined unit such as CRT; we list the unit's name in a USES statement and thereafter we can call procedures defined in the unit.

The ability to compile a unit separately from a program has several advantages. First, of course, is that it allows us to hide the source code. A user can be given the object code (which is unreadable) and a copy of the unit's interface section, and will be able to make full use of the unit without having to see how it works. Second, separate compilation saves time. The compiler has only to compile the code in the program and then incorporate the object code for the unit, which is much faster than recompiling the unit. Third, separate compilation allows us to create abstract data types that can be used directly in many different programs.

Now, let's take a closer look at the syntax of a unit. The unit heading consists of the reserved word UNIT and a name.

UNIT identifier

The name given in the heading is the same one that will be placed in a USES statement in a program. The name can be any length, but only the first eight characters are used. This is because a name in a USES statement also specifies the file where the unit's object code is stored (and DOS file names are limited to eight characters).

The interface part consists of the reserved word INTERFACE and a series of declarations:

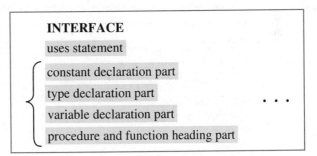

Notice that a unit can refer to other units with a USES statement. The declarations in the interface section can refer to anything made available by the units listed in the USES statement. The syntax of the constant, type, and variable declaration parts is identical to what we've seen all along in our programs.

The procedure and function heading part is what its name implies: a list of procedure and function headings. The local declarations and statements that implement the procedures and functions are omitted—they will appear in the implementation section of the unit.

Everything listed in the interface section will be visible to any program that uses the unit. Constants will become predefined constants (similar to MaxInt) in the program. The same is true for variables, procedures, and functions. The only exception is that units listed in the USES statement of a unit are not visible automatically to a program that uses the unit. If the program must also access those nested units, then their names must be listed in the program's USES statement.

Next, we consider the syntax of the implementation section.

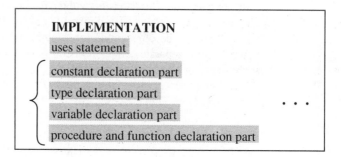

As you can see, it is the same as the interface section, except that it begins with the keyword IMPLEMENTATION, and the procedure and function heading part is instead the procedure and function **declaration** part. Although the syntax is nearly the same, the semantics are quite different. Everything in the implementation part is hidden from a program that uses the unit. These declarations are referred to as *private*.

Private   Declarations and statements that are hidden in the implementation section of a unit. Private declarations cannot be accessed by a program using the unit.

The implementation section has its own USES statement, allowing it to make use of units in addition to those listed in the interface section. The private constants, types, and variables are global with respect to the procedures and functions declared in the unit. The procedure and function declarations repeat the headings listed in the interface section and add the local declarations and statements (blocks) that form their bodies. We also can declare additional private procedures and functions in the implementation section.

The initialization part consists of either the reserved word END or a compound statement:

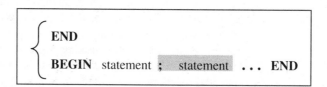

The initialization part can be empty, or it can obtain a series of statements. Statements in the initialization part are executed before the statements in a program that

Figure 19-1
A Unit as a Layered
Structure

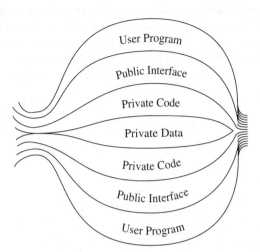

uses the unit. The initialization part typically assigns initial values to the global variables defined in the interface or implementation sections. The statements are private and are executed automatically. If a USES statement lists multiple units, their initialization parts are executed in the order that they are listed.

Let's look at a graphical representation of a unit. Figure 19-1 shows a unit inside a program, represented as four layers, something like the layers of an onion.

From the figure it is clear that the program has direct access only to the interface. It is also important to note that the interface provides a layer that hides the private code from the program. The design of the interface must not give away any information about the implementation that we wish to hide from the user. Similarly, only the private code has access to the private data.

Let's gather all of this syntactical information together into an example of a unit. The following unit provides a data type for a name and a procedure for reading a name. It also provides a function that returns True if an error was detected in reading a name. Note that the unit defines a global variable in its implementation section, making the variable private. Access to global private variables is an important aspect of the design methodology for units and will be discussed in the next section.

```
UNIT Name;

INTERFACE                          (* This part can be given to a user *)

USES
  CRT;                             (* Defines CheckEOF    *)

CONST
  Name_Length = 20;               (* Max length of a name *)

TYPE
  Name_Type = String[Name_Length];   (* Names are strings    *)
```

```
(*********************************************************************)

FUNCTION Error:                    (* Returns error status   *)
        Boolean;

(* This function returns True if the last call to Get_Name *)
(* encountered EOF before reading the name *)

(*********************************************************************)

PROCEDURE Get_Name(VAR Name:                  (* Gets a name *)
                       Name_Type);

(* This procedure gets a name from Input, checking for EOF *)

(*********************************************************************)
(*********************************************************************)
(*********************************************************************)

IMPLEMENTATION              (* This part can be hidden from a user *)

VAR
  Name_Error:            (* A private variable storing error status *)
    Boolean;

(*********************************************************************)

FUNCTION Error:          (* Returns error status *)
        Boolean;

(* This function returns True if the last call to Get_Name *)
(* encountered EOF before reading the name *)

BEGIN (* Error *)
  Error := Name_Error      (* Access private global variable *)
END;  (* Error *)

(*********************************************************************)

PROCEDURE Get_Name(VAR Name:              (* Gets a name *)
                       Name_Type);

(* This procedure gets a name from Input, checking for EOF *)
```

```
BEGIN (* Get_Name *)
  IF NOT EOF
    THEN
      BEGIN
        Read(Name);
        Name_Error := False      (* Change private global variable *)
      END
    ELSE
      Name_Error := True        (* Change private global variable *)
END;  (* Get_Name *)

(* ************************************************************** *)
(* ************************************************************** *)
(* ************************************************************** *)


(* INITIALIZATION *)

BEGIN (* Name *)
  CheckEOF := True;       (* In CRT unit enables EOF from Input *)
  Name_Error := False     (* Initialize private global variable *)
END.  (* Name *)
```

The unit is compiled like any program, with the Compile command. However, we must first set the Destination (one of the options in the Compile menu) to Disk so that the object code for the unit will be saved on a file. If the source code for a unit is stored on file NAME.PAS, then Turbo Pascal will place the object code on file NAME.TPU. TPU stands for Turbo Pascal Unit. When Turbo Pascal encounters the statement

```
USES Name;
```

in a user program, it will add the extension .TPU to Name to determine the name of the file where the object code for the unit is stored. As you can see, the name of the unit must be written consistently throughout this process. It is especially important that the source file name be the same as the unit name. Unlike Pascal data files, there is no equivalent to the Assign procedure that allows us to associate a program-dependent identifier with the system name for a unit.

Designing a Unit for an Abstract Data Type

Now that we've seen the syntax and semantics of units, let's consider how they affect our design methodology. We'll do this in the framework of developing a particular unit. By the end of the chapter we want to define an abstract data type for a date. We can lay some of the ground work for this by first defining an abstract data type for a month.

Abstract Data Types

In Chapter 12 we defined an abstract data type to be a class of data objects with a defined set of properties and a set of operations that process the data objects while maintaining the properties. Thus an abstract data type consists both of a type definition and of procedures and functions that operate on the type.

The syntax and semantics of Pascal data types partly define the properties of an abstract data type. We then add to those properties with further semantic rules. For example, in the two-dimensional array

```
TYPE
  Discount_Type = ARRAY [1..5, 1..5] OF Real;
```

we have defined a table that contains five rows of five values. The Pascal syntax does not specify what the indexes mean, only their permissible range of values. By adding more semantic information

```
TYPE
  Region_Index = 1..5;
  Level_Index = 1..5;
  Discount_Table = ARRAY [Region_Index, Level_Index] OF Real;
```

we can now see that the first index is a geographical region number and the second index is a discount level number. The data type is no different in its construction, but it is semantically closer to the actual object that it represents. Our code for manipulating the data type further adds to the semantics by placing restrictions on the values that can be stored in each element of the array. For example, a procedure that fills the array with values might verify that each successive level of discount is greater than the previous level.

The most important point in our definition of abstract data type is that any operations performed on a value of the abstract type preserve all of the properties of the type. A key to achieving this is *encapsulation*, which was defined in Chapter 6 as hiding a module implementation in a separate block with a formally specified interface. If we hide the implementation of the abstract data type and provide the user with a set of operations (procedures and functions) that are sufficient for the user to do whatever they require with values of the abstract type, then we have encapsulated the type.

The cardinal rule of abstract data types is thus to hide from the user any information that could be used to violate the properties of the type. This means that the user should not be able to see the type definition. The second rule is that the type must provide a basic set of operations that allows the user to manipulate the type in any way that doesn't violate its properties.

In the following sections we will consider in detail how to define an abstract type, its interface, and its implementation using Turbo Pascal units. While units are a significant improvement over Standard Pascal for the implementation of abstract data types, they do not directly support the hiding of type definitions. In a language such as Ada, which is designed with abstract data types in mind, we could write a type definition in the interface section as follows.

```
TYPE Discount_Table IS PRIVATE;
```

The user then cannot see the actual structure of a Discount_Table, which is only defined in the implementation section. In Turbo Pascal, however, we cannot do this. We are required to specify a type definition in the interface section. While Turbo Pascal does provide some clever ways to hide the actual type definition from the user, these do not prevent direct access to an abstract type value. An error in a Turbo Pascal program can easily violate the properties of an abstract type.

For this reason, you will see that the examples in this chapter define the data type in the interface section. It is still up to the user to carefully avoid taking advantage of this knowledge. At the end of the chapter we will briefly examine Turbo Pascal *objects*, a mechanism that allows us to fully hide the definition and implementation of a structure similar to an abstract data type.

Designing the Interface

The first step to designing an abstract data type is to stand back and consider what you, as a user of the data type, would want it to provide for you. This list of wishes will form the requirements for the interface to the unit. Obviously, the unit must define the data type, but it must also define the operations on the type. For example, we may decide that months will be represented by an enumerated type consisting of the month's names. But what operations are performed on months?

Recall from our earlier discussion of abstract data types that there are three kinds of operations on them: constructors, observers, and iterators. We can begin by considering each of these with respect to the data type.

There are two common sources from which a month might be constructed: from a number in the range of 1 through 12, and from a string containing a month's name. There are other sources, such as a string containing an abbreviation of a month's name, but we'll leave these to the exercises. The point is that a month has an internal representation in the abstract data type, and the type must provide operations that convert common representations into this form. Otherwise it would be impossible for the user to make use of the data type.

Such constructors have one additional purpose: to validate data as it is converted into the abstract representation. An abstract data type unit must not produce run-time errors, otherwise the user will regard it as unreliable and won't use it. Thus, the unit must check all data as it is converted into the internal form.

Another kind of constructor takes an existing value of the data type and returns a new value of the type, based on some operation. In other words, any operation that produces a new value of type Month is a constructor. The question is, what operations should we support? At first it may seem that there aren't any obvious operations for an abstract type. Then, once you start to see them, it often seems that there are an overwhelming number. But keep in mind that the data type doesn't have to do everything for the user; it simply has to provide a basic set of tools that enable the user to build more complex operations.

For example, Pascal doesn't provide arithmetic operators for enumerated types, but it does provide Pred, Succ, and Ord. Similarly, we needn't supply a routine for determining the difference between two abstract values, as long as we provide the ability to convert them to numeric values. The user can write

```
Abs(Num(ADT_Value_A) - Num(ADT_Value_B))
```

almost as easily as

```
Difference(ADT_Value_A, ADT_Value_B)
```

For our Month type we might want an operation that changes a month by a certain number of months. We could provide a function that takes a month and an integer (positive or negative) and returns the new month. This operation is sufficient for the user to adjust the value of a month variable by any amount.

Observers come in several forms: converting the data type to a common representation, comparing values of the data type, and providing results of operations on (or attributes of) the data type. For example, we could provide an operation that returns the name of a month as a string. We could also provide an observer that returns True if one month is less than another. Yet another observer might return the number of days in a month.

Iterators are used with structured types to permit the user to process an entire structure element by element. Because a month is a simple type, its unit won't include any iterators.

As an example, let's consider Char as an abstract data type. The type is defined by Pascal to be the list of all symbols (printing and nonprinting) in the character set of the particular computer (ASCII in the case of Turbo Pascal). Example constructors of type Char are Chr and UpCase. Chr takes an integer and returns the corresponding character in the collating sequence. UpCase takes a character and returns another (possibly different) character. Read, Readln, Pred, and Succ also serve as constructors.

Observers of type Char include Ord and the relational operators. Ord converts a character into another form—an integer representing its position in the collating sequence. The relational operators compare two characters and return True if a particular relationship (such as less-than) exists between them. We could also envision an observer function, called Letter, that returns true if a character is in the range a..z or A..Z. Whether or not a character is a letter is one of its attributes. Many attributes may be implicit in a data type, but an abstract data type interface does not have to provide observers for all of them, as long as it supplies operations that allow the user to build new attribute observers. Thus, Pascal does not supply a function called Letter but allows the user to write such a function using the relational operators.

Because Char is a simple type, iterators are not associated with it.

Now that we have looked at a standard type from the perspective of an abstract data type, let's turn our attention to user-defined enumerated types and, in particular, the Month type.

Enumerated types are a natural way to define months:

```
TYPE
  Month = January, February, March, April, May, June, July,
          August, September, October, November, December);
```

When we introduced enumerated types in Chapter 10, we noted that Pascal does not support input and output of enumerated values as text. Thus, for any abstract data type based on an enumerated type, we should provide operations that convert from a string to the type and from the type to a string. The former is a constructor, and the latter is an observer. For our Month type, we will define operations called Month_Form and Month_Name. Month_Form will take a string of up to nine characters and if it is the name of a month, return the appropriate value of type month. Month_Name will take a value of type month and return a string of up to nine characters.

Sample Call	Result	
Month_Form('January')	January	
Month_Form('august')	August	
Month_Form('MAY')	May	
Month_Form('Monday')	January	(invalid input data)
Month_Name(October)	'October'	
Month_Name(July)	'July'	

There is one small problem with these operations: we have defined type Month, but we haven't defined a string type with nine characters. It's easy enough to write.

```
TYPE
  String9 = String[9];
```

but where do we place the declaration? Because the user must be able to send and receive values of this type through the interface, the type must be declared publicly. A public type that is not the abstract type itself is called an auxiliary data type. An abstract data type interface may have several auxiliary types associated with it.

Just as Pascal provides Ord and Chr for converting characters to and from a numeric representation, it is useful to provide such operations for any enumerated type. We could use Ord, and the nonstandard Month function that Turbo Pascal automatically creates with the Month data type, but these functions do not permit us to hide their implementation—they are defined outside of the public interface layer of the unit. By defining our own functions for these operations, we can also include data validation checks. Our Month interface will thus have a constructor, called Month_Num, that takes an integer in the range 1..12 and returns a value of type Month, and an observer, called Number, that takes a value of type Month and returns an integer in the range 1..12.

Sample Call	Result	
Month_Num(5)	May	
Month_Num(11)	November	
Month_Num(47)	January	(invalid input data)
Number(June)	6	
Number(February)	2	

Here is one more advantage to writing these operations ourselves. Note that the integer ranges are 1..12. Thus, Number(January) is 1, as you would expect. Recall, however, that Ord(January) is 0. It is more natural for most people to think of January as month number one than as month number zero.

Pascal provides Pred and Succ for enumerated types, but as we mentioned above, it is sometimes more convenient to have a single operation that changes an enumerated value by any amount (positive or negative). For our present needs, Pred and Succ will be sufficient, but Programming Warm-Up exercise 1 asks you to add Function Change to the Month unit. Change will take a month and an integer number of months and return the month that is that many months away.

One attribute of a month that cannot be derived directly from its numeric or string representation is the number of days in the month. Although any user could construct a function that contains this information, it is more than just a simple formula. Thus, for the user's convenience, we should provide an attribute observer (called Days_In) that returns this value given a month. February presents a problem, however, because it can have either 28 or 29 days. The user will have to tell the function whether this is a leap year or not by passing in a second parameter that is true for leap years.

Sample Call	Result
Days_In(January, False)	31
Days_In(February, False)	28
Days_In(February, True)	29
Days_In(April, True)	30

For both Month_Num and Month_Form we said that the input values should be validated. We also showed examples of invalid input values. But how do we indicate to the user that the result is invalid? One way is to add another parameter to each function, a Boolean, that returns True whenever an error is detected. However, it is poor practice to include VAR parameters in function parameter lists. We could change these functions to procedures, but then they won't be as convenient to use.

There is another factor to consider. The user does not always want (or need) to check for an erroneous result. The user may have already validated the input. Another approach to returning error status is thus to provide an error function that returns True when the most recent abstract type operation detected an error. This gives the user the option of checking for an error. We should also provide a function that returns a string containing an error message that can be output. We'll call these functions Month_Error and Month_Error_Str. Here is how they might be used.

Sample Code Segment	Notes
`Now := Month_Form('May')`	Correctly spelled literal, no need to check
`Later := Month_Form(In_Data);`	Unvalidated user input in variable In_Data
`IF Month_Error`	Check for an error in the preceding call
`THEN`	If an error, print the error message
`Writeln(Month_Error_Str)`	

What type does Month_Error_Str return? Obviously a string, but what length? This sounds like a requirement for another auxiliary data type, and indeed it is. We'll define a type called String40 to hold error messages.

We now have enough information to write the interface section for the Month abstract data type unit. The code for the interface section is shown here. Note that we have included comments with each heading to describe the operation that will be performed by the function.

```
UNIT MonthADT;

(* This unit defines an abstract data type representing    *)
(* the months of the year. The implementation is hidden    *)
(* and instances of this type should be accessed only by the *)
(* functions provided in the interface part                *)

INTERFACE

TYPE
  String40 = String[40];
  String9 = String[9];
  Month =
    (January, February, March, April, May, June, July,
     August, September, October, November, December);

(* ********************************************************************* )


FUNCTION Month_Error:
          Boolean;          (* True if an error has occurred *)

(* This function will be True after a call to an access *)
(* function for type Month if the attempted access was  *)
(* invalid. *)


(* ********************************************************************* )
```

```
FUNCTION Month_Error_Str:
          String40;                (* Returns an error message *)

(* If Function Month_Error returns True, this function may *)
(* then be called to get an error message string that      *)
(* indicates the source of the error *)

(********************************************************************)

FUNCTION Number(In_Month:          (* Receives a month value   *)
                Month):
                  Integer;         (* Returns the month number *)

(* This function returns the number of a month (1 - 12)        *)

(********************************************************************)

FUNCTION Month_Num(Number:          (* Receives a month number *)
                   Integer):
                   Month;          (* Returns a month value   *)

(* This function returns the month corresponding to an    *)
(* integer in the range 1 - 12. If the integer is out of *)
(* range, January is used, and Month_Error is True        *)

(********************************************************************)

FUNCTION Month_Name(In_Month:          (* Receives a month number *)
                    Month):
                    String9;       (* Returns month's name    *)

(* Given a month value, this function returns the name of *)
(* the month as a string of 3 to 9 characters             *)

(********************************************************************)

FUNCTION Month_Form(Month_Str:       (* Receives a month string *)
                    String9):
                    Month;          (* Returns a month value   *)

(* Given a string, the function determines the month name *)
(* it represents and returns the appropriate month value. *)
(* Letter case is ignored. If the string is not the name  *)
(* of a month, then Month_Error returns True  *)

(********************************************************************)
```

You now could hand this interface specification to a user, who could start to write a program that uses the Month abstract type even before you have written the implementation. It is wise, however, to wait until you have completed the implementation before publishing the interface. It is not uncommon to get half-way through the implementation and discover that you've left something out of the interface. You should always try to develop the complete interface before starting the implementation. If the interface turns out to be deficient, however, it is better to correct it than to rigidly adhere to it and create a useless or cumbersome abstract data type (or even worse, an abstract data type that violates its own interface specification).

Designing the Implementation

Once the interface has been specified, the hardest part of the design is finished. What remains is simply a matter of applying top-down design principles to develop the code for the public procedures and functions in the interface. As part of that development you may create many levels of decomposition, and some of these lower level modules may turn out to be used in multiple places. It is convenient to declare these shared modules at the top level, rather than repeating them inside each module that uses them. (Recall from Chapter 3 that this is called a semihierarchical implementation.)

Procedures and functions that are declared at the top level of the implementation section but not in the interface section are private. The user program cannot access them. A typical private module is one that validates values of the abstract type. We will include a private function called Valid that checks a value of type Month to be certain it is in range.

This brings up a question about how errors are handled. If Valid detects an error, how does it signal this to Month_Error? In a normal program we would have Valid return a Boolean result that we would save in a global variable. We could then pass that value to Month_Error. However, we don't have access to the global variables in the program, nor can the user program even call Valid (it is private). Even if we could access the global variables in the program, it violates the principle that an abstract data type should be self-contained—the Month unit should not have to depend on a value stored in the user program to work correctly.

The unit does have its own private global variables; those declared in the implementation section. But how do we store the result from Valid in one of them, and then pass it to Month_Error when the user program calls Month_Error? The solution is simple, although we have carefully trained ourselves not to think of it: we must have Valid and Month_Error access the private global variables directly. This is an exception to our general rule of never accessing global variables from within a subprogram.

In a unit, private global variables are the only storage mechanism that is permanent. All local variables are created when a subprogram is called and destroyed when the subprogram returns. Because there is no top-level control structure within a unit (only the user program controls when calls to unit subprograms take place), the only way to access the private global variables once the initialization is done is by global access from within subprograms.

Thus, we will create a private global variable called Error_Flag that will be set by Valid and checked by Month_Error. Similarly, we will have Valid store an error message in a global string called Error_String, and Month_Error_Str will access this message directly.

When global variables are used to hold values between subprogram calls in an abstract data type, they are called persistent variables.

Persistent Variable   A variable declared in the outermost scope within an abstract data type implementation and used to hold values between calls to the operations that comprise the abstract data type.

Persistent variables are used whenever it is necessary to store values between calls. Error flags and messages are a simple example (Figure 19-2). For a more complex example, recall the discussion of finite state machines in Chapter 5: a finite state machine has a set of transition rules and state variables. Inputs to the machine cause transition rules to be executed that depend partly on the state variables. The effect of the rules is often to output a value and make some change to the state variables. We easily could simulate a finite state machine with a unit by providing a procedure that accepts an input and returns an output, with the state of the machine stored in persistent variables. Persistent variables can also be used to store counts (such as keeping track of the number of times a function has been called), to store a current search index into a database, to create internal files, and so on.

We do not mean to imply that global variable access is generally acceptable in units. It is still necessary to restrict the interfaces of subprograms as much as possible to their parameter lists. Accessing persistent variables is a classic example of a side effect and should be treated with great caution. However, carefully used and documented persistent variable access provides an important tool for us to use in developing units.

Because we would like to restrict direct access to private global variables as much as possible and make all such access self-documenting, we recommend that only private subprograms be allowed to change global variables. All subprograms that have public headings should call private subprograms to store persistent values.

Thus, when an error is detected by one of the public routines, it should call a private procedure (which we'll call Error) to set Error_Flag and store a message in Error_String. Of course, we also need a way to reset Error_Flag and Error_String at the start of an operation, so we will provide another private procedure (called Set_Up) that does this.

We have effectively restricted all changes to Error_Flag and Error_String to just two pieces of code. Thus, if a side-effect bug is discovered later, it will be much easier to isolate.

Of course, there is one other place that the persistent variables should be accessed: the initialization section. It is important to give initial values to all of the global variables, including any that are public.

We won't go through the algorithms used to implement the individual operations in unit MonthADT. They are all very simple. Notice that the comments from the interface section have been repeated here. It is easier for someone who is debugging or changing a unit implementation if they do not have to flip back and forth between the interface and implementation sections to see the comments. In a more complex unit, each of the operations would also have a second section of comments explaining the implementation (clearly this is not something that we want to include with the interface section).

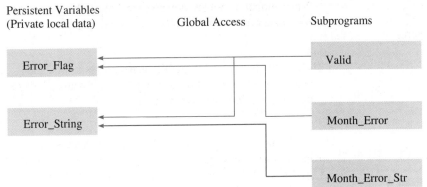

Figure 19-2
Persistent Variable
Access Within a
Unit

Here is the code for the implementation and initialization sections of the MonthADT unit.

```
IMPLEMENTATION

VAR
  Error_Flag:          (* Global variable holding error status  *)
    Boolean;
  Error_String:        (* Global variable holding error message *)
    String40;

(*********************************************************************)


PROCEDURE Set_Up;

(* This hidden procedure initializes the global variables   *)
(* Error_Flag and Error_String. It is called by most of the *)
(* functions in this unit *)

BEGIN (* Set_Up *)
  Error_Flag := False;
  Error_String := ''
END;  (* Set_Up *)

(*********************************************************************)

PROCEDURE Error(In_String:          (* Error message string *)
                  String40);

(* This procedure is used to assign an error message to the *)
(* global variable Error_String, and True to Error_Flag. It *)
(* is called by any function for which an error can occur    *)

BEGIN (* Error *)
  Error_Flag := True;
  Error_String := In_String
END;  (* Error *)
```

```
(*********************************************************************)

FUNCTION Valid(In_Month:        (* A month value        *)
                  Month):
                  Boolean;       (* True if a valid month *)

(* Checks to see if In_Month is in range. Returns False if   *)
(* not and sets global variables Error_Flag and Error_String *)
(* as a side effect *)

BEGIN (* Valid *)
  IF In_Month IN [January..December]
    THEN
      Valid := True
    ELSE
      BEGIN
        Valid := False;
        Error('Invalid or undefined month.')
      END
END;  (* Valid *)

(*********************************************************************)

FUNCTION Month_Error:
            Boolean;      (* True if an error has occurred *)

(* This function will be True after a call to an access   *)
(* function for type Month if the attempted access was    *)
(* invalid. Note that the implementation accesses global *)
(* variable Error_Flag *)

BEGIN (* Month_Error *)
  Month_Error := Error_Flag
END;  (* Month_Error *)

(*********************************************************************)

FUNCTION Month_Error_Str:
            String40;     (* Returns an error message *)

(* If Function Month_Error returns True, this function may *)
(* then be called to get an error message string that      *)
(* indicates the source of the error. Note that the        *)
(* implementation accesses global variable Error_String    *)

BEGIN
  Month_Error_Str := Error_String
END;

(*********************************************************************)
```

```
FUNCTION Number(In_Month):        (* Receives a month value    *)
                  Month):
                      Integer;    (* Returns the month number *)

(* This function returns the number of a month (1 - 12)       *)

BEGIN (* Number *)
  Set_Up;
  IF Valid(In_Month)
    THEN
      Number := Ord(In_Month) + 1
    ELSE
      BEGIN
        Error('Invalid or undefined month.');
        Number := 1
      END
END;  (* Number *)

(*********************************************************************)

FUNCTION Month_Num(Number:        (* Receives a month number *)
                    Integer:
                    Month;        (* Returns a month value    *)

(* This function returns the month corresponding to an     *)
(* integer in the range 1 - 12. If the integer is out of *)
(* range, January is used, and Month_Error is True        *)

BEGIN (* Month_Num *)
  Set_Up;
  IF (Number >= 1) AND (Number <= 12)
    THEN
      Month_Num := Month(Number - 1)
    ELSE
      BEGIN
        Error('Month number out of range.');
        Month_Num := January
      END
END;  (* Month_Num *)

(*********************************************************************)

FUNCTION Month_Name(In_Month:       (* Receives a month number *)
                    Month):
                    String9;        (* Returns month's name    *)

(* Given a month value, this function returns the name of *)
(* the month as a string of 3 to 9 characters *)
```

```
BEGIN (* Month_Name *)
  Set_Up;
  IF Valid(In_Month)
    THEN
      CASE In_Month OF
        January:   Month_Name := 'January';
        February:  Month_Name := 'February';
        March:     Month_Name := 'March';
        April:     Month_Name := 'April';
        May:       Month_Name := 'May';
        June:      Month_Name := 'June';
        July:      Month_Name := 'July';
        August:    Month_Name := 'August';
        September: Month_Name := 'September';
        October:   Month_Name := 'October';
        November:  Month_Name := 'November';
        December:  Month_Name := 'December';
      END (* CASE *)
    ELSE
      Month_Name := ''
END; (* Month_Name *)


(*******************************************************************)


FUNCTION Month_Form(Month_Str:          (* Receives a month string *)
                      String9):
                      Month;            (* Returns a month value   *)

(* Given a string, the function determines the month name *)
(* it represents and returns the appropriate month value. *)
(* Letter case is ignored. If the string is not the name  *)
(* of a month, then Month_Error returns True *)

VAR
  Index:          (* Character index into string *)
    Integer;
```

```
BEGIN (* Month_Form *)
  Set_Up;
  (* Convert input to all upper case for easier comparison *)
  FOR Index := 1 TO Length(Month_Str) DO
    Month_Str[Index] := UpCase(Month_Str[Index]);
  IF Month_Str = 'JANUARY'
    THEN
      Month_Form := January
    ELSE IF Month_Str = 'FEBRUARY'
      THEN
        Month_Form := February
    ELSE IF Month_Str = 'MARCH'
      THEN
        Month_Form := March
    ELSE IF Month_Str = 'APRIL'
      THEN
        Month_Form := April
    ELSE IF Month_Str = 'MAY'
      THEN
        Month_Form := May
    ELSE IF Month_Str = 'JUNE'
      THEN
        Month_Form := June
    ELSE IF Month_Str = 'JULY'
      THEN
        Month_Form := July
    ELSE IF Month_Str = 'AUGUST'
      THEN
        Month_Form := August
    ELSE IF Month_Str = 'SEPTEMBER'
      THEN
        Month_Form := September
    ELSE IF Month_Str = 'OCTOBER'
      THEN
        Month_Form := October
    ELSE IF Month_Str = 'NOVEMBER'
      THEN
        Month_Form := November
    ELSE IF Month_Str = 'DECEMBER'
      THEN
        Month_Form := December
    ELSE
      BEGIN
        Error('Character string not a month.');
        Month_Form := January
      END
END;  (* Month_Form *)

(* ****************************************************************** *)
```

```
( *INITIALIZATION *)

BEGIN (* Month_Unit *)
  Error_Flag := False);
  Error_String := ''
END.  (* Month_Unit *)
```

We will leave the detailed discussion of how to test a unit to the case studies and the Testing and Debugging section. However, we cannot run a unit because it has no global control structure. We can only compile it and save the code to a file (don't forget to set the Destination under the Compile menu to Disk). To test the unit we write a driver program that USES the unit and calls all of the public operations. Testing the private subprograms must be done indirectly (such as by passing invalid data to a public subprogram) or by tracing the program with the Turbo Pascal debugger and watching the persistent variables.

PROBLEM-SOLVING CASE STUDY

Abstract Data Type Date

Problem: Create an abstract data type that supports a basic set of operations on dates. In addition, it should provide operations to convert a date to and from its Julian day number (see Programming Problem 4 in Chapter 8 for an explanation of the Julian day number). The abstract type also should provide error handling functions that indicate when an error has occurred in an operation, and what caused the error.

Discussion: Because the problem asks us to create an abstract data type, there is no input or output. However, we will divide the detailed discussion into two sections: interface and implementation. First we should note that we can save ourselves some effort by using the Month abstract type developed previously. Should we also develop Day and Year abstract types? To be absolutely rigorous we could develop those types. However, their representations (integer subranges) are sufficiently simple that we can rely upon Pascal's standard facilities, together with some extra data validation code. Programming Problem 1 asks you to develop an abstract type for representing years. If you work out that problem, you may wish to incorporate it into this case study as part of testing your solution.

Interface: First we must define the data type for a date. We can represent dates in several different ways, but as we saw in Chapter 14, a record with three fields is a very natural way to store a date.

```
TYPE
  Day = 1..31;                    (* Days have the range 1..31 *)
  Year = -4713..MaxInt;           (* Julian year 0 is minimum  *)
  Date = RECORD                   (* Dates are 3-field records *)
    Month : MonthADT.Month;
    Day   : Day;
    Year  : Year
  END;   (* Record *)
```

Because we need to provide operations that convert a date to and from its Julian day number, we restrict the range of years to −4713 (Julian year zero). We also must remember to prevent storing a year numbered zero because 1 BC is followed by 1 AD (zero had not been invented at the time the calendar was devised). Days are limited to the range 1..31, but some months have fewer than 31 days, so we will have to watch out for invalid combinations of day and month.

Next we must decide what constitutes a basic set of operations on dates. The first operations that should always come to mind are those that convert between an abstract type and common external representations. We frequently represent dates as a set of three integers (month, day, and year), so it would make sense to have an operation called Make_Date that takes three integers and returns a value of type date. While it would be possible for the user to directly assign values to a date, providing a constructor is easier and also gives us the opportunity to verify that the date is valid. The interface to this operation can be written as a procedure heading with four parameters:

```
PROCEDURE Make_Date(    In_Month,     (* Number of a month *)
                        In_Day,       (* Number of a day   *)
                        In_Year:      (* Number of a year  *)
                          Integer;
                    VAR Out_Date:     (* Corresponding date *)
                          Date);
```

We also must be able to convert from an abstract date to a common form. While we could simply reverse the operation of Make_Date, it would be more useful to provide a date in the form of a string that could be printed. Because our Month ADT already provides an operation that returns the name of a month as a string, this will be easy to do. We can define the interface to this operation with a function heading containing a single parameter. Note that this definition will also require us to define a public string type with which to return the result.

```
FUNCTION Date_Str(In_Date:      (* A value of type date *)
                    Date):
                      String20;   (* Date in string form  *)
```

In addition to these conversions, the problem also specifies that the ADT should convert to and from the Julian day number. The interfaces to these operations are straightforward: a function heading that takes a value of type date and returns the Julian day number, and a procedure heading that takes a Julian day number and returns a value of type date. The Julian day number can be quite large, however, and it can include fractional parts of a day, so we must use type Real to store it.

Besides conversions, basic operations for any ordered type include comparisons. We will provide the three simplest comparisons (Equal, Less, and Greater) as functions that take two dates and return a Boolean result. The following function heading is a sample interface to a comparison operation:

```
FUNCTION Equal(Date1,          (* A value of type Date   *)
              Date2:           (* A value of type Date   *)
                 Date):
                 Boolean;      (* True if they are equal *)
```

Another set of basic operations on any ordered type is predecessor and successor. For example, the Pred and Succ functions are provided by Pascal. We can generalize these into a single operation, called Change, that takes any integer value (positive or negative) and "adds" it to a given value of the ordered type. In the case of a date, the integer value will represent a number of days. Just as with Pred and Succ, we must be careful not to exceed the limits of the data type. The interface to Change will be a procedure heading that takes a date and an integer (type LongInt).

```
PROCEDURE Change(VAR IO_Date:    (* A value of type Date   *)
                    Date;
                    Amount:      (* Number of Days to add *)
                    LongInt);
```

We now have a sufficient set of operations to work with dates as an abstract type. But we still must consider the problem of error handling. What if Make_Date is given values that make an invalid date, or the result of Change is out of range, or an attempt is made to convert a negative Julian day number to a date? We could have each of these operations return extra parameters that indicate errors, but that complicates the individual interfaces of the operations. Further, the user program will sometimes validate the data itself and should not be forced to provide error handling parameters for every ADT operation. Thus, as was done for the Month ADT, we will provide two functions for error handling. One will return a Boolean result of true if the most recent operation encountered an error, and the other will return a string indicating the cause of the error. Their interfaces are as follows. Note that the definition of the second function also requires us to define a public string type that can be used in returning the error message.

```
FUNCTION Date_Error:        (* True if an error occurs   *)
          Boolean;
FUNCTION Date_Error_Str:     (* Returns an error message *)
          String40;
```

Implementation: From the above discussion, it is clear that we will have to implement at least ten separate public subprograms on the date data type. Are there any private subprograms that we can identify prior to completing the top-down design of the implementation? Yes. Each public operation that can detect an error must be able to store an error flag and a message that Date_Error and Date_Error_Str can access. The flag and message will be stored in private global variables by calling a procedure named Error. This way, the only direct access to the global variables is from a single private procedure. The algorithm for Error is as follows.

Error (Receives Message: String40)

Set Error Flag to True
Set Error String to Message

Now consider what happens after an error occurs—suppose another ADT operation is performed that does not produce an error. If the error flag has not been reset, it will appear to the user program that the second operation also produced an error. We could have Date_Error reset the flag, but that assumes that the user program always checks Date_Error after every operation. It is better to have each operation reset the error flag itself as it starts to execute. Because every public subprogram must do this, it makes sense to write a procedure to take care of this chore. We'll call the procedure Set_Up because it sets up the initial values of the global variables. Here is its algorithm:

Set_Up

Set Error Flag to False
Set Error String to ' '

We are likely to need one other private subprogram. Because data validation is done in several of the ADT operations, we should write a function called Valid that takes a value of type date and returns True if it is a proper date. Valid must check for the proper range of years (including the absence of year zero) and that the day of the month is consistent with the number of days in the month (including the special case of leap year).

Valid (Receives In_Date: Date
        Returns Valid: Boolean)

```
IF Year is greater than or equal to −4713 and not equal to 0
  THEN
      CASE Month OF
          January, March, May, July, August, October, December
              Check that Day is in range 1..31
          April, June, September, November
              Check that Day is in range 1..30
          February
              IF Leap year
                  THEN
                      Check that Day is in range 1..29
                  ELSE
                      Check that Day is in range 1..28
  ELSE
      Valid := False;
  IF the date isn't valid
  THEN
      Call Error with message 'Invalid date.'
```

In developing this algorithm, we put off the determination of leap year to the next level of the design. We normally think of a leap year as any year that is divisible by 4. But over longer periods of time there are some special cases. A year that is also divisible by 100 (a new century year) is normally not a leap year, but when the year is also divisible by 400, it is a leap year. Thus, 1900 was not a leap year, but 2000 will be a leap year. These rules are summarized by the following algorithm.

Leap (Receives In_Year: Year
        Returns Leap: Boolean)

```
IF (In_Year MOD   4 = 0) AND NOT
   (In_Year MOD 100 = 0) OR
   (In_Year MOD 400 = 0)
   THEN
      Leap Year
   ELSE
      Not Leap Year
```

Now we are ready to start designing the public operations. We'll begin with Make_Date. Basically, Make_Date assigns the three values to the output parameter of type Date. The input Month value must be converted to type Month through the Month_Num function provided by the Month ADT. Then the date is tested with Valid. If it isn't valid, we must give it a proper value. We'll substitute Julian day zero (January 1, −4713) for the invalid value.

Make_Date (Receives In_Year: Year, In_Day: Day, In_Month: Integer,
Returns Out_Date: Date)

```
Set_Up
WITH Out_Date DO
  Set Year to In_Year;
  Set Day to In_Day;
  Set Month to Month_Num(In_Month)
IF NOT Valid(Out_Date)
  THEN
    Call Error with message 'Does not make a valid date.'
    Set Out_Date to Julian day 0
```

Converting a date into a string is straightforward with the Str procedure provided by Turbo Pascal and the Month_Name function provided by the Month ADT.

Date_Str (Receives In_Date: Date
Returns Date_Str: String20)

```
Set_Up
IF In_Date is Valid
  THEN
    WITH In_Date DO
      Convert Day to a string with Str
      Convert Year to a string with Str
      Set Date_Str to Month_Name(Month) + Day string + ', ' + Year string
  ELSE
    Set Date_Str to ' '
```

The equality comparison is also quite simple. We merely compare the values of the individual fields for equality. For good measure, we also will check that the dates are valid.

Equal (Receives Date1, Date2: Date
            Returns Equal: Boolean)

```
Set_Up
IF Date1 and Date2 are Valid
   THEN
      Set Equal to (Date1.Month  =  Date2.Month) AND
                   (Date 1.Day    =  Date 2.Day)   AND
                   (Date1.Year    =  Date2.Year)
   ELSE
      Equal : = False
```

The test for less than is a bit more complicated; we must first test the years. If they are equal, then we test the months. If the months are equal, we test the days. Again, we will start by validating the two dates.

Less (Receives Date1, Date2: Date
           Returns Less: Boolean)

```
Set_Up
IF Date1 and Date2 are Valid
   THEN
      Set Less to False
      IF Date1.Year < Date2.Year
        THEN
           Set Less to True
      IF Years are equal AND
           (Date1.Month) < Date2.Month)
        THEN
           Set Less to True
      IF Years and Months are equal AND
           (Date1.Day < Date2. Day)
        THEN
           Set Less to True
      END
   ELSE
      Set Less to False
```

Now that we have defined Equal and Less, we can simply define Greater as NOT Less AND NOT Equal. We can also skip the data validation and Set_Up because the other comparisons also perform these steps.

PROBLEM-SOLVING CASE STUDY cont'd.

Greater (Receives Date1, Date2: Date
Returns Greater: Boolean)

Set Greater to NOT Equal(Date1, Date2) AND
NOT Less(Date1, Date2)

The algorithm for converting a date to a Julian day number is given in Programming Problem 4 of Chapter 8; due to its length, it will not be repeated here. We have not previously seen the algorithm for converting from the Julian day number to a date, but some research in the library* turns up the following short algorithm, which involves some rather cryptic formulas. These formulas are a condensation of the rather complicated set of rules for determining the number of days in a month, the number of leap years preceding the current date, and the differences between old-style (Julian calendar) and new-style (Gregorian calendar) dates. Variables in the algorithm such as JD1, JD2, and so on, hold temporary values used later in the algorithm.

Date_Of_JD (Receives JD: Real
Returns Out_Date: Date)

```
Set_Up
IF JD > = 0.0
  THEN
      Set JD to JD + 0.5 (Julian day actually starts at noon)
      Set JDI to Trunc(JD)
      Set Frac to JD − JDI
      IF JDI > 2299160 (Compensate for Gregorian vs. Julian calendar)
        THEN
            Set JD1 to Trunc(JDI − 1867216.25) / 36524.25)
            Set JD2 to JDI + 1 + JD1 − JD1 DIV 4
        ELSE
            Set JD2 to JD1
      (Adjust for leap years)
      Set JD1 to JD2 + 1524
      Set JD3 to Trunc((JD1 − 122.1)/365.25)
      Set JD4 to Trunc(JD3 * 365.25);
      (Compute day of month)
      Set JD5 to Trunc((JD1 − JD4)/30.6001)
      Set Out_Day to Trunc(JD1 − JD4 + Frac − Trunc(30.6001 * JD5))
```

*Algorithm adapted from *Practical Astronomy with Your Calculator,* Second Edition, by Peter Duffet-Smith, Cambridge University Press, 1981.

(Compute month)
IF JD5 <= 13
  THEN
    Set Out_Month to JD5 − 1
  ELSE
    Set Out_Month to JD5 − 13
(Compute year)
IF Out_Month >= 3
  THEN
    Set Out_Year to JD3 − 4716
  ELSE
    Set Out_Year to JD3 − 4715
(Adjust years BC for missing year 0)
IF Out_Year <= 0
  THEN
    Set Out_Year to Out_Year − 1
IF (Out_Year < −1) OR
  (Out_Year = −1) AND (Out_Month < 3)
  THEN
    Set Out_Day to Out_Day − 1
WITH Out_Date DO
    Set Year to Out_Year
    Set Day to Out_Day
    Set Month to Month_Num(Out_Month)
ELSE
  Call Error with message 'Invalid (negative) Julian date.'
  Set Out_Date to Julian day 0

Once we have routines for converting dates to and from Julian day form, it is easy to write the algorithm for Change. We convert the date into a Julian day number, add the amount to change the date, and then convert it back into a date. Change must, of course, check that the new date is valid.

PROBLEM-SOLVING CASE STUDY cont'd.

Change (Receives/Returns IO_Date: Date,
Receives Amount: LongInt)

> Set_Up
> IF IO_Date is Valid
> THEN
>   Set Julian to Julian_Day(IO_Date) + Amount
>   If Julian < 0.0
>   THEN
>   Call Error with message 'Change results in an invalid date.'
>   Set Julian to 0.0
>   Date_Of_JD(Julian, IO_Date)
> ELSE
>   Set IO_Date to Julian day 0

The only operations remaining are Date_Error and Date_Error_Str. Each of these simply takes the value stored in the corresponding private global variable and returns it. We need not spell out these single line algorithms here. Speaking of the private global variables, however, we must not forget to initialize them. We will assign False to Error_Flag and the empty string to Error_String. Because the unit is simply a collection of modules, we will not show a module structure chart. Here, then, is the code for our Date abstract data type.

```
UNIT DateADT;

INTERFACE

USES
  MonthADT;                         (* Month abstract data type  *)

TYPE
  Day  = 1..31;                     (* Days have the range 1..31 *)
  Year = -4713..MaxInt;             (* Julian year 0 is minimum  *)
  Date = RECORD                     (* Dates are 3-field records *)
    Month : MonthADT.Month;
    Day   : Day;
    Year  : Year
  END;  (* Record *)
  String40 = String[40];            (* Error message string type *)
  String20 = String[20];            (* Date in string form type  *)

(* ************************************************************* *)
```

PROBLEM-SOLVING CASE STUDY cont'd.

```
FUNCTION Date_Error:              (* True if an error occurs *)
           Boolean;

(* This function returns True if a preceding call to one *)
(* of the other DateADT functions encounters an error    *)

(*********************************************************************)

FUNCTION Date_Error_Str:    (* Returns an error message *)
           String40;

(* If Date_Error returns True, this function provides an *)
(* error message to explain the source of the error      *)

(*********************************************************************)

FUNCTION Julian_Day(In_Date:       (* A value of type Date  *)
                        Date):
                        Real;      (* The Julian day number *)

(* This function converts a date to its Julian day. *)
(* Julian day 0 is January 1, 4713 BC *)

(*********************************************************************)

PROCEDURE Date_Of_JD(    JD:              (* Julian day number *)
                         Real;
                     VAR Out_Date:        (* Equivalent date   *)
                         Date);

(* This procedure takes a Julian day number and returns *)
(* the corresponding date *)

(*********************************************************************)

FUNCTION Date_Str(In_Date:         (* A value of type date *)
                      Date):
                      String20;    (* Date in string form  *)

(* This function converts a date into a string with the *)
(* month name spelled out in full, and the full year    *)

(*********************************************************************)

PROCEDURE Change(VAR IO_Date:          (* A value of type Date *)
                      Date;
                      Amount:          (* Number of Days to add *)
                      LongInt);
```

PROBLEM-SOLVING CASE STUDY *cont'd.*

```
(* This procedure takes a value of type Date, and adds a *)
(* number of days to it. If the result is not valid,     *)
(* the function Date_Error returns True, and the result  *)
(* of the function is Julian day zero *)


(*********************************************************************)

PROCEDURE Make_Date(     In_Month,      (* Number of a month  *)
                         In_Day,        (* Number of a day    *)
                         In_Year:       (* Number of a year   *)
                           Integer;
                     VAR Out_Date:      (* Corresponding date *)
                           Date);

(* This procedure takes three numbers representing Month, *)
(* Day, and Year, and returns a Date value after checking *)
(* that the date is valid *)


(*********************************************************************)

FUNCTION Equal(Date1,       (* A value of type Date    *)
               Date2:       (* A value of type Date    *)
                 Date):
                   Boolean;  (* True if they are equal *)

(* Given two values of type Date, returns true if they *)
(* are both valid Dates and they are equal *)


(*********************************************************************)

FUNCTION Less(Date1,        (* A value of type Date   *)
              Date2:        (* A value of type Date   *)
                Date):
                  Boolean;   (* True if Date1 < Date2 *)

(* Given two values of type Date, returns True if they *)
(* are both valid Dates and Date1 < Date2 *)


(*********************************************************************)

FUNCTION Greater(Date1,     (* A value of type Date   *)
                 Date2:     (* A value of type Date   *)
                   Date):
                     Boolean; (* True if Date1 > Date2 *)

(* Given two values of type Date, returns True if they *)
(* are both valid Dates and Date1 < Date2 *)
```

```
(**********************************************************************)
(**********************************************************************)
(**********************************************************************)


IMPLEMENTATION

VAR                    (* True if an error is encountered *)
  Error_Flag:
    Boolean;
  Error_String:        (* Holds an error message          *)
    String40;


(**********************************************************************)


PROCEDURE Set_Up;

(* This procedure initializes the global variables. It *)
(* is called by most of the other ADT functions *)

BEGIN (* Set_Up *)
  Error_Flag := False;
  Error_String := ''
END;  (* Set_Up *)


(**********************************************************************)


PROCEDURE Error(In_Str:            (* Error message *)
                  String40);

(* This procedure sets the global variables Error_Flag *)
(* and Error_String and is called by the other ADT      *)
(* functions when they encounter an error *)

BEGIN (* Error *)
  Error_Flag := True;
  Error_String := In_Str
END;  (* Error *)


(**********************************************************************)


FUNCTION Leap(In_Year:
                Year):            (* Year to test      *)
                  Boolean;        (* True if a leap year *)

(* Leap returns True if the given year is a leap year *)
```

PROBLEM-SOLVING CASE STUDY cont'd.

```
BEGIN (* Leap *)
  Leap := (In_Year MOD   4 = 0) AND NOT
          (In_Year MOD 100 = 0) OR
          (In_Year MOD 400 = 0)
END;  (* Leap *)

(**********************************************************************)

FUNCTION Valid(In_Date:          (* A value of type Date *)
                  Date):
                  Boolean;       (* True if a valid date *)

(* This function checks that the number of days in the *)
(* month is valid. Leap year is considered. It assumes *)
(* that the date was built via the ADT facilities, and *)
(* thus all the individual values have been validated  *)

VAR
  OK:            (* Temporary result *)
    Boolean;

BEGIN (* Valid *)
  WITH In_Date DO
    IF (Year >= -4713) AND (Year<> 0)
      THEN
        CASE Month OF
          January,
          March,
          May,
          July,
          August,
          October,
          December   : OK := Day IN [1..31];
          April,
          June,
          September,
          November   : OK := Day IN [1..30];
          February   : IF Leap(Year)
                         THEN
                           OK := Day IN [1..29]
                         ELSE
                           OK := Day IN [1..28]
        END (* CASE *)
      ELSE
        OK := False;
  Valid := OK;
  IF NOT OK
    THEN
      Error('Invalid date.')
END;  (* Valid *)
```

PROBLEM-SOLVING CASE STUDY cont'd.

```
(********************************************************************)

FUNCTION Date_Error:              (* True if an error occurs *)
         Boolean;

(* This function returns True if a preceding call to one *)
(* of the other DateADT functions encounters an error.   *)
(* It accesses the global variable Error_Flag *)

BEGIN (* Date_Error *)
  Date_Error := Error_Flag;
END;   (* Date_Error *)


(********************************************************************)

FUNCTION Date_Error_Str:      (* Returns an error message *)
         String40;

(* If Date_Error returns True, this function provides an *)
(* error message to explain the source of the error.     *)
(* It accesses the global variable Error_String *)

BEGIN (* Date_Error_Str *)
  Date_Error_Str := Error_String
END;   (* Date_Error *)


(********************************************************************)

FUNCTION Julian_Date(In_Date:      (* A value of type Date *)
                     Date):
                     Real;      (* The Julian day number *)

(* This function converts a date to its Julian day. *)
(* Julian day 0 is January 1, 4713 BC *)

VAR
  Year,             (* Adjusted year of date            *)
  Month,            (* Adjusted month of date           *)
  Day,              (* Day of date                      *)
  Temp,             (* Temporary variable               *)
  Leap_Factor,      (* Days to add due to leap years    *)
  Year_Days,        (* Days to add for whole years      *)
Month_Days:         (* Days to add for whole months     *)
    LongInt;
  Gregorian:        (* Date Gregorian calendar started  *)
    Date;
```

```
BEGIN (* Julian_Day *)
  Set_Up;
  IF Valid(In_Date)
    THEN
      BEGIN
        (* Convert date to separate integers *)
        Month := Number(In_Date.Month);
        Day := In_Date.Day;
        Year := In_Date.Year;
        (* Check if Year is BC, if so, add 1 so that 1 *)
        (* BC becomes year 0, eliminating gap in year  *)
        (* numbering *)
        IF Year < 0
          THEN
            Year := Year + 1;
        (* First two months are special due to leap year *)
        IF (Month = 1) OR (Month = 2)
          THEN
            BEGIN
              Year := Year - 1;
              Month := Month + 12
            END;
        (* Gregorian (modern) calendar dates must be   *)
        (* handled differently than Julian (old style) *)
        (* calendar dates *)
        Gregorian.Month := October;
        Gregorian.Day := 15;
        Gregorian.Year := 1582;
        IF Greater(In_Date, Gregorian)
          THEN
            BEGIN
              Temp := Year DIV 100;
              Leap_Factor := 2 - Temp + Temp DIV 4
            END
          ELSE
            Leap_Factor := 0;
        (* Compute days in whole years *)
        Year_Days := Trunc(365.25 * Year);
        (* Compute days in whole months *)
        Month_Days := Trunc(30.6001 * (Month + 1));
        (* Sum days and factor that makes 4713 year 0 *)
        Julian_Day := Leap_Factor + Year_Days +
                      Month_Days + Day + 1720994.5
      END
    ELSE
      Julian_Day := 0.0
END;  (* Julian_Day *)
```

```
(*********************************************************************)

PROCEDURE Date_Of_JD(     JD:              (* Julian day number *)
                            Real;
                      VAR Out_Date:        (* Equivalent date    *)
                            Date);

(* This procedure takes a Julian day number and returns *)
(* the corresponding date *)

VAR
  JDI,             (* Integer part of Julian day      *)
  JD1,             (* Intermediate Julian date result *)
  JD2,             (* Intermediate Julian date result *)
  JD3,             (* Intermediate Julian date result *)
  JD4,             (* Intermediate Julian date result *)
  JD5:             (* Intermediate Julian date result *)
    LongInt;
  Frac:            (* Fractional part of Julian day   *)
    Real;
  Out_Month,       (* Resulting month *)
  Out_Day,         (* Resulting day   *)
  Out_Year:        (* Resulting year  *)
    Integer;

BEGIN (* Date_Of_JD *)
  Set_Up;
  IF JD >= 0.0
    THEN
      BEGIN
        (* Julian day actually starts at noon *)
        JD := JD + 0.5;
        JDI := Trunc(JD);
        Frac := JD - JDI;
        (* Compensate for Gregorian vs. Julian calendar *)
        IF JDI > 2299160
          THEN
            BEGIN
              JD1 := TRUNC((JDI - 1867216.25) / 36524.25);
              JD2 := JDI + 1 + JD1 - JD1 DIV 4
            END
          ELSE
            JD2 := JDI;
```

```
          (* Adjust for leap years *)
          JD1 := JD2 + 1524;
          JD3 := Trunc((JD1 - 122.1)/365.25);
          JD4 := Trunc(JD3 * 365.25);
          JD5 := Trunc((JD1 - JD4)/30.6001);
          (* Compute day of month *)
          Out_Day := Trunc(JD1 - JD4 + Frac - Trunc(30.6001 * JD5));
          (* Compute month *)
          IF JD5 <= 13
            THEN
              Out_Month := JD5 - 1
            ELSE
              Out_Month := JD5 - 13;
          (* Compute year *)
          IF Out_Month >= 3
            THEN
              Out_Year := JD3 - 4716
            ELSE
              Out_Year := JD3 - 4715;
          (* Adjust years BC for missing year 0 *)
          IF Out_Year <= 0
            THEN
              Out_Year := Out_Year - 1;
          IF (Out_Year < -1) OR
             (Out_Year = -1) AND (Out_Month < 3)
            THEN
              Out_Day := Out_Day - 1;
          WITH Out_Date DO
            BEGIN
              Year := Out_Year;
              Day  := Out_Day;
              Month := Month_Num(Out_Month)
            END
      END
  ELSE
    BEGIN
      Error('Invalid (negative) Julian date.');
      WITH Out_Date DO
        BEGIN
          (* Set Out_Date to Julian day 0 *)
          Year := -4713;
          Day  := 1;
          Month := January
        END
  END
END;  (* Date_Of_JD *)
```

```
(***********************************************************************)

FUNCTION Date_Str(In_Date:          (* A value of type date *)
                     Date):
                     String20;       (* Date in string form  *)

(* This function converts a date into a string with the *)
(* month name spelled out in full, and the full year     *)

VAR
   Day_Str:           (* String representation of day  *)
     String[2];
   Year_Str:          (* String representation of year *)
     String[6];

BEGIN (* Date_Str *)
  Set_Up;
  IF Valid(In_Date)
    THEN
      WITH In_Date DO
        BEGIN
          Str(Day:1, Day_Str);
          Str(Year:1, Year_Str);
          Date_Str := Month_Name(Month) + ' ' + Day_Str +
                      ', ' + Year_Str
        END
    ELSE
      Date_Str := ''
END;  (* Date_Str *)


(***********************************************************************)

PROCEDURE Change(VAR IO_Date:          (* A value of type Date  *)
                        Date;
                     Amount:           (* Number of Days to add *)
                        LongInt);

(* This procedure takes a value of type Date and adds a *)
(* number of days to it. If the result is not valid,     *)
(* the function Date_Error returns True, and the result  *)
(* of the function is Julian day zero *)

VAR
   Julian:           (* Julian day of In_Date + Amount *)
     Real;
```

```
BEGIN (* Change *)
  Set_Up;
  IF Valid(IO_Date)
    THEN
      BEGIN
        Julian := Julian_Day(IO_Date) + Amount;
        IF Julian < 0.0
          THEN
            BEGIN
              Error('Change results in an invalid date.');
              Julian := 0.0
            END;
        Date_Of_JD(Julian, IO_Date)
      END
    ELSE
      WITH IO_Date DO
        BEGIN
          (* Set IO_Date to Julian day 0 *)
          Year  := -4713;
          Day   := 1;
          Month := January
        END
END;  (* Change *)

(****************************************************************)


PROCEDURE Make_Date(     In_Month,     (* Number of a month *)
                         In_Day,       (* Number of a day   *)
                         In_Year:      (* Number of a year  *)
                           Integer;
                     VAR Out_Date:     (* Corresponding date *)
                           Date);

(* This procedure takes three numbers representing Month, *)
(* Day, and Year, and returns a Date value after checking *)
(* that the date is valid *)

VAR
  Day0:        (* Julian day 0 *)
    Date;
```

```
BEGIN (* Make_Date *)
  Set_Up;
  WITH Day0 DO
    BEGIN
      Year := -4713;
      Day  := 1;
      Month := January
    END;
  WITH Out_Date DO
    BEGIN
      Year := In_Year;
      Day  := In_Day;
      Month := Month_Num(In_Month)
    END;
  IF NOT Valid(Out_Date) OR Less(Out_Date, Day0)
    THEN
      BEGIN
        Error('Does not make a valid date.');
        Out_Date := Day0
      END
END;  (* Make_Date *)
```

```
(* ********************************************************************* *)
```

```
FUNCTION Equal(Date1,          (* A value of type Date   *)
               Date2:          (* A value of type Date   *)
                  Date):
                     Boolean;  (* True if they are equal *)

(* Given two values of type Date, returns true if they *)
(* are both valid Dates and they are equal *)

BEGIN (* Equal *)
  Set_Up;
  IF Valid(Date1) AND Valid(Date2)
    THEN
      Equal := (Date1.Month = Date2.Month) AND
               (Date1.Day   = Date2.Day)   AND
               (Date1.Year  = Date2.Year)
    ELSE
      Equal := False
END;  (* Equal *)
```

```
(* ********************************************************************* *)
```

```
FUNCTION Less(Date1,            (* A value of type Date  *)
              Date2:           (* A value of type Date  *)
               Date):
                Boolean;       (* True if Date1 < Date2 *)

(* Given two values of type Date, returns True if they *)
(* are both valid Dates and Date1 < Date 2 *)

BEGIN (* Less *)
  Set_Up;
  IF Valid(Date1) AND Valid(Date2)
    THEN
      BEGIN
        Less := False;
        IF Date1.Year < Date2.Year
          THEN
            Less := True;
        IF (Date1.Year = Date2.Year) AND
           (Date1.Month < Date2.Month)
          THEN
            Less := True;
        IF (Date1.Year = Date2.Year) AND
           (Date1.Month = Date2.Month) AND
           (Date1.Day < Date2.Day)
          THEN
            Less := True
      END
    ELSE
      Less := False
END;  (* Less *)


(****************************************************************************)

FUNCTION Greater(Date1,            (* A value of type Date  *)
                 Date2:           (* A value of type Date  *)
                  Date):
                   Boolean;       (* True if Date1 > Date2 *)

(* Given two values of type Date, returns True if they *)
(* are both valid Dates and Date1 > Date2. Relies on   *)
(* Equal and Less to call Set_Up and validate dates    *)

BEGIN (* Greater *)
  Greater := NOT Equal(Date1, Date2) AND
             NOT Less(Date1, Date2)
END;  (* Greater *)
```

PROBLEM-SOLVING CASE STUDY *cont'd.*

```
(****************************************************************)
(****************************************************************)
(****************************************************************)

(* INITIALIZATION *)

BEGIN (* Date_ADT *)
  Error_Flag := False;
  Error_String := ''
END.  (* Date_ADT *)
```

Testing: Because we cannot run a unit directly, we must write a driver program that tests the unit. The driver must call each public subprogram at least once and should be tried with a planned set of test data to ensure code coverage.

For the DateADT unit we developed the following interactive driver. It begins by asking the user for a date in numeric form. Procedure Make_Date, and functions, Date_Error and Date_Error_Str are tested after this, and Date_Str is used to echo-print the input date. Then the date is converted to Julian day form (and printed) and back to date form (and printed again). Next the user is asked for an amount to change the date and Change is called. Date_Error, Date_Error_Str and Date_Str are tested again after this. Lastly, each of the comparisons is tried to determine the relationship between the new and old dates.

This is a very simple driver for testing the Date unit. To be rigorous, we should add code that calls each operation independently with invalid data and then checks Date_Error and Date_Error_String to be certain that the erroneous data was detected.

```
PROGRAM Date_ADT_Driver (Input, Output);

(* This program is used to test the operations supplied *)
(* by the Date_ADT unit. It allows a user to enter a    *)
(* date and an amount. It then prints the Julian day    *)
(* for the date, and converts the Julian day back into  *)
(* a date to print it out. Then it changes the date by  *)
(* the amount specified, and prints the new date. Last, *)
(* it determines whether the new date is less than,     *)
(* greater than, or equal to the old date *)

USES
  DateADT;
```

PROBLEM-SOLVING CASE STUDY cont'd.

```pascal
VAR
  Amount:           (* Amount of change    *)
    LongInt;
  A_Month,          (* User specified month *)
  A_Year,           (* User specified year  *)
  A_Day:            (* User specified day   *)
    Integer;
  Old_Date,         (* Original date input  *)
  New_Date:         (* Adjusted date        *)
    Date;
  Julian:           (* Julian day number    *)
    Real;

BEGIN (* Date_ADT_Driver *)
  Writeln('Enter a date in the form MM DD YYYY');
  Readln(A_Month, A_Day, A_Year);
  Writeln;
  Make_Date(A_Month, A_Day, A_Year, Old_Date);
  IF Date_Error
    THEN
      Writeln(Date_Error_Str);
  Writeln('Date = ', Date_Str(Old_Date));
  Julian := Julian_Day(Old_Date);
  Writeln('Julian day number = ', Julian:1:2);
  Date_Of_JD(Julian, New_Date);
  Writeln('Date of Julian day = ', Date_Str(New_Date));
  Writeln;
  Writeln('Enter an amount to change the date.');
  Readln(Amount);
  Writeln;
  Change(New_Date, Amount);
  IF Date_Error
    THEN
      Writeln(Date_Error_Str);
  Writeln('The new date is ', Date_Str(New_Date));
  IF Less(New_Date, Old_Date)
    THEN
      Writeln('New date is less than original date.');
  IF Greater(New_Date, Old_Date)
    THEN
      Writeln('New date is greater than original date.');
  IF Equal(New_Date, Old_Date)
    THEN
      Writeln('New date equals original date.')
END.  (* Date_ADT_Driver *)
```

PROBLEM-SOLVING CASE STUDY cont'd.

Here is a sample run of the driver.

```
Enter a date in the form MM DD YYYY
2 4 1991

Date = February 4, 1991
Julian day number = 2448291.50
Date of Julian day = February 4, 1991

Enter an amount to change the date.
10

The new date is February 14, 1991
New date is greater than original date.
```

PROBLEM-SOLVING CASE STUDY

Program Birthday Calls Rewritten

Problem: Now that we've built an abstract data type to represent dates, let's see how we can use it to rewrite Program Birthday Calls from Chapter 14. Recall that the program was to read a file of entries that included the name, phone number, and birth date of some friends. If a friend's birthday is within the next two weeks, it prints the name, phone number, and birthday so that we can remember to call them.

Input:

A file of entries (FRIENDS.DAT). Each entry contains the first and last name (15 characters each) on one line, separated by a blank. The second line of an entry contains the phone number in the form

(999)999-9999

The third line of each entry contains the friend's birth date as three numbers separated by blanks: the month, day, and year.

The current date is entered from the keyboard as numeric month, day, and year values.

Output: In addition to user prompts, the names, telephone numbers, and birth dates of each friend who has a birthday within the next two weeks. Error messages should also be output if invalid data is encountered.

PROBLEM-SOLVING CASE STUDY *cont'd.*

Discussion: We're not trying to solve a new problem here but merely recasting an old one using new and more powerful tools. We start by looking back at Program Birthday_Calls to see how we can use our Data type to simplify it. The most obvious change is that the Adjust_Date procedure (and its subsidiary function, Days_In_Month) is no longer needed. We can use Procedure Change in its place. The module that prints the date can be replaced by calling Date_Str within a Writeln statement. We can also replace Function Compare with appropriate calls to Greater, Less, and Equal.

If Compare is not to be used, we can eliminate the data type Relation. Of course, we no longer need to define our own Date type. To further simplify the program, we also will change the type of a phone number to be a string of 13 characters instead of a record. We originally used a record to provide an example of a hierarchical record (Entry_Type2) containing two other records (Date_Type and Phone_Type). However, making the phone number a single string is easier in this case because we won't be manipulating the area code and number separately. We can thus shorten the procedures for getting and printing entries.

The only other change that we'll need to make is to use Make_Date to convert input data into values of type date. We could directly store values into a Date record, but Make_Date provides data validation via the Date_Error and Date_Error_Str functions. Of course, we'll need to list DateADT in a USES statement at the start of the program. We'll also need to list MonthADT in the USES statement so that we can refer to month names. (Recall that the original program had to check for the special case of an early January birthday when the current date is near the end of December.)

The revised module structure chart follows. Notice that it is only two levels deep and that there are only four modules including the main program. In contrast, the original module structure chart had three levels and contained eight modules.

Module Structure Chart:

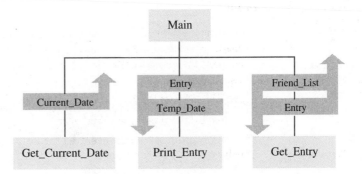

Below is the code for the revised program. Compare this to the original program, which was six and a half pages long. Not only is the new version shorter, but it has much better data validation. Clearly, the availability of a Date abstract data type has allowed us to greatly simplify and improve this program. It is true that Unit DateADT is a lengthy piece of code and itself uses one other unit. However, once it has been written, it can be used again and again in many different programs.

```pascal
PROGRAM Birthday_Calls (Input, Output, Friend_List);

(* A date is read from the keyboard, and a date two weeks away is *)
(* calculated. Names, phone numbers, and birthdays of all those   *)
(* on file Friend_List whose birthdays come on or before the date *)
(* two weeks away are printed *)

USES
   MonthADT,       (* Month abstract data type unit *)
   DateADT;        (* Date abstract data type unit  *)

CONST
   Name_Length = 15;
   Days_Hence = 14;

TYPE
   Name_Type = String[Name_Length];
   Phone_Type = String[13];
   Entry_Type = RECORD
                   First_Name,
                   Last_Name : Name_Type;
                   Phone : Phone_Type;
                   Birth_Date : Date        (* Date defined in DateADT *)
                END;   (* Record *)

VAR
   Entry:             (* Current record from Friend_List being checked *)
      Entry_Type;
   Current_Date,      (* Month, Day and Year of current day         *)
   Temp_Date,         (* Month and Day of Birth_Date, current year *)
   Target_Date:       (* Two weeks from current date               *)
      Date;
   Month,             (* Month part of Temp_Date *)
   Day,               (* Day part of Temp_Date   *)
   Year:              (* Year part of Temp_Date  *)
      Integer;
   Friend_List:       (* Input file of friend records *)
      Text;
```

PROBLEM-SOLVING CASE STUDY *cont'd.*

```
(************************************************************************)

PROCEDURE Get_Current_Date (VAR Current_Date:        (* Today's date *)
                                 Date);

(* Current date is entered from the console *)

VAR
  Month,            (* Entered month *)
  Day,              (* Entered day   *)
  Year:             (* Entered year  *)
    Integer;

BEGIN (* Get_Current_Date *)
  REPEAT
    Writeln('Please input current date as month, day, and year.');
    Writeln('Use digits for month. Separate with blanks.');
    Readln(Month, Day, Year);
    Make_Date(Month, Day, Year, Current_Date);
    IF Date_Error
      THEN
        Writeln(Date_Error_Str)
  UNTIL NOT Date_Error
END;  (* Get_Current_Date *)

(************************************************************************)

PROCEDURE Print_Entry (Entry:                 (* Valid friend record *)
                            Entry_Type;
                         Temp_Date:            (* Birthday of friend  *)
                            Date);

(* The name, phone number, and birthdate are printed *)

BEGIN (* Print_Entry *)
  WITH Entry DO
    BEGIN
      Writeln(First_Name, ' ', Last_Name);
      Writeln(Phone);
      Writeln(Date_Str(Temp_Date));
      Writeln;
      Writeln
    END
END;  (* Print_Entry *)

(************************************************************************)
```

PROBLEM-SOLVING CASE STUDY *cont'd.*

```
PROCEDURE Get_Entry (VAR Friend_List:        (* Input file of friends *)
                            Text;
                     VAR Entry:              (* Next friend from file *)
                            Entry_Type);

(* An Entry is read from file Friend_List *)

VAR
   Character:      (* Input character *)
      Char;
   Month,          (* Input month    *)
   Day,            (* Input day      *)
   Year:           (* Input year     *)
      Integer;

BEGIN (* Get_Entry *)
   WITH Entry DO
     BEGIN
       Readln(Friend_List, First_Name, Character, Last_Name);
       Readln(Friend_List, Phone);
       Readln(Friend_List, Month, Character, Day, Character, Year);
       Make_Date(Month, Day, Year, Birth_Date);
       IF Date_Error
         THEN
           Writeln(Date_Error_Str, ' File FRIENDS.DAT.');
       (* Skip over blank line *)
       Readln(Friend_List)
     END
END;  (* Get_Entry *)

(*******************************************************************)
```

```
BEGIN (* Birthday_Calls *)
  Assign(Friend_List, 'FRIENDS.DAT');
  Reset(Friend_List);
  Get_Current_Date(Current_Date);
  Target_Date := Current_Date;
  Change(Target_Date, Days_Hence);
  WHILE NOT EOF(Friend_List) DO
    BEGIN
      Get_Entry(Friend_List, Entry);
      Temp_Date := Entry.Birth_Date;
      IF (Target_Date.Year <> Current_Date.Year) AND
         (Temp_Date.Month = January)
        THEN
          Temp_Date.Year := Target_Date.Year
        ELSE
          Temp_Date.Year := Current_Date.Year;
      IF (Less(Temp_Date, Target_Date) OR
          Equal(Temp_Date, Target_Date)) AND
         (Greater(Temp_Date, Current_Date) OR
          Equal(Temp_Date, Current_Date))
        THEN
          Print_Entry(Entry, Temp_Date)
    END;
  Close(Friend_List)
END.   (* Birthday_Calls *)
```

Testing: We can use the same tests that were originally used in Chapter 14 for Program Birthday_Calls. However, now that the program includes data validation checks, we should include some invalid dates in both the data file and the keyboard input. These might include February 29th in a year that isn't a leap year, or dates such as April 31 and January 0.

Object-Oriented Programming with Turbo Pascal

Throughout this text we have used top-down design as our methodology for developing algorithmic problem solutions. Another approach to designing programs is called Object-Oriented Design. This methodology originated with the development of programs to simulate physical objects and processes in the real world. For example, to simulate an electronic circuit, you could develop a module for simulating each type of component in the circuit and then "wire-up" the simulation by having the modules pass information among themselves in the same pattern that wires connect the electronic components.

In a simulation, the top-down decomposition of the problem has already taken place. An engineer has designed a circuit, or a mechanical device, a physicist has developed a model of a physical system, a biologist has developed an experimental model, an economist has designed an economic model, and so on. Your job as a programmer is to take this problem decomposition and implement it.

The first step is to identify the simplest and most widely used objects and processes in the decomposition and implement them faithfully. Once you have done this, you can often reuse these objects and processes to implement more complex objects and processes. This hierarchy of objects is the basis for object-oriented design. As you can see, this methodology takes a bottom-up approach. While top-down design is really an extension of the divide-and-conquer problem solving technique discussed in Chapter 1, object-oriented design is based on the building-block technique.

There are three key ingredients to an object oriented design: *encapsulation, inheritance,* and *polymorphism.* We have already defined encapsulation. When one object is built on top of another object, the new object inherits the properties and processes of the older object. For example, an object representing a book might be a collection of objects representing pages. The book object inherits the properties of the page objects on which it is built. Polymorphism permits a process that is common to many objects to have a different implementation for each type of object. For example, addition can be performed on integer numbers, real numbers, complex numbers, and fractions. Although it is conceptually similar for each type of number, its implementation is different.

Inheritance   When a new object is based on an existing object, the new object inherits the properties and processes associated with the existing object.

Polymorphism   In a hierarchy of objects, it is possible for each object to define a new implementation of an operation that it has in common (through inheritance) with other objects in the hierarchy.

Turbo Pascal supports object-oriented programming with a new type called an *object.* The syntax of an object is similar to that of a record, except that the keyword OBJECT replaces the keyword RECORD, and the fields of an object can include procedure and function headings. For example,

```
TYPE
  Date = OBJECT
          Month: (January, February, March, April, May, June, July,
                  August, September, October, November, December);
          Day: 1..31;
          Year: -4713..MaxInt;
          PROCEDURE Make_Date(    In_Month,       (* Number of a month    *)
                                  In_Day,         (* Number of a day      *)
                                  In_Year:        (* Number of a year     *)
                                  Integer;
                              VAR Out_Date:       (* Corresponding date   *)
                                  Date);
          PROCEDURE Change(VAR IO_Date:           (* A value of type Date *)
                                  Date;
                                  Amount:         (* Number of days to add *)
                                  LongInt);
          FUNCTION Date_Str(In_Date:              (* A value of type date *)
                                  Date):
                                  String20;       (* Date in string form  *)
      END;  (* OBJECT *)
```

defines an object that represents a date. The first three fields contain data, and the last three fields define operations on date objects. These operations are called *methods*.

Method   An operation that is part of an object definition.

The complete definitions of the procedures and functions follow the end of the type declaration of the object. The fields of an object are accessed in the same way that record fields are, by giving the name of an object, followed by a period and the name of a field.

An object is built upon another object by giving the name of the existing object, enclosed in parentheses, following the keyword OBJECT. For example we could write

```
TYPE
  Machine_Record = OBJECT (Date)
                     Cost: Real
                   END; (* OBJECT *)
```

to define a machine record that adds a Cost field to objects of type date, to define a new type of object. Type Machine_Record implicitly contains (inherits) the fields Month, Day, and Year, and the three methods defined for dates. We could also define additional methods in type Machine_Record if we so desire.

Turbo Pascal provides many more extensions to support the use of objects. A complete discussion of object-oriented programming and the facilities provided by Turbo Pascal is beyond the scope of this text. Our purpose here is to introduce briefly the concepts and whet your appetite for further study.

Object-oriented design should not be considered as an alternative methodology to top-down design. The two approaches go hand in hand. A difficult and complex problem will often require decomposition. However, knowledge of object-oriented design may help guide the decomposition so that the solution can be built from a hierarchy of objects.

The advantage of object-oriented design is that it results in a collection of object definitions that are reused easily in other problems. Once you have a large library of objects at your disposal, writing a new program becomes largely a matter of assembling those objects. Thus, you are able to solve new problems more quickly, with less effort, and with greater confidence in the correctness of the solution.

Testing and Debugging

Because a unit cannot be run separately, like a program, you must create one or more driver programs to test the unit. All of the testing methodology for normal procedures and functions applies to those found in units, for example, trying to pass invalid data through the interface, checking the functionality of the subprogram, and verifying the preconditions and postconditions.

There are, however, some additional considerations for testing a unit. We must verify that the unit initialization is performed correctly, and we must indirectly check the private subprograms and data.

Checking the initialization of public variables is easy—we simply have the driver print their values. But we cannot directly access private variables and must instead determine their values indirectly. For example, if the length of a list is kept in a private variable, and the unit provides a function that returns the length of the list, we can call the function to determine the initial value of the variable. We also can use the Turbo debugger to watch the values of private variables.

Testing private subprograms and data also must be done indirectly. We cannot call a private subprogram, but we can call a public subprogram that uses it. By passing appropriate values to the public subprogram, we are able to exercise the private subprogram to some extent. The Turbo debugger can also help, because we can use it to trace through the private subprogram and watch the private data.

Testing and Debugging Hints

1. Check that the procedure and function headings in the implementation section match exactly their counterparts in the interface section.
2. Initialize all public variables and all private global variables.
3. Be certain that nothing has been omitted from the interface that the user will need.
4. Don't include anything in the interface that the user shouldn't have access to.
5. Just like a program, a unit ends with a period.
6. A USES statement within a unit provides the unit with access to other units. However, access to the other units is not provided automatically to the user. If the user

program also requires access to the other units, it must include them in its own USES statement.

7. Remember to set the object code destination to **disk** in the Compile menu; otherwise the object code for the unit is not saved and the user program won't be able to access it.

8. If you make a change to a unit, you must also recompile all of the units and programs that use it; otherwise they won't incorporate the change. Almost every programmer has had the experience of fixing a bug in a unit and rerunning the user program, only to see the error occur again. After much head-scratching they realize that in rushing to try out the fix, they forgot to recompile the program.

Summary

Standard Pascal does not support separate compilation and physical hiding of implementations. Turbo Pascal addresses these shortcomings with a nonstandard extension called a unit.

A unit is a separately compilable collection of declarations and code that can be used by other units and programs. It consists of three sections: interface, implementation, and initialization. The interface section gives the user all of the information required to make use of the unit but not the actual mechanism employed within the unit. The implementation section, which may be hidden from the user, contains the code that makes the unit work.

Public constants, types, variables, and subprogram headings are declared in the interface section. The implementation section contains the code bodies for the public subprograms and may also contain private constants, types, variables, and subprograms. The initialization section is executed automatically before the start of the user program and provides a way to initialize public and private variables, create files, and so on.

Private global variables are useful for holding data that persists between subprogram calls and is hidden from the user. Private global variable access is one of the few exceptions to the rule that global variables should not be accessed from within subprograms. Even so, the access must be carefully documented.

Units provide a mechanism for implementing abstract data types. Although units are much better for this than Standard Pascal, they still fail to support private type definitions as do some languages such as Ada. If we design a unit to be general, then it will be useful for many user programs and will save programming effort repeatedly in the future.

The design of a unit begins with identifying its interface requirements. Then the public subprograms are designed using top-down methodology. Subprograms that fall outside of the hierarchical decomposition (those that are called by more than one public subprogram, for example) are top-level private subprograms. Private global variables are declared whenever it is necessary to keep values, internal to the unit, between subprogram calls.

■ *Quick Check*

1. Is everything declared in the interface section of a unit accessible to a program using the unit? (pp. 890–895)

2. Which subprograms in the implementation section are private? (pp. 890–895)

3. When is the initialization section executed? (pp. 890–895)

4. What are the three types of operations found in an abstract data type? (pp. 895–910)

5. How do Turbo Pascal's units help with the implementation of abstract data types? (pp. 895–910)

Answers

1. Everything except other units listed in the USES statement of the interface section.   2. Those that do not have corresponding declarations in the interface section.   3. Before the user program.
4. Constructors, observers, and iterators.   5. By permitting the abstract data type's implementation to be hidden through separate compilation.

■ *Exam Preparation Exercises*

1. List the three main sections of a Turbo Pascal unit.

2. One unit can contain another (nested) unit. (True or False?)

3. The interface section of a unit can contain complete procedures. (True or False)

4. When a program containing a USES statement is compiled, the object code for the units is directly incorporated into the program. (True or False)

5. If you make a change to a unit, do you also have to recompile the program(s) that use it?

6. If a program uses two different units that contain the same identifier, how do you distinguish between those identifiers?

7. Describe three situations in which private global variables are especially useful.

8. How does separate compilation aid in hiding the implementation of an abstract data type?

9. When designing an abstract data type, what is the first step?

10. How do private subprograms fit into the design methodology for abstract data type units?

11. Why should an abstract data type be designed with more generality than is required for a particular program?

12. Where are private variables declared in a unit?

13. A procedure that converts a string into a month name is an example of (a) a constructor, (b) an observer, (c) an iterator. (Choose one)

14. A function that returns the number of days in a month is an example of (a) a constructor, (b) an observer, (c) an iterator. (Choose one)

15. A procedure that changes a date by a given number of days is an example of (a) a constructor, (b) an observer, (c) an iterator. (Choose one)

■ *Programming Warm-Up Exercises*

1. Add to the Month abstract data type unit a function called Change that takes as parameters a value of type Month and an integer that specifies a number of months by which the month should be changed. The integer can be positive or negative. A change that goes beyond the current year should call Error with a warning message but still return the appropriate month. For example, Change(December, 6) would return June.

2. Add to the Month abstract data type unit a function called Days_In that takes as parameters a value of type Month and a Boolean value. The Boolean value indicates a leap year when it is true, otherwise a normal year. The function returns an integer that equals the number of days in the specified Month. For example Days_In(February, True) would return 29.

3. Add to the Month abstract data type unit the functions Less, Greater, and Equal. Each function takes two values of type Month and returns a Boolean result that is true if the first month is less than, greater than, or equal to the second month, respectively.

4. Add to the Month abstract data type unit a procedure called Short_Name that takes a month as an input parameter and returns a string through a second parameter. The string should be the standard three-letter abbreviation for the month.

5. Add to the Month abstract data type unit a function called Short_Form that takes a three-letter string (the abbreviation of a month name) and returns the corresponding value of type Month. The function should validate its input and appropriately handle invalid abbreviations.

6. Add to the Date abstract data type unit a function called Week_Day that takes as a parameter a value of type Date and returns an integer value representing the day of the week. See Programming Problem 2 in Chapter 4 for an algorithm that computes the day of the week from the Julian day number.

7. Add to the Date abstract data type unit a function called Days_Between that takes two parameters of type Date and returns the number of days between them.

8. Add to the Date abstract data type unit a procedure called Short_Str that takes a value of type Date as an input parameter and returns an eight-character string representing the date in numerical form (mm/dd/yy).

9. Add to the Date abstract data type unit a procedure called Date_Form that takes an eight-character string representing the date in numerical form (mm/dd/yy), and returns a value of type date corresponding to the input date. Be sure to validate the input data.

10. Add to the Date abstract data type unit a public variable, of type Date, called Today. Change the initialization of the unit to call the procedure GetDate, defined in the Turbo Pascal DOS unit. GetDate takes four variable parameters of type Word. The parameters return the year, month, day, and day of the week. Use the values returned by the first three of these parameters to set the value of Today to the current system date.

■ *Programming Problems*

1. Develop a unit to support an abstract data type for years. A year is an integer number in the range −4713 to MaxInt, except that there is no year 0 (1 AD follows 1 BC). The unit should support the following operations: convert an integer to a value of type Year (performing data validation), convert a value of type Year to an integer, change a given year by an integer amount (making sure that the result does not violate the range of years allowed). In addition, the units should include an observer function that returns true if a given year is a leap year. The unit also should provide a Boolean function that returns true if the previous operation produced an error and another function that returns a string indicating the cause of the error.

2. Develop a unit to support an abstract data type for a time of day. The time should be represented internally by values of type LongInt in the range 0..86400 (the number of seconds in a day). The unit should provide operations that convert a set of three integers (hours, minutes, seconds) to a value of type Time (performing data validation), convert a value of type Time to a set of three integers, convert a value of type Time to a string representation (HH:MM:SS), change a time by a given number of seconds (making sure the result falls within the allowable range of values), and compute the difference between two times (with the result a value of type Time). The unit should also provide observer functions called Less, Greater, and Equal that compare two values of type Time and return Boolean results. Any operation for which an error can be detected should return an extra Boolean parameter (Error). A function, called Error_Str, should be provided that returns a string indicating the cause of the most recent error detected.

3. Develop a unit to support an abstract data type for a list of names. A name is a string of up to 30 characters. A value of type Name_List may contain up to 1000 names. You may choose whether to represent the list with an array, an array of pointers to dynamic variables, or a linked list. The unit should provide procedures that sort the list and search it for a given name (returning the position of the name in the list). It should provide constructors that take a list and add a name to it (both in-order and at the end) and another constructor that takes a list and a name and removes the name from the list. It should provide observers that return the length of the list and the name at a given position. The unit should also provide an observer function for type Name, which takes two names and returns true if they are equal (ignoring capitalization). The unit also should provide a Boolean function that returns true if the previous operation produced an error and another function that returns a string indicating the cause of the error.

   If you wish, you may implement the Name data type and its observer function as a second abstract data type unit. Separating the definition of the component type from the list type has the advantage of making it easier to later change the component type of the list.

Appendixes

Appendix A Reserved Words

AND	END	NIL	*SHR*
ASM	FILE	NOT	*STRING*
ARRAY	FOR	*OBJECT*	THEN
BEGIN	FUNCTION	OF	TO
CASE	IF	PACKED	*UNIT*
CONSTRUCTOR	*IMPLEMENTATION*	PROCEDURE	UNTIL
DESTRUCTOR	IN	PROGRAM	*USES*
DIV	*INLINE*	RECORD	VAR
DO	*INTERFACE*	REPEAT	WHILE
DOWNTO	LABEL	SET	WITH
ELSE	MOD	*SHL*	*XOR*

Reserved words shown in italics are Turbo Pascal extensions and are not part of Standard Pascal.

Standard Pascal also defines an additional word, FORWARD, which is called a required directive. Although technically not a reserved word, it may be considered to behave like a reserved word in the context of this text. Turbo Pascal additionally defines the following directives:

ABSOLUTE	EXTERNAL	INTERRUPT	PRIVATE
ASSEMBLER	FAR	NEAR	VIRTUAL

Appendix B Standard Identifiers

Identifiers printed in italics are Turbo Pascal extensions and are not part of Standard Pascal.

Standard Constants

False	True	MaxInt

Standard Types

Boolean	*LongInt*
Byte	Real
Char	*ShortInt*
Comp	*Single*
Double	*String*
Extended	Text
Integer	*Word*

Standard Files

Aux	*Lpt1*
Com1	*Lpt2*
Com2	*Lpt3*
Con	*Nul*
Input	Output

Standard Functions

Function Call	Parameter Type	Result Type	Returns
Abs(X)	Integer or Real	Same as X	Absolute value of X
Addr(X)	Identifier	Pointer	Pointer to X
ArcTan(X)	Integer or Real	Real	ArcTan of X in radians
Chr(X)	Integer	Char	Character whose ordinal number is X
Concat(S1, S2, ...,Sn)	String	String	S1, S2,...,Sn concatenated
Copy(S, P, L)	S = String; P, L = Integer	String	Substring of S starting at P, for length of L
Cos(X)	Integer or Real	Real	Cosine of X in radians
CSeg		Word	Value of CS register
DSeg		Word	Value of DS register
EOF(F)	File	Boolean	End-of-file test on F
EOLN(F)	Text	Boolean	End-of-line test on F
Exp(X)	Integer or Real	Real	e to the power X
FilePos(F)	File	LongInt	Marker position in F
FileSize(F)	File	LongInt	Size of F
Frac(X)	Real	Real	Fractional part of X
Hi(X)	Integer or Word	Byte	High order byte of X
Int(X)	Real	Real	Integer part of X
IOResult		Word	If not 0, error in last input/output operation
Length(S)	String	Integer	Characters in string S
Ln(X)	Integer or Real	Real	Natural logarithm of X
Lo	Integer or Word	Byte	Low order byte of X
MaxAvail		LongInt	Size of largest free block of memory in heap

MemAvail		LongInt	Total free memory available in heap
Odd(X)	Integer	Boolean	True if X is odd
Ofs(X)	Identifier	Word	Offset part of address of X
Ord(X)	Ordinal	LongInt	Ordinal number of X
ParamCount		Word	Number of parameters in command line
ParamStr(X)	Word	String	Xth parameter in command line
Pi		Real	3.1415926535897932385
Pos(S1, S2)	Strings	Byte	Position of S1 in S2
Pred(X)	Ordinal	Same as X	Predecessor of X
Ptr(S, O)	Words	Pointer	Converts Segment S and Offset O to an address
Random(X)	Integer	Real	Random number >= 0 and < X
Round(X)	Real	Integer	X rounded
SeekEOF(F)	File	Boolean	EOF test on F after skipping blanks, tabs and <eoln> marks
SeekEoln(F)	File	Boolean	EOLN test on F after skipping blanks, tabs
Seg(X)	Identifier	Word	Segment part of address of X
Sin(X)	Integer or Real	Real	Sine of X in radians
SizeOf(X)	Identifier	Word	Size of X in bytes
SPtr		Word	Value of SP register
Sqr(X)	Integer or Real	Same as X	Square of X
Sqrt(X)	Integer or Real	Real	Square root of X
SSeg		Word	Segment part of address of the stack segment
Succ(X)	Ordinal	Same as X	Successor of X
Swap(X)	Integer or Word	Same as X	Swaps high and low order bytes of X
Trunc(X)	Real	Integer	Integer part of X
UpCase(X)	Char	Char	Converts to uppercase

Standard Procedures

Procedure Call	Description
Append(F)	Opens a text file F and moves marker to end of file for addition of new components
Assign(F, S)	Assigns file identifier F to the DOS file name represented by the string S
BlockRead(F, V, R, C)	Reads R (integer) records into variable V from file F; number of records actually read is in C
BlockWrite(F, V, R, C)	Writes R (integer) records from V to file F, with actual number written returned in C
ChDir(S)	Changes current directory to string S
Close(F)	Closes file F
Dec(X, N)	X (an ordinal) is decremented by N (an integer)
Delete(S, P, N)	Deletes N characters starting at position P in string S

Dispose(P)	Returns to free storage variable pointed to by P
Erase(F)	Erases file F (F must be closed prior to Erase)
Exit	Exits the current block (subprogram or program)
FillChar(V, N, X)	Fills memory with N copies of X (Char or Byte) starting with first byte of variable V
Flush(F)	Ensures that all data written to text file F has actually been output prior to a Rewrite or Append
FreeMem(V, X)	Returns to free storage X bytes of memory starting at location pointed to by V
GetDir(D, S)	Gets current directory name in string S. D = 0 is current drive, D = 1 is drive A, D = 2 is drive B, etc.
GetMem(V, X)	Allocates X bytes of memory from free storage and assigns address to pointer V
Halt	Stops program execution
Inc(X, N)	Increments ordinal X by integer value N
Insert(S1, S2, P)	Inserts string S1 into string S2 at position P
Mark(V)	Assigns current heap pointer to V. Use with Release
MkDir(S)	Creates a new subdirectory specified by string S
Move(V1, V2, N)	Moves N bytes from variable V1 to variable V2
New(P)	Creates a variable of the type referenced by pointer P and assigns its address to P
Randomize	Initializes the internal random number generator with a random number (See Random function)
Read(F, V1, V2,...)	Reads data values from file F and assigns these values to the list of variables in order until all of the variables have input values. If F is not specified, Input is the default file
Readln(F, V1, V2,...)	Same as Read, except F must be a text file and the file pointer is advanced past <eoln> after the last variable has been filled
Release(P)	P is a pointer with a value assigned by Mark. Release returns to free memory all dynamic variables created with New or GetMem since P was assigned its value by Mark
Rename(F, S)	Changes the DOS file name of file identifier F to the string specified by S. File must be closed before Rename is called
Reset(F)	Sets file F to read mode and places the marker at the beginning of the file
Rewrite(F)	Sets file F to write mode, destroying any previous contents
RmDir(S)	Removes the subdirectory specified in string S
RunError(X)	Halts program execution with error code X (byte)
Seek(F, N)	Moves marker for file F to positon N (LongInt). F can be any type except Text
SetTextBuf(F, V, X)	Specifies that I/O with text file F should use X bytes of variable V as a buffer. In some cases, providing a buffer larger than the standard 128 bytes will make I/O faster. F must be closed first

Str(X, S)	Converts result of expression X to a string S. Str is analogous to writing an expression except that the output goes to a string. Fieldwidth specifiers may be used with X
Truncate(F)	Deletes all records in file F past the current position
Val(S, V, E)	Converts string S to an integer or real value V (analogous to reading from a string). If E is 0, then no error occurred during the conversion
Write(F, list)	Outputs the data specified in the list to file F. If F is omitted, file Output is assumed
Writeln(F, list)	Outputs the data specified in the list to file F and then appends <eoln>. F must be of type Text. If F is omitted, file Output is assumed

This appendix covers the most commonly used standard identifiers in Turbo Pascal. The Turbo Pascal Programmer's Guide and Library Reference list many more identifiers, including those contained in the separate units CRT, DOS, Graph, and Overlay. Most of these identifiers are beyond the scope of this text; however, many of the identifiers in Unit Graph are described in Chapter 18.

Appendix C *Pascal Operators and Symbols*

Standard Symbol	Alternate Symbol	
+		plus, set union, or string concatenation
−		minus or set difference
*		times or set intersection
/		real divide
DIV		integer divide
MOD		remainder from integer divide (modulus)
<		is less than
<=		is less than or equal to
=		is equal to
<>		is not equal to
>=		is greater than or equal to
>		is greater than
AND		Boolean conjunction
OR		Boolean inclusive disjunction
NOT		Boolean negation
IN		test set membership
:=		is assigned the value of
,		separates items in a list
;		separates statements
:		separates variable name and type; separates case label and statement; separates statement label and statement

x, y, z : Real

Standard Symbol	Alternate Symbol	
'		delimits character and string literals
.		decimal point, record selector, program terminator, unit selector
..		subrange specifier
∧		file and pointer variable indicator
@		pointer formation operator
(		starts parameter list or nested expression
)		ends parameter list or nested expression
[		starts index list or set expression
(*	{	starts a comment
*)	}	ends a comment
]		ends index list or set expression
SHL		shifts left one bit
SHR		shifts right one bit
XOR		Boolean exclusive disjunction

Appendix D   *Precedence of Operators*

Note

1. Parentheses can be used to change the order of precedence.
2. When operators of equal precedence are used, they are executed in left to right order.

NOT @	Highest precedence
* / DIV MOD AND SHL SHR	
+ − OR	
< <= = >= > <> IN	Lowest precedence

Appendix E   Syntax Templates and Syntax Diagrams

Program

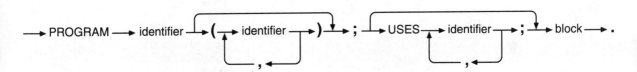

Program

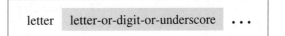

Identifier

letter   letter-or-digit-or-underscore   . . .

Identifier

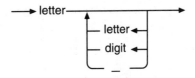

Block

simple declarations
subprogram declarations
BEGIN

   statement **;**

   statement

     .
     .
     .

END

Block

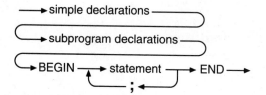

Simple Declarations

LABEL unsigned integer **,** unsigned-integer **;**
.
.
.

CONST
    identifier **=** constant-expression **;**
    identifier **=** constant-expression **;**
        .
        .
        .

TYPE
    identifier **=** type **;**
    identifier **=** type **;**
        .
        .
        .

VAR
    identifier **,**
    identifier
        .
        .
        .
    identifier **:**
     type **;**
    identifier **,**
    identifier
        .
        .
        .
    identifier **:**
     type **;**
        .
        .
        .

Subprogram Declarations

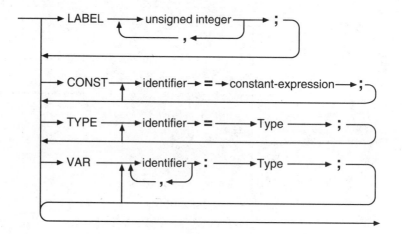

Simple Declarations

Subprogram Declarations

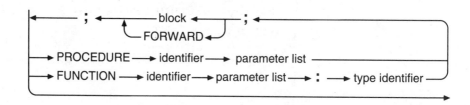

Constant

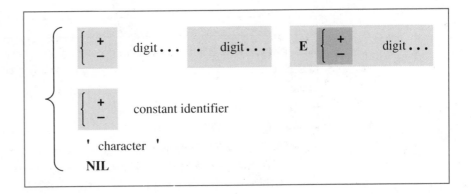

Constant

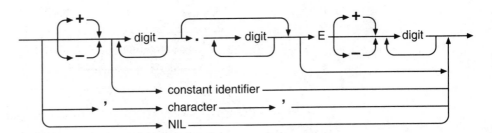

Type

{
simple type
^ type identifier
PACKED **ARRAY** [simple type , simple type ...] **OF** type
PACKED **FILE OF** type
PACKED **SET OF** simple type
PACKED **RECORD** field list **END**
STRING [constant]

Type

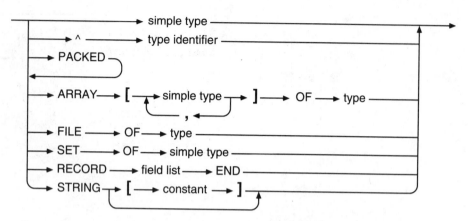

Simple Type

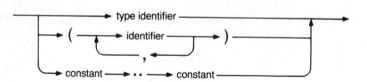

Simple Type

Field List

identifier **,** identifier **. . . :** type **;**
identifier **,** identifier **. . . :** type
.
.
.

CASE identifier **:** type-identifier **OF**

    constant **,** constant **. . . :(** field list **) ;**
    constant **,** constant **. . . :(** field list **)**
    .
    .
    .

Field List

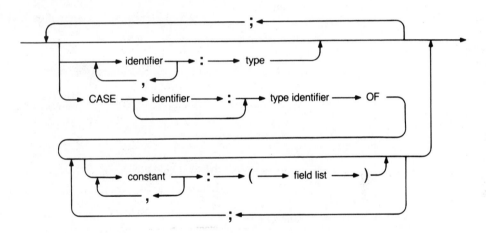

Parameter List

(VAR identifier **,** identifier **. . . :** type-identifier
VAR identifier **,** identifier **. . . :** type-identifier
    .
    .
    .
)

Parameter List

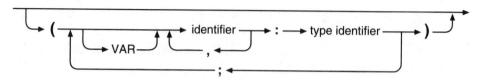

Statement

unsigned integer **:**
{
null statement

{ variable
  function-identifier } **:=** expression

procedure-identifier ({ expression
                         procedure-identifier } **,** { expression
                                                        procedure-identifier } ...)

BEGIN statement **;** statement ... **END**

IF expression **THEN** statement **ELSE** statement

CASE expression **OF** constant **,** constant ...**:** statement **;**
                        constant **,** constant ...**:** statement
                        ⋮
                        ELSE statement
                        END

WHILE expression **DO** statement

REPEAT statement **;** statement ... **UNTIL** expression

FOR variable-identifier **:=** expression { **TO**
                                              DOWNTO } expression **DO** statement

WITH variable **,** variable ... **DO** statement

GOTO unsigned integer
}

Statement

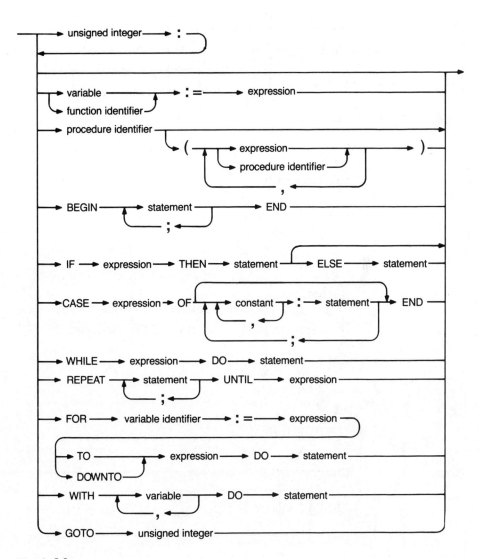

Variable

| variable-identifier
field-identifier
qualified-identifier | ^ | [expression , expression . . .]
. field-identifier | . . . |

Variable

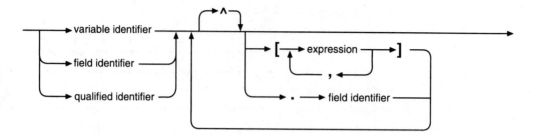

Expression

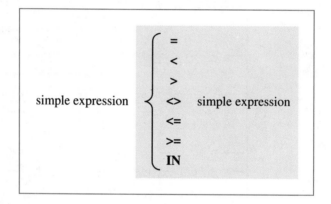

Expression

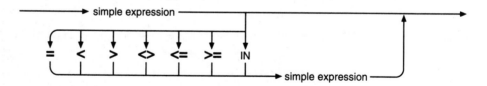

Simple Expression

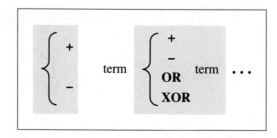

Simple Expression

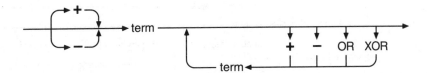

Term

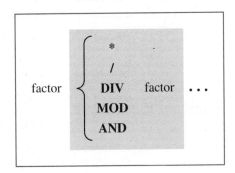

Term

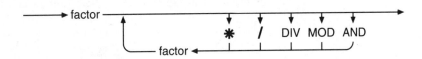

Factor

```
    ⎧ unsigned constant
    ⎪ variable
    ⎨ function identifier (expression, expression ...)
    ⎪ ( expression )
    ⎪ NOT factor
    ⎩ [ expression..expression, expression..expression ... ]
```

Factor

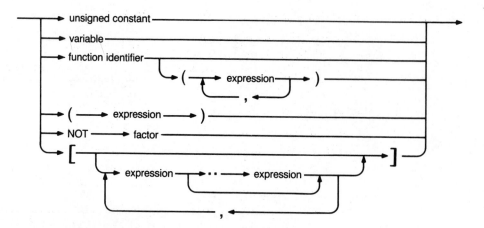

Constant Expression

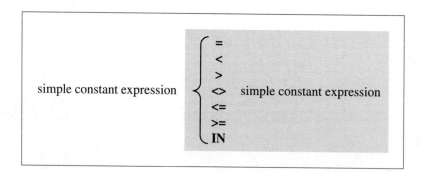

Constant Expression

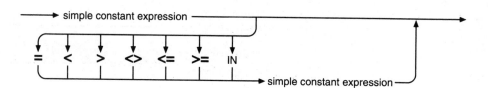

Simple Constant Expression

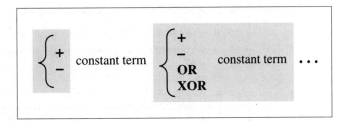

Simple Constant Expression

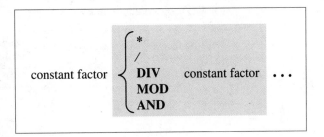

Constant Term

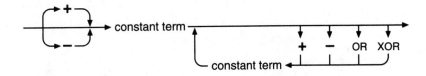

Constant Term

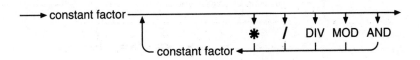

Constant Factor

$$\left\{\begin{array}{l}\text{unsigned constant}\\ \text{constant function identifier (constant expression)}\\ \text{(constant expression)}\\ \textbf{NOT}\ \text{constant factor}\\ \big[\ \text{constant expression}\ ..\ \text{constant expression}\ ,\\ \text{constant expression}\ ..\ \text{constant expression}\\ \vdots\\ \qquad\qquad\qquad\qquad\qquad\qquad\qquad \big]\end{array}\right.$$

Constant Factor

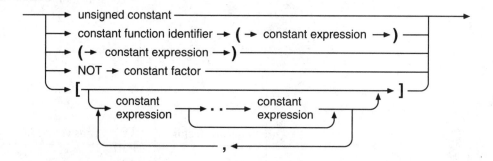

Constant Function Identifier

Constant Function Identifier

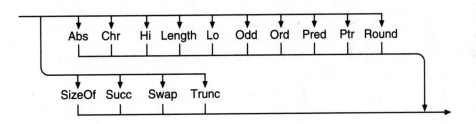

Unit

UNIT identifier **;**
interface
implementation
initialization
END.

Unit

→ UNIT → identifier → ; → interface → implementation → initialization → END → .

Interface

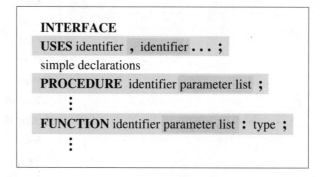

INTERFACE
USES identifier , identifier ... ;
simple declarations
PROCEDURE identifier parameter list ;
⋮
FUNCTION identifier parameter list : type ;
⋮

Interface

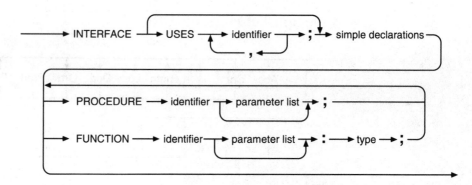

Implementation

IMPLEMENTATION
USES identifier , identifier ... ;
simple declarations
subprogram declarations

Implementation

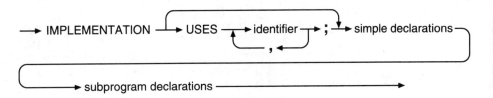

Initialization

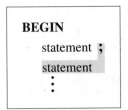

Initialization

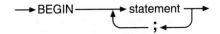

Appendix F *Compiler Error Messages*

Error Codes Produced by the Compiler

1	Out of memory.
2	Identifier expected.
3	Unknown identifier.
4	Duplicate identifier.
5	Syntax error.
6	Error in real constant.
7	Error in integer constant.
8	String constant exceeds line.
9	Too many nested files.
10	Unexpected end of file.
11	Line too long.
12	Type identifier expected.
13	Too many open files.
14	Invalid file name.
15	File not found.

16	Disk full.
17	Invalid compiler directive.
18	Too many files.
19	Undefined type in pointer definition.
20	Variable identifier expected.
21	Error in type.
22	Structure too large.
23	Set base type out of range.
24	File components may not be files or objects.
25	Invalid string length.
26	Type mismatch.
27	Invalid subrange base type.
28	Lower bound greater than upper bound.
29	Ordinal type expected.
30	Integer constant expected.
31	Constant expected.
32	Integer or real constant expected.
33	Pointer type identifier expected.
34	Invalid function result type.
35	Label identifier expected.
36	BEGIN expected.
37	END expected.
38	Integer expression expected.
39	Ordinal expression expected.
40	Boolean expression expected.
41	Operand types do not match operator.
42	Error in expression.
43	Illegal assignment.
44	Field identifier expected.
45	Object file too large.
46	Undefined external.
47	Invalid object file record.
48	Code segment too large.
49	Data segment too large.
50	DO expected.
51	Invalid PUBLIC definition.
52	Invalid EXTRN definition.
53	Too many EXTRN definitions.
54	OF expected.
55	INTERFACE expected.
56	Invalid relocatable reference.
57	THEN expected.
58	TO or DOWNTO expected.
59	Undefined forward.
60	Too many procedures.
61	Invalid typecast.

62	Division by zero.
63	Invalid file type.
64	Cannot Read or Write variables of this type.
65	Pointer variable expected.
66	String variable expected.
67	String expression expected.
68	Circular unit reference.
69	Unit name mismatch.
70	Unit version mismatch.
71	Duplicate unit name.
72	Unit file format error.
73	IMPLEMENTATION expected.
74	Constant and case types do not match.
75	Record variable expected.
76	Constant out of range.
77	File variable expected.
78	Pointer expression expected.
79	Integer or real expression expected.
80	Label not within current block.
81	Label already defined.
82	Undefined label in preceding statement part.
83	Invalid @ argument.
84	UNIT expected.
85	";" expected.
86	":" expected.
87	"," expected.
88	"(" expected.
89	")" expected.
90	" = " expected.
91	": = " expected.
92	"[" or "(." expected.
93	"]" or ")." expected.
94	"." expected.
95	".." expected.
96	Too many variables.
97	Invalid FOR control variable.
98	Integer variable expected.
99	File and procedure types are not allowed here.
100	String length mismatch.
101	Invalid ordering of fields.
102	String constant expected.
103	Integer or real variable expected.
104	Ordinal variable expected.
105	INLINE error.
106	Character expression expected.
107	Too many relocation items.

112	CASE constant out of range.
113	Error in statement.
114	Cannot call an interrupt procedure.
116	Must be in 8087 mode to compile this.
117	Target address not found.
118	Include files are not allowed here.
120	NIL expected.
121	Invalid qualifier.
122	Invalid variable reference.
123	Too many symbols.
124	Statement part too large.
126	Files must be var parameters.
127	Too many conditional symbols.
128	Misplaced conditional directive.
129	ENDIF directive missing.
130	Error in initial conditional defines.
131	Header does not match previous definition.
132	Critical disk error.
133	Cannot evaluate this expression.
134	Expression incorrectly terminated.
135	Invalid format specifier.
136	Invalid indirect reference.
137	Structured variables are not allowed here.
138	Cannot evaluate without System unit.
139	Cannot access this symbol.
140	Invalid floating-point operation.
141	Cannot compile overlays to memory.
142	Procedural or function variable expected.
143	Invalid procedure or function reference.
144	Cannot overlay this unit.
147	Object type expected.
148	Local object types are not allowed.
149	VIRTUAL expected.
150	Method identifier expected.
151	Virtual constructors are not allowed.
152	Constructor identifier expected.
153	Destructor identifier expected.
154	Fail only allowed within constructor.
155	Invalid combination of opcode and operands.
156	Memory reference expected.
157	Cannot add or subtract relocatable symbols.
158	Invalid register combination.
159	286/287 instructions are not enabled.
160	Invalid symbol reference.
161	Code generation error.
162	ASM expected.

Run-Time Error Messages

1   Invalid function number.
2   File not found.
3   Path not found.
4   Too many open files.
5   File access denied.
6   Invalid file handle.
12   Invalid file access code.
15   Invalid drive number.
16   Cannot remove current directory.
17   Cannot rename across drives.

I/O Error Messages

100   Disk read error.
101   Disk write error.
102   File not assigned.
103   File not open.
104   File not open for input.
105   File not open for output.
106   Invalid numeric format.

Critical Error Messages

150   Disk is write-protected.
151   Unknown unit.
152   Drive not ready.
153   Unknown command.
154   CRC error in data.
155   Bad drive request structure length.
156   Disk seek error.
157   Unknown media type.
158   Sector not found.
159   Printer out of paper.
160   Device write fault.
161   Device read fault.
162   Hardware failure.

Fatal Error Messages

200   Division by zero.
201   Range check error.
202   Stack overflow error.
203   Heap overflow error.
204   Invalid pointer operation.

205	Floating point overflow.
206	Floating point underflow.
207	Invalid floating point operation.
208	Overlay manager not installed.
209	Overlay file read error.
210	Object not initialized.
211	Call to abstract method.
212	Stream registration error.
213	Collection index out of range.
214	Collection overflow error.

Appendix G   Program Style, Formatting, and Documentation

Throughout this text we encourage the use of good programming style and documentation. Although the programs you write for class assignments may not be looked at by anyone except the person grading your work, outside of class you will write programs that will be used by others.

Useful programs have very long lifetimes, during which they must be modified and updated. When maintenance work must be done, either you or another programmer will have to do it. Good style and documentation are essential if another programmer is to understand and work with your program. You will also discover that, after not working with your own program for a few months, you'll be amazed at how many of the details you've forgotten.

General Guidelines

The style used in the programs and fragments throughout this text provides a good starting point for developing your own style. Our goals in creating this style were to make it simple, consistent, and easy to read.

Style is of benefit only for a human reader of your program—differences in style make no difference to the computer. Good style includes the use of meaningful variable names, comments, and indentation of control structures, all of which help others to understand and work with your program. Perhaps the most important aspect of program style is consistency. If the style within a program is not consistent, then it becomes misleading and confusing.

Sometimes, a particular style will be specified for you by your instructor or by the company you work for. When you are modifying someone else's code, you will use his or her style in order to maintain consistency within the program. However, you will also develop your own, personal programming style based on what you've been taught, your own experience, and your personal taste.

Comments

Comments are extra information included to make a program easier to understand. You should include a comment anywhere the code is difficult to understand. However, don't overcomment. Too many comments in a program will obscure the code and be a source of distraction.

In our style, there are four basic types of comments: headers, definitions, in-line, and sidebar.

1. *Header comments* appear at the top of the program immediately following the program heading, and should include your name, the date that the program was written, and its purpose. It is also useful to include the input, output, and assumptions sections from your top-down design. Think of the header comments as the reader's introduction to your program. Here is an example:

```
(* This program computes the sidereal time for a given date and *)
(* solar time.                                                   *)
(*                                                               *)
(* Written By: Your Name                                         *)
(*                                                               *)
(* Date Completed: 4/8/93                                        *)
(*                                                               *)
(* Input: A date and time in the form of MM DD YY HH MM SS       *)
(*                                                               *)
(* Output: Sidereal time in the form of HH MM SS                 *)
(*                                                               *)
(* Assumptions: Solar time is specified for a longitude of 0     *)
(*      degrees (GMT, UT, or Z time zone)                        *)
```

Header comments should also be included for all user-defined procedures. (See Chapters 6, 7, and 8.)

2. *Definition comments* accompany all declarations and definitions in the program. Anywhere that an identifier is declared, a comment should appear that explains its purpose. In programs in the text, definition comments appear to the right of the identifier being declared. For example:

```
CONST
   E = 2.718281828459      (* The base of the natural logarithms *)

VAR
   DeltaX,                 (* The difference in the X direction  *)
   DeltaY:                 (* The difference in the Y direction  *)
     Real;
```

Notice that aligning the comments gives the code a neater appearance and is less distracting.

3. *In-line comments* are used to break long sections of code into shorter, more comprehensible fragments. These are usually the names of modules in your top-down design, although you may occasionally choose to include other information. In-line

comments should be surrounded by blank lines to make them stand out. (This was not done in this text to save space. We used color printing instead.) For example:

```
BEGIN  (* Main *)

  (* Initialize *)

  Assign(Infile, 'INFILE.DAT');
  Reset(Infile);
  MinTemp := MaxInt;

  (* Get Data *)

  Readln(InFile, NumTemps);
```

Blank lines may be inserted wherever there is a logical break in the code that you would like to emphasize.

4. *Sidebar* comments appear to the right of statements in the body of the program and are used to shed light on the function of the statement. Sidebar comments are often just pseudocode statements from the lowest levels of your top-down design. If a complicated Pascal statement requires some explanation, the pseudocode statement should be written to the right of the Pascal statement. For example:

```
IF EOF(File1) <> EOF(File2)    (* If one of the files is empty *)
  THEN
     .
     .
     .
```

In addition to the four main types of comments that we have discussed, there are some miscellaneous comments that we should mention: (1) comments should be included at the main BEGIN and END of each procedure, function, and the main program; (2) a row of asterisks in a comment should appear before and after each procedure or function to help it to stand out. For example:

```
(***************************************************************)

PROCEDURE Balance (VAR Param1:     (* Definition of Param1 *)
                        Real);

BEGIN  (* Balance *)
   .
   .
END;  (* Balance *)

(***************************************************************)
```

(3) We also recommend that you comment the END associated with every RECORD declaration and CASE statement to make them easier to debug. For example,

```
CASE Command OF
    .
    .
END; (* Case *)
```

Identifiers and Keywords

The most important consideration in choosing a name for an object or process in a program is that the name convey as much information as possible about what the object is or what the process does. The name should also be readable in the context in which it is used. For example, the following names convey the same information but one is more readable than the other:

```
Date_Of_Invc   Invoice_Date
```

Identifiers for types, constants, or variables should be nouns, while names of procedures should be verbs. Because of the way that functions are called, function names should be nouns or occasionally adjectives. Here are some examples:

Variables	Address, Price, Radius, Month_Number
Constants	Pi, Tax_Rate, String_Length, Array_Size
Data Types	Names, Car_Makes, Room_Lists, Hours
Procedures	Get_Data, Clear_Table, Print_Bar_Chart
Functions	Cube_Root, Greatest, Color, Area_Of

Although an identifier may be a series of words, very long identifiers can become quite tedious, and can make the program difficult to read.

The best approach to designing an identifier is to try writing out different names until you reach an acceptable compromise—and then write an especially informative definition comment next to the declaration.

Capitalization is another consideration when choosing an identifier. In programs in the text, the first letter of every word in an identifier is capitalized.

We have written Pascal keywords in all capital letters to distinguish them from identifiers. Making the keywords stand out also helps you to quickly locate a particular statement in a long program.

Formatting Lines and Expressions

In general, it is best never to include more than one statement on a line. One exception would be when you must initialize a large array with specific values, where it is acceptable to neatly align the assignment statements in multiple columns. For example:

```
(* Initialize state abbreviations table *)

State[1]   := 'AL';        State[25] := 'MT';
State[2]   := 'AK';        State[26] := 'NE';
State[3]   := 'AZ';        State[27] := 'NV';
State[4]   := 'AR';        State[28] := 'NH';
     .
     .
     .
State[24] := 'MO';         State[50] := 'WY';
```

When a long statement must be broken in the middle and continued onto the next line, it's important to choose a breaking point that is logical and readable. Compare the readability of the following code fragments.

```
Writeln('For a radius of ', Radius:1, 'the diameter of the cir',
        'cle is ', Diameter:1);

Writeln('For a radius of ', Radius:1,
        ' the diameter of the circle is ', Diameter:1);
```

When you must split an expression across multiple lines, try to end each line with an operator. Also, try to take advantage of any repeating patterns in the expression. For example,

```
Mean_Of_Maxima := (Maximum(Set1_Value1, Set1_Value2, Set1_Value3) +
        Maximum(Set2_Value1, Set2_Value2, Set2_Value3) +
        Maximum(Set3_Value1, Set3_Value2, Set3_Value3)) / 3.0;
```

When writing expressions, also keep in mind that spaces improve readability. Usually you should include one space on either side of the := and most operators. Occasionally spaces are left out to emphasize the order in which operations are performed. Here are some examples:

```
IF X+Y > Y+Z
   THEN
     Maximum := X + Y
   ELSE
     Maximum := Y + Z;
Mileage := (Fill_Up1+Fill_Up2+Fill_Up3) / (End_Miles-Start_Miles);
```

Indentation

The purpose of indenting statements in a program is to provide visual cues to the reader and to make the program easier to debug. When a program is properly indented, the way the statements are grouped is immediately obvious. Compare the following two program fragments:

```
WHILE Count <= 10 DO      WHILE Count <= 10 DO
BEGIN                     BEGIN
Readln(Num);                Readln(Num);
IF Num = 0                  IF Num = 0
THEN                          THEN
BEGIN                          BEGIN
Count := Count + 1;              Count := Count + 1;
Num := 1                        Num := 1
END;                          END;
Writeln(Num:1);              Writeln(Num:1);
Writeln(Count:1)             Writeln(Count:1)
END;                      END;
```

As a basic rule in this text, each nested or lower-level item is indented by two spaces. Exceptions to this rule are formal parameters and statements that are split across two or more lines. Indenting by two spaces is really just a minimum. Many people prefer to indent by three, four, or even five spaces.

The remainder of this section is devoted to presenting examples of indentation for each Pascal statement, according to the style used in this book.

Declarations In the text, constant and variable declarations are indented in the same way. The keyword (CONST or VAR) appears on a line by itself, indented to the same level as the program, procedure, or function heading that immediately precedes it. On succeeding lines, each constant or variable is listed, one per line, indented by two spaces, with a defining comment to the right. For variable declarations, all of the variables of a given type are grouped together, with the data type following on a separate line, indented by two additional spaces. Here is an example:

```
CONST
  Pi = 3.141592654;    (* Ratio of circumference to diameter *)
  E = 2.718281828;     (* Base of the natural logarithms      *)

VAR
  Radius,        (* Radius of a circle        *)
  Diameter,      (* Diameter of a circle      *)
  Area:          (* Area of a circle          *)
    Real;
  Count,         (* Example number            *)
  Max_Circle,    (* Number of greatest circle *)
  Min_Circle:    (* Number of smallest circle *)
    Integer;
```

Data type declarations are generally indented like constant declarations.

In the text, two different indentation styles are used in procedure and function declarations. When space permits, the parameter list begins on the same line as the procedure or function name. Each formal parameter is listed on a separate line, in a style similar to that used for the VAR declaration. In the following example, notice that blanks are used to highlight the formal value parameter:

```
PROCEDURE Get_Sum (      Number:       (* Number of values to be read *)
                        Integer;
                  VAR Sum:          (* Sum of values read              *)
                        Real);
```

Occasionally, we need more room for the comments. In such a case, we use a second style in which the parameter list appears on lines following the procedure or function name. In the following example, note that the parameter list is indented by two spaces.

```
PROCEDURE Get_Data_Average
  (VAR Infile:      (* File of test scores                        *)
          Text;
      Num_Scores:   (* The number of scores to be read from Infile *)
          Integer;
  VAR Average:      (* The average of the test scores              *)
          Real);
```

The local declarations and body of a procedure or function follow the same guidelines as the declarations and body of the main program. The only difference is that nested procedures or functions should be indented by two spaces for each level of nesting.

Statements   In general, any statement that is part of another statement is indented by two spaces in programs in the text; including compound statements, assignment statements, procedure calls, and nested statements.

Because the IF-THEN-ELSE contains two statements, separated by the keyword ELSE, the ELSE and THEN are written on separate lines, indented two spaces to the right of the IF. The statements within the branches of the IF-THEN-ELSE are then indented by two additional spaces. The IF-THEN statement is indented like the IF-THEN-ELSE, but without the ELSE branch. Here are examples of the IF-THEN-ELSE and IF-THEN.

```
IF Sex = Male
  THEN
    BEGIN
      Male_Salary := Male_Salary + Salary;
      Male_Count := Male_Count + 1
    END
  ELSE
    Female_Salary := Female_Salary + Salary;

IF Count > 0
  THEN
    Average := Total / Count;
```

For nested IF-THEN-ELSE statements that form a generalized CASE Statement (see Chapter 9), a special style of indentation is used in the text. Here is an example:

```
IF Month = January
  THEN
    Month_Number := 1
  ELSE IF Month = February
    THEN
      Month_Number := 2
  ELSE IF Month = March
    THEN
      Month_Number := 3
  ELSE IF Month = April
    .

    .

  ELSE
    Month_Number := 12
```

The remaining Pascal statements all follow the basic indentation guideline mentioned previously. For reference purposes, here are examples of each.

```
WHILE Count <= 10 DO
  BEGIN
    Readln(Value);
    Sum := Sum + Value;
    Count := Count + 1
  END;

REPEAT
  Get_Answer(Letter);
  Put_Answer(Letter)
UNTIL Letter = 'N';

FOR Count := 1 TO Num_Sales DO
  Write('*');

FOR Count := 10 DOWNTO 1 DO
  BEGIN
    Readln(Infile, Data);
    Writeln(Outfile, Data, Count)
  END;
```

```
CASE Color OF
  Red     : Writeln('Red');
  Orange  : Writeln('Orange');
  Yellow  : Writeln('Yellow');
  Green,
  Blue,
  Indigo,
  Violet  : Writeln('Short visible wavelengths');
  White,
  Black   : BEGIN
              Writeln('Not valid colors');
              Color := None
            END
END; (* Case *)

WITH Employee_Rec DO
  BEGIN
    Writeln(Name);
    Writeln(Street);
    Writeln(City, State, Zip)
  END
```

Appendix H   *Additional Features of Pascal*

Standard Pascal has some additional features not usually covered in a first course. The syntax diagrams in Appendix E describe the complete Pascal language and show some of these additional features.

For the sake of completeness, the additional features that are available in Pascal are described in this appendix. They include the GOTO statement, another structuring option for records (variant records), and a mechanism for forward referencing procedures and functions.

GOTO Statement

A GOTO statement, or unconditional branch, is provided in most common programming languages. Pascal is no exception, but, because all the control structures already exist, the GOTO should be rarely needed. In some languages an IF and a GOTO statement must be used to construct control structures. In Pascal the IF, CASE, WHILE, FOR, and REPEAT control structures are more convenient and make programs more readable; they make the flow of control clearer.

The GOTO statement passes control directly from one point in a program to another. The GOTO must specify the label of a statement to which control is transferred. The label must be declared in the declaration section of the block. These are the rules concerning the GOTO statement:

1. All labels must be declared.
2. Label declarations precede all others in the block.
3. Labels are unsigned integers in the range 0 to 9999.
4. Each label may be declared only once, and it may be used to label only one statement.
5. A GOTO branch into a control structure or block (procedure or function) is not permitted. A GOTO branch out of a control structure or a block is permitted.
6. Labels are unsigned integers or identifiers.

In the following example, the commented statements are the equivalent control structures for the code using the GOTO.

```
PROGRAM Jump (Input, Output);

LABEL
   10, 20, 30, 40;

CONST
   N = 2000;

VAR
   Value, Sum:
     Integer;

BEGIN (* Jump *)
   Sum := 0;
10:IF EOF                       (* WHILE NOT EOF DO             *)
      THEN GOTO 20;             (*    BEGIN                     *)
   Readln(Value);               (*       Readln(Value);         *)
   Sum := Sum + Value;          (*       Sum := Sum + Value     *)
   GOTO 10;                     (*    END;                      *)
20:IF Sum <= N                  (* IF Sum > N                   *)
      THEN GOTO 30;             (*                              *)
   Writeln('Minority');         (*       THEN Writeln('Minority') *)
   GOTO 40;                     (*                              *)
30:Writeln('Majority');         (*       ELSE Writeln('Majority') *)
40:
END.      (* Jump *)
```

Structured programming is characterized by the use of control structures with only one entry and one exit. Use of the GOTO leads to unstructured programming: multiple entry and exits from control structures. This makes programs harder to read, understand, modify, and debug. Because of this the GOTO should be avoided. Use it only for exceptional circumstances and forward (not backward) jumps, such as exiting a procedure or program due to certain error conditions.

Overuse of the GOTO statement in Pascal is poor programming practice. Pascal contains all the control structures necessary to write a program without the GOTO.

Variant Records

Within a record type, there may be some fields that are mutually exclusive. That is, fields A and B may never be in use at the same time. Instead of declaring a record variable large enough to contain all the possible fields, you can use the variant record provided in Pascal.

The variant record has two parts: the fixed part where the fields are always the same and the variant part where the fields will vary. Since only a portion of the variant fields are in use at any one time, they may share space in memory. The compiler need allocate only enough space for the record variable to include the largest variant.

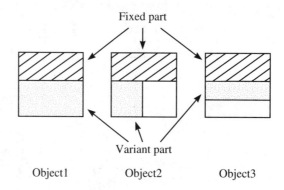

If a record has both a fixed part and a variant part, the fixed part must be defined first. The following is an example of a record definition that contains a variant part.

```
TYPE
   Item = (Assembly, Nut, Bolt, Washer, Lock);
   PartType = RECORD
              ID  : PACKED ARRAY[1..10] OF Char;
              Qty : Integer;
              Tag : Item;
              CASE Item OF
                 Assembly : (Drawing_Id : PACKED ARRAY
                                           [1..5] OF Char;
                             Code : 1..12;
                             Class : (A, B, C, D) );
                 Nut, Bolt, Washer : ();
                 Lock : (Key_No : Integer)
              END;  (* Record *)
VAR Part:
    Part_Type;
```

When using a variant record variable, the user is responsible for accessing fields that are consistent with the Tag field. For example, if the Tag field is Nut, Bolt, or Washer, only the fixed fields can be accessed. If the Tag field is Lock, Part.Key_No is a legal field reference. If the Tag field is Assembly, Part.Drawing_Id, Part.Code, and Part.Class are all legal references.

Several points should be made about defining and using variant records. We will use the above definition to illustrate.

1. A record definition may contain only one variant part, although field lists in the variant part may contain a variant part (nested variant).
2. All field identifiers within a record definition must be unique.
3. The tag field (Tag) is a separate field of a record (if present).
4. The tag field is used to indicate the variant used in a record variable.
5. The case clause in the variant part is not the same as a CASE statement.
   a. There is no matching END for the CASE; the END of the record definition is used.
   b. The case selector is a type (Item).
   c. Each variant is a field list labeled by a case label list. Each label is a constant of the tag type (Item).
   d. The field lists are in parentheses.
   e. The field lists define the fields and field types of that variant.
6. The tag type can be any ordinal type, but it must be a type identifier.
7. Several labels can be used for the same variant (Nut, Bolt, Washer).
8. A field list can be empty, which is denoted by "( )".
9. The variant to be used is assigned at run-time. The variant can be changed by assignments to other variant fields and the tag field. When a variant is used, data (if any) in a previous variant is lost.
10. The tag field does not appear in the field selectors for the variant fields.
11. It is an error to access a field that is not part of the current variant.

The case clause in the variant part of the record definition is often matched by a CASE statement in the body of the program. For example, the following program fragment could be used to print data about a record.

```
Writeln('Part Id — ', A_Part.ID);
Writeln('Qty — ', A_Part.Qty:1);
CASE Tag OF
   Assembly  : Writeln('Assembly : ', A_Part.Drawing_ID);
   Nut       : Writeln('Nut');
   Bolt      : Writeln('Bolt');
   Washer    : Writeln('Washer')
   Lock      : Writeln('Lock, Key Attached')
END;        (* Case *)
```

Forward Statement

Identifiers in Pascal must be defined before being used (the type identifier in the pointer type definition is an exception). Recursion was defined as a procedure or function calling itself. There are recursive situations where one procedure or function calls another which in turn calls the first. This is called mutual recursion.

.
.

```
(*************************************************************)

PROCEDURE One (VAR A: AType);
BEGIN
   .
   .
   Two(X);
   .
   .
END;

(*************************************************************)

PROCEDURE Two (VAR B : BType);
BEGIN
   .
   .
   One(Y);
   .
   .
END;

(*************************************************************)
```
.
.

In the above example, the call to procedure Two in the body of procedure One is not allowed because procedure Two has not yet been defined. The solution to this problem is to make a forward reference to procedure Two by using the FORWARD directive.

.
.

```
(*************************************************************)

PROCEDURE Two (VAR B : BType);
FORWARD;

(*************************************************************)
```

```
PROCEDURE One (VAR A : AType);
BEGIN
   .
   .
   .
  Two(X);
   .
   .
   .
END;

(*************************************************************)

PROCEDURE Two;
BEGIN
   .
   .
   .
  One(Y);
   .
   .
   .
END;

(*************************************************************)
   .
   .
   .
```

Notice that the parameter list (and the result type for a function) is written in the forward reference; it is *not* repeated in the actual declaration of the procedure (or function). The compiler "remembers" the parameter declarations when it encounters the actual procedure.

Appendix I   *The ASCII Character Set*

The following chart shows the ordering of the ASCII character set (American Standard Code for Information Interchange). Only printable characters are shown. The ordinal number for each character is shown in decimal. The blank character is denoted by a "□".

Left Digit(s)	Right Digit	ASCII									
		0	1	2	3	4	5	6	7	8	9
3				□	!	"	#	$	%	&	'
4		(	)	*	+	,	–	.	/	0	1
5		2	3	4	5	6	7	8	9	:	;
6		<	=	>	?	@	A	B	C	D	E
7		F	G	H	I	J	K	L	M	N	O
8		P	Q	R	S	T	U	V	W	X	Y
9		Z	[	\	]	^	—	`	a	b	c
10		d	e	f	g	h	i	j	k	l	m
11		n	o	p	q	r	s	t	u	v	w
12		x	y	z	{			}	~			

Codes 00–31 and 127 are nonprintable control characters.

Appendix J   A Graphical Tour of the Turbo Pascal Integrated Development Environment

This appendix presents the screens, menus, and dialog boxes found in the Turbo Pascal 6.0 integrated development environment. It is organized according to the order in which the main menu items appear. For each menu item, all of the submenu items are discussed and example dialog boxes are shown. We begin with the Turbo Pascal Desktop.

The Turbo Pascal Desktop screen appears whenever there are no files or other windows open in the Turbo Environment (Figure J-1). The words across the top of the screen are the main menu items. To select an item, click on it with the mouse, or press the F10 key and then the first letter of the menu name. The words at the bottom of the screen are reminders of the functions of the most commonly used function keys. F1 brings up the Turbo Help facility, F2 saves your program file, F3 opens a new program file, Alt-F9 compiles your program, F9 is used to compile programs that are divided among multiple files (see Chapter 19), and F10 allows you to select a menu item. Note that some of the function key names are highlighted while others are not. Those that are not highlighted are temporarily inactive. For example, in Figure J-1, F2 (Save) is inactive because there isn't a program on the screen that can be saved.

The Initial screen appears when you first start the Turbo environment (Figure J-2). Turbo initially does not know which file you wish to work with, so it creates an empty file called NONAME00.PAS. In this screen, the desktop is replaced by an empty edit window. A window is an area in which information can be displayed. Later we'll see several other types of windows, but for now we will use only the edit window. A window consists of the following components:

Figure J-1
The Turbo Pascal
Desktop

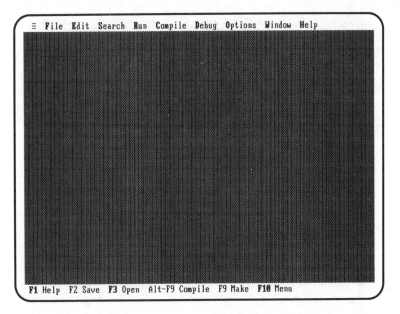

Figure J-2
The Initial Screen

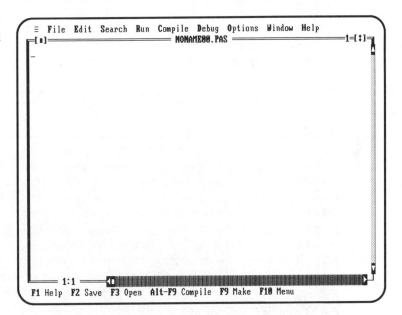

- Border (the double lines)
- Work area (the area inside of the border)
- Scroll bars (the stripes at the bottom and along the right edge)
- Close box (the box in the upper left corner)
- Zoom arrow (the double-headed arrow in the upper right corner)
- Window number (the number next to the zoom arrow)

- Title (the name centered at the top)
- Current position (the two numbers at the lower left, line:column)
- Resize corner (the single line, lower right corner)

Many of the features of a window are designed for use with a mouse; however, all can be used with the keyboard via the menu system if a mouse is not available. For example, clicking on the close box closes the window. To change the size of the window, drag the resize corner to a new position and the window will become that new size. (See Chapter 2 for an overview of clicking and dragging operations with a mouse.) To move to a new section of a file, click on the arrows at the ends of the vertical scroll bar (or press Page Up and Page Down) or drag the box in the scroll bar to a new position.

The File Submenu

Figure J-3 shows the file submenu. To select an item from a submenu, click on it with the mouse, or use the arrow keys to move the highlight down (or up) to the item and press Enter. In this example, the highlight is on Open. Turbo Pascal also provides shortcuts for many of the submenu items; these are shown to the right of the item name. For example, you can press F3 to open a file as an alternative to using the menu system. If you select a menu item by mistake, you can press the Esc key to make the submenu disappear.

Open. . . Selecting Open causes a dialog box to appear. The box is divided into several areas (Name, Files, Open, Replace, Cancel, Help, and Info). To move between areas in a dialog box, click with the mouse or press the Tab key. Different areas permit different actions. The Name area allows you to enter the name of a file to open. Clicking

Figure J-3
The File Submenu

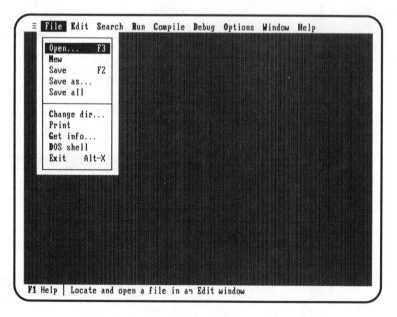

on the arrow to the right of the name area will bring up a list of most recently opened files, from which you may select. The Files area displays existing files and allows you to select one file (either by clicking or by moving the highlight with the arrow keys and pressing Enter). In Figure J-4, the file TEST.PAS has been selected. The Open, Replace, Cancel, and Help areas can only be selected (by clicking, or pressing Tab until the highlight is in that area and then pressing Enter). Areas that can only be selected are indicated by square brackets around the key word.

Note that the dialog box also has a close box. If you make a mistake, you can either select Cancel or click on the close box, and the dialog box will disappear without taking any action. You may also press the Esc key to exit a dialog box.

New   The New submenu item creates a new (empty) program file. The default name is NONAME00.PAS. If a file with that name is already present in the environment, NONAME01.PAS will be used, and so on.

Save   This submenu item saves the currently active edit window in a file with the same name as the window title. If a file has been saved previously, then this item is used to save changes to the file.

Save as. . .   If a file has not been saved previously, you must give it a name before saving it. This submenu item allows us to do just that. It brings up a dialog box, similar to that for opening a file, which allows us to name the file we are about to save (Figure J-5). The simplest method is to type the name of the file (in the "Save file as" area) and press Enter. This submenu item also is used when you have just made a major

Figure J-4
The Open a File
Dialog Box

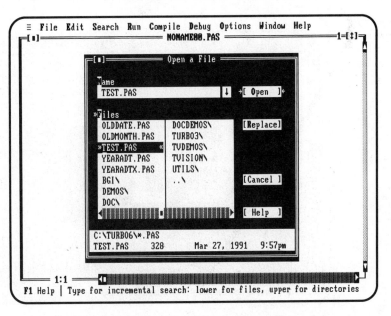

change to a file and wish to save the new version under a different name so that the old version will be preserved.

In the case of Figure J-5, the current name for the file was chosen as the new name. Turbo Pascal displays a warning dialog box to advise us that this is unusual and asks us to verify that it is really what we want to do (Figure J-6). Pressing Enter will select the highlighted area (Yes). Click on another area or use Tab and Enter to select another area.

Figure J-5
The Save File As
Dialog Box

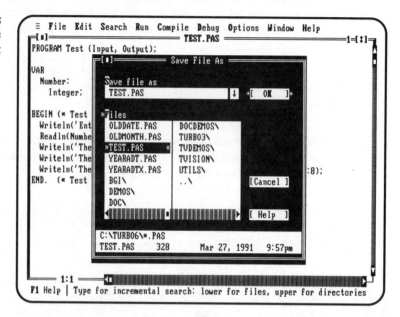

Figure J-6
A Warning
Dialog Box

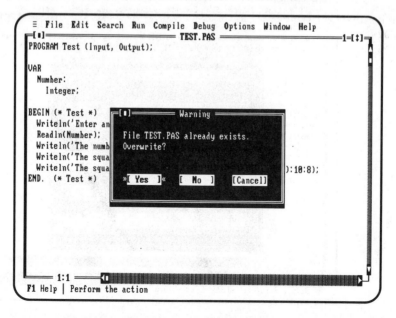

Change dir...   The File submenu items all refer to the currently selected directory on the disk, which is typically the Turbo directory. However, you may wish to work with files in other directories. This submenu item is used to change the current directory (Figure J-7). It allows us to type in the name of a directory (in the Directory name area) or to choose from a list of existing directories (in the directory tree area). Press Tab to move to the Directory tree area, and then use the arrow keys to move up and down the list. Directories that are indented further are subdirectories of those that are indented less. The Chdir area changes to the new directory without leaving the dialog box and is used if you wish to look at another subdirectory. The Revert area switches back to the previous directory.

Print   This submenu item prints the contents of the currently active window. However, you must have a printer connected to your system. Choosing this item when a printer isn't connected can cause the system to lock up, requiring you to reboot with Ctrl-Alt-Del.

Get info...   A dialog box appears that provides you with a wide range of information about the file in the currently active edit window (Figure J-8).

DOS shell   Selecting this item will temporarily suspend the Turbo environment and return you to DOS. You may enter any DOS commands that you wish, and then re-enter the Turbo environment with the DOS command Exit. The environment will reappear just as you left it.

Exit   This item shuts down the Turbo environment and returns to DOS. If you have forgotten to save any files, you will be asked if they should be saved before the environment shuts down.

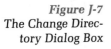

Figure J-7
The Change Directory Dialog Box

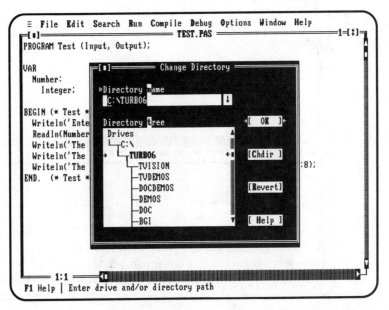

Figure J-8
The Information
Dialog Box

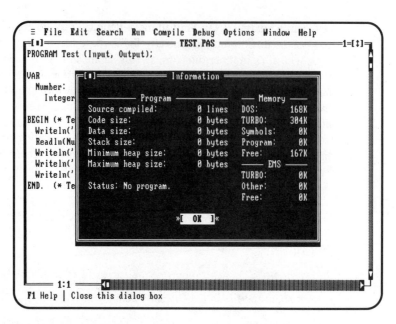

Figure J-9
The Edit Submenu

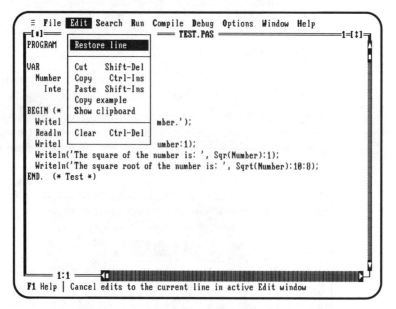

Edit

The edit menu provides a set of commands that permit us to copy and move blocks of text within and between edit windows (Figure J-9). To take advantage of these commands you must select text in the edit window. Selection with the mouse is done by simply dragging through the area that you wish to select. With the keyboard, you must position the cursor at the start of the text you wish to select, and then press the arrow keys while holding down Shift to move the cursor to the end of the text. The selected text will then be highlighted.

Restore line   The restore line item takes back the last editing command you performed on a line. For example, if you delete a line by mistake, Restore line will recover the line.

Cut   Cut deletes the selected text from the edit window and places it in a special area called the clipboard. The clipboard is basically another edit window, but with some special properties. Whenever you cut text from an edit window, it is appended to the clipboard window and remains selected in the clipboard until you cut new text.

Copy   Copy acts like Cut, except that the selected text is not deleted from the edit window. It is instead copied into the clipboard, where it becomes the selected text in the clipboard.

Paste   Paste inserts a copy of the currently selected text in the clipboard into the current edit window, at the current position of the cursor. Thus, to move a block of text to a new place in a file, select the text, cut it, move the cursor to the new location, and paste the text back into the file at that point. To make copies of some text, select the text, copy it to the clipboard, move the cursor to the new position, and paste the text as many times as necessary to create the number of copies you need.

Copy example   Copy example copies the automatically highlighted example text in a Help window into the clipboard. From there, you may paste the example into your own program.

Show clipboard   This command opens the clipboard window, allowing you to edit text that has been cut or copied. You also may change the selection in the clipboard so that previously cut or copied text may be pasted. To close the clipboard window, choose Close from the Window submenu (discussed later).

Clear   The Clear item acts like Cut, except that the selected text is not placed in the clipboard—it is deleted and cannot be recovered.

Search

When working with a large file, it is sometimes difficult to locate a particular word or phrase. Also, it can be quite tedious to replace all occurrences of a particular word with another word (such as changing a variable name throughout a program). The Search submenu provides a set of commands that help with tasks such as these (Figure J-10).

Find. . .   Selecting Find brings up the dialog box shown in Figure J-11. It provides an area to enter the text to search for. Initially, this area contains the word on which the edit window cursor is currently positioned. The Options area contains a set of check boxes that affect the search for the entered text. The Case sensitive box allows you to choose to ignore the case of characters (upper or lower). The Whole words only box

Figure J-10
The Search
Submenu

```
 ☰  File  Edit  Search  Run  Compile  Debug  Options  Window  Help
┌[■]────────────────────┐      PAS ════════════════════════1=[↕]═┐
PROGRAM Test (│ Find...          │                                  ▲
              │ Replace...       │                                  █
VAR           │ Search again     │                                  ░
  Number:     │ Go to line number...│                               ░
    Integer;  │ Find procedure...│                                  ░
              │ Find error...    │                                  ░
BEGIN (* Test └──────────────────┘                                  ░
  Writeln('Enter an integer number.');                              ░
  Readln(Number);                                                   ░
  Writeln('The number is: ', Number:1);                             ░
  Writeln('The square of the number is: ', Sqr(Number):1);          ░
  Writeln('The square root of the number is: ', Sqrt(Number):10:8); ░
END.  (* Test *)                                                    ░
                                                                    ░
                                                                    ▼
═ 1:1 ═══◄█░░░░░░░░░░░░░░░░░░░░░░░░░░░░░░░░░░░░░░░░░░░░░░░░░░░░░░░░►
F1 Help │ Search for text
```

Figure J-11
The Find
Dialog Box

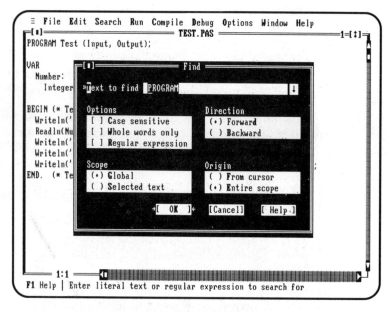

```
 ☰  File  Edit  Search  Run  Compile  Debug  Options  Window  Help
┌[■]═════════════════════ TEST.PAS ═══════════════════════1=[↕]═┐
PROGRAM Test (Input, Output);                                       ▲
                                                                    █
VAR        ┌[■]═══════════════ Find ══════════════┐                 ░
  Number:  │                                       │                ░
    Integer│ »Text to find PROGRAM           ↓ │                   ░
           │                                       │
BEGIN (* Te│ ┌Options───────────┐ ┌Direction──────┐│                ░
  Writeln('│ │ [ ] Case sensitive│ │(•) Forward    ││                ░
  Readln(Nu│ │ [ ] Whole words only│ ( ) Backward  ││                ░
  Writeln('│ │ [ ] Regular expression│              ││                ░
  Writeln('│ └───────────────────┘ └───────────────┘│
  Writeln('│ ┌Scope─────────────┐ ┌Origin─────────┐│                ;
END.  (* Te│ │(•) Global         │ │( ) From cursor││                ░
           │ │( ) Selected text  │ │(•) Entire scope││                ░
           │ └───────────────────┘ └───────────────┘│
           │      →[  OK  ]←  [Cancel]   [ Help ]   │
           └───────────────────────────────────────┘
                                                                    ▼
═ 1:1 ═══◄█░░░░░░░░░░░░░░░░░░░░░░░░░░░░░░░░░░░░░░░░░░░░░░░░░░░░░░░░►
F1 Help │ Enter literal text or regular expression to search for
```

restricts the search to instances of the text that are not embedded in text (for example, searching for *at* without checking this box will stop on words like *that*). The Regular expression check box indicates that the text can contain "wildcard" characters. The complete list of wildcards is beyond the scope of this text, but it is handy to know that the period (.) matches any character. For example, if you have identifiers with similar names (such as Temp1, Temp2, and Temp3), then checking the Regular expression box will cause the string Temp. to match any of these identifiers.

The next three areas in the dialog box contain radio buttons—only one of them may be checked at a time. Direction chooses whether to search forward or backward from the origin position. Scope indicates whether to search the entire file or just the selected text. Origin indicates whether the search should begin at the cursor or the beginning or end of the file (depending on the Direction selected). The last three areas have the usual meaning.

Replace. . .   The Replace dialog box is similar to the Find dialog box except that it allows you to specify a second text string that will replace the original text when it is found (Figure J-12). The Options area has one more option (Prompt on replace) that lets you specify whether to automatically replace the original text, or have the environment show you the text that was found and let you choose whether or not to replace it. There is one more area at the bottom of the dialog box, Change all, that will search for and replace every occurrence of the text in the area specified by the Scope. Selecting OK only replaces a single occurrence of the text.

Search again   Selecting this item causes the last Find or Replace command to be repeated. This is especially useful when you are searching for a specific occurrence of some text that appears more than once in a file.

Go to line number. . .   This item allows you to specify a line number to which the cursor will be moved (Figure J-13).

Find procedure. . .   This item is similar in appearance to the Go to Line Number dialog box but it allows you to enter the name of a procedure or function and then searches for the declaration of that subprogram.

Figure J-12
The Replace
Dialog Box

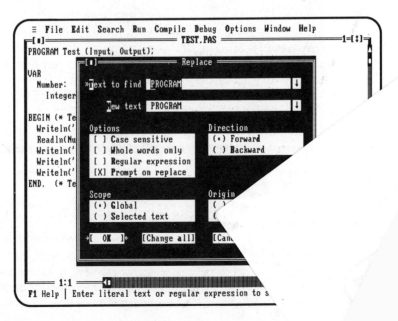

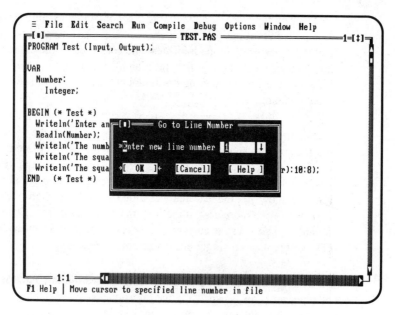

Find error. . . This item also is similar to the Go to Line Number dialog box, but it allows you to enter the location of a run-time error (as shown in the error message) and then goes to the line where the error was detected.

Run

Run This item causes your program to be executed (Figure J-14). If the program has not been compiled since it was last changed, it is automatically compiled before being run.

Program reset Program reset returns any dynamic memory that your program had allocated, resets the variable values, and closes any open files. This is especially useful if you are debugging a program with single stepping and would like to start again with everything reset to its initial state.

Go to cursor The program is executed up to the statement on which the cursor is positioned. You may then use the debugger to examine the values of variables, and so on.

Trace into This item executes your program one statement at a time. When a procedure or function call is encountered, the trace enters the called subprogram. Note that Trace into will also display execution of the initialization sections of any units declared in the USES clause of the program.

Step over This item is similar to Trace into, executing one statement at a time, except that it skips over calls to subprograms and unit initializations.

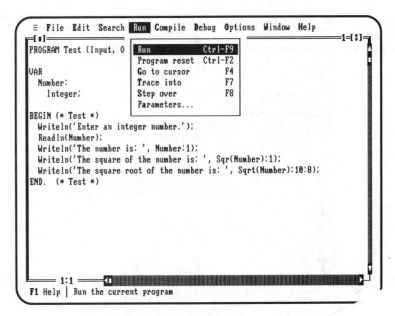

Figure J-14
The Run Submenu

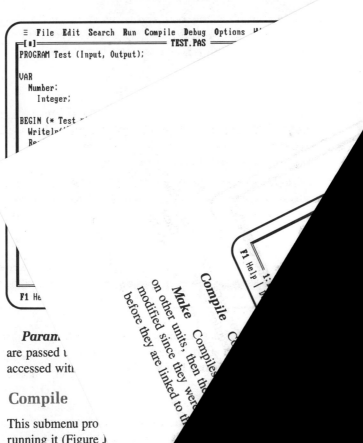

Figure J-15
The Program
Parameters
Dialog Box

Param...

are passed ι
accessed witΙ

Compile

This submenu pro
running it (Figure)

Make Compiles
on other units, then th
modified since they wer
before they are linked to th

Compile C

Figure J-16
The Compile
Submenu

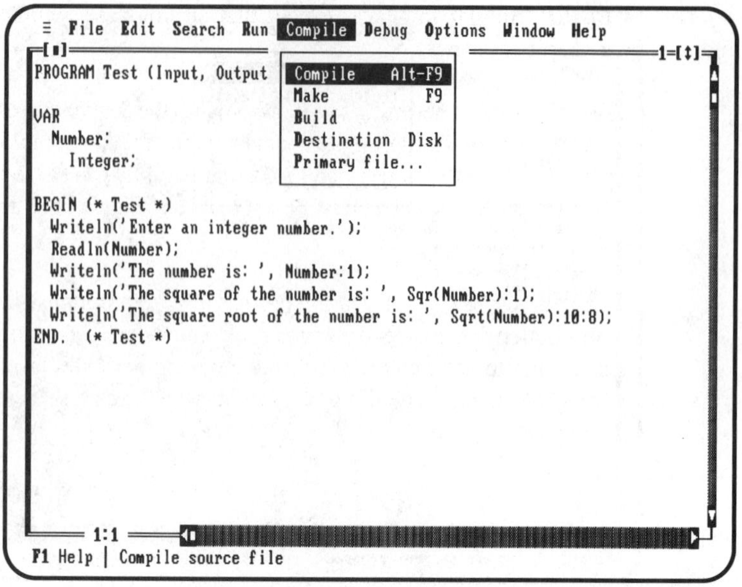

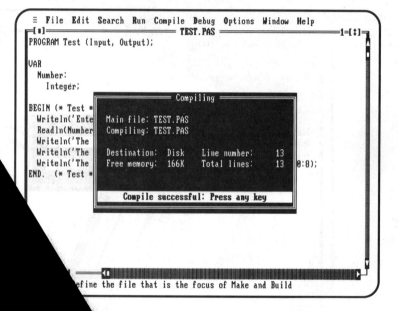

Figure J-17
A Compiler
Status Display

compiles the program in the active edit window (Figure J-17).

the program in the active edit window. If the program depends
source files for the units are checked to see if they have been
last compiled. If so, then the modified units are compiled
program.

Build Similar to Make, except that all units are recompiled whether they have been modified or not.

Destination Selecting this item switches the destination of compiled code between disk and memory. Compiling to memory is faster than compiling to disk. However, if you wish to save the object code from the compilation (as when you are compiling a unit), then the destination must be set to Disk. Figure J-16 indicates that the current destination is Disk.

Primary file. . . If you are editing a large program with several units, you can use this dialog box to specify which file contains the main program (Figure J-18). This saves having to activate the window containing the main program prior to each Make or Build command. The Compile command will, however, still compile the code in only the active window.

Debug

This submenu provides access to the Turbo Pascal Debugger (Figure J-19).

Evaluate/modify. . . This dialog box permits you to enter an expression, which will be evaluated using the current values of any program variables specified (Figure J-20). Initially, the expression in the Expression area is the word on which the cursor is currently positioned. This is useful, for example, if you wish to see the value of a variable. You may then enter a new value for the variable, if you wish, in the New Value area. If you want to copy an expression from the program into the expression area, place the cursor at the beginning of the expression prior to invoking this item,

Figure J-18
The Primary File
Dialog Box

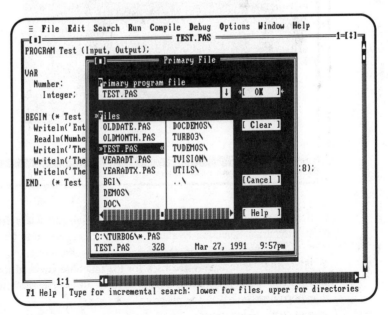

Figure J-19
The Debug
Submenu

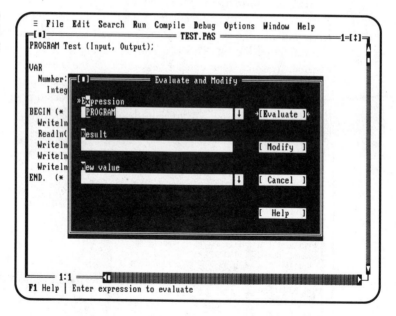

```
≡  File  Edit  Search  Run  Compile  Debug  Options  Window  Help
┌[■]══════════════════════════════ T    ╔═════════════════════════╗ ═1=[↕]═
PROGRAM Test (Input, Output);          ║ Evaluate/modify...  Ctrl-F4 ║
                                       ║ Watches                    ▶ ║
VAR                                    ║ Toggle breakpoint   Ctrl-F8 ║
  Number:                              ║ Breakpoints...             ║
    Integer;                           ╚═════════════════════════╝

BEGIN (* Test *)
  Writeln('Enter an integer number.');
  Readln(Number);
  Writeln('The number is: ', Number:1);
  Writeln('The square of the number is: ', Sqr(Number):1);
  Writeln('The square root of the number is: ', Sqrt(Number):10:8);
END.  (* Test *)



══ 1:1 ══◄█══════════════════════════════════════█►
F1 Help | Evaluate a variable or expression and display or modify the value
```

Figure J-20
The Evaluate and
Modify Dialog Box

```
≡  File  Edit  Search  Run  Compile  Debug  Options  Window  Help
┌[■]════════════════════ TEST.PAS ════════════════ ═1=[↕]═
PROGRAM Test (Input, Output);

VAR
  Number: ┌[■]════════════ Evaluate and Modify ════════════╗
    Integ ║                                                ║
          ║ »Expression                                    ║
BEGIN (*  ║  PROGRAM                          ↓  →[Evaluate ]← ║
  Writeln ║                                                ║
  Readln( ║  Result                                        ║
  Writeln ║                                      [ Modify ]  ║
  Writeln ║                                                ║
  Writeln ║  New value                                     ║
END.  (*  ║                                   ↓  [ Cancel ]  ║
          ║                                                ║
          ║                                      [ Help ]   ║
          ║                                                ║
          ╚════════════════════════════════════════════════╝



══ 1:1 ══◄█══════════════════════════════════════█►
F1 Help | Enter expression to evaluate
```

then use the right-arrow key to copy additional characters from the code into the expression area. Selecting Evaluate causes the expression to be reevaluated.

Watches   Selecting Watches brings up another level of submenu (Figure J-21). These items permit you to specify variables and expressions that will appear in the Watches window.

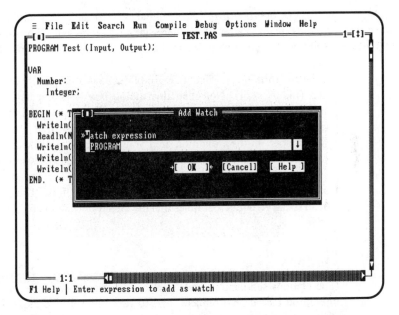

Figure J-21
The Watches
Submenu

Figure J-22
The Add Watch
Dialog Box

Add watch. . .   You may enter an expression to watch in this dialog box (Figure J-22). The default expression is the word at the current cursor position.

Delete watch   This item deletes the selected watch from the Watches window.

Edit watch. . .   This dialog box allows you to change the watch expression that is currently selected in the watch window (Figure J-23).

Remove all watches   This item clears all watches from the Watches window.

Figure J-23
The Edit Watch
Dialog Box

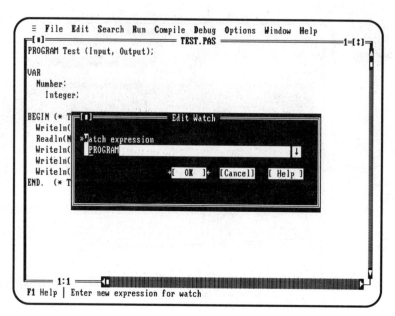

Toggle breakpoint   Sets a breakpoint at the line where the cursor is positioned. If a breakpoint is already set there, then it is removed. A breakpoint causes execution to stop at the specified point so that the values of variables may be examined.

Breakpoints. . .   This dialog box displays a list of all breakpoints set in the program (Figure J-24). Note that this dialog box does not have a cancel button—you cannot undo changes. Selecting one of the breakpoints and then Edit causes another dialog box to appear, which contains four areas: Condition, Pass count, File name, and Line number. In the Condition area you may enter a Boolean expression that will be evaluated when the breakpoint is encountered. If the expression is false, the breakpoint is skipped. For example, you may wish to examine the variables at the end of a flag-controlled loop only when the flag has been set to True. The Pass count area permits you to specify a number of times that the breakpoint should be skipped before it becomes active.

Options

The Options submenu permits you to set various options associated with elements of the Turbo Pascal environment, and to save and retrieve those option settings (Figure J-25).

Compiler. . .   You will not want to change most of the items displayed in this dialog box (Figure J-26); their discussion is beyond the scope of this text. However, in the Runtime errors area you may want to check Range checking, as this will cause the compiler to insert code to automatically check that out-of-range values are not assigned to subrange variables or used in array index expressions. You also may wish to check

Figure J-24
The Breakpoints
Dialog Box

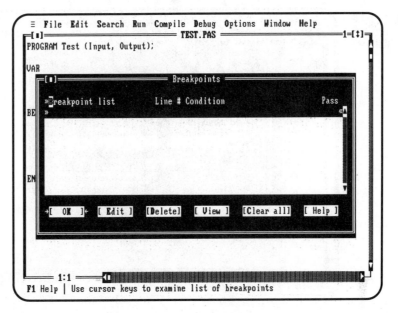

Figure J-25
The Options
Submenu

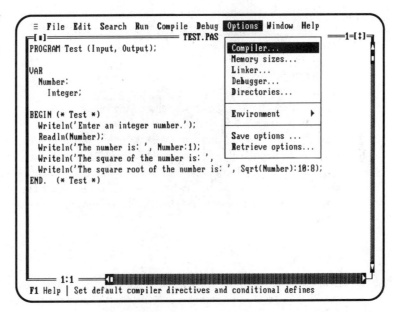

Complete Boolean eval in the Syntax options area, as this will enforce the Standard Pascal convention (no short-circuit evaluation of Boolean expressions).

Memory sizes...   In this dialog box, you can see (and change) the amount of memory allocated to the run-time stack, and the dynamic memory area (Figure J-27). It is unlikely that you will want to change these values. If you are running a program

Figure J-26
The Compiler
Options Dialog Box

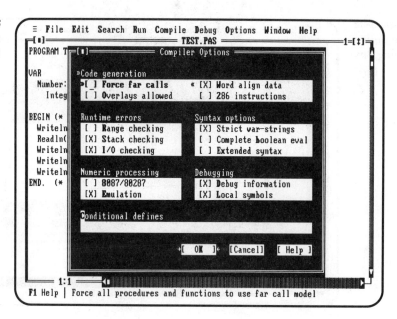

Figure J-27
The Memory Sizes
Dialog Box

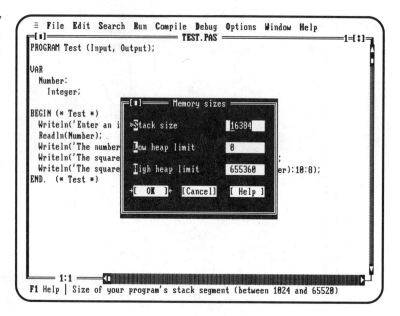

that uses recursion extensively (see Chapter 17), however, you may need to increase the area allocated to the run-time stack.

Linker. . .   Most of the options in this dialog (Figure J-28) are beyond the scope of this text. However, if you are compiling a very large program, you may find it necessary to switch the Link buffer to Disk. Although this is slower than linking with the buffer in memory, it frees up additional space for the compiler to use.

Figure J-28
The Linker
Dialog Box

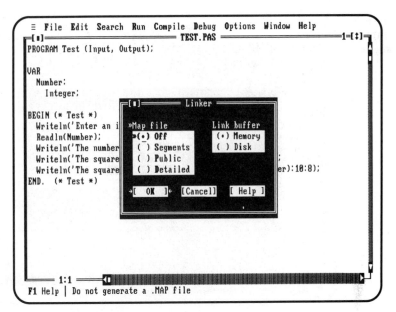

Figure J-29
The Debugger
Dialog Box

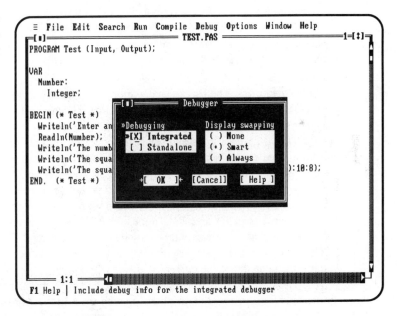

Debugger. . .   As with the Linker dialog box, most of the options in this dialog
(Figure J-29) are beyond the scope of this text. If you are debugging a graphics program,
however, you may have to change the Display swapping setting to Always. This affects
when the debugger switches between the user screen and the development environment
screen. The normal setting for Display swapping is Smart.

Figure J-30
The Directories
Dialog Box

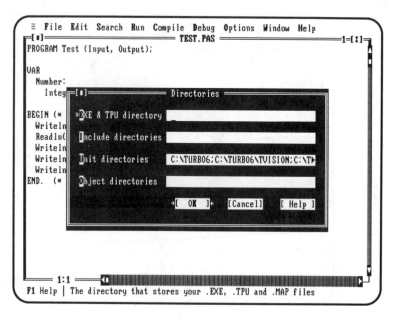

Directories. . .   This dialog box permits you to specify where object files (EXE & TPU) are stored (Figure J-30). It also permits you to specify a list of directories to be searched for Include files, Units, and Objects (see Chapter 19). Enter the names of directories, separated by semicolons.

Environment   The Environment submenu is shown in Figure J-31.

Preferences. . .   With this selection you can set general characteristics for the environment (Figure J-32). If you have a system that supports a higher resolution display than the usual 25 lines, you can select to see more lines at once. The Auto save area provides three check boxes. If you check Editor files, then your source files will be saved automatically each time you run the program. If you check Environment and Desktop, then all of your current options and preferences are saved automatically upon exiting the environment and will be restored when you next enter the environment.

The Source tracking area determines what happens when Turbo Pascal detects an error in code that is not currently in a window on the screen. For example, if an error is found in a unit that your program is using, Turbo can either open a new window or replace the contents of the current window with the code for the unit.

The Desktop file area allows you to specify where the Desktop and Environment information will be saved if you have marked them in the Auto save area.

Editor. . .   In this dialog box, you can set several options that alter the functioning of the editor (Figure J-33). If Create backup files is checked, then each time you change a file and save it, the old version is first renamed with the extension .BAK instead of .PAS. Thus, if you make a mistake, you can always recover the old version of the file. Insert mode shows whether the editor is in insert or overwrite mode (you can switch between these modes at any time by pressing the INS key; see Chapter 2 for an explanation of these modes). Autoindent mode causes the editor to indent each new line the

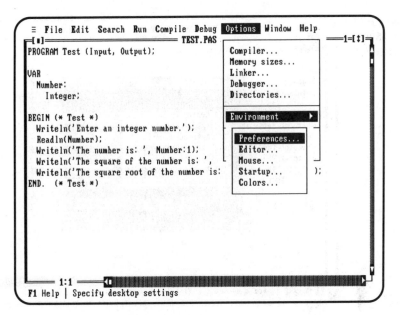

Figure J-31
The Environment
Submenu

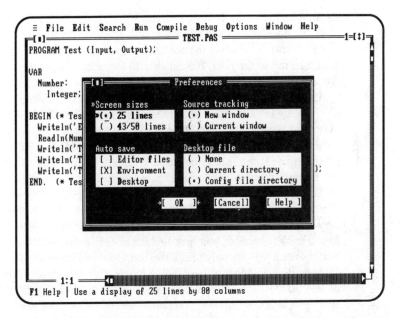

Figure J-32
The Preferences
Dialog Box

same amount as the previous line, saving time in entering heavily indented code. Use tab characters specifies that the ASCII tab character be inserted whenever the TAB key is pressed; otherwise the editor inserts spaces. Using tabs can save space in a program file but makes it more difficult to print out the file or incorporate it into documentation. Optimal fill indicates that autoindentation should be done with tab characters instead of spaces. Backspace unindents indicates that when you press the Backspace key as

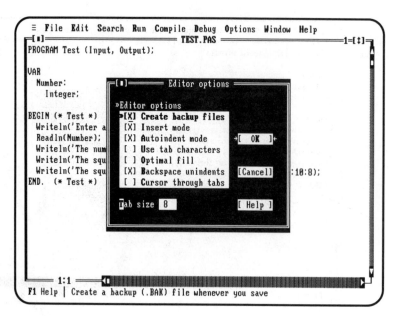

the first action on an automatically indented line, the cursor will back up to the next level of indentation (instead of backing up a single character). Cursor through tabs specifies that, when moving the cursor through a series of tabs, instead of jumping from one tab to the next, the cursor will move one character position at a time. Last, the Tab size area lets you enter the width of a tab in character positions.

Mouse. . .   If your system is equipped with a two-button mouse, the right button can be assigned a shortcut in this dialog (Figure J-34). Topic search will cause the help system to be activated with the topic being the word the mouse is pointing to. Go to cursor is the same as selecting Go to cursor from the Run submenu. Breakpoint toggles a breakpoint at the mouse position. Evaluate is the same as selecting Evaluate from the Debug submenu. Add watch causes an Add watch dialog to appear.

Several of the normal mouse actions involve clicking twice on an object (such as selecting a file name). The Mouse double click area lets you choose the amount of time between clicks in a double-click action by dragging the box toward either fast or slow. If you are left-handed, you may find it easier to work with the meanings of the mouse buttons reversed—simply check the box to reverse them.

Startup. . .   Most of the options in this dialog (Figure J-35) are beyond the scope of this text. If you are using a system with a Liquid Crystal Display (LCD) screen, such as a laptop computer, you should check LCD color set. Also, if your system is equipped with two monitors (such as monochrome and color), you should check Dual monitor support.

Colors. . .   This dialog box allows you to change the colors that Turbo Pascal selects for various items on a color display (Figure J-36). The display items are arranged into groups, so you must first select the group, and then the item within the group. This dialog is especially useful if you have color blindness or if you find the standard color scheme unacceptable.

Figure J-34
The Mouse Options
Dialog Box

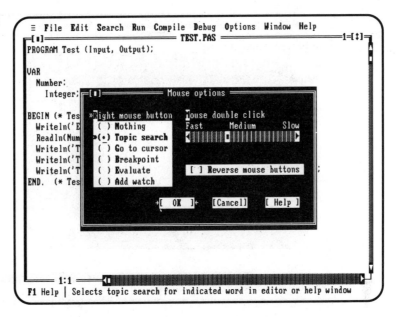

Figure J-35
The Startup
Options Dialog Box

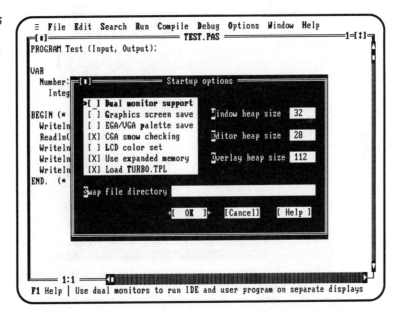

Save options. . .   Enter the name of a file in which the current option settings are to be stored and press Enter (Figure J-37).

Retrieve options. . .   Enter the name of a file in which option settings have been stored and press Enter (Figure J-38). The saved options will be recalled and the environment will be reconfigured accordingly.

Figure J-36
The Colors
Dialog Box

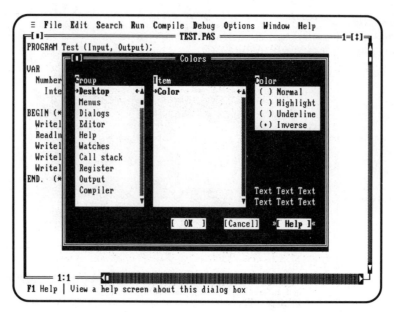

Figure J-37
The Save Option
Dialog Box

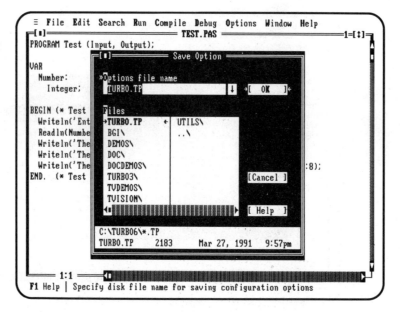

Window

The Window submenu allows you to change the way windows are displayed and to choose among the different windows available (Figure J-39).

Size/move   After selecting this item, you can move the window around the screen with the arrow keys and change its size by holding down the shift key while pressing

Figure J-38
The Retrieve
Options Dialog Box

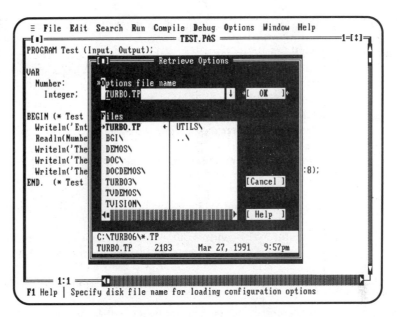

Figure J-39
The Windows
Submenu

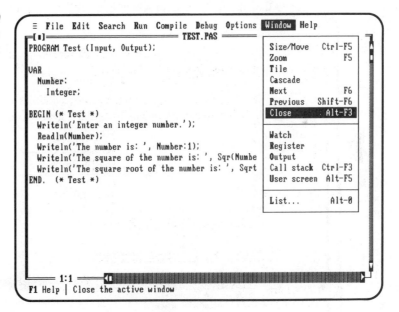

the arrow keys. These actions can be performed directly with the mouse as described earlier.

Zoom   Selecting this item causes the current window to expand to the maximum size available. Selecting this item again will return the window to its previous size. This is the same as clicking on the zoom arrow.

Tile   Tile causes multiple edit windows to be arranged so that they don't overlap.

Cascade   Cascade causes multiple edit windows to be arranged so that the current window is visible and only the title bars of the other windows can be seen.

Next   This makes the next window active.

Previous   This makes the previous window active.

Close   This item closes the current window and is the same as clicking on the close box.

Watch   Selecting Watch makes the Watch window active (Figure J-40).

Register   The contents of the hardware registers in the CPU are displayed, which is only useful if you are combining assembly language with Pascal.

Output   This selection makes the output window active (Figure J-41).

Call stack   This item brings up a window showing the chain of calls that brought execution to the current procedure, which is especially useful in debugging recursive programs.

User screen   The display switches to the user screen—a full screen showing your program's output and any interactive data entries.

List. . .   This dialog box lists all of the editor windows that have been created (Figure J-42). You can select a window from the list to become the active window.

Figure J-40
The Watches Window with a Breakpoint Set in the Program

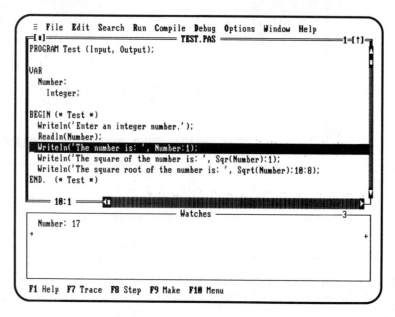

```
 ≡  File  Edit  Search  Run  Compile  Debug  Options  Window  Help
┌[■]══════════════════════ TEST.PAS ═════════════════════════1═[↑]┐
│PROGRAM Test (Input, Output);                                    ▲│
│                                                                 ▒│
│VAR                                                              ▒│
│   Number:                                                       ▒│
│    Integer;                                                     ▒│
│                                                                 ▒│
│BEGIN (* Test *)                                                 ▒│
│   Writeln('Enter an integer number.');                          ▒│
│   Readln(Number);                                               ▒│
│   Writeln('The number is: ', Number:1);                         ▒│
│   Writeln('The square of the number is: ', Sqr(Number):1);      ▒│
│   Writeln('The square root of the number is: ', Sqrt(Number):10:8); ▒│
│END.  (* Test *)                                                 ▒│
│                                                                 ▼│
├──── 10:1 ═══◄▐█████████████████████████████████████████████▌►──┤
│══════════════════════════ Watches ══════════════════════════3══│
│   Number: 17                                                    │
│  →                                                             ←│
│                                                                 │
│                                                                 │
│                                                                 │
│                                                                 │
└─────────────────────────────────────────────────────────────────┘
 F1 Help  F7 Trace  F8 Step  F9 Make  F10 Menu
```

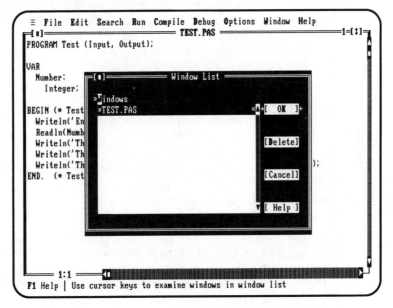

Figure J-41
The Output
Window

Figure J-42
The Window List
Dialog Box

This dialog is especially useful if you have arranged a set of editor windows on the screen such that some have been completely hidden by others.

Help

The Turbo Pascal Help facility is essentially a condensed version of the Turbo Pascal reference manuals that can be accessed while you are working on the computer (Figure

Figure J-43
The Help Submenu

Figure J-43
The Help Submenu

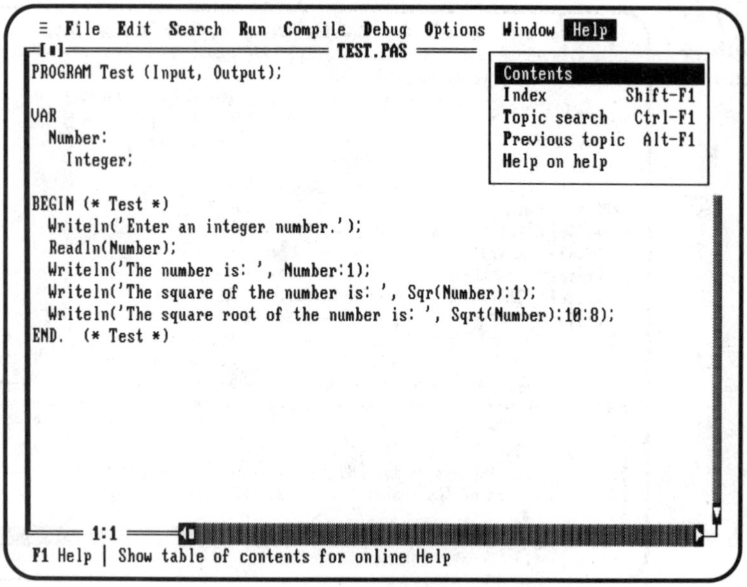

J-43). To look something up, you can select an item from the table of contents or the index, or type a topic name. You can access Help at any time by pressing F1. If you are in an edit window, you can press Ctrl-F1 and Help information will be displayed automatically for the item on which the cursor is positioned.

Contents   The table of contents for Help is divided into four sections: how to use help; how to use the menus and keyboard shortcuts; how to use the editor; and miscellaneous topics on the environment, compiler, Pascal language, and Turbo Pascal extensions (Figure J-44). Select an item (by clicking or using Tab and Enter) and help will be displayed for that topic. Help is displayed in a window that is equivalent to an editor window, so you may move through the Help text in the same way that you move through the text of a program. You also may copy material from the Help window to the clipboard and then to your program.

Index   The Help index displays a much more detailed list of topics that are available. For example, Figure J-45 shows only the first part of the index for topics beginning with D. As with the table of contents, you may select an item from the index and Help will display information on that topic.

Topic search   Selecting Topic search causes the Help system to display information on the word at the current position of the cursor. If the word isn't in the Help index, the closest match is displayed instead. This is equivalent to pressing Ctrl-F1.

Previous topic   Selecting the previous topic causes help to retrieve the last help item that you requested. The environment keeps track of the last 20 topics that you

Figure J-44
Help Contents

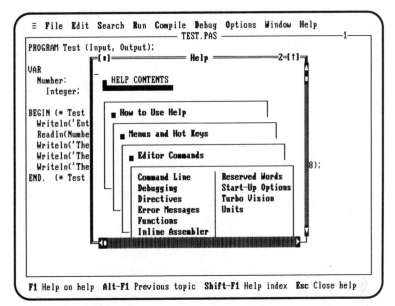

Figure J-45
Help Index

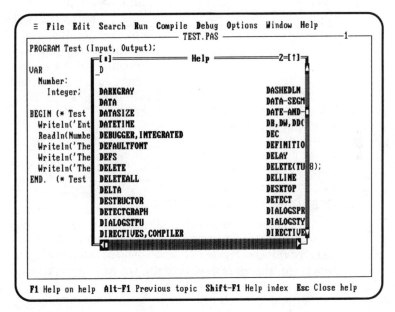

have requested; repeatedly selecting Previous topic will take you backward through this list.

Help on help   Selecting this item is a shortcut for selecting How to Use Help from the Help Contents. It takes you directly to a discussion of how the help system works.

Glossary

absolute position graphics a set of graphics operations in which everything to be drawn is specified directly by pixel coordinates

abstract data type a class of data objects with a defined set of properties and a set of operations that process the data objects while maintaining the properties

abstract step an algorithmic step for which some implementation details remain unspecified

actual parameter a variable, constant, or expression listed in the call to a procedure

algorithm a step-by-step procedure for solving a problem in a finite amount of time; a verbal or written description of a logical sequence of actions

algorithm walk-through a process for verifying an algorithm by establishing a set of preconditions and postconditions for each module and then examining the algorithm step by step to check that the preconditions and postconditions are preserved

ALU see *arithmetic/logic unit*

anonymous type a type defined in the VAR section of a program, so called because it does not have an identifier (a name) associated with it

arithmetic/logic unit (ALU) the component of the central processing unit that performs arithmetic and logical operations

array a collection of components, all of the same type, ordered on N dimensions (N >= 1); each component is accessed by N indices, each of which represents the component's position within that dimension

assembler a program that translates an assembly language program into machine code

assembly language a low-level programming language in which a mnemonic represents each of the machine language instructions for a particular computer

assignment the action that gives the value of an expression to a variable

assignment compatible condition in which the data types are compatible and the value being assigned is within the variable's subrange

assignment statement a statement that gives the value of an expression to a variable

atomic data type a data type that allows only a single value to be associated with an identifier of that type

automatic range-checking the automatic detection of the assignment of an out-of-range value to a variable

auxiliary storage device a device that stores data in encoded form outside the computer's memory

base case the case for which the solution can be stated nonrecursively

base type see *host type*

batch processing a technique for entering data and executing programs without intermediate user interaction with the computer

binary expressed in terms of combinations of the numbers 1 and 0 only

binary file a file that is created within one program to be read by another program or by the same program at a later date; such a file is written in the internal representation of a machine

binary search a search algorithm for sorted lists that involves dividing the list in half and determining, by value comparison, whether the item would be in the upper or lower half; the process is performed repeatedly until either the item is found or it is determined that an item is not on the list

binary search tree   a binary tree in which the information in any node is greater than the information in its left child and any of its children (left subtree) and less than the information in its right child and any of its children (right subtree)

binary tree   a linked data structure whose nodes each contain more than one pointer field

bit   short for binary digit; a single 1 or 0

block   the declaration and statement sections of a program, procedure, or function

Boolean   data type consisting of only two values: True and False

Boolean expression   an assertion that can be evaluated as being either True or False, the only values of the Boolean data type

Boolean operators   operations applied to values of the type Boolean; in Pascal these are the special symbols AND, OR, and NOT

booting the system   the process of starting up a computer by loading the operating system into its main memory

branch   see *selection*

branching control structure   see *selection control structure*

byte   eight bits

cancellation error   a form of representational error that occurs when numbers of widely differing magnitudes are added or subtracted

case label list   a list of values, of the same type as the case selector, appearing in the body of the CASE statement

case selector   the expression whose value determines which case label list is selected; it cannot be Real

central processing unit (CPU)   the part of the computer that executes the instructions (program) stored in memory; consists of the arithmetic/logic unit and the control unit

char   data type consisting of one alphanumeric character (letter, digit, or special symbol)

character set   a standard set of alphanumeric characters with a given collating sequence and binary representation

Chr   an operation that takes an ordinal value and returns the character at that position in the collating sequence

code coverage   a testing procedure in which each branch of a program is executed at least once

code walk-through   a verification process for a program in which each statement is examined to check that it faithfully implements the corresponding algorithmic step, and that the preconditions and postconditions of each module are preserved

coding   translating an algorithm into a programming language; the process of assigning bit patterns to pieces of information

collating sequence   the ordering of the elements of a set or series, such as the characters (values) in a character set

compatibility   a property of data types if they have the same type definition or type identifier, if they are subranges of the same host type, or if one is a subrange of the other

compiler   a program that translates a high-level language (such as Pascal, COBOL, or FORTRAN) into machine code

compiler listing   a copy of a program into which have been inserted messages from the compiler (indicating errors in the program that prevent its translation into machine language if appropriate)

composite data type   a data type that allows a collection of values to be associated with an identifier of that type

compound statement   any group of statements enclosed by the keywords BEGIN and END

computer   a programmable device that can store, retrieve, and process data

computer program   a list of instructions to

be performed by a computer

computer programming   the process of planning a sequence of steps for a computer to follow

concrete step   a step for which the implementation details are fully specified

conditional test   the point at which the Boolean expression is evaluated and the decision is made to either begin a new iteration or skip to the first statement following the loop

constant   an item in a program whose value is fixed at compile time and cannot be changed during execution

constant time   an algorithm whose Big-O work expression is a constant

control abstraction   the separation of the logical properties of a control structure from its implementation

control structure   a statement used to alter the normally sequential flow of control

control unit   the component of the central processing unit that controls actions of other components so that instructions (the program) are executed in sequence

conversion function   a function that converts a value of one type to another type so that it can be assigned to a variable of the second type; also called transfer function or type cast

count-controlled loop   a loop that executes a predetermined number of times

counter   a variable whose value is incremented to keep track of the number of times a process or event occurs

CPU   see *central processing unit*

crash   the cessation of a computer's operations as a result of the failure of one of its components; cessation of program execution due to an error

cursor control keys   a special set of keys on a computer keyboard that allow the user to move the cursor up, down, right, and left to any point on the screen

data   information that has been put into a form a computer can use

data abstraction   the separation of the logical properties of a data structure from its implementation

data coverage   a testing procedure in which all allowable data values are tried without regard to the program code

data type   the general form of a class of data items; a formal description of the set of values (called the domain) and the basic set of operations that can be applied to it

data validation   a test added to a program or a procedure that checks for errors in the data

debugging   the process by which errors are removed from a program so that it does exactly what it is supposed to do

decision   see *selection*

declaration   a statement that associates an identifier with a process or object so that the user can refer to that process or object by name

delimiter   a symbol or keyword that marks the beginning or end of a Pascal construct (e.g., statement, comment, declaration, and parameter list)

documentation   the written text and comments that make a program easier for others to understand, use, and modify

down   a descriptive term applied to a computer when it is not in a usable condition

driver   a simple dummy main program that is used to call a procedure or function being tested

dynamic data structure   a data structure that can expand and contract during program execution

dynamic variable   a variable created during execution of a program and hence not declared in the declaration section of a program

echo printing   printing the data values input to a program to verify that they are correct

editor   an interactive program used to create and modify source programs or data

empty set   the set with no members

encapsulation   the practice of hiding a module implementation in a separate block with a formally specified interface

enumerated data type an ordered set of literal values (identifiers) defined as a data type

event-controlled loop a loop that terminates when something happens inside the loop body to signal that the loop should be exited

event counter a variable that is incremented each time a particular event occurs

exception report a set of messages in a program that explains the actions taken when an invalid data item is encountered during execution

executing the action of a computer performing as instructed by a given program

execution summary a computer-generated list of all commands processed and any system messages generated during batch processing

execution trace a testing procedure that involves simulating by hand the computer executing a program

explicit matching a method of matching actual parameters to formal parameters by directly specifying their names in the actual parameter list; also called named matching

external file a file that is used to communicate with people or programs and is stored externally to the program

external pointer (to a list) a named pointer variable that references the first node in a linked list

fetch-execute cycle the sequence of steps performed by the central processing unit for each machine language instruction

field identifier the name of a component in a record

field selector the expression used to access components of a record variable; formed using the record variable name and the field identifier, separated by a period

fieldwidth the total number of columns (character positions) allotted to an output

value in a Write or Writeln statement

file a named area in the computer's memory that is used to hold a collection of data; the collection of data itself

file buffer variable a variable of the same type as the components of the file with which it is associated; it is automatically created by the system when a file variable is declared and is denoted by the file variable name followed by an up caret ($\wedge$)

file data type a collection of components, all of the same data type, accessed sequentially, one component at a time

finite state machine an idealized model of a simple computer consisting of a set of states, the rules that specify when states are changed, and a set of actions that are performed when changing states

flag a Boolean variable that is set in one part of the program and tested in another to control the logical flow of a program

flat implementation the hierarchical structure of a solution written as one long sequence of steps; also called inline implementation

floating point number the value stored in a type Real variable, so called because part of the memory location holds the exponent and the balance of the location the mantissa, with the decimal point floating as necessary among the significant digits

flow of control the order of execution of the statements in a program

formal parameter a variable declared in a procedure heading

formal parameter declaration the code that associates a formal parameter identifier with a data type and a passing mechanism

formatting the planned positioning of statements or declarations and blanks on a line of a program; the arranging of program output so that it is neatly spaced and aligned

function a subprogram that is called from within an expression, and in which a single value (for example, the square root of a number) is computed and returned to the main program through the subprogram name

functional cohesion a property of a module in which all concrete steps are directed toward solving just one problem, and any significant subproblems are written as abstract steps; the principle that a module should perform exactly one abstract action

functional equivalence the point at which a module performs exactly the same operation as the abstract step it defines, or when one module performs exactly the same operation as another module

functional modules in top-down design, the structured tasks and subtasks that are solved individually to create an effective program

functional problem description a description that clearly states what a program is to do

function call an expression in the main program requiring the computer to execute a function subprogram

function definition that portion of a function subprogram appearing in a declaration section

function result the value computed by the function subprogram and then returned to the main program; often called just the result

function result type the data type of the result value returned by a function; often referred to simply as function type

function type see *function result type*

general case in a recursive definition, the case for which the solution is expressed in terms of a smaller version of itself; also called recursive case

global a descriptive term applied to any identifier declared in the main program, so called because it is accessible to everything that follows it

hardware the physical components of a computer

heuristics assorted problem-solving strategies

hierarchical implementation a process in which a modular solution is implemented by subprograms that duplicate the hierarchical structure of the solution

hierarchical records records in which at least one of the fields is itself a record

high-level programming language any programming language in which a single statement translates into one or more machine language instructions

homogeneous a descriptive term applied to structures in which all components are of the same data type (such as an array)

host type the existing ordinal type from which a subrange type can be defined; also called base type

identifier a name associated with a process or object and used to refer to that process or object

implementation phase the second set of steps in programming a computer: translating (coding) the algorithm into a programming language; testing the resulting program by running it on a computer, checking for accuracy, and making any necessary corrections; using the program

implementing coding and testing an algorithm

implicit matching see *positional matching*

index a value that selects a component of an array

infinite loop a loop whose termination condition is never reached and which therefore is never exited without intervention from outside of the program

infinite recursion the situation in which a subprogram calls itself over and over continuously

information any knowledge that can be communicated

inline implementation see *flat implementation*

in-order traversal the order of visiting the nodes of a binary tree in which, for each node, the nodes of the left subtree are visited first, then the node, then the nodes of the right subtree

in place describes a kind of sorting algorithm in which the components in an array are sorted without the use of a second array

input the process of placing values from an outside data set into variables in a program; the data may come from either an input device (terminal keyboard) or an auxiliary storage device (disk or tape)

input/output (I/O) devices the parts of a computer that accept data to be processed (input) and present the results of that processing (output)

input prompts messages printed by an interactive program, explaining what data is to be entered

insertion sort a sorting algorithm in which values are placed one at a time into their proper position within a list that was originally empty

integer number a positive or negative whole number made up of a sign and digits (when the sign is omitted, a positive sign is assumed)

interactive system a system that allows direct communication between the user and the computer

interface a connecting link (such as a computer terminal) at a shared boundary, that allows independent systems (such as the user and the computer) to meet and act on or communicate with each other; the formal definition of the function of a subprogram and the mechanism for communicating with it

internal file a file that is created but not saved; also called a scratch file

interpreter a program that inputs a program in a high-level language and directs the computer to perform the actions specified in each statement; unlike a compiler, an interpreter does not produce a machine language version of the program

invoke to call on a subprogram, causing the subprogram to execute before control is returned to the statement following the call

iteration an individual pass through, or repetition of, the body of a loop

iteration counter a counter variable that is incremented with each iteration of a loop

leaf nodes nodes in a binary tree structure whose left child and right child are both NIL

left child (of a node) root of left subtree of the node

length the actual number of values stored in an array, list, or string

linear time for an algorithm, when the Big-O work expression can be expressed in terms of a constant times N, where N is the number of values in a data set

linked list a list in which the order of the components is determined by an explicit link field in each node, rather than by the physical order of the components in memory

listing a copy of a source program, output by a compiler, containing messages to the programmer

literal constant any constant value written in a program

literal value any constant value written in a program

local variable a variable declared within a subprogram that is not accessible outside of the block in which it's defined

logarithmic order for an algorithm, when the Big-O work expression can be expressed in terms of the logarithm of N, where N is the number of values in a data set

logging off informing a computer—usually through a simple command—that no further commands will follow

logging on taking the preliminary steps

necessary to identify one's self to a computer so that it will accept one's commands

logical order   the order in which the user wants the statements in a program to be executed, which may differ from the physical order in which they appear

loop   a method of structuring statements so that they are repeated while certain conditions are met

loop control variable (LCV)   a variable whose value is used to determine whether the loop will execute another iteration or exit

loop entry   the point at which the flow of control first passes to a statement inside a loop

loop exit   that point when the repetition of the loop body ends and control passes to the first statement following the loop

loop invariant   assertions about the characteristics of a loop that must always be true for a loop to execute properly; the assertions are true on loop entry, at the start of each loop iteration, and on exit from the loop, but are not necessarily true at each point in the body of the loop

machine language   the language, made up of binary-coded instructions, that is used directly by the computer

mainframe   a large computing system designed for high-volume processing or for use by many people at once

maintenance   the modification of a program, after it has been completed, in order to meet changing requirements or to take care of any errors that show up

maintenance phase   the modification of a program, after it has been completed, in order to meet changing requirements or to take care of any errors that show up

mantissa   with respect to floating-point representation of Real numbers, the digits representing a number itself and not its exponent

MaxInt   the predefined identifier in Pascal whose value is set to the largest integer

that can be represented in a given computer

memory unit   internal data storage in a computer

metalanguage   a language that is used to write the syntax rules for another language

microcomputer   see *personal computer*

minicomputer   a computer system larger than a personal computer but smaller than a mainframe; sometimes called an entry-level mainframe

mixed mode arithmetic   an arithmetic expression that uses both Integer and Real data types

modular programming   see *top-down design*

module   a self-contained collection of steps that solves a problem or subproblem; can contain both concrete and abstract steps

module nesting chart   a chart that depicts the nesting structure of modules and shows calls among them

named constant   a location in memory, referenced by an identifier, where a data value that cannot be changed is stored

named matching   see *explicit matching*

named type   a type defined in the TYPE section of a program, procedure, or function

name precedence   the priority treatment accorded to a local identifier over a global identifier with the same spelling in any references that the procedure or function make to that identifier

nested control structure   a program structure consisting of one control statement (selection, iteration, or procedure) embedded within another control statement

nested IF   an IF that is within another IF

nested loop   a loop that is within another loop

nested procedure   a procedure that is defined within another procedure

nodes   the building blocks of dynamic structures, each made up of a component (the data) and a pointer (the link) to the next node

nonlocal   a descriptive term applied to any

identifier declared outside of a given block

nonlocal access   access by a procedure of any identifier declared outside of its own block

null statement   an empty statement

nybble   four bits; half of a byte

object   variables and constants

object program   the machine language version of a source program

Odd   a predefined Boolean function that takes an Integer operand and gives a value of True if the operand is odd (not divisible by 2) or False otherwise

one-dimensional array   a structured collection of components of the same type given a single name; each component is accessed by an index that indicates its position within the collection

operating system   a set of programs that manages all of the computer's resources

Ord   an operation that returns the position of a value in the ordering of an ordinal data type

ordinal data types   data types in which each value (except the first) has a unique predecessor and each value (except the last) has a unique successor

overflow   the condition that arises when the value of a calculation is too large to be represented

packed array   a special type of array in which data is stored in as little memory space as possible. A packed one-dimensional array whose elements are of type Char is called a string and has special properties in Pascal

parameter list   a mechanism for communicating with a subprogram, via which data may be given to the subprogram and/or results received from it

pass by address   a parameter-passing mechanism in which memory address of the actual parameter is passed to the formal parameter; also called pass by reference

pass by name   a parameter-passing mechanism in which the actual parameter is passed to a procedure as a literal character string and interpreted by a thunk; Pascal does not support this

pass by reference   see *pass by address*

pass by value   a parameter-passing mechanism in which a copy of an actual parameter's value is passed to the formal parameter

password   a unique series of letters assigned to a user (and known only by that user) by which that user identifies himself or herself to a computer during the logging on procedure; a password system protects information stored in a computer from being tampered with or destroyed

PC   see *personal computer*

peripheral device   an input, output, or auxiliary storage device attached to a computer

personal computer (PC)   a small computer system (usually intended to fit on a desktop) that is designed to be used primarily by a single person

picture element   see *pixel*

pixel   a square on a graphics screen that may contain one displayed point

pointer   a simple data type consisting of an unbounded set of values, each of which addresses or otherwise indicates the location of a variable of a given type; operations defined on pointer variables are assignment and test for equality

positional matching   a method of matching actual and formal parameters by their relative positions in the two parameter lists; also called relative or implicit matching

postconditions   assertions that must be true after a module is executed

precision   a maximum number of significant digits

preconditions   assertions that must be true before a module begins execution

Pred   an operation that returns the unique predecessor of a value of an ordinal data type

priming Read   an initial reading of a set of data values before entry into an event-controlled loop in order to establish values for the variables

problem-solving phase the first set of steps in programming a computer: analyzing the problem; developing an algorithm; testing the algorithm for accuracy

procedural parameters a parameter-passing mechanism in which the actual parameter is the name of a subprogram and the formal parameter is a dummy subprogram heading

procedure a structure that allows replacement of a group of statements with a single statement; often called a subprogram or subroutine, it is used by writing a statement consisting of the subprogram name, often followed by a parameter list

procedure call a statement that transfers control to a procedure; in Pascal, this statement is the name of the procedure followed by a list of actual parameters

procedure declaration the procedure code, from the heading to the end of the associated block

process a program, procedure, or function; any independent collection of executable statements

programming planning, scheduling, or performing a task or an event; see also *computer programming*

programming language a set of rules, symbols, and special words used to construct a program

proper subset a subset contained within another set that holds all the elements in the subset and at least one element not in the subset

pseudocode a mixture of English statements and Pascal-like control structures that can easily be translated into a programming language

queue a data structure in which insertions are made at one end and deletions are made at the other

range the interval within which values

must fall, specified in terms of the largest and smallest allowable values

Read a statement that causes the computer to get values from a data set and place them into variables

Readln a statement that causes the computer to get values from a data set and place them into variables; the computer then skips over any extra values on the line and goes to the start of the next line

read mode the status of a file that is to be used to input data; a file is put into read mode through use of the Reset statement

real number a number that has a whole and a fractional part and no imaginary part

record a structured data type with a fixed number of components that are accessed by name, not by an index; the components may be of different types

recursion the situation in which a subprogram calls itself

recursive algorithm a solution that is expressed in terms of (a) smaller instances of itself and (b) a base case

recursive call a subprogram call in which the subprogram being called is the same as the one making the call

recursive case see *general case*

recursive definition a definition in which something is defined in terms of smaller versions of itself

referenced variable a variable created and accessed not by a name but by a pointer variable; a dynamic variable

refinement in top-down design, the expansion of a module specification to form a new module that solves a major step in the computer solution of a problem

relational operators operators that state that a relationship exists between two values; in Pascal, symbols that cause the computer to perform operations to verify whether or not the indicated relationship exists

relative matching see *positional matching*

representational error arithmetic error caused by the fact that the precision of the true result of arithmetic operations is greater than the precision of the machine

reserved word a word that has special meaning in Pascal; it cannot be used as an identifier

Reset the statement that prepares a file for reading by putting the file into read mode and setting the file marker to the first piece of data in the file

resolution the number of points that may be displayed on a screen; usually measured in terms of how many points will fit within the width and height of the screen

result see *function result*

return the point at which execution of a subprogram is completed and execution resumes with the statement immediately following the call

Rewrite the statement that prepares a file for writing by putting the file into write mode and placing the file marker at the start of the file, erasing whatever information the file previously contained

right child (of a node) root of the right subtree of the node

right-justified placed as far to the right as possible within a fixed number of character positions

robust a descriptive term for a program that can recover from erroneous inputs and keep running

root in reference to a binary tree structure, the node which is not itself the child of any other node; the tree is referenced by an external pointer to the root

scalar data type a data type in which the values are ordered and each value is atomic (indivisible)

scope see *scope of access*

scope of access all of the places from which an identifier can be accessed; often referred to just as its scope

scope rules the rules that determine where

in a program a given identifier may be accessed

scratch file see *internal file*

secondary storage device see *auxiliary storage device*

selection control structure a form of program structure allowing the computer to select one among possible actions to perform based on given circumstances; also called a branching control structure

self-documenting code a program containing meaningful identifiers as well as judiciously used clarifying comments

semantics the set of rules that gives the meaning of instructions written in a programming language

semi-hierarchical implementation a modular solution implemented by procedures and functions in a manner that preserves the hierarchical design, except that a subprogram used by multiple modules is implemented once, outside of the hierarchy, and called in each place it is needed

sentinel a special data value used in certain event-controlled loops as a signal that the loop should be exited

sequence a structure in which statements are executed one after another

set an unordered collection of distinct values (components) chosen from the possible values of a single atomic data type (other than Real) called the component or base type

siblings the left child and right child of a node in a binary tree structure

side effect any effect of one module (a procedure, a function, or the main program) on another module that is not part of the explicitly defined interface between them

significant digits those digits from the first nonzero digit on the left to the last nonzero digit on the right (plus any zero digits that are exact)

simulation a problem solution that has

been arrived at through the application of an algorithm designed to model the behavior of physical systems, materials, or processes

size (of an array)   the physical space reserved for an array

software   the computer programs; the set of all programs available on a computer

software life cycle   the phases in the life of a large software project including requirements analysis, specification, design, implementation, testing and maintenance

sorting   arranging the components of a list in order (for instance, words in alphabetical order, numbers in ascending or descending order)

source program   a program written in a high-level programming language

stack   a data structure in which insertions and deletions can be made from only one end

standard identifier   a predefined identifier in Pascal (like MaxInt); may be redefined by user

standardized   made uniform; most high-level languages are standardized, as official descriptions of them exist

stepwise design   see *top-down design*

stepwise refinement   see *top-down design*

string   a collection of characters that is interpreted as a single data item; a packed character array; a predefined type in Turbo Pascal

structured data type   a collection of components whose organization is characterized by the method used to access individual components

stub   a dummy procedure or function that assists in testing part of a program; it has the same name and interface as the procedure or function that would actually be called by the part of the program being tested, but is usually much simpler

style   the individual manner in which computer programmers translate algorithms into a programming language

subprogram   see *procedure*

subrange type   a data type composed of a specified range of any ordinal type

subroutine   see *procedure*

subset   a set including only elements that are common to the containing set

Succ   an operation that returns the unique successor of a value of an ordinal data type

supercomputer   the most powerful class of computers

syntax   the formal rules governing how valid instructions (constructs) are written in a programming language

system software   a set of programs—including the compiler, the operating system, and the editor—that improves the efficiency and convenience of the computer's processing

tail recursion   a recursive algorithm in which no statements are executed after the return from the recursive call

team programming   the use of two or more programmers to design a program that would take one programmer too long to complete

termination condition   the condition that causes a loop to be exited

testing   checking a program's output by comparing it to hand-calculated results; running a program with data sets designed to discover any errors

Text   a predefined file data type whose components are characters organized as lines that are separated by <eoln> marks. Input and output are of type Text. The subprograms Readln, Writeln, and EOLN may only be applied to files of type Text

top-down design   a technique for developing a program in which the problem is divided into more easily handled subproblems, the solutions of which create a solution to the overall problem; also called stepwise refinement and modular programming

transfer function   see *conversion function*

tree sort　a sorting algorithm that builds a binary search tree with the input data, then traverses the tree in order

two-dimensional array　a collection of components, all of the same type, structured in two dimensions; each component is accessed by a pair of indices that represent the component's position within each dimension

type cast　see *conversion function*

type coercion　an automatic assignment of a value of one type to a variable of another type

type compatible　a condition in which types have the same type definition or type identifier, they are subranges of the same host type, or one is a subrange of the other

type definition　the association of a type identifier with the definition of a new data type in the TYPE declaration section of a block

underflow　the condition that arises when the value of a calculation is too small to be represented

universal set　the set containing all the values of the component type

unstructured data type　a collection consisting of components that are not organized with respect to one another

user name　the name by which a computer recognizes the user, and which must be entered to log onto a mainframe

value parameter　a formal parameter that receives a copy of the contents of the corresponding actual parameter

variable　a location in memory, referenced by an identifier, in which a data value that can be changed is stored

variable (VAR) parameter　a formal parameter that receives the location of a variable (the actual parameter)

visible　accessible; a term used in describing a scope of access

word　groups of 16, 32, or 64 bits; a group of bits processed by the arithmetic-logic unit in a single instruction

workstation　a minicomputer designed to be used primarily by one person at a time

Write　a subprogram that causes a computer to write out the value of variables, constants, or expressions

Writeln　a subprogram that causes a computer not only to write out the value of variables, constants, or expressions but also to print the following output on the next line

write mode　the status of a file that is to be used to output data; a file is put into write mode through use of the Rewrite statement

Answers to Selected Exercises

Chapter 1 Exam Preparation Exercises

2. (a) The source file and the object code file.   (b) The source file.   (c) A listing of the program with any errors found in the source and other information relevant to the programmer.

4. The following are peripheral devices: disk drive, magnetic tape drive, printer, card reader, auxiliary storage, terminal. The arithmetic/logic unit, the memory, and the control unit are not peripherals.

Chapter 2 Exam Preparation Exercises

1. (a) invalid   (b) valid   (c) valid   (d) invalid   (e) valid   (f) invalid   (g) valid   (h) invalid

3. False

5. program—15; algorithm—14; compiler—3; identifier—1; translation phase—12; execution phase—10; variable—11; constant—2; memory—13; syntax—6; semantics—8; block—7

6. (a) Real: 13.333333   (b) Integer: 2   (c) Integer: 5   (d) Real: 13.75   (e) Integer: −4   (f) Real: 1.0   (g) Illegal: 10/3 is Real but MOD expects an integer.

8. (a) reserved   (b) user-defined   (c) user-defined   (d) reserved   (e) user-defined

13.
```
Cost is
300
Price is 30Cost is 300
Grade A Costs 300
```

Chapter 2 Programming Warm-Up Exercises

1.
```
PROGRAM Exercise (Output);

CONST
  Lbs = 15;

VAR
  Price, Cost:
    Integer;
  Ch:
    Char;
```

```
BEGIN
  Price := 30;
  Cost := Price * Lbs;
  Ch := 'A';
  Writeln('Cost is ');
  Writeln(Cost);
  Writeln('Price is ', Price, 'Cost is ', Cost);
  Write('Grade ', Ch, 'Costs ');
  Writeln(Cost)
END.
```

2. Quadratic formula. All variables are assumed to be of type Real.

```
Determinant := Sqrt(Sqr(B) - 4.0 * A * C);
Denominator := 2.0 * A;
Solution1    := (-B + Determinant) / Denominator;
Solution2    := (-B - Determinant) / Denominator;
```

Chapter 3   Exam Preparation Exercises

2. Variable E will contain 17, variable F will contain 13, and leftover values 7 and 3 will be skipped over and lost.

6. True.

8. Code segments (b) and (d) will skip one entire line of data.

11. Errors with the program are as follows: file InData is missing from the program header, file OutData is missing from the declarations section, file InData should be reset (not rewritten), and file InData is missing as the first parameter of the Read statement.

12. Assuming that the program run is the corrected version of the program in exercise 11, (a) file InData will still contain the 144 after the program is executed and (b) File OutData will also contain 144.

Chapter 3   Programming Warm-Up Exercises

1. `Read(Length, Height, Width);`

3. `Readln(Length1, Height1);`
   `Readln(Length2, Height2);`

4. `Readln(Chr1);`
   `Readln(Chr2);`
   `Readln(Chr3);`

8. `PROGRAM CopyFour (DataIn, ResultsOut, Output);`

```
        VAR
          Valuel,
          Value2,
          Value3,
          Value4:
            Integer;
          DataIn,
          ResultsOut:
            Text;

        BEGIN (* CopyFour *)
          Assign (DataIn, 'DATAFILE.DAT');
          Assign (ResultsOut, 'RESULTS.DAT');
          Reset(DataIn);
          Rewrite(ResultsOut);
          Read(DataIn, Valuel, Value2, Value3, Value4);
          Writeln(ResultsOut, Valuel, Value2, Value3, Value4);
          Close (DataIn);
          Close (ResultsOut);
        END.  (* CopyFour *)
```

9. Starting an automobile with a manual transmission and an automatic choke. Note that the problem statement said nothing about getting into the car, adjusting seatbelts, checking the mirror, or driving away. Presumably those tasks, along with starting the car, are subtasks of a larger design such as "Go to the store." Here we are concerned only with starting the car itself.

Main Module
    Ensure car won't roll.
    Disengage gears.
    Attempt ignition.

Ensure car won't roll.
    Engage parking brake.
    Turn wheels into curb.

Disengage gears.
    Push in clutch with left foot.
    Move gearshift to neutral.
    Release clutch.

Attempt ignition.
    Insert key into ignition slot.
    Turn key to ON position.
    Pump accelerator once.
    Turn key to START position.
    Release after engine catches or 5 seconds, whichever comes first.

Chapter 4   Exam Preparation Exercises

2. (a) (I = J) OR K   (b) ((I >= J) OR (I <= J)) AND K *or*
(I >= J) OR ((I <= J) AND K)   (c) (NOT K) OR K
(d) NOT (L AND L)

6. (a) 4   (b) 2   (c) 5   (d) 3   (e) 1

9. (a) IF-THEN-ELSE   (b) IF-THEN   (c) IF-THEN   (d) IF-THEN-ELSE

10. The error message is printed because there is a semicolon before the ELSE.

13. Yes; the expression X <> Y tests the same condition as (X OR Y) AND NOT (X AND Y).

Chapter 4   Programming Warm-Up Exercises

1. `Available := NumberOrdered <= (NumberOnHand - NumberReserved);`

4. `Left_Page := NOT ODD(Page_Number);`

6.
```
IF Year MOD 4 = 0
    THEN
        Writeln(Year, ' is a leap year. ');
IF Year MOD 4 <> 0
    THEN
        BEGIN
            Year := Year + 4 - Year MOD 4;
            Writeln(Year, ' is the next leap year. ')
        END;
```

8.
```
IF Age > 64
    THEN
        Write('Senior voter')
    ELSE IF Age < 18
        THEN
            Write('Underage')
    ELSE
        Write('Regular voter');
```

10.
```
BEGIN
    (* This is a nonsense program *)
    A := 10;
    IF A > 0
        THEN
            IF A < 20
                THEN
                    Writeln('A is in range')
                ELSE
                    BEGIN
                        Writeln('A is too high');
                        A := 10
                    END
```

```
            ELSE
              IF A = 0
                THEN
                   Writeln('A is null')
                ELSE
                  BEGIN
                    Writeln('A is too low');
                    A := 10
                  END
        END.
```

Chapter 5   *Exam Preparation Exercises*

3.
```
Number := 1;
WHILE Number < 11 DO
  BEGIN
    Writeln(Number:7);
    Number := Number + 1
  END;
```

4. The number of iterations executed by the loop is 6.

9. Invariant. Count is in the range of 0 to 22; Sum contains the sum of the nonnegative integers from zero up to the current value of Count minus one.

10. Telephone numbers read in with integer form have many different values that could be used as sentinels. In the United States, a standard telephone number is a positive seven-digit integer (ignoring things like area codes), and may not start with 0, 1, 411, or 911. Therefore, a "good" sentinel may be negative, greater than 9999999, or less than 2000000.

13. (a) (1) Change $<$ to $<=$; (2) Change 1 to 0; (3) Change 20 to 21. (b) Changes (1) and (3) have Count range from 1 to 20; change (2) has Count range from 0 to 19.

Chapter 5   *Programming Warm-Up Exercises*

1.
```
Danger := False;
WHILE NOT Danger DO
  BEGIN
    Read(Pressure);
    IF Pressure > 510.0
      THEN
         Danger := True
  END;
```

   or

```
          Danger := False;
          WHILE NOT Danger DO
            BEGIN
              Read(Pressure);
              Danger := (Pressure > 510.0)
            END;
  2. Count := 0;
     Count28 := 0;
     WHILE Count < 100 DO
       BEGIN
         Count := Count + 1;
         Read(Number);
         IF Number = 28
           THEN
               Count28 := Count28 + 1
       END;
  6. CheckEOF := True;
     Positives := 0;
     Negatives := 0;
     WHILE NOT EOF DO
       BEGIN
         Read(Number);
         IF Number > 0
           THEN
               Positives := Positives + 1;
         IF Number < 0
           THEN
               Negatives := Negatives + 1
       END;
     Writeln('Number of positive numbers ', Positives);
     Writeln('Number of negative numbers ', Negatives);
  7. Sum := 0;
     Count := 16;
     WHILE Count <= 26 DO
       BEGIN
         Sum := Sum + Count;
         Count := Count + 2
       END;
  9. Hour := 1;
     TenMinute := 0;
     Minute := 0;
     AM := True;
     Done := False;
     WHILE NOT Done DO
```

```
BEGIN
  Write(Hour:2, ':', TenMinute:1, Minute:1);
  IF AM
    THEN
      Writeln(' A.M.')
    ELSE
      Writeln(' P.M.');
  Minute := Minute + 1;
  IF Minute > 9
    THEN
      BEGIN
        Minute := 0;
             TenMinute := TenMinute + 1;
             IF TenMinute > 5
               THEN
                 BEGIN
                   TenMinute := 0;
                   Hour := Hour + 1;
                   IF Hour = 13
                     THEN
                       Hour := 1;
                   IF Hour = 12
                     THEN
                       AM := NOT AM;
                 END
      END;
    IF (Hour = 1) AND (TenMinute = 0) AND (Minute = 0) AND AM
      THEN
        Done := True
END;
```

Chapter 6   *Exam Preparation Exercises*

2. 13571 (the address of the cell that belongs to variable Widgets).

4. Widgets and Clunkers are synonyms for the same memory location, so after the assignment statement both Widgets and Clunkers have the value 77.

7. The answers are   12   10   3   10

10. (3) Readln(Value3, Value1);
    (4) Value2 := Value1 + 10
    (1) Writeln('Exercise');
    (2) Logical(Number1, Number2);
    (5) Writeln(Number1:6, Number2:6)

11. Only one of the marked statements is not a procedure call: the assignment to Value2.

Chapter 6   Programming Warm-Up Exercises

```
3. PROCEDURE Increment (VAR Number:
                                Integer);

    BEGIN (* Increment *)
      Number := Number + 15
    END;   (* Increment *)
```

4. (a) Procedure definition

```
PROCEDURE Scan_Heart (VAR Normal:
                          Boolean);

VAR
  Heart_Rate:
    Integer;
BEGIN (* Scan_Heart *)
  (* Initialize to impossible value *)
  Heart_Rate := -MaxInt;
  WHILE ((Heart_Rate > 80) OR (Heart_Rate < 60)) AND NOT EOF DO
    Readln(Heart_Rate);
  (* Only way to this point is if normal heart rate or EOF, *)
  (* but can't check for EOF here because after the last value in the *)
  (* file is read in EOF is set, and that last value could be normal *)
  Normal := ((Heart_Rate <= 80) AND (Heart_Rate >= 60))
END;   (* Scan_Heart *)
```

(b) Procedure invocation

```
Scan_Heart(Normal);
```

7. (a) Procedure definition:

```
PROCEDURE Rotate (VAR First_Value,    (* Receives/Returns *)
                      Second_Value,   (* Receives/Returns *)
                      Third_Value,    (* Receives/Returns *)
                      Integer);

(* This procedure takes in three variables and returns their values
   in a shifted order *)

VAR
  Temp:     (* Intermediate holding variable *)
    Integer:
```

```
BEGIN (* Rotate *)
  (* Save value in local variable *)
  Temp := First_Value;
  (* Shift next two variables *)
  First_Value := Second_Value;
  Second_Value := Third_Value;
  (* Replace final variable with saved value *)
  Third_Value := Temp
END;  (* Rotate *)
```

(b) Driver program:

```
PROGRAM Rotate_Test (Input, Output);

VAR
  Valuel,
  Value2,
  Value3:
    Integer;

(* PROCEDURE Rotate, as above, goes here *)

BEGIN (* Rotate_Test *)
  Writeln('Enter three values');
  Readln(Valuel, Value2, Value3);
  Writeln('Before: ', Valuel, Value2, Value3);
  Rotate(Valuel, Value2, Value3);
  Writeln('After: ', Valuel, Value2, Value3)
END.  (* Rotate_Test *)
```

Chapter 7   *Exam Preparation Exercises*

3. True

8. (a) False   (b) False   (c) False   (d) False, A1 is nonlocal to Block2 but isn't global   (e) False   (f) True   (g) False   (h) True   (i) True   (j) False, A1 and B1 are nonlocal to Block2 but not global

11. Variables in Sample just before Change is called: A = 10; B = 7. Variables in Change when it is first called (before any statements are executed): X = 10; Y = 7; B = undefined. Variables in Sample after return from Change: A = 10 (X in Change is a value parameter, no result returned.); B = 17.

14. 4   7   6

Chapter 7   Programming Warm-Up Exercises

1. (a) Procedure definition:

```
PROCEDURE Sum_Square (      Number1,
                            Number2,
                            Number2:
                               Integer;
                         VAR Result:
                               Integer;
                         VAR All_Positive:
                               Boolean);

BEGIN (* Sum_Square *)
  Result := Sqr(Number1) + Sqr(Number2) + Sqr(Number3);
  All_Positive := (Number1 > 0) AND (Number2 > 0) AND (Number3 > 0)
END: (* Sum_Square *)
```

(b) Calling statement:

```
Sum_Square(A, B, C, Result, All_Positive);
```

5. Procedure heading

```
PROCEDURE Get_Average (   Dept_Num:
                             Integer;
                       VAR Avg_Sales:
                             Real);
```

6. Another procedure heading

```
PROCEDURE Rocket_Simulation (     Thrust:
                                     Real;
                              VAR Weight:
                                     Real;
                                  Time_Step,
                                  Total_Time:
                                     Integer;
                              VAR Velocity:
                                     Real;
                              VAR Out_Of_Fuel:
                                     Boolean);
```

8. Skip_Blanks and Skip_First are repeated here without comments.

```pascal
PROGRAM Acronym (Input, Output);

CONST
  Blank = ' ';

VAR
  Ch:
    Char;

PROCEDURE Skip_Blanks (VAR Ch:
                             Char);

BEGIN (* Skip_Blanks *)
  Read(Ch);
  WHILE Ch = Blank DO
    Read(Ch)
END;

PROCEDURE Skip_First;
VAR
  Ch:
    Char;

BEGIN (* Skip_Non_Blanks *)
  Read(Ch);
  WHILE Ch <> Blank DO
    Read(Ch)
END;   (* Skip_Non_Blanks *)

BEGIN (* Acronym *)
  WHILE NOT EOLN DO
    BEGIN
      Skip_Blanks(Ch);
      Write(Ch);
      Skip_First
    END;
  Readln;
  Writeln
END.   (* Acronym *)
```

Chapter 8   Exam Preparation Exercises

2. False

4. Yes

5. (a) 1.4E + 12 (to 10 digits)   (b) 100.0 (to 10 digits)   (c) 3.2E + 5 (to 10 digits)

7.
```
Sum : = 0.0;                 (* Sum is now of type Real *)
WHILE NOT EOF(Data_File) DO
  BEGIN
    Readln(Data_File, Amount);
    Sum := Sum + Amount
  END;
Writeln(Round(Sum):6);
```

12. It is poor programming practice to use formal VAR parameters in a function declaration because it provides a mechanism for side effects to escape from the function. A function returns one value as its result through its name, which is then used in the expression that called the function. If a VAR parameter in a function declaration is changed, that function would be returning more than one result, which is not obvious from the way the function is used. The only time a VAR formal parameter must be in a function declaration is when a file is passed as a parameter; even then the only operations that should be performed on the file are the EOLN and EOF tests that do not have side effects.

Chapter 8   *Programming Warm-Up Exercises*

2.
```
FUNCTION Equal   (Num1,
                  Num2,
                  Difference:
                    Real):
                      Boolean;
```

5.
```
FUNCTION Hypotenuse (Side1,
                     Side2:
                       Real):
                         Real;

BEGIN (* Hypotenuse *)
  Hypotenuse := Sqrt(Sqr(Side1) + Sqr(Side2))
END;  (* Hypotenuse *)
```

6.
```
FUNCTION Same_Status (VAR File1,
                          File2:
                            Text):
                              Boolean;
```

7. Function to sum four parameters:

```
FUNCTION Compass_Heading (True_Course,
                          Wind_Corr_Angle,
                          Variance,
                          Deviation:
                            Real):
                              Real;
BEGIN (* Compass_Heading *)
  Compass_Heading := True_Course + Wind_Corr_Angle + Variance + Deviation
END;  (* Compass_Heading *)
```

11. The type of Cost_Per_Ounce and the function return type are real so that cost can be expressed in terms of dollars and cents (i.e., $1.23 = 1.23$). These types could be integer if cost is expressed in terms of cents only (i.e., $1.23 = 123$).

```
FUNCTION Postage (Pounds,
                  Ounces:
                    Integer;
                  Cost_Per_Ounce:
                    Real):
                      Real;

BEGIN (* Postage *)
  Postage := (Pounds * 16 + Ounces) * Cost_Per_Ounce
END;  (* Postage *)
```

Chapter 9   *Exam Preparation Exercises*

2. No, this is not a valid declaration of a set variable:

```
VAR Digits : ['0'..'9'];
```

This is confusing because it looks almost correct. However, the notation ['0'..'9'] refers to a set constant (not a type) that could be assigned to variable Digits, as in the following statement:

```
Digits := ['0'..'9'];
```

The proper declaration should be

```
VAR Digits : SET OF '0'..'9';
```

4. (a) ['0'..'9'] (same as Digits)   (b) ['1']   (c) ['0','2'..'9']   (d) True, expression reduces to: ['1'..'3'] <= ['0'..'9']   (e) False, expression reduces to: ['1'..'9'] > ['0'..'2','8'..'9'] and '0' is not a member of ['1'..'9']   (f) False, expression reduces to: ['0', '2', '4', '6', '8'] = ['2', '4', '6', '8']   (g) True, expression reduces to: ['0'..'9'] > ['1'..'9']   (h) ['1', '3', '5', '7', '9'] (same as Odds; Odds has no elements that are also in Evens, so no elements are removed from Odds)   (i) ['1', '3', '5', '7', '9'] (same as Odds)   (j) False, expression reduces to: [] > []; For this to be True there would have to be one element in the left-hand set which is not in the right-hand set. Note that [] >= [] is True.

8. (a) False   (b) True   (c) True   (d) False

11. False

13. False

Chapter 9   Programming Warm-Up Exercises

1. (a) I IN [1..24]   (b) Ch IN ['A', 'J', 'K']   (c) X IN [1, 51..100]

5.
```
REPEAT
   Writeln('Enter Y for Yes, N for No');
   Get_Yes_OrNo(Response);
   Write('Valid Response')
UNTIL Response = 'N';
```

10. This solution returns proper results for values of Exponent greater than or equal to zero only. It returns correct values for $(Base^0) = 1$, $(0^{Exponent}) = 0$, and the special case of $(0^0) = 1$.

```
FUNCTION Power (Base,
                  Exponent:
                      Integer):
                         Integer;

VAR
   Count,
   Temp:
      Integer;

BEGIN (* Power *)
   Temp := 1;
   FOR Count := 1 to Exponent DO
      Temp := Temp * Base;
   Power := Temp
END;   (* Power *)
```

11.
```
CASE Grade OF
    'A' : Sum := Sum + 4;
    'B' : Sum := Sum + 3;
    'C' : Sum := Sum + 2;
    'D' : Sum := Sum + 1;
    'F' : Writeln('Student is on probation')
END; (* Case *)
```

12.
```
IF Grade IN ['A'..'D', 'F']
   THEN
      CASE Grade OF
         'A' : Sum := Sum + 4;
         'B' : Sum := Sum + 3;
         'C' : Sum := Sum + 2;
         'D' : Sum := Sum + 1;
         'F' : Writeln('Student is on probation')
      END (* Case *)
   ELSE
      Writeln('Invalid letter grade');
```

Chapter 10   *Exam Preparation Exercises*

3. Pred, Succ, and Ord

6. 0, error, Dior_Essence

11. False

13. Two types are type compatible when they have the same type definition or type identifier, they are subranges of the same type, or one is a subrange of the other.

Chapter 10   *Programming Warm-Up Exercises*

2. Enumerated type definition:

```
TYPE
   National_Football = (Cowboys, Giants, Eagles, Cardinals,
                        Redskins, Bears, Lions, Packers, Vikings,
                        Buccaneers, Falcons, Rams, Saints,
                        SF_49ers);
```

4. ```
TYPE
   Upper_Case = 'A'..'Z'
```

6. ```
TYPE
   Char_Digits = '0'..'9'
```

12. Any set of procedures with meaningful information to be printed.

Chapter 11   *Exam Preparation Exercises*

1. False

4. (a) ```
TYPE
      Bird_Type = (Cardinal, Blue_Jay, Humming_Bird, Robin);
```
   (b) ```
   Siting_Type = ARRAY[Bird_Type] OF Integer;
```

   (c) ```
VAR
      Sitings:
         Siting_Type;
```

5. (a) 100    (b) 8    (c) Colors    (d) Range    (e) 8    (f) 100

## Chapter 11   *Programming Warm-Up Exercises*

1. ```
PROCEDURE Initialize (VAR Failing:
                           Fail_Type;
                      Length:
                           Index_Type);
```

```
      VAR
        Counter:          (* Loop control variable *)
          Index_Type;

      BEGIN  (* Initialize *)
        FOR Counter := 1 TO Max_Length DO
          Failing[Counter] := False
      END;  (* Initialize *)
```

3. PROCEDURE Also_Check_Score (VAR Passing:
                                      Pass_Type;
                                  Score:
                                    Score_Type;
                                  Length:
                                    Index_Type);

```
      VAR
        Counter:          (* Loop control variable *)
          Index_Type;

      BEGIN  (* Also_Check_Score *)
        FOR Counter := 1 TO Length DO
          IF Score[Counter] >= 60
            THEN
              Passing[Counter] := True
      END;  (* Also_Check_Score *)
```

6. PROCEDURE Passing_Grade (VAR Passing:
                                      Pass_Type;
                                  Score:
                                    Score_Type;
                                  Length:
                                    Index_Type;
                                  Grade:
                                    Integer);

```
      VAR
        Counter:
          Index_Type;

      BEGIN  (* Passing_Grade *)
        FOR Counter := 1 TO Length DO
          IF Score[Counter] > Grade
            THEN
              Passing[Counter] := True
      END;  (* Passing_Grade *)
```

Chapter 12   *Exam Preparation Exercises*

3. (a) valid   (b) valid   (c) valid   (d) valid   (e) invalid   (f) invalid
   (g) valid

5.   CONST
         Max_Number = 1000;
      TYPE
(a)   Car_Type = (Ford, Honda, Jaguar, Renault, Saab);
(b)   Inventory_Range = 1..Max_Number;
         Inventory = ARRAY[Inventory_Range] OF Car_Type;

(a) VAR
       Cars : Inventory;

6. (a) valid   (b) invalid   (c) valid   (d) valid   (e) valid   (f) invalid

Chapter 12   *Programming Warm-Up Exercises*

```
4. FUNCTION Found (List:
                     Real_Array;
                   Item:
                     Real;
                   Length:
                     Index_Type):
                       Boolean;

VAR
   Counter:
     Integer;

BEGIN    (* Found *)
   Counter := 1;
   Found := False;
   WHILE (Counter <= Length) AND NOT Found DO
     IF List[Counter] > Item
       THEN
         Found := True
       ELSE
         Counter := Counter + 1
END;    (* Found *)
10. PROCEDURE Set_Present (VAR Present:
                             Boolean_Array);

VAR
   Counter:
     Integer;
```

```
BEGIN    (* Set_Present *)
  FOR Counter := 1 TO Max_Length DO
    Present[Counter] := False
END;      (* Set_Present *)
```

13. Procedure Bin_Search remains the same until the last assignment statement. This statement should be replaced with the following code segment:

```
IF Found
  THEN
    Index := Middle
  ELSE
    Index := First
```

The documentation should read "Otherwise, Found is False and Index is where Item should be inserted."

14. Replace the call to Search_Ord with a call to Bin_Search.

Chapter 13   *Exam Preparation Exercises*

3. (a) 6   (b) 5   (c) 30   (d) column   (e) row

6. (a) TYPE
```
      Teams = (Lions, Tigers, Bears);
```
   (b)   Record_Type = ARRAY[Teams] OF Integer;

   (c) VAR
```
      Win_Loss : Record_Type;
```

9. (a) True   (b) False   (c) True   (d) True

10. (a) TYPE
```
      First_Index = -1..3;
      Second_Index = 'A'..'Z';
      Third_Index = 1..20;
        Three_D_Array = ARRAY[First_Index, Second_Index,
                                  Third_Index] OF Real;

    VAR
      Array_A:
        Three_D_Array;
```
   (b) TYPE
```
      Index_1_and_2 = 1..10;
      Index_3_and_4 = 'a'..'f';
      Four_D_Array = ARRAY[Index_1_and_2, Index_1_and_2,
                            Index_3_and_4, Index_3_and_4]
                            OF Real;

    VAR
      Array_B:
        Four_D_Array;
```

Chapter 13   *Programming Warm-Up Exercises*

```
2. PROCEDURE Set_Diagonals (VAR Data:
                                    Data_Type:
                                Length:
                                    Index_Type;
                                Character:
                                    Char);

   VAR
     Counter:
       Index_Type;

   BEGIN   (* Set_Diagonals *)
     FOR Counter := 1 TO Length DO
       BEGIN
         Data[Counter, Counter] := Character;
         Data[Counter, Length - Counter + 1] := Character
       END
   END;   (* Set_Diagonals *)

9. FUNCTION Sum_Row_I(Table:
                        Table_Type;
                      Which_Row:
                        Integer;
                      Col_Limit:
                        Integer):
                          Integer;

   VAR
     Col,
     Sum:
       Integer;

   BEGIN   (* Sum_Row_I *)
     Sum := 0;
     FOR Col := 1 TO Col_Limit DO
       Sum := Sum + Table[Which_Row, Col];
     Sum_Row_I := Sum
   END;   (* Sum_Row_I *)
```

Chapter 14   *Exam Preparation Exercises*

2. (a) invalid   (b) invalid   (c) valid   (d) invalid   (e) valid   (f) invalid
   (g) valid   (h) valid   (i) valid

3. (a) A_Ref := Guide[71].Chart   (b) A_Code := Guide[88].Chart.Token[1]
   (c) Guide[94].Chart.Token[23,1] := 'X'
   (d) A_Ref.Symbol[20,9] := A_Map.Map_Code[4]

5. False

7. (a) hierarchical record   (b) record   (c) record   (d) array of records   (e) array   (f) array of hierarchical records   (g) array of records   (h) packed array of Char

9. Reference to the field name in this statement is ambiguous. Friend and Self are both of type Person.

Chapter 14   *Programming Warm-Up Exercises*

1. (a)
```
CONST
    Name_Length = 20;

TYPE
    Classification = (Freshman, Sophomore, Junior, Senior);
    Sex_Type = (M, F);
    Name_String = String[Name_Length];
    SS_String = String[11];
    Person_Type = RECORD
                    Name : Name_String;
                    SS_Number : SS_String;
                    Class : Classification;
                    GPA : Real;
                    Sex : Sex_Type
                  END;   (* Record *)
```
(b)
```
VAR
    Person_Rec:
        Person_Type;

    WITH Person_Rec DO
      BEGIN
        Writeln(Name);
        Writeln(SS_Number);
        CASE Class OF
          Freshman: Writeln('Freshman');
          Sophomore: Writeln('Sophomore');
          Junior: Writeln('Junior');
          Senior: Writeln('Senior')
        END; (* CASE *)
        Writeln(GPA:5:3);
        CASE Sex OF
          M: Writeln('Male');
          F: Writeln('Female')
        END (* CASE *)
    END
```

```
(c) TYPE
      Roster = ARRAY[1..3000] OF Person_Type;
    VAR
      Roll:
        Roster;
 3. CONST
      Name_Length = 20;
      Max_Courses = 50;

    TYPE
      Course_Index = 1..Max_Courses;
      Name_String = String[Name_Length];
      Date_Type = RECORD
                      Month : 1..12;
                      Year  : 1950..2020
                  END;   (* Record *)
      Class_Type = (Freshman, Sophomore, Junior, Senior);
      Grade_Type = (A, B, C, D, F, Q):
      Grade_Record = RECORD
                        Course_Id : Integer;
                        Grade: Grade_Type
                     END;   (* Record *)
      Grade_Array = ARRAY[Course_Index] OF Grade_Record;
      Student_Type = RECORD
                        Name : Name_String;
                        Student_ID : Integer;
                        Hours_To_Date : Integer;
                        Courses_To_Date : 0..Max_Courses;
                        Course_Grades : Grade_Array;
                        First_Enrolled : Date_Type;
                        Class : Class_Type;
                        GPA : Real
                     END;   (* Record *)
10. FOR Term := 1 TO 30 DO
      WITH Term_List[Term] DO
        BEGIN
          Write(Model:16);
          Write(Rate:7);
          CASE Parity OF
            Odd : Writeln(' Odd');
            Even : Writeln(' Even');
            One : Writeln(' One');
            Zero : Writeln(' Zero');
            None : Writeln('None')
          END (* Case *)
        END;
```

Chapter 15 *Exam Preparation Exercises*

3. (a) Read   (c) EOF   (d) Write

6. Read(N), where N is a Real or Integer variable.

8. One cannot use a file type as the component type of another file.

10. The Pascal procedure Dispose releases the space reserved for a dynamic variable back to the system.

12. TYPE section, where P is defined.

Chapter 15 *Programming Warm-Up Exercises*

1. ```
Text2 = FILE OF Char;
```

2. ```
CheckEOF := True; WHILE NOT EOF DO
   BEGIN
      WHILE NOT EOLN DO
         Read(Ch);
      Writeln(Ch);
      Readln
   END
```

4. ```
TYPE
   Real_File = FILE OF Real;
```

6. ```
FUNCTION Ident(VAR File1, File2:
                        Data_Type):
                     Boolean;

VAR
   File1_Rec,
   File2_Rec:
      Rec_Type;

BEGIN
   Read(File1, File1_Rec);
   Read(File2, File2_Rec);
   Ident := File1_Rec = File2_Rec
END;
```

8. ```
TYPE
   Ptr_Ref_Rec = ^Ref_Rec;
```

## Chapter 16  *Exam Preparation Exercises*

1. True. In a linked list, elements are only logically next to each other; in an array, they are also physically next to each other.

6. (a) The top or last-entered element of a stack is the first to be removed.
   (b) The front or first-entered element of a queue is the first to be removed.
```

9. When an item is inserted into an empty queue, a front and rear pointer must be set to point to the component.

10. (b) and (c) Every element is smaller than the elements to its right and larger than those to its left.

12. An N log N sort would most likely be more time consuming than an N-squared sort because the number of elements gets smaller.

Chapter 16   *Programming Warm-Up Exercises*

```
3. PROCEDURE Dequeue (VAR Queue:
                             Queue_Type;
                       VAR Component:
                             Component_Type;
                       VAR Under_flow:
                             Boolean);

   VAR
     Pointer:
       Node_Pointer;

   BEGIN
     IF NOT Empty_Q(Queue) THEN
       BEGIN
         Pop(Queue.Front, Component);
         IF Empty(Queue.Front) THEN
           Queue.Rear := NIL
       END
     ELSE
       Underflow := True
   END;

5. PROCEDURE Q_Stack (    N:
                             Integer;
                       VAR Error:
                             Boolean;
                       VAR Stack:
                             Node_Pointer;
                       VAR Queue:
                             Queue_Type;

   VAR
     Item:
       Component_Type;
     I:
       Integer;
```

```
BEGIN
  I := 1;
  WHILE (I <= N) AND NOT Empty(Stack) DO
    BEGIN
      Pop(Stack, Item);
      Enqueue(Queue, Item);
      I := I + 1
    END;
  Error := I < N
END;
```

7.
```
FUNCTION Count_List(List:
                        Node_Pointer):
                        Integer;

  VAR
    Count:
      Integer;

  BEGIN
    Count := 0;
    WHILE LIST <> NIL DO
      BEGIN
        List := List^.Link;
        Count := Count + 1
      END;
    Count_List := Count
  END;
```

Chapter 17   *Exam Preparation Exercises*

2. False. Both procedures and functions can be recursive.

4. F(4) = 1; F(6) = −1; F(5) is undefined.

6. An IF statement is the control structure that most commonly appears in a recursive procedure.

9. The root pointer being NIL (or both descendant links being NIL) is a base case of a recursive procedure that traverses a binary tree.

Chapter 17   *Programming Warm-Up Exercises*

1.
```
FUNCTION F(N:
                Integer):
                Integer;
```

```
      BEGIN
        IF (N = 0) or (N = 1) THEN
          F := 1
        ELSE
          F := F(N - 1) + F(N - 2)
      END;
```

3. PROCEDURE Line_Print (In_File:
                                Text);

```
   VAR
     Character:
       Char;

   BEGIN
     WHILE NOT EOF(In_File) DO
       BEGIN
         WHILE NOT EOLN(In_File) DO
           BEGIN
             Read(In_File, Character);
             Write(Character)
           END
         Readln(In_File);
         Writeln
       END
   END;
```

7. PROCEDURE Print_Stack(VAR Stack:
                                Node_Pointer);

```
   VAR
     Component:
       Component_Type;

   BEGIN
     IF NOT Empty(Stack) THEN
       BEGIN
         Pop(Stack, Component);
         Print_Stack(Stack);
         Writeln(Component);
         Push(Stack, Component)
       END
   END;
```

Chapter 18   Exam Preparation Exercises

2. Modes CGAC0 through CGAC3 have a resolution of 320 pixels wide by 200 pixels high. Mode CGAHi has a resolution of 640 pixels wide by 200 pixels high.

4. The fill pattern will spill out of the region and fill the surrounding area (possibly the entire screen).

7. False. The MoveTo procedure will move the current position to a given set of coordinates.

8. False. Red can also be a background color in any of the CGA palettes, in which case it will have a numeric code of zero instead of two.

Chapter 18   Programming Warm-Up Exercises

3. Assuming that the fill pattern has been set to solid and the fill color has been set to cyan (using SetFillStyle), the following statement will fill the square from exercise 1.

```
FloodFill(159, 99, 2)
```

5. Draw a blue circle of radius 75 on a light gray background:

```
Driver := CGA;
Mode := CGAC3;
InitGraph(Driver, Mode, ''); (* Assumes driver is in current
                                         directory *)
SetBkColor(Blue);
SetFillStyle(SolidFill, 3);
FloodFill(0, 0, 3);
SetColor(0);
Circle(159, 99, 75);
```

10. Draw a checkerboard:

```
Driver := CGA;
Mode := CGAC2;
InitGraph(Driver, Mode, '');  (* Assumes driver is in current *)
                              (* directory *)
SetBkColor(Black);
SetFillStyle(SolidFill, 0);
FloodFill(0, 0, 0);                   (* Fill screen with black *)
SetColor(2);
FOR X := 1 TO 8 DO                 (* Draw a grid of red lines *)
  BEGIN
    Line(X * 40 - 1, 0, X * 40 - 1, 199);
    Line(0, X * 25 - 1, 319, x * 25 - 1);
  END;
Line(0, 0, 319, 0);                        (* Draw top edge *)
Line(0, 0, 0, 199);                        (* Draw left edge *)
SetFillStyle(SolidFill, 2);
FOR X := 1 TO 8 DO              (* Fill in the appropriate areas *)
  FOR Y := 1 TO 8 DO
    IF Odd(X) = Odd(Y)
      THEN
        FloodFill(X * 40 - 20, Y * 25 - 12, 2);
```

Chapter 19 *Exam Preparation Exercises*

2. False. Units may use other units, but they cannot be nested.

5. Yes, you must recompile any program that depends on the changed unit.

6. By using a qualified identifier: the identifier is preceded by the name of the unit and a period.

8. It prevents the user from taking advantage of knowledge about the internal workings of the abstract type.

10. They permit us to write code that is entirely hidden from the user (as opposed to public subprograms, which the user may call).

11. So that it can be used again in other programs.

12. In the implementation section.

13. A constructor.

Chapter 19 *Programming Warm-Up Exercises*

The following unit definition contains the answers to exercises 1 through 5.

```
UNIT MonthADT;
```

```
(* This unit defines an abstract data type representing   *)
(* the months of the year. The representation is hidden   *)
(* and instances of this type may be accessed only by the *)
(* functions provided in the interface part               *)

INTERFACE

TYPE
  String40 = String[40];
  String9 = String[9];
  String3 = String[3];
  Month =
      (January, February, March, April, May, June, July,
       August, September, October, November, December);


(**************************************************************)


FUNCTION Month_Error:
          Boolean;          (* True if an error has occurred *)

(* This function will be True after a call to an access   *)
(* function for type Month if the attempted access was    *)
(* invalid *)


(**************************************************************)


FUNCTION Month_Error_Str:
          String40;          (* Returns an error message *)

(* If Function Month_Error returns True, this function may *)
(* then be called to get an error message string that     *)
(* indicates the source of the error *)


(**************************************************************)


FUNCTION Change(In_Month:          (* Receives a month value *)
                   Month;
                Amount:          (* Number of months to add *)
                   Integer):
                   Month;          (* Returns adjusted month *)

(* This function takes a month value and a number of months *)
(* to change it by (either positive or negative), and       *)
(* returns the resulting month. For example, February plus  *)
(* two equals April. If the change results in going beyond  *)
(* the end of a year, Error is True and a warning message   *)
(* returned by Month_Error_Str. However, the appropriate    *)
(* value is still returned. For example, December plus six  *)
(* returns June, even though it is in the next year *)
```

```
(*******************************************************************)

     FUNCTION Number(In_Month:        (* Receives a month value *)
                     Month):
                     Integer;      (* Returns the month number *)

(* This function returns the number of a month (1 - 12)      *)

(*******************************************************************)

     FUNCTION Month_Num(Number:        (* Receives a month number *)
                     Integer):
                     Month;         (* Returns a month value *)

(* This function returns the month corresponding to an    *)
(* integer in the range 1 - 12. If the integer is out of *)
(* range, Nubmer MOD 12 is used, and Month_Error is True *)

(*******************************************************************)

     FUNCTION Month_Name(In_Month:     (* Receives a month number *)
                     Month):
                     String9;     (* Returns month's name *)

(* Given a month value, this function returns the name of *)
(* the month as a string of 3 to 9 characters          *)

(*******************************************************************)

     FUNCTION Month_Form(Month_Str:    (* Receives a month string *)
                     String9):
                     Month;       (* Returns a month value *)

(* Given a string, the function determines the month name *)
(* it represents and returns the appropriate month value. *)
(* Letter case is ignored. If the string is not the name  *)
(* of a month, then Month_Error returns True *)

(*******************************************************************)

     FUNCTION Days_In (In_Month:       (* Date being checked   *)
                     Month;
                     Leap_Year:
                     Boolean):    (* True if a leap year *)
                     Integer;

(* Days_In returns the number of days in the given *)
(* month. Leap year is considered. *)

(*******************************************************************)
```

```
FUNCTION Less (Month1,                    (* A month       *)
               Month2:                    (* Another month *)
                  Month):
                     Boolean;


(* Less returns True if the first month is less than the *)
(* second month *)


(*************************************************************)

FUNCTION Greater (Month1,                 (* A month       *)
                  Month2:                 (* Another month *)
                     Month):
                        Boolean;


(* Greater returns True if the first month is greater *)
(* than the second month *)


(*************************************************************)

FUNCTION Equal (Month1,                   (* A month       *)
                Month2:                   (* Another month *)
                   Month):
                      Boolean;


(* Equal returns True if the first month equals the *)
(* second month *)


(*************************************************************)

FUNCTION Short_Name (In_Month:               (* A month *)
                        Month):
                           String3;


(* Short_Name takes a month and returns the abbreviation *)
(* for the month as a string of three characters *)


(*************************************************************)

FUNCTION Short_Form (Month_Str:            (* A month string *)
                        String3):
                           Month;


(* Short_Form takes a month abbreviation string of three *)
(* characters and returns the corresponding month value  *)


(*************************************************************)
(*************************************************************)
(*************************************************************)
```

```
IMPLEMENTATION

VAR
  Error_Flag:          (* Global variable holding error status  *)
    Boolean;
  Error_String:        (* Global variable holding error message *)
    String40;


(*************************************************************)



(* This hidden procedure initializes the global variables   *)
(* Error_Flag and Error_String. It is called by most of the *)
(* functions in this unit *)

BEGIN (* Set_Up *)
  Error_Flag := False;
  Error_String := ' '
END; (* Set_Up *)


(*************************************************************)


FUNCTION Valid(In_Month:              (* A month value *)
                    Month):
                    Boolean;          (* True if a valid month *)

(* Checks to see if In_Month is in range. Returns False if  *)
(* not, and sets global variables Error_Flag & Error_String *)
(* as a side effect *)

BEGIN (* Valid *)
  IF In_Month IN [January..December]
    THEN
      Valid := True
    ELSE
      BEGIN
        Valid := False;
        Error_Flag := True;
        Error_String := 'Invalid or undefined month.'
      END
END;  (* Valid *)


(*************************************************************)


PROCEDURE Error(In_String:            (* Error message string *)
                    String40);
```

```
(* This procedure is used to assign an error message to the *)
(* global variable Error_String, and True to Error_Flag. It *)
(* is called by any function for which an error can occur    *)

BEGIN (* Error *)
  Error_Flag := True;
  Error_String := In_String
END;  (* Error *)

(***********************************************************)


FUNCTION Month_Error:
          Boolean;        (* True if an error has occurred *)
(* This function will be True after a call to an access    *)
(* function for type Month if the attempted access was     *)
(* invalid. Note that the implementation accesses global   *)
(* variable Error_Flag *)

BEGIN (* Month_Error *)
  Month_Error := Error Flag
END;  (* Month_Error *)

(***********************************************************)


FUNCTION Month_Error_Str:
          String40;                (* Returns an error message *)

(* If Function Month_Error returns True, this function may  *)
(* then be called to get an error message string that      *)
(* indicates the source of the error. Note that the        *)
(* implementation accesses global variable Error_String    *)


BEGIN
  Month_Error_Str := Error_String
END;

(***********************************************************)


FUNCTION Change(In_Month:             (* Receives a month value *)
                  Month;
                Amount:               (* Number of months to add *)
                  Integer):
                  Month;              (* Returns adjusted month *)


VAR
  New_Month:              (* Integer representing adjusted month *)
    Integer;
```

```
(* This function takes a month value and a number of months *)
(* to change it by (either positive or negative), and       *)
(* returns the resulting month.  For example, February plus *)
(* two equals April. If the change results in going beyond   *)
(* the end of a year, Error is True and a warning message    *)
(* returned by Month_Error_Str. However, the appropriate     *)
(* value is still returned. For example, December plus six   *)
(* returns June, even though it is in the next year *)

BEGIN (* Change *)
  Set_Up;
  IF Valid(In_Month)
    THEN
      New_Month := Ord(In_Month) + Amount
    ELSE
      New_Month := 0;
  IF (New_Month < 0) OR (New_Month > 11)
    THEN
      BEGIN
        Error('Warning: Changed more than a year.');
        New_Month := New_Month MOD 11
      END;
  Change := Month(New_Month)
END;  (* Change *)

(* ************************************************************ *)

FUNCTION Number(In_Month:              (* Receives a month value *)
                    Month):
                        Integer;   (* Returns the month number *)

(* This function returns the number of a month (1 - 12).     *)

BEGIN (* Number *)
  Set_Up;
  IF Valid(In_Month)
    THEN
      Number := Ord(In_Month) + 1
    ELSE
      BEGIN
        Error('Invalid or undefined month.');
        Number := 1
      END
END;  (* Number *)

(* ************************************************************ *)

FUNCTION Month_Num(Number:              (* Receives a month number *)
                    Integer):
                        Month;          (* Returns a month value *)
```